THE OXFORD HISTORY
OF ENGLAND

Edited by SIR GEORGE CLARK

THE OXFORD HISTORY OF ENGLAND

Edited by SIR GEORGE CLARK

THE OXFORD HISTORY OF ENGLAND

CONSOLIDATED INDEX

COMPILED BY

RICHARD RAPER

CLARENDON PRESS · OXFORD

1991

Oxford University Press, Walton Street, Oxford OX2 6DP

Oxford · New York · Toronto
Delhi · Bombay · Calcutta · Madras · Karachi
Petaling Jaya · Singapore · Hong Kong · Tokyo
Nairobi · Dar es Salaam · Cape Town
Melbourne · Auckland

and associated companies in
Berlin · Ibadan

Oxford is a trade mark of Oxford University Press

Published in the United States
by Oxford University Press, New York

British Library Cataloguing in Publication Data
Raper, Richard
Consolidated index.—(Oxford History of England, 16).
1. England, history
I. Title   942
ISBN 0-19-821786-2

Library of Congress Cataloging in Publication Data
Raper, Richard.
Consolidated indexes / compiled by Richard Raper.
(The Oxford history of England)
1. Oxford history of England—Indexes.   2. Great Britain—History—
Indexes.   3. England—Civilization—Indexes.   I. Title.
II. Series.
DA32.A1R36   1990
016.942—dc20   90–48924
ISBN 0–19–821786–2

Typeset by Context Typesetting Systems Ltd., Marlow, Bucks.
Printed in Great Britain by
Courier International Ltd,
Tiptree, Essex

PREFACE

CONSOLIDATING indexes to a series of volumes can be a prelude to chaos. Fortunately, although the *History of England* was published over a span of some fifty years, the sixteen volumes were individually indexed with thoroughness. It is a pity that records are not available for me to acknowledge the detailed and painstaking work of previous indexers.

Thanks to modern technology this consolidated index was compiled in a shorter time than if carried out entirely by hand. Even with such facilities, it was still necessary to copy each entry into electronic form, verify it for accuracy, and subject it to final editing. Eventual merging of the indexes for the sixteen volumes set up new problems of arrangement and content, all of which required personal attention. Consequently a team of associates was involved in this mammoth task and it is a pleasure to acknowledge their important contribution. They are: Stefanie Cooper; Gillian Corderoy; Gillian Delaforce; Caroline Hamilton; Janet Lawrence; Ingrid Lock; Shirley Sabin; Mary Symons; and Juli Watson.

Additionally, I wish to thank Ivon Asquith, Robert Faber, and Anthony Morris of OUP for their encouragement and patience during the course of this project; and Leofranc Holford-Strevens for his advice on order of arrangement.

STRUCTURE OF THE INDEX

It is inevitable that publishing styles change through the years. Consequently the considerable variation in the way each volume was indexed meant alteration for the sake of consistency. Where necessary, long page strings are reduced to no more than five by re-indexing. For particularly large entries, the sequence of presentation is in ascending volume order; within each volume subentries are arranged in sequential page order. It is arguable whether subentries should be presented in this order or in an alphabetical sequence as used for the main entries. The sequential style was adopted on the premise that language used for describing events is not sufficiently definitive.

Certain subjects are given different treatment. For example, *army* and *navy* are divided into volume order, because they carry many entries. *London*, similarly—the entries are sufficient to make the subject a mini-index on its own! *Parliament* is arranged in sequential order by dates; *Oxford* and *Cambridge universities* are also special cases where the entries are presented alphabetically by college rather than by volume and page sequences.

ADDITIONAL MATERIAL

Anglo-Saxon place names, listed at the end of Volume II, are included as cross-references and are also found in parentheses after current place names.

Bibliographies list details of subject areas studied, with appropriate page numbers, in a volume by volume order. *Maps*, for each volume, are also collated in a similar way.

Entries for titles, such as *Aberdare, Lord* and *Aberdeen, earl of*, are cross-referenced to the original personal names of the holders of their titles. For reasons of clarity, this rationalization in style has been followed where possible throughout the work.

SOME USER SUGGESTIONS

The correct way to use any index is usually the simplest; but occasions arise when what is sought is not immediately found. A work as comprehensive as this index probably contains that information somewhere.

For difficult search situations, especially when the information being sought is not clear, it is useful to jot down on a piece of paper the salient facts that surround it. It may be a name, a place, or an action. Subsequent use of this information as a starting point for a search, coupled with a little browsing, should go some way to finding the answer.

R. R.

Hove
May 1989

A

Aachen **VII** 170

Aandalsnes, failure **XV** 471

Aaron, martyr **Ia** 718, 721

Aaron the Jew of Lincoln **III** 228, 282, 422

Abadan **XV** 556

Abailard **III** 232, 234, 237

Abailard, Peter **VI** 679

Abbandun *see* Abingdon (Berks.)

Abberbury, Sir Richard **V** 424

Abbeville (Somme) **IV** 235; **VI** 33, 152, 250; **VII** 558; Germans reach **XV** 485

Abbeville, prior of *see* Foliot, Gilbert

Abbo of Fleury, at Ramsey **II** 450

Abbodesbyrig *see* Abbotsbury (Dorset)

Abbot, Charles (1757–1829), Baron Colchester, speaker of House of Commons **XII** 419

Abbot, George **IX** 38, 43

Abbot's Langley (Herts.) **V** 332

Abbotsbury (Abbodesbyrig) (Dorset) **II** 731; abbey 414

ABC-1 agreement **XV** 536; Americans adhere to 539

Abdication Act (1936) **XV** 402

Abdul Hamid II, sultan of Turkey **XIV** 43

Abdul Medjid, sultan of Turkey **XIII** 237, 252

Abell, Thomas **VII** 427

Aberconway, abbot of (1248) **IV** 389–90; *see also* Conway

Aberconway, Cistercian monastery, burial place of princes **IV** 389

Abercorn, English see **II** 138, 146

Abercromby, James (1706–81), general **XI** 356, 361–2

Abercromby, Sir Ralph (1734–1801) **XII** 372, 379, 386

Aberdare, Lord *see* Bruce, H. A.

Aberdeen **V** 32, 35; university **VII** 249; **X** 263; mythical landing of

Russian troops **XV** 19

Aberdeen, bishops of *see* Elphinstone

Aberdeen, earl of *see* Gordon, George Hamilton

Aberdeenshire **VII** 507

Aberdovey **III** 301

Aberffraw (Angle) **IV** 387, 392; prince of, origin of title 393

Åberg, N. **Ib** xx

Abergavenny (Monmouth) **III** 301; lordship and castle **IV** 172, 395, 396, 402, 443; parliament (1291) 346; **VI** 510; lordship 329; **X** 182

Abergavenny, Lord *see* Neville, George

Abermoyl, market town **IV** 387

Abernethy, John (1764–1831), surgeon **XI** 392

Abernethy (Perth.) **II** 606, 644; **III** 266

Aberystwyth (Cardigan) **VI** 45, 55, 65, 642; recovered for English 102

Aberystwyth, castle of Llanbardarn **III** 299–300; **IV** 394; centre of administration 410; restoration 430, 432; borough 433; revolt (1294–5) 441, 442

Abingdon (Abbandun) (Berks.) **Ia** 461, 541–2; **Ib** 61, 82, 102, 111, 156; map 3 xxxi; Barton Court 210; **II** 731; **V** 50; **VI** 520

Abingdon, abbey **II** 67, 234, 448, 455, 499; chronicle 67, 68, 346, 394, 547; foundation 68; monks 204; council 345, 349; foreign priests 444; court 499; knight service 635; **III** 18, 224, 406; **VII** 462

Abingdon, abbot of **III** 1, 30, 78, 167; Benedictine **VI** 574; *see also* Æthelwold; Athelhelm; Rudolf; Spearhafoc

Abingdon, earl of *see* Bertie, James

1

Abingdon, St Edmund of *see* Edmund

Abnormal Importations Act (1931) **XV** 328

Aborigines, committee on treatment **XIII** 390–1

abortion **XV** 165

Aboukir Bay, battle (1798) 'The Nile' **XII** 369, 378, 384

Aboukir, sunk **XV** 13

Abraham the Tinner **V** 371; **VII** 461

Abruzzi **VII** 153

absenteeism in Ireland **X** 315

Abu Klea **XIV** 82

Abyssinia **XIII** 442; Italian attack **XV** 380, 384–5, 421; political effects 397, 409, 415; recognition of Italian empire offered 423; plan for attacking Italians 460, 522; Hoare the fall guy 478; emperor restored 526, 530

Academy, Royal **XIII** 578, 587, 589

Academy of Art *see* painting and sculpture

Acadia **IX** 345; *see also* Nova Scotia

Acca, bishop of Hexham **II** 151, 187

Accursius, Franciscus **IV** 286, 469, 626

Achademy, Queene Elizabeth's **VIII** 323

Aché, A. A. d' (1700–75), comte, La Bourdonnais's successor **XI** 329

Ackerman's *Poetical Magazine* **XII** 346

Acland, Sir H. **XIII** 521, 619

Acland, Sir Thomas **XIII** 90, 268

Aclea, battle **II** 244

The Acquisitive Society **XV** 267

Acre **III** 95, 361, 362; order of Knights of St Thomas 217; fall (1291) **IV** 267

Acre, John of *see* Brienne

Acropolis **Ia** 672, 675

Act of Settlement (1701) **XV** 296

Actium **Ia** 22, 49

Acton, Lord **XIII** 339, 513, 555; **XIV** 45, 161, 551

Acton, Sir Roger, of Sutton (Worcs.) **VI** 131; squire of the household 103

Acton Burnell **IV** 337, 338, 339, 624; statute 625; *see also* statutes

actores **Ia** 530

Actors, Peter **VII** 578

Acts and Bills (1485–1558): Advancement of true religion (1543) **VII** 429; Benefit of Clergy (1489) 89; (1512) 291; Confiscation (1536) 377; (1539) 398; (1545) 399; (1547) 465, 513; Crown Debts (1529, 1544) 439; Fines (1489) 89, 124; First-fruits and tenths 359; Heresy (1539) 426; (1547) 499; (1553) 544; (1554) 549; Inclosures (1489) 450; (1515) 451; (1534, 1536) 453; Industry and Trade 467–70; Maintenance and Retainder (1487) 78; (1495, 1504) 196, 197; Navigation (1485) 65; (1489) 89; (1532, 1540) 474; Precedence (1539) 414; *Pro camera stellata* 78, 194, 196, 197, 206; Proclamations (1539) 438; Provisors (1351) 199, 329, 342; Royal Title (1485) 60; Security under a king *de facto* (1495) 123; Six articles (1539) 403, 425–7, 551, 552; (modified 1540, 1544) 427; Succession (1534) 359; (1536) 381; (1544) 366, 413–14; (1547) 499, Treasons (1531) 354; (1534) 360; (1547) 499; (1554) 541, 549; (1553) 544; Uniformity (1549) 515; (1552) 520–1; Uses (1536) 350, 378, 388; Vagabonds (1495, 1531) 453; (1536) 454; (1542) 455; (1547) 499; Wales (1536, 1543) 367–9, 436; *see also* parliament under Henry VIII; Praemunire

Acts and Bills (1558–1603): Act of Uniformity **VIII** 184; Against Catholics 170; Artificers, Labourers and Apprentices 262; assurance of queen's power, and better

2

execution of the writ *de excommunicato capiendo* 24; Felony and Sedition 185; Poor Relief 266; for recognition of queen's title 17–18; Relief of Poor and Punishment of Vagabonds 265; Supremacy and Uniformity 14, 15

Acts and Bills (1689–1760): Affirmation Acts under William III (1722, 1749) **XI** 72; Army Recruitment (1744, 1745, 1756, 1757) 221; Bill of Rights (1689) 3, 5, 30; Calendar Reform (1751) 337; 'Clan Act' (1715) 161; Combinations of Workmen, legislation against 143; Corporation Act (1661) 70; Corporation Act for Quieting and Establishing (1718) 70; Drink Traffic, legislation to restrict 132; Excise Bill (1733) 30, 191; Fox's Libel Act (1792) 323; Grace, Act of (1717) 163; Habeas Corpus (1679) 60–1; amending bill (1757) 357; Hardwicke's Marriage Act (1753) 61, 69, 137, 346; Inclosure Acts (17th cent.) 107; (18th cent.) 108; Indemnity Acts 71; Insolvent Acts 136; Ireland, Act subjecting to British Parliament (1719) 295; Irish Industries and Trade, control under Charles II 296; Jew Naturalization Bill (1753) 337; Militia (1756–7) 48, 221, 351–2, 356; Molasses (1733) 192, 313, 317; Navy Pay Act (1758) 224; Recruitment (1741) 224; Occasional Conformity (1711) 69, 80, 170; Oglethorpe's Fisheries Bill (1750) 277, 337; Peerage Bill (1719) 22, 27, 30, 164, 170–2 —debates 211; Registering the Number of People (1753) 123; Poyning's Law (1495) 295; Regency Bill (1751) 340; Riot Act (1715) 157; Savile's Relief Act (1778) 74; Schism (1714) 69, 80, 170; Scottish Industries (1718)

276; Septennial Act (1716) 29, 164; Settlement (1701) 12, 30, 151; Test Act (1673) 70; Toleration Act (1689) 69; Triennial (1694) 164; Turnpike Acts (1751) 284; Union with Scotland (1707) 276, 278; Vagrancy Acts 130

Adam, James (d. 1794), architect **XI** 287, 402, 411; **XII** 340, 341

Adam, John (b. *c*.1726) **XI** 287

Adam, Robert (1728–92), architect **XI** 287, 402, 411; **XII** 340; biography 341

Adam, son of Bartholomew the Pinder **V** 326

Adam of Usk, chronicler **VI** 4, 13, 15, 18, 55

Adamnan of Iona, biographer of St Columba **II** 89, 178

Adams, C. F. **XIII** 310–12

Adams, John (1735–1826), president of USA **XII** 474

Adams, Mr, Lord Sidmouth's brother-in-law **XII** 408

Adams, Samuel (1722–1826), Massachusetts politician **XII** 185, 191, 195, 202, 254; biography 173

Adam's Grave **Ib** 171; *see also* Wodnesbeorh

Adamson, W. **XV** 297

Adda, papal nuncio **X** 54

Addedomaros **Ia** 47

Adderley, C. B., Lord Norton **XIV** 124, 126

Addington, Henry (1757–1844), 1st Viscount Sidmouth **XII** 397, 429, 445; first lord of Treasury (1801–4) 387, 402, 404–9, 412–18, 423; biography 402; lord privy seal (1805) 418, 420, 581; lord privy seal (1806) 435, 499, 582; lord president of council (1806–7) 438, 440–3, 582; out of office 476, 484; lord president of council (1812) 492, 498, 583; list of Cabinets 581; home secretary (1812) 583

Addington, Hiley **XII** 408

Addison, Dr Christopher: biography **XV** 64; on Runciman 64; recruits Liberal support for Lloyd George 67, 70; failure of Irish negotiations 72; ungratefully treated by Lloyd George 74; minister of reconstruction 93; ideas on reconstruction 139; builds houses and is driven from office 147; Housing Act 206, 210; Agricultural Marketing Act 279; opposes cuts in benefit 297

Addison, Joseph **X** 226; advancement through writing 355, 357–9, 361, 408; the *Spectator* 357–9, 365, 382; *Cato* 370; **XI** 10, 22, 419, 421, 424; Sir Roger de Coverley 52; prose 427

Adela, daughter of William I and wife of Stephen of Blois **III** 122, 131, 179

Adelaide, sister of William I **III** 109

Adelaide, wife of Hugh de Puiset, bishop of Durham **III** 351

Adelaide, wife of Louis VI **III** 127

Adelantado of Castile **VIII** 426, 484

Adelard of Bath **III** 161, 233, 244–5

Adeliza, second wife of Henry I **III** 126, 138, 213

Adeliza, wife of Rainald I, count of Burgundy **III** 125

Adelolf, count of Boulogne **II** 344, 345

Adelphius, bishop **Ia** 340

Aden **XIII** 236, 431, 414; Cunningham instructed to send fleet **XV** 520

adiutor procuratorum **Ia** 280

Adler **XIV** 552

Adlercron (*or* Aldercron), John, colonel (d. 1766) **XI** 329

administration (Roman Britain): **Ia** 203, 323, 371, 516–37; civil service develops 78–81; provincial rule 87–9; local 88, 219, 277, 345 — officials and buildings 111–13 — education 142–3 — local responsibility 187 — Brigantes deprived 200–1 — Marcus Aurelius 203 — landowners 299, 439 — 4th cent. governors 371–2 — army's role 390 — rescripts 442–3 — town and country 573–81, 590–2; of Britain 112, 381 — 'lex provinciae' 88–9 — Severus' division 222–3, 225, 227, 231 — 4th cent. reforms 316–17 — London and Gaul 339 — military installations 390 — economic pattern destroyed 662–3; increase and decline in administrative classes 138, 143, 295, 332, 548 — governors and finance 336–9, 345, 347 — landowning officials 434–6, 728 — central administration ends 441–2 — Arles prefecture 450–1; public speaking 142–3; military and civil functions 163, 253, 295, 347, 467 — local modifications 316–17 — Constantine I 322–3, 331–3 — officials expelled 436–9; property and estates 224, 269, 530; advisory council 228–9; Diocletian's reforms 289–91, 295, 300–1, 307, 316; London as centre 317, 333, 339, 361 — building programmes 156–7, 162–3, 264; financial reforms 336–8; Constantinople 365; east and west split 415–16; Constantine III 428–9; Roman administration from Britain 434–6, 439–43, 470; industry 439, 634–5, 639; career opportunities 450–2; church 450, 463, 722; continuity of administrative system in Gaul and elsewhere 451, 478–9, 486, 448–9; control of abuses 143, 193, 219, 533–4, 536; *see also* bureaucracy; councils; *curiales*; finance; freedmen; governors; praetorian prefect; procurators; provinces; *rationalis* administration (1399–1485): Yorkist **VI** 601–4; use of the house-

4

hold in 602; receivers of estates 603; territorial regroupings 603–4; finance of Richard III's estates 635–6; docket book of Signet Office (Harleian 433), 635–6; income of Richard III 636; *see also* administrative families

administration (1660–1714): administrative system **X** 13–17; administrative offices during the French war 180

administrative families (1399–1485): Heton serving the Stafford dukes of Buckingham **VI** 601; Kidwelly and Sapcote in royal service 601; Leventhorpe of Sawbridgeworth in service of duchy of Lancaster 602; *see also* administration (1399–1485)

Adminius **Ia** 60, 67, 70

admiral of the fleet: first powers and jurisdiction **IV** 655, 656; *see also* Leyburn, William; Alard, Gervase

admiralty: **IV** 655–7; **X** 110, 186, 251; keeps control of supply **XV** 22; experiments with tanks 35; turns down German offer to restrict blockade 43; opposes convoy 84; Lloyd George 85; lays down absolute requirements 230; wants 70 cruisers 255; MacDonald imposes 50 cruisers 255; reduces economy cuts 296; fails to build aircraft carriers 341; retains control of supply 444; section goes to Bath 457; relies on Asdic 461; Churchill's experience 479; operational headquarters 486; wants attack on French bases 505; Ministry of Production 543; wants bombing of U-boats 552, 553; refuses big ships for Dieppe raid 558

admiralty, court **IV** 655; **V** 245

Admonitions to parliament **VIII** 195, 196

Adolf of Altena, archbishop of Cologne **III** 367, 450

Adolf of Nassau, king of Germany (1292–8) **IV** 659–68

adoption **Ia** 192, 290–1, 416

Adour, lower valley **IV** 650

Adowa **XIV** 243

Adrian IV, Pope **III** 195, 230, 303, 304, 326

Adrian VI (Adrian of Utrecht), Pope (1522–3) **VII** 290, 314

Adrianople, battle **Ia** 391, 400, 500

Adriatic, proposal to land **XV** 583

adultery, punishable by death **IX** 172, 305

Adventure Galley, privateer **X** 330

adventus **Ia** 328

adventus Saxonum **Ia** 471–4, 477–9; **Ib** 8; date 9–10, 13; meaning 10–11; in *Historia Brittonum* 17

Adversaria **VIII** 316

Advowsons, in English and canon law **IV** 463–4

Adwalton Moor, battle **IX** 133

Æbbe, abbess of Coldingham **II** 161

Aedan, king of Irish in west Scotland **II** 77, 86

Aedh, king of Connaught **IV** 42

Aedui **Ia** 32

Aegean islands, unsuccessful attempt to seize (1943) **XV** 573

Aegean Sea **V** 123

Ægelesburg *see* Aylesbury

Ægelesford *see* Aylesford (Kent)

Aehrenthal, Count: annexation of Bosnia and Herzegovina **XIV** 410; death 469

Ælfflæd, abbess of Whitby **II** 162

Ælfgar, son of Earl Leofric of Mercia: earl of East Anglia **II** 569, 572–4: earl of Mercia 569, 574–6; daughter of 575

Ælfgifu, wife of King Eadwig **II** 366

Ælfgifu of Northampton, wife of King Cnut **II** 397; regent of Norway 405–6; after Cnut's death 420–1

Æthelwold, St (*cont.*)
vities 451–6; author of *Regularis Concordia* 453; death 455; tradition 456; biographies 451–3; **III** 167, 259
Æthelwold, son of King Æthelred I of Wessex **II** 321–2
Æthelwulf, ealdorman of Berks. **II** 234, 249
Æthelwulf, under-king of Kent, king of Wessex **II** 236, 244–5, 272; gifts to Rome 217; sent with army to Kent 231; gives kingdom to Athelstan 233; grants land to himself 308
Aëtius (Agitus) **Ia** 474–89, 498; Saxons in his army 440; **Ib** 8–10, 13, 208; appeal to by Britons **II** 2
Ætla, bishop of Dorchester **II** 135
Afene *see* Avon, river
Afghan War, first (1839): causes **XIII** 416–17; supported by cabinet 417–18; occupation of Kabul 418; retreat from Kabul 419–20; reoccupation of Kabul 420–1
Afghan War, second (1878–80) **XIV** 62, 70
Afghanistan: Anglo-Russian agreement on **XIV** 403; British forces (1919) **XV** 138, 152
Africa **Ia** 217, 348; status 162; frontier 175; disturbances 199, 350–1, 420–1; vandals 432, 488; lands and estates 547, 600, 627, 713, 727; Christians 717, 727; **VII** 178, 224; partition **XIV** 191–4
Africa, South *see* Cape Colony
Africa, West **X** 331–3, 349; **XIII** 240–1, 267, 374–5
African Company (Royal Adventurers Trading into Africa) **IX** 319; **X** 332
African Merchant, ship **X** 285
Afrika Korps **XV** 524
Agadir, crisis **XV** 408; *see also* Morocco
Agæles threp *see* Aylesford

Agarde, Nicholas **VI** 339
Agatho, Pope **II** 136–7, 144
Agen (Lot-et-Garonne) **IV** 291, 292–3; Edward I at (1286) 256; **V** 140; Process 113; **VI** 33; town and castle 135, 140
Agen, bishop of (1279) **IV** 292–3
Agenais (Guienne) **IV** 647, 650, 654; rights 127, 128; succession 272, 273; transferred to Edward I 289, 291–3; ordinance for administration (1289) 298, 302–3; **V** 81, 109; French claim to 110, 112, 114; Edward III granted full sovereignty 140; **VI** 108, 109, 135, 178, 240
Agilbert, bishop of Wessex **II** 122; receives bishopric of Dorchester 122; bishop of Paris 122; at Synod of Whitby 122–3; joins in consecrating Wilfrid 124; entertains Theodore 132
Agincourt (Pas-de-Calais) **VI** 154–6; battle 159, 196, 241; campaign 327; battle **XV** 315
agitators **IX** 146–7, 150–3
Agitius *see* Aetius
Agnadello, battle (1509) **VII** 155, 271
Agnes, sister of Emperor Henry V **III** 127
Agostini, Agostino, Wolsey's physician **VII** 331, 332
Agra **VIII** 242
Agreement of the People **IX** 150–3
agri captivi **Ia** 104; *see also* confiscations; land allotment
agri deserti **Ia** 355, 546–8, 557
Agricola (I), Cn. Julius: campaigns in Britain **Ia** 115, 132–50, 193–4; military strategy comparison 102, 121, 207, 349; Tacitus' presentation 125, 134, 304, 310; cultural policy 142, 156, 266; recall 150, 362, 570; in Scotland 151–2, 318–19; Fishbourne palace 161; control of abuses 337, 618; education 506–7; fort 710

Agricola (II), Sex. Calpurnius *see* Calpurnius

Agricola (III), praetorian prefect **Ia** 449

Agricola (IV), British Pelagian **Ia** 449

agricultural depression: political side **XIV** 54; economic side 115–19; intensification in the nineties 284–6

agricultural labour **Ia** 595, 627, 639; agriculture *versus* military, Britons/Romans 76; hiring labour/slaves 235; soldiers or farm labourers 439–40, 509, 511; labour shortage and forced labour 546–8; slaves or tenant farmers 605–6

Agricultural Marketing Act (1931) **XV** 279

agriculture: **Ia** 554, 559–62, 586–8, 595–629; Roman development Fens 6, 189–90, 610–11; Bronze Age 8; Iron Age 13–15, 554–5, 607–8; Belgic 58; Cumbria 183, 237–8, 612–14; flooding problems 258, 267–9, 547; Saxon 461, 559–62, 611; farming product analysis 619–20; **IX** 277–84; **X** 37–9; in Scotland 265; in Ireland 299; **XI** 105–9; crops 105; inclosure 107, 109; labourers 126; prices 105, 108; **XII** 10–13, 32, 35, 374, 519–22; Board of 521; agricultural disturbances (1830) **XIII** 79–80; 20th cent. **XIV** 511–13, First World War **XV** board of 77; subsidies and quotas 341; favoured treatment 342; condition 393; Ministry set on producing meat 464; changed policy saves shipping 511; *see also* livestock; trade; exports; Ireland; Scotland

Agrius, Quintus **Ia** 33

Aguila, Don Juan del **VIII** 414, 415–16, 488, 489, 490

Ahtehe **Ib** 78

Aidan, bishop of Lindisfarne **II** 118–20, 127

aids (auxilia) **III** 418–19

aids, feudal **III** 20–1, 416, 418; in Henry III's time **IV** 32–3

Aigueblanche, Peter of, bishop of Hereford (1240–68): on a mission to western princes (1242–3) **IV** 104; and treaty of Toledo (1254) 118; during baron's war 175, 199

Aigues Mortes **IV** 224, 255; interview of Francis and Charles **VII** 341

Aiguillon **V** 132, 133, 136

Aiguillon, A. V. D. duc d' (1720–98) **XI** 362

Ailly, Cardinal Pierre d': protector of France at Council of Constance **VI** 169; animus against English at Constance 170

Ailnoth the engineer **III** 260, 338

Ailred, abbot of Rievaulx, previously *dapifer* of King David I **IV** 580

Aimer, Philip, of Tours **III** 414

Ainsworth, Henry **VII** 89

Air, Ministry of: created **XV** 96; joined to War Office 130; set on offensive 504

air photography: Cumbrian plain **Ia** 184, 613; fenland 268, 610; rural sites (Somme) 303; comparison of settlements 594; villa layouts 625; Shorden Brae 701

air raids: in First World War **XV** 43, 44; precautions, directed by Anderson 405; primitive trenches (1938) 427; whether deliberately sensational (1938) 431; seriously undertaken after Munich, false alarm at outbreak of Second World War 454; effects in Second World War 503; damage to railways 506

aircraft production, ministry: created **XV** 478; Beaverbrook leaves 509; demands violently increased

aircraft production (*cont.*)
520; Ministry of Production 543;
Cripps 599
Aire (Pas-de-Calais) river **Ib** map
xxxii; **II** 604; **III** 454; **VI** 366,
582, 583, 646; **X** 220
Aire, bishop of **IV** 295
Airmyn, William, bishop of Norwich (1325–6): keeper of the
privy seal (1323–4), treasurer
(1331–2) **V** 87, 152, 154; memoranda of the parliament (1316) 47;
taken by Scots at Myton 56; in
France with Queen Isabella 82;
great seal entrusted to 88; ambassador to Scotland 98; ambassador
to France 117, 118
Aislabie, John, chancellor of Exchequer (1718–21) **XI** 177, 179
aisled buildings **Ia** 595, 599, 609
Aisne, river: Germans defend line
(1914) **XV** 11, 33; Nivelle defeated (1917) 81
Aitchison, Craigie **XV** 294
Aitken, Max, biography **XV** 67;
brings Law and Lloyd George
together 67; urges Law not to
reveal Unionist decision to
Asquith 68; fails to become president of Board of Trade 77; *see also*
Beaverbrook
Akeman Street **Ib** xxvi, 168
Akenside, Mark (1721–70), poet **XI**
425
Akkerman, convention **XIII** 220
Alabama claims **XIV** 19; *see also*
United States of America
(1815–1870)
alabasters, English **VII** 597–8
alae (auxiliary cavalry) **Ia** 255, 293;
destruction of *ala* by Ordovices
168; *numeri* and *cunei* comparison
248; veterans in community
510–11; *ala Petriana* 528; *ala Sebosiana* 684; *see also* cavalry
Alaisagae **Ia** 667
Alamanni: attacking empire **Ia** 239,
270, 274, 370; units in Roman

armies 322, 410, 417, 446
Alamein, El: battle (1942) **XV** 316,
599; Rommel halted 555; Rommel fails to break lines 558; bells
rung 560, 563; battle for Caen
repeats 581
Alan, abbot of Tewkesbury **III**
217
Alan, Carmelite friar of Lynn **VI**
687
Alan, count of Brittany **II** 348
Alan, count of Richmond **II** 628,
632
Alan III, duke of Brittany **VI** 72
Alan, earl of Richmond **III** 142
Alan III, earl of Richmond **VI** 72
Alan the Red, count of Brittany **IV**
236
Aland Islands **XIII** 235, 274, 289
Alans **Ia** 426, 446, 447; under Aetius
against Armoricans 449, 477,
481, 493; expel Roman landlords
477
Alard, Gervase, admiral (1300) **IV**
656
Alard, Thomas, of Winchelsea **IV**
636–7
Alard family **IV** 637
Alaric **Ia** 376, 443, 447; allegiance
with Romans 417–18, 427; sack
of Rome 430–1, 477; **Ib** 6–7
Alba, battle of **IV** 225
Alba, duke of **VIII** 164; English
right to Calais 59; subjugation of
Netherlands 127–8; embargo and
blockade on English goods
129–33; resists Ridolfi plot
149–51; treaty with Scots 154;
French threat 156; Bayonne conference 159; English-Spanish settlement 163; *see also* Alva, Alvarez
de Toledo, Fernando
Albania: revolt **XIV** 462–3; independence declared 467; question
of Scutari 467–8, 573; does not
operate sanctions **XV** 380
Albano, Walter of, cardinal bishop
and legate **III** 109, 175–6

Albany: conference (1754) **XI** 320–1; plan **XII** 175

Albany, duke of, brother of James III: declares readiness to help Edward IV **VI** 585; terms for recognition as king 585; after gaining Crown, to do homage within six months 586; to marry Princess Cecily 586; approached by Scots lords 587; signs agreement with James III 589; *see also* Stewart, John

Albemarle, dukes of *see* Edward; Monck, George

Albemarle, earls of *see* Keppel, Arnold Joost van; Keppel, George

Alberbury (Salop), priory of (Grandmont) **VI** 301, 675

Albergati, Cardinal Nicholas **VI** 199–200, 235, 257; conferences held by (1432–3) 259; mediator at Congress of Arras 261; allays Burgundian scruples at Arras 262

Alberic, cardinal bishop of Ostia, and legate **III** 190, 192, 272, 274

Alberoni, Giulio, Cardinal (1664–1752) **XI** 173

Albert, cardinal archduke of Austria **VIII** 418

Albert, king of the Belgians **XIV** 493

Albert, king of Germany and emperor elect **IV** 653, 660, 667, 710; and treaty (1303) 653–4

Albert, Prince, of Saxe-Coburg-Gotha (Prince Consort of England) **XIII** 104, 178, 257, 301–2, 500; biography 106; marriage 106; character and ideas 106–8; differences with Palmerston 224, 247–50; modifies note to United States 308; death 314–15; applied arts patronage 589

Albertists **VII** 254

Albigenses **III** 257

Albigensian **III** 230, 263

Albini, Nigel de **III** 110

Albini, Ralph de **III** 319

Albini, William de **III** 479, 481

Albini I, William de, earl of Sussex **III** 138

Albini II, William de, earl of Sussex **III** 219

Albinus, Abbot, pupil of Theodore and Hadrian **II** 182

Albinus, Bernard (1652–1721) **XI** 389

Albinus, D. Clodius **Ia** 217–20, 299, 427, 517; supporters 223, 225, 227; confiscations 224, 267, 653, 721; urban improvement halted 233; effects of civil war 255, 259, 264, 319, 653

Albion's England **VIII** 286

Albrectsen, E. **Ib** 108

Albret, Alain d' **VII** 86, 88, 97, 103

Albret, Arnaud Amanieur d', Sire **V** 144, 248

Albret, Bernard d' *see* Bernard VII, count of Armagnac

Albret, Charles d', constable of France **VI** 109, 137, 152, 153, 156; renounces agreement with England (1412) 114; at Harfleur during seige 150

Albret, Charlotte d' **VII** 152

Albret, d', family **VI** 107

Albuera, battle (1811) **XII** 453, 488

Alcalá **VII** 148

Alcazar, battle **VIII** 352

alchemy and alchemists **VIII** 310, 311; **IX** 369–70

Alchester **Ia** 593–4, 608; **Ib** 168; map 2 xxx; map 3 xxxi

Alcluith *see* Dumbarton

Alcock, John, bishop of Rochester (1472–6), bishop of Worcester (1476–86), bishop of Ely (1486–1500) **VI** 634; **VII** 59, 68, 77, 203; chancellor (1485) 56, 645; founder, Jesus College, 239, 375, 570

Alcuin of York **Ib** 122; **II** 94, 163, 219, 220, 224; on Aldfrith 89; Northumbrian learning 90, 92;

Alexander III, Pope: canonizes Edward the Confessor **III** 5; Foliot's letters 203; dilemma over Becket 204, 206–7, 209–10; coronation of Henry III 213–14; ecclesiastical jurisdiction 217–18; appeals to Rome 219–20; appropriated churches 227; Bull 'Laudabilita' 303, 309; legates sanction 324; death of Adrian IV 326; recognition by Henry and Louis 328

Alexander IV, Pope (1254–61): Sicilian business **IV** 106, 120, 122–5; English baronial leaders 131, 135–6, 461; nuncios in England 159, 167; releases Henry III from oath to Provisions of Oxford 263–5; customs and privileges of Scotland 593

Alexander V, Pope **VI** 93, 300

Alexander VI, Pope (1492–1503) **VII** 112, 115, 152, 156, 175; death (Aug. 1503) 153; promised crusade (1501) 156; bull (1493) 226

Alexander, prince of Bulgaria **XIV** 195

Alexander, prior of Canon's Ashby **III** 240

Alexander II, of Serbia **XIV** 411

Alexander I, tsar of Russia **XIII** 196–8, 218; proposes Holy Alliance 199; attitude towards European revolutions 201–4, 208; death 217

Alexander II, tsar of Russia **XIII** 289; **XIV** 43

Alexander III, tsar of Russia **XIV** 197

Alexander, W. H. **XIV** 326

Alexander, Sir William **IX** 325–6

Alexander the Great **Ia** 286

Alexander of Villedieu **VII** 239

Alexandria **Ia** 588, 717; **III** 95; bombardment **XIV** 79, 123; Hamilton withdraws to **XV** 25; French ships immobilized 494;

British fleet 520; Italian human torpedoes 530; Alamein 555; Mediterranean convoy arrives 563

Alfenus Senecio, L. **Ia** 227

Alfonso II, count of Provence **IV** 112

Alfonso I, d'Este, duke of Ferrara (d. 1534) **VII** 271

Alfonso, king of Aragon (1285–91) **IV** 252; negotiations with Edward I on release of Charles of Salerno (1286–91) 256–7, 259–63, 282–4, 305; projected marriage with Eleanor, daughter of Edward I 257–8, 259, 263–4; death (Jun. 1291) 264

Alfonso VI, king of Castile **III** 185

Alfonso VIII, king of Castile **III** 329

Alfonso IX, king of Castile **III** 215, 339, 381

Alfonso X, the Wise, king of Castile (1252–85): relations with Navarre, Gascony and Henry III (1252–4) **IV** 116–18; projected crusade in Africa 118; later relations with Henry III 119–20, 122; election as king of the Romans and claim to the Empire 119, 232; relations with Edward I 226, 242–5, 656; and Navarre (1275) 241–2; quarrel with Philip III of France and the problem of the succession 242–4

Alfonso I, king of Portugal **III** 95, 149

Alfonso, third son of Edward I (1273–84) **IV** 226, 238, 429

Alfred **Ib** 4–5, 144, 146–7, 166, 172

Alfred, king of England **III** 253, 385; *Proverbs of* 253

Alfred, king of Wessex **II** 89, 243; on origin of the Angles 13; Jutish descent of mother 23–4; laws 72, 275–6, 298–9, 309, 482; payments to Rome 217; early life and education 271, 272; early campaigns 248–9; becomes king 250;

Alfred, king of Wessex (*cont.*)
driven beyond Selwood 255; at Athelney 255; wins battle Edington 255; occupies London 258, 259; becomes national leader 259; treaty with Guthrum 260–2, 317; builds warships 263–4; reorganizes militia 264; builds fortresses 265; campaign (895) 268; death (899) 269; place in history 269–79; educational design 270; translations by Alfred and his circle, *Dialogues of Pope Gregory the Great* 271, *Cura Pastoralis* 272–3, Bede's *Ecclesiastical History* 273; Orosius 273–4, Boethius 274, *Soliloquies of St. Augustine* 274–5; character of his style 275; founds monasteries 445; internal trade 528; relations with council 550, 553; charter quoted 550, 553
Alfred the Ætheling **II** 408; arrest and death 421, 562
Alfred the Englishman **III** 246
Alfred of Lincoln **II** 632
Alfrey, John, yeoman of the king **VI** 419
Alfriston **Ib** 138–9; map 2 xxx; circular brooch 60 [fig. 2(d)]; quoit brooch detail 118 [fig. 10(f)]
Algeciras conference **XIV** 370, 401
Algeria **Ia** 513
Algiers **VII** 341; Darlan **XV** 560; Churchill and Marshall 564
Alhfrith, son of King Oswiu **II** 68, 122; wife Cyneburg, daughter of Penda 151
Alhred, king of Northumbria **II** 90, 92, 174, 176
Alicante **X** 215, 219
Alice, daughter of Humbert III, count of Maurienne **III** 330
Alice, daughter of Louis VII, betrothed to Richard I **III** 329, 339, 342, 346, 359; Richard freed of obligations 360; betrothed to John 363; married to count of

Ponthieu 377
Alice, wife of William Fitz Duncan **III** 271
Alice of Brittany **IV** 92
Alice Holt *see* pottery
alien merchants **VII** 468–9, 470–2
alien priories **V** 215, 293–5, 310; **VI** 300–1; discussed at Leicester parliament (1414) 134–5; parent houses in Normandy 135
aliens, entry restrictions **XV** 164
Aliens Act (1705) **X** 287, 288
Alington, William, treasurer of Normandy **VI** 190, 205, 207, 434; in king's Council (1422) 220
Aljurbarotta, battle **V** 440
Al-Khowārizmi, algebra of **III** 245
All Quiet on the Western Front **XV** 361
All Souls College, Warden and *The Times* **XV** 193
All the Talents, Ministry of *see* Talents
Allahabad, treaty (1765) **XII** 162
Allan, Maud, libel action **XV** 103
Allan, William, general secretary of the Amalgamated Society of Engineers **XIII** 157; **XIV** 132, 133
Allas-les-Mines, wine production **Ia** 654
Allectus **Ia** 245, 300, 318, 348, 712; rise and defeat by Constantius 305–13, 470; defences attributable to 320, 327; mint 660; **Ib** 79
Alleluja Victory **Ia** 470
Allen (Alan), John, archbishop of Dublin (1529–34), master of the rolls, Ireland **VII** 364
Allen, William: staunch Catholic **VIII** 22; English college at Douai 171; invasion of England 362, 393–4; Mary Stuart 376; manifesto in support of Spain 391, 393, 400; patriotism 393, 453; death 454
Allen, William, killed in Wilkes riots **XII** 133

Allenby, Sir E.: suggested as superior to Haig **XV** 100; victories (1918) 110; Wavell 460

Aller (Alre) (Som.) **II** 257, 731

Allerthorpe, Lawrence, treasurer of England **VI** 75

Allertonshire (N. Yorks.) **VI** 544

alliances: of Edward with continental princes (1294–1303) **IV** 658–70; cost of as revealed by *computus* of Walter Langton (1298) 667

Allied Maritime Support Council **XV** 99; Executive 99

Allin, Admiral Sir Thomas **X** 64

allods and allodial tenure in Gascony **IV** 108, 297–8; claim that Gascony was itself an allod 313, 651, 652

allowance system **XIII** 1, 9, 449–50

Almack's Club **XII** 339

Almagest, of Ptolemy **VIII** 307

Almain, Henry of, son of Richard of Cornwall **IV** 41, 152; in the Lord Edward's circle 154, 253; joins baronial party (1262–3) 173, 178; rejoins Edward 177; hostage after capture at Lewes 190; goes to French court as mediator 194; released (1265) 198; at Chesterfield 209; Dictum of Kenilworth 209; mediator (1277) 214; takes the cross (1268) 219; murdered at Viterbo (Mar. 1271) 226; *see also* Béarn, Constance of

Almanza, battle **X** 215

Almeida, fortress **XII** 482, 485–7

Almond, H. H. **XIII** 484

Almondbury (Alemaneberie) **Ib** 82; map 4 xxxii

Alnham (Northumb.), manor **VI** 377

Alnwick (Northumb.) **III** 267, 277; Lord Edward at (1267) **IV** 214; barony **VI** 337

Alnwick (Northumb.), castle **VI** 9, 36, 319, 377, 528–31; yields to Queen Margaret 529; surrenders to Yorkists but proves centre of new Lancastrian revolt 530; handed over to Lancastrians by Sir Ralph Grey 530; Lancastrians from, seize Skipton castle 530; part of Henry IV's principality (1463–4) 530; surrenders to Warwick 531

Alnwick, William, keeper of privy seal, bishop of Lincoln **VI** 218, 230, 299, 301; court book 276

Alost (county) **III** 128; **VI** 169; **VIII** 357; **X** 174

Alphonse of Poitiers, brother of Louis IX, count of Poitou and, in right of his wife, of Toulouse **IV** 100–3, 127, 184; death (1271) 272; *bastides* 273, 293; problems of succession to his lands 273–4, 289–91; *see also* Toulouse, Jeanne of

Alpine tribes **Ia** 78

Alps **Ia** 50, 403, 423, 428, 452; wine trade 652–3; **VII** 150, 314; French army cross 114, 306, 315; protestantism 338

Alre *see* Aller (Som.)

Alresford, battle **IX** 137–8

Alsace-Lorraine **XIV** 6; British pledge (1917) **XV** 50; offered by Emperor Charles 115; Fourteen Points 119; agreement at Stresa, to defend 388

Alston, fort, lead-mines **Ia** 183, 570, 634

Alston Moor (Cumbria) **III** 82

altars **Ia** 201, 562, 631, 681, 711; Altar of Victory at Rome 401, 409, 682, 735; Imperial Cult 674, 683, 684; restoration 713; deliberate burial 683, 702

Alten Fiord **XV** 564

Altenwalde **Ib** 193

Althorp **X** 180

Althorp, Viscount *see* Spencer, John Charles

Altmark, stopped **XV** 470

Alton (Hants) **III** 116, 119

Alton Priors (Wodnesbeorg, Wodnesbeorh) (Wilts.) **Ib** 171; appendix II; map 3 xxxi; **II** 734; first battle 30; second battle 71
Altona, convention **X** 163
Aluberht, bishop of the Old Saxons **II** 175
Alva *see* Alba
Alvarez de Toledo, Fernando, 3rd duke of Alba (Alva) **VII** 556
Alvastra, Cistercian abbey **VI** 686
Alvetanus (de Lannoy), Cornelius **VIII** 310
Alypius **Ia** 345, 358
Amadas, Philip **VIII** 246
Amadeus IV, count of Savoy (1233–53): uncle of Eleanor of Provence and father-in-law of Manfred **IV** 123, 247; becomes vassal of Henry III 250, 679
Amadeus V, count of Savoy: disputes about succession (1285) 250–1; relations with Edward I and Philip the Fair 251, 653, 665
Amadeus VIII, duke of Savoy **VI** 163, 249, 257
Amalfi **III** 437, 439
Amalgamated Society of Engineers, treasury agreement **XV** 29
Amalric I, king of Jerusalem **III** 343
Amancier, Jean d' **VI** 486
Amaurot, Utopian city **VII** 264
Amazon **X** 236
Amber **Ia** 42
Amberwood **Ib** 213
Ambien Hill (Leics.) **VI** 643
Ambion (Leics.) **V** 332
Ambleside, fort **Ia** 141
Ambleteuse **Ia** 27; **VII** 485; **VIII** 407
Amboise, Tumult of **VIII** 46; peace of 60
Amboise, Cardinal, George de **VII** 153, 286
Amboyna, massacre **IX** 53, 222, 323; **XII** 371
Ambresbyrig *see* Amesbury
Ambrose, St **Ia** 401–8, 417, 468, 474, 728; **Ib** 15; **VI** 678
Ambrosius (II) (Aurelianus?): parentage **Ia** 461–2, 464; enemy of Vortigern 468–9, 472, 476, 501; Roman support 474; leads British resistance 483, 490
Ambrosius Aurelianus **Ib** 14–15, 18–19, 154, 158–61, 164; mentioned by Gildas 212; linked with Amesbury 213; **II** 2
Amelia, Princess (d. 1810), death **XII** 489
America: unknown **VII** 224; Cabot 226; bullion 412, 447; effect on Italy 474; English venturers 557; **IX** 107; Scots settlers **X** 281–2; colonies 333–48; **XI** 202; trade and industry 192–3, 316–17, 322 — market for English goods 112, 192 — iron-ore 114, 316 — Virginian tobacco 122, 317, 322 — naval stores 192, 317 — trading with enemy 320; list 307; government 307, 312; attitude to British government 316–17; disunion 316, 318–20, 324; French menace 316, 319, 323–4, 347–9; population 318; relations with Indians 319–21; Pontiac rebellion 319, 321; Seven Years War 319–20, 348, 357, 359; culture and education 321–3; religion 323; Choiseul negotiations 369, revolt and war of independence **XII** 86, 143, 151, 241; Grenville 104–6; Stamp Tax 115; Mutiny Act (1766) 122; import duties 127; origins 172–95; Lord North 196–219; independence negotiations and treaty 249, 252–4; American policy after independence 347, 465, 470–5, 550, 550–5; population 517, 518; *see also* United States of America
America, South **X** 325
American Civil War *see* United States
Amersham (Bucks.) **VI** 132

Amersham, Walter of, chancellor of Scotland (1296) **IV** 615

Amery, Leopold Stennett: biography **XV** 254; Law tells him Curzon will be prime minister 234; combines Colonial and Dominions Offices 254; regrets National government 293; advocates Protection 299; excluded from National government 327; favours planning 354; repudiates League of Nations 369; denounces League 381; anti-Baldwin coalition 389; remains seated 428; tells Greenwood to speak for England 452, 606; Norway campaign 472; refuses to join Chamberlain 473; 'decayed serving-men' 474

Amesbury (Ambresbyrig) (Wilts.) **Ib** 160–2, 211, 213; map 3 xxxi; **II** 349, 731; **III** 229

Amesbury, nunnery: Queen Eleanor (of Provence) retires to **IV** 73; Mary, daughter of Edward I, a nun there 268; family settlement about succession to the Crown (1290) 268, 512

Amherst, Lord, governor-general of Bengal **XIII** 413; *see also* Burmese war (first)

Amherst, Jeffrey, Baron, 1st Lord (1717–97) **XI** 221, 320, 361, 368; **XII** 130, 183, 239, 576, 580; biography 130

Amhurst, Nicholas (1679–1742), and *The Craftsman* **XI** 204

Amicable grant (1505) **VII** 304

amici **Ia** 213

Amiens (Somme): *Samarobriva Ambianorum* **Ib** 31, 125; **III** 342; award or mise **IV** 130, 182–4; treaty (1279) 235; proposed conference of kings (1294) 647; **V** 108, 111; **VI** 192, 206, 250; treaty **XII** 409–12, 413; British Expeditionary Force **XV** 6–7; British victory (1918) 108; Germans take

(1940) 485

Amiral de la mer **IV** 655

Ammianus Marcellinus **Ia** 328, 351, 375–96; restoration after barbarian incursions 345–6, 360, 411–12; barbarian threat 368–9; **Ib** 80–1, 84

Ammonio, Andrea (Ammonius): letters **VII** 238; Erasmus' letter 248; wine 256; Erasmus' aid 257, 258; papal collectorship 300

amphitheatres **Ia** 233, 544, 579, 704

amphorae **Ia** 224, 459, 641, 652–3, 704; Catuvellauni imports 57

Ampthill (Beds.), manor and advowson **VI** 330, 484; **VII** 388

Ampthill, Lord *see* Russell, Lord Odo

Amritsar, massacre **XV** 152

Amsterdam **VIII** 366; **IX** 329; **X** 84, 134; stock exchange **XII** 24

Amulree, Lord **XV** 294

Amundsen, captain **XIV** 553

amusements **XI** 135, 145; Marylebone Gardens, Ranelagh, Vauxhall 417

anabaptism **VII** 509; **VIII** 204, 205

Anacletus II, anti-pope **III** 192

Anagui **IV** 652, 661

Anastasius, Emperor **Ia** 497

anatomy **X** 376

Ancalites **Ia** 36

Ancaster **Ia** 593; **Ib** 101, 181; map 4 xxxii; map 6 88; **VII** 388

Ancaster, duke of, master of the horse (1766–78) **XII** 578

ancient demesne **III** 44; growth of the phrase **IV** 530

Ancre, river **VI** 153

Ancren Riwle **III** 253

Ancrum, battle (1545) **VII** 407

Andate, grove of **Ia** 678

Andeferas *see* Andover (Hants)

Andeli (Eure) **III** 373, 375, 377, 379

Andeli, Henri d' **III** 236

Andelle, river **III** 129, 162

Anderida *see* Pevensey

Anderson, John **XIII** 494–5

Anderson, Sir John: biography **XV** 242; directs preparations against general strike 242; enters Cabinet 405, 434; insists on war 452; combines Home Office and Home Security 456, 478; lord president's committee 482; succeeded by Morrison as home secretary 503; prepares manpower budget 512; a gatecrasher 544; chancellor of Exchequer 573; keeps manpower budget 574

Anderson, Robert **X** 42

Andevill, Hamelin de **III** 25

Andover (Andeferas) (Hants) **Ib** 149; map 3; **II** 378, 731

Andrássy, Count **XIV** 41, 42; Note 42, 48; fatal success 52

André, Bernard (*fl.* 1500): Henry VII's difficulties **VII** 67; Arthur's birth 68; Lambert Simnel 69; Perkin Warbeck 118, 119; Ireland 120; Henry VIII's tutor 234

Andreae, Johannes **VI** 678

Andredesceaster **Ib** 135, 137, 145, 148, appendix I(b); *see also* Pevensey

Andredesleag **Ib** 136; map 2 xxx; map 3 xxxi; appendix I(b)

Andredesweald *see* Weald (Sussex)

Andredsleag, wood called **II** 17

Andrelini, Fausto **VII** 26

Andrew, Richard, first warden of All Souls College (1438) **VI** 474

Andrew, Robert, of Wiltshire **VI** 343, 416

Andrew the Notary **IV** 616

Andrewes, Lancelot **IX** 68, 209, 390, 407

Andrzejewski, S., *Military Organisation and Society* **V** 253

Aneirin (Gododdin) **Ib** xxv, 17, 197; **II** 3, 77

Anencletus (*provincialis*) **Ia** 533

Anesty, Richard of **III** 409–10

Angeln **Ib** 46, 54, 72, 104, 108; *Grossstamm de Angeln* 108, 115

Angels of Mons **XV** 18

Angelsey **VI** 38, 40, 44, 55

Angers (Maine-et-Loire); taken by Saxon King Eadwacer **II** 124; **III** 378, 442, 466; **IV** 93; **VI** 191; Margaret sees René of Anjou at 532; university **VII** 348; treaty (1551) 486

Angevin: party at the French court **IV** 245; claim to Naples **VII** 84, 112, 114, 152, 154

Angle, Guichard d', earl of Huntingdon (1377–80) **V** 399, 424

Angles: royal site **Ia** 675; **Ib** 6, 17, 20, 49, 54; map 1 xxix; continental origins 28, 46–9; relations with Oberjersdal culture 55; characteristic brooches 59 [fig. 1]; wrist-clasps 63; decorative styles in pottery 63–6 [fig. 3], Saxon element in origins 69–72, 105–6; eastern England 86; dominant element in Mischgruppe 107–8; settlement in Britain 108–9; cremation cemeteries 110–11; mixed cemeteries 111; links with Jutes 115; relations with Franks 128; Ceolwulf 171–2; Penda 185; links between Deira and continental Angles 192; in Frankish embassy to Constantinople **II** 5; reverse migration from Britain 5, 6–7; origin 12–13; *see also* East Angles

Anglesey, 1st earl of *see* Annesley, Arthur

Anglesey, Isle **Ia** 110, 140, 605, 677–81; **II** 80; **III** 285, 286, 292; ravaged from Ireland (1245) **IV** 399; occupied (1277) 412; under Treaty of Conway 412–13; in the war (1282–3) 426–7, 428; Beaumaris founded in (1295) 443; **VII** 47, 52

Anglican Church **XI** 68, 70, 75, 86; benefices 76–7, 79; episcopate 76–82; incomes 79; archbishops of Canterbury 80; country clergy 80–3, 144; Bangorian controversy 82, 86–7; convocation 82–3, 86; heresies 85; Wesley's influence 99; parish registers 123; marriages solemnized 137; American colonies 323

Anglo-Burgundian alliance (1506) **VII** 163, 183–7, 535; alliance (1520) 310

Anglo-Catholicism **XIV** 34, 140–1, 306–7

Anglo-French alliance (1940) **XV** 470; Gort ends 485

Anglo-French commercial treaty (1713) **X** 237–8

Anglo-French Entente: convention (1904) **XIV** 366–8; tightening up 368–9, 371

Anglo-French union, proposed **XV** 487

Anglo-Frisian pottery **Ib** 48, 55

Anglo-German naval agreement (1935) **XV** 377; Chamberlain and Hitler praise 429; Hitler repudiates 443

Anglo-Imperial alliance (1521), terms **VII** 311

Anglo-Irish trade **VIII** 491

Anglo-Japanese alliance, ended **XV** 151

Anglo-Polish alliance: made **XV** 450; makes Hitler hesitate 451; Soviet Russia 588

Anglo-Russian Entente, convention (1907) **XIV** 402–4

Anglo-Saxon Chronicle **Ia** 483; value of early entries **Ib** 4–6, 9, 10, 19, 20; appeal to the Angles 109; London mentioned 128; South Saxons 136–7, appendix I(b); West Saxons 144–7, 153–5, 162–73, appendix II; **II** 5; value 15–17, 65; sources 15, 19–20; character of early traditions 21–5, 39; duplication of early annals 22–3; on overlords of southern English 34–5; confirmed by Aldhelm 68; chronology 246; bibliography 688–94; **III** 4, 249–50

Anglo-Saxon language **X** 381–2

Anglo-Soviet Alliance **XV** 536

Anglorum Praelia **VIII** 323

Angoulême (county) **IV** 89; *see also* Isabella

Angoulême, counts of **III** 379; *see also* Audemar

Angoulême, theatre near **Ia** 675; **V** 132; **VI** 113

Angoumois **III** 379, 466; **VI** 178

Angulus **Ib** 46; *see also* Angeln

Angus, earls of *see* Douglas, Archibald; George, earl of Angus

Anian, bishop of Bangor (1267–1305) **IV** 390–1

Anian I, bishop of St Asaph's (1249–66) **IV** 390–1

Anian II, bishop of St Asaph's (1268–93) **IV** 390–1, 434–5

animals, prevention of cruelty **XIII** 470

Anjou **II** 556; relation of William II with **III** 111–12; of Henry I with 124, 128; Angevin Empire 318, 341; plans for succession 324, 329; Henry II's campaign (1173) 326; Henry deserted by barons 345; claims of John and Arthur of Brittany 378–9, 381; **IV** 93; and Treaty of Paris (1259) 126; **VI** 114, 138, 140, 142, 241; Henry's claim to 180; Salisbury's strike at 191; Bedford's campaign 244–5; clergy 476; **VII** 50, 113, 153

Anjou, Charles of *see* Charles of Anjou

Anjou, counts of **III** 123; *see also* Fulk IV, le Réchin; Fulk V, king of Jerusalem; Geoffrey II, Martel; Geoffrey V, Plantagenet

Anjou, dukes of *see* Henry III, king of France; Louis II; RenéAnjou, Isabel of *see* Isabel of Anjou

Anjou, house of **VI** 240, 241; in Provence, Naples, and Sicily *see* Charles I; Charles II; Robert, king of Naples

Anna, king of the East Angles **II** 118

Annaghdown (Ireland), see **VI** 275

Annales . . . regnante Elizabetha **VIII** 283

Annales Cambriae **Ib** 154

Annales Londonienses, on declaration (1308) **V** 7

Annales Paulini, on coronation of Edward II **V** 4; on Gaveston 22; on the lords (1321) 63

Annales Ricardi Secundi et Henrici Quarti **VI** 19, 59, 81

Annals of the First Four Years of Queen Elizabeth **VIII** 283

Annals of Tigernach **Ib** 197; *of Ulster* 197

Annan, fort **Ia** 145

Annandale (Dumfries): signal station **Ia** 571; **III** 273; **IV** 692, 709; **VI** 586

Annates, papal **IV** 500

Anne, countess of Stafford, Edward III's granddaughter **VI** 334

Anne, countess of Warwick, takes sanctuary at Beaulieu abbey **VI** 568

Anne, daughter of John the Fearless **VI** 111

Anne, duchess of Exeter **VI** 519

Anne, Edward, lampoons the Mass **VII** 575

Anne, Princess, daughter of Edward IV: proposal for marriage to Philip, son of Maximilian **VI** 584

Anne, princess royal **XI** 195; marriage to William IV of United Provinces (1734) 260

Anne, Queen (1702–14) (b. 1665): **III** 5; as princess **X** 134, 139; question of succession 146, 190; Marlborough 183; account of 220–2; Queen Anne's bounty 221; personal distaste for her ministers 225; estrangement from duchess of Marlborough 225; electress Sophia 240; Old Pretender 241; Bolingbroke and Oxford 246–7; considerable influence 252; 'touching for the evil' 252;

the Cabinet council 255–6; Scotland 285, 287; Ireland 311, 314; communion plate presented to Mohawks by 346; at Oxford 372; illness and death 245, 248; **XI** 15, 17, 35, 152, 160; royal veto 30; ecclesiastical patronage 77, 80; grant of army commissions 218; Handel's pension 415; death **XV** 389

Anne, wife of Richard III **VI** 636

Anne of Austria, Philip II's bride elect **VIII** 145

Anne of Austria, queen of France **IX** 64, 230

Anne de Beaujeu, daughter of Louis XI, wife of Pierre de Beaujeu (d. 1522) **VII** 85, 99

Anne of Bohemia, queen of Richard II **V** 436, 465; marriage 146, 427; patron of Eye priory 294; joint founder of Coventry Charterhouse 295; her Bohemians 427; and Simon Burley 429, 458, 479; death 470; **VI** 3, 128, 480

Anne Boleyn *see* Boleyn, Anne

Anne of Brittany, daughter of duke Francis II: marriage proposals **VII** 86, 88, 103; envoy 89; Ferdinand kinsman 93; Rieux quarrel 97; Treaty of Frankfurt (1489) 99, 101; Henry VII commission 102; marriages 103–5, 326

Anne of Burgundy, daughter of John the Fearless, wife of Bedford **VI** 207, 225

Anne of Cleves: marries Henry VIII **VII** 403–4; separated 417; Cromwell testifies 415; Henry's distaste 416; parliament ratifies separation 438; accompanies Mary 529; dress 601

Anne of Denmark, queen consort, wife of James I **IX** 263, 370

Annebault, Claude de, French ambassador **VII** 409, 479

Annesley, Arthur, 1st earl of Anglesey, library **X** 15

Annesley, Francis, Lord Mountnorris **IX** 115

Annesley, Sir John **V** 443

Annesley-Voysey, C. F. **XIV** 540

annona **Ib** 14

Annual Register, quoted **XV** 311, 429

Anointing of Scottish kings **IV** 593–4

Anonimalle Chronicle, on the Good Parliament **V** 388; on the Rising (1381) 410–11

Anquetin, Richard, sheriff of Harcourt **VI** 207

Anselm, St, archbishop of Canterbury: early life **III** 190, 194, 222, 252, 268; conflict with Henry over Investitures 3, 177–9; as adviser to Crown 10; performance of military obligations 16, 176; legislates against slavery 40; at Rockingham 104, 174; quoted 109; tax for Normandy 111, 183; recall by Henry 114, 177; supports Henry in rebellion (1100) 116; respect for Anglo-Saxon clergy 167; tract from Losinga 170, 182; election as archbishop 172–3; quarrel with William II 173–5; first exile 176–7; second exile 178; agrees to settlement 179–80, 191; death 182; compared with Becket 198, 199; schools of Bec and Laon 233–4; Eadmer, his biographer 269; **V** 2

Ansger, sheriff of London and Middlesex **II** 414

Anskar, St **II** 239, 241

Anson, General George **XIII** 434–5

Anson, George, 1st Baron (1697–1762), first lord of admiralty (1757–62) **XI** 34, 224, 230, 250 262; circumnavigation 227–9, 233, 380; Cabinet member 347; Byng trial 352; **XII** 67, 576

Anstis, John (1669–1744), Garter King **XI** 396

Anthemius (I), eastern praetorian prefect **Ia** 432

Anthemius (II), Emperor **Ia** 491–3

Anthony, bastard of Bourbon **VI** 558

Anthony of Brabant, brother of John the Fearless **VI** 155

Anti-Corn Law League **XII** 358; **XIII** 89; foundation 118; activities 118–21; **XV** 330

Antigone, natural daughter of Humphrey, duke of Gloucester **VI** 486

Antigua **IX** 337; **XII** 290

Antilha **VII** 224

Antinuous **Ia** 170, 182

Antioch **Ia** 345, 358; **III** 94, 162

antiquarian and archaeological studies **XI** 394, 404

Antiquaries, Society of **VIII** 321

Antistius Adventus, Q. **Ia** 207, 209

Antius Crescens Calpurnianus, M. **Ia** 227, 526

Antonine Age **Ia** 203; Britain 232, 235, 237, 601; wars 701

Antonine Itinerary **Ia** 587

Antonine Wall **Ia** 144; 193–7; evacuation and reoccupation 200–10, 222, 226, 229, 352; settlement between the Walls 237, 543, 612; forts 260, 319; Gildas' turf wall? 405; communications by sea 562

Antoninus Pius, Emperor **Ia** 154, 223, 254, 260; invades Southern Scotland 171, 192–203, 205; confiscates Brigantian territory 277, 531, 538; Solway forts 383; provincial procurator 529, 637

Antonio, Don, of Portugal **VIII** 352, 353, 356, 406, 411

Antonius, M., triumvir **Ia** 48, 363

Antonius Primus, H. **Ia** 120–1, 133, 134

Antonius Saturninus, L. *see* Saturninus

Antony, bastard of Burgundy, visit **VI** 552

Antrim **V** 42, 43, 233

Antwerp (Andwarpe) **III** 434; English merchants **IV** 628, 663, 664; held as fief of Edward I by duke of Brabant (1298) 679; staple **V** 121, 128, 350, 352; Edward III 127, 157, 160, 162; birth of Prince Lionel 267; **VI** 351, 362; Perkin Warbeck **VII** 121; Merchant Adventurers recalled 124; trading disputes 181, 220; conference (1497) 222; Italian trade 223; *Enchiridion Militis Christiani* 250; town clerk 259; Tyndale commentaries 344; Fuggers and Welsers 412; heir to Venice 473; commercial capital 474; **X** 70, 87, 213, 218; British Expeditionary Force **XV** 6; Churchill's unsuccessful aid 11, 466; fall (1914) 11–12; Germans plan garrison 65; captured (1944) 583; Hitler plans to take 589

Anund, king of Sweden **II** 403

Anwykyll, John **VII** 239, 577

Anyder **VII** 264

Anzac beach, evacuated **XV** 48

Anzio: landing (1944) **XV** 575, 579; does not aid main front **XV** 576; war cabinet not told date 580

Aosta, valley **III** 172, 330

Aper, Gallic landowner **Ia** 453

Apollinaris (I) **Ia** 436

Apollinaris (II), Sidonius *see* Sidonius

Apollinaris (III), bishop **Ia** 498

Apollodorus, architect **Ia** 181

Apology, bishop Jewel's **VIII** 32–33

Apology of the Commons **IX** 6–7

apothecaries **VIII** 313; **X** 419

Apothecaries, Society **IX** 365–6

appeal to Rome: by province **Ia** 419, 442–5, 534; by citizens 526

appeals: to *parlement* of Paris **IV** 311–15, 647; from Gascony to the king of England 307–8, 315–18; to judges of appeal in Gascony 314–15, 317; Nicholas Segrave's attempt to appeal from English to

French court 332–3; tutorial 466, 492–4; from Scottish court to English king 608–12, 616; regulations in parliament 610

appellants **VI** 5, 6, 20, 472

Appian **Ia** 525

Appius Bradua, M. **Ia** 182

Appius and Virginia **VIII** 296

The Apple Cart **XV** 305

Applebaum, S. **Ia** 468, 619, 626–9, 663–4

Appleby, castle **III** 277

Appleby, Thomas, bishop of Carlisle (1363–95) **V** 389

Applecross, lay priest of, later first earl of Ross **IV** 580

Appledore (Apuldre) (Kent) **II** 266, 731

Applegarth, Robert, secretary of the Amalgamated Society of Carpenters and Joiners (1862–1871) **XIII** 613; **XIV** 132

Appleton, brother William **V** 262, 412

apprentices, statute **IX** 294–5

Approver **III** 396–7, 397

Apsley, Baron *see* Bathurst, Henry

Apuldre *see* Appledore (Kent)

Apuleius **Ia** 598; **III** 235

Apulia, estates **Ia** 600; **VII** 153, 175

Aquae Sulis see Bath

aqueducts **Ia** 577

Aquileia: defeat of Constaine II **Ia** 348, 349, 368; defeat of Magnus Maximus 404; church 718

Aquilinus, freedman **Ia** 254

Aquinas, St Thomas **IV** 230; **V** 509; **VI** 309, 315, 680, 683; **VII** 239; **IX** 360

Aquincum (*canabae*) **Ia** 582

Aquitaine, duchy **II** 407, 585; William II's ambition to acquire **III** 111; acquired by Henry Plantagenet 163, 318; Queen Eleanor's position 243; Richard I recognized as successor 325, 329–30; wars 340–1, 344; Richard I's relations with 349,

351, 360, 374; barons do homage to Eleanor on Richard's death 378; John's relations with 381, 466; extent of in Edward I's time **IV** 273–4, 291–2; administration of 273–80; temporary sale to Louis IX of King Henry's rights in bishoprics and their surrender by Edward I (1279) 280–1, 289; 'privileged' in 290–1, 298; *recognitiones* 295–6; ordinance of Condom 298–304, 524; discussions on status 647, 650–1; process of Périgueux (1310–11) 291, 292; **V** 1, 4, 105, 115; lands granted to Gaveston 8; Plantagenet claim to 107; source of Anglo-French animosity 151; wheat shipment to (in 1338) 242; principality granted to Black Prince (1362) 267; duke of Gloucester's acquisition 469; **VI** 23, 67, 70, 74; Beaufort, Thomas, admiral of 104; English claim to territories in 110–11, 140; Bishop Beaufort's ultimatum 142; payment to keeper 222; administration 432; René of Anjou's land in 475; Suffolk's promise to deliver to Charles 492; **VII** 95, 96, 111, 131

Aquitaine, dukes of *see* William

Aquitania **Ia** 435, 448, 481

Arabi Pasha **XIV** 78, 79

Arabic numerals **III** 245; science 232, 244–6, 257

arable: farming **Ia** 281, 604, 613, 620–4, 626–8; treatment in early times **II** 280–2; regular shares 471–2, 474–5

Arabs: revolt **XV** 49, 56; Lloyd George 116; Palestine 152, 407; resist immigration of Jews 276

Aragon **III** 325, 381, 458; fief of the Holy See **IV** 252; connection with Provence and Toulouse 100, 101, 252; liberties and royal needs (1283) 255; Edward I and nobles of 269; **V** 428, 464; Louis XI tries

to prevent alliance with England **VI** 533; threatens to leave Louis 534; title to Naples **VII** 84; in Naples 112; Ferrante apprehensive 113; Catherine's succession rights 148; Henry VII's marriage projects 177, 187; Henry VIII's treaty 273; Charles's wish to secure 306

Aragon, Catherine (Katharine) of *see* Catherine

Aragon, kings of *see* Alfonso; James; John II

Aragon, Sanchia of, wife of Raymond VII of Toulouse **IV** 99, 100

Aragon, Yolanda of *see* Yolanda of Aragon ('Queen of Sicily')

Arbeitsgemeinschaft für Sachsenforschung **Ib** xx

arbitration: boards suggested (1264) **IV** 194; treaty with the United States **XIV** 448

Arbogastes (I), Flavius **Ia** 408–9, 416, 417, 496, 736

Arbogastes (II), bishop **Ia** 496

Arbury Road, Cambridge, cemetery **Ia** 700

Arbuthnot, Charles **XIII** 53, 107

Arbuthnot, John **X** 258

Arbuthnot, Dr John (1667–1735) **XI** 204, 390, 421

Arc, Joan of *see* Joan of Arc

Arcadia **VIII** 292–3

Arcadia conference **XV** 536–40, 551, 553

Arcadius, Emperor **Ia** 409, 415, 420, 428; marriage 417; government's involvement with Alaric 423, 427; death 430

arcani see areani

Arch, Joseph **XIV** 35, 117

archaeology: precision of dating **Ia** 196, 206–7, 232–4, 300; barbarian hypotheses 221–3, 333, 386–8; demolition and fire damage 232, 312–13; stratigraphy 296, 458; villas 602–3, 609–10;

archaeology (*cont.*)
cult practices 668, 705–7; Cogidubnus, appendix IV; historical value **II** 1, 38, 44; obsolescence of cremation 13; of Anglian, Saxon, and Jutish burials 13; Jutish burials 23, 59; Isle of Wight and Hants 23; Middle Thames 24–6; Peak District 41; Trent basin 41–2; Middle Anglia 42; East Anglia 50–2; Thames basin 55; Yorkshire 74–5; *see also* fire damage
Archangel **VII** 507; British forces **XV** 138
archbishops of Canterbury *see* Canterbury, archbishops of
archdeacons and archdeaconries: Anglo-Saxon **II** 440; Anglo-Norman 676; **IV** 445, 454; of Berkshire 448; publication of canons of councils 473; inquiries ordered by Pecham 475; clerical taxation 502; **VI** 277; *bursalitas* attributed to 277
Archenfield (Erging, Ircingafeld) **II** 213, 341, 573
Archer, John, member of council of duke of Exeter **VI** 419
Archer, William **XIV** 329
archers **IV** 422; **V** 239, 243, 253; Bruce's 34; at battle of Bannockburn: Welsh 35, English 38; Edward III's deployment of longbow after Bannockburn 39, 148, 150: at Halidon Hill 117; Sluys 129; Crécy 134–5; Neville's Cross 136; King John's tactics at Poitiers 139; training 148; grant redemption (1335) 155; practice by ordinary citizens 203, 241; Bourchier's company of one hundred 210; indenture 235–6; mounted 240; national sport 240; Cheshire 447, 449, 475, 481, 484, 487
archery, decay **VIII** 278
Arches, court, at St Mary-le Bow, as Court of Canterbury **IV** 492;

black book of 492; court official **VI** 265
arches, monumental **Ia** 232, 326
Archibald, earl of Douglas **VI** 35, 36, 45, 46; Henry Percy 48; son and heir 244; son-in-law *see* Buchan
architects **Ia** 157, 181, 390, 578, 667; under Agricola 142; *see also* Royal Institute of British Architects
architecture **Ia** 234, 302, 325–7, 342, 674; monumental scale 156; perpendicular or rectilinear style **VI** 647–50; porches 649–50; roofs 650; castle building 651–2; **VII** 591–7; **VIII** 303–5; **IX** 377–81; **X** 388–96; and landscape-gardening **XI** 147, 398, 401, 411–14; **XII** 340–2, 544–7; (to 1886) **XIV** 152–3, 154, 155–6; (to 1900) 323–5; (to 1914) 540–2; **XV** 178
archives, royal **VI** 36
archpriest controversy **VIII** 454–6
Arcis-sur-Aube, battle **XII** 561
Arcos, raid **XV** 255
Arcy, Thomas, Lord D' of Chiche, lord chamberlain of the household (1551) **VII** 649
Ardagh, bishop of (Henry Nony) **V** 301
Arden, forest of **II** 40, 43; law **III** 32; **V** 312
Arden of Feversham **VIII** 296–7
Ardennes, German offensive (1944) **XV** 589–91
Ardoch: fort **Ia** 151, 206; road 175
Ardres **VII** 310
ards **Ia** 8, 623 *see also* ploughs
Ards of Ulster **VIII** 394
Ardwick-le-Street **VII** 519
areani **Ia** 351–3, 377, 385
Argenson, René Louis, marquis d' (1694–1757) **XI** 263
Argentan **III** 134, 135, 307
Argentein, Sir William **VI** 473
Argentine, *medicus* **VI** 624, 625

Arghun, khan of Persia **IV** 252, 265
Argonne **VI** 245
Argyle, dukes of *see* Campbell, Archibald; Campbell, John
Argyle, earl of/marquess of *see* Campbell, Archibald
Argyll **V** 32
Argyll, Alexander of **IV** 657
Argyll, 8th duke of **XIV** 45
Argyll, dukes of: political influence **XII** 69, 70, 282; *see also* Campbell, Archibald; Campbell, John
Argyll, earl of *see* Campbell, Archibald
Argyll, John of **IV** 716
Argyll, marquis of *see* Campbell
Arians **Ia** 341, 450, 489, 494, 736; Constantius 357
Aricia, shrine **Ia** 673
Ariminum, Council of **Ia** 343, 727
Aristides, orator **Ia** 569
Aristippus, Sicilian scholar **III** 237
aristocrats: native British **Ia** 15–16, 57–8, 566, 599, 605; attitudes to business 57–8, 617, 631, 659–60, 662–3; contribution to public works 112, 142, 266, 331, 372; provincial and local 113, 153–5, 158–60, 235, 264, 277; rise and fall of Roman aristocrats 272, 320, 344–5; Roman 356, 370, 394, 489; religious adherence 356, 400, 409, 736, 739 — symbolic role 681–3 — burials 697–8, 731–2 — church 723–6; avoidance of duties 388, 430–1, 442, 463; enforcement of duty 398, 463, 728; reluctance to maintain army 439, 537; life-style in 4th and 5th cent. 498, 738–9 — post-Empire survival 449–53, 454 — merchant classes 457 — influential Britons 462–7 — Pelagians 470 — villas 596–7 — philosophy 709–10; *see also curiales*; estates; imperial courts; land-owners; magistracies; senatorial order

Aristotelianism **Ia** 716
Aristotle (384–322 BC) **III** 3, 232, 235, 236, 246; medieval commentaries of his *Politics* **IV** 521–2; **VI** 307; **IX** 361, 364; influence in 18th cent. **XI** 91
Ark Royal: aeroplanes cripple *Bismarck* **XV** 506; sunk 530
Arkwright, Sir Richard (1732–92), engineer, manufacturer and exploiter of inventions **XII** 333, 347, 509, 511
Arlen, Michael **XV** 311
Arles, kingdom: administrative centre **Ia** 429, 451, 518, 662 — Britons serving 447 — writ enforced 448; mint 446; Council 340, 723; Council of the Gauls 449; sieges 433–4, 443, 476; water-mill near 632; **III** 367; **IV** 98–9; plans for restoration 246–7
Arlington, 1st earl of *see* Bennet, Henry
armada, Spanish: original idea **VIII** 389; negotiations concerning 390, 391; Santa Cruz favours combined naval and military attack 392; Mendoza's military plan 392; king's plan assumes help from English Catholics 393; Parma's striking force 393; English preparations to oppose 394; instructions to Parma 394; partial destruction of Spanish fleet by Drake at Cadiz 395; departure from Lisbon 396; banner 396; strategy 397–8; disposition of English fleet 398–9; dispersal by gale 400; arrives off Lizard 400; pursued to Calais 401; attacked by English fire-ships 402; battle of Gravelines and escape into North Sea 402–3; reason for defeat 402–3; rumours of whereabouts 403; authentic news of remnant and arrival at Santander 404; Philip II's reception of the

armada(*cont.*)
  news 404; Rome shows no sympathy 404
Armageddon: naval, expected by Fisher **XV** 6; battle (1918) 49, 110
Armagh, archbishop of **III** 222; **XI** 293–4; *see also* Fitzralph, Richard; Gelasius; Palatio, Octavian de
Armagh: book **III** 302; primacy 304; see 304; **XV** 597
Armagnac **IV** 291, 292
Armagnac, Bonne d' *see* Bonne d'Armagnac
Armagnac, count of **IV** 293; *see also* Albret, Bernard d'; John I, count of Armagnac
Armagnac, Gascon family of **VI** 107
Armagnacs: offered (1412) to Henry IV for recovery of Aquitaine **VI** 113; Henry V's use of this (1415) 114; party led by Bernard VII 139; bidding against Burgundians (1414–15) 139; agreement with (1412), copies circulated to Council of Constance 146; internecine war with Burgundians 174; control Pont de l'Arche until captured by Henry V 174; control Marne and Seine (July 1418) 175; seize Compiègne 175; recreating strength on and beyond Loire (Feb. and Mar. 1419) 177; Spanish and Scottish negotiations, and consolidation in Touraine 177; garrisoning Maine frontier 178; excluded from truce (15 May 1419) between Henry and king and queen of France 180; centres of resistance (1419) 183; in region between Paris and Chartres (1424) 239; infiltrating from right bank of Seine 239; on north bank of Somme estuary 239
Armenia **Ia** 110; Lloyd George **XV** 116
Arminianism, opposed by Puritans **IX** 71–7

Arminians **IX** 44; support prerogative 32, 74–5, 94–5; tenets 71–2, 213
Arminius **Ia** 374
Armistice: Russo-German (1917) **XV** 94; with enemy powers (1918) 110, 111–13; Franco-German (1940) 488, 493; British conditions with Germany (1940) 489
Armistice Day **XV** 163, 164, 594
Armorica **Ia** 24; independence 434, 444–5, 448; St Germanus' appeal 449, 477, 481; British settlement 492–3; *see also* Brittany; Normandy
armour and arms **Ia** 74, 77; development **IV** 549, 553; **V** 238–41
Arms, Assize of *see* Assize of Arms
arms, coats and rolls **IV** 551–2
army (to AD 500) **Ia** 505–30; security and intelligence 27, 36, 374–5, 377, 419, 571; discipline 54, 60, 391, 683 — systems 75–6 — Albinus 217 — arrogance 242–3 — order restored 379–81 — politically unreliable 439–40; pre-Roman in Britain 76–7; political importance 164–5, 230, 310, 402 — civil wars 129–36 — Trojan favoured 154–5, 169 — Commodus 211–12 — Caracalla 242–3 — Tetrarchy 307 — reconstruction 324; recruitment and manpower 197, 376, 450, 470, 477 — barbarian incorporation 311–12, 418–19, 424–6, 480–93, 509–10 — food production 618–30; strategy and campaigns 198, 200, 228, 239 — auxiliaries 74–5, 260–1 — British conquest 242 — troops placated 247–8 — Welsh security 254–5 — political influence 271 — Constans' British visit 349–55 — regrading 367 — pagan regime 409 — Hunnish threat 482–3; pay 230, 425, 438, 440,

26

660; and agriculture 237–8, 511, 613–14; unpopularity 253, 439–40; reforms, Diocletian 291–5, 331 — Constantine 333–5, 347, 349–51; supplies 332, 337, 529–30, 615–22, 659–60 — grain control 58, 76 — intra-mural zone 613 — pottery 641; towns 388, 511, 595, 605, 612–14 — garrisons 330 — artillery 390–1 — mining 633–4; departure of troops from 390–410, 422–4, 425–7, 435–40; sub-Roman 434, 438, 471, 491–3; religion 667–71, 683–6, 701, 711–13, 721–5, 736; *see also* artillery; *auxilia*; barbarians; cavalry; cohorts; *comitiatenses*; conscription; *foederati*; *laeti*; legions; military; veterans

army (*c.* AD 550–1087): composition under King Harold **II** 582–4; assembled 588; disbanded 588

army (1216–1307), Edward I's **IV** 603, 612–13, 686–7; contrast with Henry III 409; numbers and weapons 411, 422, 445; paid levies 422, 519–20; vanquishes Llywelyn 428; recruit source 439–43; development of paid army as reflection of social change 542–56, 669–70, 681; Welsh rebellion 649; war with Flanders 666, 668–70, 678–82; levies from clergy 680–1; war with Scotland 688–94; Galloway campaign 700; feudal host at Berwick 706; Scots submit 708–10; siege of Stirling 710–11; and Robert Bruce 715; *see also* feudal host; knights; money fief; service, military

army, feudal: summoned against Welsh (1263), then directed against Lord Edward in Windsor (1263) **IV** 175, 176; general levy (1264) 192–3

army, English (1415–22): recruitment of **VI** 143; indentures, master rolls and Exchequer procedure 143; king's retinue in Agincourt campaign 144; tradesmen in 144; period of service of 144; cost of maintaining 144–5; size on first expedition to France 148; number at Agincourt 154; use of archers 155; mobility 155; French prisoners taken 155–6; losses at Agincourt 156

army (1603–60): under Mansfeld **IX** 36, 60; Cadiz expedition 61–2; expedition to Isle of Ré 65–6; disorders 67; plot 101; how armies were raised (1642) 130–1; formation of New Model 138–40; scheme to reduce 145–6; political intervention 145–52; dissatisfied with Rump 171–3; draws up Instrument of Government 176; debates on control 178–9; arrears of pay 187–8; dissensions 189; champions toleration 194; intervenes in politics 237–52; Restoration 259–60

army (1660–1714): pay due to Monck's army under Charles II **X** 4, 6; James II's (1688) 132; under James II 122, 168; under William III 138, 151–2, 168–9, 178; Crown and parliament 152; growth 167–9; operations in French war 167–74; reduction after the peace 188; compulsory service 261; Scottish professional soldiers 264; in Ireland 305, 307; Irish soldiers transported to France 309, 315

army (1714–60) **XI** 213–22; impressment 61, 221, 357; police duties 213; numbers 214, 335; pay and pensions 214–15, 217, 338; barracks 215; officers 215–18; administration 217–18; reforms 217–18; drilling and tactics 218–19; artillery 219–20; engineers 220; Woolwich

army (1714–60) (*cont.*)
Academy 220; recruitment 220–1; militia 221, 356, 365; medical services 221, 392; Highland regiments 281, 283, 356; North American stations 318; supply 334–5; Chelsea pensioners 338; Articles of War and court martial 352; *see also* Ireland; subsidies

army (1760–1815): state of **XII** 363, 369, 415, 481; recruitment schemes 365, 376, 415, 418, 454; Windham, short enlistments 437; reductions (1764) 103, (1802) 412

army, British (1815–70): condition (1815–54) **XIII** 180, 265–71; reforms after Crimean war 291–3; *see also under* Crimean war

army (1870–1914): 20,000 men added (1870) **XIV** 9; Cardwell's reforms 8–16; commander-in-chief put under secretary of state 9; abolition of purchase 9–12; flogging 9; shortening of service 13; first breech-loaders 14; regiments made territorial 14; linked battalions 15; muzzle-loading cannon 15; Hartington Commission 290; general staff plan omitted 291; Campbell-Bannerman's attitude 291; commission on South African War 292–3; Haldane's reforms 385–96, 525–6; general staff 395; Expeditionary Force 396; Territorial Force 396; Officers' Training Corps 396; mobilization reform 525

army (1914–45): Kitchener's **XV** 20; strength (1916) 59; conservative character 62; songs 62; dependent on horse transport 109; medical services 121; mechanized transport 122; in Ireland 155; leaves Ireland 159; Geddes axe cuts 184; neglected between the wars 231–2; non-existent as European force 365; 'limited liability' 375; 32-division target for 433, 460; German air force threat 470; disputes over strategic use 481; strength doubled 490; excessive requirements 509; put at end of queue 512; comparison with First World War 515

army, French: at Agincourt **VI** 156; cavalry against English archers 155; footmen 155

army, Norman *see* knight service

army, Old English *see* ceorl; fyrd service; housecarles; thegns

Army Bureau of Current Affairs **XV** 550

Arnaud, Marshall **XIII** 275–8

Arnaud-Guilhem **VI** 188

Arne, Thomas Augustine (1710–78) **XI** 305, 417

Arnemuiden **VIII** 339

Arnesby (Leics.) **VI** 376

Arnhem, failure to take (1944) **XV** 583

Arni, battle (1782) **XII** 316

Arnold, American general **XV** 537

Arnold, Benedict (1748–1801) **XII** 202, 203, 216–18

Arnold, John, merchant of London **VI** 110

Arnold, Matthew **XIII** 481, 531, 533, 623; biography 499; poetry 538; **XIV** 142, 145, 362

Arnold, Robert, of London: harbours Sir John Oldcastle **VI** 132

Arnold, Dr Thomas **XIII** 486–7, 498, 507; biography 486; **XV** 313

Arnold-Forster, H. O. **XIV** 362, 396

Arnould, Cardinal **V** 29

Arnulf, bishop of Lisieux **III** 216, 334, 357

Arnulf, count of Flanders **II** 344

Arnulf de Hesdin **II** 629

Arques (Seine-Inf.) **II** 558; **III** 335, 382, 384, 430, 432; castle 161; **VI** 152

Arraignment of Paris **VIII** 296

Arran, earls of *see* Hamilton, James; Stewart, James

Arras (Pas-de-Calais): medallion **Ia** 310; **III** 86, 91; constable **IV** 11; **VI** 111, 260; formality of council 143; Burgundian estates 183; Anglo-French peace 261–2; delays peace with Hansa 358; Suffolk a delegate 473; **VII** 116, 598; **VIII** 346; **X** 220; battle (1917) **XV** 81; (1940) 486

Arras (Yorks.), manor **VI** 337

Arras, treaties: (1429) **VI** 256, 465, 487; between Louis XI and Maximilian (1482) **VI** 587; **VII** 85, 99, 101; between Louis XII and Philip (1499) 152; *see also* treaties

Arras Culture **Ia** 10, 670

arras work **VIII** 272

Array, commissions **IV** 554

Arrentation **IV** 546

Arrian **Ia** 513

Arsenic and Old Lace **XV** 542

Arsuf **III** 361

art: Iron Age **Ia** 15; Mediterranean 81; Augustan 682; funerary 697; criticism of Victorian age **XIV** 152–5; rival diagnoses 322; *see also* architecture; arts and crafts; paintings; Royal Society of Art; sculpture

Art Collections Fund, National **XIV** 543

art galleries, multiplication of public **XIV** 326

Art of Navigation, Martin Cortes **VIII** 238

Arteveldt, Jacques von **IV** 669

Arteveldt, James van **V** 127–8, 130, 131, 132

Arteveldt, Philip van **V** 430

Arthur (Artorius) **Ib** 15–16

Arthur, count of Brittany **VI** 222

Arthur, duke of Brittany (1305–12) **IV** 598

Arthur, King **Ia** 485; in history and legend **II** 3–4; legend **III** 254–6; his crown **IV** 429, 516; and

Arthurianism 515–16; **V** 97, 150, 251; Malory **VI** 656–8; 'Frensshe Booke' 656

Arthur, Prince of Wales (1486–1502): b. Winchester (1486) **VII** 68; marriage to Catherine 81, 115, 148, 172, 173; regent (1492) 108; death (1502) 169, 174; marriage consummated 175, 328; Philip's daughter 182; knighted (1489) 192, 215; president, Council at Ludlow 204, 366, 385; warden in the north (1489) 205; tutor 242; cupboard 597

Arthur, son of Geoffrey of Brittany **III** 281; overlordship of wardship 342; appointed heir by Richard I 355; Walter of Coutance's role 356; betrothed to Tancred's daughter 360; accession of King John 378–9, 381; murdered 382–3, 483; **IV** 92, 116, 242

Arthurian legend *see* Arthur, King

articles: in opposition to Edward I's Flemish campaign **IV** 682; of bill presented to Edward I at Lincoln (1301) 704–5

Articles, Forty-two and Thirty-nine **VII** 521–2

articuli super cartas: *cleri* statute (1316) **IV** 484; (1300) 697, 698, 700–1, 704; **V** 9

Artificers, Statute **IX** 294

artifices **Ia** 314, 359; *see also* craftsmen

artillery **Ia** 74, 281, 300, 325, 387; use of army manpower 390–1; animal husbandry 620

artisans **Ia** 457, 663

Artois **III** 361, 376, 454; **IV** 12; **V** 134, 143, 350, 432; Robert of, Edward III's ally 115, 120, 124, 126, 138; forged claim to Artois 120; attacks St Omer 129; **VI** 178, 263, 588; estates 250; **VII** 85, 110, 316; **VIII** 346

Artois, Charles d', count of Eu **VI** 141, 222, 257

Artois, Jean d', count of Eu: Congress of Arras **VI** 260

Artois, Robert of **IV** 239, 240, 241, 242; command of French forces in Gascony (1296–7) 649, 666

Artorius Castus, L. **Ia** 213

arts and crafts **XIV** 325, 540; *see also* art

Arun, river **Ia** 627

Arundel (Sussex): castle **II** 615, 628; **III** 117, 138

Arundel, Charles **VIII** 362

Arundel, countess of *see* Eleanor, countess of Arundel

Arundel, earl of: joins Edward IV at Pontefract **VI** 557; *see also* Albini I, William de; Albini II, William de; Fitzalan, earls of Arundel; Fitzalan, Edmund; Fitzalan, Henry; Fitzalan, Richard; Fitzalan, Thomas; Howard, Thomas; Sussex, earls of

Arundel, John, see of Durham **VI** 270

Arundel, Sir John **V** 405

Arundel, Sir John of Cornwall **VI** 572

Arundel, Lady *see* Lovell, Maud

Arundel, Lord, duke of Touraine **VI** 484

Arundel, Thomas, bishop of Ely (1378–88) **V** 471, 473, 474, 478; archbishop of Canterbury (1396–7) 298; archbishop of York (1388–96) 299, 462, 465; with Richard II at Eltham 443–4; Suffolk's trial 445; on commission (1386) 451; chancellor (1386–9, 1391–6) 462; chancery reforms 462; removed from chancery 464; provokes king 470; on Richard II in Ireland 472; deprived 480; in France with Henry of Lancaster 491; interview with Richard II at Conway 493; support of Henry of Lancaster 495–6, 522; Oxford university 503; support of Henry Lanark 522

Arundel, Thomas FitzAlan, archbishop of Canterbury: **VI** 271; dispossessed 1; Richard's abdication 11, 13, 14; Henry's title to crown 15–16; chancellorship 17–18, 86, 105, 112; Lollardy 19, 94–9; appealed of treason 21, 59; Richard's fate determined in secrecy 22; Henry's son declared prince of Wales 23; Thomas Langley's promotion 33; Scrope's trial 61; Calais crisis (1407) 87; Henry's illness 99–100; confidant of prince of Wales 102; English position in Aquitaine 113; friend of king 116; humanity 273; preaching constitutions 283; Lynn mediation 388; king's councillor 429; book collection 666; interviews Margery Kempe 686

Arundel Society **XIII** 594

Arundell, Henry, 3rd Baron Arundell of Wardour **X** 123

Arundell, Sir Thomas **VII** 492

Arviragus **Ia** 165

Arwe *see* Orwell, river

Arwystli, cantref of West Powys, claimed by Llywelyn ap Gruffydd (1278–82) **IV** 417–20

Asaf-ud-daula, nawab of Oudh **XII** 310, 318

Ascham, Roger (1515–68), Edward VI's tutor **VII** 479; secretary 487; St John's College 571; animadversions 573; liberal ideas 576; approach to Latin 577; *Toxophilus* (1545) 583; **VIII** 4, 278, 279, 324–7

Asclepiodotus **Ia** 307, 308–9, 320

Ascot **XV** 551

asdic **XV** 461; betrayed by French to Germans 504

Asenby (N. Yorks.), manor **VI** 337

Ashanti: kingdom **XIII** 375; war (1873–4) **XIV** 27–9; campaign (1896) 226; revolt (1900) 382; railway to Kumasi 382

Ashbee, C. R. **XIV** 540
Ashbourne (Derby.) **V** 370
Ashburton (Devon) **V** 500; **VI** 649
Ashburton, Lord *see* Baring, Alexander; Dunning, John
Ashby de la Zouch (Leics.) **VI** 339
Ashby v. White **X** 254
Ashdown (Berks.) **II** 66; battle 249
Ashdown Forest **VI** 10
Ashenden, John **V** 508
Ashfield, Richard **IX** 239
Ashford, manor of (Derby.) **IV** 326
Ashill, well-shaft **Ia** 691
Ashingdon (Assandun)(Essex) **II** 731; battle 391; **VI** 345
Ashley (Wilts.) **III** 61
Ashley, 1st Baron *see* Cooper, Anthony Ashley
Ashley, Nicolas **VII** 145
Ashmole, Elias (1617–92) **X** 414; **XI** 394
Ashton, Christopher **VII** 146
Ashton, Sir Robert, treasurer (1375–7) **V** 386–7, 395
Ashton, fonts **Ia** 729, 730
Ashton-under-Lyme, Aitken's seat at, needed for Stanley **XV** 77
Asia **VII** 224, 226
Asia Minor **Ia** 109, 234, 364, 673–4, 717; Pergamum 114; **III** 244; **VI** 353
Asiatic Society **XII** 308
Asiento **X** 221, 250; **XI** 177, 196, 207, 265, 314–15
Aske, Robert, Yorkshire rising **VII** 389, 390, 391; executed (1537) 392
Askes **VII** 414
Askew, Anne **VII** 428
Askham (Yorks.) **III** 92
Askrigg (N. Yorks.) **VI** 328
Askwith, Lord **XIV** 441
Aspatria (Cumbria), manor **VI** 9
Aspern, battle (1809) **XII** 478
Asquith, Herbert Henry, 1st earl of Oxford and Asquith **XIV** 208, 210, 223, 390, 399; biography 210; declines Liberal leadership

in the Commons 239, 249; attacked for Featherstone shooting 299; chancellor of the Exchequer 384; sole conflict with Campbell-Bannerman 392; budget (1906) 396; becomes premier 406; personality at that time 407–8; budget (1908) 408; supports Lloyd George on budget 416; dealings with Edward VII over 'guarantees' 419; draft list of 250 new peers 431; meets rail unions 441; miners' strike 442; attitude to Carson's movement 453–4; to Redmond 454; comment on German offer 462; memorandum to the king 474; interviews with Bonar Law 474; negotiation with Carson 474; announces proposals for Ulster 476; becomes war minister 479; Germany's Belgium policy 492; favours intervention 492; neglect of the Press 492, 526, 573–4; biography **XV** 3; ultimatum to Germany 3; summons council of war 6; agrees British Expeditionary Force shall go Maubeuge 7; advises Kitchener 10; negative attitude 14; parliamentary position 15; Home Rule Act 16; promises not to coerce Ulster 17; against conscription 20; attitude of Irish and Labour 27; challenged by Lloyd George 28, 466; fall of Liberal government 30; Coalition prime minister 32, 34; abstention from King's Pledge 37; on Suvla bay 45; sends Kitchener to Near East 46; sets up war committee 47; conscription 53–5; in Dublin 57; yields to Lansdowne 57, 71–2; declining authority 58; conflict with Lloyd George and Law 65–9, 224; resigns 69; leads Opposition 92; hesitates over franchise reform 93; women's suffrage 94;

Asquith, Herbert Henry (*cont.*)
approves Lloyd George's statement of war aims 97; supports Robertson 98, 99; named in Black Book 103; Maurice debate 105, at armistice 114; refuses to join Lloyd George's government 125; complains of 'coupon' 126; demands reparations 127; on 'Troubles' 155; distribution of honours 188; mistakes repeated by Lloyd George 189, 192; Curzon desertion 195, 202; general election (1922) 197; undisputed Liberal leader 208; puts Labour in office 209; hesitates to attack Russian treaty 218; Campbell case 218–19; defeat and passage to Lords 220; committee of imperial defence 228; prime minister 231; angry with Lloyd George over general strike 246; resigns Liberal leadership 252; Neville Chamberlain more generous than 475

Asquith, Margot: on Kitchener **XV** 47; named in Black Book 103

Assam, Japanese failure **XV** 586

Assandun *see* Ashingdon (Essex)

assart **III** 34, 49, 51

Asser, bishop of Sherborne **II** 271–3, 439

Assertio Septem Sacramentorum **VII** 311

assessments, of clerical revenue **IV** 221, 498, 505, 509; *see also* taxation

Assheton, Sir Ralph **VI** 626

Assheton, Sir William **VI** 449

Assier, Rigaud d', bishop of Winchester (1320–33) **V** 275, 286

assignment of revenue **IV** 524; English customs to citizens of Bayonne 650

Assize of Arms **III** 41, 339, 369–70; and distraint of knighthood **IV** 552–3

Association, island of **IX** 338

Astarte **Ia** 667

Astley, Sir Jacob **IX** 142

Aston (Yorks.), manor **VI** 323

Aston, John **V** 518, 519, 520

Aston Rowant (Oxon.) **III** 51

Astor, John J., buys *The Times* **XV** 193, 418

Astor, Lady Nancy, elected MP **XV** 128

Astor, Viscount: and *Observer* **XV** 194; dismisses Garvin 573

Astrakhan **VII** 507; **VIII** 238, 239

astrology **VIII** 308–9; **IX** 369–70

astronomer royal **X** 412

astronomy **VIII** 307–8; **IX** 369; **X** 373; **XI** 379–81

Astrophel and Stella **VIII** 288

Astures **Ia** 511

Astwood, Thomas **VII** 165, 166

Atbara, railway **XIV** 382

Ateius Coceianus **Ia** 684

Ath **X** 174

Athanasian Creed **Ia** 357

Athanasius, St **VI** 678

Athaulf **Ia** 431, 446, 447

Athée, Gerard de **III** 372, 477; **IV** 22

Atheist's Tragedy **VIII** 301

Athelhelm of Jumièges, abbot of Abingdon **II** 677

Athelm, archbishop of Canterbury **II** 446

Athelney (Æthelingaig) (Som.) **II** 255, 731; monastery 271, 445, 455

Athelstan **Ia** 495

Athelstan, bishop of Hereford **II** 425, 573

Athelstan, King: style of Athelstan's solemn charters, quoted **II** 322, 353–4; laws quoted 316, 354–5; educated in Mercia 339; accession 339; marriages of sisters 339, 344, 344–7; overlordship in Britain 340–2; Welsh princes at his court 341–2; attacks Scotland by land and sea 342; wins battle of Brunanburh 343; foreign relations 343–7, 443–4 —with France 344–7 —with Germany

345-7 —with Northmen on Loire 348 —with Brittany 348 —with Norway 349; royal style 349; councils 349-51; attended by magnates from remote parts 351-2; personality and achievements 354-7; death 356

Athelstan, Mercian scholar **II** 271

Athelstan, under-king of Kent **II** 236

Athelstan the Half-King **II** 351

Athenaeum, absorbed by *Nation* **XV** 310

Athenry, battle of **V** 44

Athens **Ia** 364, 672, 675

Athequa, George de, bishop of Llandaff **VII** 350

Atherstone (War.) **VI** 643

Athlone **X** 308, 309

Athol, earl of: appointed warden of Scotland north of Forth (1304) **IV** 711; Bruce's coronation (1306) 714; hanged 716; *see also* David of Strathbogie; Ginkel

Atholl, duke of *see* Murray, John

Atholl, earls of *see* Stuart, John

Atholl, marquess of *see* Murray, John

atillator **IV** 303

Atkin, Edmund (*fl.* mid-18th cent.), and North American Indians **XI** 321

Atkinson, Matthew (d. 1729), Roman Catholic priest **XI** 74

Atlantic: ocean navigation **VII** 188; islands 224; 'blue ribbon' **XIV** 279, 505; battle (1941-3) **XV** 505, 564

Atlantic Charter (1941): made **XV** 529-30, 536; terms 534-5; unconditional surrender 562

Atlantic fleet, Invergordon mutiny **XV** 296

Atlantic Triangle, trade system **XII** 20-2, 289

Atlantis **VII** 224, 264

Atlas Mountains **Ia** 110

Atlay, Dr, bishop **XIV** 307

atomic bomb: refugee scientists **XV** 491-2; used against Japan 598; reasons for use 601

Atrebates: in Gaul **Ia** 27, 143; British 43, 56, 59, 583; coins 43, 47; Verica 70, 90; client kingdom 91; **Ib** 149-50, 152, 160, 167, 172

Atrius, Quintus **Ia** 33

Attacotti **Ia** 369, 375

Attainder, Act of **X** 306

Attalus III, King **Ia** 114

Atterbury, Francis (1662-1372), bishop of Rochester **XI** 73, 77, 82, 86, 291; action following Queen Anne's death 150; implicated in Jacobite plot, banished (1722) 182-4

Attica **Ia** 667

Atticus, Aulus **Ia** 148

Attila **Ia** 448, 475, 481-3, 486, 489

Attlee, Clement: biography **XV** 199; survivor of lost generation 120; condemns armaments 199; member of Simon Commission 254; Liberal unity 281; sits on Labour front bench 328; no agreement on foreign policy 360; combines support for League and disarmament 368; grudgingly supports Covenant 381; becomes Labour leader 382; opposes rearmament 393; opposition to arms estimates 414; blesses Chamberlain's mission to Munich 429; opposes conscription 445; absent at outbreak of war 452; favours Halifax as prime minister 473; meets Chamberlain 474; in War Cabinet from first to last 477; Churchill's deputy 478, 509; Defence Committee (Operations) 481; chairs Cabinet committees 482; against formal rejection of Hitler's peace offer 489; becomes deputy prime minister 546; succeeds Anderson as lord president 574; hesitates to end coalition 595; maintains

Attlee (*cont.*)
peacetime Cabinet 596; becomes prime minister 597
attributi **Ia** 115
Attwood, Thomas **XIII** 134, 137, 607
Atwater (Water, Waters), John, mayor of Cork **VII** 117, 133, 144, 165; son 165
Atwater, William, bishop of Lincoln (1514–21) **VII** 586
Aubenas, Raymond d' **V** 114
Aubers Ridge, battle **XV** 26
Aubigny, Sieur de *see* Stewart, Bernard
Aubrey, John **VI** 649; **IX** 269–70, 386
Aubrey de Coucy, earl of Northumbria **II** 614
Auch, city and ecclesiastical province of **IV** 292
Auchinleck, Sir C.: biography **XV** 527; becomes commander-in-chief, Middle East 527; refuses to take offensive 528, 554; orders desert offensive 530; defeated in Libya 541; takes over command at front 555; displaced 556
Auchmuty, Samuel (1756–1822) **XII** 489
Auckland, Baron *see* Eden, William
Auckland, earl of *see* Eden, George
auctoritas **Ia** 49–50, 80, 287, 365, 572
Aucwrweew-en-Béarn **IV** 242
Audacious, sunk **XV** 13
Audemar, count of Angoulême **III** 379–80
Auden, Wystan Hugh: representative poet **XV** 311; leads revolt 347; anti-Fascism 395; on Spain 396; departs for United States 437
auditors: bailiffs' accounts **IV** 366–7; the 104 auditors in parliament, of Scottish succession case (1292) 605–8; Flemish cases under treaty of Montreuil (1274) 623; Spanish and Portuguese

complaints against merchants of Bayonne (1293) 644; cases at Montreuil (1305–6) 657, 658
Audley, Baron *see* Touchet, James; Tuchet
Audley, Edmund, bishop of Salisbury (1502–24) **VII** 175
Audley, Hugh, earl of Gloucester (1337–47) **V** 47; Middle Party 52; Partition of Gloucester estates 58–9; imprisoned in Berkhamsted castle 73; earl of Gloucester 153, 165
Audley, Hugh of **IV** 283
Audley, Sir Humphrey **VI** 569
Audley, James of **IV** 190, 196
Audley, Sir James **V** 252
Audley, James, Lord **VI** 234
Audley, John, Lord **VI** 515, 634
Audley, Sir Thomas, Baron Audley (1538): chancellor (1533) **VII** 355, 646; Treason Bill 360; land received 400; parliamentary oration (1542) 433, 441; Magdalene College founded 570; speaker of House of Commons (1529) 653
Audley estates **V** 4
Aufidius Lemnus, M., freedman **Ia** 688
Aufidius Maximus **Ia** 687
Augbsburg **VII** 599
Auge (Calvados) **VI** 174
Aughrim **X** 309
Augsburg **VI** 356; Confession (1530) **VII** 340, 382; **VIII** 31; league of (1686) 128, 134; negotiations at (1759) **XII** 73
Augst, temple and theatre **Ia** 695
augur **Ia** 702
Augusta (London) **Ia** 317, 575
Augusta of Saxe-Gotha, princess of Wales, mother of George III **XI** 340, 421
augustales **Ia** 580, 653
Augustalis (Romano-Briton) **Ia** 688
Augustine, St, of Canterbury: **Ia** 340, 452, 724; **Ib** 1, 20, 157, 173, 184; mission established 128;

Austria (*cont.*)
380; incorporated into Germany 413, 415, 419, 424, 441; Halifax's assurances to Hitler 422; *see also* Charles VI; Maria Theresa

Austria, archduke of *see* Charles

Austria, dukes of *see* Leopold

Austria-Hungary: **XIII** 195, 197–200, 217–18, 223, 227; and Italy 202–3, 245–8, 298–304; eastern question 233–5, 237–8; slave-ships 240–1; Crimean war 254, 259, 261–4, 288–91; Franco-Austrian war 301; Polish rebellion 315–16; Schleswig-Holstein question 319–23; Austro-Prussian war 323–5; policy **XIV** 42, 46, 194–6; joins Salisbury's Mediterranean pact 198; annexation of Bosnia-Herzegovina 410; threatens ultimatum to Serbia 411; interest in the Balkans 465; keeps Balkan Allies off Adriatic 467; champions Albania 467; project to attack Serbia 469; ultimatum to Serbia 486; declaration of war against **XV** 2; attempt to make peace with 115; Lloyd George does not wish to destroy 97; ceases to exist 113; Fourteen Points and 119; Grey thinks Serbia should yield to 370; administration takes place of government; *see also* Hötzendorf, Conrad von

Autun **Ia** 314, 354, 375; temple 671

Auvergne **Ia** 453; **III** 318, 329, 330, 347; **VI** 241

Auvergne, count of **III** 463

Auxerre **Ia** 448, 462–3, 479; **III** 92; **VI** 248, 257; *bailliage* 191, 239; county 263

Auxerre, bishop of *see* Germanus

auxilia (auxiliaries) **Ia** 34, 74–5, 255, 374, 508–10, 528, 583; campaigns 27, 101–7, 120–1, 133–4, 140, 146–7; status 102, 293, 335, 583; changes in organization 248–9,

260–1; fort garrisons 149–50, 163, 221, 231, 260; recruitment 167, 197, 208, 220, 260–1

auxilia (Late Roman élite units) **Ia** 335, 366–7, 404

auxiliary settlements **Ia** 208

'Auxis' **XV** 155

Avaux, count d' **X** 134

Avenches, *civitas* at **Ia** 581

Aversa, French defeat (1528) **VII** 319

Avesnes, John of, count of Hainault **IV** 622; and Philip IV of France 664, 665

aviary **Ia** 614

Avicenna **VIII** 312

Avidius Cassius **Ia** 207–9, 212

Avidius Quietus, T. **Ia** 163–4

Avignon, imperial city, united under Charles II of Sicily, later acquired by the papacy **IV** 99, 272–3; negotiations at (1344) 652

Avignon, papacy **V** 118, 219; Middle Party 52; Montagu's mission to 101; Clement VI 130; Urban V 142; Clement VII 146; Edward's confidential mission 167; Clement V 272; 'Babylonish Captivity' and Great Schism (1378) 272, 405; patronage 273; benefices 277–9; provisions 281; William of Ockham 509

Avison, Charles (*c.*1710–70), musician **XI** 417

Avon **Ia** 43, 68

Avon, river (Bristol) **Ib** 161, 168, 170, 172; map 2 xxx; map 3 xxxi; (Salisbury) 161; map 3 xxxi; (War.) 139; **III** 163

Avonmouth, port **Ia** 585

Avranches (Manche) **III** 120, 136; capture 160, 384; ecclesiastical jurisdiction 216, 218–19; **VI** 173, 177, 190; diocese 192; German counter-attack (1944) **XV** 582

Avranches, Hugh of, earl of Chester *see* Hugh I; Hugh II

Avranchin **III** 104

Axbridge (Som.) **II** 533, 535; **III** 85

Axel **VIII** 368

Axholme, Isle of (Lincs.) **II** 603; rebels in (1265–6) **IV** 206, 208, 210; **VII** 36, 40

Ayala, Pedro de, Spanish ambassador **VII** 165, 179, 224; in Scotland 138, 144

Aylesbury (Ægelesburg) (Bucks.) **Ib** 165–7, 170; map 3 xxxi; appendix II; **II** 27, 536, 731

Aylesbury, Franciscans *see* Franciscans of Aylesbury

The Aylesbury Men **X** 254

Aylesdon, Robert, treasurer (1332–4), keeper of the privy seal (1334) **V** 154

Aylesford (Ægelesford, Agæles threp) (Kent) **Ib** appendix I(a); **II** 16; lathe 499, 731

Aylesford-Swarling Culture **Ia** 11

Aylmer, John (1521–94), tutor to Lady Jane Grey **VII** 571, 583; bishop of London (1577)

Aylsham (Norfolk) **V** 9

Ayr: castle **IV** 694, 707; garrison 695; **VII** 144

Ayscough, William, bishop of Salisbury **VI** 495, 496

Ayscue, Sir George **IX** 223, 344

Ayton (Yorks.) **VI** 9; silk manufacturer **XII** 511

Ayton, treaty **VII** 115, 147, 148

Azay le Rideau (Touraine) **III** 346

Azim-ul-Umara **XII** 382

Azincourt *see* Agincourt

Azo **III** 247

Azores **VII** 224; **VIII** 353, 395, 411, 412, 426; Portugal allows use **XV** 564

B

Baa, *bastide* nr. Bordeaux **IV** 309–10

Babington, Anthony, Babington plot **VIII** 380–2

Babington, William, Chief Justice of the Common Pleas **VI** 343

Bablockhythe (Oxon.) **V** 453

Babwell (Suffolk): Franciscan friary **IV** 363; Franciscan convent **VI** 484

Babylon, name for Cairo **IV** 82

Babylonish captivity **VII** 336

Bacaudae **Ia** 283, 287, 444–5; *see also* peasants

Bacchus *see* Dionysus

Bach, Johann Sebastian **X** 407

Bachelors **IV** 152, 153–4

Bachelor's Walk, shooting **XIV** 481, 494

bachinator **IV** 303

Backbarrow Company's ironworks, Furness **XI** 117

Backwell, Edward **IX** 286

Bacon, Anthony **VIII** 421, 423

Bacon, Sir Francis, Lord Verulam, Viscount St Albans (1561–1626): history of Henry VII **VII** 7, 46, 593; sceptical of Henry's sincerity 52; on Henry's behaviour 54; furtiveness 55; 'coronation pardon' 62; treasury demands 63; Lambert Simnel 69, 73; Innocent VIII's Bull 77; foreign policy 82; Northumberland's death 91; 'parliament of war' 106; Warbeck uncertainty 117–18, 120; Clifford and Stanley 122; Warbeck conspiracy fails 123; Audley's nature 141; Darcy Commission 146; Scottish treaty 162; Curzon and Suffolk conspiracy 168; marriage prospects 177; 'Intercursus Malus' 186; mercantilist policy 214; Empson and Dudley 216; savings 218; estimation of Henry

VII 230; triple subsidy debate **VIII** 229–30; on plantation 246–7; on windows 304; view of Spain 407; protégé of Essex 421–5, 440–1; *Observations on a Libel* 453; on knighthood **IX** 1; assessment of Cecil 2; case against purveyance 4; urges union 9; on licentious speech 23; impeachment 26; on religion 71; yeomanry 282; scientist 362–3, 410–11; curricula of Oxford and Cambridge 356; pleasure of a garden 383–4; works of literature 390, 406; lord chancellor **XI** 65

Bacon, John (1381–5) **V** 437

Bacon, John (1740–99), sculptor **XI** 402

Bacon, Nathaniel **X** 347

Bacon, Sir Nicholas **VII** 479; **VIII** 10, 14, 27, 96, 144

Bacon, Robert, Dominican **IV** 55

Bacon, Roger **IV** 230

Bacon, Sir Roger **V** 345, 417, 419

Bacons' ironworks, Merthyr Tydvil, Glamorgan **XI** 117

Baconthorpe, John, Carmelite **VI** 297

Badajoz **XII** 453, 482, 487, 493

Badajoz, bishop of, imperial ambassador **VII** 290

Badbury **Ib** 159–60; map 3 xxxi

Badbury Rings (Baddanbyrig) (Dorset) **II** 321, 731

Badby, John, Lollard **VI** 95

Badda **Ib** 159

Baddanbyrig *see* Badbury Rings (Dorset)

Badecanwiellon *see* Bakewell (Derby.)

Baden, margrave of **X** 208

Baden, peace **X** 243

Baden-Powell, R. S. S., afterwards Lord **XIV** 236, 253, 554

38

Badenoch, the caput of the senior branch of the house of Comyn **IV** 581

Badlesmere, Bartholomew, Lord **V** 65; Middle Party envoy (1316) 52; secret indenture (1317) 52–3; Steward of (royal) household 55–6; constable of Dover Castle and warden of Cinque Ports 58; hanged 73; Burghesh (bishop), role in downfall 80

Badminton, Queen Mary at **XV** 457

Badoer, Andrea, Venetian ambassador (1509–15) **VII** 232

Badoglio, forms government **XV** 572

Baedeker raids **XV** 553

Bænesingtun *see* Bensington (Oxon.)

Baeshe, Edward **VIII** 260

Baetica **Ia** 553–4

Bagehot, Walter **XIV** 145, 342

Bagenal, Sir Henry **VIII** 428, 485

Bagendon, mint, pottery **Ia** 59, 83

Baghdad: advance on **XV** 49; taken 98

Bagimond's Roll **IV** 585

Bagley, Thomas, Lollard **VI** 283

Bagley Wood (Berks.) **III** 30

Bagot, Sir William **V** 475, 491, 492; **VI** 1, 21

Bagworth (Leics.) **VI** 339

Bahamas **X** 331, 334; duke of Windsor, governor **XV** 402

Baiamundus de Vitia, papal collector in Scotland **IV** 583

Bailey, Nathaniel (d. 1742), lexicographer **XI** 432

Bailey, Philip James **XIII** 534; **XIV** 330

bailiffs **Ia** 507, 600, 602, 637; their lords and the law **IV** 366–8; auditors of their accounts 366–7; **V** 169, 200, 258, 317–19, 344; *see also vilicus*

Baillie, Robert **IX** 87, 97, 135, 193

Bailly, Charles **VIII** 151

Bainbridge, Christopher, Cardinal, archbishop of York (1508–14) **VII** 257, 272, 277, 289, 300; master of the rolls (1504) 648

Bainbridge (N. Yorks.), lordship **VI** 321

Baird, Sir David (1757–1829) **XII** 46

Bairnsfather, Bruce **XV** 62

Baker, Geoffrey le, on *alumpni Iezebelae* **V** 80; on Edward II at Kenilworth 90

Baker, Sir Herbert **XIV** 540

Baker, Sir John, speaker of the House of Commons (1547) **VII** 498, 654

Baker, Robert **V** 337

Baker, Thomas (1656–1740), nonjuror **XI** 75

Baker, William (1668–1732), bishop of Bangor **XI** 78

Bakewell (Badecanwiellon) (Derby.) **II** 334, 731

Bakewell, Robert, farmer (1725–95), of Dishley **XI** 106; **XII** 33

Bakewell (Blackwell) Hall **IX** 290

Baku: occupied **XV** 138; French wish to bomb 467

balance of payments: First World War **XV** 42; nineteen-twenties 249; Macmillan Report 287–8; blamed for financial crisis 292; exact 336; nineteen-thirties 343; Second World War 566, 599

Balasore **X** 349

Balchen, Sir John, Admiral (1670–1744) **XI** 227, 236

Baldock, Ralph, bishop of London (1306–13) **V** 10

Baldock, Robert, keeper of the privy seal (1320–3), chancellor (1323–6) **V** 57, 84, 86; thirteen years' truce negotiator 75–6; offices 77, 277; loyalty to Edward II 93; dispossessed of land 97

Baldred, king of Kent **II** 231

Baldred patricius **II** 67

Baldwin, abbot of Bury St Edmunds **II** 649
Baldwin, Alfred **XIV** 113
Baldwin, archbishop of Canterbury **III** 221, 225, 296, 344
Baldwin II, count of Flanders **II** 344
Baldwin V, count of Flanders **II** 422, 428–9, 565; shelters Tostig 579; becomes regent 585; dies 607
Baldwin VI, count of Flanders **II** 607
Baldwin VII, count of Flanders **III** 124
Baldwin IX, count of Flanders **III** 367, 376, 379, 381, 454
Baldwin VI, count of Hainault **III** 3
Baldwin I, king of Jerusalem **III** 94, 189
Baldwin II, king of Jerusalem **III** 128, 343
Baldwin III, king of Jerusalem **III** 343
Baldwin IV, king of Jerusalem **III** 343
Baldwin V, king of Jerusalem **III** 343
Baldwin, Richard (?1672–1758), provost of Trinity College, Dublin **XI** 305
Baldwin, son of count Gilbert of Brionne **II** 632
Baldwin, Stanley **XV** 131, 173; biography 125; reduces War Loan 125; parliament (1918) 128–9; opposes continuance of coalition 191–3; chancellor of Exchequer 196; settlement of American debt 202–335; prime minister 204–5, 224; espouses Protection 206–7; approves Chelmsford in Labour government 210; Campbell case 219; renounces Protection 220; again prime minister 221; achieves quiet time 227; successful on radio 235; resists attack on political levy 236; reduction of wages 239; negotiates with General Council 243; general strike 244; Churchill on *British Gazette* 246; end of general strike 247; condemns mine-owners 248; attack on unions 250; appoints Irwin viceroy 254; Arcos raid 255; Safety First 267; resigns as prime minister 271; agrees with MacDonald over India 277; breach with Churchill 278; backbenchers' mistrust 281; Beaverbrook's campaign against 282; victorious 283; accepts National government 292; relieved at exclusion of Churchill 293; only Christian prime minister 317; League of Nations 318; National government 323; co-operates with MacDonald over India 326; praises Labour for not seceding 327; attends Ottawa conference 329; dominion status for India 355–6; Lloyd George 357; agrees with MacDonald over foreign affairs 359–60; fails to inform TUC on foreign affairs 361; future war fears 364; East Fulham election 367; justifies rearmament 369; promises air parity 375; prime minister again 378; pious phrases 380; steals Labour's thunder 381; has parliament dissolved 382; promises no great armaments 383; gives Hoare his blessing 386; statement on rearmament 387; rides out unpopularity 392–3; Spanish Civil War 397–8; Edward VIII 400–1, 403; prestige restored 404; resigns 404; keeps promise of no great armaments 412; Chamberlain's impatience 414; Jewish refugees appeal 420; Eden provides smokescreen 421
Baldwin Docheman (Dutchman) **VI** 652
Bale, Bishop John **VI** 297
Balearic Isles: and Aragon **IV** 256,

40

Baliol, John, son of John (*cont.*)
himself heir 601; position as a
Scottish magnate 602; fealty to
Edward I, installed at Scone, and
does homage at Newcastle 608;
reign and relationships 608–9,
610, 611, 613; renounces his homage 614; abdication 615; later life
615

Baliol, William, one of Scottish
embassy in France (1302–4) **IV**
697

Balkan League **XIV** 463

Balkan provinces, ordnance factories **Ia** 423

Balkans: alleged project to invade
XV 573; myths about importance
576–7

Ball, John **V** 253, 338, 418; released
by rebels 408; sermon at Blackheath 409; communism 413, 421;
executed 419; Wyclif 514; Langland 527

ballads **VIII** 187, 289; **IX** 274–5,
320–1, 389, 415

Ballard **VIII** 380, 382

Ballard, John **V** 248

Ballin, Albert **XIV** 461

Ballinahinch, battle (1798) **XII** 398

Ballinamuck, French surrender **XII**
399

Balliol, Bernard of **III** 271

Balliol, Edward, titular king of Scots
V 115–19, 142, 234, 256

Balliol, Guy of **III** 70

Balliol, Jocelin of **III** 211

Balliol, John **VII** 135

Ballot Act **XIV** 23–4; effect in
Ireland 24

Balmerino, Arthur Elphinstone, 6th
Lord (1688–1746) **XI** 256

Baltic **III** 89; **VI** 1, 69, 70, 347;
European diplomacy **VII** 83;
trade 111; Merchant Adventurers
excluded 221; Riga treaty 222;
shipbuilding imports 470; Easterlings exclude English 471;
altar-piece exports 598; Baltic

Powers **XI** 13, 165, 167, 172,
174–6; trade 122, 165, 176; British fleets 222; trade (1760) **XII** 24

Baltic Sea **V** 358, 359, 360; **IX**
225–9, 318–19

Baltimore, Ireland **IX** 111

Baltimore, Lord *see* Calvert

Baltinglas, Viscount *see* Eustace,
James

Bamborough **Ib** 199; map 4 xxxii

Bamborough, Morel of **III** 267

Bamborough castle **III** 109, 270,
272, 431; in the settlement (1265)
IV 198, 199; **V** 12, 13, 24

Bambow, Francesco, Italian merchant exporting for Edward IV
VI 591

Bambridge, Thomas (*fl.* 1729), and
Fleet prison **XI** 135

Bamburgh (Bebbanburg) (Northumb.) **II** 74, 92–3, 253, 362;
castle **VI** 9, 528–31, shire 529,
burnt 584, 731

Bampton (Oxon.), church **II** 365;
III 145, 154

Banaster, Adam **V** 50, 204

Banbury (Oxon.) **II** 438; **IX** 132;
parliamentary representation
XII 52, 59, 147; inadequate railway link **XV** 507

Bancroft, Richard **VIII** 455, 456;
pluralism 190; suppression of
puritanism 194, 202–3, 457, 460;
IX 7, 69

Banda **XII** 371

Banff castle **IV** 693

Bangor **III** 299; **IV** 428; alleged
attempt on Llywelyn's life 427;
liberties of diocese confirmed by
Edward I 434; Edward I at
(1294–5) 442, 443

Bangor (Caernarfon) **VI** 40; *see also*
Byford

Bangor (Ireland) **X** 307

Bangor, bishops of **IV** 390–1; **XI** 23;
see also Anian, Richard; Baker,
William; Bird, John; David;
Dean, Henry; Gilbert; Hervé;

42

Hoadly, Benjamin; Sherlock, Thomas
Bangor Iscoed, monastery **II** 78
Banister, John **X** 376, 404
Bank Charter Acts (1833) **XIII** 60, 112; (1844) 112
Bank of England **XII** 418; charter renewed 105; payment suspended 372, 406; Gold **XV** 5; restricts credits 140; issues paper money 223; financial crisis (1931) 289–90; reports that credits exhausted 296; sterling area 337; national-ization announced 597
Bankes, Henry (1757–1834) **XII** 440, 447
Bankes, Richard **VI** 664, 665
banking **IX** 286–7; amalgamations **XIV** 114
banking facilities **XII** 24, 28, 406, 464
Bankruptcy Act (1883) **XIV** 87
banks: of England **X** 172, 176–8; of Scotland 265, 284
Banks, Sir Joseph (1743–1820) **XII** 339
Banks, Thomas (1735–1805), sculptor **XI** 402
Bann, river **III** 315
Bannerets **V** 237–8
Bannister, duke of Norfolk's agent **VIII** 151
Bannockburn, battle **III** 317; **V** 35–40, 41, 100, 107, 139, 169
Banquefort, near Bordeaux **IV** 264
Banqueting House, Whitehall **IX** 380
Banquo **III** 273
Banstead, clock **XV** 534
Banstead, John of, king's clerk **IV** 337
Bantam **X** 69, 349, 350
Bantry Bay **X** 164
Bapaume (Pas-de-Calais) **VI** 152, 153
baptism **Ia** 402, 410, 470, 729–30, 737
Baptists **X** 19, 27

Bar **III** 453
Bar, counts of *see* Henry III; Theobald
Bar, duchy **VI** 256, 579
Bar, duke of **VI** 156
Bar, John de **IV** 690
Bar Hill, fort **Ia** 260
Bar Kochba **Ia** 182
Bar Moor **VII** 281
Barates **Ia** 514, 659
Barbados **IX** 179, 232, 240, 321, 344; proprietorship dispute 337–8; **X** 325, 327; Anglo-French war 329, 330; slave-owners biggest landowners 331; negro slaves 345
Barbanera, Genoese captain **V** 128
barbarians: definition **Ia** 236, 239–41; incursions, Cimbri and Teutones 11; in or allied with Roman army 67, 417–19, 426, 440 —Theodosius 404–6 —Pyrenean defence 432–3; campaigns against 122, 391, 395, 470, 476 —Claudian invasion 86 —Caractacus captured 106 —Agricola's campaign 140 —Scottish campaign 194 —Severus 228–30 —Saxon shore forts 299–300 —Julian 'the Apostate' 359, 363 —defences 421–2 —Stilicho 425–6; attitudes towards 173, 218, 288, 291 —absolute moral right 66 —divide and rule 81 —glory and slaughter 211, 419 —fair game 240 —Constantius campaign 315 —troops transferred 330–1 —British army fears 427 —Jews and Christians 717 —wrath of God 728 —pagan elements 738; settlement within empire 204–8, 210, 274, 355, 418; British frontier 221–2, 227, 368, 421–3, 426; Rhine-Danube frontier 239, 274, 429, 438 —Alamanni penetrate Italy 270–1 —Trier link 302

Barker, H. Granville **XIV** 547

Barking (Berecingas) (Essex) **II** 599, 601; monastery 161; abbess of *see* Hildelith

Barksore (Kent) **V** 321

Barkway, near Royston, votive offerings **Ia** 689

Barletta, battle (1502) **VII** 153

barley **Ia** 234

Barlings **VII** 397

Barlow, agitator **XII** 359

Barlow, Arthur **VIII** 246

Barlow, Francis **X** 399

Barlow, Jerome **VII** 344

Barlow, William, bishop of St Asaph (1536), bishop of St David's (1536), bishop of Bath and Wells (1548–54), bishop of Chichester (1559): texts presented **VII** 363; Cranmer's supporter 382, 431; reformation sermons 512; imprisoned 543

Barnack (Northants) **III** 80

Barnard, Sir Henry **XIII** 435

Barnard, Sir John (1685–1764) **XI** 187, 336

Barnard Castle (N. Yorks.) **IV** 466, 580; **VI** 609; Beauchamp lordship 329; Richard of Gloucester's college 609; **VIII** 140

Barnardo, Dr T. J. **XIV** 163, 335

Barnes, G. N. **XIV** 265, 300

Barnes, George Nicoll: biography **XV** 90; War Cabinet 90; leaves Labour party 125, 293; wishes to hang Kaiser 127; attends peace conference 130, 132

Barnes, Joshua, on Edward III **V** 148

Barnes (Bernes, Berners), Juliana **VI** 665; **VII** 581

Barnes, Robert **VII** 257, 345, 382, 416, 427

Barnes, Thomas **XIV** 310

Barnes (Barons), William, later lord keeper, master of the rolls (1 Feb. 1502) **VII** 648

Barnet (Herts.) **V** 337, 414; battle **VI** 546, 568

Barnet, John, bishop of Worcester (1362–3), of Bath and Wells (1363–6), of Ely (1366–73), treasurer (1363–9) **V** 211, 227

Barnet, John, official of the Court of Canterbury **V** 265

Barnevelt, John Van Olden **IX** 395

Barnham (Sussex) **VI** 279

barns **Ia** 458, 595, 610, 611

Barnstaple (Bardanstapol) (Devon) **II** 532; **III** 85; **IX** 133, 731

Barnwell priory (Cambs.) **III** 186; **V** 83, 417

baronial committees **IV** 78–9; plans for reforms (1238–58) 77–9; leaders' sworn agreement (1258) 130–1; later developments 135, 140, 146

baronial families of old English descent **II** 684–5

Baronies and Knights' Fees **IV** 550

barons, honorial **II** 618, 636

barons and baronage: Edward I and **IV** 516–19, 521; households and military aspect 519–20; political thought about status 520–3; and the Crown 542–3; in Scotland and its Scottish and English affiliations 579–83; literature on 768–9; extravagant households **VII** 17; weakened after Bosworth 13, 22; *see also* seignorial administration

barons of the conquest: origin **II** 629–31; king's court 632–4; sheriffs 633–4; tenants by knight service 634–6; numbers 634–5

Barons' War (1264): begins in the Marches **IV** 185; dated from attack on Northampton or *diffidatio* at Lewes 187, 209; end 204, 209; ordinances for peace and restoration of order 204–5; restoration of peace (1266–7) 206–15

Barons' Wars **VIII** 286

barracks **Ia** 256, 605, 695

Barré, Colonel Isaac (1726–1802) on Chatham **XI** 363; **XII** 143, 149, 260; fights American stamp duties 106; Shelburne 232, 244; navy treasurer 578; paymaster 579

Barrett, W. A. **XIV** 544

Barrie, Sir J. M. **XIV** 546, 547, 554

Barrier Treaty (1709) **X** 218

Barrington (Cambs.): cruciform brooch detail **Ib** 58 [fig. 1(f)]; map 2 xxx; map 5 68

Barrington, Hon. Samuel (1729–1800), Admiral, and naval training **XI** 225

Barrington, 2nd Viscount *see* Wildman, William

barristers **Ia** 394, 448, 467

Barrow, Henry **VIII** 200, 201, 203, 204

Barrow, Sir John **XIII** 45

Barrow, river **V** 472

Barrow, William, bishop of Carlisle **VI** 51

Barrow on Humber (Bearwe) (Lincs.) **II** 452; **VI** 351, 731

barrows **Ia** 10, 605, 670, 697

Barry, Sir Charles: biography **XIII** 583; work of 583–4

Barry, Gerald **XV** 310

Barry, 11th lord of Buttevant **VII** 133

Barry, Spranger (1719–77), actor **XI** 304

Barstable (Essex) **V** 340

Bart, Jean **X** 172

Bartholomew, bishop of Exeter **III** 216, 222, 229

Bartholomew, bishop of Girgenti **III** 331

Bartholomew, Harry Guy, and *Daily Mirror* **XV** 548, 632

Bartholomew the Englishman **V** 524

Bartholomew Fair **VIII** 301

Bartlett, Vernon, victor at Bridgwater **XV** 436

Bartlow Hills, barrows **Ia** 605, 697, 700, 704

Barton, Andrew **VII** 144, 270

Barton, Elizabeth, Holy Maid of Kent **VII** 361–2; executed (Apr. 1534) 362

Barton, John, Bedford's treasurer **VI** 205

Barton, John junior, of Bucks **VI** 416

Barton, Robert **VII** 144, 270

Barton, William **V** 513

Barton Regis (Som.) **V** 79

Barton-on-Humber **Ib** 177; map 4 xxxii; **III** 77, 96

Barwell, Richard (1741–1804) **XII** 169, 170, 310, 313, 315

Basel (Basle) **V** 301; council **VI** 135, 259, 260; French members of English nation at 259; **VII** 162, 258, 273, 336, 600

Basengum *see* Basing (Hants)

basilica **Ia** 141, 157–8, 168, 325, 582; Exeter 138; St Peter's 326, 724; feature of large towns 589, 591, 592; as church 724

Basilicata **VII** 153

Basin, Thomas, chronicler **VI** 207, 252

Basing (Basengum) (Hants) **II** 249, 731

Basing House **IX** 142

Basingstoke (Hants) **II** 301

Basingwerk (Flint) **II** 214, 230; castle **III** 293; Cistercian abbey **IV** 412

Baskerville, John (1706–75), printer **XI** 414

Baskerville, Sir Thomas **VIII** 417, 419

Baslow (Derby.) **V** 333

Basra **VIII** 242; **X** 349

Bass Rock **VI** 64

Bassae, sanctuary **Ia** 672

Bassein, port **XII** 158

Basset, Alan **III** 473

Basset, Fulk, bishop of London (1244–59) **IV** 125, 133, 150

Basset, Gilbert **IV** 53–4, 60, 66, 150

Basset, Philip (d. 1271), justiciar:

biography **IV** 150; 'friend and ally' of Lord Edward 153; closes London to Lord Edward 157–9; barons' community broken 161; earl of Leicester's claim 164; appointed judiciar 165–6; loses grip on home affairs 171; captured by Earl Simon 190; last days of Earl Simon 203–4; peace settlement 214; potential guardian for Edward's children 224–5

Basset, Ralph **III** 388, 404

Basset, Ralph, of Drayton **IV** 202; **V** 451

Basset, Sir Ralph, seneschal of Gascony **V** 109

Basset, Reginald **III** 430

Basset, Thomas **III** 473

Basset, William **III** 390

Bassingburn, Warin de **IV** 153

bastardy, law **IV** 70–1, 453

bastides **IV** 309–10, 431; built by Edward I **VI** 107

bastions **Ia** 281, 325, 352, 387–9

Baston **Ib** 176, 193; map 4 xxxii

Bastwick, John **IX** 72, 75

Batavi (Late Roman unit) **Ia** 361, 381

Batavia(ns) **Ia** 130, 133, 144, 148, 684; prefect 711; **Ib** 75, 106

Bate, John **IX** 10

Bateman, industrialist **XII** 508

Bateman, William, bishop of Norwich (1344–55) **V** 299, 300, 507

Bath (Bathum) (Aquae Sulis) (Som.) **Ia** 96, 238, 280, 484; baths 635; cult centre 514–15, 686–8; altar 631; guild 659; **Ib** 155, 158, 163, 168–70, 172; map 3 xxxi; appendix II; **II** 29, 264, 368, 385, 731; abbey 447, 455, 680; **III** 101, 233, 244; **VI** 569; **VII** 40, 591, 593; **X** 409; Haile Selassie at **XV** 385; admiralty 457

Bath, bishopric **III** 226

Bath, earls of *see* Bourchier, John; Chandé, Philibert de; Pulteney, William

Bath, 3rd Viscount *see* Thynne, Thomas

Bathampton Down, Celtic fields **Ia** 621

Bath and Wells, bishops of *see* Barnet; Bourne, Dr; Bowet, Henry; Droxford; Erghum, Ralph; Fox, Richard; Godfrey; Jocelin; John; Savaric; Shrewsbury; Skirlaw; Stafford, John

Bath and Wells, diocese **V** 277, 371; see **VI** 268; **VII** 238, 294, 461

baths: public **Ia** 571, 578–9, 635, 687; social pleasure 160, 514–15; Flavian period 185–6; private 459, 610; military 223, 537, 733; **X** 409

Bathum *see* Bath (Som.)

Bathurst, Allen, 1st Earl (1684–1775) **XI** 150, 421

Bathurst, Catherine, Lady Bathurst **X** 221

Bathurst, Earl **XIII** 367

Bathurst, 3rd Earl, president of the Board of Trade (1807–12) **XII** 582; foreign secretary (1809) 582; secretary of war and colonies (1812) 583

Bathurst, Henry, 2nd Earl (1714–94): biography **XII** 149; lord chancellor (1771–8) 149, 576; lord president of the council (1779–82) 225, 575

Battersea North **XV** 200, 271

Battle (Sussex) **II** 593–4; **III** 226

Battle, abbot of **III** 10; *see also* Odo

battle, trial by **III** 387, 396–7, 411, 413

Battle Abbey (Sussex) **II** 594, 673; **III** 169, 247, 295; abbot of 10, 200; administration of justice 7, 12; monastic reform 185; **V** 328, 341; **VI** 460

Battle Axe offensive **XV** 527

battles: Agnadello (1509) **VII** 155, 271; Ancrum (1545) 407; Aversa (1528) 319; Bicocca (1522) 312; Blackheath (1497) 142; Bosworth battles (*cont.*)

(1485) 7–9, 52–3; Cerignola (1503) 153; Dixmude (1489) 98–9; Dussindale (1549) 490; Flodden (1513) 280–3; Fornovo (1495) 115; Garigliano (1503) 153; Gravelines (1558) 559; Guinegate, Spurs (1513) 279; Haddon Rig (1542) 405; Knocktue (1504) 133; Landriano (1529) 319, 328; Marignano (1515) 306; Mohacz (1526) 320; Mühlberg (1547) 483; Nancyl (1477) 84; Novara (1500) 152; Pavia (1525) 315, 340–1; Pinkie (1547) 483–5; Ravenna (1512) 274; St Aubin du Cormier (1488) 87, 99; St Quentin (1557) 558; Sauchieburn (1488) 76, 135; Seminara (1503) 153; Solway Moss (1542) 405–6; Stoke (1487) 8, 73–5; Arcot (1751) **XI** 328, 347; Beauséjour (1755) 347, 349; Belle Île (1762) 368; Cape Passaro (1718) 173, 209; Chinsura (1759) 329; Chotusitz (1742) 240; Condore (1758) 330; Crefeld (1758) 361; Culloden (1746) 256; Dettingen (1743) 220, 242, 251, 266; Falkirk (1746) 255, 259; Fontenoy (1745) 220, 251, 281, 291; Glenshiel (1719) 173, 182, 280; Hyères (or Toulon) (1744) 229, 247–8, 262, 266; Kolin (1757) 359; Künersdorf (1759) 364; Laffeldt (1747) 260; Lagos (1759) 359, 365; Leuthen (1757) 350; Minden (1759) 220, 364; Minorca (1756) 230, 352; Montreal (1760) 368; Naval operations (1747) 262; (1755) 349, 351; (1757–8) 361; raids on French coast 359, 362–3; Ohio (Monongahela) (1755) 349, 351; Plassey (1757) 329, 330, 366; Preston (1715) 162; Prestonpans (1745) 254; Quebec (1759) 220, 365; Quiberon (1759) 230, 359, 366; Rheinberg (1758) 360, 361, Rochefort (1757) 360; Rossbach (1757) 360; Roucoux near Liège (1746) 260; St Foy (1760) 356; Sheriffmuir (1715) 162; Ticonderoga (1758) 356, 361; Trichinopoly (1752) 347; Vellinghausen (1761) 369; Wandewash (1760) 330; Warburg (1761) 220; Zorndorf (1758) 364; *see also* naval operations; military actions

Baudihillia **Ia** 667

Baugé (Maine-et-Loire), battle **VI** 194, 200

bauson **IV** 644

Bauto **Ia** 417

Bautzen, battle (1813) **XII** 556

Bavaria: sees founded by Boniface **II** 169; elector of **X** 197; **XI** 350; *see also* Charles Albert; subsidies

Bavaria, duke of *see* Lewis, duke of Bavaria

Bavaria, prince of *see* Philip

Bavinchove, battle **II** 607

Bawd, Peter **VII** 408

Bax, Arnold **XIV** 545

Baxter, Richard **V** 517; **X** 20, 32, 54, 224, 269

Bayard, Chevalier **VII** 153, 279, 311

Baydon **Ib** 159–60; map 3 xxxi

Bayeaux (Calvados) **II** 577, 586; **III** 119, 120, 384; **VI** 172; diocese 192

Bayeux Tapestry **II** 577–8; **III** 264

Bayham (Sussex), abbot of **V** 155

Bayle, William of Wareham **VII** 196

Baylen, battle (1808) **XII** 459

Bayley, Lancashire JP **XI** 52

Baynard's castle (London) **III** 63, 455; **VII** 43, 44, 293, 528, 594

Bayonne (Basses-Pyrénées) **III** 92; **IV** 244; Treaty of Paris (1259) 126; meeting between kings of France and Castile (1290) 262; barons' war 281; court of mayor and jurats appeals from 316, 317; Channel Islands 318; feuds with sailors of Cinque Ports 644, 646; Philip IV demands punishment

48

for damages 645; citizens during the war (1294–1303) 622, 650, 659; ship-building 656; **V** 114, 145, 433; **VI** 107, 108, 222, 470; **VII** 274; conference **VIII** 159

Bayston (Salop) **II** 483

Bazadais **V** 112

Bazaine, Marshal **XIV** 7

Bazan, Alonso de **VIII** 412

Bazas (Gironde): court **IV** 109, 285, 301; bishop, chapter and commune 275; **VI** 107, 113

BBC: orchestra **XV** 234; voice 234

Beach, Sir Michael Hicks, viscount, then Earl St Aldwyn: **XIV** 33, 49, 60, 76, 89; biography 32; becomes chancellor of Exchequer 91; Coercion Bill 96; Home Rule Bill 98; Irish secretary 172; resigns for eyesight 176; Tenants' Relief Bill 178; evictions 179; returns to Exchequer 225; speech on civil list 344; war finance 349–50; on Lord Salisbury 353–4; resigns office 354; opposed to Chamberlain's fiscal policy 373; Licensing Bill 409; fiscal controversy 415; chairman of royal commission on ecclesiastical discipline 529–30

Beachy Head: battle **X** 165, 308; German plan to land **XV** 498

Beaconsfield, earl of *see* Disraeli, Benjamin

Beaker People **Ia** 8, 17

Beale (Beal), Dr, canon of St Mary's Hospital **VII** 298

Beale, Dorothea **XIII** 497; **XIV** 149, 150

Beale, John **X** 42

Beale, Mary **X** 401

Beale, Robert **VIII** 376, 387

Beamfleot *see* Benfleet (Essex)

beans **Ia** 234

Beansale (War.) **VI** 379

bear-baiting and bull-baiting **VIII** 276–7; **IX** 180, 264, 311

Beard, Thomas **IX** 414

Beardanig *see* Bardney (Lincs.)

Beardmore's **XV** 40

Beardsley, Aubrey **XIV** 333

Béarn, Constance of, countess of Marsan, daughter of Gaston, wife of Henry of Almain **IV** 284, 287, 316

Béarn, Gaston, viscount of **IV** 108, 109, 112, 284; family relationships 112; Simon de Montfort 112–13; Alfonso X of Castile 116, 118; sent to help Alfonso X 245; treaty of Canfran (1288) 282, 283; rebellion against Edward I and reconciliation (1273–8) 285–7; the succession to Bigorre 287

Bearstead (Berghamstyde) (Kent), council **II** 62

Bearwe *see* Barrow-on-Humber (Lincs.)

Beaton, David, Cardinal, archbishop of St Andrews (1539–46) **VII** 405, 406, 407, 408

Beaton, James, archbishop of Glasgow **VIII** 101, 106, 357

Beaton, James, archbishop of St Andrews (1522–39) **VII** 405

Beaton, John **VIII** 83–4

Beatrice, daughter of Amadeus of Savoy, wife of Manfred **IV** 247

Beatrice, daughter of Henry III (d. 1275), wife of John of Brittany (1260) **IV** 97, 159, 235

Beatrice of Provence, wife of Charles of Anjou **IV** 119, 234

Beatrice of Savoy, wife of Raymond-Berengar of Provence **IV** 74, 107, 119

Beatty, Sir David: biography **XV** 63; at Jutland 63

Beauce, district **VI** 175, 191

Beauchamp, Anne **VI** 336

Beauchamp, family possessions **VI** 329, 416; Despenser lands 336

Beauchamp, Sir Giles **V** 153, 159

Beauchamp, Guy, earl of Warwick (1298–1315) **V** 1, 6, 304; 'black dog of Arden' 9; an Ordainer 10, 11, 24; seizure of Gaveston 26–8;

paign continuation 159; loans (1421) 195; efforts to be made cardinal (1418) 198–9; subsequent penal loan 199; free to serve papal interest 200; salary 220; friendly to Burgundians 224; chancellor's special salary (1425) 226; loans estimate 226; Exchequer's indebtedness 227; claims port control 228; Verneuil campaign loans 228; Gloucester's complaints committee appearance 230; repudiates disloyalty 231; worsted by Gloucester 231; made cardinal (1426) and legate (1428) 234–5, 236–7; preaches crusade (June 1429) 237; crusade diverted 238; crusade enrolment 238; support after Troyes 238; prelate of Garter 252; Windsor visit postponed 253; loyalty upheld (1431) 253–4; restores king's jewels 254; buys out of quandary 254; Calais peacemaking visits 258; Arras ambassador 260–1; treaty of Troyes 263; council attendance 431; customs lien 440; total crown loans 442; York's enmity 467; council following 468; tomb in Winchester 650

Beaufort, Henry, bishop of Lincoln (1398–1404) **V** 473

Beaufort, Henry, earl and duke of Somerset **VI** 517, 523, 526, 529, 530; beheaded 531

Beaufort, Henry, marquis of Dorset, declines to surrender Maine **VI** 480

Beaufort, John, brother of duke of Somerset, killed at Tewkesbury **VI** 569

Beaufort, John, earl of Somerset and marquis of Dorset (1373?–1410) **V** 185, 473, 479, 483, 489; **VI** 21; chamberlain 22; 68, 104, 105; captain of Calais 103; **VII** 158

Beaufort, Margaret *see* Margaret

Beaufort, Thomas, admiral **VI** 63, 163, 211, 218, 230; character and judgement 104; prince of Wales' chancellor 105; French expedition 114; French ambassador (1415) 141; Harfleur captain 157; Harfleur operations 157, 158; negotiations with France 180; Bois-de-Vincennes 201; interim council 212; instruction of Henry VI 213; justice of N. Wales 220; commons lawyers 417; council member 431, 433

Beaufort, Thomas Grey *see* Grey, Thomas

Beauforts, legitimization **VI** 105

Beaufront Red House, Corbridge, Agricolan base **Ia** 144

Beaugency (Loiret) **III** 163; **VI** 245, 247, 250

Beaugué, Jean de **VII** 484

Beaujeu, Pierre de, brother of John II, duke of Bourbon **VII** 85

Beaujolais **VI** 240

Beaulieu (Hants), abbey **III** 229, 428; abbot 456; **VI** 295; **VII** 145

Beaulieu (New Hall), near Chelmsford **VII** 595

Beaulieu in Vermandois (Oise) **VI** 248

Beaumanor (Leics.) **VI** 376

Beaumaris (Anglesey): castle **IV** 431, 432, 443; borough 423–3; **VI** 39, 40, 55, 499

Beaumont, Francis **VIII** 301; **IX** 392–4

Beaumont, Henry de, titular earl of Buchan (1312–40) **V** 46, 93, 99, 115; Edward II's cousin 13; Isle of Man 13, 24; king's council 81; exile in Paris 82

Beaumont, Henry, Lord **VI** 7

Beaumont, house of **III** 137, 160

Beaumont, John (*fl.* 1550) **VII** 501; master of the rolls (13 Dec. 1550) 648

Beaumont, John, Viscount, constable of England **VI** 481, 483, 494, 503, 508; and Edward IV 567

Beaumont, Louis de, bishop of Durham (1318–33) **V** 40, 61, 75, 80, 275

Beaumont, Richard, vicomte of **III** 279

Beaumont, Robert de **II** 630

Beaumont, Robert de, earl of Leicester (d. 1190) **IV** 75; daughters Amicia and Margaret 75

Beaumont, William, Viscount, killed at Northampton **VI** 520; attainder (1461) 539; with Oxford in Cornwall (1473) 571

Beaumont Palace (Oxford) **III** 236, 348

Beaumont-le-Vicomte (Sarthe) **VI** 189

Beaumont-sur-Oise (Oise) **VI** 172, 186, 189

Beaupie, Peter, Edward IV's clerk **VI** 604

Beauport Park, inscription **Ia** 637

Beaurain **II** 577

Beaurevoir (Aisne), castle **VI** 248

Beauvais (Oise) **II** 327, 328; **VI** 111, 168; county 170; conference **XV** 102

Beauvais, bishop of **III** 467

Beauvais, Vincent of *see* Vincent of Beauvais

Beaverbrook, Lord: Northcliffe **XV** 27; Birkenhead 57; minister of information 107; Maurice debate 117; favours capital levy 125; urges Law to destroy coalition 191; dismayed by Law 197; Curzon 204; Baldwin competes for Law's inheritance 207; doubts whether Law recommended Baldwin 224; giant of Fleet Street 234–5; campaigns against Baldwin 282–3; promotes livelier newspapers 309; social classes 310; Churchill attempts to surpass 356; supports Edward

VIII's marriage 401; backs Churchill 473; becomes minister of aircraft production 478; Defence Committee (Operations) 481; provides aeroplanes for fighter command 490; urges release of Mosley 492; orders dispersal of factories 502; a pirate 507; battle with Bevin 509; minister of supply 509, 510; Churchill consults on Soviet alliance 528; advocates Soviet cause 529; American war effort 530; minister of war production 543; leaves government 544; *Daily Express* 548; on Cripps 559; returns to office 573–4; against Labour 596; *see also* Aitken

Beaworth (Hants) **III** 111

Bebbanburg *see* Bamburg (Northumb.)

Bec: abbey **II** 662–3; **III** 172, 190, 233; priory **V** 329; **VI** 174, 301

Bec, abbot of **III** 173; **V** 344–5

Becca Banks **Ib** map 4 xxxii

Beche, Sir Nicholas **V** 168

Becherel **V** 385, 391

Bechuanaland **XIV** 228

Beck, Polish foreign minister, accepts British guarantee **XV** 442; refuses to admit Red Army 447; refuses to negotiate with Hitler 451

Becket, Gilbert **III** 197

Becket, St Thomas, of Canterbury: at Northampton **III** 11, 207–8; chancellor 171, 198–200, 322, 323, 326, 327; in archbishop Theobald's household 196; youth and education 197; archdeacon of Canterbury 197–9; character 198; made archbishop 200–1, 228; relations with Henry II 200–1; resigns chancellorship 202; quarrels with him 202, 331; at Clarendon 205–6; in exile 209–14, 445; his murder 214, 221, 229, 252, 309, 336–7; his cult 215,

340; **IV** 489; new shrine 14, 24; Pecham on his martyrdom 478; **V** 2, 69, 169, 170, 173; **VI** 235, 292; pilgrimage 132; contemporary English gentleman 281; **VII** 90, 286, 489; shrine despoiled 396

Beckford **Ia** 14

Beckford, John **VI** 103

Beckford, Roger **VI** 103

Beckford, William (1709–70) **XI** 22, 368; lord mayor, MP **XII** 96, 131, 140

Beckford, William (1760–1844), author of *Vathek* **XII** 352, 545

Beckfords, the **XI** 145, 313

Beckley (Oxon.) **II** 381; **IV** 160; **V** 337

Beckwith, Sir William **V** 469

Becon, Thomas (1512–67) **VII** 457, 542

Beda of Lindsey **Ib** 178

Bedcanford, battle **II** 27, 29

Bedchamber crisis **XIII** 105–6

Beddgelert (Caernarfon) prior **VI** 39

Bede: *Ecclesiastical History*...: importance for early English history **Ib** 6–7; on Gildas' dating 9; on continental origins of the invaders 28–9, 46–9; use of *vicus* and *villa* 35; Saxon Shore 86; *Adventus Saxonum* 109; Jutes in Kent 114, 122, 127; Horsa's tombstone 114; London 128, 130, 133; Ælle as first bretwalda 137; on Isle of Wight 146; use of term Northumbria 175; Deira 184, 189, 191–2, 196; Ad Gefrin 199; Æthelfrith 200; ignores tradition of reverse migration **II** 8; analysis of English peoples 8–10; continental Saxons 10–11; value of traditions recorded 13–16, 17, 19, 23–4, 27; overlordship of the southern English 33–4; chronologist 76, 186; heathen festivals 96–8; family monasteries 161; literary background 185; literary

works 185–7; historian 186–7; teacher 187–8

Bedford (Bedanford) **Ib** 165; **II** 260, 324, 325–7; **III** 67, 92, 164, 418, 471; castle 319; Faukes de Breauté **IV** 26; siege 27; **V** 97; earldom of *see* Coucy, Enguerrard de

Bedford, dowager duchess of *see* Jacquetta, dowager duchess of Bedford

Bedford, dukes of **XIII** 96, 100; **XIV** 49, 119; *see also* John; Russell, John; Tudor, Jasper

Bedford, earls of *see* Russell, Francis; Russell, John

Bedford, John, 4th duke of *see* Russell, John, 4th duke of Bedford

Bedford group **XI** 29; **XII** 128; joined government 129, 150; part in Douglas case 135, 136

Bedfordshire **Ia** 43, 608; **II** 327, 338; **III** 465; **V** 268, 414; **VII** 505

Bedlam Hospital, London, foundation **XII** 11

Bedriacum, battles **Ia** 129, 131

Bedwellty, guardians suspended at **XV** 256

Bedwyn, Great (Wilts.) **II** 482, 534

Bedwyn, Little (Wilts.) **II** 307

Bedyll, Thomas **VII** 377

Beecham, Sir Thomas **XIV** 543; **XV** 234

beer **Ia** 655; **IX** 294, 306

bees **Ia** 614

Beesly, E. S. **XIV** 132

Beeston Castle (Cheshire) **IV** 202

Beetgum **Ib** map 5 68

Beethoven, Ludwig van **XV** 268

begums of Oudh **XII** 310, 318, 322

Behn, Aphra **X** 418

Béhuchet, Nicolas, Admiral **V** 128

Bek, Antony, bishop of Durham (1284–1311) **IV** 290, 493–6; mission to Aragon (1282) 257, 294; Isle of Man 596; Scottish affairs 613, 615, 689, 690, 697; Brigham treaty 599–600; **V** 3

Bek, Antony, bishop of Norwich (1337–43) **V** 178
Bek, John **IV** 623, 624
Bek, Thomas, bishop of St Davids (1280–93) **IV** 418, 435
Bekesbourne (Kent), Jutish pottery **Ib** 67 [fig. 4(a)]; map 5 68
Bekynton, Thomas, bishop of Bath and Wells, king's English secretary **VI** 272, 470, 539
Bela III, king of Hungary **III** 362
Bela Kun **XV** 135
Belatucader **Ia** 685
Belcher, John **XIV** 324
Belers, James, JP **VI** 455
Belfast: no strike against conscription **XV** 104; parliament 156
Belfast Lough **XV** 159
Belgae **Ia** 9, 10–12, 23–4, 42–3, 58; *civitas* 93; flock 627; mounds 700; **Ib** 149–50, 152
Belgium: **Ia** 494, 496, 623, 653; **XIII** 8, 194; independence 226–30; neutrality **XIV** 3, 490, 491, 492, 493; Bonar Law 494; German invasion 495; Gladstone's view 574–5; German invasion (1914) **XV** 3, 32, 244, 370; invasion foreseen by Kitchener 7; its effect on Liberal party 17; refugees 19; Ireland 21; liberation as principal British war aim 50–1, 97, 115, 489; German plans for 65; Fourteen Points 119; Locarno 221, British guarantee offered to (1936) 386; RAF needs bases 391; British Expeditionary Force on frontier 460; German invasion (1940) 474, 483–4; Allied forces enter 484–5; Belgian army capitulates 486; its government in England 494; more valuable than Czechoslovakia 577; liberation 600; *see also* Leopold of Saxe-Coburg; Schlieffen Plan
Belgrade **VII** 314; **X** 169
Belisarius **Ia** 447, 632
Belknap, Sir Robert **V** 407, 449

Bell, Revd Andrew, educationalist (1753–1832) **XII** 524, 525; biography **XIII** 475
Bell, Graham **XIV** 110
Bell, Henry **X** 391
Bell, Lady (Hugh) **XIV** 513
Bell, Richard **XV** 143
Bell, Robert **VIII** 97
Bell, Robert, confessor-general of Syon **VI** 687
Bell, Stephen **V** 520
Bell, Thomas, of Iffley **VI** 370
Bellamy, Edward **XIV** 334
Bellamy, George Anne (?1731–88), actress **XI** 304
Bellarmine, Robert **IX** 209
Bellasis, John Lord **IX** 136
Bellasis (Belasyse), Thomas, Earl Fauconberg **IX** 242, 245
Bellasyse, John, Baron **X** 123
Belle Isle **VI** 72; **XI** 368, 372; capture by England **XII** 73; returned to France 85; expedition (1800)
Bellebell, mistress of Henry II **III** 332
Bellegarde, defeat at *bastide* (1297) **IV** 666
Belleisle, C. L. A., duc de, maréchal (1684–1761) **XI** 237
Bellême (Orne): house of **II** 554; lordship **III** 124; **IV** 93, 94; **VI** 114
Bêlleme, Robert of: at siege of Rochester **III** 101; position and character 105–6; oppression 108; builds castle of Gisors 112; capture and exile 117–19; at Tinchebrai 120; capture and death 123; in Wales 288–9
Bellenden, William (d. 1633), and classical scholarship **XI** 393
Bellers, Roger **V** 204
Belleville **V** 140; **VI** 135
Bellingham **XII** 497
Bellingham, Sir Edward, lord deputy of Ireland (1548) **VII** 651
Bellovaci **Ia** 24

Bell's copper cylinder **XII** 333

Belmayne, John **VII** 479

Belmeis, John, bishop of Poitiers and archbishop of Lyons **III** 196, 202, 204

Belmeis, Richard de, bishop of London **III** 92, 181

Beltingham, dedication **Ia** 538

Belvoir Castle **II** 631

Belyngham, Henry **VI** 459

Bembridge **XII** 260

Bemersyde, Haigs **IV** 580

Benares *see* Chait Singh

Benauges **IV** 288

Benauges, viscount of *see* Grilly, John de

Benbow, John, Vice-Admiral **X** 330

Benburb **VIII** 470; battle **IX** 162

Bench, King's: king's council **IV** 326–8, 334; rolls 334; judges 341; state trials 362

Bencoolen **X** 349, 350

Benedetti, Count V. **XIV** 3

Benedict, abbot of Chiusa **III** 330

Benedict, abbot of Peterborough **III** 390

Benedict VIII, Pope **II** 407

Benedict X, Pope **II** 465–7

Benedict XII, Pope (1334–42) **V** 130; efforts for peace 118, 122, 124, 161; postpones the crusade 124; and Philip VI 125; letter of Edward III to 164; provisions 278; statute against *proprietas* **VI** 197

Benedict XIII, Pope **VI** 68, 91, 163, 167

Benedict of Aniane **II** 453

Benedict Biscop **II** 68, 132, 159, 162, 180; foundation of Wearmouth and Jarrow 184–5; abbot of St Peter and St Paul at Canterbury 184; granted estate by king 301

Benedictines **V** 300, 305–6, 308–9, 507, 511

Benedictional of St Æthelwold **II** 462

Benefice **IV** 466

beneficiarii consularis **Ia** 213, 521, 522, 537, 597

benefit: of clergy **VII** 291; 'uncovenanted' **XV** 148–89; statutory 237; cuts demanded 291–2; cuts opposed by Labour 293, 297; cuts made 286; cuts restored 351; unemployment assistance 352–3

Beneš, Eduard: invents collective security **XV** 299; negotiates with Germans 425–6; Anglo-French ultimatum 427; succeeded by Hacha 439; recognized as head of provisional government 494

Benevento **III** 176; **IV** 120

benevolence **VII** 213; **IX** 18, 23

Benfield, Paul (d. 1810) **XII** 159

Benfleet (Beamfleot) (Essex) **II** 258, 266, 731

Bengal **IX** 323; **X** 350, 352, 353; failure of harvest **XV** 563; governor-general of *see* Bentinck, Lord William Cavendish

Bengeworth (Worcs.) **II** 650

Benghazi, taken **XV** 524

Benhall (Suffolk), manor **VI** 472

Benn, Wedgwood, opposes revenue tariff **XV** 297

Bennachie **Ia** 146

Bennet, Henry, 1st earl of Arlington **X** 56, 71, 72, 75, 77; hopes for Spanish alliance 63; pro-papist 80

Bennett, Arnold **XIV** 160, 548; as feature writer **XV** 235, 311

Bennett, R. B., at Ottawa conference **XV** 333

Bennett, Sir William Sterndale **XIII** 561

Bennington, battle **XII** 210

Benolt, Thomas, Clariencieux herald **VII** 312, 318

Bensington (Bænesingtun, Benson) (Oxon.) **Ib** 165–6; map 3 xxxi; appendix II; **II** 27, 30; battle 209, 730

Benson, Dr E. W., archbishop **XIV** 142, 307

Benson, Martin (1689–1752), bishop of Gloucester **XI** 81, 88

Benstead, John **V** 3

Bentham, Jeremy (1748–1832) **XI** 57; **XII** 330–2, 440, 450, 532; **XIII** 19, 216, 368, 384, 451; character and ideas 35–7; county courts 472; Paropticon 476; invention of terms 529; ethical system 544

Bentinck, Lord George Cavendish **XIII** 626; biography 123; attacks Peel 123–4; support of Jewish claims 162; death 163

Bentinck, William (Hans Willem), 1st earl of Portland **X** 187, 189, 195, 316, 393; Rye House Plot 113; hires troops from Germany 134; offices conferred by James II 180

Bentinck, William, earl of Portland (1649–1709) **XI** 153

Bentinck, Lord William Cavendish (1774–1839): biography **XII** 385; governor general of Madras 385; in Italy 557, 563, 569; **XIII** 415; governor-general of Bengal 415–16

Bentinck, William Henry Cavendish, 3rd duke of Portland (1738–1809) **XII** 121, 250, 258; title to lands 144; biography 243; lord lieutenant of Ireland (1782) 243, 578; first lord of the Treasury (1783) 269, 579; home secretary (1794–1801) 356, 361, 381 — (1801–4) 581 — Portland Whigs 325, 368, 394 — opposes Pitt 401; lord president of council (1804–5) 418, 581; first lord of Treasury (1807–9) 443–5, 451, 455, 466, 476–8; death 483; list of Cabinets 580, 582–3

Bentley, J. F. **XIV** 325, 507

Bentley, Richard (1662–1742) **X** 361, 375, 383–4, 415; **XI** 10, 23, 57, 140, 393

Bentworth, Richard, bishop of London (1338–9); keeper of the privy seal (1337–8); chancellor (1338–40) **V** 157, 158, 159

Benvenuto da Imola **VI** 680

Benwell **Ia** 568; **Ib** map 4 xxxii

Beoforlic *see* Beverley (Yorks.)

Beorchore (Oxon.), new town **II** 537

Beorhford, battle **II** 204

Beorhhamstede *see* Great Berkhamstead (Herts.)

Beorhtfrith, Northumbrian ealdorman **II** 88

Beorhtric, king of Wessex **II** 209, 220, 225

Beorhtwulf, king of Mercia **II** 234, 244; charters quoted 289

Beorn, Earl, brother of Swein Estrithson **II** 427, 429

Beornhæth, Northumbrian ealdorman **II** 88

Beornred, abbot of Echternach, later archbishop of Sens **II** 176, 219

Beornwine, nephew of St Wilfrid **II** 138

Beornwulf, king of Mercia **II** 231

Beowulf **Ib** 55, 109; **II** 192–9; story outline 194; historical allusions 195; script 199

bequest **II** 307–8

Beranbyrg *see* Barbury Castle

Berchtesgaden, Chamberlain meets Hitler **XV** 426, 477

Berchtold, Count **XIV** 469

Bere, castle and borough **IV** 429, 432, 441

Bere Alston (Devon) **V** 371

Berecingas *see* Barking (Essex)

Bereford, Chief Justice **IV** 373

Bereford, Sir Simon **V** 96, 102

Berehaven **XV** 159

Berengar, Raymond, count of Barcelona **III** 325

Berengaria, daughter of Sancho, king of Navarre, and wife of King Richard I **III** 360; **IV** 109

Berengarius Moyne, castle **VII** 38

Beresford, John (1738–1805), first commissioner of Irish revenue **XII** 393–5

Beresford, Viscount *see* Carr, William

Berg, count of **V** 121

Bergen: German bridge **VI** 69; Hansa factory 358; **VII** 221; **X** 65

Bergen op Zoom **VI** 362

Bergerac (Dordogne) **IV** 292, 293; **V** 132, 254; **VI** 108; Henry IV's protection 110

Bergerac, lord of **IV** 293

Berghamstyde *see* Bearsted (Kent)

Bergman, and scientific discovery **XII** 334

Bergson **XIV** 551

Berhtwald, archbishop of Canterbury **II** 142–5

Berhtwald, nephew of King Æthelred of Mercia **II** 69, 151

Bericus *see* Verica

Berkeley (Glos.) **III** 26, 101; **V** 94, 263, 344, 492; castle **VI** 8

Berkeley, George (1685–1753), bishop of Cloyne **XI** 10, 77, 85, 89, 94; career, characteristics and ideas 90–3; epitaph at Christ Church, Oxford 93; Irish famine 298; literary society 305; scheme for college in Bermuda 323

Berkeley, George, 1st earl of Berkeley **X** 323, 347, 387–8

Berkeley, James, canon of Exeter **V** 276

Berkeley, James, Lord **VI** 212, 329, 336

Berkeley, Sir John **IX** 147–8

Berkeley, Sir John, of Beverstone (Glos.) **VI** 331

Berkeley, Sir Maurice de **V** 253

Berkeley, Sir Robert **IX** 84–5

Berkeley, Thomas de, appointed constable (1297) **IV** 680, 681

Berkeley, Thomas, Lord **VI** 7, 8, 329, **VI** 429, 650, 664–5

Berkeley, Thomas II, Lord **V** 259, 316, 320, 321, 322, 344

Berkeley, Thomas III, Lord **V** 94

Berkeley, Thomas IV, Lord **V** 341, 422

Berkeley, Sir William **VI** 626, 627; keeper of king's Isle of Wight castles 635

Berkeley, Sir William **IX** 345

Berkeley, William, earl of Nottingham, later marquess of Berkeley (d. 1492), earl marshal (1486) **VII** 650

Berkhamsted (Herts.) **II** 597–8; honour **III** 203, 208; manor and castle **IV** 9, 40, 160; **V** 73, 329, 424

Berkley (Glos.) **III** 26, 101

Berkshire **Ia** 43; **Ib** 43, 139, 149, 152, 170; East Wansdyke 155–6; **II** 25–6, 28, 63, 65–6; becomes West Saxon shire 245; land division 283; division of West Saxon sees 439; Swein's earldom 561; military obligations of peasants 583; Downs 731; **III** 350, 406; **V** 312, 316, 365, 429; sheriff amerced (1457–8) **VI** 513; **VII** 452, 505, 528

Berksted, Stephen, bishop of Chichester (1262–87) **IV** 176, 186, 487; as a Montfortian 189, 191–2, 208

Berlin: republic proclaimed **XV** 113; Zinoviev letter 225–6; cultural centre 260, 347; commission after Munich 429; congress 430; Polish plenipotentiary 451; British begin to bomb 499; bombed 570–1; first target for Thunderclap 591; Churchill wishes to take 593; unconditional surrender 594

Berlin Decrees (1806) **XII** 464; Congress (1878) **XIV** 49–54; Conference (1884) 191

berm **Ia** 180

Bermingham, John de, earl of Louth (1319–29) **V** 229

Bermingham, Sir Walter de **V** 231

Bermondsey (Surrey): hoard **Ia** 459;

Bermondsey (Surrey) (*cont.*)
II 391; priory then abbey (Cluniac) 160, 165; **III** 169, 185, 321; prior and Adam de Stratton **IV** 365; **V** 293, 294; **VI** 300; convent **VII** 69

Bermudas **IX** 327; **X** 331

Bernadotte, Charles **XII** 426, 556, 558, 561

Bernal, J. D. **XV** 508

Bernard, bishop of St David's **III** 296

Bernard VII, count of Armagnac **VI** 109; supports French dukes in offer to Henry 113; operations against English at Harfleur 157–8; determined to starve out the garrison 163; intransigent about Harfleur 165; taken prisoner 174

Bernard, Raymond, lord of Montpezat **V** 109

Bernard de Neufmarché **II** 632

Bernardi, Major John **X** 185

Berners, Sir James **V** 458

Berners, John, Lord **VI** 525

Berners, Lord *see* Bourchier

Bernham, W. de, a Scottish scholar, letters **IV** 742

Bernicia **Ib** 175, 188, 197–201; map 4 xxxii; **II** 81–2, 91; kingdom **III** 265

Bernicians, *Bernice* **II** 37–8, 74–83; royal dynasty 75

Bernoulli, Daniel (1700–82) **XI** 379

Bernstorff, Andreas Gottlieb von (1649–1726) **XI** 20, 153, 175

Berri **III** 347, 374, 375, 379; siege 343–4

Berridge, Revd John (1716–93), of Everton **XI** 88

Berry **VI** 240, 241

Berry, duchess of *see* Marie, duchess of Berry

Berry, duke of *see* John, duke of Berry

Bertano, Gurone **VIII** 28

Bertha, fort **Ia** 175, 206

Bertha, wife of King Æthelberht of Kent **Ia** 724; **Ib** 10, 127; **II** 59, 105, 109, 112

Berthelet, Thomas **VII** 578

Bertie, James, 1st earl of Abingdon **X** 139

Bertie, Robert, earl of Lindsay **IX** 216

Bertrade, wife of Philip I, king of France **III** 124

Berwick (Salop), nr. Shrewsbury **VI** 52

Berwick, castle, burgh, and shire: **III** 277, 278, 279, 282, 283, 480; Edward I (1291–2) **IV** 604, 606, 685, 687, 700, 716; appeal of burgess to Edward I 608; petition of burgesses 609–10; captured (1296) 614; new town planned 614, 636–7; centre of Edward's Scottish administration and exchequer 614, 686, 712; parliament 615–17; in war time 706; **V** 11, 35, 39, 70; port 23; castle 33; falls to Scots (1318) 41; siege (1319) 56–7; capture (1333) 117; Richard II 439–40; **VI** 9, 35, 36, 40, 54; northern rebellion 63; government debts 221; Margaret offers surrender 523; surrenders to Scots 527; Edward IV's right recognized 585; East March incorporation 587; defences **VII** 37; Richard III retakes 53; Scottish parliament (Jan. 1488) 76; defence reorganized 78; Warbeck's promise 140; James' offer 147; Scottish marriage treaty (1502) 159, 160, 161; Gloucester captures 204; expenses 214; revenue 218; Scottish invasion (1513) 280, 281; English invasion (1544–5) 407; garrison reduced 487; defence costs 500; **VIII** 42, 44, 46, 47, 370; treaty **IX** 90; **XII** 44

Berwick, duc de *see* Fitzjames, James

61

Bigod, Hugh (d. 1266), son of Earl Hugh: justiciar (1258–60) **IV** 41, 54, 124, 125; sworn agreement (12 Apr. 1258) to king 130–1, 135, 140; made judiciar 137; thoroughness 146; grievances in the shires 148; council of regency 150; pursues course of justice 150–1; during royal absence (1259–60) 150, 156–8; kings' orders (Apr. 1260) 156–7; ceases to be justiciar 162, 163; wavers over loyalty to Henry 164–5, 173–4; drafting of concessions 175; escape to Pevensey 190

Bigod, Sir John **VII** 392

Bigod, Roger, earl of Norfolk **III** 12, 100, 283

Bigod, Roger, earl of Norfolk and earl marshal (d. 1306) **IV** 518, 707; leader of opposition to the king's policy (1297) 666, 678–83; summoned by Edward (1305) 689; preparation for war 690; demands firm observance of Charters 697

Bigod, Roger (d. 1270), eldest son of Earl Hugh: and his successor as earl of Norfolk **IV** 41; sworn agreement to king (12 Apr. 1258) 130–1, 135, 140; council of regency 150; died 174; drafting of concessions 175

Bigorre, county of **IV** 112; claimed by Constance of Béarn 287; count of 293; seneschal of 292, 294; **VI** 108

Bilbao **VIII** 369

Bildeston **Ib** 170

Bill, William **VII** 571; **VIII** 9

bill, or written petition **IV** 352

Bill of Rights **X** 153, 188

Billericay (Essex): Romano-Saxon urn **Ib** 93, 94 [fig. 8]; map 2 xxx; map 6 88; **V** 418

Billfrith the anchorite **II** 191

billiards **XV** 19

Billing, Pemberton, 'member for air' **XV** 44, 95; libel action against 103, 170

Billingham **Ib** 197

bills **IV** 355; in eyre 355

bills of supremacy and uniformity, opposition to **VIII** 11, 12; *see also* Acts and Bills

Bilney **VIII** 29

Bilney, Thomas **VII** 257, 345, 572

Binchester, inscription **Ia** 522

Bindon (Dorset) **III** 226

Bing Boys **XV** 52

Bingham, George Charles, 3rd earl of Lucan **XIII** 280–1; biography 280

Bingham, Robert, bishop of Salisbury (1228–46) **IV** 60

Bingham, William, founder of Godshouse **VI** 669; rector of Carlton Curlieu (Leics.) 669

Bingley, Mr, printer **XII** 140

Binham, William **V** 511

Birch, John **IX** 273

Birchington, Stephen (chronicle ascribed to), on Edward III and Stratford **V** 176

Bird, Francis (1667–1731), sculptor **XI** 402

Bird, John, bishop of Bangor (1537–41); bishop of Chester (1541–54) 545

Bird, Thomas, bishop of St Asaph **VI** 539

Birdoswald (Camboglanna): coin **Ia** 377; fort 178; inscriptions 314, 315, 317; water-mill 632; **Ib** 77, 198; map 4 xxxii

Birinus, bishop of the West Saxons **Ib** 157, 168, 172; **II** 102, 117–18

Birkbeck, George **XIII** 494–5

Birkenhead, Lord *see* Smith, Frederick Edwin

Birkwood Park (Yorks.) **VI** 330

Birmingham: **IX** 280; local government **XI** 47; metal industry 121; industry **XII** 28, 30, 334, 507; enfranchisement project 278; riots (1792) 324; population 517;

XIII 2, 26, 65, 81, 83–4; Political Union and reform agitation 78, 84, 134; chartist movement 134, 137; Convention of Industrious Classes 137–40; Complete Suffrage Union 142; Orsini plot 170; franchise 182; Reform Act (1867) 187–80; water supplies 463; Rowland Hill school 485; college of medicine 493; ironworks 603; Trade Union Congress 615; municipal activities **XIV** 127, 129; population **XV** 256; Neville Chamberlain its lord mayor 256; Joseph Chamberlain's work 266; repertory theatre 314; speech by Chamberlain 440–1; Germans bomb 501

Biron, duc de **VIII** 357

Birrell, Augustine **XIV** 385, 392, 393, 479; **XV** 56

Birrens (*Blatobulgium*): fort **Ia** 176, 211; inscription 667; **Ib** 75; map 4 xxxii

Birth of a Nation **XV** 315

birth-control **XIII** 2

birth-rates **XIV** 103–4, 270–2, 499; **XV** 165, 301–2

births, registration **IX** 202

Birtley (Northumb.), Belgian town **XV** 20

Biscay, bay of **III** 149; **XV** 564

Biscop **Ib** 178

Bisham (Berks.) **V** 73

bishops: **Ia** 462, 469, 470–81, 496, 498; Ambrosius 401; Chrysanthus, son 407; authority and status 410, 451, 580, 722–31; Sidonius 453; British 340, 343, 491–2, 738–9; duties **II** 147–8; English **IV** 340–1, 485–8; in English political life 23–4, 46–7, 55–60; charges against Simon de Montfort (1260) 161; the Monfortian (1263–5) 176, 186, 189, 192–5, 208; Welsh 390–1; rulers in their dioceses 451–6, 474–5; elections 468; monastic 485; family connec-

tions 486–7; jurisdiction and the metropolitan 489–93; clerical taxation 501–9; appointment **VI** 268–9; Thomas Gascoigne's view 269; relations with clergy 272; sees vacated **VII** 350; *congé d'élire* introduced 358; subjected to vicar-general 359; six new sees created 400; appointed by letters patent 513; attack on Catholic bishops 516–18; Catholic, treatment **VIII** 16; excluded from parliament **X** 10; the seven 141; Scottish *see also* Canterbury; Church, Scotland; London

Bishops' Book (Institution of a Christian Man) **VII** 395, 428, 568, 573

Bishop's Lynn *see* King's Lynn

Bishop's Stortford (Herts.) **II** 642

Bishopstone **Ib** 138; map 2 xxx

Bishopthorpe (N. Yorks.) **VI** 61

Bismarck, Otto, Prince (1815–98): **XIV** 3, 4, 6, 38, 495; at Berlin Congress 49–50; his policies (1875 to 1881) 84; their consequences 84–5; yields to colonial party 188; at Berlin Conference 191; foreign policies (1881 to 1890) 194–6; 'Re-insurance' Treaty 196; letter to Lord Salisbury 198; offers alliance against France 199; dismissed by William II 199; exceptional authority 570; **XIII** 175, 225, 265, 315, 323; Polish rebellion 315–16; Schleswig-Holstein question 319–21, 323; and Luxemburg 324–5; on Balkans **XV** 577

Bismarck, sunk **XV** 505–6

Bithynia **Ia** 566, 569, 577

Bitterne (*Clausentum*) (Hants) **Ia** 384; **Ib** 92, 151; map 2 xxx; map 3 xxxi; map 6 88

Blacader, Robert, archbishop of Glasgow **VII** 158, 161

Blachford, Lord *see* Rogers, Frederic

Black, Joseph (1728–99), chemist
XI 287, 385, 386–7, 391; XII 334
Black Book XV 103, 170
Black Book (1820) XIII 28, 508, 512
'Black Book of the Household',
unfinished treatise VI 595–6
Black Death V 219, 220, 289, 301,
328–9; criminal activities 205;
trade 224, 225, 357–8, 362; effects
on clergy 297, 299; nature and
incidence 331–3; monasteries
306, 308; population 313, 331–2,
347–8; labour situation 333–6,
369; tin-mining in Cornwall 371;
in Lincoln 380; VI 368, 370, 372,
381; X 66
Black Friday XV 146, 240
Black Monks: suggested reforms VI
197; *proprietas* 197; numbers 294
Black Patch Ib 149; map 3 xxxi
Black Rubric VII 520
Black Sea clauses XIV 4–5
Black and Tans XV 155, 161
Blackborough VII 527
Blackbourton (Oxon.) III 148
Blackburn, Nicholas, mayor of York
VI 403, 404
Blackburn, population XV 167, 304
Blackburne, Lancelot (1658–1743),
archbishop of York XI 78, 81;
unclerical behaviour 81
Blackburnshire (Lancs.) VI 369
Blackett family XII 52
Blackfriars, London: burial Ia 526;
ship 564; king's council meeting
VI 220; council (1410) 96
Blackheath (Kent) V 408, 409; VI
496; VII 142
Blackloists IX 211
Blacklow hill (War.) V 26
Blackpool: population XV 167;
Labour conference 595
Blackstone, Sir William (1723–80)
XI 6, 10; *Commentaries on Laws of
England* 56–7, 64; on king's bench
59; capital punishment 62;
teacher at Oxford 140; English
common law 274; XII 338; bio-

graphical note 145; mystique of
law 330
Blackwater (Ireland), fort VIII 485
Blackwater river (Essex) VI 63
Blackwell, George, archpriest VIII
454, 455, 456; IX 208
Blaecca Ib 178–9
Blaen Llyfni (Glam.) V 74
Blaenllyfni (Brecon) VI 42
Blagden, Sir Charles (1748–1820)
XII 339
Blage, Sir George VII 428
Blair, James (1656–1743), commis-
sary in Virginia XI 323
Blair, Robert (1699–1746), poet XI
425
Blair Atholl X 277
Blake, John V 449, 458
Blake, Robert XV 224
Blake, Robert (1599–1657) IX 141,
222–3, 225, 231, 235; blockade of
Spanish coast 233
Blake, Sexton XV 312
Blake, William (1757–1827), Eng-
lish poet XII 460, 535, 537;
XIII 32, 35; death 530; symbol-
ism 593
Blakeney (Norfolk) VI 363
Blakeney, William, Lord (1672–
1761) XI 255, 352
Blamont, count of VI 156
Blanca, Count Florida XII 460
Blanche, daughter of Henry IV VI
68
Blanche, duchess of Lancaster V
255, 267, 531
Blanche of Artois, wife of Henry,
count of Champagne and king of
Navarre, later wife of Edward of
Lancaster IV 236, 238–41
Blanche of Castile, wife of Louis
VIII, king of France III 379, 483;
IV 102; husband's claim to
English throne 8; defeat off Sand-
wich 12–13; regent for Louis IX
88, 91–4; revolt by La Marche
97; death (Nov. 1252) 114
Blanche of Champagne, marries

John, later duke of Brittany **IV** 109, 236, 237
Blanche Taque (Somme), ford **VI** 152
Bland, Hubert **XIV** 334
Blandinium, abbey **II** 344; *see also* Ghent
Bland's regiment **XI** 227
Blankenberghe **VIII** 402
Blanket, Thomas **V** 368
Blanketeers **XIII** 64; **XV** 349
Blanquefort (nr. Bordeaux) **IV** 264
Blatchford, Robert **XIV** 334
Blathwayt, William **X** 186
Blatobulgium see Birrens
Blavet **VIII** 414
Blaye (Gironde) **IV** 103, 650, 666; **VI** 108, 109
Blean (Kent) **III** 79
Blenheim: battle **X** 207–9; palace 389, 390
Blériot, Louis, Channel flight **XIV** 433, 510
Bletchingley (Surrey) **VI** 417
Bligh, Edward (1685–1775), General **XI** 362
blitz: conscientious objectors **XV** 457; effects 501–3; improvized act 517; demand for retaliation 518, 528, 534
blockade: of Germany in First World War **XV** 14; effect exaggerated 319, 369; proposed against Japan 372–3; conducted by Ministry of Economic Warfare 456; exists mainly on paper 461
Blockade, Ministry of **XV** 76, 130
Bloemfontein: conference **XIV** 248; occupation 255
Blois (Loir-et-Cher) **VI** 114, 246, 474
Blois, Charles of **V** 131, 136, 143, 146, 247
Blois, Henry of, bishop of Winchester: as abbot of Glastonbury **III** 44, 224; supports Stephen 132–3; made legate 138, 193; joins the Empress 138–9, 143; rejoins

Stephen 144; in ecclesiastical affairs 190–1, 193, 194; estimate of character 193; his interest in antiques, art and literature 193, 250, 259; relations with Becket 199–200, 208; his castles 322; privilege in favour of 400
Blois, house of **III** 122, 318
Blois, Peter of **III** 196, 247, 332, 334; on Henry II 321; Longchamp's downfall 358
Blois, treaty: between Maxmilian, Louis XII, and Philip (1504) **VII** 154; between Louis and Ferdinand (1505) 154; **VIII** 154, 155, 163
Blois, William of **III** 257
Blomfield, Dr C. J. **XIII** 450, 463, 506, 508
Blomfield, Sir R. **XIV** 540
Bloody Assize **X** 139
'Bloody Sunday' **XIV** 180–1
Blore Heath (Staffs.) **VI** 515
Blount, Sir Charles **VIII** 419, 428; Lord Mountjoy 486, 487, 490
Blount, Sir Christopher **VIII** 433, 441
Blount, Elizabeth **VII** 325
Blount, Sir James, lieutenant of Hammes (d. 1493): joins Henry Tudor **VI** 640; **VII** 50
Blount, John, Lord Mountjoy **VI** 340
Blount, Sir Thomas **V** 91; **VI** 25
Blount, Walter, Lord Mountjoy: Pontefract **VI** 557
Blount, William, 4th Lord Mountjoy (d. 1543) **VII** 249, 250, 251, 252, 256
Blounts, the **XI** 73
Blow, John (*c.*1649–1708) **XI** 399, 417
Bloxham (Oxon.), church: Milcombe chapel **VI** 648
Blücher **XII** 558, 560, 567
Bluet, Thomas, priest **VIII** 455, 456
Blum, L., and non-intervention **XV** 394

Blumental, pottery types, Saxon *Buckelurnen* **Ib** 71 [fig. 6(c)]

Blund, John **IV** 56

Blundell, William **IX** 211

Blunden, Edmund **XV** 61, 549

Blundevill, Ranulf de, earl of Chester **IV** 2, 3, 11; position in England 20; charter of liberties 20; royal castles 24–5; and Fawkes de Breauté 27; and Richard of Cornwall (1227) 40; and Llywelyn ab Iorwerth 45, 392; and Hubert de Burgh 51; in Normandy 96; death and successors 51, 197

Blundus, Robert **III** 17

Blunt, Wilfrid Scawen **XIV** 180

Blyth (Notts.) **III** 25

Blythe, John, later bishop of Salisbury (1494), master of the rolls (5 May 1492) **VII** 648

board of trade *see* trade, board of

Boar's Head Tavern **VI** 125–6

Bocardo **VII** 377, 551

Boccaccio, Giovanni **V** 531; **VI** 679

Bochastle, fort **Ia** 149

Bocher, Joan **VII** 520, 524, 549, 552

Bocking (Essex) **V** 345

Bocking, Dr Edward **VII** 361

Bodiam Castle (Sussex) **V** 263; **VI** 651

Bodley, G. F. **XIV** 325

Bodley, Sir Thomas **VIII** 320; **IX** 353

Bodmin (Corn.): Moor **Ia** 4; fort 93; **III** 85, 233; **VI** 419; **VII** 145

Bodrugan, Henry **VI** 572

Bodunni *see* Dobunni

Bodvoc **Ia** 68, 83

body politic **IV** 522, 527, 528

Boece **III** 276

Boece, Hector (1465?-1536) principal, Aberdeen university **VII** 249

Boehme, Jakob (1575-1624): influence on William Law **XI** 94

Boenammus **III** 457

Boer war, concentration camps **XV** 418

Boerhaave, Herman (1668–1738) **XI** 389, 396

Boerio, John Baptist **VII** 251

Boethius **III** 246; **V** 531

Bohemia **V** 427; **VII** 104; **IX** 22–3, 55

Bohic ('Bowyk'), Henry, canonist **VI** 666

Bohum, Eleanor de, duchess of Gloucester **V** 268, 460

Bohun, Humphrey de **III** 277, 336

Bohun, Humphrey de, earl of Hereford (d. 1275), captured at Lewes **IV** 190

Bohun, Humphrey de, junior, his son: a Montfortian **IV** 182, 185; on council of nine (1264) 192; captured and dies 202

Bohun, Humphrey de, grandson of previous earl, earl of Hereford (d. 1298), constable: recovers Brecon (1277) **IV** 409, 411; on trial (1290) 329; on trial (1294) 441; not present in parliament at Salisbury (1297) 680; joins earl marshal in opposition to Edward I's policy 680, 681–3; Edward summoned from Berwick 689; Scottish war 690; demands observance of Charters 697–8; dies 697

Bohun, Humphrey de, earl of Hereford and Essex (1302–22) **V** 1, 264; an Ordainer 10, 23, 24; and Gaveston 26, 28; and negotiations (1312) 29; on Bannockburn campaign 35, 40; and Middle Party 52, 61; at Sherburn-in-Elmet 62; on Boroughbridge campaign 65; killed 66; forfeiture of estates 73

Bohun, Humphrey de, earl of Hereford and Essex (1336–61) **V** 256

Bohun, Humphrey de, earl of Hereford, Essex, and Northampton (1363–73) **V** 256, 260, 268; **VI** 74

Bohun, Joanna, later countess of Hereford **VI** 26, 63

Bohun, John de, earl of Hereford and Essex (1326–36) **V** 75, 260

Bohun, Mary de, countess of Derby **V** 460

Bohun, William de, earl of Northampton (1337–69) **V** 134, 159, 176, 177, 205, 238; loyalty to Edward III 148, 256; created earl 153; indenture for Brittany (1345) 236; knight, Order of the Garter 252–3

Bohun family **V** 503

Bohun heiresses **VI** 334

Bois-de-Vincennes **V** 82, 112

Boisratier, Guillaume, archbishop of Bourges **VI** 137, 141

Boitard, Louis Peter (*fl.* 1750), engraver **XI** 414

Boke named the Governor **VII** 576, 582

Bokenham, Osbern **VI** 659

Bokhara **VII** 507, 561; **VIII** 238

Bole, Richard, fellow of Balliol college **VI** 679

Boleyn, Anne: attracts notice of Henry **VII** 322–6; Francis' view 331; marquess of Pembroke (1532) 339; fall (1536), and execution 341, 379; pregnancy 357; act of succession 359; result of death 382, 404; Catherine Howard's cousin 416; Cranmer intercedes 552; **VIII** 2

Boleyn, Elizabeth, wife of Sir Thomas Boleyn, daughter of 2nd duke of Norfolk **VII** 323

Boleyn, George, Viscount Rochford (d. 1536) **VII** 379

Boleyn, Margaret, wife of Sir William Boleyn, daughter of Thomas, 7th earl of Ormond, grandmother of Anne **VII** 323

Boleyn, Mary **VII** 323, 325, 380

Boleyn, Thomas, Viscount Rochford, earl of Wiltshire and Ormond: City stock **VII** 323; created Viscount Rochford

(1525) 324; keeper of the privy seal (1530) 352, 647; treasurer of the household (1522) 649

Bolingbroke (Lincs.) **II** 525; honour **VI** 2

Bolingbroke *see* Henry IV

Bolingbroke, Henry St John, 1st Viscount: Harley's new country party **X** 188; anti-Dutch policy 235; account of 236; October club 238; jealousy of Harley 239; old pretender 243; foreign policy 245; culmination of quarrel with Harley 245–8; leaves England 249; Irish parliament 321; Brothers Club 358; **XII** 6

Bolingbroke, Roger **VI** 482

Bollati, Christopher de, Milanese ambassador **VI** 574

Bologna **III** 239, 247, 330, 369; university **V** 144; **VII** 348; Colet reads law 242; Erasmus visits 251; Pace visits 257; Julius besieges 274; Leo and Francis come to terms 306; Charles crowned (24 Feb. 1530) 320; Clement issues brief 331; pope recalls council (Mar. 1547) 482

Bologna, John of, *summa notarie* **IV** 490

Bolton (Northumb.) **VI** 328

Bolton (Lancs.) **VII** 280; weavers **XII** 509

Bolton, Baron *see* Orde (Orde-Powlett), Thomas

Bolton, dukes of *see* Paulet, Charles; Paulet, Harry; Powlett, Charles

Bolton Castle **VIII** 112, 114, 118

Bolton Priory **VII** 592

Bombay **IX** 322; **X** 60, 349, 350, 351

Bomber Command: created **XV** 391; incapable of damaging enemy 392; headquarters 480; opposes attacks on U-boats 517; night bombing 518; breaks off strategic offensive (1941) 519; Harris becomes commander 520; initiates indiscriminate bombing

Bomber Command (*cont.*)
534; conducts compaign against enemy morale (1942) 552–3; third offensive (1943–4) 570–2; under Eisenhower 572; Thunderclap 591; receives no acknowledgement 592

Bona of Savoy 534, 535; unacceptable bride **VI** 550

Bona Vista, cape **X** 343

Bonaparte, Joseph **XII** 459, 494–6, 557

Bonaparte, Louis **XII** 452

Bonaparte, Napoleon *see* Napoleon

Bonaventura **VI** 680

Bond of Association **VIII** 377

Bondfield, Margaret **XV** 271

bones: animal **Ia** 613, 620; analysis 655; human 551; evidence of funerary customs 691–2, 696, 701, 704

Bonet, André Louis F., Prussian envoy under George I and II **XI** 38

Boniface (Wynfrith) **II** 91, 111, 159, 161; compared with Willibrord 167–8; early life 168; joins Willibrord in Frisia 168; consecrated bishop 168; receives pallium 169; bishoprics in Germany 169; consecrates Pippin, king of Franks 170; reforms Frankish church 170; last mission to Frisia and death 171; significance of career 171; correspondence 171–2, 205; invites English followers to Germany 172; place of women in his mission 172–3; introduces English learning into Germany 173; writer of Latin prose 183; letter to King Æthelbald 205

Boniface, count of Savoy (1253–63) **IV** 249, 250

Boniface IV, Pope **II** 112

Boniface V, Pope **II** 114

Boniface VIII, Pope (1294–1303) **IV** 233; intervention in Scottish war 228–9, 685, 693, 701–2; financial arrangement with Edward I and change of attitude to Scottish affairs 500, 709, 710; bull *Noveritis nos* 523; attitude to Anglo-French war (1294–8) and his efforts for peace 661–2, 668; arbitration in his private capacity (1298) 650–3; bull *Clericis laicos* 666, 674–6; bull *Etsi de statu* (1297) 674, 677; replies to him from Edward I and the barons of England 697, 702, 705–6

Boniface IX, Pope (1389–1404), translations of bishops **V** 277; anti-papal legislation 282; Richard II 282–3, 477, 478, 486; demands for subsidies 285, 297; lollards 522; **VI** 26, 94, 97, 268, 300

Boniface of Savoy, uncle of Queen Eleanor (of Provence), archbishop of Canterbury (d. 1270) **IV** 118; closeness to Eleanor 74; Plan of the Magnates 79; royal justice 143; council of fifteen 145; council of regency 150; papal injunctions about Provisions of Oxford 165; provincial councils and constitutions 165, 167, 451, 453, 456–7, 472–3; leaves England (1263) 175, 178; at Boulogne 179; baronial council orders his return 199; death 225

Bonington, Richard Parkes **XIII** 590

Bonluc, nr. Bayonne **IV** 238

Bonmoulins (Orne) **III** 345

Bonn **Ia** 587, 695; capture **X** 204

Bonne d'Armagnac, first wife of Charles of Orléans **VI** 484

Bonnegarde, Edward I's Christmas at (1288) **IV** 284

Bonner, Edmund, bishop of London (1540–59): chaplain to Wolsey **VII** 331; London consecration 416; 'Il Cortigiano' 417; surrenders 512; deprived (1549) 518; released from Marshalsea (1553)

Bordeaux (Gironde) (*cont.*)
145; court established 143; wine trade 361–3; **VI** 10, 34, 107, 148, 240; centre of wine trade 106; district (*Bordelais*) 107, 109; loyalty to England 107; appeal (1406) ignored by Henry IV 109; *jurade* 110; imports 364–5; Bekynton's visit 470; French troops enter (1451) 504; requests English aid (Mar. 1452) 505; welcomes Shrewsbury's forces (Oct. 1452) 505; expels French garrison 505; municipality 506; trade with Bristol 506; trade with London and Southampton 506; English mercantile colony 506; **VII** 312; **X** 237; French government at **XV** 487; Churchill wants landing 583

Bordeaux, archbishop of *see* Uguccione, Francis

Borden, Sir Robert **XV** 82

border, Scottish **IV** 574, 588–9, 600; **VI** 221; Richard III's defence principles 637; franchise and administration 637; treaty to regulate disputes (1502) **VII** 158

borders (Marches): treaty (1502) **VII** 159; raid of Eskdale (1504) 162–3; council 204, 385; light horse 268; 'incidents' 270; Scots cross (22 Aug. 1513) 280; Dacre's truce 312–13; Pilgrimage of Grace 385–6; Somerset invades (1547) 484

Bordesholm, Anglian pottery **Ib** 65 [fig. 3(a)]

Bordesley Abbey (Worcs.), monks **III** 447; **V** 258

Boreham (Essex) **IV** 339

Borgard, Albert (1659–1751) **XI** 220

Borgia, Cesare (Caesar), son of Pope Alexander VI, duke of Valentinois (d. 1507): Italian core **VII** 83; temporal principality 112; deposition urged 114; betrothed to Charlotte d'Albret 152; ill in crisis (1503) 153; misfortunes 155

Borgia, Rodrigo *see* Alexander VI, Pope

Borgstedt, Anglian pottery **Ib** 65 [fig.3(c)], 72, 192; map 1 xxix

Born, Bertrand de **III** 340

Borodino, battle (1812) **XII** 497

Boron, Robert de **VI** 657

borough: as a trading centre **II** 336, 526; eleventh century 292; pre-Alfredian 526–30; plots enclosed 529–30; plots attached to rural manors 531; customary law of *burhriht* 530–2; varied conditions of tenure 533–4; earl's third penny 534; court separate from the hundred 534–5; minting place 535–8

Borough, Stephen (1525–84) **VII** 507, 561

Borough, William **VIII** 318

'Borough English' **III** 41

Boroughbridge **Ib** 188; battle **V** 66, 69, 73, 80; **VII** 35

boroughs and market towns: literature on **IV** 771–2; representation of selected cities (1265 and 1273) 197, 225; development and taxation 529–34; Welsh 432–3; *see also* towns

Borowara (Boroware) **Ib** 125; map 2 xxx

Borowe, Thomas, *custos rotulorum*, prebendary of St Stephen's, Westminster **VI** 634

Borrow, George: biography **XIII** 553; writings 553

Bosa, bishop of York **II** 135, 139

Bosanhamm *see* Bosham (Sussex)

Bosanquet, Bernard **XIV** 330

Boscawen, Sir Edward, admiral (1711–61) **XI** 224, 229, 359, 361, 365; attack on Pondichery (1748) 327; skirmish with French fleet in America 349

Bosham (Bosanhamm) (Sussex) **II** 429, 565, 731; monks 128, 731

Bosnian crisis **XIV** 410–11

Boso, Cardinal **III** 195

Boston (Lincs.) **III** 80, 82, 96; St Botolph's fair 77, 87; **V** 357, 380; **VI** 221, 360, 418; **VII** 181, 221, 471

Boston (Mass.) **X** 338, 340, 347; massacre **XII** 193; Tea Party 196

Boston Newsletter **X** 347

Boswell, James (1740–95) **XI** 141, 305, 427, 430; **XII** 135, 271, 325, 353; biography 325; man of letters 339; influence on society 347

Bosworth, battle **V** 332; **VI** 643–5; contemporary indifference **VII** 7; new dynasty 8, 22; Richard's death, Henry's crowning 46; Scottish aid 51; Croyland chronicler 58; Henry already king 62; papal support 66; Richard's army 75; Stanley 122; attainders 124; Poynings 128; Henry's reign begins 191; council 205; magic of crown 562

Bosworth Psalter **II** 462

botany **VIII** 316, 317; **X** 376

Boteler, Henry, recorder of Coventry **VI** 604

Botetourt, John de **V** 23

Botha, L. **XV** 31, 82

Botha, General Louis **XIV** 253, 255, 256, 345, 346; Kruger communication 347; European visit 348; prime minister 390; fiscal system 405

Bothmar, Count **X** 242

Bothmer, Johann G., Graf von (1656–1732) **XI** 152, 153

Bothwell: castle **IV** 693, 694; bridge **X** 100, 271

Bothwell, earls of *see* Hepburn, Patrick; Stewart, Francis; Herbert, James

Bothwell, Lord *see* Ramsay, John

Botreaux, William, Lord **VI** 212, 480

Bottisham, Bottlesham, John, master of Peterhouse, bishop of Rochester **VI** 79, 272

Bottomley, Horatio: biography **XV** 21; recruiting agent 20; denounces liquor control 37; War Cabinet consults 103; demagogue 106; Lloyd George identified with 137; called in to quell mutinies 138; convicted 180

Botulf of Icanhoh **II** 117

Botwine, abbot of Ripon **II** 174

Bouchain **X** 219, 220; capture 230, 234

Boucicaut, Jean le Meingre de, marshal of France **VI** 152, 153, 222; at Caudebec 150

Boudicca (Boudica) **Ia** 113–22, 124–5, 127–8, 155, 261; crop sowing failure 76; Colchester correction 89–90; rebellion 94, 95, 101, 109; sack of Verulamium 233, 659–60; massacre 544, 582, 692, 699; **Ib** 97

Bougainville, Louis Antoine de (1729–1811) **XI** 365

Boughton, Rutland **XIV** 545

Bouillon, duke of **VIII** 57

Boulenois, treasurer of **VI** 257

Boulogne (Pas-de-Calais): **Ia** 27, 308, 563; Carausius' base 288, 298, 304–5, 320; *classis Britannica* 529; **II** 263, 265, 347; county **III** 132, 453; honour 132, 165, 440; **IV** 12; *émigrés* and conferences (1263–5) 178, 179, 181, 193–5; **V** 4, 492; peace conference **VI** 1, 67, 152, 166; **VII** 102; besieged (1492) 108–9; defence 111; expedition 141, 211; siege 208; Battle of Spurs (1513) 279; siege intended 313; taken by Suffolk (1544) 409; Henry II covets 482; cession offered 483; guarantee hopes 485; treaty (1550) 486; troops dismissed 487; defence costs 500; **VIII** 407; entrenched camp proposed **XV** 12

Boulogne, counts of **III** 433, 440; *see also* Adelof; Eustace; Dammartin, Renaud of; Matthew

Boulonnais **II** 629

Boulter, Hugh (1672–1742), archbishop of Armagh **XI** 288, 289, 293, 297–8, 302

Boulton, Matthew, manufacturer (1728–1809) **XII** 28, 30, 334, 506, 508; biography 28

Boundary Commission, Irish **XV** 158, 162, 218

Bouquet **II** 14

Bourbon, Antoine, king of Navarre **VIII** 60

Bourbon, Cardinal, archbishop of Lyons **VI** 578

Bourbon, Charles, count of Montpensier and duke of, constable of France: Suffolk alliance 313; besieges Marseilles 315; reinstated 316; killed (1527) 317

Bourbon, Charles de, archbishop of Lyons: treaty of Picquigny **VI** 577

Bourbon, duc de **XII** 423; *see also* Louis; Louis Henri

Bourbon, Henry, of Navarre **VIII** 147, 158, 160, 344; succession 364–5; *see also* Henry IV, king of France

Bourbon, Jean, count of La Marche **VI** 56

Bourbon, Louis, prince of Condé: defies house of Guise **VIII** 54–8; signs peace of Amboise 60; **IX** 230, 234

Bourbon, Louis de, count of Vendôme **VI** 141, 204, 222; Scottish embassy 177

Bourbon, Louis Henri, duc de (1692–1740) **XI** 185, 194, 195, 200

Bourbon Powers **XI** 213, 241, 244; marriage alliances 193–4, 200, 209, 232; Family Compact 206, 209, 232, 263; secret treaty (1761) 369; *see also* France; 'Gallispans';

Spain

Bourbourg **V** 431, 432

Bourchier, Sir Edward **VI** 516

Bourchier, Fulk, Lord Fitzwarren **VI** 602

Bourchier, Henry, 2nd earl of Essex (d. 1540) **VII** 414

Bourchier, Henry, Viscount, earl of Essex **VI** 512, 538; joins Edward IV at Pontefract 557; made member of Warwick's council 562; wool importer and exporter 591

Bourchier, John **VI** 516

Bourchier, John, 2nd Baron Berners (1467–1533) **VII** 581

Bourchier, John, 3rd earl of Bath (d. 1561) **VII** 528

Bourchier, Sir Robert, Chancellor (1340–1) **V** 168, 176, 210

Bourchier, T., cardinal of Canterbury **VI** 595

Bourchier, Thomas, bishop of Ely, later archbishop of Canterbury (1454–86) **VI** 270, 420, 504, 513; chancellor 510; accompanies earls to Northampton 520; sequestrates Edward IV's goods 614; pleads with queen for duke of York 619; **VII** 77

Bourchier, Sir Thomas **VI** 643

Bourchier, Sir Thomas **VII** 169; constabulary, Windsor Castle 57

Bourchier, Sir William, count of Eu **VI** 213, 234, 434; ambassador to France (Mar. 1415) 141; constable of Tower (1416) 141

Bourchier family **VII** 50

La Bourdonnais, Bertrand de (1699–1755) **XI** 261, 326

Bourg (Gironde) **III** 442; **IV** 650, 666; **VI** 108, 109

Bourgeois, Émile, on French participation in Austrian Succession war **XI** 268

Bourges (Cher) **Ia** 493; inscription 580; assembly of French clergy (1225) **IV** 502; assembly (1283) 254; ecclesiastical province 292;

VI 113, 244; besieged by Charles VI 114; university **VII** 348

Bourges, archbishop of *see* Bois-ratier, Guillaume

Bourgneuf Bay (Brittany) **V** 360; **VI** 71, 359

Bourgtheroulde (Seine-Inf.) **III** 127

Bourne (Lincs.) **V** 526

Bourne, Dr Gilbert (d. 1569), bishop of Bath and Wells (1554) **VII** 542

Bourne, Sir John, principal secretary of state (Aug. 1553–Mar. 1558) **VII** 649

Bourne, W. Sturges **XIII** 75

Bourne, William **VIII** 318

Bournemouth (Dorset): beginning **XIV** 114; population **XV** 167; Labour conference 474

Bourton, John, merchant of Bristol **VI** 418

Boutellier, Guy, captain of Rouen **VI** 173, 176

Bouvines: battle **III** 91, 122, 343, 440, 449; King John desperate 300; great coalition broken 367; Poitou campaign 465; allies clash with enemy 467

bovata see oxgang

Bovate **III** 43

Boves (Somme) treaty **III** 342; **VI** 153

Boves, Hugh of **III** 471, 477

Bow Street Runners **XII** 45

Bowcombe **Ib** 213

Bowen, Lord **XIV** 299

Bower, Scots historian **VI** 34

Bowes, bath-house **Ia** 685

Bowes, Sir George **VIII** 140

Bowes, John (1690–1767), lord chancellor of Ireland **XI** 289

Bowes, Sir Robert (1495?–1554) **VII** 405; master of the rolls (1552) 648

Bowet, Henry **V** 490

Bowet, Henry, bishop of Bath and Wells, later archbishop of York **VI** 76, 268

Bowley, Robert, master of the coinage of groats **VII** 56

bowls **IX** 311

Bowness-on-Solway: fort **Ia** 177, 178; inscription 659

Boxall, John (d. 1571), secretary of state (1557) **VII** 649

Boxgrove (Sussex) **VI** 279

boxing **X** 258

Boxley (Kent): abbey **III** 189; **VII** 395

boy scouts **XIV** 554

Boyce, William (1710–79), composer **XI** 417

Boycott, Captain **XIV** 72

Boyd, William, 4th earl of Kilmarnock (1704–46) **XI** 256

Boydell, John (1719–1804), printseller **XII** 346

Boyer, Abel (1667–1729) **X** 379; **XI** 31

Boyle, Hon. Charles **X** 384

Boyle, Charles, 4th earl of Orrery (1676–1731) **XI** 182

Boyle, Henry, earl of Shannon (1682–1764) **XI** 294, 303

Boyle, Richard, 3rd earl of Burlington (1695–1753) **XI** 396, 402, 404, 411, 421

Boyle, Richard, earl of Cork **IX** 115

Boyle, Hon. Robert (1627–91), chemist **IX** 364; **X** 323–4, 346, 375, 376; scientific movement 30, 43; **XI** 385

Boyle, Roger, Lord Broghil **IX** 242, 414

Boyne: river **V** 472; battle **X** 165, 307–8

Boynton, Christopher **VI** 323

Boynton, Yorkshire family **VI** 327

Boys, Commodore, blockades Dunkirk (1759) **XI** 365

Brabançon mercenaries **III** 335, 337, 372, 373, 377

Brabant **III** 381; merchants **IV** 519; wool trade 622, 637, 659, 662; Edward I 647, 661, 664, 665; beginnings of English staple 663,

Brabant (*cont.*)
679; **V** 22, 111, 165; merchants
170; Order of the Garter, membership 253; Lion of 267; wool
trade 350; estates **VI** 169; county
351, 553, 582, 583; **VII** 473

Brabant, Anthony of *see* Anthony of
Brabant

Brabant, dukes of *see* John I; John
II; John III; Henry

'Brabant, lines of' **X** 211

Brabant, Marie of, queen of France
see Marie of Brabant

Brabazon, Roger, Judge: spokesman
of King Edward's demands in
Scottish case **IV** 603, 608; pronounces judgement in favour of
Baliol 608

Bracey, Roger, constable of Chester
VI 55

Bracken, B., persuades Churchill to
remain silent **XV** 473

Brackenbury, Sir Henry **XIV** 11,
29, 290

Brackenbury, Sir Robert: keeper of
Tower **VI** 635, 643; Gloucester's
household treasurer 605; killed
VII 58

Brackley (Northants) **III** 25, 470;
negotiations (1264) **IV** 186

Brackley, Baron, later viscount *see*
Ellesmere, Thomas Egerton

Brackley, Thomas, Dominican **VI**
296

bracteates **Ib** 26, 115–16

Bracton **III** 4, 44, 78, 409

Bracton, Henry de, Judge **IV** 212,
374; writs of consultation 477; on
kingship 512; **V** 5; **VI** 313

Bradanforda *see* Bradford-on-Avon
(Wilts.)

Bradbury, Thomas (1677–1759) **XI**
88

Braddock, Edward (1695–1755),
General **XI** 218, 220, 348, 349,
351

Bradford (Yorks.) **VI** 366; **IX** 132;
XII 513; **XIV** 128

Bradford, countess of **XIV** 30

Bradford, John (1510?-55), prebendary of St Paul's **VII** 542, 546,
550, 571

Bradford, William **IX** 330

Bradford-on-Avon (Bradanforda)
(Wilts.) **II** 374, 731; monastery
160; later church 443; **VI** 365

Bradlaugh, Charles: biography **XIV**
67; oath controversy 67–8; Mal-
thusian propaganda 104; as free-
thinker 141

Bradley, A. C. **XIV** 551

Bradley, F. H. **XIV** 329

Bradley, James (1693–1762), astronomer **XI** 380, 381

Bradshaw **XII** 147, 151

Bradshaw, John **IX** 156, 174

Bradstreet, John (1711–71), colonel
XI 362

Bradwardine, Thomas, archbishop
of Canterbury (1349) **V** 296, 508,
509–10; **VI** 677, 680

Bradwell (Suffolk), manor **VI** 345

Bradwell on Sea (Ythancæstir)
(Essex) **Ib** 89, 102; map 2 xxx;
map 6 88; church **II** 111, 121, 152
VI 63, 634

Brady, William, bishop of Meath
VIII 468

Braganza, duke of **VIII** 352

Bragge **XII** 408, 492

Bragge-Bathurst, C., chancellor of
the duchy of Lancaster (1812)
XII 583

Brahe, Tycho **VIII** 307

Braidshaigh, John **IX** 210

Brakelond, Jocelin of **III** 78, 228

Bramah, Joseph (1748–1814), inventor **XII** 511; biographical note
XIII 5

Bramber (Sussex), castle **II** 628

Bramham Moor (N. Yorks.) **VI** 65

Brampton (Hunts.) **III** 4

Brampton, Sir Edward **VI** 592–4;
one of the king's converted Jews
592; induces Genoese surrender
593; marries Isabel, Tresham's

widow 593; trading in *malaguetta* 593; destroys morale of Wood-ville's fleet 615; **VII** 118, 119

Brampton, William, London alder-man and burgess **VI** 70–1, 429

Bramston, James (?1694–1744), poet, quoted **XI** 411

Brancaster *Branodunum*: fort **Ia** 257, 281, 300, 320, 530; civil settle-ment 258, 594; **Ib** xxvi, 89, 91, 97; map 2 xxx; map 6 88

Brancepeth (Co. Durham), lordship **VI** 8, 319, 321, 528; **VIII** 138, 139, 140

Brand, Sir Henry, Viscount Hamp-den **XIV** 67–8

Brand, Thomas (1774–1851), 20th Baron Dacre: biography **XII** 450; introduction of reform bill 450

Brandenburg **VI** 69; **VII** 159; **X** 74, 113; alliance with Dutch 85; with French 107; 'great elector' 123; coalition 161

Brandenburg, elector (Lewis V) **V** 121, 127

Brandenburg, Swiss and *landsknechts* **VII** 83

Brandon, Charles, 1st duke of Suf-folk (d. 1545): marriages **VII** 284, 300, 305; 'Amicable Grant' revolt 304; attacks France (1523) 313; marriage dispensations 326; great seal 330; Pilgrimage of Grace 388–9; land received 400; be-sieges Boulogne (1544) 409; dies (1545) 419; great master of the household (1540) 649

Brandon, Eleanor, countess of Cumberland **VII** 523

Brandon, Frances, duchess of Suf-folk **VII** 523

Brandon, Reginal de **IV** 491, 496

Brandon, villa **Ia** 607, 610

Brandon, Sir William (d. 1485): killed **VII** 53

Brandt, Sebastian **VII** 252, 253

Brandywine, battle **XII** 209

Brantingham, Thomas, bishop of Exeter (1370–94), treasurer (1369–71, 1377–81, 1389) **V** 211, 228, 389, 446; removed from Exchequer (1371) 291, 385; rein-stated (1389) 464

Branxton **VII** 282

Braose, Eva de, daughter of William the Marshal and wife of William, son of Reginald de Braose **IV** 395

Braose, Giles de, bishop of Hereford **III** 221, 301, 446

Braose, Graeca de, daughter of William Brewer, first wife of Reginald de Braose and mother of William **IV** 395

Braose, Isabella de, daughter of William de Braose (hanged 1230) **IV** 395–6

Braose, John de, lord of Bramber and Gower (d. 1232) **IV** 396

Braose, Matilda de **IV** 201

Braose, Philip de **III** 314

Braose, Reginald de, lord of Aber-gavenny and Builth (d. 1227): marriage **III** 301; **IV** 394, 395, 396

Braose, William de (d. 1211), father of William junior (d. 1210) and Reginald, and grandfather of John, lord of Gower: the strongest baron **III** 297; downfall 299; and William de Burgh 314; fled to Ireland 315; exile in France (1210) 383; wife and son starved by King John 427; estates 434; **IV** 396

Braose, William de, son of Reginald, lord of Abergavenny **IV** 45; hanged (1230) 395–6; succession to his lands 396–7

Braose family **III** 288, 297, 301

Braquemont, Robert de **VI** 175

Brasil (Brazil) **VII** 224, 259; **X** 236; independence **XIII** 211

Braughing **Ia** 556

Braxfield, 1st Baron *see* Macqueen, Robert

Bray (Berks.) **II** 301; **VI** 600

77

Bright, John (*cont.*)
of Lords 88–96; letter against Home Rule 99; individualism 124; Quakerism 137

Brighthampton **Ib** 156; map 3 xxxi

Brighton **XII** 546

Brill **VIII** 155, 338, 365, 416

Brimpsfield (Glos.) 404

Brindisi **IV** 107

Brinlow, Henry (d. 1546) **VII** 423, 431, 456, 583

Brinsley, John **IX** 350

Brinton, Thomas, bishop of Rochester (1373–89) **V** 300

Brionne, county **II** 558; count of *see* Gilbert

Bristol (Brycgstow) (Som.): **II** 565, 576, 600, 731; **III** 36, 67, 121, 233, 452; private exchequer 12; slave trade 40; trial by jury prohibited 73; port 93, 94, 389, 437, 484; headquarters of Empress Matilda 138, 140, 143, 146, 151; Robert, earl of Gloucester, died at 148; Henry Plantagenet 161, 244; relations with Ireland 303, 307, 308; castle 382, 417; Jew of 423; castellans **IV** 3, 22; confirmation of Charter of Liberties (1216) 4; centre of the Lord Edward's household administration (1254) 118, 159, 401; feudal army summoned to (1257) 138; the Clare claim to 173, 519; Edward fails to hold (1263) 176; held by his friends (1264) 196; ceded to Simon de Montfort 197, 198; burgesses support Earl Simon, but make terms with Henry III after Evesham 200, 202, 203; military and naval base 422, 442; parliament of magnates and Christmas feast (1284) 430; castle, town, barton, and Dublin 565; *Little Red Book* 626; town development 635; **V** 8, 47, 79, 493; revolt of burgesses 50; surrendered by Despenser 85; Prince Edward keeper of the realm 88; tax assessment 192; deaths from plague 332; staple 351, 353; cloth exports 357–8, 360; cloth industry 365, 369; population 379; expansion 381; government 382; meeting of committee of eighteen 487; surrenders to Bolingbroke 492; **VI** 4, 8, 25, 50, 72; relations with Bordeaux 110; Lollard artisans (1414) 132; scriveners 132; Henry V's visit 194; loan from 204; county status 386, 392; merchants 386; citizen divisions 387; oligarchs and community disorders 387; St Mark's church 650; Canynges' mansion 653; merchants' houses 653; **VII** 35, 41, 68, 142; castle 57; merchants 188; shipping 219–20; trade routes 224–5; John Cabot 225–6; adventurers 227, 473; *see* 400; manufacturing 458; cloth trade 462; mint 488, 501, 607; architecture 596; treaty **VIII** 164; **IX** 133, 141, 196; **X** 40, 53, 119; workhouse 53; newspaper; charity schools **XI** 142; relief of the poor 137; trade, import and export 121; **XII** 25; population 13, 517; politics 48, 53, 59; docks 515; riots **XIII** 83

Bristol, bishop of *see* Conybeare, John

Bristol, earls of *see* Digby, George; Hervey, George William

Bristol Channel **Ia** 137, 683; navy yard? 384

Britain, battle of (1940) **XV** 392, 498–500; Dowding's pencil incident 485; plans for victory 515

Britannia **VIII** 282–4, 319

Britannia, Roman diocese **Ib** 48

Britannicus **Ia** 89

Britannicus Maximus (title) **Ia** 287, 315

Britford (Wilts.) **II** 578; church 151

British Association for the Advancement of Science **XIII** 566, 569–70, 575

British Broadcasting Company **XV** 232

British Broadcasting Corporation: created **XV** 233; effects on culture and politics 233–5; during general strike 246; model for regulated capitalism 278; increased caution 307; broadcasts in 43 languages 516; plays the *International* 542; archival material 610–11

British Expeditionary Force (1914): decision to send to France **XV** 6, 7; equipment 8; at Mons 9, 17; retreat from Mons 9; on Marne 10, 32–3; on Aisne 11; at Ypres 12

British Expeditionary Force (1939): promised **XV** 436; sent to France 459; Belgian frontier 460; advances into Belgium 484–5; evacuated from Dunkirk 486; losses 487

British and Foreign Bible Society **XII** 354

British Gazette 246

British Legion **XV** 163

British Medical Association **XIII** 619

British Museum **XI** 396–7

British provinces: *Superior* (Upper Britain) **Ia** 231, 249, 253, 256, 258; *Inferior* (Lower Britain) 251–2, 258, 520, 522, 580 — administration 231 — governors 249–50; troops in 260; *Flavia Caesariensis* 317; *Maxima Caesariensis* 317; *Prima* 317, 714; *Secunda* 317; status 523, 528; status of governor 523, 655; capital 583; *see also* Valentia

British Socialist party: organizes Leeds convention **XV** 89; sets up Communist party 142

British Somaliland: offered to Abyssinia **XV** 380; conquered by Italians 523

British survivals in Anglian society **II** 315

British Union of Fascists **XV** 374; members interned 492

British Weekly **XV** 28

British West Indies **XV** 151; American bases 496

British Worker **XV** 246

Brito, Walter **III** 23

Britons: **Ia** 51, 55–6, 86, 127; **Ib** 142, 148, 151–2, 164, 197–201; appeal to Honorius 7; movement to Brittany 8; appeal to Aetius 8, 10, 13, 207; victory at Mons Badonicus 14–15, 162; Pelagian controversy 20; scarcity of archaeological evidence 21–3; scarcity of surviving place-names 30–2; appeal to the Angles 109–10; personal names: Caedbaed 140–1, 182; Cerdic and Caedwalla 147; Natanleod 148; Cuthwulf's conquests 167; concentration in lower Severn area 169; Ceolwulf 172

Brittania, Goddess **Ia** 531

Brittany (Armorica): **Ia** 24, 44, 213, 283, 288; population movement 738; **Ib** 8, 18; *see also* Armorica; Bretons; migration **II** 5; relations with England in 10th cent. 347–8; relations with Normandy 565, 577, 585, 608; barons 629; English conquest **III** 14, 124, 323–5, 329; duchy held by earls of Richmond 18; supports Henry I 119–20; mercenaries 154; Geoffrey of Monmouth's connection with 255; rebellions 334, 383–4; liability for foreign service 371, 471; Arthur recognized 378, 381; pirates on coast 433, succession **IV** 92; Peter of Dreux and 92–4, 96; Henry III's expedition (1230–4) 94–7; dynastic relations with Champagne and Navarre 236–8; origin of the Montfort claim 598; *see also* Dreux, Peter of;

Brittany (Armorica) *(cont.)*
V 138, 147, 149, 242; war 137, 143, 210, 403 — claimants to duchy 131 — Pembroke's defeat at La Rochelle 145; war indentures 235–6; active service, Pembroke and Lancaster 254, 256; Gaunt absent but blamed for abbey raid 404; Thomas of Woodstock 443; salt trade with 360; VI 71, 135, 140, 180, 348; attack on English wine cargoes 72; truce (1417) 173; English ambassadors 474; ships 432; VII 50, 81, 115, 598; Henry and France's quandary over 84–7; English interest 86–9; Spain, Britain, and France vie for 91–3, 95, 103–6; English expedition lands (1489) 97; Henry's coalition breaks up (1489) 101; treaty between Henry and Anne (Feb. 1490) 102; Breton independence 109–11; Henry VII's expenditure in war 109, 209, 211, 217; Henry VIII and war 274–6; ravaged by Surrey 312

Brittany, Alice of *see* Alice

Brittany, Arthur of *see* Arthur, son of Geoffrey

Brittany, counts of *see* Arthur; Fergant, Alan; Geoffrey; Thouars, Guy de

Brittany, dukes of *see* Alan III; Arthur; Conan III; Conan IV; Francis II; John, married Beatrice, daughter of Henry III; John, son of Peter of Dreux John V; Montfort, John de

Brittany, Eleanor of *see* Eleanor, sister of Arthur

Brittany, Yolande of *see* Yolande

Britton, John XIII 583

Britton, Thomas X 404

Brittones Ia 197

Briudun *see* Breedon-on-the-Hill (Leics.)

Brixworth (Northants) Ib map 2

xxx; church II 112, 152; monastery 160

Broadhurst, Henry XIV 101, 128

Broadwood, Lucy XIV 544

Broc, Rannulf de III 211, 214

Brock, Colonel XII 52

Brockenhurst (Hants) III 113

Brockley Warren Ia 611

Brodhull, Cinque Ports court IV 645

Brodie, Mr, of Moray XII 282

Brodrick, St John, Viscount Mideton XIV 267, 345, 346, 362, 375; Younghusband treaty 383; general election (1906) 386; army reform 396

Brodrick, Thomas (d. 1769), Admiral XI 365

Broghil, Lord *see* Boyle

Broglie, Victor François, duc de, maréchal XI 219

Brogne, Gerard of II 447

Brois, Philip of, canon of Bedford 202

Brome, Adam de V 507

Bromfield (Maelor) IV 410, 424

Bromfield (Salop) II 668

Bromholm Priory (Norfolk) IV 49

Bromley, Sir Henry VIII 226, 227

Bromley, William (1664–1732) XI 154

Bromswold Forest (Bruneswald) (Hunts.) II 284–5

Bromyard (Hereford) V 339

Bromyard, John V 505; *Summa praedicantium* VI 299

Bronescombe, Walter, bishop of Exeter IV 485

Brontë, Anne XIII 557

Brontë, Charlotte XIII 556; biography 557; works 558

Brontë, Emily: biography XIII 557; works of 557–8

bronze Ia 657, 689

Bronze Age Ia 8–9, 44, 46

brooches: long Ib 56–7; square-headed 56–7, 116; cruciform 57, 59, 115; style 1 animal ornament 57, 61, 116–17; development 58

80

[fig. 1]; applied 59, 61–2, 133; button 59, 138; equal-armed 59, 61–2; round 59; saucer 59, 61–2, 86–7, 138–9; circular types 60 [fig. 2]; Stützarmfibel 61; *tutulus* 82; Quoit 118 [fig. 10] (*see also* Quoit Brooch Style)

Brooke (Norfolk), cruciform brooch **Ib** 58 [fig. 1 (g)]

Brooke, Sir Alan: resists Churchill **XV** 481; commands in France 487; commands home forces 497; Chief of Imperial General Staff 536; advocates Mediterranean campaign 555, 556

Brooke, Henry, 8th Lord Cobham **IX** 3

Brooke, Henry (1703–83) **XI** 305

Brooke, John, 7th Lord Cobham (d. 1512) **VII** 142

Brooke, Lord *see* Greville

Brooke, Sir Robert, speaker of the House of Commons (1554) **VII** 654

Brooke, Rupert **XV** 20, 61

Brook's club **XII** 339

Brooks, James, bishop of Gloucester (1554–8) **VII** 551

brothels **Ia** 657; **IX** 180

Brothers Club **X** 358

Brotherton, Margaret, countess of Norfolk **V** 261

Brotherton, Thomas, earl of Norfolk (1312–38) **V** 59, 75, 80; marshall 52; joins Isabella 83; Despenser's trial 85; hatred of the Despensers 93

Brough-on-Humber (*Petuaria Parisiorum*): military **Ia** 136, 281; town development 187, 278; mosaicists 656; **Ib** xxvi, 176–7, 187, 189, 195; map 4 xxxii; map 6 88

Brough-on-Noe, fort **Ia** 260

Brough-by-Sands **Ib** 77

Brough-under-Stainmore, seals **Ia** 570

Brougham, Henry Peter, Lord (1778–1868), 1st Baron

Brougham and Vaux: **XI** 144; **XII** 436, 446, 541, 572; biography 437; **XIII** 31, 37, 68–9, 75, 78; biography 56; character and ideas 56; and Queen Caroline 66–7; Reform Bill 84; Ten Hours' movement 148; Parizzi 300; Irish church 346; Poor Law report 452; introduces legal reforms 472, 473; improvement of education 478, 491, 493–5; scientific discovery 569

Brougham Bridge (Westmorland), Clifford castle **VI** 59

Broughton (Oxon.), castle **VI** 333

Broughton, Sir Thomas **VII** 68, 69, 73; killed (1487) 74

Broughty Castle **VII** 484

Brouns, Thomas, chancellor of archbishop Chichele **VI** 287

Brown, Anthony, Lord Montague **VIII** 131

Brown, Charles, Commodore (d. 1753) **XI** 233

Brown, Ford Madox **XIII** 593

Brown, George, bishop of Dunkeld **VII** 9

Brown, Lancelot ('Capability Brown') (1715–83) **XI** 413; **XII** 341, 546

Brown, Thomas **III** 331

Brown, W. J. **XV** 548

Browne, Anne **VII** 284

Browne, Sir Anthony, standard-bearer of England and constable of Calais **VII** 169, 284

Browne, Sir Anthony, son of Sir Anthony, standard bearer of England KG (1540), Esquire of the Body to Henry VIII (d. 1548) **VII** 494, 496

Browne, George, count de (1698–1792) **XI** 291

Browne, John **VII** 599

Browne, Robert **VIII** 200–1

Browne, Sir Thomas **IX** 407; **X** 357, 359

Browne, Valentine **VIII** 143

Browne, William **VIII** 302
Browning, Mrs Elizabeth Barrett **XIII** 537
Browning, Robert (1812–89) **XIII** 300, 529–30, 532, 536–8, 539; biography 537; mentions matches 624; **XIV** 136, 161
Brownists **IX** 125
Brownrigg, Sir John **XIII** 412
Brownsea Island **Ia** 558
Bruce, Christina de, sister of Robert, king of Scots, wife of Christopher Seton, later of Andrew, son of Andrew of Moray junior **IV** 687, 716
Bruce, Edward **III** 317; **V** 33, 38, 40; campaigns in Ireland 42–4, 228, 231
Bruce, H. A., Lord Aberdare: biography **XIV** 20; licensing bills 21, 25
Bruce, Isabel, sister of Robert, king of Scots, married Eric, king of Norway **IV** 611, 613
Bruce, Margery, infant daughter of Robert, king of Scots, demanded as hostage (1297) **IV** 685; later wife of Walter the Steward and mother of first Stuart king 685
Bruce, Marjorie **VII** 406
Bruce, Mary, sister of Robert: imprisoned in a cage (1306) **IV** 716
Bruce, Robert **III** 271
Bruce, Robert the **VII** 406
Bruce, Robert, the claimant, lord of Annandale (1245–95), recognized as his heir by Alexander II (1238) **IV** 587, 602; captured at Lewes (1264) 190; judge in England (pre 1269) 190; compact with Richard de Burgh and Thomas de Clare (1286) 597–8; one of commissioners appointed to arrange for succession of Margaret of Norway (1289) 598; action after her death 600–2; claims to throne 606–7, 611;

indenture with Florence, count of Holland 611; death (1295) 611
Bruce, Robert, earl of Carrick, son of the claimant **IV** 595, 598, 613, 695; claim to throne 611, 616
Bruce, Robert, earl of Carrick, grandson of the claimant, the future King Robert II **IV** 602, 611; insurrection (1306) 514–15, 713–16; fealty and homage for his Scottish lands to Edward I (Mar. 1296) 613–14; revolt (1297–8) 684–5, 687, 692; guardian of Scotland (1299–1300) 694, 696, 697; return to King Edward I 694–5; campaign (1303–4) 709; advises the king (1305) and becomes a counsellor in Scotland 712, 713; flight and return (1306–7) 718–19
Bruce family **III** 273
Brudenell, Thomas James, 7th earl of Cardigan **XIII** 280–2; biography 280
Bruges (Flanders) **II** 422, 565; **III** 90, 91, 461; partisans of Philip IV (1297) **IV** 669; **V** 22, 128, 165, 285; trade with 120, 359; truce of 145, 386; wool staple 224, 351, 352; in French hands 355, 430, 432; Wyclif 511; **VI** 72, 351, 362; Hansa merchants 69; negotiations (1377) 136; **VII** 98, 181, 297, 311, 599; **VIII** 357, 364; **X** 233; Walter of *see* Walter of Bruges
Brugha, Cathal **XV** 154
Bruide mac Beli, king of the Picts **II** 87–8
Bruis, Peter de **III** 481
Brummel, George (1778–1840) **XII** 419, 548
Brunanburh, battle **II** 342–3
Brunel, Isambard Kingdom **XIII** 46, 579
Bruneswald *see* Bromswold Forest (Hunts.)
Brunhild, Queen **II** 105

Bruni, Leonardo **VI** 677; **VII** 239
Brunnus **Ia** 270
Bruno of Sayn, archbishop of Cologne **III** 450
Brunswick **III** 215; house 376
Brunswick-Lüneburg, duchy of **XI** 11; electorate of *see also* Hanover, territories of
Brussels **V** 127; **VII** 307, 548; **VIII** 357; **X** 173; conference (1937) **XV** 421
Brussels Declarations on the Laws of War **XIV** 35
Brute, and his fellowship **VII** 189, 565
Brute, Walter **V** 301, 519, 520
Bruton (Som.) **II** 535, 536
Bruttium **Ia** 443
Brutus of Troy **III** 255; **VI** 42, 316
Bryce, James, afterwards Viscount **XIV** 178, 249; biography 211; chairman of royal commission on education 318, 320; Irish secretary 385; ambassador at Washington 393
Brycgstow *see* Bristol
Brycheiniog *see* Brecknock
Brydges, James **X** 247
Brydon, John McKean, architect **XIV** 324
Brydon, W. **XIII** 420
Bryngherst, Bringhurst (Leics.) **VI** 500
Brytford *see* Britford (Wilts.)
Brythonic (Brittonic) language **Ia** 17
Bubba **Ib** 178
Bubwith, Nicholas, bishop of Bath and Wells **VI** 105, 112, 195, 430
buccaneers **X** 326–9
Buccingahamm *see* Buckingham
Buccleuch, countess of *see* Scott, Anne
Buccleugh, dukes of **XII** 135, 329
Bucer, Martin **VII** 423, 509, 516; critic of Prayer Book 520; exhumed and burnt 553; given chair at Cambridge 574; **VIII** 29

Buchan, countess of, sister of the earl of Fife, and installation of Robert Bruce at Scone **IV** 714, 716
Buchan, earldom of **V** 32
Buchan, earls of *see* Comyn; Stewart, John
Buchan, J. **XV** 312
Buchanan, George **VII** 313
Buchenwald, German murder camp **XV** 600
Buckelurnen **Ib** 69, 71 [fig. 6], 72, 193
Buckhurst, Lord *see* Sackville, Thomas
Buckingham (Buccingahamm) **II** 325, 731; shire 338, 431, 574; council 351; county **III** 31
Buckingham, dowager duchess of *see* Katherine
Buckingham, dukes of *see* Stafford, Henry; Villiers, George
Buckingham, earldom of *see* Thomas of Woodstock
Buckingham, John, bishop of Lincoln (1363–98) **V** 211, 276
Buckingham, Katherine, duchess of (1683–1743) **XI** 99, 148
Buckingham, 1st marquis of *see* Temple 2nd earl
Buckingham and Chandos, 3rd duke of **XIII** 384
Buckingham Palace: conference **XIV** 480–1; Privy Council **XV** 2; Haig married in its chapel 46; conference after Asquith's resignation 69; Lloyd George at 70; demonstrations for Edward VIII outside 401; war rations 403; Neville Chamberlain resigns 474; George VI practises revolver shooting 493; damaged 502
Buckinghamshire **Ia** 43, 484; **V** 2, 312, 510; **VII** 452, 505, 528; **IX** 4
Buckinghamshire, earls of *see* Hobart, John; Hobart, Robert
Buckland, Hugh of **III** 388
Buckland, W. **XIII** 572

Buckle, Henry Thomas: biography **XIII** 549; works 549–50, 558

Bucklersbury **VII** 248

Buda *see* Ofen

Budapest, Rothermere fountain **XV** 282

Budé, Guillaume **VII** 258

Budget: Lloyd George's first war (Nov. 1914) doubled income tax **XV** 28–9; second war (May 1915) added no new taxes 29; McKenna's duties (Sep. 1915) 40–1, 212, 237; Law's (1918) National Savings 88–9; surplus (1920–1) 144; estimates fall (1922) 163; Snowden's (1924) 'free breakfast table' 212; Churchill's first (1925) contributory old age pensions 237; Churchill's balancing act 253; Snowden's (1930) 286 —stop-gap budget (Apr. 1931) 287 —emergency budget (Sep. 1931) 295–6, 331, 332; Chamberlain's (Apr. 1932) disarmament and War Loan conversion 331–2, 338; economy, not spending (1933) 338; Chamberlain's (1934 and 1935) recovery of prosperity 351; Thomas' (1936) budget leak 359; Chamberlain's last budget (Apr. 1937), National Defence Contribution 412; Wood's (July 1940) purchase tax 491 —(Apr. 1941) closing of 'inflationary gap' 511–12

Budin, Dr **XIV** 519

Buenos Aires, republic **XII** 85, 453, 466; **XIII** 211

Buffon, Georges-Louis Leclerc de (1707–88) **XI** 396

Bugenhagen, Johann **VII** 395

building, industry **Ia** 390, 422, 514, 629, 638; programmes 124, 138, 142, 232, 576 —chartered status 112 —Colchester 117; Wroxeter 185, 584; Flavian 156–163; 3rd cent. 265–7; Trier 302; Constantinian 325–8; 4th cent. 372;

late use of Roman buildings 495; materials 562–3, 602–3, 609, *see also* timber; stone, etc.; **V** 95, 263–4, 300, 508; Lancaster enhances value of castles 67; Edward III expands Windsor home 226; Savoy Palace 254; Canterbury Cathedral nave 298, 341; York Minster additions 299; reckless expenditure by Richard 488; Westminster Hall 498

Builth (Brecknock) **III** 297, 301; borough of **IV** 433

Builth (Radnor): castle **VI** 641; Mortimer estates 510

Builth, constable of *see* Hywel ap Meurig

Builth, district and castle besieged by Llywelyn **IV** 155; endangered by Welsh campaign 394; promised as marriage portion by William de Braose 395–6; regained by Llywelyn 397, 402, 404, 406; given to Edward 401; rebuilt (1277) 403, 410–11, 430, 432; earl of Lincoln reoccupies 409; war (1282) 422, 428; John Giffard in 438; attacked by Madog (1294) 441

Buironfosse **V** 127

Bulgar people **III** 454; Exarch granted **XIV** 41; 'Bulgarian atrocities' 44, **XV** 385; 'Big Bulgaria' 50–1; treatment at Berlin Congress 51, 52

Bulgaria: villa and village **Ia** 610; united with Eastern Rumelia **XIV** 195; kidnapping and abdication of Prince Alexander 195; election of Ferdinand 196; complete independence proclaimed 410; joins Balkan League 463; victories over Turkey 464; spoliation by Serbia, Greece and Rumania 468; enters First World War **XV** 50; signs armistice 110; peacemaking with 132; favours Hitler 524; pure burden 577

85

Burgh, Margaret de (*cont.*)
of Hubert de Burgh **IV** 23, 41, 43, 73

Burgh, Richard de, nephew of Hubert and justiciar of Ireland (1228–32) **IV** 42–3, 54, 58

Burgh, Richard de, earl of Ulster (1283–1326) **IV** 564, 565; compact with Robert Bruce (1286) 597–8; serves with Edward I in Scotland 614, 709; **V** 1, 41, 43, 44

Burgh, Sir Thomas **VI** 627; local rebellion 558

Burgh, Ulich de, 5th earl of Clanricarde **IX** 163

Burgh, Walter de, earl of Ulster, son of Richard, earl of Ulster **IV** 43

Burgh, Walter, Lord **VI** 480, 507

Burgh, William de **III** 313–14

Burgh, William de, brother of Hubert **IV** 43

Burgh, William de, earl of Ulster (1330–3) **V** 228, 267

Burgh, Sir William de **V** 449

Burgh Castle (Gariannorum): fort **Ia** 281, 300; **Ib** 89, 97; map 2 xxx; map 6 88

Burgh family, in Connaught and Ulster **IV** 562, 564

burghal hidage **II** 265, 646

Burgh-by-Sands, fort **Ia** 166

Burgh-upon-the-Sands (Cumbria): Edward I dies at **IV** 719; **V** 1

Burghersh, Sir Bartholomew **V** 101, 152, 219, 245, 254; seneschal of Ponthieu (1332) 117

Burghersh, Henry, bishop of Lincoln (1320–40), treasurer (1237–8, 1334–7), chancellor (1330) **V** 87, 92, 98, 121, 154; Edward II's animosity 80; intercedes between Isabella and Edward 81; formal request to king 89; made treasurer 152; removed from Chancery 152; in the Low Countries 159

Burghill, John, bishop of Coventry and Lichfield **VI** 272

Burghley, Lord *see* Cecil, Sir William

Burghs, Scottish **IV** 572, 575

Burgin, Leslie, minister of supply **XV** 444

Burgos **IV** 118

Burgoyne, John (1722–92), General **XII** 76, 168, 202, 208–11, 314; biography 76

Burgoyne, Sir John **XIII** 278

Burgred, king of Mercia **II** 245, 248, 251, 252, 259

Burgum Regine, bastide **IV** 310

Burgundian fleet **VI** 559

Burgundians: prisoners of war **Ia** 282; permanent kingdom 433; settled in Roman territory 446, 453, 477, 491, 499; some expelled 490; in Britain 549; **Ib** 79, 81, 117; **VI** 173; upper Seine (Feb. 1418) 173; during Normandy conquest 174; *baillages* (summer 1418) 177; enter Paris 174; truce (June 1418) 174; Rouen/Pont de l'Arche understanding 175; embassy (July 1433) 177

Burgundy: monastic reform **II** 444–5; free country, and Philip IV **IV** 667, 668; English relations with **VI** 90; commercial treaty (to Nov. 1464) 534; Edward IV treaty confirmed 584; **VII** 82, 85, 117, 188, 598; betrothal of Charles and Claude 153–4; ambitions in the Netherlands 163; Henry's marriage proposals 172; claimants to Castile 178; Charles' succession 309; treaty of Madrid 316; Francis and Charles make peace 319; Mary and Philip betrothed 537

Burgundy, bastard of *see* Antony, bastard of Burgundy

Burgundy, counts of *see* Otto IV; Rainald I; Rainald II; William I

Burgundy, duchess of *see* Margaret, duchess of Burgundy

Burgundy, duchy of **V** 140, 143,

212, 253; county of 143; **VI** 169, 588

Burgundy, dukes of **III** 341; attitude towards Calais **VI** 106; *see also* Charles the Bold; Hugh IV; John the Fearless; Philip the Bold; Philip the Good; Robert II

Burgus (Bourg-sur-Gironde) **Ia** 450

burh see borough; fortresses

Burhham *see* Burpham (Sussex)

burial, prohibition of Anglican services **IX** 202

burial customs: grave goods as dating evidence **Ib** 25–8; meaning of 'heathen burials' 38; cremation superseded by inhumation 93; practices of continental Angles 108, 110–11; mixed cemeteries 111–12; significance of cremation 112; inhumation areas in southeast 112–13; scarcity of cremation in Kent 122; male burials in prehistoric round barrows 149; Lankhills cemetery 150; practices in Mercia 185

burials **Ia** 514, 520–1, 522, 526, 693–703; Iron age 10, 46, 670; aristocratic 56, 417, 461, 471, 494; numismatic information 358–9; Germanic officers 375; live 682; sacred objects 683, 702, 712, 719; Christian 731; heathen *see* archaeology; *see also* cemeteries; grave goods

Burials Act (1880) **XIV** 86

Burke, Edmund (1729–97) **X** 312; **XI** 31, 67, 305, 338, 407; **XII** 65, 236, 272, 284, 348; on banking 28; patronized by Verney 36; social advance 37; on punishments 39; on magistrates 47; patronized by Rockingham 62; on King's friends 120; on Pitt 125; on Junius 145; political affiliations 165; on America 200, 203; on Ireland 224; attempts at economic reform 231, 240, 418, 439; Gordon riots 237; paymaster of forces (1782)

243, 246–9, 260, 578; civil list act (1782) 246–9, 259, 286; board of trade 276; regency crisis 304; *Reflections* on French Revolution 323–5, 437; social life 338; Portland Whigs 368; paymaster of forces (1783) 579; **XIII** 39, 118, 531, 544

Burke, house of **VII** 125, 132

Burke, William **XII** 262, 313

Burke family **III** 313

Burkes, of Ireland **VIII** 464

Burley, Sir Simon **V** 408, 428, 438, 446, 465; *magister* of Richard II 424, 425; gifts to 429; deprived 454; impeachment and execution 458; queen intercedes 479; condemned by Lord Cobham Commission 482

Burley, Walter **IV** 523; his commentary on Aristotle's *Politics* and his views on kings and magnates 521–2; **VI** 680

Burlingjobb (Radnor) **II** 214

Burlington, earl of *see* Boyle, Richard

Burma: Upper, War and annexation **XIV** 91; lost **XV** 542, 544; India needed for reconquest 546; Alexander summoned from 556; offensive promised 562; no rice from 563; Americans demand invasion 572; invasion prepared 586

Burmese War, first (1824) **XIII** 270, 413–15; second (1852) 426–7

Burnaby, Revd Andrew (1734–1812): on differences between colonies **XI** 321

Burne-Jones, Sir E. **XIII** 593–4; **XIV** 45, 155, 157, 158

Burnell, Hugh, Lord **VI** 38, 87, 336, 430; captain of Bridgnorth 7; averts Welsh crisis (Sep. 1400) 40; prince of Wales' council 105

Burnell, Philip **IV** 339

Burnell, Robert, king's clerk, chancellor, bishop of Bath and Wells

Burnell, Robert (*cont.*)
(1275–92) **IV** 225; Gascon mission (1278) 287–9, 297, 338; at Paris (1286) 290–1; bastide of Baa 309; chancellor 335–8, 558; life and character 338–9; lands and barony 339; state trials (1289) 362; elected archbishop of Canterbury (1278) but rejected by Pope Nicholas III 469–70; bishop 485–6; chancellor (1274–92) **V** 264

Burnes, Sir Alexander **XIII** 419

Burnet, Alexander, Archbishop **X** 270, 275

Burnet, Gilbert, Bishop **X** 32, 156, 379–80, 412, 413

Burnet, Sir J. J., architect **XIV** 540, 541, 542

Burnett, George (1776?–1811) **XII** 532

Burnett, Gilbert (1643–1715), bishop of Salisbury **VII** 328, 383, 416, 433, 479; Anne of Cleves divorce 417; Henry's executors 493; on Cranmer 510

Burnett-Hurst, A. R. **XIV** 515

Burney, Dr Charles (1726–1814) **XI** 417; musician **XII** 349

Burney, Fanny (Madame D'Arblay) (1752–1840) **XII** 304, 322, 349, 538

Burnham, John **VI** 685

Burnham, river **II** 587

Burnham committee **XV** 184

Burning Babe **VIII** 289

Burns, John: biography **XIV** 100; 'Bloody Sunday' 181; London dock strike 206; on the LCC 296; president of local government board 385; administration 516–18, 519; resigns office on eve of war 493; **XV** 200

Burns, Robert (1759–96) **X** 263, 293; **XII** 351

Burnside (Westmorland) **VI** 459

Burntisland **VIII** 43, 44

Burpham (Burhham) (Sussex) **II** 265, 731

Burrard, Sir Harry (1755–1813) **XII** 460

Burrough, Stephen **VIII** 237, 238, 241

Burroughs, Samuel (*History of Chancery*) **VI** 458

Burrows, Sir John **VIII** 413

Burrus, Sex. Afranius **Ia** 116, 119

Burstwick (Holderness) **IV** 716; **V** 76

Burton, annals, documents contained in **IV** 125, 136, 453, 454–6, 503

Burton, Henry **IX** 75, 79, 415

Burton, Sir R. **XIII** 552

Burton Down **Ia** 627

Burton Latimer (Northants) **III** 124

Burton upon Trent (Byrtun) (Staffs.), abbey **II** 455, 496, 553, 731; **III** 45; **V** 66; **VI** 51; **VII** 36

Burwell (Cambs.) **III** 147

Bury (Lancs.) **XII** 511

Bury, Adam **V** 391

Bury, Richard, bishop of Durham (1333–45) **V** 159, 160, 161, 177; keeper of the privy seal 100; letter to Curia 101; chancellor 153, 154; bibliophile 300

Bury St Edmunds (Sanctæ Eadmundes Stow) (Suffolk): Benedictine abbey **II** 491; liberty of 501; knight service 635, 731; **III** 7, 78, 185, 259, 336; the forty knights 18; jurisdiction controversy with shire 156; death of Eustace 164; financial ruin 228; knight's council (1197) 371; confiscation of clergy's property 447; parliament (1267) **IV** 213, 221; ecclesiastical council at (1267) 504; parliament (1296) 636, 674, 675, 676; **V** 83, 275, 290, 306; rebels run amok 415–16; rebellion ends 418; reasons for dispute 419; **VI** 196, 294, 483; **VII** 528

Bury St Edmunds (Sanctæ Ead-

Buttington (Buttingtum) (Montgomery) **II** 213, 267, 731

Buttingtum *see* Buttington (Montgomery)

Button's Coffee-house **X** 358

Butts, Sir William, royal physician **VII** 330, 419, 479

Buxar, battle (1764) **XII** 161

Buxhill, Sir Alan **V** 403

Buxton **Ia** 673; **X** 408, 409

Buxton, Sydney, afterwards Viscount, later Earl **XIV** 385

Buxton, Sir Thomas Fowell **XIII** 370

Buys, Paul **VIII** 338

Buzenol, relief **Ia** 623

Bwlch y Dinas, castle **V** 74

Bycarrs Dyke, convention made at **IV** 206

Byerly Turk, horse **X** 408

Byfleet (Surrey) **V** 253

Byford, Lewis, bishop of Bangor **VI** 39, 65

Byland (Yorks.) **V** 75

Byng, George **XII** 228

Byng, George, Viscount Torrington (1663–1733) **XI** 161, 173

Byng, John, Admiral (1704–57) **XI** 229, 230, 352

Byng of Vimy, Lord, and constitutional crisis in Canada **XV** 261

Byrd, William (1543–1623) **VIII** 306; **IX** 387; **XI** 399

Byrhtferth of Ramsey **II** 396, 450, 457

Byrhthelm, archbishop of Canterbury **II** 367

Byrhtnoth, ealdorman of Essex **II** 364, 366, 377, 455

Byrom, John (1692–1763), poet **XI** 420; *Pastoral* 425

Byron, Lord George (1788–1824) **XII** 538, 543, 548; **XIII** 32–5, 38, 215, 217, 366; religion 533; Italy 537

Byron, John, admiral and explorer (1723–86) **XI** 229; **XII** 17, 212

Byrtun *see* Burton-on-Trent (Staffs.)

Byset, John **V** 325

Bythan Castle **IV** 21, 22

Bywell (Northumb.), manor **VI** 323

Byzantine emperors **Ia** 325

Byzantium, Byzantine **Ia** 521; **III** 4, 259; *see also* Constantinople

C

Cabal **X** 77, 81–2

Cabinet **X** 13–14, 152, 254–6; **XII** 1, 7, 97, 123, 124; ministerial difficulties 116, 225; Lord North 149, 203; and America 210; Shelburne 257; solidarity with Pitt 273, 279, 300; surrender of colonies 410; Lord Liverpool 503; list of office holders and Cabinets 574–83; not consulted on ultimatum to Germany **XV** 2; authorizes mobilization of army 6; insists two divisions must remain in England 7; swept away by Lloyd George 130; casually restored 173; prime minister's power 197; overrules Law over American debt settlement 203; Campbell case 225; secretary for air in 229; Bondfield first woman in 271; rejects Mosley's proposals 285; committee on May Report 288; economy demands 291–2; votes taken in 297; small National Cabinet 293; decides dissolution for last time 323; normal size restored 326; committee on balance of trade 328–9; agreement to differ 330; ignores chiefs of staffs' advice 364; waters down White Paper on defence 376; approves Hoare-Laval plan 384; endorses increase in fighters 391; receives statutory recognition 404; Anderson first civil servant 405; supports Neville Chamberlain's foreign policy 420, 423; acquiesces in Hitler's demands 426; interviews *News Chronicle* correspondent 442; insists on German withdrawal from Poland 451; ultimatum to Germany 452; restored by Churchill 596; list of (1914–45) 649–59; *see also* ministers of state

Cabinet Council **IX** 31; *see also* Scottish committee

Cabinet Secretariat: organized by Hankey **XV** 75; preserved by Law 196

Cabot, John **VII** 225–6; **VIII** 235

Cabot, Sebastian **VII** 227, 228, 507

Cabrera of Cordova **VIII** 398

Cadafael, king of Gwynedd **II** 84

Cadbury (Som.): Congresbury Hillfort **Ia** 453; **Ib** 140; **II** 536–7

Cade, Jack **VI** 496, 499; caught by Iden 497; comparison of revolts (1381) 496–7; **VII** 142

Cade, William, financier **III** 423

Cadell, co-founder of Carron ironworks (1759) **XI** 117

Cader Idris **VI** 44

Cadewallon **III** 300

Cadiz **VII** 273; **VIII** 395, 418–19; expedition to **IX** 35, 61–3; **X** 171, 233; expedition against 204, 206

Cadogan, Sir Alexander, draft of Atlantic Charter **XV** 535

Cadogan, William, 1st Earl (1675–1726) **XI** 162, 203

Cadorna, Italian general **XV** 80

Cadsand **V** 128

Cadwaladyr **VII** 54, 55, 208

Cadwallon, king of Gwynedd **Ib** 197; **II** 80–2, 116; death 118

Cadwgan **III** 286, 289, 290

Caecina Alienus, A. **Ia** 128–9

Caedbaed **Ib** 141, 182

Cædmon **II** 196, 200

Cædwalla, king of Wessex **Ib** 147; **II** 37, 69–73; baptism 69–70; charter quoted 70, 303; kills Æthelwalh of Sussex 138

Caelichyth *see* Chelsea

Caelius, M., centurion **Ia** 701

Caen (Calvados) **III** 136, 197; stone 80–1; *Consuetudines et Justicie* 107;

Caen (Calvados) (*cont.*)
Henry I's conquest of Normandy 119; Theobald of Étampes 237; progress of Philip Augustus 384; **V** 133, 178, 212, 219, 246; prisoner sold 247; **VI** 137, 171, 172, 189, 190; put in defence state 171; *bailliage* 189; *camera compotorum* 191; Norman estates summoned 206; free fairs 565; siege 666; **VII** 219; battle (1944) **XV** 581-2

Caen (Calvados), abbeys **II** 585; Holy Trinity **III** 45, 54, 105, 169; St Stephen's 414

Caen, John Arthur of, notary **IV** 283, 495, 602

Caerellius Priscus **Ia** 210

Caerleon (on Usk): legionary fortress **Ia** 98, 137, 152, 231, 255; rebuilding 163, 256; inscriptions from 250, 512; status 512, 583; *canabae* 575, 583; amphitheatre 579; martyrs? 718, 721; castle **Ib** 121; **II** 627; **IV** 397

Caernarvon: waterside fortifications **Ia** 384; troops from 404; **IV** 429; castle and borough 430-2; destroyed and rebuilt (1292-5) 441, 443; Edward II born at 429; **VI** 77; county 41, 55; French attack 55; **XV** 198

Caerphilly Castle **V** 50

Caerwent **Ia** 138, 185, 186, 586; inscriptions 251, 534, 659; gates 262; plague 552; weaving-mill? 656; pagan gods 666, 668; church 724

Caerwys, borough of **IV** 433

Caesar (title) **Ia** 516

Caesar, Caius Julius: Britain and Gaul in his time **Ia** 1-18; constitutional position and motives for invasion 22-5, 38-9, 396; Druids 24, 677; invasion of Britain 25-38; economic factors and the invasion 37, 41, 630, 652; relations with British tribes 42, 57; example and source of *auctoritas*,

to Augustus 48-50, to Claudius 71, to Julian 359-363; Julian family 68, 71, 155, 291; contrast with Claudian invasion 75-84; handling of resistance 102, 106, 126, 669, 680; as military historian 304; **Ib** 3; **VI** 307

Caesarea, title for London? **Ia** 328

Caesennius Paetus, L. **Ia** 117

Caetani, Benedetto *see* Boniface VIII; Gaetani, Benedict

Caetani, Cardinal **VIII** 454

Cafncarnedd **Ia** 105

Cahors (Lot) **III** 326; bishopric: treaty of Paris (1259) **IV** 127, 128, 280-1, 289, 292; merchants 281; town and castle **V** 122, 140; **VI** 135; *see also* Quercy

Caine, Hall **XIV** 331

Caird, Edward **XIV** 329

Cairns, 1st Earl **XIII** 117

Cairns, Earl **XIV** 17, 18, 32, 39, 91; settled Land Act 87; low church 137

Cairo **IV** 82; Wavell and Longmore **XV** 520; Smuts 525; Lyttelton minister of state 528; Mussolini prepares to enter 555; Churchill (1942) 556-7; conference (1943) 574-5

Caister (Norfolk), castle **VI** 345; besieged by Duke of Norfolk 557; built by Fastolf 651

Caister-by-Yarmouth (Norfolk): military? **Ia** 258; **Ib** xxvii, 89, 97; map 2 xxx; map 6 88

Caistor-by-Norwich (*Venta Icenorum*) (Norfolk): forum and *civitas* **Ia** 156, 593; weaving-mill? 696; **Ib** xix, xxvii, 72, 87, 89, 110; Anglian pottery 65 [fig. 3(d, f)]; Saxon pottery [fig. 5(b)]; map 2 xxx; map 5 68; map 6 88; development 96-101; barbarian *laeti* 178

Caistor-on-the-Wolds (Lincs.) **Ib** 89, 176, 179-81; map 4 xxxii; map 6 88

Caithness **II** 342

Calais (*cont.*)
47, 56–61, 418; British Expeditionary Force **XV** 11; Anglo-French conference (1915) 45; (1917) 80; mutiny at camp 138; falls (1940) 486

Calamy, Edmund (1671–1732) **X** 264; **XI** 88

Calamy, Edmund (?1697–1755), son of the above **XI** 88

Calcraft, John (1726–72) **XII** 62, 65

Calcutta **X** 351

Calder, river **VI** 366, 646

Calder, Sir Robert (1745–1818) **XII** 431

Calder Abbey (Cumbria) **III** 271

Caledonia **Ia** 147, 229; *see also* Scotland

Caledonian Canal **XII** 519, 522

Caledonians **Ia** 225–7, 230, 241, 318

calendar, reform **XI** 337, 381

Calgacus **Ia** 146–8

Calhau, Bertrand de **V** 22; family 14

calico **IX** 323; printing **X** 49

Calicut **VII** 224, 259

Caligula, Emperor *see* Gaius

Caliver **VIII** 278

Calixtus II, Pope **III** 124–5, 125, 180, 184, 187; **VI** 270

Calleva Atrebatum see Silchester

Callières, François de **X** 173

Callistus, Andronicus **VII** 237

Calpurnius, St Patrick's father **Ia** 463

Calpurnius Agricola, Sex. **Ia** 203, 205, 207, 635

Calpurnius Piso, C. **Ia** 128

Calthorpe, William, squire of the body **VI** 448–9

Calveley, Sir Hugh **V** 278, 295, 431, 432, 469

Calverley (Yorks.) **VI** 366

Calvert, Cecilius, 2nd Lord Baltimore **IX** 343–4

Calvert, George, Lord Baltimore **IX** 325, 343

Calvert, Leonard **IX** 344

Calvin, Jean (1509–64) **VII** 516; *Institution of the Christian Religion* 338; **XI** 89

Calvin (Colvill), Robert **IX** 10

Calvinism: relation to capitalism **VII** 444; Arminians against **IX** 71–2

Calvisius Rufus **Ia** 251

Cam, river **Ib** map 2 xxx; **II** 26, 28

Camboglanna see Birdoswald

Cambon, Paul **XIV** 245, 366, 490, 491, 493; exchange of letters with Grey 462; Entente 567

Cambrai **Ia** 493; **III** 450; **V** 127; **VIII** 355, 418; **X** 220; battle **XV** 88, 109

Cambrai, bishops of *see* Henry of Bergen

Cambrai, Congress (1724) **XI** 193

Cambrai, 'Ladies Peace' (1529) **VII** 112, 319, 328, 329, 339

Cambrai, League of (Dec. 1508) **VII** 155, 188, 271; 2nd League of (1517) 307

Cambridge (Grantanbrycg) (Cambs.): Iron Age shaft **Ia** 692; cemeteries 693, 700; **Ib** 87, 101, 166, 178; region 38–9, 87, 112; map 2 xxx; map 5 68; **II** 252–3, 324, 328–9, 338; shire 279, 561; pontage 291; borough courts 533; divided into wards 540; castle 601; battle 612; **III** 76, 147, 225; church of St Peter 225; a scholar, son of earl of Ross (1306–7) **IV** 580; castle 9; **V** 83, 416–17, 418, 420; parliament (1388) 281, 339, 355, 374, 462; **VI** 483, 587; earldom 465; **VII** 526, 528, 529, 553; White Horse Tavern 'Germany' 343, 572; population doubles **XV** 167

Cambridge (Mass.) **X** 347

Cambridge, duke of **XII** 447; **XIV** 9, 11, 16, 130, 220, 290; *see also* George II

Cambridge, earls of *see* Langley, Edmund; Richard of York

Cambridge, university: **III** 239; chancellor **IV** 701; **V** 279, 500, 505–8, 512, 519; peasants attack 416; exclusivity 501; **VI** 421, 671; conciliar views 91; letter against William Russell 298; Godshouse College 669; **VII** 251, 256, 257, 348, 377; early reformers 343; physicians' status 466–7; professor of divinity 516; classical tradition 571–2; chancellors 572; public professorships and lectureships 572–3; regius chairs founded (1540) 573; printing press 579; Barclay's education 585; colleges 594; **IX** 131, 199, 355–7, 368; **X** 106, 124, 390, 414, 415; latitudinarians, attempt to rationalize religion 32; professorships of modern history **XIII** 196; condition (1815) 489–90; unequal treatment of women **XV** 166; Anglican chapels 169; modern universities contrasted 171, 308–9; University Grants Committee 186; *see also* universities

Cambridge University, colleges: Balliol **VII** 257; Christ's **VII** 570; Clare Hall **V** 264, 506; **VII** 574; Corpus Christi **V** 374, 416, 506; **VII** 571; Gonville **V** 300, 506; **VII** 575; Jesus **VI** 669; **VII** 239, 348, 375, 571, 575; founded 570; King's **V** 97; **VI** 669, 670–1, 674, 675; **VII** 229, 571, 589, 592; King's Hall **VI** 385; Magdalene **VII** 570, 575; Michaelhouse **V** 506, 507; Pembroke Hall **V** 264, 506; **VII** 571; Peterhouse **VI** 287; Queen's **VI** 648, 669, 672; **VII** 571; St Catharine's **VI** 669, 671; St John's **VII** 242, 375, 570, 571, 594; Trinity **V** 300, 506; **VII** 257, 570, 571, 574; Trinity Hall **VII** 571, 572, 574

Cambridge Platonists **X** 32–3, 386

Cambridgeshire **Ia** 12, 43, 101; river communications 252, 562; **III** 144, 147, 276; **V** 47, 341, 418, 419, 487; cultivation figures 329; revolt 416

Cambyses **VIII** 296

Camden, battle (1780) **XII** 215

Camden, earls of *see* Pratt, Charles; Pratt, John Jeffreys

Camden, William (1551–1623) **VII** 12, 433; **VIII** 205, 241, 267, 275; *Britannia, Remains Concerning Britain* and *Annales . . . Regnante Elizabetha* 282–5, 318–19; **IX** 354, 406; **XI** 112

Camelon, fort **Ia** 144, 205

Camelot *see* South Cadbury

Cameron, Richard **X** 273

Cameronians **X** 273, 275

Cameroons, conquered **XV** 23

Camerton, pewter moulds **Ia** 595, 636

Camoys, Thomas, Lord **VI** 7, 155

Camp (nr. Ardres), treaty (1546) **VII** 410

Campania, estates **Ia** 600

Campaspe **VIII** 296

Campbell, Alexander, 2nd earl of Marchmont (1675–1740) **XI** 273, 428

Campbell, Hon. Alexander Hume (1708–60) **XI** 353

Campbell, Sir Archibald **XIII** 414

Campbell, Archibald, 1st duke of Argyle **X** 277

Campbell, Archibald, 3rd duke of Argyll, earl of Islay (1682–1761) **XI** 24, 253, 273, 275, 280; brewers' strike 278; Appin murder trial 283

Campbell, Archibald, 2nd earl of Argyll **VII** 282

Campbell, Archibald, 5th earl of Argyll **VIII** 82, 93, 99, 101

Campbell, Archibald, 8th earl and 1st marquis of Argyll **IX** 90, 166, 168

Campbell, Archibald, 9th earl of Argyle **X** 118

Campbell, Sir Archibald (1739–91), governor of Jamaica **XII** 214

Campbell, Archibald, marquis of Argyle **X** 266

Campbell, Brian **Ia** 510

Campbell, Colin (d. 1729), architect **XI** 403

Campbell, Sir Colin (1776–1847) **XII** 481

Campbell, Sir Colin (1796–1863) **XIII** 280, 438; biography 438

Campbell, Commander **XV** 550

Campbell, J. R., projected prosecution **XV** 218, 225

Campbell, John (?1720–90), Admiral **XI** 229, 382

Campbell, John, 2nd duke of Argyll (1678–1743) **X** 248; **XI** 161, 203, 204, 253, 273, 280

Campbell, John, 1st earl of Breadalbane **X** 281

Campbell, John, 4th earl of Loudoun (1705–82) **XI** 255, 360, 361

Campbell, Mrs Patrick **XIV** 329

Campbell, Thomas **XIII** 491

Campbell-Bannerman, Sir Henry **XIV** 16, 211, 223, 249, 392; biography 209; secures resignation of duke of Cambridge 220; defeat on cordite vote 221; sits on Raid Inquiry 233, 234; becomes liberal leader in the Commons 239; opposed to establishing general staff 291; 'methods of barbarism' 346, 390; eventual breach with Lord Rosebery 380; becomes prime minister 381; position at that time 384; demurred to by Grey 384; Cabinet 385–6; settles South Africa 389–91; 'enough of this foolery' 391; sanctions Anglo-French military conversations 399, 400; *Nation* article on armaments 401; '*Vive la Douma!*' 404; death 406; declaration about poverty 515

Campbell Clan **XI** 253, 279, 283

Campbell *see also* MacGregor

Campeggio, Lorenzo, Cardinal and bishop of Salisbury **VII** 290, 308, 345; Catherine of Aragon's fate 325, 327–9

Camperdown, battle (1797) **XII** 373, 398

Campion, Edmund S. J., Jesuit campaign 179–82; *Decem Rationes* 183; martyr 179, 187

Campion, Thomas **VIII** 306

Campo Formio, peace of (1797) **XII** 372

Campodunum (nr. Leeds) **II** 115

Campus Martius, inscription **Ia** 86

Camulodunum see Colchester

Camville, Gerard de, constable of Lincoln Castle **III** 355, 366, 485

Camville, Roger de **III** 25

canabae **Ia** 511, 575, 581–4, 591; **Ib** 76; *see also* civil settlement; *vicus*

Canada (1485–1558) **VII** 227; (1603–60) **IX** 326, 342; (1714–60) **XI** 262, 323–4, 368–9, 372; French involvement 202, 311, 317–18, 347, 361; forts 202, 318, 362; expedition (1746) 261; Seven Years War 362, 365, 368; Choiseul negotiations 368; (1760–1815) attraction for England **XII** 18, 175; acquisition 85–7; feelings of Canadians 177; constitution 198; American invasion 202; settlement (1783) 253, 256; 1791 act 302; sources of wood 466; boundaries 374; coveted by America 551; attacked by America 552–4; (1815–70) **XIII** 205–6, 308, 383, 384; delimitation of frontier with United States 206–7, 305–6, 327; with Russia 210; development 375–6, 377–9; Canadian discontent 379–80; disturbances (1837) 380; Lord Durham's mission and report 380–1; grant of responsible government 381–3; federation of 383–4; (1914–1945) approves declaration of war (1914) **XV** 3;

forces take Vimy ridge 81; enter Mons 113; representation at peace conference 132; troops mutiny 138; compliant with United States 150; model for Ireland 157, 160; no support at Chanak 191; constitutional conflict 261; Ottawa conference 333; Munich 430; approves declaration of war (1939) 452–4; maintains relations with Vichy France 495; million dollar gift and mutual aid from 514; troops at Dieppe 557–8

Canaletto, Antonio (1697–1768) **XI** 406; **XII** 279

canals **Ia** 562–4; **XII** 26, 518; **XIII** 4; defects 47, 596–7

Canary Islands **VIII** 123, 369, 417

cancer **XV** 164

Canche, river **II** 132; **VI** 153

Candover **Ib** 149, 162; map 3 31

Canfran, treaty (1288) **IV** 260, 269, 282–4

Caniziani, Gerard de, Edward IV's merchant **VI** 591–2; sent to recruit Scottish financial help 592; Burgundy's attorney 592; Medici bank 592

Cannae **XIV** 7

cannibalism **Ia** 369

Canning, Charles John, Earl (1812–62): biography **XIII** 434; governor-general of India 434–5, 439–40, 442; *see also* Indian Mutiny

Canning, George (1770–1827) **XII** 408, 436, 441–3, 461; biography 408; foreign secretary (1807–9) 444–6, 457, 477, 483, 582; opposition to Castlereagh 477, 483; out of office 485, 492, 498–500; political opinions 529; social style 549; **XIII** 24, 55–6, 78, 196–7, 200; biography 55; leader of the House of Commons 69; influence upon the Tory party

69–70; prime minister 74; death 75; views on foreign policy 207; French intervention in Spain 208; the Polignac memorandum 209; the Monroe declaration 210–11; recognition of Buenos Aires, Mexico and Colombia 211; relations with Portugal 211–12; eastern policy 212, 217–18, 220; on Palmerston 222; instructing public 224; abolition of slavery 371; Durham report 381

Canning, Stratford, Viscount Stratford de Redcliffe: biography **XIII** 252; early views about Turkey 252–4; negotiations before the Crimean war 255–63, 264

Canningites **XIII** 76–8

Cannings (Wilts.) **II** 439

Cannings family, Bristol shipowners **VII** 472

Cannock Chase (Staffs.) **II** 40, 326; **VII** 34

Cannon, Colonel **X** 277

Cannon Street, London: inscription **Ia** 533; hotel **XV** 142

Canon, Edward, master stone cutter **VI** 381

canon law **IV** 450, 452, 462–6; study and practice 485, 489–92; importance in Scotland 584–5; *see also* law; legislation

canons (1571) **VIII** 190; *see also* clergy, communities

Canrobert, Marshal **XIII** 278–9, 286

Cantacuzenus, Demetrius **VII** 237

cantarists **VI** 290

Canterbury (Cantwaraburg) (Kent) **Ia** 590; theatre 233, 579; walls 263, 265; skeletons 296; church 724; **Ib** 9, 31, 66, 99, 122–5, 146, 204, 209, 213; map 2 xxx; map 5 68; name derivation 31; Jutish pottery 66; Germanic settlement of Kent 122–5; tribal lands 146; **II** 106, 206, 244, 537, 596; attacked by Danes and betrayed

Canterbury (*cont.*)
to them 383, 731; early history
526–8; city 535; **III** 109, 132,
215, 279, 479; chapmen's gild 74;
coronation 145, 407; royal Christmas (1262) **IV** 171; meeting of
bishops (1263) 176; peace (1264)
194–6; Henry III awaits arrival
of queen and legate (1265) 206;
and Wales 406; appeals to provincial court 466, 491–4; provincial and diocesan 490–3; trial
between foreign and Gascon merchants (1293) 644; *see also*
appeals, tutorial; **V** 73; see 30;
wool staple 353; **VI** 116, 141, 159,
193, 417; Pisa representation 92;
metropolitical jurisdiction 253;
Use 264; Consistory court 275–6;
Christ Church priory 294; Kentish estates 372; leases 372; Yeomen of the Crown 418; Rose case
460; St Sepulchre's prioress 460;
Province 502; **VII** 229, 239, 310,
361, 459; school and college 236,
237; convocation 417; see vacant
on Cranmer's condemnation 545;
'Bell Harry' tower 592; mint
604–6, 607; **VIII** 355; **X** 49;
population **XV** 256; *see also* Convocation of Canterbury
Canterbury, archbishopric **III** 181,
194, 216, 251, 422; feudal service 12–16; controversy over its
vacancy 171–3; Anselm forfeits
see 176–9; as *legatus natus* 184;
contest with York over primacy
184, 213, 269; Thomas appointed
archdeacon 199; recovery of
alienated lands 202; administration 211, 214; election 221,
443–5; contest with Wales over
primacy 295–7; **VII** 381; Davidson appeals for compromise during general strike **XV** 246; Lang
attracts less notice than Harold
Davidson 316; protests against
Hoare-Laval plan 385; triumphs

over laxity 403–4; Temple and
indiscriminate bombing 592
Canterbury, archbishops of *see*
Ælfheah; Ælfric; Æthelheard;
Æthelnoth; Anselm; Arundel;
Athelm; Baldwin; Becket; Berht-
wald; Boniface of Savoy; Bour-
chier; Bradwardine; Bregowine;
Burhthelm; Ceolnoth; Corbeil;
Courtenay; Cranmer; Cuthbert;
Dean; Deusdedit; Dunstan; Ed-
mund (St) of Abingdon; Grant;
Honorius; Islip; Jaenberht;
Jubert; Justus; Kilwardby;
Langham; Lanfranc; Langton;
Laurentius; Meopham; Morton;
Oda; Pecham; Plegmund; Ralph;
Reynolds; Rich; Richard; Robert
of Jumièges; Sigeric; Stephen;
Stigand; Stratford; Sudbury; Tat-
wine; Theobald; Theodore; Wal-
den; Warham; Whittlesey; Winchelsey; Wulfred
Canterbury, archdeacon of *see*
Harpsfield, Nicholas
Canterbury, 'Cardinal' *see* Bourchier, T.
Canterbury, cathedral church of
Christ **II** 36, 456; Lanfranc composes *consuetudines* 672; early organization 107–10, 146–7; relations
with York 108–9, 435, 664–5;
early history of see 111–13; projected removal of archbishopric
226; knight service 634; **III**
226, 262, 264; school 196, 233
V 298, 341; Henry IV's tomb **VI**
116–17
Canterbury, Christ Church **III**
222–3, 267, 358; Lanfranc's Constitutions 185; Becket's appointment 200; monks' excesses 228;
number of monks 229; *Anglo-
Saxon Chronicle* 249–50; library
235, 249; **VII** 236, 398; prior of *see*
Eatry
Canterbury, convent of St Sepulchre **VII** 361

Canterbury, Gervase of **III** 248, 325

Canterbury, Henry of, Gascon records **IV** 278

Canterbury, monastery of St Peter and St Paul (St Augustine's) **II** 109–11, 455; knight service 635; abbots of *see* Albinus; Benedict Biscop; Hadrian; Peter; Scotland

Canterbury, prior of *see* Chillenden, Thomas

Canterbury, priory of (Christ Church) **V** 69, 297, 316–45; documents against Despensers 62; Black Death 306

Canterbury, St Augustine's **III** 185, 191, 225, 250, 483

Canterbury, St Gabriel, chapel of, in crypt **III** 264

Canterbury, St Gregory's priory **III** 186

Canterbury, Thomas *see* Becket, St Thomas

Canterbury, William of **III** 252

Cantilupe, George de, heir to Abergavenny **IV** 172, 402

Cantilupe, Sir Nicholas **V** 169, 170

Cantilupe, St Thomas de, chancellor of the university of Oxford: bishop of Hereford (1275–82) **IV** 475, 488–90; at Amiens (1264) 182; chancellor of king (Feb. 1265) 198; withdraws from court (May 1265) 200

Cantilupe, Walter de, bishop of Worcester (1237–66) **IV** 164, 192, 200; *dictatore* 113; as Henry's commissioner 124; as reformer 125; council of regency 150; 'form of peace' 176; seeks agreement with King Louis 178; mediates at Gloucester 185; peace attempts 186, 189; restoration of order in Church 193; 'peace of Canterbury' 194; death 208; constitutions (1240) 452; and pluralism 459

Cantiones Sacrae **VIII** 306

Cantref Bychan **V** 61

Cantref Mawr **IV** 436, 438, 440; **V** 59, 61

Cantwara(burg) (-byrig/burh) *see* Canterbury (Kent)

Cantware (Cantiaci, Cantii) **Ib** 115, 122–3, 126, 173, 209

Canute VI, king of Denmark **III** 363

Canute, king of England **III** 385

Canynges, John **VI** 350

Canynges, London branch **VI** 351

Canynges, William the Elder, cloth merchant **VI** 350

Canynges, William the Younger, shipowner **VI** 350, 351; **VII** 220

Cap Saint-Mattieu (Brittany), Cinque Ports fleet defeats Norman (1293) **IV** 664

Cape Breton Island **X** 343; British acquisition **XII** 85

Cape Coast Castle **X** 63, 332, 333

Cape Colony **XIII** 194; development 396–7, 399; frontier problem 397–8; the 'great trek' 398; annexation of Natal 398; policy of Sir Harry Smith 400; Sand River Convention (1852) 401; grant of responsible government 401–2

Cape Finisterre, battle **XII** 431

Cape of Good Hope **VII** 188, 224; **XII** 256, 371, 377, 409, 563

Cape route **XV** 520, 523

Cape St Vincent, battle (1797) **XII** 369, 372, 428, 431

Cape Verde Islands **VII** 224; **VIII** 369; **X** 332

Capel, Arthur, earl of Essex **X** 95, 105

Capel, Sir Henry **X** 180

Capel, William, 3rd earl of Essex (1697–1743) **XI** 146

Capello, Francesco, Venetian ambassador **VII** 218

Capetians **III** 367, 449

Capgrave, John, Austin canon **VI** 658

capital, availability **XII** 24, 27, 332, 504

capital levy: proposed after First World War **XV** 125; repudiated by Labour 197

capitalism, development **VII** 461–3; **IX** 128, 285–6, 289–93, 317; growth **X** 179

Capitanata **VII** 153

Capitaneus **IV** 173, 649

Capitol, Rome **Ia** 51

Capitoline Triad **Ia** 515

Capitolinus **Ia** 194

Capitula itineris **IV** 16, 39, 353–4

Caporetto, battle **XV** 94

Cappuck, fort **Ia** 165, 211

Captain Poverty **VII** 392

Captal de Buch, French commander **VI** 107

Capua, cathedral **III** 215; **VII** 153

Capua, Peter of, cardinal legate **III** 377

Car Dyke **Ia** 258, 564, 620

Caracalla, Emperor **Ia** 259, 531, 590; Antonine Wall 201, 211; Scotland abandoned and frontier consolidated 228–31, 241–5, 256, 324; German frontier 274; extension of citizenship 293; ambitions 363; II Augusta Antoniniana 520

Caractacus *see* Caratacus

Caraffa, Cardinal **VIII** 391

Caraffa, Giovanni Pietro *see* Paul IV, Pope

Caratacus **Ia** 67, 68, 70, 83, 103–6; career ended 133, 239

Carausius (I), M. Mausaeus **Ia** 245; proclaims himself emperor 287, 288–90, 295–300, 639; relations with barbarians 288, 381; displacement from Gaul, and death 303–5; minting of coins 313, 532, 660; forts 300, 320, 327; **Ib** 53, 79, 83–4, 91

Carausius (II), coins **Ia** 358

Carberry hill **VIII** 106

carbon dioxide **XII** 334

carbonic acid **XII** 334

Carcassonne, viscount of **IV** 99; **V** 138

Cardean, fort **Ia** 149

Cardenas, Alonso de **IX** 232

Cardiff, fort **Ia** 378; **III** 121, 295; **V** 351; **VI** 510

Cardiff Castle **III** 288; **VII** 57

Cardigan: Welsh revolt (1094) **III** 288–9; Richard Fitz Gilbert replaces Cadwgan 290; Fitz Gilbert dies 291; Rhys ap Gruffydd's conquest 293–4; occupied by Falkes de Bréauté 299; strategic centre 301, 305; **VI** 57

Cardigan, 7th earl of **XIV** 11; *see also* Brudenell, James Thomas

Cardigan Castle **III** 294; and honour **IV** 393, 394, 396, 397; Hubert de Burgh's lordship 42–4; Peter des Rivaux as castellan 52; shire 397–8; granted to the Lord Edward (1254) 401; centre of royal administration 406, 410; attacked (1294) 441

Cardiganshire **VII** 37

Cardinal of St Peter **VI** 259

Cardurnock, fort **Ia** 177–8

Cardus, Neville **XV** 313

Cardwell, Edward, afterwards Viscount **XIII** 270, 359; **XIV** 79; biography 8; army reforms 8–16

careers: Late Empire **Ia** 338–9; separation of civil and military 400, 435–6; in Gallic prefecture 450–2; army 520–2; patronage 518–19; Church 450, 722–3; *see also* senatorial order

'caretaker' government **XV** 596

Carew, Sir Francis **VIII** 191

Carew, Sir George **VIII** 419, 487, 488

Carew, Sir Peter **VII** 528; **VIII** 474

Carew, Richard **VIII** 282

Carew, Thomas **IX** 401

Carew, Thomas, Lord, checks Glyn Dŵr's forces (1403) **VI** 54

Carew family **III** 310; **VII** 538

Carey, Sir George **VIII** 259

Carey, Henry (d. 1743), *Sally in our Alley* **XI** 425

Carey, Henry, 1st Lord Hunsdon leads against rebels **VIII** 139–42; 316, 358

Carey, Sir Robert **VIII** 388

Carey, William **XIII** 408

Cargill, Donald **X** 273

Carham on Tweed (Carrum) (Northumb.), battle **II** 418, 419, 731; **VI** 36

Carhampton, earl of *see* Luttrell, H. L.

Carib tribes **X** 331

Caribbean Sea **X** 174, 325

Carinthia, Herman of **III** 245

Carisbrooke (Wihtgarabyrig) (IOW) **Ib** 145–6, 213; map 2 xxx; map 3 xxxi; map 6 88; castle **V** 478; **VI** 635; **VII** 57; **IX** 153

Carlaverock Castle, siege (1300) and poem on **IV** 693

Carleton, Mr, MP **VIII** 221

Carleton, Sir Dudley **IX** 263, 413

Carleton, Sir Guy, 1st Baron Dorchester (1724–1808) **XI** 364; **XII** 207

Carlile, Captain Christopher **VIII** 244

Carlile, Richard **XIII** 80, 82, 133; biography 31

Carlingford **VII** 130

Carlini, Agostino (d. 1790), sculptor **XI** 408

Carlisle (Luguvallium): military bases **Ia** 136, 144–5, 174; *civitas Carvetiorum* 200, 277, 613; *Notitia Dignitatum* 392, 412; Imperial Cult 683–4; burial 699; tomb relief 705; St Patrick from? 463; **Ib** 18, 205; map 4 xxxii; **II** 186, 332; mines **III** 82; honour 141; Henry II knighted 162; cathedral 186, 226; capture by William Rufus 266; granted to Henry, son of King Stephen 270; King David escapes to 272; Henry of Anjou visits 273; King David claims 275; court of Henry II 278; surrender by Alexander 283; King

John visits (1201) 431; capture by Scotland in reign of King John 484; the Scots **IV** 574; Scottish wars 613, 692, 698, 715–19; parliament (1307) 712, 718; **V** 2, 87, 440; parliament (1307) 184, 273, 281, 331, 493; **VI** 45, 63, 337; charter of incorporation 392; castle defies Lancastrians 528; promised to Scots 528; **VII** 392; fortress 37; state ownership of liquor traffic **XV** 37

Carlisle, bishops of *see* Appleby; Barrow, William; Halton, John; Mauclerc, Walter; Merke, Thomas; Strickland, William

Carlisle, countess of, wife of 5th earl **XII** 275

Carlisle, earls of *see* Harclay; Hay; Howard, Charles; Howard, Frederick

Carlisle, see **IV** 574; bishop elections and parliamentary proceedings (1279) 347; **VI** 272; **VII** 399

Carloman, son of Charles Martel **II** 170

Carlos, Don (1715–88), king of Naples, Charles III of Spain (1759–88) **XI** 193–4, 201, 240, 244, 263; exchanges Parma and Tuscany for Sicilies 172–3, 206; marriage bargain 199; acquires Irish regiment 291; succeeds King Ferdinand (1759) 369

Carlos, Don, prince of Spain **VII** 537; **VIII** 55, 74, 75, 76; **XIII** 230–2

Carlow (Ireland) **III** 12; **V** 232, 471; county **VI** 425; castle **VII** 128

Carlton (Cumbria) **III** 283

Carlton Club **XIII** 88; Conservative meeting **XV** 192, 195, 204

Carlyle, Alexander (1722–1805) **XI** 286

Carlyle, Thomas (1795–1881): on war of Austrian Succession **XI** 265; Seven Years War 270; Adam

Carlyle, Thomas (*cont.*)
Smith 430; **XIII** 109, 188, 300, 374, 474; works 530–1, 545; biography 542; writings 542–4; Ruskin 546; Dickens 555; **XIV** 45, 136; quoted by Lloyd George **XV** 69

Carmarthen: town development **Ia** 180, 372; amphitheatre 579; **III** 110, 112, 114, 288; in possession of Rhys ap Gruffydd 294; religious cell 295; strategical centre 301; Hubert de Burgh's lordship **IV** 42–4; Peter des Rivaux as castellan 52; honour and castle 393, 394, 396, 397; shire 397–8, 438; granted to Lord Edward (1254) 401; centre of royal administration 406, 410; Welsh victory (1257) 137; **V** 351, 353; **VI** 54, 642; castle 44, 57

Carmarthen, marquis of *see* Leeds, duke of; Osborne, Thomas

Carmarthenshire **V** 59, 61

Carmeliano, Pietro **VII** 237

Carmelites **V** 35, 90, 161, 417, 439; John Latimer, informer 434; Nicholas of Lynn, calendar 509; John Kenningham, theological controversy 511

Carnarvon, 4th earl of **XIII** 186; biography **XIV** 12, 32, 35; resignation 48; South African policy 57–9, 61; Irish policy 76, 92, 112; interview with Parnell 92, 93, 560, 561; interviews with Lord Salisbury 90, 560, 561; resigns viceroyalty 95

Carnarvon Castle **V** 153

Carne, Sir Edward **VIII** 9, 10

Carnegie, Andrew **XIV** 322

Carnot **XII** 366

Carnwath, earl of *see* Dalzell, Sir Robert

Carolan (d. 1737), Irish bard **XI** 303

Carolina **X** 334, 339, 344; North 345; South 281, 339, 344

Carolinas, the **XI** 308–9

Caroline, princess of Wales and queen **XII** 368, 445, 447

Caroline, Queen (1683–1737) **XI** 10, 77, 84, 152, 202–3; 'guardian of the realm' 40, 42; ecclesiastical patronage 77–8; influence on George II 202–3, 206; with reference to Porteous 278 — to Frederick, prince of Wales 338–9; death 354; Walpole's defence 374; art criticism 406; Swift received 421; *see also* Walpole, Sir Robert

Caroline, Queen (wife of George IV) **XIII** 66–9, 466

Carolingian minuscle **III** 259

carols **VI** 660–1

Carolus-Duran **XIV** 326

Caroz, Luis de Villeragut, Spanish ambassador **VII** 231, 232, 235

Carpenter, Edward **XIV** 101, 161

Carpenter, George (1657–1732), General **XI** 119, 162

Carpenter, Robert: legal collections **IV** 150, 366, 370; *La court de baron* 730

carpets **VIII** 272; **IX** 382

Carpow: temporary camp **Ia** 146; legionary fortress 229–31; under Caracalla 246; campaign of Constantius 319; evacuation 530

Carr, Robert, Viscount Rochester **IX** 16, 19–20

Carr, William, Viscount Beresford (1768–1854) **XII** 453, 487

Carrawburgh (*Procolitia*): fort **Ia** 178, 183, 260; Coventina's shrine 666, 671, 691, 733; Mithraeum 668, 711, 733; **Ib** 75, 79; map 4 xxxii

Carreg Cennen Castle **IV** 410, 414, 419, 437, 439

Carrhae, battle **Ia** 272–3

Carrick, near Wexford **III** 306; **X** 300

Carrick, earldom of **V** 42

Carrick, earls of *see* Bruce...

Carrickfergus (Antrim) **III** 315; **V** 43, 228, 232, **VII** 130; **X** 307
Carrickfergus Bay **XII** 222
Carrog (Denbigh) **VI** 40, 65
Carron ironworks, Falkirk **XI** 116, 285; **XII** 31, 508
Carrum *see* Carham (Northumb.)
Carson, Sir Edward Henry, afterwards Lord, biography **XIV** 452; organizes Ulster resistance to Home Rule 453; reviews 80,000 volunteers 453; delusion about Southern Ireland 455; contrives Ulster Covenant 456; negotiates with Asquith 474; demands exclusion without time-limit 476; negotiates through Lord Murray 480; at Buckingham Palace Conference 480; biography **XV** 31; first coalition 31; negotiates with Lloyd George over Ireland 57, 71; leads attack on Asquith 66; gives information to Dawson 69; excluded from War Cabinet 75; at admiralty 76; Lloyd George and Irish convention 83; opposes convoy 84–5; resigns 86; opposes women's suffrage 93; Maurice debate 105; expediency of prosecuting considered 225
Carstairs Castle **IV** 707
Carswell, William of Witney, approver **VI** 133
Carta Caritatis **III** 187, 188
Carta mercatoria (1303) **IV** 620, 630–1
cartae baronum (1166) **III** 13–14
cartage service **II** 289
Cartagena (Colombia) **VIII** 125, 248, 369; **X** 174; **XI** 222, 223, 224, 231, 234–6
Cartagena (Spain) **XI** 361
Carter, Elizabeth (1717–1806) **XI** 148
Carteret, Lord John, Earl Granville (1690–1763) **XI** 10, 19, 22, 39, 41; career and characteristics 2, 34, 146, 148, 239 — career

impeded 246 — president of council 343 — Newcastle's ministry 347 — scholar 394; on power of Crown 17, 21; on powers of House of Lords 24; relations with George I 32, 185 — with George II 18, 239, 249, 258, 259 — with Walpole 204, 272; resignations 34, 185–6, 203, 249; lord lieutenant of Devon 48; on Roman Catholics 73, 183; gin drinking 134; education 140; ambassador to Stockholm 175; Walpole's ministry 182; secretary of state (1742) 238–49, 301–2, 305; foreign affairs 239–49, 268; battle of Dettingen 242; Scottish affairs 272; Scottish herrings 277; regent thanked 291; lord lieutenant of Ireland 292, 294, 298; Bahamas and Carolinas 308, 309; lord president of council 343, 347, 354–5; Seven Years War 348; on Pitt and crisis (1762) 370; 'Essay on Homer' 394; lord president of the council (1751–63) **XII** 575
Carteret, Philip, explorer (d. 1796) **XII** 17
Carthage **Ia** 162, 400, 600, 718
Carthusians, **III** 86, 229; **V** 308; order **VI** 295; English houses 295–6; **VII** 244, 247; martyred 362
Cartimandua **Ia** 106, 108, 133, 134, 199
cartoons **XII** 265, 346
carts **Ia** 542, 562
Cartwright, Edmund (1743–1823), inventor **XII** 333, 510–13
Cartwright, Major John (1740–1824), agitator **XII** 571; **XIII** 63
Cartwright, Dr Thomas **VIII** 194, 195, 199, 203, 457
Carucage **IV** 27, 29, 31
Carvoran: fort **Ia**; inscription 203; **Ib** map 4 xxxii
Cary, John (d. *c.*1720) **XI** 137

Castlemaine, earl of *see* Palmer, Roger

Castlereagh, Lord **XV** 132, 202; *see also* Stewart, Robert

castleries in England **II** 625, 627, 628, 683

Castlerosse, Lord **XV** 235

castles: Norman **II** 559; nature of 556–7; preconquest in England 562; founded by William I 625; **III** 25–7; in Wales 285; in Ireland 316; in warfare **IV** 8–9; royal and private 20; resumption of control over royal 21–5; Hubert de Burgh and 48, 50; royal castles (1232) 52 — (1258) 137 — (1261) 164–5 — (1263) 176, 181 — (1264–5) 190, 191, 196, 198–9; building in Aquitaine 292, 300, 303 — in Wales 430–2 — in Scotland 589, 616, 686, 694–6; King David 575; restored to Edward 600, 604, 608; Baliol ordered to surrender 613; Edward seizes Lochmaben 692; garrisons 707

Castlesteads (*Uxellodunum*) 75; map 4 xxxii

Castor, industries near **Ia** 644, 730; villa 720

Castro, Philip de **IV** 269

casualties: British Expeditionary Force **XV** 12; air raids in First World War 44, 121; Somme 61; battle of Arras 81; Flanders offensive 87; final offensive (1918) 109; First World War 120–1; actual air raids in Second World War 411; air raid fears 437–8; Alamein 559; Anzio 576; Allied casualties compared 577; Second World War 597

Catalans **X** 234, 244–5, 266

Catalaunian Plains, battle **Ia** 439, 440, 475, 487

Catalina of Lancaster, queen of Castile **V** 464

Catalonia: and the war (1285) **IV**

255; **V** 354; **X** 172, 220

catapults *see* artillery

Cateau-Cambrésis, treaty (1559) **VII** 112, 560; **VIII** 17, 37, 38

Catelet, Le **VIII** 355

Catesby (Northants.), nunnery **IV** 182

Catesby, Robert **IX** 8

Catesby, William, killed (1485) **VII** 58

Catharan sect **III** 230

Catharine of Braganza **X** 60, 349

Cathay **VII** 224, 226, 227; **VIII** 237, 240, 241

Cathay Company (Frobisher's) **VIII** 241

Cathcart, Charles, 8th Baron (1686–1740) **XI** 235

Cathcart, Charles, 9th Baron (1721–76) **XI** 275

Cathcart, 1st earl of **XIII** 197

cathedrals, organization **II** 440–1, 676

Catherine of Alexandria, St **VI** 250

Catherine (Katharine) of Aragon **VII** 234, 339, 380, 474; marriage treaty with Prince Arthur 81, 93–6, 115, 148, 172–4; reception in London 158, 192; marriage 'made in blood' 166; proposed bride for Henry 174; proxy marriage to Henry (1503) 175; papal dispensation 175–6; unhappy plight 178–80; marriage to Henry (June 1509) 180, 231; James' death 283; produces no heir 314; Wolsey's plans for power 318; separation planned 320, 322–5, 356; marriage against divine law 326, 357; Wolsey no longer her enemy 331; death (1536) 341, 370, 382; divorce 348; cult of Elizabeth Barton 361; Pope decides in her favour 362; Tunstall's support 386; confessor 396; Featherstone, Powell, and Abell hanged 427; Master Michiel painting 598

Catherine of Burgundy, daughter of John the Fearless **VI** 139

Catherine of France, wife of Henry V **VII** 228

Catherine the Great of Russia (1762–96), picture galleries at the Hermitage **XI** 181

Catherine Howard *see* Howard, Catherine

Catherine Parr *see* Parr, Catherine

Catherine of Siena, St **VI** 296

Catherine of Valois, daughter of Charles VI, queen of Henry V **VI** 138, 139, 140, 182, 183; discussions on her dowry 141, 142, 180, 184; marriage negotiations 178; leaves Rouen 192; in London 193; coronation 194; loan to Crown (1421) 195; son born 200–1; queen dowager 214, 226

Cathie (Catherine), wife of Peter Martyr **VII** 553

Catholics *see* Roman Catholics

Catiline **Ia** 396

Catiline, Roman play **VIII** 300

Catinat, Marshal **X** 170

Cato, Angelo **VI** 610

Cato the Elder **Ia** 601, 605, 625

Catterick (*Cateractonium*, Cetreht) (Yorks.): town **Ia** 412, 593; governor's staff 521–2; **Ib** 197; map 4 xxxii; **II** 115; battle 77; 731

Catterick, John, bishop of Coventry and Lichfield **VI** 253; Burgundian embassy 111

cattle **Ia** 42, 58, 191, 620, 627; Boudiccan revolt 120; exports 630; Irish trade **X** 299–301; Scottish 300

Catto, Lord **XV** 118

Catton (N. Yorks.), manor **VI** 337

Catullus **III** 235

Catusminianus **Ia** 688

Catuvellauni: origins and territory **Ia** 10, 12, 43; resistance to Rome 33, 70; anti-Roman policies 35–6; coinage 47; economic control 57–9, 652; Adminius expelled 60; domination of British tribes 68–70, 83, 89, 105, 589; *see also* Verulamium

Caucasus, German advance feared **XV** 521, 528, 530, 531

Cauchon, Pierre, bishop of Beauvais **VI** 249–50, 251

Caudebec (Seine-Inf.) **VI** 158, 173

Caudray, Richard, archdeacon of Norwich **VI** 237

Caulfeild, James, 1st earl of Charlemont (1728–99) **XI** 404; **XII** 224

Caussin, Nicholas **IX** 210

Causton (Norfolk) **V** 9

cautionary towns **VIII** 365, 367; **IX** 49, 52

Caux, Chef de (Seine Estuary) *see* Chef de Caux

Caux, Issac de **IX** 384

Caux, John of, abbot of Peterborough: treasurer (1260–3) **IV** 162

Cavagnari, Sir Louis **XIV** 63

Cavalcade **XV** 314

Cavalier, Jean **X** 211

Cavallari, Antonio **VII** 592

cavalry: Britain and Gaul **Ia** 77, 120, 122, 137, 148; stranded 27; Commius 30; shatters resistance 34; Batavians 134; on borders 151, 207, 223, 255; élite troops 292–3, 335; horse-breeding centre? 536; officers 683–4; *see also* knights; men-at-arms

Cave, Lord **XV** 3

Cavendish (Suffolk) **V** 415; **VI** 647, 649

Cavendish, Lord Frederick **XIV** 75

Cavendish, George, Wolsey's gentleman usher and biographer (1500–61?) **VII** 287, 288, 332, 352

Cavendish, Henry (1731–1810), scientist **XI** 385, 387

Cavendish, John, fishmonger **V** 437

Cavendish, Sir John **V** 415–16

Cavendish, Lord John (1732–96) **XII** 197, 237; chancellor of the

Cecil, Sir William (*cont.*)
English right to Calais 61; Randolph 76; mediates with Scots and Scottish disappointment 79–80; David Rizzio murder 92–4; Elizabeth urged to marry 96–7, 219; Elizabeth incensed by Scots 109; Mary detained in England 111; 'conference' at York (1568) 112–13, 115; de Quatra conflict 122–3; relations with Spain 124; Alva and de Spes 129–34; Norfolk's imprisonment and subsequent rebellion 137–8; punishment of the North (1570) 142–3; urges subjection of Scotland 144; Elizabeth and Anjou marriage proposals 148, 349–50, 354; becomes Baron Burghley (1571) 152; France and the Netherlands 153–4, 156; Huguenot massacre 160; recommends concord with Spain 163–4; bull of excommunication 169; penal code against Catholics 186; impropriations of episcopal lands 190; Puritanism 195, 199; council work 209; voyages of discovery 240; chancellorship at Cambridge 320; Spain and the Netherlands 338, 342, 365; Netherlands campaign 366; Mary's execution 387; successor 421, 423; death 427
Cecil, William, 2nd earl of Salisbury **IX** 83
Cecil family, control of Stamford **XII** 52
Cecily, daughter of Edward IV, betrothed to Prince James of Scotland **VI** 574–5
Cedd, bishop of East Saxons **II** 111, 121, 452, death 29–30
Ceiriog (Wales) **Ia** 103
Ceiriog, poet **XIV** 335, 336
Celestine II, Pope **III** 194
Celestine III, Pope **III** 278, 358, 366

Celestine V, Pope (Jul.–Dec. 1294) **IV** 671
Celtic: art **Ia** 15; language 17, 385, 507; cavalry 77, 84; term for sub-Roman society 484; writers 485, 498; mirrors 599; fields 619–21; coins 661; religion 666–75, 691–2; languages **X** 409–10
'Celtic fringe' **XIV** 207
Celts, sack of Rome **Ia** 270
Cely, Sir Benedict **VI** 25
Cely, George **VI** 354
Cely, Richard **VI** 361, 362
Cely firm **VI** 361–2
cemeteries **Ia** 461, 550–1, 611, 693, 700–5; churches 724; Christian 729–32; sub-Roman 737–8
Cemona **III** 331
Cenimagni **Ia** 36
Cenotaph **XV** 163, 164
cenotaphs **Ia** 701–2
Cenred, father of King Ine and of Ingeld, ancestor of King Alfred **II** 65, 72
Cenred, king of Mercia **II** 142, 203–4
Censuarius **III** 45–6
Census Act (1800) **XII** 419; census (1801) 517, 532
Census of Production **XIV** 506–7
Central Economic Information Service **XV** 329
Central Electricity Board **XV** 240, 278
centurions **Ia** 513, 514, 521, 522, 666; appointment 536; slaughtered 681; monument 701; shrine dedicator 713
Centwine, king of Wessex **II** 68–9
Cenwald, bishop of Worcester **II** 366, 444
Cenwalh, king of Wessex: warfare with Britons **II** 63; relations with other kings 66–7, 72; succeeded by his widow Seaxburg 68; exiled 84, 118; conversion 118; founds see of Winchester 122; supports

108

Roman usages 122, 125; quarrels with Bishop Wine 132

Cenwulf, king of Mercia **II** 94, 217–18, 224–9, 230–2, 237; limitation of authority 225; dispute with Archbishop Wulfred 229–30; attacks Wales 230; charter quoted 292, 298, 305

Ceoddor *see* Cheddar (Som.)

Ceol, king of Wessex (591) **Ib** 171; **II** 30

Ceolesig *see* Cholsey (Berks.)

Ceolfrith, abbot of Wearmouth **II** 117, 185; anonymous life 187

Ceolnoth, archbishop of Canterbury **II** 440

Ceolred, bishop of Leicester **II** 234

Ceolred, king of Mercia **II** 71, 203–5

Ceolwulf I, king of Mercia **II** 230–2; charter quoted 92

Ceolwulf II, king of Mercia **II** 250, 254, 259; royal style 545

Ceolwulf, king of Northumbria **II** 91; reads draft of *Historia Ecclesiastica* 8, 187

Ceolwulf, king of Wessex **Ib** 157, 171–2, 597; **II** 63

Ceorl: as rent-payer **II** 261–2; in Kent 277–8, 282; in Wessex and Mercia 278–9; nature of his holding, in Wessex 279–80, in Kent 281–2; as farmer 279–80; military duties 290–1, 583; as slave owner 314; gradual depression 470–2; in 11th cent. 476; *see also* peasants

ceramics **XI** 414

Cercamp **VII** 559; **VIII** 35

Cerdagne and Roussillon **IV** 255; **VII** 84, 88, 95, 96, 110; secured by Spain 172

Cerdic, king of Wessex **Ib** 150–2, 155, 161, 163–4, appendix II; captures Isle of Wight 145; status 146–8; **II** 27, 28, 69, 72, 277; traditions 19–23; name 24–5

Cerdicesford **Ib** 147, appendix II; map 3 xxxi

Cerdicesleaga **Ib** 147, appendix II

Cerdicesora **Ib** appendix II

Ceredigion **IV** 398, 401, 410

Ceri (Kerry), cantref **IV** 44, 45; **VI** 335

Cerignola, battle (1503) **VII** 153

Cerne Abbas (Dorset) **II** 396, 455, 458

Cerotæsei *see* Chertsey (Surrey)

Certic, Cerdic, king in Elmet **II** 80

Cervia **VII** 271

Cervianus, Aurelius **Ib** bronze plate 120 [fig. 11]

Cesalpino **VIII** 317

Cesarini, Cardinal Giuliano **VI** 236

'cessation' **IX** 135–6, 161

Cesterwara **Ib** 125; map 2 xxx

Cetewayo *see* Keshwayo

Cetreht (Catreath) *see* Catterick (Yorks.)

Ceux de l'Evangile **VII** 338

Cevennes, the, revolt **X** 211

Ceylon **VII** 259; **IX** 324; **XII** 255, 371, 377, 409; **XIII** 412–13; fear of Japanese attack **XV** 544

Cezimbra **VIII** 490

Chabotrie, la **V** 138

Chaceporc, Peter, king's clerk **IV** 113

Chadderton, Master Edmund, king's chaplain: and lands of Buckingham **VI** 605; Gloucester's treasurer 634, 636

Chadwick, Edwin **XIII** 150, 452, 463–4, 466, 598; biography 452; **XV** 353

Chadworth, John, bishop of Lincoln **VI** 520

chairs **VIII** 272

Chait Singh, zemindar of Benares **XII** 317, 320

Challoner, Richard (1691–1781), Roman Catholic bishop **XII** 235

Challoner, Sir Thomas **VIII** 44, 59

Chalmers, Thomas **XIII** 526–7; biography 526

Châlons (Marne): battles **Ia** 276; tournament **IV** 226, 233; **VI** 184
Chalton **Ia** 611
Châlus (Limousin), castle **III** 378
chamber, royal **IV** 323−4; king's **V** 3, 424, 428, 437, 448; souce of revenue 76; Henry Ferrars, surveyor 159; lands 215−16; controlled by Exchequer 218, 225; of the Black Prince 258
Chamberlain, Arthur **XIV** 361
Chamberlain, Austen, afterwards Sir: **XIV** 422, 442, 446, 493; biography 374; **XV** 68; deputizes for Lloyd George 5; during conflict between Asquith and Lloyd George 68; resigns (1917) 70; War Cabinet 104; parliament (1918) 129; chancellor of Exchequer 130; Unionist leader 158; Irish boundary 158; offered premiership by Lloyd George 189; attempts to continue coalition 191−2; refuses to join Law 195; refuses premiership 204; joins Baldwin 205, 207, 220; proposed as prime minister 208; foreign secretary 221; against commitment in eastern Europe 222, 415; Cabinet (before 1914) 236; foreign policy successful 255; impetus lags 272; at odds with Lord Lloyd 276, 359; joins Mussolini for holiday 317; not in National government 326; consulted by MacDonald 360; against Hoare-Laval plan 385; anti-Baldwin coalition 389
Chamberlain, John **IX** 413
Chamberlain, Joseph: **XIII** 446, 483; origins **XIV** 33, 71; mayoralty of Birmingham 36, 127; enters Parliament 55; opposes coercion in Cabinet 73; at Board of Trade 86, 87; radical speeches (1883) 87; forces franchise extension 88; Irish devolution scheme 89; abortive negotiation

with Parnell 89; tenders resignation 89; 'unauthorized programme' 92; differs from Gladstone over Home Rule 96; resigns 97; circular on relief works 111; last conference with Gladstone 176; deadliest critic of second Home Rule Bill 211; votes for Welsh disestablishment 223; takes Colonial Office 224; negotiates with Rhodes over Bechuanaland 228; ultimatum to Kruger over 'drifts' question 229; tries to stop Raid 231; question of his responsibility 233−6; unhappy speech 234, 236; passes Workmen's Compensation Act 237; advocates old age pensions 237; organizes West African Frontier Force 243; more diplomatic than Milner 248, f250; last attempts to avert war 249; offers alliance to Germany 260; second offer and Leicester speech 261; reforms Boer concentration camps 346; relations with Boer generals' mission 348; third offer 352; cab accident 354; attitude to Balfour's Education Bill 357; proposal to Paul Cambon 366; rebuff at Colonial Conference (1902) 371−2; visits South Africa 372; thwarted by Ritchie 372; declares for fiscal preference 373; resigns office 374; conducts tariff agitation 375−6; paralysis and retirement 388−9; estimate 389; mayor of Birmingham **XV** 256; Balfour's Education Act 256; Neville Chamberlain reference 406, 420
Chamberlain, Sir Neville: **XIV** 62; biography **XV** 79; fails as director of National Service 79; sets mark on record 174; Inner Cabinet 197; buried in Westminster Abbey 204; chancellor of Exchequer 205; man of No Luck 206; Housing Act 206, 210, 279; minister of

health 221; social reform 237; reforms local government 255–7, 266; dislikes derating 258; ignores multiplier 268; tricked by Baldwin 282–3; relies on natural forces 299; preserves appearance of National unity 323; becomes chancellor of Exchequer 326; committee on balance of trade 328; introduces Protection 330; budget (1932) 331; converts war loan 332; Ottawa 333; keeps pegging away 345; budgets (1934 and 1935) 351; reforms unemployment assistance 352–4; excludes Lloyd George 357; introduces lowest arms estimates 364; East Fulham by-election 367; fails to foresee cost of rearmament 385; proposed memorandum to Edward VIII 398; prime minister 404–5; Eire 406–7; outlook on foreign affairs 408, 414–16; introduces NDC 412; general support 421; disputes with Eden 421–3; Czechoslovakia 424–5; visits Hitler 426–7; Munich conference 428, 429; announces peace for our time 430–1; urges rearmament 432; resists drastic steps 435; visits Mussolini 436; changes course 439–41; gives guarantee to Poland 442–4; sceptical of Soviet alliance 445–6; refuses to send Eden to Moscow 448; personal failings 449; forced into war 450–4; sets up War Cabinet 456; fails to unite country 458; dismisses Hore-Belisha 460; relies on blockade 461; subsidies most valuable legacy 467; says Hitler has missed the bus 470; attacked over Norway 472; favours Halifax as prime minister 473; recommends Churchill as prime minister 474; serves under him 475; in Churchill's War Cabinet 478; Defence Committee (Operations)

481; heads civil side of war 482; against formal rejection of Hitler's peace offer 489; resigns 509; pledge against indiscriminate bombing 517

chamberlains **Ia** 519

Chambers, Ephraim (d. 1740): *Cyclopaedia, Proposals for a Dictionary* **XI** 395

Chambers, Richard **IX** 43, 83

Chambers, Robert **XIII** 573

Chambers, Sir William (1726–96), architect **XI** 304; **XII** 544

Champagne **Ia** 654; **III** 86; house of 342; **IV** 236–41; administration by Edmund of Lancaster 240; survey (1276–8) 241; **VI** 191, 206, 248, 573

Champagne, Blanche of *see* Blanche of Champagne

Champagne, counts of *see* Henry; Odo; Theobald IV, V; *see also* Jeanne, queen of France

Champagny, envoy of Requesens **VIII** 338

Champernoun, Sir Henry **VIII** 131

Champlain, lake **X** 342

Chanak, crisis over **XV** 190–2, 207, 228–9

Chanceaux, Andrew of **IV** 22

chancellor: position in Edward I's reign **IV** 335–9; jurisdiction **VI** 456; royal prerogative 456; *sub poena* summonses 456; Kent and Essex cases 457; of Exchequer **XI** 33

Chancellor, Richard (d. 1556) **VII** 507, 561; **VIII** 237

chancery **II** 353, 641–3; and the wardrobe **IV** 336–8; under Edward II **V** 11, 20, 23, 76, 77; under Edward III 152, 154, 158, 199, 213–14, 291; St Mary's church 154; source of expertise 194; of the Black Prince 258; of the duchy of Lancaster 259; Richard II, Lambeth records

chancery (*cont.*)
burnt 409; court of **IX** 3, 172, 175; *see also* writs

Chanda Sahib, nawab of the Carnatic (1749) **XI** 327; **XII** 159

Chandé, Philibert de, earl of Bath **VII** 51

Chandler, Samuel (1693–1766) **XI** 84, 89

Chandos, James Brydges, 1st duke of (1673–1744): paymaster of the forces **XI** 338; palace at Canons 338, 412, 415; music 415

Chandos, Sir John **V** 238, 241, 249, 252, 265

Chandos, Lord **XIII** 82

Chandos herald, admirer of the Black Prince **V** 143, 265

Channel, English: in war (1216–17) **IV** 9–10; defence **VI** 72; **VII** 307, 311, 557; German plans to cross **XV** 498; closed to shipping 506; German battleships sail through 542

Channel Islands **III** 384, 484; **IV** 9, 10, 14, 31; granted to Lord Edward 118, 318; social and administrative developments 318–21; inquiry into state (1274) 320, 358; Norman ecclesiastical courts 350; **V** 119; under German occupation **XV** 493

Chantrey, Sir Francis Legatt **XIII** 587

chantries **V** 297, 304–5, 311, 499–500; dissolved (1545) **VI** 290, 291; York municipality 403–4; **VII** 399; act renewed (1547) 513–14

Chapel Izod **X** 300

chapels, king's and diocesan rights **IV** 326

chaplains, stipendiary **VI** 284

Chaplin, Charlie **XV** 181, 633; children's parties 314; *The Great Dictator* 316

Chaplin, Henry, **XIV** 238, 286, 512; on Opposition front bench **XV** 32

Chapman, George **VIII** 301; **IX** 392, 400

Chaptal, J. A. **XII** 413

Chapuys, Eustace, Imperial ambassador **VII** 331, 332, 352, 370, 408; Elizabeth Barton affair 361

charabancs **XV** 305

charcoal **Ia** 631

Charente, river **III** 466; Saintonge border **IV** 102–3, 127; **V** 112; **VI** 107, 140

Charenton (Seine) **VI** 201

Charford-on-Avon **Ib** 149

Charing (London), Inn **VI** 331

chariots: battle **Ia** 34, 76, 84, 120, 147, 165; burials 10, 46, 670; racing 579

Charité, La, Cluniac priory **VI** 300

Charity Organization Society **XIV** 164

charity schools **X** 123, 158, 416–17

Charlbury (Oxon.) **II** 297

Charlemagne *see* Charles, king of the Franks

Charlemont (Ireland) **X** 307

Charlemont, earl of *see* Caulfeild, James

Charleroi **X** 171

Charles, archduke of Austria **VIII** 49, 74, **XII** 426, 433

Charles, Archduke, king of France (Emperor Charles VI) **X** 206, 211, 218–20, 231, 234; defends Barcelona 213

Charles, cardinal of Lorraine **VII** 599

Charles the Good, count of Flanders **III** 125, 127

Charles, Dauphin, son of Charles VI: financial position **VI** 142–3, 241; Burgundy relations (June 1418) 175; Rouen 176; Scots in army 177; partisan mind 178; Burgundy rapprochement 180–1; Burgundy Montereau meeting (28 Aug. 1419) 181; murder of duke 181–2; treaty of Troyes 187; besieges Chartres 200; *roi de*

Charles I, king of England (1625–49) **VII** 608; as prince of Wales, belief in divine right **IX** 33; succession 34; trial and execution 34, 156–60, 219–20; relations with early parliaments 34–6; assents to Petition of Right 39–45; seeks Spanish bride 58, 395; marriage 60; helps Huguenots 65–6; makes peace 67; effects of foreign policy 67; wants to control sermons 75; ideals of government 81–2; Scottish policy 87–97; dissolves parliament 93; sacrifices Strafford 102; in Scotland 105–6; on Irish parliament 112–13; tries to arrest five members 122–3; position (1642) 124, 129; rejects Nineteen Propositions 126; elements in his party 126–7; tries to get aid from Ireland 134–5, 142; surrenders to Scots 143; negotiations with Irish and Scots 143–4; Presbyterianism 143–4; delivered to the English 145; seized by army 146; accepts Scottish terms 146, 153–4; negotiates with army 147–8; denounced as man of blood 152–4; *Eikon Basilike* 159; burial 202–3; attitude to Roman Catholics 205–6, 210; asserts sovereignty at sea 215–18, 235; his court 264; created peerages wholesale 266; and the colonies 328; interferes with trade 333–5; touches for the king's evil 367; a patron of art 377; and the drama 393–5; **XI** 35, 160; statue of 398; Lansbury's threat to George V **XV** 209; parliamentary stir of 1927 and 1928 comparison 259

Charles II, king of England (1660–85): proclaimed in Scotland **IX** 166–7; defeated but escapes to France 168–9; in Flanders 186; treaty with Spain (1656) 233–4; restoration 233–4, 259–60; cavaliers' support 246; issues Declaration of Breda 257; 'touching for the evil' 367; portraits 375–6; character **X** 1; at Restoration 2–3; land restoration 5; debts 6–8; contributions to exchequer, attitude to Church 19–20; science 28, 43, 411; Ogilby's road book 51; opposition to 57; ruled without parliament 58; attitude to foreign affairs 58; marriage 60; fire of London 66; relations with France 75–7; agreement with Louis XIV 86–7, 91; 3rd and 4th parliaments 99; dependence on France 102–3; interest in navy 110; death 115; and Scotland 266–7; and Ireland 302–3; slave-trade 328; William Penn 340; Bombay 349; St Évremond 359; letter-writer 360; character of court 369; buildings 388–9; painting 397; music 406; horse-racing 408; **XI** 35, 152

Charles IV, king of France (1322–8) **V** 81, 115, 151; homage of Prince Edward to 82; Queen Isabella 83; relations with Edward II 108–11

Charles V, king of France (1364–80) **V** 130, 140, 393, 497; allies with Scots 142–3; diplomacy 143, 385–6; appeal of Gascon lords 144–5; French successes 145; death (1380) 146; **VI** 108; violates Calais peace 136

Charles VI, king of France (1380–1422): and Richard II **V** 146–7, 151, 444, 456, 488; and papal schism 282; invades Flanders 430; Gaunt concludes truce with (1384) 434; threat of invasion of England by 442; **VI** 113, 165, 166, 167, 175; Glynn Dŵr alliance 56; requests Queen Isabel's dowry repayment 67; Richard II truce (1396) 109; Bourges pact 114; English diplomats 137; Henry V embassy 141; council 165, 166; Calais embassy (Sep. 1416) 168; negotiates with Henry V 179; to retain French throne 182; English truce 183; treaty of Troyes 183, 184, 185–6; *ministri* 185; death 201

Charles VII, king of France (1422–61) **VI** 256, 476; gains prestige from English failures 250; described by English as Dauphin 258; Council of Basel 259; Burgundy alliance discussed 260; Henry VI's French claims 262; denounces John the Fearless' murder 263; Somme towns 263; withdraws English safeconducts (1455) 365; Orléans' release 469; attacks Tartas and St Sever (June 1442) 470; peace negotiations 474; Metz war 476; urges Maine surrender 479; irritated by Henry VI's failure to fulfil promise 479; Le Mans surrender 480; takes Rouen (Oct. 1449) 491; 'Kyng of Fraunce' 492; sends armies to Bordeaux 505; Gascon allegiance to England 505; opens Norman harbours to Queen Margaret 523; dies (22 July 1461) 532; **VII** 84; *see also* Charles, Dauphin

Charles VIII, king of France (1483–98): supports Henry Tudor **VI** 628; **VII** 85, 88, 99, 117, 124; Medina del Campo (1489) 94–5; marriage to Anne (1491) 104–5; Henry prepares for war 106–7; treaty of Étaples (1492) 109–10; interest in Italy 113–14; League of Venice (1495) 115; death 116, 149; Perkin Warbeck 121; English/Scottish relations 136

Charles IX, king of France **VIII** 48, 74, 131; Treaty of St Germain 147; Anjou marriage 152; Treaty of Blois 154; Coligny 157; the king's 'stratagem' 158; christening of daughter 160; death 162; opinion of Mary Stuart 373; Shane's appeal 470

Charles X, king of France **XIII** 218, 226–7, 389

Charles, king of the Franks (Charlemagne) **II** 90, 93–4, 176, 189, 219–21; kingdom of the Danes 239, 240; **III** 5, 254

Charles IV, king of Germany *see* Charles of Moravia

Charles II (the Bad), king of Navarre (1322–87) **V** 138, 140, 254

Charles II, king of Spain **X** 71, 161, 173, 192, 194

Charles X, king of Sweden **IX** 226–9

Charles XI, king of Sweden **X** 162

Charles XII, king of Sweden (1697–1718) (b. 1682) **X** 201; **XI** 166, 173

Charles the Simple, king of the West Franks (d. 929) **II** 344–5, 346; imprisonment (923–9) **IV** 104

Charles, lord of Ivry **VI** 141

Charles, 2nd marquis of Rockingham (1730–82) **XI** 49, 106

Charles Albert, elector of Bavaria (1697–1745), Emperor Charles VII (1742–5) **XI** 237, 238, 243–4, 249, 268; death 261; *see also* subsidies

Charles of Anjou, count of Provence, king of Sicily (d. 1285) **IV** 119, 121, 231, 232, 531; relations with Guy de Montfort 225–6 — and Edward I 234, 248; party in the French court 245, 248; dealings with Rudolf of Habsburg and resistance to claims of Margaret of Provence 247–9; Sicilian revolt against 249, 253; feud with Aragon 253; proposed duel with Peter of Aragon 254; death 255; the Venaissin 272; **VI** 474, 479

Charles Edward, the Young Pretender (1720–88) **XI** 41, 248; characteristics 251–2, 257; rebellion (1745) 252–7, 258, 269, 283

Charles of Egmont, duke of Gelders **VII** 103, 159, 163, 170, 183; Holy League (1511) 273

Charles Emmanuel III, duke of Savoy, king of Sardinia (1730–73) (b. 1701) **XI** 237, 241, 244–5, 247, 261; Maria Theresa alliance 263; subsidies 265; aims 266; *see also* subsidies

Charles Gustavas, king of Sweden **X** 73

Charles Martel **II** 167, 169

Charles of Mayenne (d. 1481) **VII** 113

Charles of Moravia, later Charles IV, king of Germany (1346–78) **V** 120

Charles of Salerno, count of Provence, king of Sicily, son and successor of Charles of Anjou: friendship with Edward I **IV** 234, 247, 248; Alfonso X of Castile (1280) 243–4; defends Provence (1282) 249; captured in naval battle off Naples (1284) 253; negotiations for his release 256–7, 258–63, 283; acquires Avignon (1290) 272; Pope Boniface VIII and 661

Charles III of Spain *see* Carlos, Don

Charles Town **X** 339

Charles of Valois, son of Philip III of France: invested by the pope with Aragon **IV** 254–5; receives Anjou and Maine 262

Charlotte, daughter of Francis I **VII** 307

Charlotte, Princess, daughter of George IV **XIII** 66–7, 104

Charlotte Augusta, Princess (1796–1817) **XII** 563

Charlotte Sophia, Queen (1744–1818): marriage to George III **XII** 7; regency crisis (1788–9) 305

Charlton, Edward, Lord Powys **VI** 64, 65

Charlton, John **V** 22, 50, 76, 86; Lord Powys **VI** 44

Charlton, Lewis, bishop of Hereford (1361–9) **V** 278

Charlton, Thomas **V** 49

Charlton Island **X** 340

Charnels, John **V** 157

Charnock, Richard **VII** 250

Charnwood, forest **VII** 35

Charolais, count of *see* Charles the Bold, duke of Burgundy

charter, Old English, derived from private Roman documents **II** 141, 307; introduced by Theodore 141; as evidence of gift 307–8; religious background 308–9; type continued under William I 642; *see* writ

Charter of Liberties, Great **III** 5–6, 20; Henry I's 114, 115, 386, 462, 471–2; Stephen's 133, 182, 190, 388–9; the unknown 371, 471–2; **IV** 142; significance of reissue (1216) 4–5; second confirmation (1217) 15, 40; confirmation (1225) 28–30; taxation 31; appeal to (1233–4) 53, 55, 59–60; legislation 67–70; confirmation (1237) 75, 78, 536 — (1253) 79, 453 — (1297) 536–7, 683 — (1300) 700–1; excommunication of infringers 75, 198, 217, 222, 473, 476, 697 — (1264–5) 194, 198, 217 — (1267) 216–18; emphasis on statutory nature (1267 and 1300) 217–18; in pleadings in the king's court 326, 329–30; copies affixed in churches 473, 476; and the forest (1297) 676, 682; ignored 682; local justices elected to deal with infringements (1300) 701, 704

charters: as materials for early history **II** 45; script 179; as evidence for reign of Offa 210–11; issued for laymen 301–2, 307–8; rights granted 307–10; of Athelstan 352–4; of Æthelred II 395–6; royal and private **IV** 38–9; interpretation by the courts 328; municipal **X** 12, 108, 136, 182

chartism: character **XIII** 120, 127–8; People's Charter 133–4; first national petition 134, 137–9; Convention of the Industrious Classes 137–9; Newport rising 139–40; second national petition 141; 'New Move' 141–3; O'Connor's land schemes 143–6; third national petition 144–5; results 146–8, 159

Chartley **IV** 212; castle **VII** 38; manor **VIII** 379, 380, 381, 383

Chartres (Eure-et-Loire) **Ia** 496, 514; **III** 234–5; Henry III in **IV** 235, 243, 262; **V** 138, 212; **VI** 172, 173, 191, 200, 239; siege of Orléans 250

Chartres, Bernard of **III** 235, 243, 262

Chartres, Ivo, bishop of *see* Ivo

Chartres, Renaud de, Chancellor, archbishop of Rheims **VI** 168; heads embassy 164; Scottish embassy 177

Chartres, Thierry of **III** 235

Chastel, Guillame du, Breton nobleman **VI** 72

Chastel, Tanneguy du **VI** 181, 188

Chastellain, G., chronicler **VI** 481

Château Gaillard (Seine-Inf.) **III** 375, 379, 383, 384; **VI** 183

Château-Thierry **VIII** 364

Châteauneuf-sur-Charente **VI** 113

Châteauroux (Berri) **III** 328, 343, 344, 466

Châtelherault, duke of *see* Hamilton, James

Chatfield, Admiral Lord **XV** 456

Chatham (Kent) **VIII** 407; harbour **X** 67

Chatham, earls of *see* Pitt, John; Pitt, William

Châtillon, Gaspard de Coligny, seigneur de **VII** 485

Châtillon, Jacques de, admiral of France **VI** 156

Châtillon negotiations (1814) **XII** 560

Châtillon, Walter of **III** 242

Chatsworth **VIII** 146; **X** 391

Chatteris (Cambs.) **V** 341

Chatterton, Thomas (d. 1770) **XII** 350, 353

Chatti **Ia** 167

Chaucer, Alice (later Montagu), countess of Salisbury (later de la Pole), duchess of Suffolk **VI** 473, 501

Chaucer, Geoffrey **III** 241; **V** 379, 446, 500, 522, 527; quotations 123, 196, 199, 508; on the Age of Gold 249; *Book of the Duchess* 267; on the village parson 302; on chantry priests 304; on friars 309; on reeves 319; on a poor widow 342; on a schoolboy 499; *Sir Thopas* 525; life and works 529–32; **VI** 277; local variations in English speech 658; **VII** 579, 583–4, 587; **X** 361

Chaucer, Philippa **V** 530

Chaucer, Thomas, of Ewelme **VI** 31, 199, 220, 417, 473; Commons speaker (1407, 1410, 1414, 1421) 31, 84, 112, 140; councillor 434; son of Geoffrey and Philippa Roet 473

Chauci **Ib** 50–5, 66–7

Chaumont **III** 108, 112, 127; *bailliage* **VI** 189; treaty (1814) **XII** 561; treaty **XIII** 195, 197

Chauncey, American commodore **XII** 553

Chaundler, Ralph, MP Grimsby **VI** 419

Chaundler, Thomas **VII** 236

Chauny (Aisne) **VI** 250

Chauvelin, Germain Louis de (1685–1762) **XI** 202

Chaworth, Pain de, lord of Kidwelly **IV** 196, 409, 410, 415

Cheam, John de, bishop of Glasgow (1259–67): claims for his see **IV** 574

Cheddar (Ceoddor) (Som.) **II** 446, 731

Chedworth (Glos.) **VI** 647

cheese, Stilton **XII** 34

Chef de Caux (Seine Estuary) **VI** 149, 559; *bailliage* 174, 189

Cheke, Sir John **VII** 520, 523, 527, 529, 552; tutor to Edward VI 479; education 571, 573; additional principal secretary of state (1553) 649

Chellaston **VII** 36, 597

Chelmsford (Essex): *mansio* **Ia** 567, 597; Romano-Saxon urn **Ib** 94–6, 95 [fig. 9]; map 2 xxx; map 6 88; **V** 418, 500

Chelmsford, Lord, in Labour government **XV** 210; *see also* Thesiger, General

Chelsea (Caelichyth) (Middx.) **II** 731; contentious synod (787) 218; (789) 237; (816) 237; synods (788) 309; speech by Hoare **XV** 437

Chelsea Hospital **X** 389

Cheltenham (Glos.) **VI** 56; **X** 409

chemistry **IX** 364; **X** 376

Chemistry, Royal College of **XIII** 566–7

Chepstow (Monmouth) **Ib** 18; castle **II** 615; **III** 287, 290; **V** 86; honour and castle 74

Chequers **XV** 481

Cherbourg (Manche) **III** 107, 123, 160, 384; **V** 403; fortress **VI** 137, 176, 190; captain 233; American plan to take **XV** 554; American objective 581

Cheriton, Odo of (d. 1247), sermons **IV** 765

Cherokee Indians **XII** 73

Cherré, theatre **Ia** 675

Chertsey (Cerotæsei) (Surrey) **II** 731; abbey 55, 455; founded by Egbert 61, 501, 635; abbey charter 67; monks appointed 451; **III** 30; **VII** 515

Cherwell, Lord *see* Lindemann, F. A.

Cherwell, river **Ia** 60; **Ib** map 3 xxxi

Chesapeake, battle **XII** 217

Cheselden, William (1688–1752), surgeon **XI** 390–1

Cheshire **Ia** 45; **II** 389, 503, 604; origin of shire 337; raided by Danes 375; devastated by William I 605; **III** 258, 394; **V** 178, 187, 447, 492; risings 204, 469; archers 447, 449, 475, 484, 487 — escorts for Arundel's beheading 481; **VI** 78; archers 21, 48, 52; king's forests 497

Cheshunt **Ib** 33; map 2 xxx

Chesney, Sir George **XIV** 8

Chesney, Robert, bishop of Lincoln **III** 160, 387

Chester: fortress **Ia** 152, 163, 231, 255, 329; Cartimandua? 133; construction 138; II Adivtrix transferred 150; *canabae* 575; amphitheatre 579; tile-factory 631; water-pipe 635; inscriptions 512, 683, 702; **Ib** 121; **II** 267, 326, 333, 339, 533; battle 78; bridgework 291; Edgar 369–70; castle 605; *judices* 532–3; see 666; rural conditions **III** 58; fixed sum paid to sheriff 65; trial by jury 73; waterways 80; German merchants 90; collection of taxes 94; surrender of northern counties by Scotland (1157) 275; earldom 285–6; campaign by Owain Gwynedd 291–2, 299; castle and honour, succession (1232 and 1237) **IV** 197, 606–7; shire and city granted to Lord Edward (1254) 118; as a base in war 138, 411, 422, 441; rights in shire acquired by and annexed to Crown 197; acquired in exchange by Simon de Montfort 197–8; recovered by Edward 203; legislation in county court (1260) 379; Exchequer 412, 414; justice 414; taxation of community (1291) 443; **V** 47, 153, 453, 474, 493; literature and miracle plays 526; **VI** 4, 32, 42, 47, 55; border county 44; justiciarship accepted by Henry Percy 50; Rhys ap Tudor dies 65; archdeaconry 421–2; **VII** 35; county 94; see 400; **IX** 351; chamberlain *see* Daniel, Thomas

Chester, bishop of **III** 160; *see also* Bird, John

Chester, earldom of **III** 285; **V** 258, 259, 266

Chester, earls of *see* Blundevill; John the Scot; Edward II; Edward of Woodstock; Hugh I; Hugh II; Rannulf I, le Meschin; Rannulf II, de Gernon; Rannulf III, de Blondeville; Richard; Richard II

Chester, Captain Edward **VIII** 338

Chester, Robert of, archdeacon of Pamplona **III** 244

Chester-le-Street (Cuncacestir) (Durham) **II** 731; cathedral church 342, 433, 666; bishop of 352; guardians suspended **XV** 256; *see also* Ælfsige

Chesterfield (Derby.), defeat of disinherited **IV** 208, 210

Chesterfield, dowager countess of **XIV** 30

Chesterfield, earl of *see* Stanhope, Philip Dormer

Chesterholm (Vindolanda): fort **Ia** 165; inscriptions 203, 521, 522; *vicus* 380; writing-tablets 508; *mansio* 568; bacteriological material 551; **Ib** 77; map 4 xxxii

Chesters: fort **Ia** 178; inscriptions 227, 250; water-mill 632; infant burial 695; **Ib** map 4 xxxii

Chesterton (Durobrivae) **Ia** 644; industrial centre 595; mosaicists 656; *see also* Water Newton

Chesterton, Gilbert of, wool merchant **IV** 632, 662

Chesterton, Gilbert Keith **XIV** 527, 531; quoted **XV** 40

Chevington, Richard, builder of All Souls College **VI** 648

Cheviot **III** 226, 283

Cheviot Hills **Ia** 4, 145

Chew Green, temporary camp **Ia** 145

Cheyne, Drayton Beauchamp family: Lollard revolt **VI** 132

Cheyne, Sir Edward **VI** 664

Cheyne, Sir John **V** 521; **VII** 89

Cheyne, Sir John, of Beckford **VI** 79, 91, 413, 429

Cheyne, Matthew **V** 429

Cheyne, Sir Thomas **V** 247

Cheyney (Cheyne), Sir Thomas (d. 1558), nephew of Sir John, treasurer of the household (1541) **VII** 494, 531, 650

Chezy (Loire) **VI** 246

Chiang Kai-shek: at Cairo **XV** 474; Roosevelt goes back on promise 575

Chichele, Henry, bishop of St David's (1414), archbishop of Canterbury: **VI** 91, 92, 93, 96, 97; council member 106; embassies 111, 136, 168, 179; fall of Rouen 176; royal marriage negotiations 180; crowns Catherine 193; Beaufort's Red Hat 198; John Langdon's promotion 199; Bedford's council summons 232; explains council's position 232; anti-papalism 235; legation and metropolitical power 236; prorogues convocation 237; register 268; Winchelsey's constitution 284; Lollardy trials 298; Convocation 303, 407–8; *domini de consilio* 485; Eleanor Cobham's trial 485; All Souls College statutes 673

Chichele, Sir Robert **VI** 664; son in Queen Margaret's household 481

Chichele, Sir William **VI** 664

Chichester (Cisseceaster) (Sussex) **Ia** 83, 96, 97; Cogidubnus 91; amphitheatre 579; inscriptions 659, 666, 669; (*Noviomagus Regnensium*) **Ib** xxvi, 31, 134–5, 137–8; map 2 xxx; map 3 xxxi; **II** 265, 531, 536, 731; rape 628; knight service 635; see 666; **III** 96, 247, 428; bishopric 446; **VII** 396

Chichester, Sir Arthur **V** 233

Chichester, Arthur, Lord **IX** 109

Chichester, bishops of, and the chapel in Hastings castle; *see also* Berksted, Steven; Christopherson, John; Day, George; Hilary; Medford; Nevill, Ralph; Poore, Richard, of Salisbury; Rede; Rushook; Sampson, Richard; Stratford; Waldby; Wych, St Richard

Chichester, diocese, register of acts *sede vacante* **VI** 279

Chichester, earls of *see* Pelham, Thomas

Chicken, Parson, *alias* Thomas Sowdley **VII** 545

chickens **Ia** 614

Chicklade (Wilts.), manor **VI** 462

Chiddingfold (Surrey) **VI** 654

Chief Diplomatic Adviser **XV** 405

Chief Economic Adviser **XV** 174, 329

Chief of the Imperial General Staff: Robertson **XV** 47; Henry Wilson 100; position 174, 228; Ironside replaces Gort 459; Dill 487, 497; Brooke becomes 536

Chiefs of Staff's Committee: origin **XV** 229; Singapore 230; bombing strategy 231; urges rearmament 363–4; promotes Germany to more immediate danger 375; favours surrender of Irish ports 406; anticipates defeat of France 407; low opinion of Soviet strength 416, 466; opposes war over Czechoslovakia 424–35; favours attack on Trondheim 471; Churchill directs 472, 479–80; estimate of prospects of invasion 490, 498; sends out Cromwell signal 499; plans for victory 515; Britain in Egypt 520; authorizes bombing against morale 551; rules out invasion of France (1942) 555; authorizes withdrawal from Egypt 556; Cripps wants different system 558–9; supports Montgomery in vain 590; atomic bomb 598

Chieregato, Lionel, papal nuncio **VII** 101, 102; threatened with rack by Wolsey 301

Chigwell, Hamo de **V** 84, 375

chilblains **XV** 306

Child, Sir John (d. *c.*1690), governor of Bombay **XI** 331

child workers *see* Factory Acts

Childeric **Ia** 493–6

Childerich, king of the Franks **II** 12

Childers, Hugh **XIV** 8, 17, 97

children, employment of **XI** 125–6, 141; pauper 131–2, 137

Childs **XI** 145

Chillenden, Edmund **IX** 314–15

Chillenden, Thomas (1391–1411), prior of Christ Church, Canterbury **V** 340–1; **VI** 92, 372

Chillingworth, William **IX** 213

Chilperich, king of the Franks **II** 14

Chiltern Hills (Ciltern) **II** 731; **III** 64

Chilterns (*Ciltern saetan*) **Ib** xxvi, 129–30, 167, 170; map 2 xxx; map 3 xxxi; **II** 28, 43, 54, 58, 67

chimneys **VIII** 272

China **IX** 334; **X** 350; **XIII** 8, 168; first and second China war 296–8; war with Japan **XIV** 219; Powers scramble for her ports 259–60; Lancashire's concern in her markets 260, 350; Boxer outbreak, siege and relief of the

121

ment for munitions 465; cautious political tactics 466–7; wishes to mine Norwegian lead 467; hopes to divert Finnish expedition 468; says German ships will be sunk 470; responsible for Norwegian campaign 471; defends Chamberlain government 472; ready to serve under anyone 473; remains silent 474; becomes prime minister and announces victory at all costs 475; Conservative leader 477; government 478; makes himself minister of defence 479; chiefs of staff 480; army plans 481; War Cabinet 482–3; regrets advance of British Expeditionary Force 484; sees Gamelin 485; warns of heavy tidings 486; sees Reynaud 487; speaks on radio 488–9; announces finest hour 491; checks measures of panic 492–3; orders attack on French fleet 494; appeals to Roosevelt 495–6; Dowding resists 497; acknowledges the 'few' 500; Lindemann 501, 508; after air raid 502; proclaims Battle of Atlantic 505; supports Beaverbrook 509; army and labour famine 512; thinks Germans can be defeated by local populations 515; thinks bombing only way 518; objects to withdrawal from Mediterranean 520; pursues Turkish alliance 522; war in Mediterranean 523; doubts Wavell's offensive spirit 524; warns against Greek campaign 525; discredited by failure in Greece 526; demands immediate action from Wavell 527; announces solidarity with Soviet Russia 528–9; Placentia Bay 529; sends battleships to Singapore 531–2; on Pearl Harbour 533; Grand Alliance 536; Arcadia conference 537–40; share of responsibility for fall of Singapore 541; mutterings against 542; attempts to buy off Cripps 543; loses Beaverbrook 544; India 546; wishes to suppress *Daily Mirror* 548; restores transport of cut-flowers 551; sceptical of strategical bombing 552; agrees to second front in principle 553; vote of no confidence in 554; argues with Marshall 555; Cairo (1942) 556; meets Stalin 557; bores House of Commons 558; shakes off Cripps 559; not anti-fascist 560; at Casablanca 561–2; at Washington (1943) 563–4; counts on friendship with Roosevelt 566; rejects nationalization of mines 567; at Quebec (1943) 572–3; at Cairo and Teheran (1943) 574–5; unconditional surrender 576; Balkans 576–7; opposes Transportation plan 580; does not go to France on D-day 581; still has Mediterranean plans 582–3; faces problems of future 585; at Quebec (1944) 586–7; at Moscow (1944) 588; in Athens 589; at Yalta 590–1; indiscriminate bombing 592; sounds anti-Bolshevik alarm 593; announces victory 594; proposes continuance of coalition 595; resigns 596; consents to use of atomic bomb 598; polemics against him 621

Churchill, Mrs Winston, raises fund for Aid to Russia **XV** 543

churchwardens (*economi*) **VI** 281

Churchyard, Thomas **VIII** 253–4

churchyards, markets and fairs in **IV** 369

Cibber, Colley (1671–1757) **XI** 145, 306, 421, 423

Cibber, Colley, sculptor, son of the above **X** 397

Cibò, Giambattista *see* Innocent VIII, Pope

Cicero, M. Tullius **Ia** 38–9, 53, 527; **III** 235, 236, 250

Cicero, Q. Tullius **Ia** 39

Cîeaux, abbot of **IV** 12

Cigogné, Engelard de **III** 393, 477; **IV** 22, 25, 544

Cilgerran (Wales) **IV** 443; lordship **VI** 77; castle 641

Ciltern *see* Chiltern Hills

Cilternsætan **II** 43–4, 296

Cimbri **Ia** 11, 126

Ciminian forest **Ia** 5, 555

cinema **XV** 180–1, 313–14; talkies 315; on Sundays 316

Cingetorix **Ia** 36

Cinque Ports **II** 430–2, 567; **III** 63, 382, 433–4, 484; instability (1216–17) **IV** 9–10; the Shipway 86; in Welsh wars 138, 409, 411, 422; and the Crown 158, 523, 531, 646, 655–6; during the years (1263–5) 175, 187, 193, 200; Edward I 207, 531, 619, 635, 655; war and piracy 644, 645; Brodhull court 645; in the Scottish war 657, 692–3; **V** 16, 58, 90, 390, 454; receives Ordinances from Edward II 17; Despenser's base for piracy 65; representatives at York parliament (1322) 71 — and Westminster (1327) 88; William Clinton warden 153; fleet 243; decline 380; Lord Latimer warden **VI** 18, 104, 418, 526; service 112; barons 158; **VII** 108, 219, 234; **X** 222; warden *see also* Humphrey, duke of Gloucester

Cintra, convention of (1808) **XII** 460

Ciolheard, Offa's gold coin **II** 224

Cipangu, Japan, Marco Polo's report **VII** 224

Cippanhamm *see* Chippenham (Wilts.)

Cippenham (nr. Windsor) **IV** 170

Cipriani, G. B. (1727–85), painter **XI** 406

circumnavigation, Drake's voyage **VIII** 249–51

Circumspecte agatis **IV** 482–3

Cirenceaster *see* Cirencester (Glos.)

Cirencester (Cirenceaster) (Glos.): military site **Ia** 96–7, 105; forum 138, 158; basilica 168; defences 218–19, 262, 329; gates 232; size of town 265, 593; mosaicists 280, 656; inscriptions 347, 718; end of town life 460, 484, 552; relationship with environs 584–6; provincial capital 585–6; donkey-mill 632; *macellum* 658; 'Jupiter column' 669, 714, 733; cemetery 704; **Ib** xxvi, 152, appendix II; map 3 xxi; Mons Badonicus 159–69; Ceawlin saga 163, 168, 170, 172; **II** 29, 44–5; Danes at 257; 731; **III** 61, 145; abbey 186; **V** 65, 453; **VI** 25, 367; **VII** 596

Cirencester, Robert, abbot of **III** 190

Cissa **Ib** 137, appendix I(b)

Cissbury **Ib** 137; map 2 xxx

Cisseceaster *see* Chichester (Sussex)

Cistercians: estates **III** 37; sheep farming industry 84; monastic influence 186–8, 295; opposition to William Fitz Herbert 191; refuge of Becket 211; decline 227, 229; architectural development 262; ransom of Richard I 366; royal revenue for building abbeys 422; privilege of exemption 446; monies paid to Exchequer 449; in Wales **IV** 389–90; in Ireland 568; Pecham's opinion of 434; **V** 42, 185, 308, 507, 511

Cîteaux **III** 185, 186, 188, 227, 229; abbot of **IV** 12

citizenship: army recruitment **Ia** 102, 271, 508, 510; extension 173, 175, 272, 293; and culture 505; rights 525–6; membership of community 534, 581–3, 591; *see also* barbarians; *peregrini*; Romanization

Clare, Gilbert of, earl of Gloucester and Hertford (d. 1230) **IV** 41; his son and heir *see* Richard de Clare

Clare, Gilbert of, earl of Gloucester and Hertford, son of Richard **IV** 152, 327, 519; his difficult succession (1262–3) 173, 175, 181; baronial leader (1264) 184, 187; knighted by Simon de Montfort 188; one of the three (1264–5) 191, 194, 196; defection (1265) 199, 201; intervention on behalf of the disinherited (1267) 213–15; takes the cross 219; co-operation in council during Edward's absence 225; marries Joan, daughter of Edward I 268, 329, 512; the liberties of the Marches 329–30; writs of *quo warranto* 378; builds Caerphilly Castle 406; defeated at Llandeilo (1282) 420, 422; joins in suppression of Rhys ap Mareddud (1287) 439; rebellion in Glamorgan against 440, 443; son Gilbert 517

Clare, Gilbert of, earl of Pembroke **III** 137

Clare, Gilbert, lord of **III** 109, 114, 290

Clare, Margaret de: married (1) Peter Gaveston, (2) Hugh Audley **V** 3, 59

Clare, Richard of, earl of Gloucester and Hertford (d. 1262) **III** 76; **IV** 41, 43, 44, 76; baronial movement (1258–60) 130, 140, 147–8, 150, 154–8; relations with Simon de Montfort 147; bachelors 152; compact with Lord Edward 152; royalism (1260) 161; death 171; succession 173; Scottish affairs (1255) 590, 591

Clare, Richard of, earl of Pembroke (Strongbow): capture of Cardigan Castle **III** 294; conquest of Ireland 294, 304, 305, 310, 312; estates inherited by William Marshall 297, 347; death 313

Clare, Richard Fitz Gilbert, lord of **III** 291

Clare, Roger of, brother of Gilbert **III** 114

Clare, Roger of, earl of Hertford **III** 260, 294

Clare, Thomas of: Edward's escape from Hereford (1265) **IV** 200–1; compact with Robert Bruce the claimant (1286) 598

Clare, viscount of *see* O'Brien, Charles

Clare, Walter of, brother of Gilbert **III** 290

Clare family **III** 114, 290; **IV** 519, 561

Clarel, John, king's clerk **IV** 136

Clarence, dukes of *see* George; Neviile, George; Lionel; Thomas

Clarence, Phillippa of, countess of March **V** 256, 267, 384

Clarencieux, herald at arms *see* Benolt, Thomas

Clarendon **III** 7, 29, 88, 321; assize, freemen and villeins 39; manorial court 57; demolition of houses 65; investiture contest 180; constitutions 201, 202, 211, 327, 447; council 205, 207; customs enforced by Norman kings 205–7, 385, 406, 409; coronation of Henry III 214; renunciation of customs 216–19; law against receiving heretics 230; Scottish police regulations 280; legislative acts of Henry II 327, 339; system of frankpledge 395; jury presentment 398–9; compurgation and ordeal 402; novel disseisin 407 **IV** 512

Clarendon, 4th earl of **XIV** 4; *see* Hyde, Edward; Hyde, Henry; Villiers, George William Frederick

Clarendon, Lord **XV** 242

Clarendon Code **X** 21–5, 106, 155

Clark, John **VII** 345

Clarke, Sir Edward **XIV** 64, 249, 443

Clarke, Sir George, Lord Sydenham
XIV 362
Clarke, John, archdeacon of Colchester, master of the rolls (20 Oct. 1522) VII 648
Clarke, Mrs Mary Anne (1776–1852) XII 447–9
Clarke, Revd Samuel (1675–1729) XI 10, 77, 84, 140, 396
Clarke, William XIV 334
Class XV 170–5
Classes, Act of IX 168
classical: studies X 383–4; scholarship XI 393–4
Classicianus, C. Julius Alpinus Ia 121–4, 156, 530, 630
Classicus (I), Julius, revolt Ia 127, 411
Classicus (II) Ia 533–4
classis Britannica Ia 258–9, 529, 559, 570, 637; disappears 639; see also fleets; Ib 79, 83
classis Germanica Ia 529
Clastburh see Glasbury (Brecon)
Claude, daughter of Louis XII VII 323; betrothed to Charles of Burgundy 153, 154; betrothed to Francis of Angoulême (later Frances I) 154
Claudia Martina, Anencletus' wife Ia 533
Claudian Ia 382, 405, 419–21, 423; Ib 84; V 531
Claudius, Emperor: motives for invading Britain Ia 3, 69–72, 107; formation of province 16, 87–99; economic activity 39, 115; tribes 40; accession 68; citizenship and army 75; administrative reforms at Rome 79–81; conquest of Britain 82–7, 286, 517, 539, 661; resistance under Caratacus 101–6; Colchester 104, 112, 115; death 108–9, 111; development of London 112; policy against Druids 711; deification 715
Claudius Appelinus Ia 251
Claudius Paulinus, Tiberius Ia

250–1
Claudius Postumus Dardanus see Postumus
Claudius Xenephon Ia 251
Clausentum see Bitterne
Claverhouse, John Graham of, 1st Viscount Dundee X 271, 276–8
Clavering, John (1722–77): in India XII 170, 310–13
Claverley (Salop) III 264
clay Ia 188, 602
Clay, Henry (1772–1852), American politician XII 551
Claydon, John, skinner of London, Lollard VI 133
Claypole, Elizabeth IX 266
Clayton, Charlotte, Lady Sundon (d. 1742) XI 78
Clayton, Robert, bishop of Killala (1695–1758): and Mrs Clayton XI 304
Cleland, William X 278
Clemenceau, G.: on Balfour XV 31; angry at Turkish armistice 113; and Paris peace conference 132; accepts League of Nations 133; yields over Rhineland 134; attempted assassination of 135; and intervention in Russia 137; and Fiume 162; Churchill echoes 475
Clement, John (d. 1572) VII 570, 571
Clement III, antipope II 674; III 173
Clement III, Pope: vices of clergy III 225; Scots, ecclesiastical independence 269, 278; William Longchamp, papal legate 354, 356, 358
Clement IV, Pope (1265–8), former cardinal legate to England IV 180; and Charles of Anjou 121, 531; and Simon de Montfort 199; excommunication of disturbers of the realm 681; see also Gui, Foulquois

Clement V, Pope (1305–14): castle-builder **IV** 444; the writ of caption 465; clerical *gravamina* (1309) 483–4; taxes English clergy (1305) 500; coronation (Nov. 1305) 514; court of claims at Montreuil 657; absolves Edward I from his oath 703–4; suspends archbishop Winchelsey 718; **V** 3, 29, 30, 33, 275; pleads for Gaveston 8; settles at Avignon 272; protest of English barons 273; provisions to benefices 277; *Si plures* 280; taxation of clergy 283–4; claim to annates 285; dissolution of Order of the Templars 291–2, 298

Clement VI, Pope (1342–52) **V** 123, 130, 211; provisions to benefices 276, 278, 296, 299

Clement VII, Pope (1378–94) **V** 146, 405, 429

Clement VII, Pope (1523–4) (Giulo de' Medici): **VII** 290, 311; new holy league formed (1524) 314–15; league of Cognac (1526) 316–17; imprisoned by imperialists and released (1527) 318, 327; makes peace at Barcelona with Charles (June 1529) 319, 328; hesitates about 'divorce' 326, 327, 329, 349; recalls case to Rome 328; in touch with Wolsey 331; death 340; attack on Vienna (1529) 341; Henry's struggle against 353; forbids Henry to remarry 354; Thomas Cranmer 356; prepares to excommunicate Henry (1533) 357; decides for Catherine 362

Clement VIII, Pope **VIII** 453, 459, 480

Clementia, mistress of King John **III** 428

Cleobury Castle **III** 322

Cleopatra **Ia** 49

clergy: communities **II** 149, 152, 441, 451, 668; works written for guidance **IV** 764–5

clergy, English: and laity **IV** 86; Hubert de Burgh 46–7; representation (1254) 117; in wartime (1264) 193, 195; taxation (1266–73) 220–4; views of on crusade (1291–2) 267; numbers 445–6; types 458–9; Edward I and 666, 671–5; taxation (1294–8) 672, 673, 675, 676–7, 678, 681, 688; and Pope Boniface VIII 673, 676; *see also* clerks; convocation; dioceses; *Gravamina*; representation; taxation

clergy, French **IV** 267, 674, 676, 677

clergy, parochial: condition **II** 456–7; *Catholic Homilies* 458–60; effect of Conquest on parish clergy 668–9; marriage 668; learning **VI** 279–80; celebration of sacraments 281; dependent on farming and livestock 285

Clerical Disqualification Act (1801) **XII** 132

Clericis laicos: Bull of Boniface VIII (1296) 458, 666, 674; Edward I and 675, 676–7; infringements in England 676

Clerk, Thomas, draper, MP Reading **VI** 418

clerk of the peace **XII** 43

Clerke, G., Wilkite **XII** 133, 140

Clerkenwell, London **III** 190; workhouse **X** 53

Clerk-Maxwell, James **XIII** 570; **XIV** 136, 151

clerks **Ia** 507, 519–20; foreign, in English churches **II** 443–4; promoted to bishoprics 464; beneficed, Adam Marsh on **IV** 445; status 447–9, 458–9; confessions 447; discipline 449, 451–3; problem of crominous 462–3; resort to king's court by 467–8; king's 478–9, 340–1, 458–60

Clermont, council (1095) **III** 110

Clermont-Ferrand **Ia** 494, 498

Cletoft (Yorks.) **VI** 9

Clitheroe **III** 271; honour **VI** 1

Clitheroe, Richard, admiral of England **VI** 82

Clitumnus, river, shrine **Ia** 690–1

Clive, Robert, 1st Baron (1725–74) **XI** 327–32, 347, 366, 412; achievements in India **XII** 17, 159, 162–4, 306, 311; political affiliations 83, 150, 163; attacks on 164, 166, 168

Clives, the **XI** 145

clocks **X** 398

Clodius Albinus, D. *see* Albinus

Clofeshoh, annual synod **II** 133; council held (746) 150, 237; (803) 134, 227; legatine council (786) 155

Clogher, bishops of *see* Courcey, John Edmund

Clonmel **VII** 72

Clontarf, battle **III** 302; **VII** 364

Clopton, William, abbot of Thorne (1305–22) **V** 321

Clopton, Sir William, of Kentwell Hall **VI** 473

Clorach (Angle) **VI** 39

cloth manufacture **V** 150, 336, 356–60, 379, 381; export growth **VI** 349; vendor selling 350; church building 647; **VII** 462–3, 469; **VIII** 237; **X** 317–18

cloth tax **V** 221, 357, 359, 369

cloth-workers, riots **X** 258

Clothall, nr. Baldock, curse **Ia** 689

clothes **XII** 548

Clough, A. H. **XIV** 138–9

Clough, Anne Jemima **XIII** 497, 498; **XIV** 150

Clough, Arthur Hugh **XIII** 497, 539–40; biography 539

clover crop **XII** 34

Clovis, Frankish king **Ia** 462, 494–501; **Ib** xviii, 119, 126–7; **II** 12

Clowes, William **VIII** 313, 314

Clown, William **V** 308, 316

Cloyne (Ireland), see **VI** 275

clubs, social **X** 357–9; importance **XII** 338–9; *see* societies and clubs

La Clue, Sabran de, Admiral, in Seven Years War **XI** 361, 365

Cluentius Habitus, A. (I), defended by Cicero **Ia** 711

Cluentius Habitus, A. (II) (*praefectus cohortis*) **Ia** 711

Clun (Salop) **VI** 335

Cluniac Order **VI** 299–300; Great Schism 300; abbots 300

Cluny: monastery **II** 574, 673; **III** 185–6, 262, 322; church 185; abbey **V** 293

Cluny, prior of *see* Foliot, Gilbert

Clux, Hartank van **VI** 161

Clwyd **Ia** 45, 631; river 144, 197, 229; **II** 230, 447–8, 576, 615; **III** 285, 287, 393; *see also* Antonine Wall

Clydesdale, signal station **Ia** 571

Clydeside: discontent **XV** 39; Red Flag 199

Clydesiders **XV** 198, 201, 209

Clymme, Adam **V** 416

Clynes, J. R.: supports general strike **XV** 144; defeated as Labour leader 201; opposes cuts in benefit 292, 297

Clyro **Ia** 95, 105, 107

Cnebba **Ib** appendix II

cniht **II** 527–8

Cnut, Danish king, coins found at York **II** 262, 263

Cnut, King, son of King Swein: **II** 386–9; joined by Thorkell the Tall 388; invaded England with Danish army (1015) 389; received fealty of assembly at Southampton 390; began siege of London 391; came to terms with Edmund Ironside 392; chosen as king when Edmund died (30 Nov. 1016) 393; attitude to English Church 396–8, 410–12; marries Emma, widow of Æthelred (1017) 397; European position 397, 407; wives 397–8; character 398–9; nature of his English gov-

132

ernment 398; dismissal of fleet 399; northern expeditions and conquest of Norway 399–404; daughter 406; visits Rome 407; relations with Emperor 408; obtains Slesvig from Emperor 408; relations with Normandy 408–9; code 409–10; relations with English Church 410; invades Scotland 419; laws quoted 489, 499, 694; writ quoted 497

Cnut, St, king of Denmark **II** 611; invasion of England 617

Co-operative Wholesale Society, early growth **XIV** 134

coaches and caroches **VIII** 264; road **XIII** 4, 42

coal **Ia** 631; **III** 81; mining **V** 371–2; **VIII** 236; **IX** 280, 294, 301, 333–4; tax **XII** 26; output and use 27, 31, 334, 505, 516; **XIV** 108, 276, 503

coal industry: **V** 349; **X** 48, 305, 322; taxes, in Scotland 289; in Ireland 322; nationalized **XV** 78; effects of First World War 122; Sankey commission 140; drags nation into turmoil 142; strike (1920) 144; collapse of exports 145; returned to private ownership 145; lock-out (1921) 145–6; subsidy to 146; decline 182, 305; renewed conflict 239–41; lock-out (1926) 243; Samuel's recommendations 247; defeat of miners 248; royalties rationalized 340; royalties nationalized 406; traffic a burden on railways 506; shortage 546; proposed rationing defeated 547; nationalization announced 597; loss of workers 599

Coal Mines Act (1931) **XV** 278–9

coal mines legislation *see* Factory Acts

Coalbrookdale (Salop) **X** 50; ironworks **XI** 115, 117; **XII** 31, 507

coalition, first: made **XV** 30–2; Asquith's conduct 34; and Dardanelles 44; end 69; second: made **XV** 70; maintained after war 112; Lloyd George tries to extend 125; wins general election 128; changed character 131; proposal to continue 189, 191; dissolved 192

coastal command (1939–45 war) **XV** 504–5, 517

coastal defences **Ia** 306–9, 420–1, 423, 528–30; Cumbria 170, 260, 384; S. and E. coasts 257–60, 281–2; W. coast 378; N.E. coast 383–4; *see also classis Britannica*; fleets; Saxon Shore; Solway Firth

coastline changes **Ia** 555–6

Coatham (Yorks.) **III** 96

Cobbett, William (1762–1835) **XI** 125, 144; **XII** 368, 522, 571; **XIII** 21–2, 30, 80, 92, 127; biography 21; ten hours' movement 149; pauper definition 453; prose comparison 531; conifers 598; tea drinking 623; **XV** 186, 240

Cobden, Richard **XIII** 124, 176, 180; biography 120; works for repeal of the corn laws 120–2; negotiates commercial treaty with France 179–80; views on the Crimean War 258; **XIV** 118, 186

Cobden-Sanderson, T. J. **XIV** 540

Cobham, Edward, Lord **VI** 520

Cobham, Eleanor: lady in waiting to Jacqueline of Hainault **VI** 226; wife of Humphrey of Gloucester examined for heresy 482; 485

Cobham, Lord Henry **VIII** 151, 347, 348, 440

Cobham, Joan **VI** 103 *see also* Old-castle

Cobham, Sir John **V** 186

Cobham, Lord John **V** 446, 451, 462; returns from Guernsey **VI** 7; *see also* Brooke, John

Cobham, Sir Reginald **V** 148, 159

Cobham, Thomas, bishop of Worcester (1317–27) **V** 30, 275, 300, 503

Cobham, Lord Thomas **VI** 504

Cobham, Viscount *see* Temple, Sir Richard

Coblenz **V** 122

Cobos, Alonzo de **VIII** 484

Cocham *see* Cookham (Berks.)

Cochin **XII** 409

Cochrane, Sir Alexander (1758–1832) **XII** 554

Cochrane, C. B. **XV** 250

Cochrane, Thomas, 10th earl of Dundonald (1775–1860) **XII** 478

Cocidius (Vernostonus) **Ia** 685

cock-fighting **VIII** 276, 277; **IX** 180, 311

Cockayne, William **IX** 317–18, 333

Cockbrook, Towton (Yorks.) **VI** 526

Cockburn, captain **VIII** 86

Cockburn, Claude **XV** 397

Cockburnspath (Berwick) **VI** 35

Cockerell, Charles Robert **XIII** 583

Cockermouth (Cumbria): honour and castle **IV** 21, 364, 707; **VI** 9, 63, 337, 376

Cockerton surcharges **XIV** 355–6

Cocklaws Castle, Teviotdale **VI** 47

Cockson, Thomas **VIII** 302

Cocos Island, *Emden* sunk **XV** 13

cod-liver oil, use **XII** 11

Codex Amiatinus **II** 179, 191

Codex Aureus **II** 433

Codex Theodosianus **Ia** 398, 408, 568, 598, 622, 732

Codrington, Admiral **XIII** 218–19, 271

Codrington, General Christopher **X** 348

Codrington College **X** 348

Coehoorn, Menno **X** 43

coffee: trade **X** 349, 358; houses 358–9; **XI** 419

coffins **Ia** 636, 697–8, 700, 701, 703; nails 706; Christian 731–2; *see also* sarcophagi

Cogan, Miles of, constable of Dublin **III** 306, 312, 313

Coggeshall (Essex): cloth production **VI** 366

Coggeshall, Ralph of **III** 469

Cogidubnus (Cogidumnus) **Ia** 87, 91, 97, 111, 161–2; emperor's representative 659; identity and career 748–52; **Ib** 135

Cognac (Charente) **IV** 124; league (1526) **VII** 316, 317

cohorts **Ia** 129, 247, 256, 293, 322; unsuitable against Britons 34; urban cohorts, Carthage 162 — London? 162 — Lyons 162, 220 — Rome 334; Baetasians 258, 260; first cohort of Aquitani 260; Tungri 683; Lingones 684; Thracians 685; Batavians 711

Coifi, heathen priest of Deira **II** 114

coinage: **Ia** 68, 90, 101, 506, 681; Belgae 11–12, 23; Venetic scarcity 24; lack of silver 39; distribution 40–1; Catuvellauni 43; confused conditions 47; Tincommius 52; Colchester mint 55; Atrebates 56, 59; Roman occupation 202, 206, 211, 212, 337 — Domitian's triumph 167 — victory in Britain 194 — Antorinus Pius 199 — celebratory 231 — Bitterne base 384; difficulties of dating hoards 244; significance 259; Carausius 297, 299, 312–13, 660; Arras medallion 310–11; *adventus* from London mint 327; validity throughout empire 415; decline and cessation of use in Britain 424–5, 454–6, 457–9, 479, 660–1; other ritual uses 564, 704; money economy 616, 625, 660; in shrines 690–1, 708; barbarous, minted in London **II** 57, 222; *sceatta* currency 222; origin of penny 222–5; gold *mancus* of King Offa 223; struck for Egbert in London 232; in honour of St Edmund 249; Viking, minted in London 250; minted in York 262, 263, 338; historical importance 535–8; Old English, discovered and imitated in Scandinavia 542–3; of Harold II 581; Norman campaigns **III** 111; Stephen 154–5; baronial issues 158–9; Irish 315; reform (1180–1) 339; 'new statutes' 385; debasement 414–15; Edward I's new (1279–80) **IV** 632–4; in Gascony 306; judicial action against debased and false coins 632, 633; farthing 633, 634; debasement **VII** 412, 475, 502; Appendix 604–8; reform **VIII** 262; *see also* currency; groat; maille; minting places; mints; Morlaas

Coinmail, British king **Ib** 168, appendix II; **II** 4, 29

Coke, Sir Edward (1552–1634): manuscripts of the Provisions of Oxford **IV** 147; **V** 202; Lord Chief Justice **VII** 415; **VIII** 212, 422, 423; **IX** 3, 10, 111, 390; his fall 20–1; imprisoned 27–8; Petition of Right 40; **XI** 65

Coke, Dr John, Edward IV's envoy to Netherlands **VI** 583

Coke, Thomas William, 1st earl of Leicester (1752–1842) **XI** 106; **XII** 33

Col, Gontier **VI** 168

Colbert, Jean Baptiste **X** 91, 163; *see also* Torcy

Colchester (Colneceaster) (Essex): British capital **Ia** 55–7, 589, 674; captured by Claudius 70, 86, 97; provincial capital 89, 112, 117, 124, 530; *colonia* 103, 127, 574, 585, 599 —first established 104, 112 —Trinovantes' hatred 115 —resentment 153 —stone walls 262 —importance 510; Imperial Cult 115, 515, 683; trade 652; coins 660; Facilis' tombstone 699; (*Camulodunum*) **Ib** 89, 107,

129–30, 214; Romano-Saxon pottery 90 [fig. 7(e)]; map 2 xxx; map 6 88; **II** 325, 329, 533, 731; council 352, 351; **III** 96, 418, 480; castle 26; St Botolph's priory 186; castle **IV** 9; abbey **V** 248; **VI** 460; municipal register 282; cloth manufacture 366; **VII** 67, 199, 398, 500; **IX** 155; workhouse **X** 53; riots 258

Colchester, 1st Baron *see* Abbot, Charles

Colchester, Viscount *see* Savage, Thomas

Colchester, William, abbot of Westminster **VI** 22, 25, 26, 91, 234

Coldham-in-Elm (Cambs.) **V** 321

Coldingham (Berwick): monastery **II** 135, 162; **VII** 160, 407; abbess of *see* Æbbe

Coldstream, truce (1488) **VII** 137; 147, 281

Coldwell, John, bishop of Salisbury **VIII** 191

Cole, G. D. H. **XV** 142, 331, 347

Cole, Revd William (1714–82), antiquarian **XI** 396

Cole, William Willoughby, 1st earl of Enniskillen (1736–1803) **XI** 298

Colebrooke, John (*c*.1720), and Ostend Company **XI** 196

Coleman, Edward **X** 104

Coleraine **V** 233; *see also* Londonderry

Coleridge, Sir John, later 1st Lord **XIV** 12, 17, 23, 25

Coleridge, Samuel Taylor (1772–1834) **XII** 534, 539, 542, 544, 549; biography 539; **XIII** 3, 32, 35, 37–8, 503; latitudinarians 506; death 530; **XIV** 328

Coleshill (Berks.) **V** 337

Colet, Sir Henry (d. 1505) **VII** 242

Colet, John (1467–1519) **VII** 43, 240, 241, 242–7, 576; Erasmus 250–1, 256–7; on war 269;

135

Colet, John (*cont.*)
schools 577; dean of St Paul's **XI**
139
Coleville, William de **IV** 21, 22
Colfox, Richard, of London **VI** 131
coliberti **II** 475–6
Coligny, Gaspard de, admiral of
France **VIII** 54, 57, 60, 131;
summons to the council 147;
Lewis of Nassau 153; shot 157
Colin, Peter van **VII** 408
Colin Clout's Come Home Again **VIII**
291
Collcutt, T. E. **XIV** 324
Collective security and Oxford
Union resolution **XV** 362; Attlee
on 368; an impressive phrase 369;
a divisive force 374; depreciated
in White Paper 376; for ostenta-
tion, not for use 379; Hoare
pledges support 380; in action
381; Labour 382, 420; its failure a
cause of war 453
College, Stephen **X** 103, 106
College of Physicians **VII** 242
Colleges: Acaster **VI** 668; Winches-
ter 668; Eton 668–9; Rotherham
668; *see also* universities
collegia **Ia** 659, 666, 696–7
Colley, Sir George **XIV** 11, 29,
69
Collier, Jeremy (1650–1726) **X** 369;
XI 419
Collier, Sir R., later Lord Monkswell **XIV** 17, 20
Collingbourne, William **VII** 53
Collings, Jesse **XIV** 97, 128
Collingwood, Cuthbert, 1st Baron
(1750–1810), admiral **XII** 429,
459
Collingwood, R. G. **Ia** 100, 138,
167, 312, 542; **XV** 398
Collins, Anthony (1676–1729) **XI**
85
Collins, John **X** 42; **XIII** 140
Collins, Michael: leads IRA **XV**
154–5; confesses IRA near defeat
157; killed 159; hint to him con-

cerning boundary 162; orders
assassination of Henry Wilson
188; died in vain 358
Collins, William (1721–59), poet
XI 426
Collis, John **Ia** 6, 10, 544
Colloquia (Erasmus) **VIII** 323
Colloquium speciale **IV** 688, 689, 701
Collyweston **VII** 161
Colman, bishop of Lindisfarne **II**
123–4
Colne (Essex) **V** 476
Colne (Lancs.) **XV** 304
Colne Roger (Glos.) **III** 393
Colneceaster *see* Colchester (Essex)
Colnet, Nicholas, Henry V's physician **VI** 287, 288
Cologne (Köln) **Ia** 73, 127, 409, 587;
administrative centre 517; fleet
base 282; Frankish kingdom 456,
493, 494, 496, 497; cult of *matres*
669; **II** 462; **III** 83, 89–90, 92,
327, 450; **V** 119, 359, 476–7; dean
477; **VI** 70; principality 84, 113,
129, 565; Hansa 358; Hanseatics
compensate for alleged piracy
554; archbishopric 574; **VII** 219,
343; bombed **XV** 553
Cologne, archbishop of **IV** 660;
Engelbert 73; **V** 476; *see also* Adolf
of Altena; Bruno of Sayn; Reinald
of Dassel
Cologne, elector **X** 197
Colombia, republic of **XIII** 211
Colombières **III** 346, 347
Colombo **XV** 545
Colon, Gaillard **IV** 109
Colon family **IV** 109, 111
Coloni **Ia** 546, 561, 606, 644
colonia **Ia** 94, 510, 534, 574–5,
580–91; Colchester 87, 101, 104,
112, 674; first established 104;
Lincoln 152, 262; Gloucester 153,
232, 262, 584–6; buildings 159;
stone walls 262; London? 582;
Caerleon? 586; Cologne 669
colonial: legislatures **X** 335–7;
policy **XI** 311, 316–19; contin-

German fascism 418; discredited by opposing Second World War 458; summons People's convention 503; membership increases after German attack on Russia 542

Communitas, proctors of at the papal court (1245) **IV** 133, 150

'community of the realm' **IV** 131-7, 141-2, 146, 192, 528; definition 67

community of the vill **IV** 143

Commutation Act (1784) **XII** 288

Comnenus, Alexius I, eastern emperor **III** 94

Comnenus, Isaac of Cyprus **III** 360

Comnenus, Manuel I, eastern emperor **III** 339

Como, cardinal of **VIII** 173, 176, 177, 178

companies: British Linen Company (Scotland) **XI** 277; Free British Fishery Company 277; Royal African 313; *see also* East India Company; South Sea Company

companies, growth of limited **XIV** 112-14

Company, the **IX** 286, 318-19

Compiègne (Oise) **VI** 175, 239, 248, 249, 257; Louis' army 576; **VII** 318

Complaints **VIII** 291

'Composition' of Connaught **VIII** 472

Compostella **III** 94, 215

Compromissio, compromissum **IV** 182-4, 650-1

Compton, Henry, bishop of London **X** 118, 121, 124

Compton, Sir Spencer, earl of Wilmington (?1673-1743) **XI** 17, 202, 238, 246

Compworth, Thomas **V** 520, 521

Comyn, Alexander, earl of Buchan (1233-89) **IV** 581, 582, 589, 592

Comyn, John **V** 32, 33

Comyn, John, of Badenoch (d. 1274) **IV** 190, 581, 582

Comyn, John, of Badenoch, the claimant **IV** 582; guardian of Scotland (1286) 597, 598; supports John Baliol 601

Comyn, John, earl of Buchan (d. 1308) **IV** 581-2, 606, 608, 696, 697; wife 714, 716

Comyn, John, the Red, of Badenoch, guardian of Scotland, slain (1306) **IV** 694; captured at Dunbar (1296) 614; King Philip's letter 695, 697; dispute over Wallace's lands 696; routs Segrave 708; capitulates at Strathorde 709, 711; made counsellor 713; murdered 713-14

Comyn, Richard **IV** 581

Comyn, Walter, of Badenoch, earl of Menteith (d. 1258) **IV** 581, 582, 589, 592

Comyn (Cumin), William, clerk, chancellor of David I **IV** 581

Comyn, William, earl of Buchan (d. 1233) **IV** 581

Comyn, William, of Kilbride **IV** 582

Comyn family, Scottish genealogy **IV** 581-3

Con, George **IX** 210

Conan, citizen of Rouen **III** 106

Conan, duke of Brittany **II** 577

Conan III, duke of Brittany **III** 324; **VI** 72

Conan IV, duke of Brittany, earl of Richmond **III** 281

Concarneau **VII** 97, 102, 104

concentration camps **XIV** 345, 346

concessionaires *see conductores*

Conches, lordship of **III** 107

Conches, William of **III** 161, 235, 243

concilium see councils

Concordat of Bologna (1516) (Francis I and Leo X) **VII** 336

Concordia **VII** 272

Concressault, Alexander Monypenny, Sieur de **VII** 121, 138

concrete **Ia** 609

139

Condat (nr. Livourne), ordinance for the Agenais (1289) **IV** 298, 302–3

Condé, prince of **X** 83; **XII** 423; *see* Bourbon, Louis

Condidan, British king **Ib** 168, appendix II; **II** 4, 29

Condom, Agenais **IV** 298; ordinances (1289) 298–301, 303–4; *paréage* 308

Condover **IV** 339

conductores: on estates **Ia** 268, 604; mines 633–4

Conduit, Reginald **V** 156, 168

coney-catching tracts **VIII** 293

Conference about the Next Succession **VIII** 454

confession of faith **IX** 193

confiscations: territory of conquered tribes **Ia** 89, 104, 224, 277, 531 — territory 538, 604; resulting from civil war 266–8; pagan temple property 341–2, 401, 730; to raise money for army 405; misappropriated funds 534

Conflans, Hubert de Brienne, comte de, and battle of Quiberon (1759) **XI** 365

Congested Districts Board, creation **XIV** 187, 450

Congregation, Lords of the **VIII** 40, 42, 43

Congregational ministers, holders of benefices **X** 17

Congress, Indian: led by Gandhi **XV** 152–3; declares Indian independence 275; and Round Table conference 275–6; demands immediate self-government 545

Congress, United States: lend-lease **XV** 538, 587; Roosevelt seeks to influence elections 555, 560; atomic bomb used 601

Congress of Philadelphia **XII** 199, 201, 204, 207, 214

Congresses: Vienna **XIII** 194–5, 198; Aix-la-Chappelle 200–2; Troppau 203; Laibach 203;

Verona 204, 207–8; Paris 290–1, 304

Congreve, William (1670–1729) **X** 323, 358, 362, 369; **XI** 421

Conisbrough (Conisburgh) (Yorks.): castle **III** 27; **VI** 147

Connaught **III** 305, 308, 311, 313, 314; conquest **IV** 42, 43, 54; shire and cantrefs 564; expedition (1286) 598; **V** 41, 44, 229, 232, 267; **VI** 425; **VII** 125, 130, 131; **IX** 114, 164

Connaught, earls of *see* Mortimer, earls of March

Connecticut **IX** 342; **X** 333, 334, 337

Connolly, James **XIV** 473

Conolly, William (d. 1729) **XI** 294

Conopios, Nathaniel **X** 358

Conrad, count palatine of the Rhine **III** 367, 376

Conrad, duke of Swabia **III** 367

Conrad, Emperor **II** 407

Conrad III, Emperor **III** 149

Conrad, Joseph **XIV** 548, 549

Conrad of Hohenstaufen, son of Frederick II **IV** 122

Conrad of Jungingen, master of Teutonic Order **VI** 71

Conrad the Peaceable, king of Burgundy **II** 346

Conradin , son of Conrad of Hohenstaufen **IV** 122

Conroy, Sir John **XIII** 103–4

conscientious objectors: First World War **XV** 53; disfranchised for five years 116; Second World War 457

conscription **Ia** 114, 197, 283, 294, 548; unpopular with land-owners 439, 457, 487–8, 509–10; in France **XII** 365; First World War **XV** 53–56; proposed extension to Ireland 103–4; planned for labour 375; demand for (1939) 433; introduced 444–5; extended 456; moves slowly 457; based on national register 464; in operation

Consentius, land-owner **Ia** 450

Conservative Party: Unionists revert to name **XV** 161; maintains ban on divorce 170; businessmen and aristocrats 172; turns against Lloyd George 188; ends coalition 190–2; Law becomes leader 193; twice wins absolute majority 195; wins general election (1922) 198; Curzon unpopular 204; Baldwin becomes leader 205; and Protection 206–7; attacks Russian treaty 217; Campbell case 218–19; benefits from increase in women voters 262; organization 263–4; offers Safety First 267; does not threaten Free Trade 270; in confusion 271; agrees with Labour's foreign policy 277; annoyed at lapse of safeguarding duties 286; supports National government 293, 296; pretends inquiry into Protection 324; wins general election (1931) 326; MacDonald an excuse for its shortcomings 334; Churchill attempts to drive Baldwin from leadership 356; has no plans for war against Soviet Russia 359; welcomes London naval treaty 360; and League of Nations 368–9; wins general election (1935) 383; Hoare-Laval plan 385; distrusts clever men 389; Spanish Civil War 397–8; resignation of Eden 423; and Munich 430; Popular Front 435; turns against appeasement 440; Nazi-Soviet pact 450; Churchill aims to capture 466–7; enthusiastic for Finland 468; attack on Chamberlain 472–3; does not cheer Churchill 475; preponderance in Churchill's government 478; revolts against coal rationing 547; rejects electoral reform 568, 569; Yalta 591; general election (1945) 596–7; *see also* Unionist party

Conservator of the Church in Scotland **IV** 583
conservators of liberties **IV** 77–8
Consilium de Emendanda Ecclesia **VII** 555
consilium principis **Ia** 192
conspiracy **Ia** 306, 309–10; suspicion of religious groups 344, 411, 665; the 'barbarian conspiracy' 375–82; Valentia? 395–6; writ and ordinance **IV** 354
constable: office of **V** 53, 265, 452, 479; court of chivalry 96, 265, 443, 489; high, of county **XII** 45; of watch 46; *see also* Thomas of Woodstock; Edward of York
Constable, John, painter (1776–1837) **XI** 401; **XII** 543; **XIII** 536; biography 589; work 588–90
Constable, Marmaduke **V** 207
Constable, Robert, of Holme (Yorks.) **VI** 345
constables, police **III** 392, 439
constabulariae, in Scotland **IV** 575
constabularies of burghers (1265) **IV** 200
Constance, council **VII** 336
Constance, countess of Gloucester, widow of Thomas Despenser **VI** 26, 56; tries to abduct two Mortimers 56
Constance, daughter of Conan IV of Brittany **III** 281, 325, 337, 378
Constance, General Council **VI** 121, 161, 200, 295, 327; Spanish delegates 162; nations in 170
Constance, queen of Aragon, daughter of Manfred and wife of Peter of Aragon: claim to Sicily **IV** 252, 253
Constance, sister of Louis VII **III** 147, 162, 326
Constance, wife of Emperor Henry VI **III** 360
Constance of Castile, duchess of Lancaster **V** 267, 441, 473

141

Constance of Castile, wife of Louis VII **III** 329

Constans (I), Emperor **Ia** 348–54, 368, 377, 384, 386–7; imperial visits 517; **Ib** 78, 84

Constans (II) (Caesar) **Ia** 428, 432, 433

The Constant Nymph **XV** 311

Constantine, donation of **III** 303; **IV** 98

Constantine I, the Great, Emperor **Ia** 322–47; proclamation and rise to power 4, 323–5, 331, 340, 733; army reforms 291–5, 331–4, 349–50; defence policy 291–2, 330, 348, 387; coinage 318, 327–8; arrangements in Britain 323, 330, 345–7; religious policy 323, 340–5, 354, 356, 577 — pagans 713, 716; York 325–8; architecture 326; financial effects of his policies 342, 345, 663; Constantinople 364–6; **Ib** 79–81, 83

Constantine II, Emperor **Ia** 348, 354, 358

Constantine III, Emperor **Ia** 428–9; Justinianus 384; military campaigns 428–9, 431–4; Arles 433–4, 451, 453, 518; Britain 434, 436, 437–41, 469, 661; Gallo-Romans 436; Sidonius Apollinaris 498

Constantine, king of Dumnonia **II** 4

Constantine, king of Greece **XV** 190

Constantine, king of Scots **II** 333–4, 340, 342

Constantine, Pope **II** 165

Constantine Pogonatus, emperor of Constantinople **II** 137

Constantinople **Ia** 362, 369, 391, 407, 408; establishment of new city 285, 326, 364–6; distant authority 401, 517; Stilicko's claim 423; *Vicarius* 435; Aetius 475; maintenance of imperial tradition and army 486, 489–594; food supplies 588; **III** 89, 94;

conquest by the Latins (1204) **IV** 82; **V** 248; defence against Turks **VI** 76; **VII** 151, 236; Kitchener expects fall **XV** 25; promised to Russia 50; Allied occupation 132; shadow sultan 190; Turks recover 202

Constantius IV, author **Ia** 465, 466

Constantius I, Chlorus, Emperor **Ia** 245, 259, 293, 301–6; Britain 304–5, 307–15, 317–20, 322, 323; death 324; York 325, 328; religious policy 340, 712–13, 716, 721; **Ib** 78–80

Constantius II, Emperor: at Constantinople **Ia** 285, 348, 365–6; military successes 348, 350, 354–6; relations with Julian 359, 361, 373; economic control 577, 663

Constantius III, Flavius, Emperor **Ia** 446, 447, 474

Constantius, *Vita Sancti Germani* **Ib** 8, 23, 206

constitutio Antoniniana **Ia** 575, 581

Constitutio Domus Regis **III** 8–9

constitution, at Restoration **X** 8

constitutional conference **XIV** 422–4; membership 422

constitutional development under Queen Anne **X** 252–62

constitutional problem in Ireland **X** 319–21

constitutional theory, English **XII** 55–63, 117, 137, 357–9, 361; place of opposition 80, 87; Burke believes in common sense policy 125; in America 173, 176, 184–7, 191, 205; in Ireland 223

constitutions of the Archbishops: *Presbyteri stipendarii* (1305) **VI** 284; *Effrenata* (1378) 284

Constitutions of Clarendon **VII** 342

consular (status) **Ia** 223, 331, 344; governors of British provinces 346, 523, 528; Ambrose 401, 469; Clovis 497 consultation, writs and statute **IV** 477–8

Consumer Needs Department **XV** 510

Contades, Louis George Erasme, marquis de (1704–95), marshal of France **XI** 364

Contagious Diseases Acts, agitation to repeal **XIV** 171

Contarini, Gasparo, Cardinal **VII** 547

contenmentum **IV** 6

continent *see* Europe

continuity: between Romano-British and Saxon settlements **II** 25–6; between Anglo-Saxon and Norman England 683–7

Contis, Arnold de, of Bayonne, warden of the Channel Islands (1271) **IV** 318

contraceptives: use **XV** 165–6, 297; in plain covers 306

contracts, seals of *see* seals

Controverted Elections Act (1770) **XII** 139

Conventicle Acts **X** 22

conventus **Ia** 582

Convers, Alexander le, clerk **IV** 705

Conversana, Geoffrey of **III** 113

conversion, comparison between Irish and continental influences **II** 125–7

convocation **V** 65, 155, 164, 178, 403; tax-granting assembly 185; clerical taxes 285, 288–9; Archbishop Courtenay 291; John Wyclif 396; **IX** 94; **IV** 479, 496–508, 665, 674; (1295) 483; 1299–1316) 483–4; (1297) 675–7; (1298) 678

Convocation of Canterbury **VI** 203; Henry IV grants 118–20; papal collector's address 234; procedure 302–4; royal needs 420; exemption from tenth 420; charitable subsidies 420–1; clerical subsidy 421; generous grant (1475) 422; grants (1461–3) 543; York's

grants (1460–2) 543; 'caritative' subsidy 543

convoy: opposed by admiralty **XV** 84; imposed by Lloyd George 85; instituted on outbreak of Second World War 462; stopped in Channel 498; battleships accompany 504; increasingly successful 505; Americans neglect 546; renewed through Mediterranean 563; Americans provide destroyers for 564

Conway (Caern): river **II** 615; **III** 285, 286, 298, 299; castle and borough **IV** 430–3; mayor 430–3; Cistercian abbey moved to Maenen (1284) 434–5; **V** 493, 494; treaty (1277) **IV** 412–13, 415, 416; Welsh revolt (1294–5) 442; agreements with continental princes (1295) 661; Archbishop Winchelsey takes oath of fealty 672, 673; **V** 493, 494; Richard II **VI** 13; castle 39, 40, 44, 65

Conway, Abbot **VI** 40

Conway, Hon. Henry Seymour General (1719–95): **XI** 360; biography **XII** 102; dismissal (1764) 102; secretary of state (1765–8) 111, 115, 117, 124, 327 —joins Pitt 121 —opposes anti-American policy 128 —state office holders 575; lieutenant general of ordnance 129; commander in chief (1762–3) 578, 579

Conway, Hugh **VII** 131, 132, 169–70

Conybeare, John (1692–1755), bishop of Bristol **XI** 84

Conyers, Christopher **VI** 323, 558

Conyers, Sir John **VI** 516, 555; Robin of Redesdale 558; attacks Edward IV at Edgecot 556

Conyers, William, 1st Baron Conyers **VII** 215

Conyers, Sir William, of Marske **VI** 555

194; *civitas?* 200; inscription 203; few Carausian coins 313; town 380, 412, 594, 659; Barates 514; official buildings on road to 538; Shorden Brae treasure 701–2, 729; (*Corstopitum*) **Ib** 78, 198; map 4 xxxii; battles **II** 333, 731; church 151; **V** 16, 32

Corbulo, Cn. Domitius **Ia** 110, 140, 154, 677

Cordell, Sir William, solicitor-general (1553): master of the rolls (1557) **VII** 648; speaker of the House of Commons (1558) 654

Cordoba, Gonsalvo de **VII** 115, 153

Cordova, Luis de, Spanish admiral **XII** 226

Corelli, Marie **XIV** 331

Corfe (Corfesgeat) (Dorset) **II** 373, 731; castle **III** 138, 382, 484; **IV** 1, 22, 23, 53, 331; restored to Edward 198; **V** 94; **VII** 195

Corfesgeat *see* Corfe (Dorset)

corie **Ia** 45

Corio **Ia** 68

Coritani **Ia** 43, 95; *see also* Leicester

Coritani **Ib** 183

Cork (Ireland) **III** 302, 308, 312; **V** 351, 353, 470; **VII** 116, 119, 125, 132, 144; **X** 308, 322

Cork, earl of *see* Boyle

Cork and Orrery, Lord **XV** 471

Cormantine **X** 332

corn: collection **Ia** 30, 518, 522; exported 42, 630; shortage 70, 121, 124, 234; bought back by Britons 141; Julian's bulk shipment 359; Constantinople (corn-dole) 365; drying 458–9; trade **V** 349, 360; **IX** 301; **X** 38, 178, 299; duty **XIV** 349, 372, 512

corn laws **XII** 520, 572; (before 1832) **XIII** 60–2; (after 1832) 101; Peel's views upon 113; agitation for repeal 118–22; Russell's Edinburgh letter 122; repeal 124; effect of repeal 124–5; **XV** 330

Cornburgh, Avery **VI** 599

Cornbury, Viscount Lord *see* Hyde, Henry

Cornelius of Chelmsford **VIII** 271

Corner, William de la, bishop of Salisbury, letter to Henry Eastry **IV** 262

Cornewall, James (1699–1744), Commodore **XI** 227, 248

Cornhill **VIII** 275

Cornhill, Gervase of **III** 144, 214

Cornhill, Henry of **III** 358, 434, 435

Cornhill, Reginald of **III** 390, 435, 479

cornicularius **Ia** 520

Cornish language **Ia** 507; **X** 409–10

Cornovii **Ia** 45, 159; *civitas* 186; *see also* Wroxeter

Cornwall: **Ia** 17, 44–5; tin 16, 44; **II** 439–40, 603; conquered by Egbert of Wessex 235; Tamar boundary 341; raided by the Danes 375; forest **III** 30; 76, 255, 348, 355, 399; tin mines 83; *Vicearachidiaconus* 224; county court 401; burglary case judgement 402; tin pledged (1297) **IV** 667; **V** 22, 192, 259, 312, 350; tin mining 371; Castilian attacks 403; **VI** 77, 498; county constituency 497; rising **VII** 141–5, 215, 217, 461; **IX** 269; **XV** 551; *see also* St Germans

Cornwall, Charles Wolfran (1735–89) **XII** 204; speaker of House of Commons 240, 276

Cornwall, duchy **V** 258, 266; **VI** 77, 80, 446, 477; **VII** 64, 94

Cornwall, dukes of *see* Edward of Woodstock; Henry V; Richard II

Cornwall, earldom **V** 2, 3, 266

Cornwall, earls of *see* Edward of Woodstock; Edmund of Almaine; Gaveston; Reginald; Richard

Cornwall, John **V** 524

Cornwall, Sir John, later Lord Fanhope **VI** 330, 469, 484; Aquitaine expedition (1412) 114;

Cornwall, Sir John (*cont.*)
financial demands 115; Brittany
ambassador 474
Cornwallis, Charles, 2nd Earl and
1st Marquis (1738–1805) **XII**
397, 402; biography 209; American campaigns 209, 214–18; governor general in India 275, 306,
322, 382, 385; viceroy of Ireland
399; master general of the ordnance (1795–1801) 580
Cornwallis, Sir Thomas, comptroller (1557) **VII** 650
Cornwallis, Sir William (1745–
1819), Admiral **XII** 431
Cornyshe, William **VII** 588, 589
Coromandel Coast **X** 349
coronation: oath **IV** 1, 7, 75; award
of Amiens 183; Scottish kings and
the papacy 593–4; of George VI
XV 402, 404, 420
Coronel, battle **XV** 14
coroners: origin and duties **III**
390–1; **V** 169, 189, 200; **XII** 43
corporal oath or oath *ex officio* **VIII**
199
Corporation Act (1661) **X** 12, 21–4;
proposal to modify **XII** 301
Corpus Christi, feast **VI** 281
correctores **Ia** 536, 597
corregidor of Biscay **VIII** 368, 369
Corresponding Society **XII** 324,
356, 361, 525, 571
Corringham (Essex) **V** 407
Corrupt Practices Act (1883) **XIV**
87
corruption **X** 85, 259; *see also*
influence of government
Corsica: capture by France **XII** 108;
capture by England 217, 371;
British evacuation 372
Corstopitum see Corbridge
Cort, Henry (1740–1800) **XI** 115;
inventions **XII** 31, 332, 505
Cortegiano **VIII** 324
Cortenuova, battle **IV** 98
Cortes, Martin **VIII** 238
Cortigiano, Il **VII** 417, 582

Corunna **VIII** 400, 411, 412; **XII**
453, 461, 554
Corvinus, Matthias, king of Hun-
gary (1485–90) **VII** 85
Corvus, Johannes (Jan Raf) **VII** 599
Corwen (Meri) **III** 293; **VI** 40, 66
Cory, William **XIV** 140
Cosa, temples **Ia** 735
Cosenza **IV** 240
Cosgrave, W. T. **XV** 357
Cosin, John **IX** 200
Cosmo III, grand duke of Tuscany
IX 382
Cosne-sur-Loire (Nièvre) **VI** 201
Cospatric, son of Maldred, earl of
Northumbria **II** 601, 604, 606,
610, 614
Cospatric, son of Uhtred: charter **II**
503; murder 578
cost plus **XV** 35–6, 78
costume (to 1886) **XIV** 167–9; (to
1900) 337–8; (to 1914) 554–5
Cosway, Richard (1740–1821),
painter **XI** 408
Cotentin **II** 379; **III** 104, 107, 108,
119, 120; Geoffrey of Anjou, mas-
ter of 161; **V** 133; **VI** 172; penin-
sula **XV** 554, 581
Cotes, Francis (?1725–70), painter
XI 410
Cotes, hamlet of Winchcombe
(Glos.) **VI** 367
Coting, William, rector of Titchwell
VI 288
Cotman, John Sell (1782–1842),
painter **XI** 401; **XIII** 590
Cotswolds **Ia** 607; **V** 315, 350, 358,
365, 381; **VI** 348, 362, 524; towns
354; broadcloth 365; population
changes 367; **VII** 462
cottarii, Kotsetla **II** 473–4, 475
Cottars **III** 38, 40, 43
Cottenham (Cambs.) **VI** 375
Cotterstock (Northants.), church,
college conversion **VI** 291
Cottesmore, John, justice of assize
VI 343
Cottingham (Yorks.) **VI** 288

Cottington, Francis, Lord **IX** 100
cotton **IX** 288, 338; famine **XIII** 312–14; control in First World War **XV** 78; distorting effects of control 122; collapse of exports 145, 182; decline 305; destruction of spindles 340
Cotton, Sir John Hynde (d. 1752) **XI** 250
Cotton, Sir Richard, comptroller (1552) 650
Cotton, Sir Robert **IX** 408
Cotton, Sir Robert Bruce (1571–1631) **XI** 394, 397
Cotton, Sir Roger **VII** 57, 127
cotton industry **X** 49, 331; **XII** 29, 332–5, 406, 466, 505; technical advances and changing fortunes 508–12; trade **XIV** 110, 277–8
Coucy, Enguerrand de, earl of Bedford (1366–77) **V** 268
Coucy, Isabella de **V** 268
Coucy, Marie de, second wife of Alexander II, king of Scots **IV** 573, 585, 587; queen-mother in Scotland 591, 592; *see also* Brienne, John de
Coucy, Philippa de, countess of Oxford **V** 268, 425, 447
Couesnon, river **II** 348, 577
Council, Crown and, under Tudors **VII** 563–4; Henry VII, composition 56, 202–2; development and competence 203–8; factions 419–20, 480, 491, 531; under Henry VIII, Mary, and Edward *see* Council and Courts of Star Chamber, Requests; Chancery; Augmentations; First Fruits and Tenths; Surveyors; Wards; and Liveries
council, Anglo-Norman, the King's Great **II** 556, 631, 640–2
Council, Great **IV** 66, 67; taxation 29, 536; legislation 67; and the king 74–9; (1258–62) 131–7; Edward I 331, 382; military action in Gascony (June 1294)

648, 649; **V** 9, 155, 182, 191, 466; Winchester (1371) 385; Westminster, Good Parliament (1376) 394; loans authorized during financial troubles (1379) 405; counter-offensive against France 442
Council, King's (*witan, witena gemot*) **II** 552, 554; origins 236–7, 302; ecclesiastical element 236–8, 464; development 237–8; mobility 349–53; size and composition 550–4; takes initative in choice of king 551–4; weakness 554; king obliged to govern under advice 554; **IV** 3, 30, 66, 74–5; oath taken by members 74, 125, 133; king's right to appoint members 77–8, 130, 132–4, 180, 183, 186; as reformed (1258) 136–7, 139, 147; committees 150; the Three and the Nine (1264) 191, 192; suggested compromises on appointments 194–5; directed by the guardians of Edward's children and lands (1270–4) 224–5; Gascon affairs 275; as a court 326–8, 334; parliament 329–30, 331–4, 346; records of proceedings 346; under Edward II **V** 16, 45–9, 54, 81, 82; in minority of Edward III 96, 100–1; under Edward III 158–9, 172, 180, 214, 391 — taxation and debts 160 — Bishop Stratford principal councillor 164, 176, 178 — ten-shilling levy 193 — compared to parliament 193–4 — petitions and delegations of business 198–9 — representational council 222–3 — reform 390 — 'great roll of indictments' 387; under Richard II 402, 442, 462, 465 — Gaunt excluded 400 — Northampton's trial 435 — 'continual council' 446 — nomination of councillors 459 — king's freedom from tutelage

147

courts, ecclesiastical (*cont.*)
434, 564; **X** 21; *see also* Canterbury; York; King's Bench, Common Pleas, and Exchequer **VII** 193–5; Wolsey's interference 297; *see also under* law, justices; popular: pre-Alfredian **II** 297–8; in Danelaw 510–1

courts of justice, reform **XIII** 471–3; higher, reconstituted (1873) **XIV** 17–19

Cousinot, Guillame, Réné of Anjou's envoy **VI** 479

Coutances (Manche) **VI** 173

Coutances, bishop of **III** 101: in Channel Islands **IV** 350; diocese 318

Coutances, Walter of, archbishop of Rouen: bishop of Lincoln **III** 70, 242, 354, 355–6, 357; chief justiciar 358; besieged Windsor 364; career 369; manor of Andeli 375

Coutts's bank **XII** 418

covenant **IX** 88, 140

Covenant *see* League of Nations, Covenant

Covent Garden **IX** 380

Coventina, water goddess **Ia** 666, 671, 691, 733; **Ib** 79

Coventry (War.): abbey **II** 635; **III** 151, 160, 164; bishopric 172, 182, 226; plan of Dictum of Kinilworth **IV** 209; **V** 65, 78, 314, 360, 519; prior 185; charterhouse 259; diocese 303; population 379; rise to prominence 381; intended duel between Hereford and Norfold 487–8; **VI** 115, 194, 366, 367, 504; parliament (1404) 70, 81; 'blue cloth' 366; crafts participate in plays 397, 398; crown loans (1400, 1416) 398–9; Mercers' arms 398; Trinity Gild 400–2; gild of Nativity suppressed (1384–1449) 404; yeoman gilds of St Anne and St George 404; less craft support for pageants 405;

court centre (from 1456) 513; parliament (1459) 516, 522, 538; Yorkist fortunes (after 1400) 547; Lancastrian demands 547; Edward IV's expenses 548; Warwick's present 548; Cheylesmore Park 548; City's liberties 548; Warwick's withdrawal 567; Richard III and Buckingham 626; **VII** 73, 455, 465, 504; trading and gilds 458–9; cloth trade 462–3; **VIII** 140; local politics **XII** 48, 49; strike **XV** 106; population 167; bombed 501–2

Coventry, bishops of *see* Gerard la Pucelle; Langton, John; Limesey, Robert of; Muschamp, Geoffrey; Nonant, Hugh of; Northburgh; Peche, Richard; Skirlaw; Stretton

Coventry, Henry **X** 56, 102

Coventry, Thomas, 1st Baron (1578–1640), lord keeper **XI** 65

Coventry, Sir William **X** 102

Coventry and Lichfield, bishops of *see* Longespée, Roger; Patteshall, Hugh; Sampson, Richard; Stavensby, Alexander; Weseham

Coverdale, Miles, bishop of Exeter (1551–3) **V** 524; **VII** 397, 432, 518, 520, 600; declaration of steadfastness and loyalty 546

Coward, Noel **XV** 260, 314

Cowdray, Richard, notary **VI** 178

Cowell, John **IX** 13

Cowes (IOW) **VI** 355

Cowhall (Suffolk) **VI** 345

Cowick Ordinances **V** 77

Cowley (Oxon.) **III** 189

Cowley, Abraham **X** 359, 364

Cowley, Earl **XIII** 249, 300

Cowley, Thomas, of Iffley **VI** 370

Cowper, Lord **XIV** 73, 75, 173, 179

Cowper, William, Earl (d. 1723) **XI** 25, 50, 57, 154

Cowper, William (1731–1800) **XII** 351

Cowper-Temple, W. **XIII** 483

cowpox, inoculation **XII** 11

Crowmarsh (Oxon.) **III** 164

Crowmer, William, sheriff of Kent **VI** 333, 497; widow 497

Crown, state: succession to **IV** 1, 225, 268; responsibility of king's vassals 5–6; king's duty 7–8, 28, 38–9; commission of *capitula itineris* 16; Peter des Rivaux 48–9, 53; Great Charter 67–8; sheriffs' duties 144–5; council of regency 150–1; lands inalienable from the Crown 274–5, 381, 530; relation to lords of liberties 368, 376–9; feudal relations with Scotland 381; and with Wales 381–2; ecclesiastical system 453–69, 475–85; Dictum of Kenilworth 530; boroughs 530–1; knight service 542, 546; public safety 551, 701; and Ireland 562, 564; expression of national power **VII** 22, 189; sacrosanctity and splendour 191–3, 560, 562, 563; power canalized 201; law as instrument 287, 564; instrument of politicians 480, 481, 491–2; continuity in government 532; power enhanced 567–9; finance **X** 6; opposition to 12; under Queen Anne 252–3; colonial legislatures 335–7, powers **XI** 2–5, 8, 15–19, 21, 30; royal arms 12; relations with ministers 16–18, 30, 32, 258–9, 370; royal veto 30; local 46–8, 53; constitutional restrictions 152; favour of king 239; Pelham's triumph 259; Irish budget surplus 295; colonies 308, 312; Walpole and Pitt 375; *see also* George I; George II; George III

Crowther, G., quoted **XV** 301

Croxton (Leics.), abbot of **III** 485

Croydon (Surrey) **Ib** 102, 138; map 2 xxx; **V** 414

Croyland chronicle, continuator **VII** 46, 52, 58, 61, 62

Crozon, fort **VIII** 415, 416

crucible, steel, invention of Hunts-

man's **XII** 31

Crudwell (Wilts.) **III** 62

Crudwell, Richard of **III** 61–2

Crugland *see* Crowland (Lincs.)

Crumpe, Henry **V** 511

crusade, Bohemian **VI** 252

crusade, first **III** 97, 102, 113, 176

crusade, projects for **V** 105, 123–5, 142, 463, 478; of the bishop of Norwich 146, 246, 355, 429–33, 438

crusade, second **III** 149

crusade, third **III** 149, 279, 296, 343–4, 373; expectation of Richard's death 356; his departure and capture (1192) 359–62; costs of enterprise 350–1, 434

crusade, thirteenth century **IV** 80–3; (1236) 105, 107; Louis IX 110, 114 *see also* Louis IX; Henry III and 106; Alfonso X 118; Lord Edward's 221–4, 264–7, 281–2; preaching 219, 231–2; against Aragon (1284) 254; English clergy 267; against Sicily 660–1; *see also* taxation, papal

crusaders, commutation of vows **IV** 760

crusades, effects of **III** 94–5, 244, 434–5

Crutched Friars **VI** 296

Cuba **IX** 337

Cuckhamsley Knob (Berks.) **II** 381

Cuckmere, river xxvi, 138; map 2 xxx

Cuckoo, Warbeck's ship **VII** 144

Cuddesdon **Ib** 170; map 3 xxxi

Cudworth, Ralph **X** 32

Cuerdale hoard **II** 248

Cuesta **XII** 482

Cuichelm (Cwichelm) **Ib** 171, 184

Culham **VII** 68

Cullen, Cardinal **XIV** 24

Cullen, William (1710–90) **XI** 286, 385, 389, 391

Cullompton (Devon) **VI** 650

Culpepper, Sir John **IX** 121

Culpepper, Thomas **VII** 418

Cumberland **II** 503; **III** 82, 265, 275, 422; William the Lion's claim 280, 281; coast-guards 437; local levies and Scottish disturbances (1297) **IV** 684, 689; overrun by Scots 686 **V** 1, 32, 66, 192, 440; **VII** 68, 385, 392, 461; **IX** 281; **XV** 122, 352; *see also* Northwestern England

Cumberland, countess of *see* Brandon, Eleanor

Cumberland, duke of, son of George III **XIII** 102

Cumberland, earl of *see* Clifford, George; Clifford, Henry

Cumberland, Henry Frederik, duke of (1745–90) **XII** 155

Cumberland, William Augustus, duke of (1721–65) **XI** 20, 72, 221, 342, 346; and council of regency 40, 340; military command 217, 218, 250–1, 260, 355 — Weser army 358; rebellion (1745) 255, 281, 282; unpopularity 340; Irish regiments 348; duke of Devonshire 354; and Pitt 360; Watson's electrical demonstrations 383; armies 393; **XII** 81; political position (1762) 82; advice to king (1765) 110

Cumbraland (Strathclyde) **II** 359

Cumbria **Ia** 4; coastal defences 145, 177, 206, 260, 683; agricultural development 184, 237–8, 589, 613; Valentia? 393; palaeobotany 571; font? 730; **III** 165, 266, 268

Cumenesora (*Cymenesora*) **Ib** 136–7; appendix I(b); map 2 xxx

Cumin, John, archbishop of Dublin **III** 210, 309, 328

Cumin, William **III** 191, 275; **IV** 581; *see also* Comyn

Cumnor (Berks.) **III** 30

Cumnor Place **VIII** 50

Cunault, priory **III** 21

Cuncacestir *see* Chester-le-Street (Durham)

Cunedda **Ia** 404

Cuneglassus, king of unnamed British kingdom **II** 4

cunei (army units) **Ia** 248; **Ib** 77, 79; *Frisiorum* 77

Cunetio see Mildenhall (Wilts.)

Cunipert, king of the Lombards **II** 70

Cunliffe-Lister, P. (Lloyd-Greame), Lord Swinton **XV** 378; radar 392

Cunningham, Archdeacon **XV** 331

Cunningham, General Sir Alan **XV** 530

Cunningham, Admiral Sir Andrew: refuses to abandon Mediterranean **XV** 520; takes offensive 523; refuses to block Tripoli 526; commands in Mediterranean 563

Cunningham, John (1729–73), poet **XI** 420

Cunningham, William, 4th earl of Glencairn **VII** 406

Cunningham, William, 9th earl of Glencairne **IX** 169

Cunobelinus **Ia** 55–7, 67–8, 104–5; coinage 55, 56, 681; Colchester 56–7, 589

Cup Final **XV** 313

Curaçao **X** 325

curates, temporary and perpetual **IV** 459

Curbridge, cemetery **Ia** 704, 706

Cure of the diseased, in remote regions **VIII** 314

cure of souls **IV** 449

curia Regis **II** 556, 640–1

curia Textoverdorum **Ia** 45, 538

curiales **Ia** 235, 426, 463, 510–1, 538; financial burdens 345, 372, 537, 577–8, 663; forbidden to move to country 398, 598–9; council members 575; small towns 595; *see also* decurions; *irdo*

Curiatius Saturninus, C. *see* Saturninus

Curie, Madame **XIV** 551

Curle, Hippolytus **VIII** 380

Curragh, the (Kildare) **IV** 58; episode **XIV** 477–9

Curran, John Philpot (1750–1817)
XII 422

currants **IX** 11

currency, Old English: continuous
history begins in reign of Offa **II**
223; imitated in Scandinavia 543;
centralized control 535, 581;
debased **IV** 670, 671; in Scotland
573; restoration **XIII** 58–9; *see
also* coins; coinage; minting places

curses **Ia** 679, 688–9

Curson, John, of Derbyshire **VI** 429

Cursor Mundi **V** 523, 526

cursus honorum **Ia** 79

Curtis, L. **XV** 418

Curtis, Piers, burgess of Leicester
VI 599

Curwen's Act **XII** 449

Curzon of Kedleston, Lord (1859–
1925) **XIV** 382, 403; procures defeat of Diehards 429–30;
as chancellor at Oxford 537; biography **XV** 19; entertains king of
the Belgians 19; disloyal to Law
34; supports Gallipoli campaign
to last 46; pledges himself against
Lloyd George 68–9; joins Lloyd
George 70; in War Cabinet 75;
accompanies Lloyd George to
admiralty 85; supports Haig 87;
supports Robertson 99; wishes to
try Kaiser 127; remains in London 130; runs Foreign Office 132;
establishes British protectorate
over Persia 152; temporarily
replaced by Balfour 190; favours
agreement with Kemal 190;
remains foreign secretary under
Law 195–6; at Lausanne conference 202; does not become prime
minister 204, 224; on Baldwin
205; death 228

Curzon, Sir Robert **VII** 167, 168

Curzon line **XV** 590

Cusack, Nicholas, bishop of Kildare
IV 569

Cusance, William **V** 217

Cusanweoh **II** 102

Cust, Henry **XIV** 296

Cust, Sir John (1718–70), speaker of
House of Commons **XII** 99, 143,
149

Cust family, control of Grantham
XII 52

Custodes pacis, in the shires **IV** 176,
182

customs: on trade **IV** 619, 628–31;
'new aid' (1266) 619, 629–38;
'great custom' on wool and
leather (1275) 629–30; maltolte
(1294–7) 630, 659, 663, 683;
'petty' custom dues and *ad valorem*
duties (1303) 630–1; **VII** 214,
219, 475–7, 502; **IX** 10–11, 14,
187; *see also* taxation

Customs, Assize of (1203) **III** 93–4,
96

cut-flowers, attempt to stop **XV** 551

Cutha, West Saxon leader **Ib** 163,
165, 169; **II** 29

Cuthbert, St, archbishop of Canterbury **Ib** 18; **II** 86, 126–7, 148,
161, 174; career as monk 126;
retirement to Farne island 126;
Celtic usages 126; bishop of Hexham 126, 139; bishop of Lindisfarne 126, 139; prior of Lindisfarne 126–7; conception of
bishop's duty 126–7, 148; attitude towards archbishop of Canterbury 127; composes rule for
Lindisfarne 159; anonymous life
186; social position 290; relics 435

Cuthred, brother of Cenwulf, king of
Kent **II** 225

Cuthred, king of Wessex **II** 204

Cuthwine, West Saxon leader **Ib**
163; **II** 29

Cuthwulf, West Saxon leader **Ib**
163, 165–6, 168; **II** 27

cutlery **X** 179

Cutteslowe (Cudeslowe) **Ib** 169–70;
map 3 xxxi

Cuxham **Ia** 542

Cuxhaven (Germany) **Ib** xxx, xxi,
xxvii, 51; map 1 xxix; **II** 7, 31

Cuyck, John, lord of **IV** 664

Cwichelm, son of Cynegils, king of Wessex **II** 45, 63, 66

Cwichelm, West Saxon leader who perished with Ceawlin **II** 30

Cwm Hir, Cistercian abbey, burial place of Llywelyn ap Gruffydd **IV** 428

Cybele **Ia** 668

cycling **XIV** 166, 338; first 'safety' bicycles 338

Cyfartha **XII** 506

Cyil *see* Kyle

Cymen **Ib** 137, appendix I(b)

Cymenes ora **II** 17-18

Cyneburg, daughter of Penda and wife of Alhfrith, son of Oswiu **II** 151

Cynegils, king of Wessex **II** 45, 63, 66; baptism 67, 118; gives Dorchester to Birinus 82, 118

Cyneheard, archdeacon at Canterbury **II** 440

Cynesige, archbishop of York **II** 466

Cynewulf, king of Wessex **II** 174, 204, 208, 216; relations with Offa 209; daughter 209; charters quoted 286, 307

Cynewulf, religious poet **II** 19, 197, 199-200

Cynibre *see* Kinver Forest (Staffs.)

Cynigils **Ib** 172

cyninges tun **II** 482

Cyningrstun *see* Kingston (Surrey)

Cynllaith (Meri) **VI** 37

Cynllaith, Owain *see* Glyn Dŵr, Owain; Sycarth

Cynric, king of the West Saxons **Ib** 145-6, 148, appendix II; genealogy and rule 152-5; fight with Britons 162, 164; **II** 19-22, 27-8

Cynuit *see* Countisbury Hill (Devon)

Cynwrig, Maredudd ap **VI** 55

Cyprus **III** 94, 360, 373; **V** 123

Cyprus, king of *see* James I, king of Cyprus

Cyrenaica: captured **XV** 524; lost 525-6, 541; Rommel launches offensive 554; Rommel abandons 559

Cyricbyrig *see* Chirbury (Salop)

Cyrtlinctum *see* Kirtlington (Oxon.)

Czecho-Slovakia: falls to pieces **XV** 439; post-Munich guarantee meaningless 443

Czechoslovakia: independence recognized **XV** 108; Lloyd George blamed for its creation 137; French treaty with 222; Labour thinks frontiers should be revised 373, 417; crisis over 408, 415, 424-8; Halifax's assurances to Hitler over 422; partitioned at Munich 429; debate over 430; Hitler's treatment 431; military strength 432, 433; collapses 439; Chamberlain on invasion 440; not within British range 470; German generals 476; liberation a British war aim 489; provisional government recognized 494; less valuable than Belgium 577

D

D-day (6 June 1944): lessons from Dieppe **XV** 558; at right time 578; preparations 579; takes place 581; welcome effects in England 583

Dachau, German murder camp **XV** 317, 600

D'Aché, A. A. *see* Aché, A. A. d'

Dacia **Ia** 74, 150, 169, 521, 526

Daciens, on reliefs **Ia** 77

Dacre, 20th Baron *see* Brand, Thomas

Dacre (Dacres), Edward **VIII** 141

Dacre, Humphrey, Lord **VI** 539, 643

Dacre (Dacres), Leonard **VIII** 136–7, 141, 142

Dacre, Ralph, brother of Humphrey **VI** 539

Dacre, Thomas, of Gillisland **VI** 320

Dacre, Thomas, Lord of the North, services against Scots (d. 1525) **VII** 276, 312–13

Dacre, Thomas Fiennes, Lord of the South, hanged (1541) **VII** 418

Dacre, William, son of Lord Dacre of the North March, Warden of the West March (1528) **VII** 381

Dacre of Gillisland (Gillesland) family **VI** 319, 464

Daenningas **Ib** map 2 xxx

Dafydd ap Gwilym **XIV** 336

Dafydd Benfras, poet **IV** 386, 390

Dagan, Irish bishop in Kent **II** 112, 125

daggers **VIII** 271, 272

Dagobert I, king of the Franks **II** 81

Dagobert II, king of the Franks **II** 136

Dagualdus **Ib** 78

Dagworth, Sir Nicholas **V** 463

Dahl, Michael (1656–1743) **X** 400; Swedish painter **XI** 406

Dahlerus, spreads rich banquet before Hitler **XV** 456

Dail: set up **XV** 128, 153; declares republic 154; second elected 156; and treaty 158–9; devises constitution 159; oath for members 160; De Valera enters 357

Daily Chronicle: supports Lloyd George **XV** 28, 66; bought by Lloyd George fund 118; absorbed by *Daily News* 309

Daily Courant 356

Daily Express: supports Lloyd George **XV** 66; unimportant during First World War 107; building 178; wins greatest circulation 235; joins newspaper war 309; tops 2 million 310; says no war this year or next 408; created by Beaverbrook 548

Daily Herald: appears **XV** 142; limited appeal 172; does not pay 181; stopped during general strike 246; TUC and Odhams acquire 251; starts newspaper war 301; reaches 2 million 310; Lansbury 328

Daily Mail: Northcliffe **XV** 27, 548; war aims 52; supports Lloyd George 66; Northcliffe rates above *The Times* 187; compositors refuse to set 224; Zinoviev letter 225; sponsors Melba 232; staff recruited to *Daily Herald* 256; supports Empire Free Trade 282; enters newspaper war 309

Daily Mirror: wins circulation race during Second World War **XV** 172, 548

Daily News: does not support Lloyd George **XV** 66; amalgamates with *Daily Chronicle* 118, 309; *see also News Chronicle*

Daily Telegraph, Lansdowne's letter **XV** 94

Daily Worker: politically tied **XV** 251, 397; opposes Munich 430; banned 503

Daimler, Gottfried, inventor **XIV** 281

Dakar **XV** 516

Daladier, E.: appeals to Chamberlain **XV** 426; advocates resistance 428; at Munich 429; falls 470

D'Albret *see* Albret

Dale, David (1739–1806) **XII** 533

Dale, Milford Haven (Pembroke) **VI** 641

Dale, R. W. **XIII** 483

Dalege, Marco, Italian merchant **VI** 591

Dalginross, fort **Ia** 149

Dalham (Suffolk) **V** 9

Dalhousie, marquis of *see* Ramsay, James Andrew Broun

Dalkeith **VII** 161

Dallingridge, Sir Edward **V** 467

Dalmatia **Ia** 49, 287, 488; treaty of London **XV** 50, 161–2

Dalnaspidal, battle **IX** 169

Dalry, Bruce defeated (1306) **IV** 716

Dalrymple, Sir Hew (1652–1737) **XI** 273

Dalrymple, Sir Hew Whitefoord (1750–1830) **XII** 460

Dalrymple, Sir John (1726–1810) **XI** 275

Dalrymple, Sir John, 6th earl of Stair (1749–1821) **X** 280, 281; **XII** 193

Dalswinton, fort **Ia** 145, 151, 165

Dalton, Hugh John Neale: biography **XV** 213; condemns Keynes 213; regarded as moderate 347; supports Covenant 381; opposes any action over Rhineland 386; supports rearmament 393, 414; proposes coal rationing 547; chancellor of Exchequer 597

Dalton, John **XIII** 566, 568

Dalzell, Sir Robert, 5th earl of Carnwath (1685–1737) **XI** 162

Dalziel: and Lloyd George **XV** 28; buys *Daily Chronicle* 118

Dalziel, Sir Thomas **X** 268

damages: naval warfare (1294–1303) **IV** 657; court of claims at Montreuil-sur-mer (1305–11) 657–8; claims against Scots 658

Damascus, Allenby enters **XV** 110

Damascus, Hugh, archbishop of (1344–51) **V** 301

Damaskinos, Archbishop **XV** 589

Damerham (Hants, formerly Wilts.) **III** 54

Damian, bishop of Rochester **II** 128

Damietta, crusaders **IV** 90

Dammartin, count of **VI** 156

Dammartin, Renaud of, count of Boulogne **III** 376, 381, 440, 453, 457; at battle of Damme 461; English allegiance 464; capture at Battle of Bouvines 467

Dammartin, Simon de, count of Ponthieu **IV** 73

Damme, battle **III** 461

damnatio memoriae **Ia** 250

Damon and Pythias **VIII** 296

Damony, Sir Roger **V** 52–3, 59, 73, 96

Damory, Sir Richard **V** 337

Dampier, William, pirate (1652–1715) **XI** 228; **XII** 17

Dampierre, Guy of, count of Flanders (1280–1305), son of the countess Margaret: Philip IV and **IV** 612, 659, 668–9; relations with Edward I (1274–92) 622–3, 648, 659; appeal to Boniface VIII 652; becomes Edward's ally and is deserted 664–5, 667–9

Danby, Christopher **VIII** 138

Danby, earl of *see* Osborne, Thomas

Danby, Robert, chief justice **VI** 547

Danby, Mr, of Swinton, and land reclamation **XI** 106

Dance, George (1741–1825), architect and painter **XI** 412

dancing **IX** 265, 311, 358

Danebury: hill-fort **Ia** 13, 589; landscape survey 611

Danegeld: origin **II** 376, 412–13; **III** 151–2, 158; payment in north-eastern counties 37; immunity of 'sokes' 69; levied by William Rufus 110–11; origin 418; by Stephen 154; **IV** 31

Danelaw **II** 242, 257, 260; autonomy granted 371; Northern 387; heathenism 433–4; monastic foundations 452; meaning of word 505; distinctive features 506, 525; principal divisions 506–7; legal customs 506–12; written statements of legal customs 508; Northumbrian wergilds 508–9; Wantage code of Æthelred II 508–12; Northumbrian Priests' Law 508–12; monastic foundations 452; social conditions 513–15; agrarian system 513–15; peasant classes 515–17; territorial in sokes 515–18; **III** 37, 38

Danes: motives for early Danish raids **II** 239–43; size of armies 243; great army (865) 246–56; significance of its conquests 257; army (878) 257; on Continent 257; alliances with other Danes 257, 263, 266; treaty with Guthrum after invasion (886) shows relations between Danes and English 261, 262; army (892) 263; Alfred's remodelling of defences 264–6; settlement 319–21; East Anglian 321, 323–7; Northumbrian 321–2, 322; land bought from 322–3; army (914) 325; settlement by shires 338; attitude to Norse raiders 358; later invasions 374; settled in England by Cnut 413–41; **III** 88–9, 271, 293

Dangan Hill, battle **IX** 162

Dangerous Positions **VIII** 202, 203

d'Angle, Guichard *see* Angle

Daniel, bishop of Winchester **II** 147, 168

Daniel, Elizabeth, sister of Thomas **VI** 449

Daniel, Samuel: on Edward III **V** 145; **VIII** 283, 286, 287; **IX** 400

Daniel, Thomas **VI** 449, 497, 501, 508, 547; opposes duke of Suffolk 497; Cade's followers 497; attainted 600; constable of Castle Rising 600

D'Annunzio **XV** 162

Dante **IV** 85, 230, 232–3, 643; **V** 531; *Commentaria* **VI** 679; *Divine Comedy* 679

Danube: river **Ia** 49, 72, 130; M. Aurelius' policy 66, 203–4, 207–10, 271, 549; frontier zone 166–8, 178, 269–70; Gallienus 271–4; Aurelian 276; Maximian 307; Gothic raids 364, 423; Jovian 369; Theodosius 401; barbarian kingdoms 438; Huns 481, 500; life on the frontier 270, 457, 582; **VII** 341

Danyel, John **VIII** 306

Danzig **V** 359; **VI** 69, 70, 356; merchantmen 64; **VII** 221; **IX** 227–8; established as free city **XV** 134; Halifax's assurances to Hitler 422; Poles negotiate with Hitler over 422; British sympathize with Hitler's claim 443; British hope to forget 448; tension mounts 449; Anglo-Polish alliance 450

Daoulas **VII** 469

Darby, Abraham I (1677–1717) **X** 50; **XI** 109, 115, 117

Darby, Abraham II (1711–63) **XI** 115, 117

Darby family **XII** 31

Darcy, Sir John **V** 159, 175, 176, 231

Darcy, Lord **VIII** 139

D'Arcy, Robert, 4th earl of Holderness (1718–78) **XI** 350, 354, 356, 368; Yorkshire landowner 106; succeeds Bedford 342–3

Darcy, Thomas, baron of Templehurst (1467–1537) **VII** 146, 273, 386, 389, 437; beheaded 392

Darcy v Allen, case **IX** 24

Darcy of Platten **VII** 72

Dardanelles: closing of the **XIII** 234; plan for expedition **XV** 23–4; naval action 25; committee of inquiry 44, 46, 47, 58; Fourteen Points 119; discredits Churchill 466; Finnish expedition equally slapdash 469; *see also* Straits Convention

Darien scheme (Company of Scotland trading to Africa and the Indies) **X** 47, 250, 281–5, 290

Darlan, Admiral, in Algiers **XV** 560; assassinated 561

Darley Arab, horse **X** 408

Darling, Mr Justice **XV** 103

Darlington (Durham) **Ib** 197; map 4 xxxii; **II** 496

Darlington, earl of *see* Vane, Henry

Darlington, John of, Dominican royal confessor **IV** 156, 176; his oath of fealty as archbishop of Dublin 348

Darlington, Sophia Charlotte von Platen, Baroness Kielmansegge, countess of (?1673–1725) **XI** 152, 185, 354

Darnel, Sir Thomas, case **IX** 38

Darnhall (Cheshire) **V** 344

Darnley, Lord *see* Stuart, Henry

Darrein presentment, assize **III** 406, 408–9, 409, 412

Darrell, William, of Littlecote **VIII** 261

Dartford (Kent) **V** 408; **VI** 2, 504

Dartmoor **Ia** 4; **III** 30

Dartmouth (Devon) **III** 96, 149, 441; **VI** 56, 72, 560; Brittany treaty 554; **VII** 476

Dartmouth, 1st Baron *see* Legge, George

Dartmouth, earl of *see* Legge, William

Darvell Gadarn **VII** 396

Darwin, Charles Robert **XIII** 549, 564, 567, 569, 577; biography 573; work of 573–5; opposition 575–6; **XIV** 45, 136

Darwin, Erasmus (1731–1802) **XII** 536

Dashwood, Sir Francis (1708–81), 15th Baron le Despenser: chancellor of Exchequer (1762–3) **XII** 92, 577; friend of Wilkes 98

D'Assonleville, agent of Alva **VIII** 163

Datchworth **XV** 584

Daubeney, Sir Giles, 1st Baron Daubeney (d. 1508) **VI** 599, 627; **VII** 108, 141, 142, 145, 169–70; joins Henry VII's council 56; obtains Bristol Castle 57; captain of Calais 98, 99; fined by Henry 215

Daubeney, William **VII** 122

Daubeney, William, jewel house clerk **VI** 614

Daubeny, Philip **IV** 9–10, 13, 40, 91

Daubigny, Sire **V** 247

Daudan (Seine-et-Oise) **VI** 111

Daundesey, John, of Trowbridge (Wilts.), constable of Bristol **VI** 419

Dauntsey, Walter, clothier **VI** 365

Dauphin *see* Charles; John; Louis

Dauphiné, county **VI** 240

Davenant, Charles (1656–1714), pamphleteer, on cost of poor-rates **XI** 131

Davenant, Sir William **IX** 389, 398–9

Davenport (Devennport) (Cheshire) **II** 334, 732

Daventry (Northants) **V** 436; **IX** 278–9

David, bishop of Bangor and St David's **III** 295, 296

David, duke of Rothesay **VI** 35, 36

162

Declaration of Independence **XII** 191, 205

Declaration of Indulgence (1662) **X** 58, 79; (1672) 23, 79; (1687) 125; (1688) 126

Declaration of London **XIV** 447–8

Declaration of Rights **X** 145–6

decorative arts **X** 397–9

decurions (*decuriones*) **Ia** 398, 575–6, 598, 604, 723; municipal 727; *see also ordo*; *curiales*

Deddington (Oxon.) **V** 25–6

Dedham (Essex) **VI** 472, 647

dedications **Ia** 666–7, 680, 699–700; *see also* votive offerings

Dee, Dr John (1527–1608): mathematician **VII** 571; **VIII** 241, 307, 310, 331; **IX** 369

Dee, river (Chester) **II** 369–70, 574; **III** 286, 294; **VI** 40, 66; Glyn Dŵr's properties 42

deer-hunting **VIII** 277

Deerhurst (Doerhyrst) (Glos.) **II** 392, 732

defence: minister for co-ordination of instituted **XV** 390; abolished 456

Defence, minister of: suggested after First World War **XV** 229; created by Churchill 479; demand for independent minister 542, 554

defence, synonym for war **XV** 363

defence committee: for operations **XV** 481; for supplies 482

Defence of Poesy **VIII** 286, 294

Defence of the Realm **VIII** 407

Defence of the Realm Acts: and censorship **XV** 18; and Labour 29; and requisitioning 36; Lansdowne insists on for Ireland 72; perpetuated by Emergency Powers Act 144

Defence of Rime **VIII** 294

Defensores, ducal rights in Aquitaine **IV** 303–4

Deffand, Madame du (d. 1780) **XI** 147

Defoe, Daniel (?1661–1731) **VII** 258; **X** 226, 228, 362–3, 366, 411; leading literary figure 24; *True Englishman*, political satire 196; **XI** 10, 74–5, 89, 112, 131; *Tour through Great Britain* 102, 105, 110, 113, 118 — leading ports 121 — wages 125 — Tunbridge Wells 145; population estimates 121; Chandos palace 412; union promotion 420; *Robinson Crusoe* 422, 427

Deganwy, fortress **II** 230–1; **III** 285, 300; castle **IV** 137, 172, 178, 398–9, 432; rebuilt by Henry I 339, 400, 402, 404; in Welsh war (1277) 412

Degsastan, battle **II** 77

Deheubarth **III** 205, 287, 289, 291; **IV** 386, 393

Deira **Ib** 107, 173, 196; map 4 xxxii; origins 175, 187–9; **II** 81–2, 91

Deirans, *Dere* **II** 37–8, 74

deism **XI** 83–7, 429

Dekker, Thomas **VIII** 268, 293, 300, 301; **IX** 392, 414

Delafaye, under-secretary (*c.*1732) **XI** 187

Delamere, 2nd Baron *see* Booth, Henry

Delancey, Oliver (1749–1822), American loyalist **XII** 177, 182

Delane **XV** 26, 234

Delane, J. T. **XIII** 276; **XIV** 24, 45, 144, 310

Delany, Mrs Mary (1700–88) **XI** 304, 305

Delany, Dr Patrick (1685–1768) **XI** 304, 305

Delavals, the **XI** 118

Delaware: bay **VII** 228; **X** 334, 340; river 340

Delcassé, E. **XIV** 244, 366, 367, 368, 370; entente 567

Delft **VIII** 364

Delhi **X** 348

delinquents, cost of war **IX** 130

Delius, Frederick **XIV** 545; **XV** 178

Deloney, Thomas **IX** 416

Delopis, John **VI** 362

371; **VI** 693; **VII** 461

Dere Street **Ia** 145, 166, 193, 246, 697

Dereham, Elias of **IV** 8, 12, 14

Dereham, Richard, chancellor of Cambridge University **VI** 91, 93

Dermot, king of Leinster: descendants **IV** 561, 562

Dervorgil, wife of Tiernan O'Rourke **III** 302, 305

Derwent, river **Ib** 78, 196; map 2 xxx; map 4 xxxii

Derwentwater, earl of *see* Radcliffe, Sir James

Desaguliers, John T. (1683–1744), scientist **XI** 383

Desborough **Ib** 48

Descartes, René (1596–1650) **X** 32; **XI** 83, 378

Description of Britain **VIII** 283

deserters **Ia** 221, 283, 379, 381

designers, mosaic **Ia** 656–7

Desirade, returned to France **XII** 85

Desmond, earldom **VIII** 464

Desmond, earls of *see* Fitzgerald, Gerald; FitzMaurice, Gerald; FitzThomas, Maurice

Desmond, James, earl of *see* James, earl of Desmond

Despard, E. M. (1751–1803), his plot **XII** 417

Despenser, Edward **V** 386

Despenser, Edward le **VI** 271

Despenser, Edward, Lord **VI** 22

Despenser, Henry, bishop of Norwich (1370–1404): crusade in Flanders **V** 146, 246, 429–33, 436, 478; in the Good Parliament 389; suppresses revolt in eastern counties 418; attempts to raise force for Richard II 492; **VI** 26–7, 271

Despenser, Hugh, the elder, earl of Winchester (1322–6) **V** 8, 56, 68, 102, 110; removed from council 46; early career 58; exiled and recalled 64–5; in power 73–83; overthrown by Isabella and Mor-

timer 83–5; sentenced at Bristol 85–6; unpopularity 93; Charles IV 111; judgement invalid 480

Despenser, Hugh, justiciar (1260–1) **IV** 162, 163; judiciar (1263) 176, 194, 198, 200; slain at Evesham 202

Despenser, Hugh, prince of Wales' governor **VI** 44–5, 101

Despenser, Hugh, the younger **V** 68, 93, 110, 111, 480; given lands in Scotland 35; expelled from court 46; husband of Eleanor de Clare 52, 58; territorial gains 58–9; confederation against him 58–63; exiled and recalled 64–5; in power 73; work as chamberlain 76–7; staple policy 78, 351–2, 366; charges against 81; tries to annul Edward II's marriage 81; overthrown by Isabella and Mortimer 83–6; sentenced at Hereford 87; administrative reorganization 104; financial aims 215

Despenser, Isabel, countess of Worcester **VI** 329

Despenser, Richard, Lord **VI** 321

Despenser, Thomas, earl of Gloucester (1397–9) **V** 386, 479, 480, 483; **VI** 6

Despenser, Thomas, Lord, attainder reversed (1461) **VI** 540

Dessau, Bridge of, battle **IX** 65

D'Estaing, French admiral **XII** 212, 214

Deusdedit, archbishop of Canterbury **II** 122, 124, 128–30; date of death 129

Deventer, Holland **II** 169

Deveraux, Walter **VI** 643

Devereux, Sir John **V** 446, 451

Devereux, Robert, 2nd earl of Esssex **VIII** 407, 419–41, 444–6; attack on Lisbon 412; siege of Rouen 414–15; assault on Cadiz 418–19

Devereux, Robert, 3rd earl of Essex **IX** 16, 97, 131–2, 134, 138

Devereux, Walter, 1st earl of Essex **VIII** 474, 481

Devereux, Sir Walter, Lord Ferrers (1461), killed **VII** 58

Devereux, Sir William **VI** 516

Devis, Arthur (?1711–87), painter **XI** 410, 413

Devizes (Wilts.) **III** 121, 148, 153, 159; castle 121, 137, 148, 153, 154, 159; **IV** 1, 9, 331, 422; Hubert de Burgh 51, 53, 60; **V** 58; **X** 207

Devizes, Richard of **III** 436

Devon **Ia** 44; **II** 4, 64, 235, 281; English conquest 64, 68, 73; raided by Danes 375; revolt (1069) 602–3; **III** 39, 134, 348, 399; forest 30–1; tin mines 83; tin pledged (1297) **IV** 667; **V** 22, 171, 312, 331, 368; lead-mining 371; **VII** 145, 467; **IX** 18, 289; ealdorman of *see* Ordgar

Devon, earl of **III** 134, 157; *see also* Courtenay, Edward de; Courtenay, Hugh; Courtenay, Thomas

Devon, earldom of, Fawkes de Breauté and lands **IV** 26; *see also* Forz, Isabella de

Devonport, Lord **XV** 78; *see also* Kearley, H. E.

Devonshire, duchess of *see* Georgiana

Devonshire, duke of: in cabinet **XV** 196; *see also* Cavendish, William

Devonshire, 7th duke of **XIII** 491, 570

Devonshire, 8th duke of, marquess of Hartington (till Dec. 1891): becomes Liberal leader **XIV** 33; accepts policy of franchise extension 55; declines premiership 66; influential in sending out Gordon 81; urges relief expedition 82; opposed to Chamberlain 88, 89; differs from Gladstone over Home Rule 96; again refuses premiership 172; third refusal 175; chairman of royal commission on

army 290, 291–2; succeeds to dukedom 208; joins Unionist Cabinet 224; opposed to Chamberlain's fiscal policy 373; resigns office 374; death 415

Devonshire, 9th duke of *see* Cavendish, Victor

Devorguilla, daughter of Alan of Galloway and Margaret, daughter of David of Huntingdon: brings part of Galloway to her husband John Baliol **IV** 581, 606; death (1290) and relief of her lands 602, 610; founder of Sweetheart Abbey 693

Devoy, John **XIV** 57

D'Ewes, Sir Simonds, quoted **IX** 46, 83, 130, 402, 410

Deyncourt, William **V** 61

D'Havré, Marquis **VIII** 343

dialects, local **X** 411; disappearance **XV** 167

Dialogue of the Exchequer **III** 29, 393

Diana, sanctuary **Ia** 673

diaphragm, contraceptive **XV** 165

Diaz, Bartholomew **VII** 224

Dibblee, G. Binney **XIV** 507

Dibdin, Charles (1745–1814) **XI** 417; **XII** 544

Dicalydonae **Ia** 375

Diceto, Ralph de, dean of St Paul's **III** 249

Dickens, Charles **XIII** 530; biography 554; novels 554–6; **XIV** 136; sets of works given away **XV** 310, 351

Dickinson, G. L. **XV** 51

Dickinson, John (1732–1808): Farmer's Letters **XII** 191; efforts for conciliation 201

dictator **Ia** 48

dictatores, Simon de Montfort's Gascon accounts **IV** 113

dictionaries **XI** 395–6, 431–2

Dictum of Kenilworth **IV** 209–13, 216, 370, 530; King Edward's conditions for enforcement (1276) 209–10

Didcot (Berks.) **III** 319
Diderot, Denis (1713–84), philosopher **XI** 395
Didius Gallus, A. **Ia** 107–9
Didius Julianus **Ia** 217
'Die-hards' **XIV** 429, 441
Dieppe (Seine-Inf.) **III** 161, 373, 430, 459; **VI** 173; **VIII** 56, 57, 414; **X** 64; raid on **XV** 557–8
Dietrich, count of Holland (Lincs.) **III** 367
Dieulacres, Chronicle **VI** 4, 13, 14
diffidatio **IV** 55, 189, 203, 614, 661
Diffinitores **IV** 86–7
Digby, George, 2nd earl of Bristol **X** 71
Digby, John, earl of Bristol **IX** 36, 43
Digby, Kenelm **XIII** 114–15
Digby, Sir Kenelm **IX** 63
Digby, Simon, bishop of Limerick **X** 401
diggers **IX** 129, 171, 198
Digges, Thomas **VIII** 307; **IX** 369
Dijon **III** 110; **VII** 279
Dilettanti Society **XII** 338
Dilke, Sir C. **XV** 170
Dilke, Sir Charles W. **XIII** 402; **XIV** 33, 66, 89; concerned in divorce case 97, 169–70, 183; chairman of royal commission on housing 128; appoints women poor-law inspectors 130; treaty with Portugal 190, 191; opinion of Edward VII 342–3; pioneer of anti-sweating legislation 515
Dill, General Sir J., worn down by Churchill **XV** 481; becomes Chief of Imperial General Staff 497; urges Greek campaign 525; on combined chiefs of staff committee 536, 538
Dillenius, John James (1687–1747), botanist **XI** 388
Dillon, Arthur (1670–1733) **XI** 182
Dillon, John **XIII** 349; **XIV** 75, 76, 179, 180, 182; Parnell support 184; Boulogne negotiations 186

Dillon commanders **XI** 292
dilution **XV** 29
Dinant **III** 83
Dinas Bran Castle **IV** 410, 424
Dinefwr Castle **IV** 391; centre of administration 410, 420, 438; capture and recovery (1287) 439, 440
Dinham, Dynham, Charles, of Devon **VI** 599
Dinham, Dynham, John, Lord **VI** 517, 602, 635; joins Edward at Pontefract 557; steward of Duchy of Cornwall 615
dining rooms (*triclinia*) **Ia** 609, 725
Dinwiddie, Robert (*c.*1690–1770), governor of Virginia **XI** 320
Dio (Cassius Dio Cocceianus), historian: Augustus' projected campaigns **Ia** 48, 50, 61; Celtic tribes 68, 69, 84; Claudian invasion 70, 82, 85–6; Boudicca 114–16, 119, 659–60, 678; Commodus 210, 212–13; Severus 217–20, 226, 229, 230, 318; Caracalla 231
dioceses: administrative unit **Ia** 295, 316–17, 337–8; Britain 368, 381, 391, 426, 435; treasuries 442; Britain 517, 714; **IV** 445; assemblies of clergy 448, 478–9, 501–9; archives 490; medieval English territorial unit **VI** 274; vicars general and assistant bishops 274; bishop's official diocese 275
Diocletian, Emperor **Ia** 243, 244, 285–318; tetrarchy 290–1, 301, 307, 314; succession 291, 322–3, 532; army reorganization 291–5, 333–4, 376; administration 316–17, 332, 576; York? 325; palace at Split 452; British goods in price edict 655, 656
Diodora, priestess **Ia** 667
Diodorus Siculus **Ia** 44
Dionysius, Areopagite **VII** 240, 243, 244
Dionysus **Ia** 675, 711–12, 735

169

Dioscuri **Ia** 712
diploma **Ia** 153, 181
diplomacy **Ia** 225, 417–19, 425, 430–1, 457; in E. and W. empires 419, 490; St Germanus 466, 469, 476, 492; among Welsh chieftains 680; Renaissance period **VII** 82
diplomatic revolution **VIII** 154
Directory, the **IX** 193, 198–201
Dirksen, German ambassador **XV** 476
Dirleton Castle **IV** 573, 689
disarmament: German **XV** 135; not initiated by Britain 227; control commission withdrawn from Germany 235; three-party agreement 271; Great Britain pledged 318; springs from economy 331; will prevent war 361; higher loyalty 362; Labour's central demand 369; divides opinion 374; failure a cause of war 453
disarmament conference **XV** 255; Henderson promotes 273; meets 351, 362, 364; Henderson president 360; MacDonald pins faith on 364; fails 365–6, 376; debate 408
Disbrowe, John **IX** 183, 237, 247–9, 260
Disciplina Augusta, cult **Ia** 683
discipline *see* army
Discourse of the Common Weal of this Realm of England **VII** 503, 504, 507, 583, 585
Discourse to Prove a North-West Passage **VIII** 240
discoveries, geographical **VII** 4, 188, 224–8, 507, 561
Discovery of a Gaping Gulf . . . **VIII** 350
diseases **Ia** 551; *see also* plague
Disenchantment **XV** 61
Diserth Castle **IV** 137, 172, 178, 399, 400; destroyed by Llywelyn ap Gruffydd (1263) 402, 403, 404
Disinherited, the: action against (1265–7) **IV** 206–9, 213–15; *see*

also Dictum of Kenilworth
disorder **X** 258–60
dispensaries **X** 419
Dispensary for Sick Children **XII** 12
Disraeli, Benjamin, earl of Beaconsfield **XIII** 89, 90, 156, 163, 166–9; biography 115; character and ideas 115–18; attack on Peel 118, 123; later attitude towards Protection 161, 163; chancellor of the Exchequer (1852) 164–5, (1858–9) 171–2, (1866–8) 184–8; introduces Reform Bill (1859) 171–2; and Gladstone 176–7; Franchise Bill 183; introduces Reform Bill (1867) 184–7; prime minister (1868) 188–90; novel-writing 191, 531; and Bismark 315; and Irish church bill 361; Irish problems 362–4; Canada 367; public health 446; education 483, 493; **XIV** 5, 137, 353, 377, 387; political duel with Gladstone 1–2, 71; declines office 25; prospects and policy (1874) 30; Crystal Palace speech 31; relations with Lord Salisbury 31–2; *sanitas sanitatum* 36, 125, 126; purchase of Suez Canal shares 37–8; 'empress of India' 39; takes peerage 40; view of Eastern Question 41–2; rejects Berlin Memorandum 43; wavers and approaches Russia 43; attitude to Bulgarian atrocities 44; orders fleet to Constantinople 48; orders Indian troops to Malta 49; at Berlin Congress 49–50; 'peace with honour' 50; aim to break up *Dreikaiserbund* 52–3; Cyprus policy 53; refusal to help agriculture 54; failure to control Frere 60; and Lytton 62; defeated at polls and resigns 64; Salisbury's criticisms 64–5; death and character 70–1; indifference to Africa 188; inter-House conflict 430; on Belgian neutrality 575; **XV** 70

170

dissection **VIII** 313

dissent *see* nonconformity

dissenters, Protestant, **XI** 62, 69, 70–2, 74, 87–8; heresies 85, 88; education 88–9, 139; Whitefield's preaching 98; marriage banns 137; Tory Acts repealed 170; *see also* Nonconformists

Distraint **IV** 368, 372; and investigations (1279) 359; of knighthood 546–8, 552–3

Districciones Scaccarii statute **IV** 325

Ditchley, villa **Ia** 560–2, 608, 628, 629

Diuma, Bishop **II** 120

diverticulum **Ia** 608, 626

Dives, river **II** 588

Diviciacus **Ia** 24

divine right of kings: theory **IX** 31–34, 68, 94, 412; **X** 34

divorce (nullity suit of Henry VIII and Catherine of Aragon): origin **VII** 322–6; precedents 326; Decretal Commission (1528) 327; legatine court (1529) 328; case recalled (1529) 328

divorce, still a barrier in public life **XV** 170, 399

Divorce Act (1937) **XV** 403

Dixmude (Dixmuiden) (Flanders) **V** 431; **VI** 111; battle (1489) **VII** 98, 99, 208; **VIII** 357; fall **X** 112

Djem, brother of Sultan Bayazid **VII** 101

Dobneck, John (Cochlaeus) **VII** 343

Dobson, John, citizen of London **VI** 653–4

Dobson, William **IX** 374–5

Dobunni **Ia** 43, 59, 83, 103, 159

dockers inquiry **XV** 141; refuse to load *Jolly George* **XV** 143

Docking, Thomas **VI** 680

docks **Ia** 564, 631

Dockum, Holland **II** 171

Docura, Sir Thomas, prior of St John of Jerusalem **VII** 291

Docwra, Sir Henry **VIII** 487, 490

Doddridge, Philip (1702–51) **XI** 88;

academy at Northampton 89

Dodington, George Bubb (1691–1762), Lord Melcombe **XI** 26, 28, 337, 428, 431; diarist 2, 148; sycophant 10

Dodona **Ia** 672

Dodsley, James (1724–97) **XII** 353

Doenitz, Admiral, and end of war **XV** 593

Doesborowe, John of *see* John of Doesborowe

Doesburg **VIII** 368

Doget, Andrew **VI** 672

Dogger Bank, battle (1781) **XII** 241

Doggett, Thomas (d. 1721), founder of race for Doggett's Badge **XI** 133

dogs **Ia** 42, 58

Doherty, John **XIII** 128

Dohna, Baron Christopher, Frederick's envoy **IX** 56

Dohna, Count **X** 74

D'Oilli, Robert **III** 143, 388

Dol, Brittany **II** 608; **III** 273, 334; castle 335

Dolaucothi, gold mines **Ia** 632, 634

D'Olbreuse, Eleanor, morganatic wife of George William, uncle of George I **XI** 11

Dolfin, son of Earl Gospatric **III** 266

Dolforwyn: battle? **Ia** 105; castle **IV** 387, 406, 409

Dolgelly, parliament of Glyn Dŵr **VI** 56

Dollart **Ib** 54; map 1 xxix

Dolley, Michael **II** 222, 337, 581

Dollond, John (1706–61), optician **XI** 382

Dollond, Peter, son of the above **XI** 382

Dolwyddelan Castle **IV** 428, 441

Dombes, prince of **VIII** 414

Domesday Book **Ia** 543–4; **Ib** 30, 82, 183, 190; compared with *Rectitudines* **II** 473–8; social terminology 476–80; compilation 655–7; the two volumes 656; *see* Exon Domesday; use made of **III** 1;

171

Domesday Book (*cont.*)

  analysis of land 2; peasants 36, 38–40; proof of ancient demesne 44; evidence for destruction caused by Conquest 64–5; jury used for 405; assessment used for levy of carucage 418; evidence cited 12, 66, 72, 81, 170, 258, 287; **IV** 6, 530, 703; **V** 312, 313, 338

'Domesday of the Ports' **IV** 646

Domesday Survey: antecedents 61; contemporary description 618–19; occasion for pleas of land 626; function of the jury (649) 652; instructions to commissioners 652–3; their interpretation 653–6

domestic and foreign policy: (1661–8) **X** 55–74; (1668–78) 75–91

domestic servants, decline in number **XV** 38, 52, 177, 305

Domfront (Orne): castlery **II** 554; **III** 108, 116, 119, 134, 453; **VI** 176

Dominica **VIII** 369; British capture **XII** 73; free port 187; French capture 212, 289; British victory at 217; restored to England (1782) 255

Dominicans **IV** 24; Edward I's letter to the provincial of, on the outbreak of Gascon war (1294) 648; summoned (1300) to Lincoln parliament (1301) 702; **V** 26, 47, 90, 504; Thomas Dunhead rescues king 94; Robert Holcot 510; *see also* Hotham, William of

Dominion status: Indian demand for **XV** 153; Smuts urges for Ireland 156; Irish treaty 157; gives increasing rights 160, 191; defined by Balfour 253; promised to India 275, 277, 355; French regard union as 488

Dominions: not consulted on declaration of war (1914) **XV** 3; war debts 42, 123; military contribu-

tion 81; refused to be subordinated to Imperial War Cabinet 82; endorse Lloyd George's statement of war aims 97; representation at peace conference 132; reject Lloyd George's economic plans 150; insist on agreement with United States 151; Chanak crisis 191; Imperial Preference 207; oppose Protocol 221; want status defined 253, separate Department of State 254; separate secretary 285; and Ottawa conference 333; sterling area 337; trade with 339; agriculture 342; reject morganatic marriage for Edward VIII 401; legislate for abdication 406; support appeasement 420; approve Munich settlement 430; free to decide for themselves 452; declaration of war (1939) 453; support from 495; military contribution in Second World War 515

Domitian, Emperor **Ia** 149–154; recall of Agricola 141, 149–53, 167, 362, 570; persecution of senate 154, 171–2, 531, 715; frontier works 166; triumph 167; Colosseum completed 156; Lincoln *colonia* 157; palace 161; coin 564; vine-growing edict 652–3; punishment of Vestal 682

Domitius Ahenobarbus, L. **Ia** 25

Domitius Corbulo, Cn. *see* Corbulo

domus see houses

Don, river **Ib** 175; map 4 xxxii; **VII** 394

Donald, R.: and Lloyd George **XV** 28; dismissed as editor of *Daily Chronicle* 118

Donald Bane, king of Scotland, ancestor of the Comyns **III** 267–8; **IV** 581

Donatus **III** 232

Doncaster (Yorks.): garrison **Ia** 392; **III** 232, 270; **V** 61, 64–5; **VI** 3, 4, 53; **VII** 39, 389–91; monastery

397; **VIII** 139; last county borough created **XV** 256

donkeys: draught **Ia** 563; power 632

Donnchad Ua Longargain, archbishop of Cashel **IV** 568

Donne, John **VIII** 302; **IX** 362, 401–3, 407

Donnington (Lincs.) **V** 47, 73

Donnington Castle **IX** 138

Donoughmore, earl of **XIII** 348

Donum **III** 153, 418–19

Doomsday, coming foreshadowed **XV** 598

Dopping, Anthony, bishop of Meath **X** 310

Dorchester (Dornwaraceastor) (Dorset) **Ia** 280; amphitheatre 579; mosaicists 655; Christian cemetery 551, 700; Christian community 735; **II** 239, 337, 536, 732; council 349; **III** 65; **V** 239; **IX** 339

Dorchester, Lord (Baron) *see* Carleton, Guy

Dorchester Abbey (Oxon.) **III** 263; abbot of 169

Dorchester-on-Thames (Dorciccæstrae): *beneficiarii* **Ia** 523, 597; **Ib** 61, 82, 129, 170; map 3 xxxi; barbarian presence 86, 99; Saxon pottery and buckles 102–3, 156–7, 167–8; Roman altar found 167; Birinus and bishopric 172; West Saxon see **II** 35, 82, 118; Mercian see 68, 135; late Old English see 437, 468, 664, 732; **VI** 656; abbey (Austin canons) 302; bishop of *see* Ætla; Agilbert; Birinus; Remigius; Ulf; Wulfwig

Dordogne: wine-growing **Ia** 654; river **III** 442; **V** 112, 361; **VI** 364, 506; archives 107; lordship 107

Dordrecht **IV** 663, 664, 667; **V** 83, 156–7; **VI** 71; **VIII** 338

Dore (Dor) (Derby.) **II** 232, 732

Doreward, John, Speaker (1399) **VI** 19, 79, 413, 429

Doria, Andrea, admiral of Genoa, terms with Charles V (1528) **VII** 319

Dorislaus, Issac **IX** 219, 222, 356

Dormer, Jane, duchess of Feria **VII** 480

dormice **Ia** 614

Dorpius, Martinus **VII** 255

Dorset **Ia** 44, 280; conquest 93, 97; pottery industry 645–6, 650; Christians 342, 725, 735; **Ib** 150, 215; **II** 63, 279, 375, 379, 603; meaning of name 336; **III** 146, 241, 348; **V** 22, 67, 315, 331, 368; **VII** 145, 146

Dorset, 3rd duke of, and cricket **XII** 337; *see also* Lionel

Dorset, marquesses of *see* Beaufort, Edmund; Beaufort, Henry; Beaufort, John; Beaufort, Thomas; Grey, Thomas

Douai **VI** 582, 583; seminary **VIII** 171–2, 346; **X** 220, 234

Doughty, C. M. **XIV** 549

Douglas, Archbishop, 6th earl of Angus **VII** 305, 326, 406, 407, 484

Douglas, Archibald, 1st earl of Angus, 'Bell the cat' **VII** 136

Douglas, Archibald, 8th earl of Angus **VIII** 361

Douglas, Archibald, 3rd marquis and 1st duke of (1694–1761) **XII** 135; case **XII** 135

Douglas, C. H. **XV** 222

Douglas, Charles, 2nd earl of Selkirk (1663–1739) **XI** 272

Douglas, earl of *see* Archibald

Douglas, James, earl of (1384–8) **V** 463

Douglas, James, earl of Drumlanrig, 2nd duke of Queensberry **X** 139

Douglas, James, 4th earl of Morton: conspirator **VIII** 92–3; hatred of Darnley 99; Scottish settlement 144–5; Mary's return to Scotland 146; regency 161, 352, 357; prosecution 358

Douglas, James (1675–1742), surgeon **XI** 389

Douglas, Sir James ('Black Douglas'), son of William Douglas **IV** 685, 708; **V** 38, 39, 40, 56, 65

Douglas, Lady Jean (1698–1753) **XII** 135

Douglas, Margaret, daughter of Angus and Margaret **VII** 407

Douglas, Sylvester, 1st Baron Glenbervie (1743–1823) **XII** 401, 406, 409

Douglas, William **IV** 684, 685

Douglas, William, 1st duke of Queensberry **X** 275

Douglas-Home *see* Dunglass

Douhet, General **XV** 390

Doulcereau, agent of Piers de Brézé **VI** 514

Doullens (Somme) **VI** 192, 576; **VIII** 418; conference **XV** 101–2

Doumergue, G. **XIV** 483

Dove, river **Ib** map 2 xxx

Dover (Dofras) (Kent) Caesar **Ia** 28; fleet 258–9, 308, 529, 563, 637; base demolished 639; **Ib** *Dubris* 31, 83, 113, 124, 126, 204; map 2 xxx; map 6 88; Straits of 91; **II** 431, 562–3, 567, 603, 732; port **III** 96; priory of St Martin 104, 136, 141, 159, 163, 356; lighthouse 107, 166, 175, 283, 340, 437; refused admission to Stephen 132; capitulates to Stephen 136; Henry V lands 193; withholding permission to papal legates 219; lieutenant 236; church of St Martin le Grand 260; Sigismund's advice 347; Geoffrey taken in custody to castle 356; John returns 359; Stephen Langton's stay 448; negotiations for end of interdict 456–7; foreign troops 477; mercenaries 479; loyal to John 484; straits 494, **V** 5, 58, 90, 136, 243, 370, 548; Gaveston sails into exile from 13; French attacks 128; Wil-

liam Clinton constable (1334) 153; Lord Latimer constable (1372) 390; Anglo-Imperial alliance (1522) 310–12; **VII** 35, 108, 370, 548,; Anglo-Imperial alliance (1522) 310–12; **VIII** 355, 398–9, 418; strait 145–6; treaty **X** 76, 78, 79; straits of, convoys attacked **XV** 498

Dover, 1st Baron *see* Jermyn, Henry

Dover, William of **III** 149, 153

Dover Castle **II** 526, 599; **III** 18, 333, 338, 356, 433; besieged (1216–17) **IV** 1, 4, 9, 10, 12; held by justiciar 48; and by Peter de Rivaux 52; baronial disturbances 163, 165, 176, 181, 187, 198; Lord Edward (1265–6) 206, 207; constable and Nicholas Segrave 332; attacked by French galley (1294) 655; court of constable 701; **V** 454

Dow, Alexander (d. 1779) **XII** 166

Dowdeswell, William, MP (1721–75) **XII** 62; chancellor of Exchequer (1765–6) 111, 577; loyalty to Rockingham 121; attack on Townshend 127

Dowding, Air Marshal, appointed to fighter command **XV** 391; appeals to War Cabinet 480, 485; thinks front line strength adequate 490; resists demand for dramatic action 497; refuses to defend convoys 498; has cause for anxiety 499; receives little acknowledgement 500

dower, law of **IV** 326

Dowgate, London **III** 89, 92

Dowing, Sir George **X** 62, 67, 348

Dowland, John **VIII** 306, 307

Down, county **V** 233

Down Survey **X** 297

Downhouse (Devon) **VI** 372

Downie, American commander **XII** 554

Downpatrick **III** 311

Downs **VII** 270, 312; **VIII** 399

174

Downshire, marquis of *see* Hillsborough, Viscount

Downton (Wilts.)) **III** 54; **VI** 418

Dowsing, William **IX** 357

Doyley, Sir William **IX** 314

D'Oysel, M. **VIII** 39, 68

Dragonby **Ib** 180

drainage: land **Ia** 153, 267–8, 555–6; buildings 578, 610; mines 632; **XII** 34; *see also* fens

Draining **IX** 281–2

Drake, F. (1696–1771), antiquarian **XI** 395

Drake, Sir Francis: expeditions with Hawkins **VIII** 124, 416–17; feud with Spain 247, 370, 394–5, 411–12, 416–17; pirate 248, 249, 369, 411; circumnavigation 249–50; armada 399, 411; death 417

Drake, governor of Calcutta (1756) **XI** 328

drama: Elizabethan **VIII** 294–301; **IX** 367–70, 391–9; **XIV** 328–9, 546–8; reforms of stage production 547

Draper, Sir William (1721–87) **XI** 330

draught animals **Ia** 563, 627

Drawswerd, Thomas **VII** 591

Drayton, Michael **VIII** 286, 287; **IX** 399–400

Dream of the Rood **II** 196–7

Dreikaiserbund **XIV** 42, 52–3, 84; renewed (1881) 194–5

drengs **II** 503

Drengsted **Ib** 72; map 1 xxix; map 5 68

Dresden: negotiations **XII** 556; battle (1813) 558; bombed **XV** 591–2

dress **VIII** 268, 269, 270, 271; **XII** 548; effects of First World War **XV** 38, 52; becomes more uniform 173

Dreux (Eure-et-Loire) **VI** 173, 179, 200, 256; battle **VIII** 60

Dreux, Peter of, count of Brittany **IV** 15, 73; relations with Blanche of Castile and Henry III 91, 92–7; fights for Louis IX (1242) 103; descendants in Brittany 159, 235–6; attempt to secure the succession to Navarre for his son 237; *see also* Brittany

Driberg, T.: invents William Hickey **XV** 235; Independent MP 548

Driffield **Ib** 81; map 4 xxxii

drinks and drinking **VIII** 273–4

Drinkwater, J. **XV** 314

Droeshout, Martin and John **VIII** 302–3

Drogheda **V** 351, 353; **VII** 131; parliament (1494) 128–9, 130, 133; **IX** 162–3; **X** 307

Drogo, count of the Vexin **II** 619–20; married Godgifu, daughter of Æthelred **II** 560

Droitwich, house **Ia** 276

Dropt, river **VI** 109

Drouet, French commander **XII** 488

Droxford **Ib** 148; map 3 xxxi

Droxford, John, bishop of Bath and Wells (1309–29) **V** 9, 80, 300, 304

Droxford, John, keeper of wardrobe **IV** 662

Druell, Master John **VI** 288

Druidism **Ia** 24, 110, 677–9, 680

Drumclog **X** 271

Drumlanrig, earl of *see* Douglas, James

Drummond, Mr, MP and contractor **XII** 247

Drummond, James, 6th Earl, 3rd 'duke' of Perth (1713–47) **XI** 254, 282

Drummond, John, 1st earl of Melfort **X** 275

Drummond, Lord John, 4th duke of Perth (1714–47) **XI** 255

Drummond, Robert Hay (1711–76), archbishop of York **XI** 81

Drummond, Thomas **XIII** 334, 347–8

Drummond, William, of Hawthornden **VIII** 302
Drumquhassle Ridge, fort **Ia** 149
Drunemeton, Asia Minor **Ia** 673
drunkenness **IX** 180, 305–6
Drury, Robert, privy councillor (d. 1536), speaker of House of Commons (1495) **VII** 653
Drury, Sir William **VIII** 144, 145, 161–2
Drury House **VIII** 439
Drusslan (Carmarthen) **V** 59
Dry Drayton (Cambs.) **V** 343
Dryburgh **VII** 407
Dryburgh Abbey (Berwicks.) **III** 273
Dryden, John (1631–1700) **IX** 393–4, 402; **X** 355, 358, 360–2, 365–7, 370; *The Hind and the Panther*, catholic persuasion (1867) 54; translates Virgil 356; book on painting 401; poetry commissioned 404; **XI** 419–20, 427
Dryslwyn·(Carmarthen) **VI** 54
Dryslwyn Castle **IV** 410, 421, 438; siege 439–40; under a royal castellan 440
Du Croc **VIII** 101
Du Maurier, Daphne **XV** 312
dual system in India **XII** 161, 307, 384
Dublin: **II** 334, 340, 342–3; **III** 311; Danes of 293; coastal town for Ostmen 302; master of O'Conor 303; invasion (1170) and fall to English 306–7; archbishop of 308; royal palace 308; Hugh de Lacy deprived of custody 312; shipping **IV** 442; division of county 564, 569; connections with Bristol 565; mint and exchange 633; collection of customs 650; **V** 44, 45, 232; Edward III establishes control 231; wool staple town 351, 353; Sir William of Windsor 387; Richard II's pacification plan 472–3; Irish

parliament **VI** 423–5; constituencies 423; Commons participation 423–5; local community grants 424; political and administrative business 424; the Pale 499; **VII** 70, 72, 79, 128, 130, 132, 364; **IX** 162; **X** 305, 308, 322–3; Philosophical Society 322–3, **XI** 293, 298, 303–4, 415; militia 300; Smock Alley Theatre 304; society 304–6; Trinity College 304; books and newspapers 306; *see also* societies and clubs; rebellion **XV** 55, 56; Asquith 57; convention meets 83; Joyce remembers 179; British threaten to intervene 188; bombed in mistake for Belfast 501
Dublin, archbishops of **III** 308; **XI** 294; *see also* Bicknor; Cranley, Thomas; Cumin, John; Darlington, John of; Henry; Hotham, William; London, Henry of; Waldby; Wikeford
Dublin, county **VI** 425
Dublin Castle **III** 315; **X** 391; rules **XV** 16, 57, 153; ignored 154; Collins has agents in 155
Dublin university, members **XV** 128, 156
Dubois, Guillaume (1656–1723), Cardinal **XI** 73, 166, 182, 185, 193, 291
Dubois, Pierre **IV** 82–3
Dubourg, Matthew (1703–67), violinist **XI** 304
Dubris see Dover
Ducarel, Andrew (1713–85), antiquarian **XI** 395
Duchess of Malfi **VIII** 301
Duckett, John **VI** 127
Duckham, Sir A. **XV** 140
Ducklington, villa **Ia** 461, 607
Duddon, river **III** 265
Dudington, Lieutenant **XII** 195
Dudley (Worcs.), castle **II** 627, 629; **V** 78
Dudley, Ambrose, earl of Warwick

176

VIII 60, 61, 62, 140, 142

Dudley, Sir Andrew VII 484, 492, 524, 529

Dudley, Catherine VII 524

Dudley, Dud (1599–1684) XI 113

Dudley, earl of XIII 220

Dudley, Edmund (1462?–1510), speaker of House of Commons (1504) VII 200, 299, 442, 582, 653; financial methods 213, 501; charges and execution 216–17, 267; named as scrutineer 229; sent to Tower 231–2; his *Tree of Commonwealth* (1509–10) 266, 566, 581, 582; on war 269

Dudley, Ferdinando, Lord (1710–57) XI 118

Dudley, Guildford VII 523, 530, 539

Dudley, Lord Henry VII 487, 529

Dudley, John, duke of Northumberland VIII 49

Dudley, John, Viscount Lisle, earl of Warwick (1547), duke of Northumberland (1551) VII 400, 409, 410, 542, 561; absence on military duty 419, 431; strikes Gardiner in council 420; influence in Privy Council 435; becomes earl of Warwick 480–1, 494; council ascendancy (1549–51) 481; duke of Northumberland 481, 491, 492; subservience to France 486–8, 491; suppresses Kett's rebellion (1549) 490; advances to power (1550–1) 491; control of Star Chamber 497; dissolves parliament (1553) 498; second parliament (autumn 1553) 499; taxation 500; shaky finances and foreign debt 501, 503; Protestantism 512; sees of Durham and Newcastle 518; Knox's sermon 519; Lady Jane Grey 522–5; failure and death 526–30, 536; Ridley in Tower 543; Cranmer condemned 544; spoliation 546; recantation 552; academic reform 574; great master of the household (1550) 649; lord admiral (1543–7, 1549) 650; earl marshal (1551) 651

Dudley, John Sutton, Lord VI 501, 511

Dudley, Lord Robert VII 526, 529; VIII 107, 108–9, 370; Elizabeth's favourite 49, 75; Cumnor tragedy 49–52; marriage with Mary Stuart 75, 77–81; created earl of Leicester 81; succession debate 97, 134; Norfolk-Arundel plot 133; pro-French party leader 148; Anjou marriage confidant 155–3, 355; backs Frobisher's voyages 240; chancellor of Oxford 320; war-party leader 342; Netherlands expedition 343, 365–8

Dudley and Ward, 2nd Viscount, profits from industry XII 32

Duduc, bishop of Wells II 464

duelling IX 305; X 420–1

duels: Gaston of Béarn to Edward I IV 285; Charles of Anjou and Peter of Aragon 254; canon law 254

Dufay, F. de C. (1698–1739), electrician XI 383

Dufferin, 1st marquess of XIV 83

Dufford, Sir Ralph V 231

Duffy, Sir Charles Gavan XIII 349

Dufnal *see* Dunmail

Dugga (Tunisia), street plan Ia 92

Duguesclin, Bertrand V 130, 131, 144, 145, 247

Duiveland VIII 338

Duke of York sinks *Scharnhorst* XV 564

Dulcitius Ia 382, 395, 411

Dumbarton (Alcluith) II 86, 92; VII 485; castle VIII 109, 144, 151, 358, 361

Dumbarton Oaks XV 487

Dumbell, John VII 519

Dumfries, castle and burgh: truce with Scots (1300) IV 693; meeting of Bruce and Comyn (1306)

Dunmail, king of Strathclyde **II** 359, 369; sons blinded by orders of King Edmund 359

Dunmore, 4th earl of *see* Murray, John

Dunning, John (1731–83), Baron Ashburton: biography **XII** 232; solicitor general (1768–70) 135; opposition to North 232–4, 252; chancellor of the Duchy of Lancaster (1782–3) 578, 579

Dunois, *bailliage* **VI** 191, 239

Dunois, Count, natural son of duke of Orléans **VI** 245, 247, 474, 492; treaty of Picquigny 577

Dunraven, earl of **XIV** 358, 359

Duns Scotus **VII** 377

Dunstable (Beds.): burial **Ia** 696, 706; **III** 166, 202, 258; priory 186; justices of assize **IV** 27; **V** 83, 306; prior of 414; **VI** 134; Cranmer's court **VII** 357

Dunstable, John (d. 1453) **VII** 266, 588

Dunstable, William **V** 242

Dunstanburgh (Northumb.) **VI** 528; surrenders to Warwick 531

Dunster Castle (Som.) **III** 138

Dunton (Essex) **V** 329

Dunwich (Dommocceaster) (Suffolk): bishop's seat **II** 116, 132; diocese 134, 146, 433, 732; **III** 90, 96; burgesses **IV** 484

Dupleix, Joseph (*c.*1700–63) **XI** 326, 328, 347, 372

Duplessis-Mornay **VIII** 206

Dupplin, Viscount *see* Hay, George

Dupplin Moor, battle **V** 116, 154

Duquesne, Ange, Marquis **XI** 361

Durand, Templar **III** 456

Duras, Louis de, 2nd earl of Feversham **X** 119

D'Urban, Sir Benjamin **XIII** 396–9; biography 396

Dürer, Albrecht (1471–1528) **VII** 265

Durham (Dunholm) **II** 602, 732; foundation of cathedral 435; origin of county 435, 503, 732; monks introduced 678; **III** 55, 270, 272; monks 171, 408; **V** 32, 136, 439; **VI** 33; violence 127; *see* 270; priory 294; St Nicholas rectory 288; Ralph Neville's lands 323; sequestrated temporalities 603; attacked (June 1461) 528; **VII** 75, 161, 280, 386, 393; proposal to divide 518; **IX** 136, 351; unemployment **XV** 351

Durham, bishop of **III** 280, 282; *see also* Æthelwine; Beaumont, Louis de; Bek, Anthony; Bury, Richard; Butler, Joseph; Ealdhun; Flambard, Rannulf; Fordham; Fox, Richard; Hatfield; Kirkham, Walter of; Langley, Thomas; Marsh, Richard; Philip; Poore, Richard le; Puiset, Hugh de; Ruthall, Thomas; St Calais, William of; Skirlaw; Tunstall, Cuthbert; Walcher; William

Durham, bishopric **III** 182, 192, 226, 275

Durham, cathedral church **III** 260, 261–2, 445, 448; **IV** 495; dispute about rights of administration 469, 493–4; and the bishop 493, 495–6; prior and Alexander II, king of Scots (1239) 586; bishop of and John Baliol 266; monks at Oxford 485; *see* **V** 3, 80, 275; palatinate 40, 187, 254

Durham, cathedral priory **V** 305, 317, 320–36, 372

Durham, city and county **VI** 133; **X** 12; **XII** 52

Durham, earl of *see* Lambton, John George

Durham, palatinate **VI** 329; **VII** 194; **VIII** 135, 139, 188

Durham, see **II** 659, 660, 665, 666; **VII** 294, 399, 546

Durham Castle **II** 611; **III** 103, 223; **VII** 37

Durham House, Strand, mint **VII** 606–7

Durno, temporary camp **Ia** 146

Durobrivae see Rochester

Durocortorum Remorum see Reims

Durotriges **Ia** 44, 45, 59, 92–3, 97

Durovernum Cantiacorum **Ib** 125, 146, 209; *see also* Canterbury

Durward, Alan (*Ostiarus*) **IV** 590, 592

Dussindale, Kett crushed **VII** 490, 541

Dustchucks **XII** 160

Duston, cemetery **Ia** 706

Dutch, the: workers in England after Restoration **X** 41; Dutch East India Company 46; rivalry with England 61–4; second Anglo-Dutch war 63–8; navy 64–5, 78, 80–1, 164, 218; alliance with England 68, 73; third Anglo-Dutch war 78–83; European coalition 84; Louis XIV's commercial measures against 132; French war 160; Spanish succession 193, 194, 203; English support 196; subsidies to foreign rulers 214, 221, 253, 264; demands (in 1709) 218; peace negotiations (1710–13) 234–6; South America 325, 327; West Indies 328, 329, 330; coast of West Africa 332–3; in India 348–50; influence on English architecture 393; barrier fortresses **XI** 165, 196, 265, 350; relations with Britain 165, 172, 173, 202, 241 —defence 258, 350; East India Company 193, 196, 325, 329; with Maria Theresa 237; invasion (1747) 260; with French 260, 263–4; fishing fleets 276; *see also* Holland; Netherlands

Dutch cap, contraceptive **XV** 165

Dutch East Indies **XV** 351, 485; lost 544

Dutch shipping, seizure **VIII** 339

duties *see* taxation

Dutigern, British king **II** 76

Dutton, Hugh of **III** 258

Duttons family **IX** 268

dux, military rank **Ia** 333–4, 350–1, 443, 517; Fullofaudes **Ia** 377, 411; Dulcitius 395; Theodosius the Great 401

dux Britanniarum **Ia** 333, 377, 392–3, 402, 411; *Notitia* 412; **Ib** 187, 189, 195–6

Duxford (Cambs.) **V** 416

Dyer, Sir James, speaker of the House of Commons (1553) **VII** 654

Dyer, John (*c.*1700–58) **XI** 420; *The Fleece* quoted 111; *Grongar Hill* 425

Dyer, General R. E. H., at Amritsar **XV** 152

Dyfed **Ia** 45; **II** 215, 230; kings of 330, 359

Dyffryn Clwyd (Denbigh): one of the Four Cantrefs **IV** 400; granted by Edward I to David of Wales 414; later barony of Ruthin 424; **VI** 37

Dyke, Sir W. Hart **XIV** 95, 204

Dykeveld, lord of *see* Weede, Everard van

Dyle, river, battle **II** 263

Dymock, Sir Thomas, king's champion **VI** 19

Dynant, Alan **III** 124

dynasties in England **II** 36–8; their extinction 232; decline 304–5

Dynefor *see* Dinefwr

Dynham, Sir John (Lord Dynham 1467): Henry VII's council **VII** 56; treasurer (1486) 56, 646

Dynne, West Saxon friend of Boniface **II** 173

Dyrham (Deorham) (Glos.) **Ib** 163, 168, appendix II; map 3 xxxi; **II** 731

Dyrham in Marshfield (Glos.): battle **II** 45; importance 29

Dyson, Jeremiah (1722–76) **XII** 153

E

earldoms, Anglo-Danish **II** 414–16; not autonomous under Edward the Confessor 549–50; suppression 612; of the Welsh marches 615–16

Earle, John **IX** 415

earls, *Danish*, in England, under Athelstan **II** 351; under Cnut 414–16, 417; revenues 535, 547–8; nominated by the king 547–8; nature of functions 547–8

earls, *English* **IV** 40–1, 50–1; personnel (1306) 516–17; relations with Edward I and Edward II 517–19; theory of earls (*comites*) as peers and companions of the king 521; Scottish 577, 578–82; during Alexander III's minority 590–2; claim authority during interregnum (1291 and 1296) 601–2, 613, 614; rebellion **VIII** 136–44

earls, *Scottish* **IV** 577, 578–82; during Alexander III's minority 590–2; claim authority during interregnum (1291 and 1296) 601–2, 613, 614; rebellion **VIII** 136–44

Earls Barton (Northants) **II** 442

Earnwig, master of school at Peterborough **II** 462

earthworks **Ia** 218–19, 222, 262–3, 264, 694–5

East Anglia **Ia** 6, 36, 100, 602, 677; **Ib** 40, 59, 176, 193; map 2 xxx; late Roman and early Germanic remains 82; Saxon presence 86; Wuffingas 97; Anglo-Saxon amalgam 100; early Saxon settlement 107; Frisian law codes 143; scanty political history records 173; **II** 9, 18, 37; **II** 50, 243; royal dynasty 50; conversion 116–17; chose Egbert as protector 231; Danish invasions 247–8, 250, 257; agrarian system 281; Danish kings 328; earldom 561, 572, 574; later see 437–8; social peculiarities 491; social organization **III** 37, 49, 164, 469; ports **IV** 659, **V** 83, 314, 375, 436; industrial population **VI** 365; **VII** 219, 304, 462, 464, 526; Mary's Protestant following 533; invasion feared **XV** 498; *see also* Eohric; Essex; fens; Guthrum; Norfolk; Suffolk

East Bergholt (Essex) **VI** 647

East Brandon (Northumb.), manor **VI** 323

East Fulham, by-election **XV** 367, 387

East Grinstead (Sussex) **VI** 419

East Hertfordshire, by-election **XV** 44

East India Company **VIII** 250–1; **IX** 52, 286, 318–19, 322–51, 334–5; **X** 46, 107, 249, 258, 348–54; Bombay 60; duke of York buys stock 61; loans to state 249; trading monopoly in Asia 250, 282, 301; protests against silk importation 258; falling stocks 283; power in the East 348–54; Hon. Robert Boyle, director 375; New East India Company 353–4; **XI** 21, 27, 176, 178, 193; interlopers 196; disputes 265; prosperity and territory 324–7, 329; imports and exports 325; changed status 331–3; French conflict 366; **XII** 303; trade 14, 25, 196, 383; settlement (1767) 124; in politics 131, 157, 164–6, 170, 282 —private money for Pitt's cause 271 —allegations of corruption 448; position and development up to (1774) 157–72; termination of charter (1780) 232; history (1773–84) 261–5, 268, 305–22 —(1784–93) 274, 322; monopoly reaffirmed 277; acquisitions (1799) 384; revision of charter (1813) 570; **XIII** 567; charter (1813) 8, 405, (1833) 405–6, 409; territories under control (1815)

403; position and policy 404–5; trade 405–6; educational policy 406–8; reforms 408; change in character of British administration 409–10; transfer of territories and jurisdiction to the Crown 441–2; *see also* India

East Indies: Anglo-Dutch rivalry **IX** 52, 85; massacre of Amboyna 53; formation of East India Company 85; *see also* East India Company

East Linton (Kent), Haddington **VI** 37

East Lothian, Scotland **VI** 37

East Meon (Hants), tenants dispute **VI** 540–1

East Saxons **Ib** 130, 173; map 2 xxx; **II** 9, 10, 37

East Shefford (Berks.), cruciform brooch **Ib** 58 [fig. 1(c)]

Eastbourne **XII** 549

Eastbridge (Kent), hospital **III** 79

Easter **Ia** 480; **Ib** 5; tables **II** 15; methods of determining 112; controversy over 119–20, 123–4

Easter rebellion **XV** 55–7, 72

Easterlings **VI** 515

Eastern Association **IX** 133, 137, 139–40, 199

eastern empire: L. Verus' campaign **Ia** 207; defeat of Valerian 272–3; wealth and culture 273, 364; Constantinople 348; Honorius and Stilicho 366, 423, 426, 430; unity of the empire 400, 430–2, 486, 489–90, 497; support of Danubian king 438; Vandals and Huns 475, 481, 483; English contacts **II** 4–8, 51–2, 137, 175, 182; English art 443; Englishmen in the service of 680–1

eastern religions **Ia** 676, 715

Eastland Company **VIII** 239; **IX** 318–19; **X** 47

Easton Neston (Northants) **V** 345

Eastorege *see* Eastry (Kent)

Eastry (Eastorege) (Kent) **Ib** 123; map 2 xxx; map 5 68; **II** 55, 293, 732; monastery 47

Eastry, Henry, prior of Canterbury **IV** 485, 717; letters to 261–2; **V** 81, 93, 345; questions parliament without king 91; control of estates 316–17; crop farming 319–20, 321

Eastward Ho! **VIII** 301

Eata, abbot of Melrose **II** 124, 126; bishop of Hexham 125–6, 139; influence on the life of Cuthbert 126; prior of Lindisfarne 126, 136, 139; death 139

Eaton (Hereford.) **V** 339

Ebbesborne Wake (Wilts.) **III** 79

Ebbsfleet (Ypwines fleot) (Kent) **Ib** appendix I(a); **II** 16, 734

Ebchester: inscription **Ia** 685; **Ib** 79; map 4 xxxii

Eboracum see York

Eborius, Bishop **Ia** 340

Ebrington (Glos.), manor **VI** 310

Ebroin, mayor of the Palace in Neustria **II** 132

Ecclesfield priory **V** 295

Eccleshall (Staffs.) **VI** 515

ecclesia (ecles) **Ib** 32–3

Ecclesiasticae disciplinae . . . explicatio **VIII** 195

ecclesiastical organization *see* Church of England

Ecclesiastical Polity, Of the Laws of **VIII** 458–60

Ecgfrith **Ib** 175

Ecgfrith, king of Mercia **II** 217–20, 225

Ecgfrith, king of Northumbria **II** 85–8, 134–5, 138, 184; death 139

Echternach, monastery **II** 167, 176

Eck, John **VII** 338

Eckardstein, Baron von **XIV** 260, 352

Eckhart, Meister **IV** 230

Economic Advisory Council **XV** 329

The Economic Consequences of the Peace **XV** 136

economic development: **Ia** 615–64; Flavian 159–60; Severan? 233–7; villa economy 282, 584–5, 614,

Edgcumbe, Richard, 1st Baron (1680–1758) **XI** 48

Edgecombe (Edgecumbe), Sir Richard (d. 1489): Henry VII's council (1485) 56; comptroller of the household (1485) 56, 650; king's friend 57; negotiates with Scotland 76; mission to Ireland (1488) 79–80, 125; envoy to Brittany (1488) 89

Edgecot (War.), battle **VI** 422, 555, 556

Edgehill, battle 131–2

Edgeworth, Maria (1767–1849), *Castle Rackrent* and *The Absentee* **XI** 299

Edgeworth, R. L. **XIII** 476

Edgware (Middx.) **VI** 675

Edict of Milan **Ia** 285

Edinburgh (Etain, Etin) **Ib** 197–8; **V** 33, 35, 98, 440; **VI** 34; held against Henry VI 35; **VII** 161, 275, 405, 407; **IX** 87; **X** 263, 278–9; medical school 264; **XI** 391; rebellion (1745) 254, 283; population 274; Porteous riots 278–9; theatre 286; convention (1793) **XII** 359; growth 517, 523; **XIII** 3, 26; university **XV** 128; *see also under* societies

Edinburgh, castle (*Castrum Puellarum*) **III** 278, 279; **IV** 571, 589–90, 614, 686, 692; parliament (1258) 592; capture **VIII** 161–2; treaty 47, 70

Edinburgh Philosophical Society **XII** 327

Edinburgh Review **XII** 541

Edington (Wilts.): battle **II** 255, 343; **V** 213; **VI** 495, 496

Edington, William, bishop of Winchester (1346–66), treasurer (1344–56), chancellor (1356–63) **V** 211–27, 301, 316

Edison, Thomas Alva, inventor **XIV** 151

Édit de Janvier **VIII** 54

Edith, wife of Edward the Confessor **II** 425, 502, 568, 578, 596

Edith, wife of Henry I *see* Matilda

Edmund II (Ironside): received in Five Boroughs **II** 389; harries English Mercia 388; chosen king of Wessex 390; war with Cnut 390–3; death 393; sons 397; **III** 115, 265

Edmund, duke of York **VI** 6, 8, 25, 292

Edmund, earl of Cornwall **III** 169; **IV** 57, 344, 507, 511, 519

Edmund ('Crouchback'), earl of Lancaster (1267–96) **V** 495

Edmund, earl of Rutland, second son of Richard duke of York, receives Welsh revenue **VI** 522

Edmund, earl of Stafford **VI** 7

Edmund, king of East Anglia **II** 236, 248

Edmund, king of Wessex **II** 343, 356–60, 446–7, 552; reconquest of Northern Mercia 357–8; invades Strathclyde 359, 369; laws quoted 299

Edmund, second son of Henry III, later earl of Lancaster: crown of Sicily offered to by the pope and accepted for him by Henry III **IV** 121–3; released by Pope Alexander IV from obligations (1258) 136; later history of claim 167, 168; sent to England from Paris as *capitaneus* (1262) 171, 172, 173; surrenders Dover 176; created earl of Leicester and seneschal of England (1265) 206; receives lands of earl of Derby 212; takes the cross 219; career, character, lands and loyalty to Edward I 235–6, 239, 240, 518; marriage to Blanche of Artois and position as vassal of Philip III 236–41; joins league of Mâcon 248; acquires Peter of Savoy's house 250; with mother in France (1263–5) 280; with Edward I in Paris (1286) 290; in west Wales 406, 410, 414;

Edmund, son of Henry III (*cont.*)
regent in England (1286–9), puts down rebellion of Rhys ap Mareddud 439; negotiations in Paris (1293–4) 646–8; leads expedition to Gascony and dies (1296) 649; founder of Dominican priory at Leicester 519

Edmund, son of Henry VII (d. 1500) **VII** 169

Edmund, son of Malcolm III, king of Scotland **III** 268

Edmund of Almaine, earl of Cornwall (1272–1300) **V** 507

Edmund of Lancaster (1245–96) **VI** 13

Edmund of Woodstock, earl of Kent (1321–30) **V** 59, 80, 85, 93; pursuit of Lancaster, siege of Pontefract 66–7; Edward II's halfbrother 75; trial and execution 100; ambassador to France 109, 115

Ednyfed, son of Tudor ap Goronwy **VI** 39

Ednyfed Fychan, seneschal of prince of Snowdonia **IV** 391

Edric the Wild **II** 603–4

education: provincial policy **Ia** 142–3, 160, 506, 507; traditional 297, 304, 319, 338–9, 347; Julian's 355; Valentinian 370; Germanus 466; provided by army 508; **VIII** 320–7; **X** 157, 264, 347, 412–18; legal **XI** 62–3; dissenters 69, 88–9, 99, 170; schools 139–41; charity schools 141–2; Woolwich Academy 220; Portsmouth Naval Academy 225; science 385, 388; **XII** 39–41, 354, 437, 524; Irish **XIII** 350–1; technical 475, 500–1; adult: work of Brougham and Society for Diffusion of Useful Knowledge 494–5; mechanics' institutes 494–5; Working Men's College 496; women's: girls' schools 496–7; higher 497–8; technical **XIV**

151, 203–4, 318–20; (till 1886) 146–52; women's 148–50; elementary made free 204, 316; Cross Commission 317; work of A. H. D. Acland 317–18; Bryce Commission 318, 320; public schools 322, 537; (after 1900) 536–9; growth of secondary schools (after 1902) 536–7; before First World War **XV** 1; increases class division 170–1; Geddes axe 184–5; Trevelyan's proposed reform 211; share of national income 237; local authorities 257; proposed raising of schoolleaving age 280, 406; state of 308; discussions 408; evacuation 455; *see also* American colonies; Education Acts; Ireland; literacy; Ruskin College; Scotland; school buildings; universities; university colleges; university extension; Workers Educational Association

Education, Board of **XV** 257, 433

education, primary: religious societies **XIII** 14, 477–8, 506; position (1815) 14, 475–6; monitorial system 475–6, 479; ideas of reformers 476–7; grants of state aid 478, 480; privy council committee 479; Newcastle Commission 481; 'Payment by results' 482; Act (1870) 482–3

education, secondary: position (1815) **XIII** 484–6; reform of the public schools 486–7; Clarendon and Taunton commissions 487–8, 496–8, 501; Woodard schools 488; teaching of science 498–501; *see also* universities, separate schools

Education Acts: (1870) **XIV** 3, 19, 146; (1902) 355–8; (1902) effect on religion **XV** 168; Fisher's Act (1918) 'Education for all' 170 — school-leaving age raised 184, 308, 568; Trevelyan's Bill (1931)

estates 603; Chamber main treasury 604; Warwick, Salisbury, and Spencer estates 604; Chamber also centre of audit 605; receivers 606; Neville grants 606; Elizabeth Woodville executor 607; wills and codicils 607; death (9 Apr. 1483) 610; **VII** 7, 11, 14, 61, 170; accession 60; popularity in Ireland 71; foreign treaties 81, 108; Sir Edward Brampton 118; Edmund de la Pole 167; royal dignity 191; attempts to curb sheriff's power 194; statutes compiled for JPs 195; parliament, prorogations 199; fleet 210; alienation of crown lands 213; goodwill towards Easterlings 221; cloth trade 462, 469; *see also* Edward, earl of March

Edward V, king of England (1483), son of Edward IV, Prince in the Tower: father's death **VI** 611; at Stony Stratford with Vaughan and Grey 613; ministers' arrests protest 613; supposed illegitimacy 619; death rumour (Oct. 1483) 623; forecasts death 624; Henry Tudor's silence 625; **VII** 7, 11

Edward VI, king of England (1547–53) **VII** 238, 339, 551, 569, 574; birth (1537) 394, 478; projected marriage to Scottish queen 406–7; Henry's succession 413; duke of Norfolk imprisonment 422; book of homilies 431; religious gilds 465; foreign trade charter 473; Hansards' privileges revoked 475; pass to Protestantism 478; *Journal* 479, 494, 580, 581; youth 479–80; devises Crown to Lady Jane Grey (1553) 481, 522–3, 530; betrothed, order of St Michael (1551) 486; frailty 488; sits in council (1551) 491; brought to London (1547) 493; coronation 494; regulations for

council 497; military expenditure 500; debasing currency 502; economic stringency 503; agrarian difficulties 504; religious issues 507–8; character 524–5; death (6 July 1553) 526, 535; Judge Hales 530; Privy Council 531, 566; obsequies 533; weak government 536; Nine Statutes repealed by Mary 544; heresy executions 549; divine right 562; sheriff's power 563; ecclesiastical ornament 568; 'printer to the king' 578–9; music 590; royal painter 601; health precautions 602; coinage 606–7

Edward VII, king of England (1901–10) (till 1901 prince of Wales) **XIII** 300, 320; **XIV** 352, 383, 410; illness (1871) 26; on royal commission on housing 127; hedonist 142–3; accession 342; characteristics and contrasts with Queen Victoria 342–3; part in Anglo-French Entente 367; appoints new prime minister at Biarritz 406; pleads against Lords' rejecting Licensing Bill 409; and budget (1909) 417; dealings with Asquith over 'guarantees' 419; death 420; role in foreign affairs 567–9

Edward VIII, king of England (1936): succeeds to throne **XV** 398; wishes to marry Mrs Simpson 399–401; abdicates 402–4; Chamberlain rigorous towards 414, 430; Dawson against 418; public taken by surprise 430; Churchill's support 466; Hitler proposal 489

Edward, Prince, son of Richard III: declared heir apparent **VI** 631; dies at Middleham (Apr. 1484) 636

Edward, prince of Wales, son of Henry VI and Margaret of Anjou **VI** 217, 310, 509; marriage arranged 523; proposed marriage

Edward, son of Henry VI (*cont.*)
559; return not allowed 559;
killed 569

Edward, son of Amadeus V **IV** 251

Edward, son of Edmund Ironside
III 115

Edward the Ætheling, son of
Edmund Ironside **II** 397, 560,
571

Edward of Angoulême **V** 424

Edward of Caernarvon *see* Edward
II, king of England

Edward of Salisbury **II** 633

Edward of Woodstock (the Black
Prince), earl of Chester (1333–
76), duke of Cornwall (1337–76),
prince of Wales (1343–76),
prince of Aquitaine (1362–76)
V 238, 244, 246, 248, 390;
first 'naval despatch' from Edward III 129; Crécy campaign
134, 255; Poitiers campaign
137–40; Gascony 143–4; Castile
144, 149; siege of Limoges 145;
zeal for war 150, 249, 253; keeper
of the realm 159, 160, 212; dukedom bestowed by king 185; suppresses Cheshire rising (1353)
204; knighthood financing 221;
extravagances 228; sale of prisoners 247; a knight of the Garter
252; Fitzalan, loans 256; organization of his appanage 258–9;
his life by Chandos herald 265;
marriage 266, 424; affection for
Gaunt 268; papal mandates 276,
279; convocation harangues 289;
Crown dues claim challenged
296; friendship with Abbot de la
Mare 308; demesne leases 329;
runaway serfs 337; relations with
tenants 344; income from the
stannaries 371; decline 384;
Latimer 390; death during the
Good Parliament 392; Hungerford 395; dependants 400; education of his son 424; **VI** 23, 145

Edward of York, earl of Rutland

(1390–1415), duke of Aumale
(1397–9) **V** 465, 471, 473, 478,
479; dukedom received from
Richard II, cousin 483; share of
Lancastrian lands after Gaunt's
death 490; traitor 492–3

Edwards, Edward **XIII** 494

Edwards, J. Passmore **XIV** 322

Edwards, Jonathan (1703–58) **XI**
323

Edwards, Owen M. **XIV** 336

Edwards, Thomas **IX** 197

Edwin, brother of Athelstan **II**
355

Edwin, earl of Mercia **II** 576, 581,
596–7, 599, 687; defeats Tostig
587; Norwegian assault 589;
leaves court with Morcar 601;
death 606

Edwin, king of Northumbria **II** 38,
78–81; overlord of southern
English 34, 79–81; death 81, 116;
conversion 113–15; assists Paulinus 114–15

Edwin of Deira **Ib** 184, 195–6, 199

Egbert, Bishop, afterwards archbishop of York **II** 92, 160–1, 175;
pupil of Bede 8, 188; receives
pallium 145–6

Egbert I, king of Kent **II** 61, 130,
132; founder of Chertsey Abbey
61

Egbert II, king of Kent **II** 36,
207–9, 216

Egbert I, king of Northumbria **II**
248, 251

Egbert II, king of Northumbria **II**
253

Egbert, king of Wessex, overlord of
the southern English **II** 34, 71,
95, 207, 259; expelled by Offa
220; becomes king 225; defeats
King Beornwulf 231; king of Mercia 232; receives submission of
Northumbria 232; supremacy
232; temporary nature 232–3;
conquers Cornwall 235; historical
importance 235; compared to

Æthelwulf 244; charter quoted 301
Egbert, organizer of mission to Frisia II 166
Egerton, Thomas IX 194
Egerton, Thomas, Baron Ellesmere, later Viscount Brackley (?1540–1617) XI 65
Eglesfield, Robert of V 500, 507
Eglinton, earl of see Montgomerie, Hugh
Eglinton tournament XIII 115
Egmont, earls of see Perceval, Sir John
Egnatius Lucilianus Ia 251
Egonesham see Eynsham (Oxon.)
Egremont (Cumbria), barony and manor VI 337
Egremont, 2nd earl of see Wyndham, Charles
Egremont, Sir John VII 91
Egremont, Lord XIII 92
Egremont, Thomas (Percy), Lord VI 508, 510; killed at Northampton 520
Egypt: Ia 130, 199, 207, 234, 340; decurions prohibited from moving to country 398; ruler cults 667; sultan (1239–40) IV 105, 110; Mamlūks 167; VII 113, 224; campaigns XII 378, 384, 386, 454; British occupation XIV 77–86; Bismarck's part 84; consequences of Gladstone's refusal to guarantee loan (1884) 85; whip-hand for Germany 85–6; removed by Anglo-French (Entente) Convention 367, 368; British forces during First World War XV 49; nominally independent 275; failure to secure treaty with 276, 318, 359; Mussolini 380; British forces during Second World War 460, 520; Hitler wants 489; Australia and New Zealand jealous 495; American aeroplanes sent to 513; Britain's continued presence 521; Italy invades 522; remains neutral 523; Eden 524; Wavell defends 526; servicemen 549; British army stirred up 556; secured 559

Ehret, Georg Dionysius (1710–70), botanist XI 388
Eichstätt, bishopric II 169, 175
Eider, river Ib map 1 xxix; II 13
eighteenth-century characteristics XI 1–3, 9–10
'Eik' VIII 116, 117
Eikon Basilike IX 159
Eikonoklastes IX 159
Eilaf, Viking leader II 382; rebellion 403; earl under Cnut 403, 404, 416
Einkreisung, colour lent to idea by Edward VII's tours XIV 569
Einsiedeln, abbey II 453
Einstein, Albert XIV 552; XV 259, 268
Eire: created XV 406; neutrality 430, 453, 504; no conscription in Northern Ireland 444
Eisenhower, Dwight David: supreme commander in North Africa XV 556; Mediterranean 563; for Overlord 573, 575, 579, 580; Harris put under 573; decides to invade France 581; urged to dismiss Montgomery 582; favours broad advance 583; conducts war against Germany 587; gives Montgomery temporary command in Ardennes 589; disputes with Montgomery 590; strategic air forces released from control 591; accepts German surrender 593, 594
Eisteddfod III 294
El Mina VIII 123
Elafius (British 'tyrant'?) Ia 480
Elagabalus, Emperor Ia 280, 531; Unconquered Sun 715
Elba: British surrender XII 372; French acquisition 411, 566
Elbe, river Ia 52, 89; Ib xxvii, 46, 50–1, 105; map 1 xxix; migration

193

governor-general of Canada 382; viceroy of India 442

Elgin, 9th earl of **XIV** 385, 406

Elias, J. S. and *Daily Herald* **XV** 251, 309

Elibank, master of, Lord Murray of: biography **XIV** 426; Marconi affair 457; attempts to settle Ulster conflict 480

Eliot, Sir Charles **XIV** 381

Eliot, George (Mary Ann Evans) **XIII** 533, 549; biography 557; works 557–8; **XIV** 158, 160

Eliot, John **X** 346

Eliot, Sir John **IX** 38, 111; on Cadiz expedition 36, 62–3; leadership in House of Commons 41–5; anti-Spanish 59

Eliot, Thomas Stearns **XV** 179

Eliot, William, joint master of the rolls (1485) **VII** 648

Elizabeth, countess of Warwick, wife of Beauchamp **VI** 343

Elizabeth, daughter of Edward I, marries John, count of Holland (1297) **IV** 665, 680

Elizabeth, daughter of Edward IV, queen of Henry VII (1465–1503) **VII** 49, 54, 65, 228; crowned (25 Nov. 1487) 78; Perkin Warbeck affair 142; died (1503) 151, 175, 230; death of Arthur 174; feast of St George (1488) 191; character 234

Elizabeth, daughter of Henry II of France **VII** 486

Elizabeth, Princess **IX** 17, 54

Elizabeth, queen consort **XV** 403

Elizabeth, queen of Edward IV (1437?–92) **VII** 61

Elizabeth I, queen of England (1558–1603) **III** 73; as princess **VII** 475, 493, 517, 562, 583 — England awaits 603; coronation 193; Nicholas Sander's attack 322; act of succession (1544) 413; and Thomas Seymour 421, 488; Edward's rela-

tion to 480; England's expanding trade 507; Lady Jane Grey 523, 527; accompanies victorious Mary 529; Wyatt's rising 538, 540; Mary's marriage 541; 'conforming' to Rome 547; Mary's unpopularity 557, 559; Mary's death 560; *Ecclesia Anglicana* 567, 569; coinage 607–8; appearance, character and qualities **VIII** 1–5; accession 5–6; treatment of de Feria 6–7; chooses Cecil as secretary 7–8; council 8; retains Sir Edward Carne at Rome 9; official 'style' 9; instructs Oglethorpe to omit elevation of Host 9; favours Protestants, but prohibits preaching 10; coronation 10; proclaimed 'defender of the faith' 10; recalls Carne from Rome 10; approves Acts of Supremacy and Uniformity 14–15; claims only *potestas jurisdictionis* 15; 'only supreme governess of the church' 16; title to Crown confirmed 18; rejects Commons' petition to marry 19; shuns Catholic revival, bars papal envoys 27; chooses Parker as archbishop of Canterbury 29; indifference to Church 30; keeps control of ecclesiastical matters 31; prohibition of destruction of monuments and family memorials 33; takes over ecclesiastical lands 33; resolves to recover Calais 35; refuses marriage offer of Philip II 37; agrees to Treaty of Cateau-Cambrésis 37–8; suspicious of French and Guises 38–9; secretly assists Scottish rebels 42; alliance with Lords of 'Congregation' 44; hears of turmoil in France 46; intervenes openly in Scotland 46; upbraids Cecil 48; falls in love with Lord Robert Dudley 49; Amy Robsart affair 49, 50, 51; seeks allies abroad 52;

Elizabeth I (*cont.*)

her object 53; offers to mediate in France 55–6; secret Treaty of Richmond with Huguenots 57; sends expedition to Le Havre 60; abandons Le Havre and makes Peace of Troyes 62; discusses Stuart claim to English Crown with Lethington 70–1; Treaty of Edinburgh and 'amicable conference' proposals 71–3; opposes Mary's proposed match with Don Carlos 74; offers Lord Robert Dudley to Mary 75; sanctions return of earl of Lennox and Lord Darnley to Scotland 78; opposes marriage of Mary and Darnley 83; sends Throckmorton to arrest the marriage 84; offers to mediate in Scotland 84–5; Thomworth follows 85; trounces Murray 87; knowledge of plot against Rizzio 94; falls ill of the smallpox 95; trouble with parliament over succession 95–9; hears of birth of Prince James 100; implores Mary to bring Darnley's murderers to justice 105; intervenes in Scotland to liberate Mary after Carberry Hill surrender 107; declines to receive Mary after her escape from Loch Leven Castle 108; makes an offer to Mary through Lord Herries 112; arranges 'conference' of York 113; and Westminster 114–15; Scottish queen sent to Tutbury Castle 118; stirs up trouble in the Netherlands 120; professes sympathy with Philip II 121; patronizes Hawkins 124; refuses to check piracy in the channel 126–7; supports the *gueux de mer* 128; seizes Spanish treasure 129; receives ultimatum from French ambassador 132; forbids marriage of Norfolk and Mary Stuart 134; instructs Sussex to order the northern earls to repair to court immediately 138; sends army against them 140; moves Mary Stuart to Coventry, orders arrest of Leonard Dacre 141; congratulates Lord Hunsdon on Battle of the Gelt 142; instructs Sussex concerning punishment of the northern rebels 143; sends punitive expedition into Scotland 144; reverses Scottish policy 145; takes precautions against Spain 145–6; attempts settlement with Mary 146; duke of Anjou marriage proposals 147–8, 348–50; learns of Ridolfi plot, sanctions execution of Norfolk 151; refuses to grant Anjou freedom of worship in England 152; makes Treaty of Blois with France 154; expels *gueux de mer* from England 155; permits assistance to Netherlands 156; attitude to Massacre of St Bartholomew 160; retains ambassador in Paris 160; offers to hand over Mary Stuart to Scots to be judged 161; helps the Rochellois 162; but obtains confirmation of Treaty of Blois 163; favours Anjou marriage but achieves friendly settlement with Alva 164–5; is excommunicated by Pope Pius V 166–7; indifference to the bull 169; protected by statutes 170; overthrow planned by Pope Gregory XIII 173–5; Gregory XIII authorizes her assassination 178; measures against Catholics and the 'persecution' 184–8; instructs Canterbury and York to make strict rules for church service 192; but does not support them 193; resists parliamentary intervention in ecclesiastical affairs 196; orders suppression of 'prophesyings' 197; suspends Archbishop Grindal 198; appoints Whitgift

Elizabeth I (*cont.*)
and another to Ferrol and Azores 426; appoints Essex Lord-Lieutenant of Ireland 428; angered by his failure 433; condemns his unexpected return to London 436–7; punishes him 437–8; sanctions his trial for treason and execution 440–1; refuses to nominate James VI as her successor 442; writes to duke of Florence about the prosperity of England 453; refuses liberty of conscience to Catholics 455; orders all Jesuits and secular priests to leave the kingdom 456; Irish policy 465–76; holy war in Ireland against her 476–7, spreads to Munster 478; opposed by Hugh Roe O'Donnell and Hugh O'Neill, earl of Tyrone 480–90; last years, illness, and death 493–6; **IX** 1, 10, 24, 47, 263; **XI** 110; **XV** 259

Elizabeth, Tsarina **XV** 593

Elizabeth, Tsaritsa (1741–62) (b. 1709) **XI** 350, 371

Elizabeth of Bohemia **X** 190

Elizabeth Charlotte, duchess of Orléans **X** 128

Elizabeth Farnese (1692–1766), queen of Spain **XI** 172, 194, 199

Elizabeth of Valois, daughter of Henry II of France, offer of marriage to by Philip II **VIII** 37

Elizabeth of York, Richard III's niece **VI** 636

Elizabetha (poem) **VIII** 323

Elizabethae Angliae Reginae haeresim Calvinianam propugnantis etc. **VIII** 407

'Elizabethan', literary meaning **VIII** 281, 282

Ellenborough, earl of, 1st baron *see* Law, Edward

Ellendun, battle **II** 231

Ellesmere (Salop) **IV** 399; **VI** 291; canal **XII** 519

Ellesmere, Baron *see* Egerton, Thomas

Elliot, Sir Gilbert, 3rd baronet of Minto (1722–77) **XII** 79; treasurer of the navy (1770–5) 577

Elliot (Elyot), Hugh **VII** 225, 227

Elliot, Jean (1727–1805), poet, *Flowers of the Forest* **XI** 425

Elliot, W., insists on war **XV** 452

Elliott, Sir Henry **XIV** 42, 43, 44

Ellis, Mr **XII** 161

Ellis, Dom Philip **X** 54

Ellis, Thomas E. **XIV** 336

Ellis, Welbore, 1st Baron Mendip (1713–1802): secretary at war **XII** 577; treasurer of the navy 577; secretary of state 576

Ellough (Suffolk) **II** 434

Ellwood, Thomas **IX** 309–10

Ellys, John (1701–57), painter **XI** 399

Elmet (Elmete) (Yorks.), British kingdom **II** 33, 74, 732; Anglian conquest 80

Elmete *see* Elmet (Yorks.)

Elmetsætan **II** 296

Elmham, North (Norfolk): see **II** 134, 146, 433; revived see 437, 667; ruined church 441; bishops of *see* Æthelmær; Herfast; Stigand

Elmham *see* North Elmham (Norfolk)

Elmham, Thomas, prior of Lenton **VI** 122; *liber metricus* 122; vicar-general and chamberlain 122

Elmham, Sir William **V** 431, 432

Elmham, Sir William de **VI** 473

Elmina **X** 332; **XIV** 27, 28

Elmley (Worcs.) **V** 305

Elne, bishop of **VI** 582, 584

Elphinstone, Mountstuart **XIII** 407–8, 410, 411; biography 407

Elphinstone, William, bishop of Aberdeen (1489–1514) **VII** 249

Elphinstone, William George Keith **XIII** 419–20; biography 419

Elrington, John, household treasurer **VI** 596, 597

Elsham **Ib** 180-1; map 4 xxxii

Elstob, Elizabeth **X** 382

Eltham (Kent) **V** 442-4, 454, 462; royal residence **VI** 116, 131, 189, 229, 230; Margaret's arrival 477; and Henry V 480; **VII** 234, 249; ordinances (1526) 303, 434

Ely (Elge) (Cambs.) **II** 732; **III** 147; bishopric 182, 226; cathedral 263; disinherited in Isle of (1266-7) **IV** 208, 210, 213-15, 331; episcopal exemplars 57; convocation of clergy (1290) 513; cathedral **V** 499; diocese 286, 332; priory 308; see 317, 320-1, 323-4, 327, 330; **VI** 381; see **VII** 399

Ely, abbess of *see* Æthelthryth; Seaxburg

Ely, Archdeacon **VI** 670

Ely, bishop of **III** 78, 224; *see also* Arundel, Thomas; Barnet; Bourchier, Thomas; Burgh, Geoffrey de; Cox, Richard; Eustace; Fordham, J.; Goodrich, Thomas; Hotham; Langham; Longchamp, William; Lyle; Montagu, Simon; Morgan, Philip; Morton, John; Nigel; Thirlby, Thomas; West, Nicholas

Ely, Isle of **II** 53, 421, 605; double monastery 162; significance of name 293; abbey 373, 452, 455, 491, 649, 635; **V** 416 abbess of *see* Æthelthryth; Seaxburg

Ely, Nicholas of, chancellor **IV** 176, 181

Ely, Reginald, chief mason of King's College, Cambridge **VI** 648

Ely, Symeon, abbot of **III** 171

Ely, Thomas Green, bishop of (1658-1738) **XI** 23; Bentley's opponent 393

Ely, William of, treasurer **IV** 65

Elyot, Sir Thomas **VII** 576, 582, 600, 601

Elys, John **V** 437

Elys, William **V** 391

emancipation, Catholic *see* Roman Catholics

Emanuel of Constantinople **VII** 237

embargoes **VIII** 129, 130

embassies **Ia** 29, 35-6, 457

Emden (Germany) **VIII** 239

Emden, sunk **XV** 13

Emergency Powers Act (1920) **XV** 144, 213; (1939) 450; (1940) 479

Emerson, Ralph **VIII** 183, 184

emigration **IX** 319-21; **XIII** 366, 601; **XIV** 271, 500; *see also* Ireland

Emlyn, new castle **IV** 439, 440

Emma of Normandy: marries Æthelred II **II** 379; holds Exeter in dower 380; marries Cnut 397; supports Harthacnut 420; expelled to Flanders 422; relations with Edward the Confessor 426-7

Emma, sister of Roger, earl of Hereford, wife of Earl Ralf **II** 611-12

Emma, wife of Ralf II, earl of East Anglia **II** 612

Emmanuel, Philip, duc de Mercoeur **VIII** 414

Emmet, Robert (1778-1803) **XII** 421

Emo, historian of Frisia **III** 238

Empire, historical period **Ia** 22; political unit 523-5

Empire Free Trade: and Lloyd George **XV** 150; and Beaverbrook 192, 235, 282-3; dream shattered at Ottawa 333

Empresa **VIII** 175, 176, 352, 453

Empson, Richard (d. 1510) **VII** 200, 208, 213, 442, 501; fraudulence and execution 216-17; Henry's will executed 229, 231-2; executed 267; speaker of House of Commons (1491) 652

Ems, river **Ib** 50-55; map 1 xxix

Enborne, river **Ib** 149

Encinas, Francisco de (Dryander) **VII** 516

Enckhuizen **VIII** 338, 365

enclosure: of common pasture **IV** 69; movement **XII** 34, 37, 520

enclosures *see* inclosures

Endymion **VIII** 295

Enfield (Middx.) **V** 365; manor **VI** 562; **VII** 493

engagement: army **IX** 146; Scottish 153–4

Engaine family **III** 31

Engels, Friedrich **XIII** 144, 150; **XV** 173

Engenulf de Laigle **II** 630

Enghien, duc de **XII** 423

engineering **Ia** 555, 578, 695

engineers **Ia** 138, 142, 267, 547, 577

Englafeld *see* Englefield (Berks.)

England, kingdom **II** 211; description **VII** 25–41

Englefield (Englafeld) (Berks.) (Tegeingl) **II** 249, 732; one of the Four Cantrefs **IV** 400, 414

Englefield, Thomas, speaker of House of Commons (1497, 1510) **VII** 653

English Channel: not a cultural barrier **Ia** 19, 23, 81; invasions, (Caesar) 27, 31, (Gaius) 61, (Claudius) 71, 78, (Severus) 228, (Constantine III) 427–8; communications 122, 563, 570–1; defences 259, 289, 320–1, 384, 474; raiders in Channel 259, 283, 320–1, 375; navigation 306, 307, 308; **VII** 87, 115, 171; *see also* coastal defences; communications; Saxon Shore; trade

English Journey **XV** 301

Englishry **III** 393

engraving *see* printing and engraving

Eniskillen **X** 304, 307

Enniskillen, 1st earl of *see* Willoughby Cole, William

Enriquez, Don Martin **VIII** 125

Ensor, Sir Robert **XV** 361

Enstone (Oxon.) **V** 322

'enterprise of Flanders' **VIII** 154

entertainment, king and his servants

II 288–90

entertainments **Ia** 106, 311, 579; *see also* amphitheatres; theatres

Entre-deux-mers, district **VI** 108, 240

Eofeshamm *see* Evesham (Worcs.)

Eohric, Danish king of East Anglia **II** 322

Eorcenberht, king of Kent **II** 61, 113, 128

Eorcenwald, bishop of London **II** 73

Eorforwic *see* York

Eorpwald, king of East Anglia **II** 222

Eostre, Goddess **II** 97–8

Eowa, brother of Penda **II** 203, 206

Epaphroditus Claudianus, Claudius, dedication **Ia** 684

Epaticcu **Ia** 56, 59

Epernon (Seine et Oise), castle **III** 112

Ephemeris anni 1557 currentis juxta . . . canones **VIII** 307

Epicene **VIII** 301

Epicureanism **Ia** 710, 728

Epidauros, theatre **Ia** 675

epimenia **Ib** 14

Epirus **Ia** 423

episcopacy, unpopularity **IX** 72–3; in Scotland 86, 89; debates 104; restrictions 124; abolition 172, 190–1

Epithalamion **VIII** 291

Epona, cult **Ia** 669

Eppillus **Ia** 47, 56

Epte, river **III** 112, 162, 324, 377, 382

Epworth (Lincs.) **V** 294

equestrians: equestrian order **Ia** 79, 505; administrative posts 79, 88; growing importance 88, 153–4, 681; procurators 88, 193, 224, 337; military commanders 88, 213, 251–2; Vespasian 94, 155; senatorial attitudes 123; governors 251–2, 337, 519, 530; finance 659; Senicianus 689

equity **IV** 328

Erasmus, Desiderius (1466–1536) **VII** 216, 259, 282, 576, 587; opinions of England 26; Eltham nursery 234; humanism 235; beliefs and scholarship 240–1; on Colet's piety 243; assists Lily 245; biography of More 247; biography and career 248–52; early life 249; visits to England 249–52; *Praise of Folly* 252–5; reaction to it 255–6; humanist tradition 257; liberal reformation hopes 265; anti-war teaching 269; 'Germany' in Cambridge 343–4; linked to Luther 346; Edward VI's education 479; denounced by Gardiner 511; 'Erastianism' 511–12; Mary's education 534; Cambridge's classical tradition 571; book imports 578; English reputation for music 590; Hans Holbein 600; **VIII** 323; **XI** 139

Erastianism **X** 278

Erce **II** 98

Erdberg (Austria) **III** 362

Erddreiniog (Angle) **VI** 39, 40

Erdington (War.) **VI** 379

Erenbald, William **III** 82

Erghum, Ralph, bishop of Salisbury (1375–88), Bath and Wells (1388–1400) **V** 400; **VI** 271

Erging *see* Archenfield

Eric, duke of Pomerania **VI** 69

Eric, king of Norway **IV** 599, 606; marries Isabel Bruce 611; his treaty with Philip IV of France and understanding with the Scots (1295) 613

Eric, king of Norway, Sweden and Denmark **VI** 69, 70, 326

Eric IX, king of Sweden **III** 230

Eric, prince of Sweden **VIII** 49

Eric Bloodaxe, king of Norway **II** 360; king of York 360–2; death 362

Eric of Hlathir, Norway, joins Cnut **II** 387, 402; earl of Northumbria 390, 398, 418–19

Erle, Sir W. **XIV** 131, 132

Ermenfrid, bishop of Sion **II** 659, 662; penitential canons 661–2

Ermentrude, wife of Fulk V, count of Anjou **III** 113, 343

Ermine Street **III** 78

Ernest Augustus, elector of Hanover (d. 1698), father of George I **XI** 11

Ernost, bishop of Rochester **II** 649

erotic verse **VIII** 289

Erpingham, Sir Thomas, king's chamberlain **VI** 1, 18, 19, 31, 390; Henry IV's administration 429

Erse language **VIII** 463, 492

Erskine, John, 1st earl of Mar **VIII** 144, 161, 373

Erskine, John, 2nd earl of Mar **VIII** 361

Erskine, John, 6th or 11th earl of Mar (1675–1732) **XI** 157–162, 163, 185

Erskine, Thomas (1750–1823), 1st Baron **XII** 57, 409, 499; biography 409; lord chancellor (1806–7) 435, 582

Escanceaster *see* Exeter (Devon)

Esce *see* Exe, river

escheats and escheators **IV** 63–47; **V** 77, 154, 169

Escombe (Co. Durham), church **II** 151

Escudo **VIII** 417

Esher (Surrey) **VII** 330

Esher, 2nd Viscount **XIV** 362, 371, 525

Esingwold, Robert, York court proctor **VI** 62

Esk, river **VII** 405, 483

Eskdale (Cumbria) **VI** 585; raid (1504) **VII** 163

Esnecca **III** 434

Espagne, Jean d', French commander **VI** 55

España, General Don Carlos d' **XII** 558

Espléchin, truce of **V** 130, 165

Esquerdes, seigneur d' *see* Crève-coeur, Philippe de
Esquiline Hill, treasurer **Ia** 431
Essays and Reviews **XIII** 575–6
Essé, André de Montalenbert, sieur d' **VII** 485
Essen, Wood refuses to bomb **XV** 459
Essex **Ia** 12, 41, 43, 47, 84; Bartlow Hills 605; **Ib** 93, 130, 140; *-ingas* names 37–41; Romano-Saxon pottery 90–1 [fig. 7(d, e)]; Saxon naming 106; early Saxon settlement 107; cultural assimilation in 5th cent. 111, 113; **II** 428, 591, 633; forest **III** 30; marsh 53, 146, 393, 469; **V** 256, 316, 329, 358, 476; Hereford entrusted with defence 24; Rising (1381) 204, 413, 415, 419, 422; woodlands 208, 312, 322; rebels 338; labour conditions 339–40; Sir John Hawkwood 346; peasants against tax-collectors 407; Wat Tyler leads attack on London 408; **VI** 7, 26; Ralph Neville's lands 321, 323; **VII** 504; **IX** 83, 131, 154, 280; riots **X** 258; population **XV** 167
Essex, countess of *see* Howard
Essex, earl of **III** 157; *see also* Bohun, Humphrey de; Bourchier; Capel, Arthur; Capel, William; Cromwell, Thomas; Devereux, Robert; Devereux, Walter; Fitz Peter, Geoffrey; Geoffrey de Mandeville I; Geoffrey de Mandeville II; Geoffrey de Mandeville III; Henry, Viscount Bourchier; Thomas of Woodstock; William de Mandeville
Essex, Henry of, constable **III** 292, 326
Essex, kingdom **II** 36, 53, 281; genealogy of royal house 53; pagan reaction 113; conversion 121; later kings names 204; relations with Offa 210; submission to Egbert 231, 236
Essoins **III** 400, 407
estates, private **Ia** 439–40, 599–600, 628–9; church 341–2, 600, 730; Gaul 435; Britain 457, 738; administration 530, 625; economic importance 624–5; imperial *see* imperial estates; *see also* landowners; villas
Estcourt, John, Chichele's commissary-general **VI** 287
Este family **VI** 126
Estella, castle in Navarre **IV** 238, 239, 241
Estonia (Esthonia), accepts Soviet control **XV** 466
Estoutville, Lord, prisoner **VI** 223
Estrada, Ferdinand, duke of: Spanish ambassador **VII** 174, 176
Estremadura **XII** 488
Estrete, John **VII** 72
Estrith, daughter of King Swein **II** 382
Esturmy, Thomas **III** 23
Etal **VII** 280, 281
Étampes (Seine-et-Oise) **VI** 111, 239
Étampes, Theobald of **III** 232, 237
Étaples (Pas-de-Calais) **VI** 152; treaty (1492) **VII** 108–9, 110, 112, 115, 136; Perkin Warbeck 121; treaty renewed (1498) 149, 152; Henry's pension 284
Etherege, George, classical scholar **VII** 571
Eton College **V** 500; King's College (Cambridge) link **VI** 670; **VII** 246, 571, 576, 577, 588; **X** 415; **XII** 39; **XV** 171, 271
Étretat (Seine-Inf.) **VI** 158
Etsi de statu, papal bull **IV** 674, 677
Ettrick forest, William Wallace established (1297) **IV** 684, 686, 690
Etty, William **XIII** 588, 590; biography 590

cese 277, 332; **VI** 569; 'fellowship' 388; St James estate 675; **VII** 35, 119, 232, 476, 489; Perkin War- beck 145–6; **IX** 131; bombed **XV** 553; **X** 53; newspaper 356

Exeter, Anne, duchess of *see* Anne, duchess of Exeter

Exeter, bishops of **III** 13; *see also* Bartholomew; Brantingham; Courtenay, Peter; Coverdale, Miles; Fox, Richard; Grandisson; Leofric; Neville, George; Osbern; Stafford, Edmund; Stapledon; Warelwast

Exeter, duchess of, Richard III's sister **VI** 631

Exeter, dukes of *see* Holand, Henry; Holland, John; Percy, Thomas

Exeter, Gertrude, marchioness of **VII** 362, 414, 529

Exeter, marquess of *see* Courtenay

Exeter, marquis of *see* Percy, Thomas

Exeter Book **II** 199, 443, 677

Exhibition, Great (1851) **XIII** 49, 164, 295, 500, 570; hall 579; excursions 624

Exhortation to Her Majesty for Establishing the Succession, A Pithy **VIII** 226

Exmoor **Ia** 4; **III** 30

Exmouth **III** 96

Exning, villa **Ia** 604

Exon Domesday **II** 644, 654

Explanatio **VIII** 174

Explanation, Act of (1665) **X** 297

exploration in South Pacific **XII** 17

exploratores **Ia** 249

exports **X** 48, 235, 252, 265, 299–301; **XIV** 110; graphs **XV** xxi–xxii; yield from 42; collapse after boom 145; permanent decline of old staples 182–3; gold standard 223; demand not expanding 238; do not reach pre- war figure 249; effect of Depres- sion 284; Protection expected to increase 322; do not increase 336; effect of tariffs 339; buy more 343; restricted by lend-lease 513; reduced after war 566, 599

Exsupereus **Ia** 688

extenta, survey of Champagne (1276–8), possible English in- fluence **IV** 241

Exuperantius **Ia** 448, 476

Eye (Suffolk), castle **II** 639; priory **V** 294

Eye, honour **III** 132, 165, 203, 208, 368; awarded to duke of Brabant 376–7, 453

Eyemouth **VIII** 47

Eynesford, William of **III** 202

Eynsham (Egonesham) (Oxon.) **Ib** 165–6; appendix II; map 3 xxxi; **II** 27, 732; abbey 396, 455, 458, 551; Benedictine abbey **VI** 302, 672

Eynsham, abbot of *see* Æfric

Eyre **III** 399–401

eyre, articles of the **III** 390, 399, 400, 413; general **V** 168–9, 175, 199, 201

Eyton, Fulk **VI** 479

Eyvill, John d' **IV** 208, 213–15

Ezinge **Ib** map 5 68

F

faber **Ib** 125–6; *see also* Faversham
Faber, Frederick William **XIII** 114
Fabian Society **XIV** 100, 222, 296
Fabier, Lodovico, Venetian ambassador (1528–31) **VII** 218, 301
Fabius Rusticus **Ia** 538
Fabyan, Thomas **VII** 580
factories: development **XII** 28–32, 333, 510, 513, 524; effect of mechanization 529–31; canteens **XV** 37; inspectors 491
Factory Acts: poor law apprentices (1802) **XIII** 12, 13; child labour limited to twelve hours (1819) 13; Hobhouse's bill (1831) 148; Ashley and Sadler (1833) 151–2; Mines Act (1842) 152–3; textile industry (1844) 153–5; calico-printing (1845) 154; ten hours' day (1847) 154–5; coal mines inspection act (1850) 155–6; coal mines (1860, 1862 and 1872) 156; protected industries (1860 and 1861) 610; revised definition of factory and workshop (1864, 1867) 611; **XV** 36, 406
Faerie Queene **VIII** 290, 291–2, 445
Fagal, Gaspar **X** 131
Fagius, Paul **VII** 516, 553, 574
fair pleading **IV** 217
Fairfax, Ferdinand, Lord **IX** 133
Fairfax, Guy, of Steeton (Yorks.) **VI** 62
Fairfax, Robert **VII** 588
Fairfax, Sir Thomas **IX** 133, 136–7, 140–1, 148–9, 155
Fairfeld **Ib** map 5 68
Fairfield, John, Brecon receiver **VI** 54
Fairford (Glos.) **Ib** 139, 140, circular brooches 60 [fig. 2 (g, h)]; map 3 xxxi **VI** 367, 647
fairs **Ia** 281
Fakenham (Norfolk) **V** 9

Falaise (Calvados) **III** 119, 121, 148, 336; treaty 277–8, 351; Arthur imprisoned at 382; capitulation 384; **VI** 172, 173; castle 327; Germans encircled **XV** 582
falconry **VIII** 276, 277
Falkirk **II** 614; battle (1298) **IV** 433, 689–90, 694, 695; **V** 35, 36
Falkland (Scotland) **VII** 406
Falkland, Viscount *see* Cary
Falkland Islands **XII** 154; battle (1914) **XV** 14, 462
Falmouth **VII** 186
Falside Bray **VII** 483
family (*familia*) **Ia** 53–4, 81; soldiers' families 277, 511; *lares and penates* 408, 685, 708; survival of families 436; Lullingstone, busts 601; death 694, 697–9; birth 696; importance in Roman religion 707–9; 'royal duties' (Latin quote) **IV** 151; *see also* imperial family
Family Compacts *see under* Bourbon Powers
family land **II** 318
famine **Ia** 234; (1315–17) **V** 43, 49–50, 329
Fane, John, 10th earl of Westmorland (1759–1841): lord-lieutenant of Ireland **XII** 392–4; lord privy seal (1798–1806, 1807) 401, 408, 580, 581, 582, 583; biography 408
Fane Fragment (Lords Journals) **VI** 541–2
Fanhope, John, Lord *see* Cornwall, Sir John
Fantosme, Jordan **III** 38, 250, 277
fanum **Ia** 673; *see also* sanctuaries; shrines
Faques, William **VII** 578
Far East: Australia and New Zealand anxious over **XV** 485; neg-

lected for sake of Mediterranean 520–1; alarm 531–2; war 537, 538; disasters 540, 541, 544; British participate in war 586; Stalin offers aid 590

Faraday, Michael (1791–1867) **XI** 384; **XIII** 501, 568, 569; biography 565

Faremoutiers-en-Brie, monastery **II** 162

Farinelli, Carlo (1705–82), singer **XI** 416

Faringdon (Berks.) **III** 148

Faringdon, Thomas **V** 411

Farinmail, British king **Ib** 168, appendix II; **II** 4, 29

Farley, John, Oxford University registrar **VI** 679; **VII** 236

farm, borough **III** definition 67; Oxford 65; London and Middlesex 69, 70, 71; fee-farm, definition 71; county 415, 417, 421; sheriff's **IV** 62–3

farming *see* agriculture; arable; stock-raising

farms: buildings **Ia** 235, 595, 609–10; siting 586–8, 602–7, 612–14; Pliny's farms 601; ownership 602–4; farmyard burial 696; *see also* agriculture; villas

Farnaby, Giles **IX** 387

Farndon (Cheshire) **II** 339

Farne *see* Farne Island

Farne Island **II** 126

Farnese, Alessandro *see* Paul III, Pope

Farnése, Alexander, duke of Parma **VIII** 344–5, 383; governor of Netherlands 351; Portuguese succession, claimant 352; defeats Anjou 355–7; Netherlands campaign 364; role in armada campaign 392, 394–401; supports Catholic League 414–15

Farney, Master Richard **VI** 276

Farnham (Fearnhamm) (Surrey): pottery **Ia** 645, 646; **II** 70, 102, 147, 266, 303; manor 483;

V 332, 334

Farnley Wood **X** 22

Faro **VIII** 419

Farquhar, George **X** 370

Farthington **VIII** 270

Fasciculus de superioritate maris **IV** 655–6

fascism: demonstrations against **XV** 350; divides parties 374; Spanish Civil War 395; Edward VIII 401; Labour against 418–19; war a crusade against 453, 458; Churchill not fighting war against 560

Fashoda incident **XIV** 244–5

fast days **IX** 308

Fastolf, Sir John **VI** 244, 247, 263, 330, 342; Normandy raiding (Nov. 1415) 157; and Paston 344–5; cloth industry 356; pretended heir 449; grand jury panel 462; charged with diminishing English garrisons in France 498; 'traitor' 498; title deeds investigated 600

Fastolf, Thomas **VI** 345

Fauconberg, Earl *see* Bellasis

Fauconberg, Eustace de, treasurer, later bishop of London (1221–28) **IV** 16

Fauconberg, Joan **VI** 324

Fauconberg, John of **V** 61

Fauconberg, Sir John **VI** 59; death 324

Fauconberg, lordship **VI** 8, 323–4

Fauconberg, Sir Thomas, Lord **VI** 324, 464

Faughart, battle at hill of **V** 44

Faulkner, George (?1699–1775), bookseller **XI** 306

Faulkner's Journal **XI** 306

Fauquembergue, Clément de, *greffieur* of *parlement* **VI** 186

Fauroux, Marie **II** 651

Faustina the Elder, Empress **Ia** 192

Faustus, Doctor **VIII** 297, 308

fautores of Simon de Montfort: treatment **IV** 204; *see also* Dictum of Kenilworth

Fava, Lewis de la **VII** 214

Favent, Thomas, on favourites of Richard II **V** 447; on appeal of Gloucester (1388) 455; on proceedings against Brembre 457; on Burley 458

Faversham (Kent): mausoleum **Ia** 731; **Ib** 124–5; Jutish pottery 67 [fig. 4(h)]; quoit brooch style 118 [fig. 10(b)] map 5 68; council **II** 349; priory **III** 185

Faversham, Eustace of, chaplain and biographer of St Edmund **IV** 57

Favianae **Ia** 467

Favonius Facilis, M., tombstone **Ia** 94, 699–700

Fawcett, Prof. Henry **XIV** 10, 12, 24; biography 66

Fawcett, 'Mr Attorney' (b. ?1712) **XI** 37; recorder of Newcastle 341

Fawdon (Northumb.) **VI** 377

Fawkes, Guy **IX** 8

Fearndun *see* Farndon (Cheshire)

Fearnhamm *see* Farnham (Surrey)

feather beds **VIII** 272

Feathers Tavern petition **XII** 155, 228

Featherstone, Richard **VII** 427

Fécamp (Seine-Inf.) **III** 120, 370, 459; abbey 107, 185; **VI** 152, 158

Feckenham (Worcs.), royal manor **IV** 512, 706

Feckenham, John de (1518?–85), dean of St Paul's **VII** 551

Feddersen Wierde **Ib** xxi, 51–2, 72; map 1 xxix

federation **X** 337

Federigo II, duke of Mantua **VII** 340

Federigo, king of Naples (1496–1501) **VII** 152; surrenders to France (1501) 153

fee system **XII** 61, 260, 284

Felix, biographer of St Guthlac **II** 178, 203, 210

Felix, bishop of East Anglia **II** 116–17, 119, 125

felix **Ia** 23

Felixstowe **Ib** 89

Fell, Samuel **IX** 357

Felmingham (Norfolk), Abraham of **III** 337

Felmingham (Norfolk), Isaac of **III** 337

felony, those charged invited to volunteer in Gascony (1294) and Scotland (1296) **IV** 648

Felton, John **VIII** 167; kills Buckingham **IX** 43, 63

Felton, Sir Thomas **V** 253

Feltwell, villa **Ia** 604

Fen Causeway **Ia** 101, 258

fencibles **XII** 365

fencing, schools **VIII** 278

Fendoch, fort **Ia** 149, 150

Fénelon, La Mothe **VIII** 132, 134, 144, 146; Huguenot flight to England 159–61

Fenhouse Farm, Brandon, villa **Ia** 607

Fenians and Fenianism **XIV** 56, 57, 75, 451; *see also* Ireland

Fenn, Thomas **XII** 54

fens (Fen Edge, Fenland) **Ia** 41, 102; Iron age 6, 189; Roman development 6; flooding and drainage 6, 243, 258, 267–9, 276 — canals 564 — burials 696; Hockwold treasure 101; exploitation 189–90, 237–8, 547–8, 644; pottery industries 237, 643; agricultural production 238, 619–20; settlement patterns 557, 602–7, 610; coastlines 558–9; Mildenhall treasure 607; amphora stamp 653; Church estate? 730; **IX** 281–2; *see also* imperial estates

Fenwick, Sir John **X** 185; executed (1697) for plotting to assassinate William III **XI** 183

feorm see food-rent

Feppingas **II** 44, 297

Ferdinand, Archduke (afterwards Emperor Ferdinand I 1556–64) **VII** 535

Finch, Daniel (*cont.*)
boundary of Church of England
154; secretary of state 181, 222,
224; difficult to work with 182;
joins the Whigs 232; Spanish
treaty 247; **XI** 154, 164
Finch, Heneage, 1st earl of Nottingham (1621–82), lord chancellor
XI 65
Finch, Sir John (created Lord) **IX**
92
Finchale (Co. Durham) **III** 94, 256
Finchale Priory **V** 372
fine art **VIII** 302–6
Finedon (Northants) **III** 485; **IV**
704
fines *see* finance and taxation
Fingreth-in-Blackmore (Essex) **V**
332, 333
Finistere, Cape *see* Cape Finistere
Finland **III** 230; Soviet Russia
invades **XV** 468; Anglo-French
plan to aid 468, 469; makes peace
469
Finn, Frisian king **II** 193
Finnegan's Wake **XV** 179
Finnsburh fragment **Ib** 55
Firbank, Ronald **XV** 312, 606
fire brigade **Ia** 344; metropolitan
XIII 467
fire damage **Ia** 312–13; London 119,
186; Verulamium 119, 232–3;
bath-houses 223, 686; S. coast
282; towns 658
Fire of London **X** 66
fire-ships *see* armada
fireworks **XII** 339
firma unius noctis **II** 483
The First Hundred Thousand **XV** 52
First International **XIII** 612
fiscal preference **XIV** 241–2, 373–6,
405–6, 426
fish **Ia** 620
Fish, Simon **V** 295; **VII** 301, 346,
372, 456; *Supplication for the Beg-
gars* 344
fish sauce **Ia** 652
Fishacre, Richard **VI** 680

Fishbourne: military structures **Ia**
91, 160; palace? 161–2, 597,
749–52; fire 282; courtyard 609
Fisher, Admiral Lord: biography
XV 6; battle of Falkland Islands
14; Dardanelles 23–4; resigns 30
Fisher, H. A. L. **XV** 184, 568
Fisher, John, bishop of Rochester
(1504–35) **VII** 251, 256, 257,
357; opposes 'divorce' 326–8;
tried and beheaded (1535) 362–
3, 423; aids St John's College 375, 570; execution justified
379; Cranmer intercedes for 552;
Cambridge scholarship 571, 572;
Holbein portrait 600
Fisher, John A., afterwards Lord
XIV 123, 362; co-operation with
Lord Cawdor 363–5; fleet redis-
tribution 363, 522–3; Dread-
nought policy 364, 522–3; unwise
about general staff 523–4; oil-fuel
524
Fisher, Sir Warren **XV** 174
fishing industry **IX** 51, 216–17, 325,
338–9; **X** 301, 317
fishponds **Ia** 614; private **IV** 69,
367
Fiskerton (Lincs.) **III** 391
Fitch, Ralph **VIII** 242
Fitton, Sir Edward **VIII** 472
Fitz Ailwin, Henry, mayor of Lon-
don **III** 64, 71
Fitz Audlin, William **III** 311
Fitz Bernard, John, son of Eugenia
Picot **III** 23
Fitz Bernard, Thomas **III** 23, 390
Fitz Brien, Robert **III** 402
Fitz Count, Brian **III** 133, 139, 144,
159
Fitz Duncan, William **III** 271
Fitz Geoffrey, John **IV** 130, 173–4
Fitz Gerald, house **III** 288
Fitz Gerald, Maurice **III** 294, 305,
313
Fitz Gilbert, John **III** 15
Fitz Gilbert, Richard *see* Clare,
Richard Fitz Gilbert, lord of

Fitzgerald, James (Fitzmaurice) (*cont.*)
  125, 128, 132; **VIII** 177, 352, 476, 478, 479; 'sugane' earl of Desmond 485
Fitzgerald, James, 1st duke of Leinster and 20th earl of Kildare (1722–73) **XI** 303
Fitzgerald, Maurice, 9th earl of Desmond (d. 1520) **VII** 71, 72, 80, 125, 128; Perkin Warbeck 119, 120, 132, 138
Fitzgerald, Maurice, 7th earl of Kildare (1342–90) **V** 229, 231
Fitzgerald, Maurice, justiciar of Ireland **IV** 58
Fitzgerald, Thomas, chancellor of Ireland, killed at Stoke (1487) **VII** 72, 74
Fitzgerald, Lord Thomas, 10th earl of Kildare, rebellion **VII** 364–5
Fitzgerald, Thomas Fitzthomas, 11th earl of Desmond (d. 1534) **VII** 364
Fitzgerald, W. Vesey **XIII** 76–7, 343
Fitzgibbon, John (1749–1802), earl of Clare **XII** 393; Irish chancellor 393–5, 401
Fitzgibbon, Maurice, archbishop of Cashel **VIII** 476, 477
Fitzharris, Edward **X** 95
FitzHerbert, John, king's remembrancer (1485) **VI** 605; **VII** 56
Fitzherbert, Master **VII** 451, 456
FitzHugh, Henry, lord of Ravensworth, Henry V's chamberlain **VI** 196, 211, 212, 218, 326; royal service 327–8, 433; son-in-law 417; grandson Henry 523
FitzHugh, William **VI** 323, 328
Fitz-James, James, duke of Berwick (1670–1734) **X** 209, 211, 213, 215, 243; **XI** 153, 154, 158, 160
Fitzjames, Richard, bishop of London (1497–1522) **VII** 291
Fitzmaurice, Edmond, 8th Lord Kerry and Lixnaw **VII** 80

FitzMaurice, Gerald, earl of Desmond (1359–98) **V** 232, 233
Fitzmaurices, barony in Kerry **IV** 564
FitzNicholas, Ralph **IV** 95
FitzOtto, Hugh **IV** 323
Fitzpatrick, Barnaby **VII** 479
Fitzpatrick, Richard (1747–1813), secretary at war (1783) **XII** 579
FitzPeter, Geoffrey **IV** 23
Fitzralph, Richard, archbishop of Armagh (1348–60) **V** 504, 511; **VI** 680
FitzRandolph, Sir John, of Spennithorne **VI** 59
Fitzroy, Augustus Henry, 3rd duke of Grafton (1735–1811): secretary of state (1765–6) **XII** 111, 114–16, 575; refusal to go bail for Wilkes 100; resignation 117, 146, 148, 203; first lord of Treasury (1766–70) 121, 125, 128, 130, 134–8, 143–6, 149, 193, 575; on India 125, 162, 165; lord privy seal (1771–5) 151, 575; lord privy seal (1782–3) 243, 578, 579
Fitzroy, Charles, 2nd duke of Grafton (1683–1757) **XI** 34; lord lieutenant of Ireland 292, 301
Fitzroy, Henry, 1st duke of Grafton **X** 139, 141
Fitzroy, Henry, duke of Richmond, natural son of Henry VIII (1519–36) **VII** 297, 299, 364, 420; potential successor to throne 325; death 380; lieutenant general north of the Trent 385–6; lord admiral (1525) 650; lord lieutenant in Ireland (1529) 651
Fitzsimons, Walter, archbishop of Dublin (d. 1511) 133; lord deputy of Ireland (1492) 127, 651
Fitzthedmar, Arnold **III** 89–90
FitzThomas, Maurice, earl of Desmond (1329–56) **V** 229, 231
FitzThomas, Thomas, mayor of London **IV** 186
Fitzwalter, John, Lord **VI** 558

214

FitzWalter, Robert **IV** 8, 11

Fitzwalter, Walter, Lord **VI** 7, 8, 68

Fitzwarren, Lord *see* Bourchier, Fulk

Fitzwater (Fitzwalter), Lord *see* Radcliffe, John

Fitzwilliam, 2nd earl **XIII** 65; *see also* Wentworth, William

Fitzwilliam, Sir Thomas, speaker of the House of Commons (1489) **VII** 652

Fitzwilliam, Sir William, 1st earl of Southampton (1537): comptroller of the household (1526) 650; lord admiral (1536) 650; treasurer of the household (1537) 650; keeper of the privy seal (June 1540) 647

Fitzwilliam family **XII** 271

Fiume (Rijeka, Yugoslavia): not promised to Italy **XV** 50; dispute at peace conference 132, 135, 161-2

Five Boroughs **II** 358, 385, 388-9, 504-5, 508; assembly 510-12

Five Mile Act **X** 22, 268

Flacius, Matthias, commonly called Illyricus (d. 1566) **VII** 33

Flamank, Thomas, lawyer **VII** 141, 142, 143

Flambard, Rannulf, bishop of Durham **III** 104; granted protection in his forests 34; king's agent 106, 114, 170-1; imprisonment and escape 114, 115; church building 260

Flamborough Head **Ib** 186-7; map 4 xxxii

Flamsteed, John (1646-1719), astronomer **XI** 380

Flanders **Ia** 283; **II** 420, 422, 428, 540; influence on urban development **III** 73; trade with 81, 84, 90-1, 376; treaty with 118; Henry I at war with 124; William Clito put forward as count of 127-8; takes part in Portuguese crusade 149; John subsidizes knights of 381, 471; money lenders of, used

by Richard I and John 423; John forms alliance with 454-5, 464; attacked by Philip Augustus 455, 459-61; political crisis (1122) **IV** 132; Henry III and 621; Hansa in London 621; break with Edward I and English wool embargo (1270-8) 621-3, 645; wool exports 637; Philip IV's hold 648, 659, 669; Edward I (1297) *see* Edward I; French invasion and defeat at Courtrai (1302) 653, 669, 697; later relations with France 669; **V** 22, 39, 205, 235; Edward III's negotiations 119-20; alliance 130, 132; loss of English control 137, 143, 146, 355; Edward's influence 147-8; military activity 149; trade 350, 352-3, 364, 366, 367; crusade of bishop of Norwich 430-3; **VI** 70, 135-40, 180, 351, 366; 'Four Members' 72-3; truce 137; Burgundian 348; civil war (1379) 352; Burgundian treaty 553; **VII** 85, 123, 166, 288, 559; cloth trade 182, 186; galleys 223, 471, 475; treaty of Madrid 316; English wool exports 449; Merchant Adventurers 473; music 588; artists 598; French wars **X** 167, 168; British Expeditionary Force **XV** 11; offensive (1917) 86-7, 515; *see also* Arnulf; Baldwin II, V, VI; Robert

Flanders, countess of **III** 356; *see also* Margaret

Flanders, counts of **III** 123, 433; *see also* Baldwin VII; Baldwin IX; Charles the Good; Dampierre, Guy; Ferrand; Matthew; Philip of Alsace; Robert II; Thierry of Alsace

Flanders, Philippe of, daughter of Count Guy **IV** 659

Flatman, Thomas **X** 400

Flavians **Ia** 130-68; supporters 131, 132-4; opposition 164, 662, 709;

Flavians (*cont.*)
  town development 156–62, 660;
  Romanization 156–63, 185; town
  defences 162–3, 262; Bath 686;
  London 162, 517, 530; Wroxeter
  584; Fenland settlement 189; con-
  trol of mining 635; military text-
  books 319
Flavius Antigonus Papias **Ia** 700
Flavius Arbogastes *see* Arbogastes
Flavius Constantius *see* Constantius
  III
Flavius Longinus, T. **Ia** 510–1
Flavius Martinus **Ia** 345, 358
Flavius Sabinus **Ia** 73, 84
Flavius Sanctus **Ia** 346–7
Flavius Senilis, T. **Ia** 384
Flavius Stilicho *see* Stilicho
Flavius Valerius Severus, Emperor
  Ia 316, 322, 324
Flavius Virilis, T. **Ia** 513
flax **IX** 286
Flaxman, John (1755–1828) **XI** 414;
  XIII 587
Fleet marriages **XI** 136–7
Fleet prison **III** 338; **IV** 356, 364,
  366; **IX** 135, 309
Fleet Street **VIII** 275; *see also* Lon-
  don, boroughs and place-names
fleets: Agricola **Ia** 146, 149;
  Carausius and Constantius 289,
  305–7, 319; use of barbarians
  310–11; against pirates 320–1;
  Julian's grain fleet 359–60;
  Theodosius 382–4; Maximus and
  Theorodius the Great 403–4; no
  navy in N. Sea 455; built by
  Alfred **II** 263–4; assembled by
  Athelstan 347; by Edgar 369;
  built by Æthelred II 382; standing, of Cnut 399, 413; assembled
  by Edward the Confessor 429;
  and closed narrow seas to Flemish ships 429; used against raiders
  from Ireland 430; dispersed by
  Edward the Confessor 431;
  assembled against Earl Godwin
  566; assembled (1066) 581;

assembled by Harold II 587–8;
  IX 302–3, Dutch and English **X**
  64–5, 78, 80–1, 164, 218; French
  81, 165; *see also classis Britannica;
  classis Germanica;* ships
Fleetwood, Charles **IX** 163, 183,
  186, 260; Wallingford House
  Party 237–8; effects end of pro-
  tectorate 241; commander-in-
  chief 244, 247–8; submission of
  army 252; landowner 273
Fleetwood, William, Bishop **X** 381
Fleetwood, Sir William, London
  recorder **VI** 265
Fleming, Nicholas le **V** 368
Fleming, Richard, bishop of Lincoln
  VI 97, 194, 234–5, 299, 434;
  translation to York 269; Lincoln
  College foundation 672
Fleming, Sir Thomas **IX** 11
Flemings: mercenaries **III** 59, 135,
  277, 363; attack England for the
  sake of wool 84, 274, 335;
  Stephen's reliance upon 140, 154;
  colonize Pembrokeshire 290, 291,
  322; Welsh invasion 293; expelled
  321–2; settlement in England
  336; battle of Bouvines 467; **VI**
  223; raiding (1404) 73; in Eng-
  land **VIII** 121
Flemish weavers **V** 120, 367–8
Fleta **IV** 356, 521
Fletcher, Andrew, of Saltoun **X** 286
Fletcher, Giles, the elder **VIII** 319
Fletcher, Giles, younger brother of
  Phineas **VIII** 302; **IX** 400
Fletcher, John, cousin of Phineas
  and collaborator with Francis
  Beaumont **VIII** 301; **IX** 392–5
Fletcher, Revd John William of
  Madeley (1729–85) **XI** 88
Fletcher, Phineas, elder son of Giles
  VIII 302; **IX** 400
Fletcher, Richard, bishop of Bristol
  and London, father of John **VIII**
  190
Fleurus **X** 169; battle (1794) **XII**
  369

Fleury, André Hercule de (1653–1743), Cardinal **XI** 200, 202, 206, 232, 237

Fleury, Hugh of **III** 179

Fleury, monastery of **II** 447–50, 452, 462

Flint **III** 285; royal headquarters (1277) **IV** 412; new town 432; county 435; **VI** 14, 38; lordship 78

Flint Castle **IV** 412, 430–2; **V** 493

Flintshire **Ia** 631

Flitcroft, Henry (1697–1769), architect **XI** 404

Flodden: battle (1513) **VII** 161, 268, 312, 323, 389; campaign 279–83

Flood, Henry (1732–91) **XII** 223, 229, 389

flooding **Ia** 6, 243, 258, 267–9, 276; sea level 555–7; canals 564; burial 696

Flore, Roger, steward **VI** 413; Speaker (1422) 413

Florence: battle near **Ia** 426; city: life reflected in a lawsuit **IV** 626; merchants 641; **V** 346, 530; **VI** 348; **VII** 223, 242, 251, 306, 351; treaty (1490) 102; politics of Italy 112–13; occupied by French (1494) 114; League of Cognac (1526) 316; French aid 340; *see also* Bardi; Frescobaldi; Pegolotti

Florence, count of Holland: claimant of kingdom of Scotland **IV** 606; compact with Robert Bruce 611; pensioner of Edward I and Philip IV 659, 664; murdered (1296) 664

Florence, duke of **VIII** 375

Florence, dukedom **VIII** 133

Florentines, in Southampton **VI** 353, 354

Florentius **Ia** 373

Flores, Island **VIII** 412, 413

Florida **VIII** 369; **XI** 309, 372; boundaries 209

Florus **Ia** 677

Flower, Bernard **VII** 591

Flowerdew, Edward **VII** 490

Floyer, Charles, governor of Fort St George (*c.*1750) **XI** 327

Flushing **VIII** 156, 338–9, 347, 355, 365; **IX** 60

flying bombs **XV** 578, 583–4

Flying Fortresses **XV** 570

flying shuttle **XII** 28, 513

Fobbing (Essex) **V** 407

Foch, F.: becomes Allied commander **XV** 102; orders offensive 108–9; armistice 111–13; Churchill on 480; Weygand and 485

Foe, James **X** 363

foederati: **Ia** 386–7, 406, 417–18, 440, 446; interventions 448; commanders 467; settlements 477, 484; British as *foederati* 491–3; **Ib** 8, 14–15, 79, 82, 156; Thanet 123; land tenure 124

foedus **Ib** 14, 110

Fogge, Sir John, of Ashford (Kent) **VI** 599, 631; Gloucester reconciliation 621

Foggia, Charles of Anjou dies at **IV** 253

Foglia (Italy), alum **VI** 353

Fog's Weekly Journal **XI** 205

Foilan, Irish ascetic in East Anglia **II** 117

Foix **V** 122; county **VI** 175

Foix, count of **VI** 249

Foix, Gaston de **VII** 274; *see also* Gaston II, count of Foix

Foix, Germaine de, betrothed to Ferdinand **VII** 154, 177

Foix, Jean de, earl of Kendal **VI** 519, 520, 532

Foix, Paul de **VIII** 87, 152

Folcanstan *see* Folkestone (Kent)

folcgemot **II** 298; *see also* London

folcriht **II** 310

Foley's ironworks, Stourbridge, Worcestershire **XI** 117

Foliot, Gilbert, bishop of Hereford and afterwards of London: approves of John of Crema **III** 183, 322; election to Hereford

Foliot, Gilbert (*cont.*)
192; opposes Becket 197, 200, 203, 208; translated to London 203; early career 203–4; excommunicated 212; suspended 214
Folkestone (Kent): villa **Ia** 128; **II** 567; **V** 128; mutiny **XV** 138
folkland **II** 309–12
Folville family **V** 204–5, 207
Fonaby **Ib** 180; map 4 xxxii
Fondi **VII** 341
Fonnereau, Thomas, MP **XII** 54
Fontainebleau decree (1812) **XII** 468
fontana **Ib** 32–3
Fontevrault **III** 229, 346, 425; order of 188; prioress and convent **IV** 268; Isabella of Angoulême's last years 103; Henry III (1254) 119; Edward I (1286) 256
Fontmell (Dorset) **II** 65
fonts? **Ia** 729–30
food **VIII** 273
Food, Ministry of: created in First World War **XV** 76; final profit 121; ended 130; created in Second World War 456; Colwyn Bay 457; introduces rationing 463–4; threatens to raise prices 466; adopts points 510; exaggerates needs 512, 546; regional government 569
food policy committee **XV** 482
Food Production, Department of **XV** 76, 77
food-rent 278–9, 287–9, 294, 297–8, 472; folkland 311; *firma unius noctis* 483
football **IX** 311; development **XIV** 164–5; **XV** 181, 245, 313
Foote, Samuel (1720–77), actor **XI** 304; **XII** 350
Forbes, Duncan, of Culloden (1685–1747) **XI** 253, 255, 273, 278, 281
Forbes, John (1710–59), General **XI** 321, 362
Forcalquier, county **IV** 112, 246,

247; Garsenda of and her daughter, mother of Gaston of Béarn 112
Ford **VII** 279
Ford, John **IX** 392
Forde, Francis (d. 1770), Colonel **XI** 218, 329, 330
Forden Gaer, fort **Ia** 150
Fordham, John, bishop of Durham (1382–8), of Ely (1388–1425), keeper of the privy seal (1377–81), treasurer (1386) **V** 410, 443, 445, 449
Fordun **III** 276
Fordun (Kincardinesh) **II** 342
Fordwic *see* Fordwich (Kent)
Fordwich (Kent) **II** 431
Fordyce, Alexander (d. 1789), banker **XII** 62, 167
foreign affairs: basic considerations of British relations with European powers **XII** 71–88, 107–9, 154, 210–19, 225 — hostility 240 — America 254–7 — United Provinces 293–9; war with France 363–74, 377–87, 403, 451–89, 493–7, 555–70 — emphasizes Irish problem 387 — fall of Pitt 403 — Addington hopes for peace talks 406 — Britain restores conquests 409–13 — French mismanagement 421–34 — Fox attempts to end hostilities 437 — England in state of blockade 443
foreign and domestic policy (1661–8) **X** 55–74; (1668–78) 75–91
foreign enlistment act (1819) **XIII** 231, 232, 310
foreign investments: loss and gain in First World War **XV** 42, 123; show surplus 249; hit by Depression 287; reduced 343; sold in Second World War 599
Foreign Office and diplomatic service (1815) **XIII** 196–7
forest, law of: introduced into Eng-

land **II** 683–4; **III** 29–30, 102, 339, 420, 456; **V** 17, 24, 207–9; **IX** 83, 103

Forest of Dean, iron **Ia** 637–8

forestry **Ia** 631

Forestry Commission **XV** 84

forests **Ia** 5, 83, 141, 554–6, 560–1; palaeobotany 571; greater cover 613; forest sanctuaries 672–3; **II** 284–6, 683–4; **III** 29–35; charter of the 29, 33, 475; beasts 30–1; officers 32; eyre 32–4, 338–9; royal **IV** 767–8; charter (1217) 15, 40; disputes about perambulation 40, 697, 699, 700–3; hunting tours (1290) 512–13; confirmations (1297–1300) 683, 700; Edward I's inquiries into malpractices 698, 699, 702, 703; wardens **V** 22; keepers 153, 226

Forêt de Lyons **III** 129

form of government (June 1264) **IV** 191–4, 198; *see also* Canterbury, peace of

Forma pacis (1263) **IV** 176

Forman, Andrew, bishop of Moray (1502–14), later archbishop of St Andrews (1515–22) 144, 158, 271, 273, 276

Formigny (Calvados), battle **VI** 491

Formosus, Pope **II** 435, 438

Forncett (Norfolk), manor **VI** 375; **V** 317, 325, 333, 337, 339

Fornham St Genevieve (Suffolk) **III** 336

Fornovo, battle (1495) **VII** 115, 152

Forrest, Friar **VII** 396

Forster, John, shipping merchant **VI** 591

Forster, Sir John **VIII** 141, 144

Förster, M. **II** 199

Forster, Rowland, jewel house yeoman **VI** 614

Forster, Thomas (?1675–1738) **XI** 119, 161, 162

Forster, William Edward **XIII** 176; biography 482; introduces education act 482–3; **XIV** 19, 33, 333;

coercion policy 73; its failure 74; resignation 75; president of Imperial Federation League 178, 362

Forsyte Saga **XV** 178

Fort Albany **X** 340, 342

fort annexes **Ia** 195, 247

Fort Belvedere **XV** 400

Fort Churchill **X** 340

Fort Duquesne **XI** 348, 362

Fort James **X** 332, 333

Fort St George **IX** 323; **X** 349

Fort Schuyler **XII** 210

Fort Severn **X** 340

Fort Stanwix **XII** 210

Fort Wayne, treaty (1809) **XII** 550

Fort William **X** 278

Fort York **X** 340

Fortescue, Sir John **VI** 309–16; *Governance of England* 309, 310; *De laudibus legum Anglie* 310–11; *De natura legis naturae* 311; *Dominium politicum et regale* theory 314–15; council lords' rapacity 435; Towton escape 526; Roman legal procedure 563; Lancastrian raiding 528; Flanders 530; attainder (1461) 539; **IX** 4; **VII** 12, 189, 259, 450, 603; law of England 564–5; **VIII** 283

Forth, earl of *see* Ruthven

Forth, Firth of, **Ia** 248, 319; Northumbrian boundary **II** 86, 95; **III** 265, 266, 268

Forth, river **Ia** 144, 146, 197, 202, 229; Tyne-Forth province 612; **V** 11, 34, 38, 40, 70, 440; landing for Scottish defeat 116

Forth-Clyde line **Ia** 144–5, 197, 202, 211, 226; Severus 229; *see also* Antonine Wall

forts **Ia** 75; pre-Roman 44; Claudian 89–95, 97, 101, 104; legionary fortresses 90, 103, 135, 152–3, 157 — York 325 — fortifications 328–9, 407; vexillation (half-legion) fortresses 95, 101, 103, 105; Wales 103, 104, 137, 150, 255 — abandonment 404;

Fowey (Corn.) **III** 96; **V** 403; **VI** 354; **VII** 476

Fowke, Joseph **XII** 311

Fowler, H. H., Viscount Wolverhampton **XIV** 305; biography 209; passes Local Government Act (1894) 213–14; speech on Indian cotton duties 220

fowling **VIII** 277–8

Fox, Charles James (1749–1806) **XI** 72, 333; **XII** 150, 155, 286, 301, 368; biography 137; character 137, 303, 338, 353; and Jebb 228; secretary of state for foreign affairs (1783) 243, 246, 249, 578, 579; opposition (1782–3) 250, 253, 257; coalition with North (1783) 258–67; India 263–5, 319–21; opposition to Pitt 268–72, 275, 277, 294, 436 — and George III 267 — Libel Act (1792) 302 — with prince of Wales against king 303 — social behaviour 304 — tax 305 — Hastings' impeachment 322–6 — criticism of new Acts 360–2 — French war 374, 381 — failure of opposition 404; on Scotland 281; French Revolution 323–5, 357, 362; urges for peace 371; regency issue 390; Ireland 392–4, 401; peace and retrenchment 409, 410; approves disarmament 413; exclusion from office 417–20; secretary of state for foreign affairs (1806) 435, 437, 582; election consequences 439–41; death 438; **XIV** 1; **XV** 52, 327

Fox, Edward (1496?–1538) **VII** 348, 382

Fox, George, founder of Quakerism **IX** 195–7, 410

Fox, Henry, 1st Lord Holland (1705–74) **XI** 22, 34, 39, 61, 338; marriage 137; Cumberland faction 340; Bedford and Sandwich 342; Pelham's leadership 345; abilities 346; cabinet action 348;

Newcastle–Pitt negotiations 349; resigns 353; Devonshire 354; Pitt's alliance 355; bribery 373; character and aims **XII** 8, 82, 90, 94; patronage of Calcraft 62, 65; paymaster of forces 67, 110, 164, 247, 260 — victory against Pitt 419 — state office holders 577; leader of court party in Commons 82; views on dismissal of Devonshire 84; promotion to Lords 95

Fox, John **V** 520

Fox, Richard, bishop of Exeter (1487–92), bishop of Bath and Wells (1492–4), bishop of Durham (1494–1501), bishop of Winchester (1501–28) **VII** 37, 94, 108, 232; joins Henry VII's council (1485) 56; keeper of the privy seal (1487) 56, 647; Scottish marriage negotiations (1495 and 1499) 139, 157; negotiations with Scotland 143–4; truce of Ayton (1497) 147–8; successor 233; Erasmus seeks advancement 251; assists Wolsey 288, 293; resigns privy seal 297; Wolsey's ambition 299, 306; Corpus Christi College 570, 572, 599; Johannes Corvus portrait 599; secretary to the king (1485) 648

Fox, Thomas (d. 1763), naval captain **XI** 262

Foxe, John (1516–87) **VII** 511; *Acts and Monuments* or *Book of Martyrs* 301; English New Testaments 345; Thomas More 346–7; Thomas Cromwell 352, 590; readership of kings 352–3; code of canon law (1571) 424; Edward VI and Joan Bocher 524; Mary's protestant following 533, 541–2; *Faithful Admonition to the Professors of God's Truth in England* 553

Foxe, John, martyrologist **VIII** 283

Foyle, river **X** 305

Framlingham (Suffolk) **VI** 472; castle 63; **VII** 526

221

Framlingham, John, of Debenham **VI** 419

Frampton, villa **Ia** 342, 725

France (to *c.* AD 500) **Ia** 303

France (1087–1216): French influence on town constitutions **III** 72–3; trade with 82–3, 88, 90–2; William II's relations with 111–12; Henry I's wars with 122–7; Henry II's relations with 162, 323–6, 333; Investiture contest 179; Becket in 199, 211, 214; Richard I and 350, 364–7; under Interdict 377; John's excommunication pronounced in 448; alliances formed against 451–3, 464; effect of victory of Bouvines 465–8

France (1216–1307): peers **IV** 55–6; Henry III becomes peer (1259) 84, 126, 313; Edward I as peer 243; royal domain increases after Alphonse of Poitiers dies 272–3; barons' alleged influence on English opposition to episcopal discipline 455; clergy's action adopted by English bishops (1225, 1261, 1297) 502, 457, 676; patriotic propaganda 527

France (1307–99): relations of Edward II with **V** 81–3, 107–11; Edward III 111–26, 127–45, 147–50; allied with Scots 117–19, 124, 136, 146–79 —Franco-Scottish League (1371) 142–3 —prelude to invading England 439–40; Richard II 146–7, 444, 456, 488, 492 —Charles opposed to Anglo-Scottish agreement 439 —peace negotiations 463 —marriage alliance and ensuing problems 475–7; literary influence 525, 531

France (before 1422): expenditure (1400–1408) **VI** 30; agreement (1396) 34; hostility (1399–1403) 50; Welsh expedition 57; court (1405) 64; truce (1399–1403) 72;

raiding England 73; Welsh alliance 74; aliens in household 80; 'adamantine hardness' 142; defence problems 170; Treaty of Troyes 186; estates general meeting 188; prisoners 218, 222; *see also* Henry V; Troyes, treaty

France (1485–1558) **VII** 67, 141, 178, 559; Henry VII's truce (1485–6) 81, 95; nationalism 83; claims in Italy 84; ambitions in Netherlands 85; designs upon Brittany 86–7, 91; Ferdinand's plans against 93–4; Medina del Campo treaty (1489) 94–5, 96; Henry VII at war with (1490) 97; tries for peace with England (1489–90) 101; coalition against (1490) 102–3; Ferdinand negotiates with 104, 283; marriage of Charles and Anne (1491) 105; Henry prepares for war 106–7; invasion by Henry VII (1492) 108–9, 110, 111; Italian states 112, 113; Louis XII succeeds to throne 114; beaten by League of Venice (1495) 114–15; death of Charles VIII 116; Perkin Warbeck 120–2; 'Auld Alliance' and triple *entente* 135–7, 269; Ferdinand's machinations 143, 149–50, 174, 283; French failures in Naples (1503–4) 152–3; marriage treaties with Ferdinand 154; League of Cambrai (1508) 155–6, 188; Henry's *entente* 157; treaties (1502) 159; intimacy with Scotland 163–4; Anglo-Burgundian treaties (1506) 185; Henry's war costs (1492) 217; in Mediterranean 220; *perfectae literae* 237; Erasmus 249; Henry VIII's relations with 267; Henry VIII renews treaty (1510) 269, 272; Holy League (1511) 273; war preparations (1511) 273–4; fleet attacked by Howard 275; urges Scotland to war (1512)

275-6; truce with Ferdinand (1513) 276; invasion by Henry VIII (1513) 277-9; marriage treaty with Henry (1514) 284-5; Wolsey and Louis (1525) 301; pensions to Henry VIII 303; death of Louis XII 305; victory at Marignano 306; almost encircled by Habsburgs 309; Anglo-Imperial alliance (1522) 310-11; Charles and Henry sign invasion treaty (1522) 312; triple attack (1523) 313; Battle of Pavia (1525) 314-15, 321; Treaty of Madrid (1526) 316; Wolsey's negotiations 316, 318, 321, 327; Anglo-French alliance (1527) 316-17; League of Cognac 316-17; Wolsey hopes for French bride for Henry 324-5; Henry and Catherine's divorce 328-9, 356; shuns Wolsey 331; Reformed Church 338-9, 516; Peace of Cambrai (1529) 339; Italian ambitions 340; alliance with Turks 341; Truce of Nice (1538) 341; Scottish relations 363-4; Gardiner as ambassador (1535) 382; possible marriage alliance with Henry 402-3; invasion by Henry VIII (1544) 409; hat-making 463; *entente* with Henry VIII 474; Henry's will 493; religion 509; supports Northumberland 523-4, 528; death of Edward VI 535; succession of Mary 536-7; risings against Mary 538, 557, 558; allies with Paul IV against Spain 556; regains Calais 558-60

France (1603-60) **IX** 216, 218; marriage alliance with 58-9; war with 63-5; unfriendly to commonwealth 219-20, 231; position in Europe 230; alliance with England 233-4; makes Treaty of Pyrenees 234

France (1660-1714): hostility towards Spain **X** 59-60, 69; aggression 69, 111; navy 81, 134, 164; Dutch wars 83; trade with England prohibited 91; reaction 109; (in 1686) 128-9; at war 159-74; Spanish succession 193, 194; commerce with Spain 197; Marlborough's war (1702-10) 198-218; allies in war of Spanish succession 200; and the peace (1710-13) 234-5; Anglo-French commercial treaty (1713) 237; and Ireland 303-4, 306; West Indies 325, 327; coast of West Africa 332-3; in North America 338, 340-3; in India 348; influence on English literature 359; on English theatre 368-9; on English architecture 392-4; on English music 405

France (1714-60): and Jacobites **XI** 158, 162, 166; relations with Britain 166-8, 172, 178, 193-5, 197; Fleury's aims 200; and Irish 202, 290-2; Chauvelin 202; British influence weakened 206; Spanish negotiations 232; power and prestige 233; with Maria Theresa 237, 351; Pragmatic army 241; Spanish sheltered 247; Breda and Aix 264-5; colonial disputes 268, 347; in Newfoundland 307, 368, 372-5; in West Indies 308, 347, 364, 372; in India 325-31, 347, 372; threats of invasion 351, 359, 365; in West Africa 359, 363, 372; *see also* Bourbon Powers; Frederic II; 'Gallispans'; Louis XIV; Louis XV; wars

France (1760-1815): peace (1783) **XII** 155; trade in India 159, 166, 255, 314-16; help to America 205, 208, 212, 214-19, 254; trade treaty with 256, 288, 463, 504; in South America 453; population 517; *see also* foreign affairs

France (1870-1914): defeated by Prussia **XIV** 7-8; dissolution of condominium with Great Britain

France (1870–1914) (*cont.*)
in Egypt 79, 84; breach with Italy over Tunis 84; intrigues in Burma 91; further weakened through static population 102–3, 269, 498; activity on Congo 188; on Niger and in West Africa 189; annexationist plans and aggressive methods 192; Anglo-French agreement (1890) 194; joins with Russia 197; Anglo-French controversy and settlement over Siam 213; rivalry in West Africa 242; Anglo-French Convention 243; Fashoda dispute 244–5; Anglo-French Entente 366–9; military conversations 400; naval co-operation 368; foreign office minute (1911) on Anglo-French relations 435; British state visit (1914) 483; *see also* Cambon, Paul

France (1914–45): British Expeditionary Force goes to **XV** 7; trench line 12; war debt 42; British army 48; partition agreement 50; general offensive 109; casualties 120; peace terms 134–5; regarded as militaristic 137; aid to Poland 143; makes peace with Kemal 190; refuses aid at Chanak 191; settles American war debt 203; Ruhr 203–4; MacDonald 214; Locarno 221–2; currency depreciation 223; not a serious danger 227; air rival 231, 391; Henderson 272; Italy wants naval parity with 273; financial crisis 289; MacDonald hopes to reconcile with Germany 324; does not pay war debt 335; currency agreement 337; rejects compromise with Germany 365–6; League 369; Manchurian affair 370; gives no support against Italy 384; no Rhineland policy 386–8; wants non-intervention in Spain 394; defeat expected 409; Chamberlain regards as secure 415; army

men cool towards 417; Czechoslovakia 424–6; ultimatum to Beneš 427; military strength 432; strategic position 435, 455; staff talks 436; declaration of joint resistance 442; committed to support Poland 443; pushes Soviet alliance 447; thought strong enough to hold balance 449; stands aside 450; mobilizes 451; declares war 452–3; British Expeditionary Force sent to 459; Finland 467–70; battle 485–7, 492, 493; proposal for union with 487; makes armistice 488; liberation a British war aim 489; fleet destroyed 494; American contracts taken over 496; Atlantic bases used by Germans 504–5; proposed landing (1942) 515, 554–5; fall 518, 520, 536; British feel stronger without 522; United Nations 537; occupied by Germans 560; proposed landing (1943) 562; preparations to invade (1944) 564–6, 572; landing 576, 579, 580; landing in south 575, 582

Franche, Comté **VII** 85, 110

franchise: parliamentary **X** 11–12; reform (1918) **XV** 93–4, 115–16; (1928) 262; proposed (1931) 280; proposed (1944) 568–9

Francis I **VII** 290, 322, 348, 370, 599; as count of Angoulême betrothed to Claude, daughter of Louis XII (1506) 154; pensions to Henry VIII 303; renews treaty with England (1515) 305; Treaty of Noyon (1516) 307–8; meets Henry VIII at Field of Cloth of Gold (1520) 310; distrains English merchants' goods 312; wanton conduct 313; terms with pope 314; Battle of Pavia (1525) 315; Treaty of Madrid (1526) 316; Anglo-French alliance (1527) 317; 'peace' of Cambrai

Fraser, William, bishop of St Andrews (1280–97), guardian of Scotland (1286) **IV** 597, 598, 599, 606; letter to King Edward (Oct. 1290) 268, 600–1; supports John Baliol 601; queries Edward's right to receive appeals from Scotland 608; Scottish plenipotentiary in France 612; dies (1297) 616

Frasers **XI** 254

Frazer, J. G., afterwards Sir **XIV** 329, 551, 552

Frederic II, king of Prussia (1740–86) (b. 1712) **XI** 198, 263, 343, 345; attacks on Silesia 210, 231, 236, 249, 268; military tactics 218; *Mémoires* quoted 233; to France 233, 268; Austria and Maria Theresa 237, 239–41, 244, 261; Carteret 239; attacks on Bohemia 246; aims of 266, 269, 270; Seven Years War 270, 350, 359–60, 364; to George II 344; to Russia 351; English alliance 351, 357–62, 368, 371; attacks on Saxony 353; deserted by England 372, 373; *see also* subsidies; treaties; Aix-la-Chapelle and Klein-Schnellendorff

Frederick I, Barbarossa, Emperor **III** 5, 210, 339, 367; relations with Henry II 327–9, 332

Frederick, duke of Swabia **III** 127

Frederick III, Elector **X** 161

Frederick V, Elector Palatine **IX** 215; driven out of Palatinate 22–3, 58; marries Elizabeth 54; accepts Bohemian crown 56; Charles attempts to aid 57

Frederick II, Emperor (d. 1250) **III** 19, 246, 452; **IV** 233; as crusader and relations with papacy 48, 83, 88; marries Isabella, sister of Henry III (1235) 59, 72, 593; Henry III's letter 59, 132; relations with Henry III 97, 98, 103; break with papacy and policy in

Arelate 98–9, 247; Richard of Cornwall 105, 106; Simon de Montfort 107; regarded as Anti-Christ, in league with Tartars 110

Frederick III, Emperor (father of Maximilian) (d. 1494) **VI** 572; Hansa support 554; **VII** 121

Frederick, prince of Saxe-Coburg **XII** 364, 366

Frederick, prince of Wales (1707–51) **XI** 20, 21, 147, 198, 204; war (1739) 210; Pelham's triumph 259; Fishery governorship 277, 337; relations with parents 338–9; death 338, 340, 342; merits 340, 406; Stephen Hales 384; wedding anthem 415; patronage of literature 421; reputation 428; **XII** 70

Frederick, son of the Emperor Frederick I **III** 328

Frederick of Aragon, brother of James II, king of Aragon, elected king of Sicily **IV** 661

Frederick Augustus, duke of York (1763–1827) **XI** 12

Frederick III of Denmark **X** 382

Frederick the Great **XV** 593

Frederick Henry, prince of Orange **IX** 218–19

Frederick William, elector of Brandenburg **IX** 227, 229

Frederick William I, king of Prussia (1713–40) (b. 1688) **XI** 218; deserts Hanover alliance 199; relations with George I 19, 175, 197–8

Free, John **VII** 236

Free Churches **XV** 168, 169, 254

Free County of Burgundy *see* Burgundy

Free French **XV** 494, 516, 527

free men **II** 261, 473, 475; in East Anglia 517–18

Free Trade: (1914) **XV** 15, 17; coalition Liberals support 131; Lloyd George indifferent 150; last triumph 195; reunites Liberal party 208; secured by Baldwin 220; flaws 224, 258; (1929) 270; Liberal unity 281; Lloyd George defends 321; MacDonald seeks to reconcile with Protection 324; dead issue 325; Ottawa conference 334; archaic principles 335

freedmen **Ia** 505, 525, 576; imperial 79, 280, 530, 567; prejudice against 122–3; control of abuses 193, 217; tasks 508, 511, 580, 600, 659; relationship with former master 514, 688, 699; individual inscriptions 254, 697; **II** 475–6; *coliberti* 475–7

Freeman, E. A. **XIV** 45, 145, 161

Freiburg **X** 243

Freind, Dr John (1675–1728) **XI** 390, 421

Freising, Otto of **IV** 85

French *see* France

French, Sir John, earl of Ypres (1852–1925) **XIV** 254, 255, 478, 479; council of war **XV** 6; biography 7; first instructions 7–8; Battle of Mons 9; ordered to remain in line 10; at Ypres 12; opposes Dardanelles expedition 24; complains of shell shortage 26; put under Joffre 45; Battle of Loos 46; recalled 47; becomes viceroy of Ireland 104

French Pacific Company **X** 250

French people **VII** 450, 602

French Revolution: compared with Puritan Revolution **IX** 312; principal discussion of reactions in England **XII** 323–5, 353, 356–9, 361, 537

freols boc **II** 307; *see also* bookland

Frere, Sir Bartle **XIV** 59, 60, 61, 62

Frere, John Hookham (1769–1846) **XII** 461

Frescobaldi, Amerigo dei, Edward I's yeoman **IV** 632, 639–42

Frescobaldi, Amerigo dei & Co: control of local exchanges in England **IV** 633–4; **V** 7, 14–15, 22

Fresnel, Pierre, bishop of Noyon **VI** 141; bishop of Lisieux 141, 261

Fréteval (Loir-et-Cher) **III** 213, 375

Freud, Sigmund **XIV** 552; **XV** 259–60; comes to England 419–20

Freycinet, Monsieur de **XIV** 78–9

Friagabis **Ia** 667

friars **V** 309–10, 311, 502, 512, 514; conflict with university 503–4

Frideswide, St, constitution for feast **VI** 303

Friedland, battle (1807) **XII** 455

friendly societies **XIII** 617–18

Friesland, dukes of *see* Saxony

friezes, woollen **X** 317

Frig, Goddess **II** 98–9

Frigidus, river, battle **Ia** 409

Frilford (Berks.): shrine **Ia** 671; **II** 25

Frion, Stephen **VII** 121

Frisby, Richard, Leicester minorite brother **VI** 28

Frisby, Roger, minorite of Leicester **VI** 28

Frisia **Ib** 55, 63, 107, 126; English mission **II** 165–9, 175

Frisians **Ib** 47–9, 52, 54–5, 109, 134; in Roman army 77–8; *laten* 143; map 1 xxix; in Britain **II** 5–6; early trade with England 56–7, 221; sea power 240

Frisii **Ia** 116, 208

Frith, John (1503–33), Protestant martyr **VII** 346, 571

Frithugisl, abbot of Tours **II** 189

Fritigern **Ia** 391

Friuli **VII** 151

Frobisher, Sir Martin **VIII** 240, 241, 412, 416

Frocester, abbot of Gloucester **VI** 647

Frocester Court, villa **Ia** 278

Froidmont, Helinandus of *see* Helinandus

Froissart, Jean (1335–1410), French chronicler **V** 269, 531; on 'bachelors' at Valenciennes 126; on

227

Froissart (*cont.*)
Sluys 129; on Geoffrey of Harcourt 133; on church-burning 246; on Black Prince and Edward III 249; on the Order of the Garter 251; on heralds 265; on Richard II's knowledge of French 524; **VI** 240; **VII** 581

Frome (Som.), council **II** 349; monastery 160

Fronsac (Gironde), castle **VI** 110, 222

Fronsac, viscount of, *parlement* of Paris **IV** 311–12

Frontenac, compte de **X** 341

frontiers **Ia** 523–5, 617, 618, 622; German 24, 197, 229, 274 —raiders 288, 428 —Burgundians settle 433; British 198, 241–3, 245–7, 260, 298 —security 313, 427 —Constantius 317–18 —troops withdrawn 330 —*Notitia* 412; barbarian settlement within 204; Danube 276, 288, 438; Diocletian and Constantine compared 291–2, 330; *see also limes*

Frontinus (I), Sex. Julius **Ia** 43, 137–8, 156, 168, 319

Frontinus (II) (exile in Britain) **Ia** 395

Fronto, M. Cornelius **Ia** 174, 182

Froom *see* Frome (Som.)

Frost, John (1750–1842), secretary of Corresponding Society **XII** 358

Frost, John, JP (d. 1877) **XIII** 139–40

Frost, William, mayor of York **VI** 62

Froude, James Anthony (1818–94) **VII** 541; **XIII** 551–2; **XIV** 45, 58, 178

Froude, Richard Hurrell **XIII** 514–15, 518

fruit industry **X** 299, 359

frumentarii **Ia** 522

Frundsberg, Georg von **VII** 317

Fry, Elizabeth (1780–1845) **XII** 39;

XIII 467–8, 621; biography 467

fuel **Ia** 631

Fuel and Power, Ministry of **XV** 547, 569

Fuensalida **VII** 149, 172, 179, 180

Fuenterrabia **VII** 274, 311, 313

Fuentes de Oñoro, battle (1811) **XII** 487

Fuggers of Augsburg **VII** 412; **VIII** 45, 236

Fuhlsbüttel **Ib** 54, 66; map 1 xxix

Fulco, archbishop of Rheims **II** 271

Fulda, monastery **II** 172–3; traditions preserved 7, 8, 30–1

Fulford (Yorks.), battle **II** 589–90, 687

Fulford, Sir Baldwin **VI** 615

Fulford, Sir Thomas **VI** 615

Fulham (Middx.) **II** 204, 257

Fulhope Law, battle **VI** 35

Fulk IV, le Réchin, count of Anjou **II** 607; **III** 111, 113

Fulk V, king of Jerusalem, count of Anjou **III** 123, 124, alliance with Maine 112, 113; on crusade 125; cause of the Clito 126; his title 128, 343

Fulk the Good, count of Anjou **V** 5

Fullanhamm *see* Fulham (Middx.)

Fuller, Thomas: alien priories 295; on Flemish weavers **V** 367; Wyclif 517; **IX** 282, 409

Fuller-Maitland, J. A. **XIV** 544

Fulling-mills **V** 365–6

Fullofaudes **Ia** 377, 382, 411; **Ib** 196

Fulthorp, Sir Roger **V** 449, 450

Fulton, Robert (1765–1815) **XII** 515

funta **Ib** 32

fur trade **X** 340

Furies **Ia** 678–9

Furneaux, Philip (1726–83) **XI** 88

Furnell, Alan de **III** 390

Furnell, William de **III** 435

Furnes **VII** 99; **X** 171 *see* Veurne

Furness (Lancs.) **V** 40; **VII** 397

furniture: English **VII** 597; **IX** 382–3; household **X** 398; **XI**

412–13; **XII** 29, 339
Furnival, Joan **VI** 8, 324
Furnival, Lord *see* Neville, Thomas
Furnival, Thomas, lord of Sheffield **V** 61
Furnival family **VI** 9; lordship 8, 323–4
Fursa, Irish ascetic in East Anglia **II** 117, 121, 125
Fürstenberg, William von, bishop of Strasbourg **X** 129, 135, 161
'Fury': Spanish **VIII** 340; French 357

Fuscus, Cornelius **Ia** 130
Fuseli, H. (1741–1825) **XII** 537, 543
Fusoris, Jean, Henry V notes **VI** 126
Fychan, Ednyfed **VI** 38
Fychan, Gruffyd, son of Gruffyd of Madog **VI** 39, 40
Fyn **Ib** 47, 54–5, 108, 192; map 1 xxix
Fyrd **III** 102
fyrd-service **II** 290–1, 308, 583

G

Gabaston (Béarn) **IV** 276
Gabbard, naval battle **IX** 223
Gæignesburh *see* Gainsborough (Lincs.)
Gaelic language **X** 410
Gaeta **VII** 153
Gaetani, Benedict, Cardinal, later Pope Boniface VIII **IV** 263; arbitrates between Edward I and Philip IV **IV** 650
Gage, Sir John (d. 1556) **VII** 494, 531; lord chamberlain (1553) 649; comptroller (1540) 650
Gage, Thomas (1721–87) **XII** 195, 199–202
Gaguin, Robert **VII** 580
Gaiety theatre, Manchester **XV** 314
Gainsborough (Gæignesburh) (Lincs.) **II** 385, 732; **IX** 134
Gainsborough, Thomas (1727–88) **XI** 10, 401, 410, 412, 414; his artistic style 404; included in *The Art of Painting* 407; **XII** 343, 346
Gairdner, Dr James **VI** 640
Gairdner, James **XIV** 145, 161, 329
Gaiseric **Ia** 473
Gaius, Emperor: invasion preparations **Ia** 60–1 — cancellation 3, 67, 306; assassination 68; extravagance 72; reign 80; army problems 82
galanas **IV** 389
Galatia **Ia** 673
Galatians, council **Ia** 673–4
Galba, Emperor **Ia** 128, 209
Gale, John **VIII** 313
Gale, Samuel (1682–1754), antiquarian **XI** 395
Galen **Ia** 234, 549; **III** 246; **VII** 242; **VIII** 312; **IX** 364
Galen, Bernhard von, bishop of Münster **X** 64, 75–6
Galerius, Emperor **Ia** 293, 301, 315, 318, 322; persecution 721

Galgenberg bei Cuxhaven **Ib** xx 111, 193
Galicia **VII** 274
Galilei, Galileo **VIII** 307; **IX** 360–1; **X** 43
Galissonié, Roland-Michel Barrin, marquis de la (1693–1756) **XI** 352
Galitzin, Prince D. A. (1753–1803) **XI** 368
Galla Placidia **Ia** 447, 474–5, 471, 481, 492
Gallacher, W.: imprisoned **XV** 139; elected 384; remains seated 428; opposes Munich 429
galleries *see* art galleries
Gallic: Chronicle **Ia** 472–3, 474; councils 736
Gallic prefecture *see* prefecture of the Gauls
Galliéni, General, and battle of Marne **XV** 32–3
Gallienus, Emperor **Ia** 202, 251, 269, 270, 273–4; military exclusion 275
Gallipoli: landing **XV** 25–6; evacuation 18, 46, 48; reinforcements 30, 44; second landing 45; estimate 49, 96; Churchill discredited 74, 526, 556, 573; Finnish expedition repeats 469; Norwegian campaign repeats 483; Dieppe repeats 558; Anzio repeats 575, 579
'Gallispans' **XI** 249, 261
Gallo-Romans: predominate in administration **Ia** 435–6, 451, 737; life-styles 451–4, 662; culture 464; detachment of Loire area 477, 493; Trier 480; Visigothic march on Rome 488; Syagrius in N. Gaul 494; Sidonius Apollinaris and son 494, 498; comparison with Britain 498–501

230

Galloway **II** 86, 87; **III** 271, 274, 276, 278; Edward I in **IV** 692–4, 707; **V** 32; *see also* Dumfries and Galloway
Galloway, Joseph **XII** 199
Galloway, Roland of, and successors **IV** 580–1
gallowglasses (mercenaries from Scotland), in Ireland **IV** 566–7
Gallows Hill, inscription from **Ia** 298
Galsted **Ib** map 5 68
Galsworthy, John **XIV** 546, 548, 549; **XV** 52, 177–8, 314
Galvani, Luigi (1737–98) **XI** 384
Galway **V** 233; **IX** 114, 163; **X** 312, 321
Galway, earl of (1648–1720) **XI** 216, 220; *see also* Massue, Henri de
Gama, Vasco da **VII** 4, 224
Gamaches (Somme) **VI** 205
Gambetta **XIV** 78
Gambia, river **X** 333
Gambier, James (1756–1833), 1st Baron **XII** 456
gambling **IX** 180, 304–5
game-laws **X** 15
Gamelin, bishop of St Andrews (1255–71) **IV** 592, 593
Gamelin, General: British Expeditionary Force **XV** 459; decides to advance into Belgium 484; explains defeat 485
games, development and invention **XIV** 164–6
Gammer Gurton's Needle **VIII** 296
Gandhi, Mohandas K. (Mahatma): starts civil disobedience **IV** 152–3; breaches salt monopoly 275; attends Round Table conference 276, 356; Halifax and 420; refuses postdated cheque 545
Ganganelli, Lorenzo, Cardinal **III** 353
Ganges, river **X** 349
Gannoc, campaign (1245) **IV** 399; *see also* Degannwy

Gant, Gilbert de **III** 485
gaol delivery **IV** 361
'Garaussing' **VIII** 273
Garbett, Samuel (1717–1805) **XI** 117
Garde, Antoine Paulin, Baron de la, French admiral **VII** 487
'Garden Suburb' (Lloyd George's) **XV** 75–6, 131, 196
gardeners, Scottish **X** 253
gardens **Ia** 278, 620; **VIII** 274, 275; **IX** 384–5; **X** 396
Gardiner, Samuel Rawson **IX** 92, 118; **XIII** 552; **XIV** 161, 329
Gardiner, Stephen (1483?–1555), bishop of Winchester (1531–51, 1553–5) **VII** 329, 352, 479, 563, 593; Erasmus 346; Henry's divorce from Catherine 348; Henry's quarrel with Rome 350; replies for convocation (1532) 354; forfeits royal favour 355–6; commissioner for valuation of ecclesiastical revenue (1535) 371; *De Vera Obedientia* (1535) 379, 423; ambassador in France (1535–8) 382; translates gospels from Greek 397; supports imperial alliance 408; promotes Henry's marriage with Catherine Howard 416; Cleves marriage dissolved (1540) 417; power struggles and religious division 419–20; struck by Lisle 420; statute of six articles (1539) 427; reading of Bible restricted (1543) 429; 'his highnes Pryvey Counsaill' 435; 'packing' parliament 437; suspicious of Proclamations Act 439; retires from council 496; opinion of parliament 498, 499; accepts transubstantiation 508–9; death of Henry 510; opposes changes during royal minority 511, 513; imprisoned in Fleet (1547) 513; released (1548) 514; imprisoned in Tower (1548) 514, 524; accepts first Prayer

231

Gardiner, Stephen (*cont.*)

Book 515; deprived (1551) 518; and royal supremacy 522; released (1553) 530; in council 532; chancellor (1553-5) 531, 543, 646; mass for Edward VI 533; Edward Courtenay 536; opposes Mary and Philip marriage 537; Wyatt rising and consequences 538-40; proposes exclusion of Elizabeth 541; Catholicism gains ground 542; persecution of heretics 550; last oration and death 554-5; estimate 555; education at Cambridge 571-3; chancellor of Cambridge and visitor to Oxford colleges 575

Garendon (Leics.), abbey **III** 183

Garenter, Thomas, Lollard **VI** 283

Gargrave, George, Marshal **VI** 419

Gargrave, Sir Thomas **VIII** 18, 138, 142, 143-4

Gariannonum see Burgh Castle

Garibaldi, Giuseppe **XIII** 302-3, 615; Churchill echoes **XV** 475

Garigliano, battle (1503) **VII** 153

Garmon, St **Ib** 17

Garnett, Mr **XII** 513

Garnier, Arnulf **V** 285

Garonne, lordship **VI** 107

Garonne, river **Ia** 448, 450; **III** 442, 466; **V** 112, 114; **VI** 364

Garrard (Gerrard, Garrett), Thomas **VII** 346, 427

Garrett, Edmund **XIV** 227

Garrick, David (1717-79) **XI** 10, 145, 304, 407, 419; **XII** 338

Garsiis, Louis de **VI** 263

Garter, order of **V** 226, 251-3, 491; **VI** 252; **VII** 493; German knights struck off **XV** 43; Balfour earns 151

Garth, Sir Samuel (1661-1719) **XI** 390

Garth, Captain Thomas **VII** 121, 127

Garvin, J. L.: **XIV** 536; briefed by

Fisher **XV** 23; during First World War 27; inherited by Astor 194; dismissed by Astor 573

gas: used by Germans **XV** 26; masks distributed 427, 454; not used in Second World War 427-8; masks carried 459

gas-lighting **XIII** 49

Gascoign, George **VIII** 287

Gascoigne, Thomas, Oxford University chancellor **VI** 96, 269, 270, 476, 681; bishops 269, 495; faith 685

Gascoigne, Sir William, chief justice of the King's Bench **VI** 61; register 62

Gascony **III** 92, 379, 442, 484; attacked by Louis VIII and saved (1224-6) **IV** 90-1; Henry III (1227-30) 94-5; Henry III in (1242-3) 100, 103, 557; conditions and administration 108-10, 274-80, 295-318; Simon de Montfort as *custos* (1248-52) 110-13; Henry's expedition to (1253-4) 116-19; Henry's plans for Edward 118-19; Edward's establishment 118-19; Henry's lordship recognized in treaty of Paris (1259) 126, 128; affairs (1262) 170-1; settlement (1265) 198; Edward I in (1273-4) 226, 295-6; conference of kings of France and Castile (1280) 243-4; hostages and pledges under treaty of Canfran 260-1; status, before Henry III's death 274-5; lieutenants of duke 275, 279; close relations with England 276, 280-4, 294; dioceses 292; homages of vassals 295; King Edward in (1286-9) 295, 298; finances 296, 304; court 297; allods 297-8; exchequer 300; seneschal 300-1, 312; administrative division of 301; coinages 305; *paréages* and *bastides* 308-10; Channel Island 318; contingents in Welsh war

(1282) 421, 422, 427; Philip IV claims immediate jurisdiction over disturbers of his peace and declares the duchy confiscated 645–8; war and truce (1294–1303), discussions of status 648–58; wine exports 669; contingent at Falkirk (1298) 689, 690; **V** 90, 191, 256, 428; Edward II 57; Prince Edward invested with duchy of 82; Hundred Years War 106–15, 123–7, 210, 246, 253, 430 — Edward III's attempts to divert French troops 132, 133 — struggle for possession 136, 137, 138, 147–9; truce of Brétigny 140; Black Prince 138, 143–5; in French wars 254, 268; trade 349, 357–63; John of Gaunt 464, **VI** 30, 104, 106, 222; king's lieutenant 75; financial demands 88; English boundaries 107, 108; operations (1403–5) 109–10; English settlers 110; wine trade 364; wine exports 418; perilous condition (1442) 470; shipping licences 533; **VII** 220, 470; *see also* Bordeaux

Gascoyne-Cecil, Robert Arthur Talbot, 3rd marquis of Salisbury, Lord Robert Cecil and Viscount Cranbourne: biography **XIII** 183; views on parliamentary reform 183; resigns on reform question 186; views on Schleswig-Holstein question 320, 324

Gask Ridge: forts **Ia** 175; signal station 570

Gasparino of Betgamo **VI** 680

Gaspée incident **XII** 193, 197

Gaston II, count of Foix **V** 114

Gatacre, Sir W. **XIV** 253

Gatcombe, villa **Ia** 329, 453

Gatehouse of Fleet, fort **Ia** 145

Gates, General **XII** 210, 215

Gates, Sir John **VII** 492, 497, 529, 530

Gateshead (Rægeheafde) (Co.

Durham) **II** 614, 733; **V** 372; population **XV** 167; industrial estate 352; evacuation 434

gateways, town **Ia** 232, 262–3

Gatton (Surrey) **VI** 419

Gaucelin of Eauze, Cardinal **V** 40, 52

Gaucourt, Sieur de, Harfleur captain **VI** 150, 165, 166, 223; English prisoner 157

Gaul: Caesar's campaigns **Ia** 22–6, 37; Augustus' visit 51; communications 58, 259, 455, 466, 495 — Tacitus 539; relations with Germany 126, 497, 549; disturbances in 128, 282–3, 287, 303, 425 — self-sufficiency 454–5 — fatal policy 473 — insurgency and warfare 477 — troops withdrawal 488 — kingdoms form 490; towns 160, 219, 263, 275–9, 327 — weakening 412; Britain and Gaul compared 160–1, 324, 339, 342, 348 — economy 454, 635 — Vortigern's policy 472 — differences between barbarians 499–501 — Tacitus 540; Albinus 219, 225, 312; Imperium Galliarum 244; Carausius 289, 297, 304–5; sea raids 289, 375, 380; sea defences 320, 384, 529; Valentinian 351, 369, 379; Julian 353, 359, 361–2, 367; Gallic prefecture 353; Silvanus 358; barbarian invasions 359, 426, 439, 475; St Jerome 369; Ammianus 379; villages 383, 610; Ausonius at court 400; Magnus Maximus 402; loss of control by Rome 424, 445, 454–5, 473, 477 — army withers 488 — barbarian kingdoms 447–55, 491–501; army in Gaul 427, 473, 488, 549; civil war 428; St Gemanus 466; Aetius 475–7; Majorian 491; British settlement in Gaul 492–3; Saxons 498; economic relations with Britain 600, 635–6, 639, 642–3, 652–4

196, 270 — urgency of campaign 325 — 'a fraud and a freak' 327 — reparations 383 — electors felt cheated 596; (1922) 195, 196–8; 1923) 195 — Labour given 'a fair chance' 208–9; (1924) 195, 270, 327 — effect of Zinoviev letter on Labour 219 — Conservative victory 220–1; (1929) 269–71; (1931) 270, 321 — Conservative majority 195, 326 — National government 324–7, 370; (1935) 383–4 — Churchill without a future 357 — dominant themes 383 — collective security failure 389 — armament begun after 409; (1945) Churchill's prestige exploited 270, 595 — Labour's first great majority 569, 597 — Beaverbrook 574, 596; *see also* elections

general strikes: demobilization in Glasgow (1919) **XV** 139; plans made (1920) 143, 199; (1926) 227, 233, 242–7; fails to help miners 248; made illegal (1927) 250

general warrants **XII** 99–100, 114, 139

Geneva, lake **III** 330; **VII** 340

Geneva, League **XV** 255; naval conference 273; speech by Hoare 380; Haile Selassie 385

Geneville, Geoffrey de, lord of Ludlow and Trim **IV** 201, 517; Edward I's agent in Paris (1280) 244; appointed marshal (1297) 680, 681; one of Edward's commissioners 653

genius **Ia** 682, 683, 684, 707, 708; *see also* Imperial Cult

genius loci **Ia** 671

Genlis **VIII** 157

Genoa **III** 86, 95; galleys **IV** 637; Philip IV's naval activity (1293–4) 646; **V** 530; **VI** 158; woad exports 354; loan to

Edward IV 592; **VII** 112, 220, 271, 309, 319; **X** 111, 113; conference **XV** 189–90, 334

Genoese: bowmen **III** 372; **VI** 348; carracks 615–16; **VII** 225

Genouni, Genounian district **Ia** 199

Genrich, A. **Ib** xxi, 192

Gentiles **Ib** 79

Gentle Craft **VIII** 293

Gentleman Pensioners **VII** 269

Gentleman's Magazine **XI** 31, 422, 431

gentry, country, Edward I and military development **IV** 546, 548, 551–6, 678–81

Geoffrey 'with the beard' **III** 407

Geoffrey, bishop of Coutances **II** 623, 630, 632, 637, 649–50; at William's coronation 598; suppresses revolt in south-west 603; holds pleas in England 610; historical importance 632, 633; heir of his vast fee 637

Geoffrey, chancellor of Henry I **III** 421

Geoffrey, count of Brittany, brother of King Henry II **III** 129, 324

Geoffrey, count of Brittany, son of King Henry II **III** 281, 325, 332, 341, 351; inherited Brittany 329; death 342; income 337

Geoffrey, husband of Constance of Brittany **IV** 92

Geoffrey, natural son of Henry II, archbishop of York **III** 445, 446; proved a lawful son 347–8; abduction and release 356–7

Geoffrey, natural son of King John **III** 428, 441

Geoffrey V, Plantagenet, count of Anjou **III** 21, 129, 135, 145; knighted 24; marriage with Matilda 113, 115, 126, 128, 131; conquest of Normandy 160–1; ceded Gisors 162, 323; literacy 243; house of Anjou 343

Geoffrey Alselin **II** 626

Geoffrey de Choques **II** 629

Geoffrey de Mandeville **II** 633

Geoffrey de Mandeville I, earl of Essex **III** 69, 144, 146–8, 150, 256; sheriff 155–6; adjudicator 408

Geoffrey de Mandeville II, earl of Essex **III** 24

Geoffrey de Mandeville III, earl of Essex **III** 472

Geoffrey Fitz Peter *see* Fitz Peter, Geoffrey

Geoffrey Martel, count of Anjou **II** 585, 607; **III** 318

Geoffrey of Monmouth (1100?–54) **VI** 657; **VII** 27, 33

geography **VIII** 317–19

Geological Museum, conference **XV** 334–5

geology **X** 376

George, bishop of Ostia **II** 215–16

George, David Lloyd *see* Lloyd George, David

George, duke of Clarence (1449–78) **VII** 49, 71

George, earl of Angus **VI** 45

George, Henry **XIV** 334

George I, king of England (1714–27): question of succession **X** 190; in Netherlands 207; growing importance 242; Ireland 311; ministers **XI** 2, 17, 32, 38, 153 — Pitt 376; descent 11; Hanoverian career and interests 11–15, 19–20, 166, 174; position and powers in Great Britain 15–16; and army 18, 217–18; foreign affairs 19, 165, 167, 195, 200; absences in Hanover 40, 41, 152, 166, 197; unpopularity 42, 152, 157; peaceful succession of 55, 152–4, 157; religious toleration 77, 170; ecclesiastical patronage 77, 80; history professors instituted 140; characteristics 152, 340; mistresses 152, 185, 354; and Whigs 153, 156; and George II 167, 172, 202; and Gibraltar 174; and Prussia 175, 197–9; and South Sea Bubble 177; death 202; and 'Wood's halfpence' patent 303; art and music patronage 406, 414–15; **XIII** 196; *see also* Carteret; Crown; Hanover; Walpole

George II, king of England (1727–60): writ of summons to House of Lords (as duke of Cambridge) **X** 246; Ireland 311; **XI** 11, 14, 341, 345; bribery 16; and ministers 17, 32, 38, 258, 259 — Newcastle 342 — Pelham 345 — Pitt 354, 355–6, 364, 376 — Walpole 367; with Walpole 17, 202–3, 206, 339, 367; relations with Carteret 18, 239, 249, 367; army and navy 18–19, 217, 218, 225, 234; foreign affairs 19, 237–8; characteristics 19, 147, 152, 203, 340 — political independence 367; and Hanover 20, 21, 237–8, 240, 350 — preference 367; as prince of Wales 38, 40, 167, 171, 198 — Walpole 202; absences in Hanover 40, 41, 231, 253, 258 — Newcastle in Hanover 342, 344 — Amalie Wallmoden 354; unpopularity 42, 152, 339; ecclesiastical patronage 77, 80; robbed in Kensington Palace Garden 138; Prussia 175; at Dettingen 242; Black Watch 281; and Georgia 309; with Frederick prince of Wales 338–9; with Newcastle 339, 344, 367; with earl of Sandwich 341; with Pelham 345, 367; with reference to Byng 352; Cumberland dismissed 360; death 367; and University at Göttingen 389; medical treatment 390; and Society of Antiquaries 394; with reference to British Museum 397; art and music patronage 406, 414–16; *see also* Caroline, Queen; Crown; Hanover; Pitt; Yarmouth, countess of

George III, king of England (1760–1820) **XI** 9, 18, 21, 57,

340; as prince of Wales 38, 355, 383; and Pitt 367; and lightning conductor 384; drawing teacher 406; and Hogarth 406; art patronage 408; and Dr Johnson 430, 431; ministers **XII** 1, 65, 125, 225; character and personal views 2–7, 59, 82, 117, 120; marriage 6; task of (1760) 7, 66; patronage of Eton 39 —of art 340, 345; county appointments 43; finances 61, 208, 232, 247–9, 286; Bute 67, 69; speech from throne (1761) 71; part in fall of Pitt (1761) 74; dislike of Newcastle 79, 82 —of Grenville 79, 128 —of Fox 82, 95, 243, 303, 417 —excludes from coalition 420; charge of subverting constitution 92; Grenville's control 97; attacks of madness 109, 304, 416, 489–91, 501 —security of throne 503; Burke's pamphlet 126; relations with North 148, 152, 225, 233; relief of Nonconformists 156; America 185, 213, 244; Gordon Riots 238; 'influence of the Crown' and Shelburne 244, 250; views on French war 244, 368, 373; dislike of Fox-North coalition 258–60, 266, 272; relations with Pitt 266, 273, 302, 323, 401–5 —agrees to bill for reform 278; on Catholic emancipation 395, 401, 405, 441–3, 484; mourns Fox 438; Canning and Castlereagh 477; **XIII** 23, 26, 66–7, 104

George IV, king of England (1820–30) (also Prince Regent) **XII** 324, 347, 349, 391, 419; friendship with Fox 243, 304; given private establishment 260; political significance 303–5; regency, crisis 304, 490; marriage 368, 447; Prince Regent 490–2, 498–501, 547; character **XIII** 23, 24, 33–4, 38, 63; and his queen 66–9; Tory cabinet 74–5; death

77; Victoria's governess 103; unofficial private secretary 104; architecture 108; interest in foreign policy 196, 208; and Castlereagh 204; and Madame Lieven 250; '*Humanity Martin*' 470

George V, king of England (1910–36): accession **XIV** 422; negotiation with Asquith 424; criticized by Lord Hugh Cecil 431; Conservative demand he dismiss Asquith 473–4; convenes Buckingham Palace Conference 480; state visit to Paris 483; prince of Wales 501; biography **XV** 2; sanctions state of war 2; takes King's Pledge 37; protests against reprisals 44; on Haig 46; summons conference 69; makes Lloyd George prime minister 70; makes Haig field marshal 74; Haig appeals to 80; approves Lloyd George's war aims 97; supports and deserts Robertson 98–9; objects to Beaverbrook 107; agrees to general election 112; objects to Birkenhead 130; opens parliament in Belfast 156–7; protests at Riddle's peerage 170; appoints Baldwin prime minister 204, 224; appoints Labour government 209; wants fair play for Labour 220; moderating influence during general strike 247, 250; never visited Dominions as king 254; Lansbury 271; objects to meeting Soviet ambassador 274; welcomes National government 292; Christmas broadcasts 307; attends Cup Final 313; opens world economic conference 334; Jubilee 377–8; death 398; conflicts with Lloyd George 623

George VI, king of England (1936–52): coronation **XV** 307; becomes king 402; wants Halifax as prime minister 474; appoints

George VI (*cont.*)
Churchill prime minister 475; will not leave England 493; institutes George Cross 503; perturbed over Darlan 560; does not go to France on D-day 581; at St Paul's 594; appoints Attlee prime minister 597

George of Cappodocia, St **VI** 126

George Cross **XV** 503

George of Denmark, Prince **X** 29, 139, 224, 251

George of Hesse-Darmstadt, Prince **X** 196, 209, 211

George William, duke of Brunswick-Lüneburg (d. 1705), uncle of George I **XI** 11

Georges, General **XV** 459

Georgia **XI** 99, 307, 309, 310, 384; Wesley's evangelism 95; colony (established 1732) boundary disputes 207, 209; money and protection from England 318

Georgiana, duchess of Devonshire (1757–1806) **XII** 275, 338, 445

Geraint, king of Dumnonia **II** 64, 73, 182

Gerald, earl of Kildare **VI** 629

Gerald of Wales, on Welsh, Normans and English **IV** 384, 385; *see also* Giraldus Cambrensis

Geraldines: of Kildare **VI** 425; of Ireland **VIII** 464

Gerard, Balthazar **VIII** 364

Gerard, Charles, 1st earl of Macclesfield **X** 139

Gerard, John **VIII** 317

Gerard, John (1545–1612), author of *Herbal* **XI** 388

Gerard de Athée **III** 372, 383

Gerard the chancellor, bishop of Hereford, archbishop of York **II** 642; **III** 174

Gerard of Brogne **II** 447

Gerard la Pucelle, bishop of Coventry **III** 242

Gerberoy, castle **II** 609

Gerbrand, bishop of Roskilde **II** 463

Gerento, abbot of St Benignus **III** 110, 175, 176

Germain, Lady Elizabeth **XII** 203

Germain, Lord George *see* Sackville, Lord George

German East Africa **XV** 23, 133

German language **Ia** 499

German South West Africa **XV** 23, 133, 137

Germania of Tacitus **II** 11

Germanic peoples, early movements **II** 11

Germanicus **Ia** 681, 701

Germans: invasions **Ia** 11–12, 127, 204, 207, 270 —deterioration 274–5 —usurpers 427–8 —revolts 432–4; in Roman army 322, 335, 374, 387, 427 —anti-Hun forces 482; settled on lands within empire 349, 355, 549; in Britain 385–8, 484–5, 499, 506; cults in Britain 667, 679, 736; use of Roman titles 486, 496; **VII** 156, 557, 592; *see also* Germany

Germanus **II** 450

Germanus, bishop of Auxerre **II** 1

Germany: invaders from **Ia** 11, 25, 427; Caesar's attitude 23; Roman provinces 78, 353; Varus 89, 681; army 128–9, 173, 200, 221, 273; Saturnius 152; towns 160, 302; Britain and Germany compared 160, 166–7, 175, 270, 296; frontiers 166–77, 175, 274–5, 307; British units in 197–9; Caracalla 244, 270; communications 259, 304, 359, 539; Germany and Gaul 273, 303, 353; villas 302; Julian's corn supply and campaigns 359–60, 363; troops unwilling to transfer 513; imperial estates 524; wine-trade 653; cemeteries and temples 695; English mission **II** 90, 92–3, 165–76; trade **III** 83, 89–90; Henry I's relations with 126–7; mentioned 131, 149, 171, 192, 230, 271; influence on English decorative art 262; Henry

II's relations with 326–8; Richard I captive in 362–7; later relations with 376–7; John's relations with 449–52; double election of king (1257) **IV** 119; merchants invited to pursue trade with 'safe Scotland' 687; **V** 119, 122, 427; **VII** 237, 263, 307, 316, 343; peasants' revolt 304, 394, 490; imperial election 309; Lutherism and advance of Turks 309, 319–20, 340; schismatics 327; humanism in allies with Luther 338; religious disputes 340, 509; Cranmer sent (1532) 356; Henry rejects Augsburg Confession (1536) 382; Gardiner ambassador to 435; silver mines 447; Merchant Adventurers 473; Hansards 475; anti-papal churches 509; Charles alienates Catholics 535–6; artwork 599–600; **X** 111, 112, 129, 192, 205; Louis XIV's ambitions 113–14, 161; Electoral Palatinate 128; influence on English music 406–7; policies (till 1881) **XIV** 84–5; colonial expansions 188, 189, 191, 193; Anglo-German Agreement (1890) 193–4; European policies (1881–90) 194–6; relations with Great Britain at that time 198–200; courts Turkey by condoning Armenian massacres 220; Kruger telegram 232; starts building great navy 258; embarks on Berlin-Baghdad scheme 258, 270; seizes Kiaochau 259; blackmailing methods 259; Chamberlain's first and second offers of alliance rejected 260, 261; Navy Law (1900) 262; effect of Boxer expedition 262; Anglo-German convention (Yangtse agreement) 262; its breakdown 351; Chamberlain's third offer rejected 352; Anglo-German co-operation against

Venezuela 365–6; first Morocco crisis 369; Anglo-German relations after Algeciras 404–5; Germany backs Austria in Bosnian dispute 411; veiled ultimatum to Russia 411; second Morocco crisis 412; Germany makes tepid bids for British neutrality 432; precipitates third (Agadir) Morocco crisis 433; nature of her interest in Balkans 465–6; backs Austria at the London Ambassadors' Conference 467; capital levy for armament 469; preparations for early war 470; negotiations through Lichnowsky 471–2; financial preparations 482; *carte blanche* to Austria 485–6; ultimatum to Russia 490; ultimatum to Belgium 493; war declared against **XV** 2; party attitude towards 17; atrocities alleged 19; no policy for 50; and Ireland 56; war aims 65, 95; United States declare war 84; Labour wants reconciliation with 97; Northcliffe's propaganda to 107; seeks armistice 110–12; revolution in 113; demand to make pay 127; peace terms with 131, 133–6; Genoa conference 189; Ruhr occupation 203; MacDonald's attitude towards 214–15; Locarno 221–2; gold rate 223; has no navy 227; remakes air force too soon 231; in League 255; hatred of, forgotten 260, 359, 373; Hague conference 272; unemployment 284; British lending to 289; inflation 290, 325; MacDonald seeks to conciliate 324; recovery 336; competition from 339; Hitler becomes chancellor 350; First World War causes 361; chiefs of staff fear 363; leaves Disarmament conference 365–7; blockade 369; Manchuria 370; White Paper 376; conscription

Germany (*cont.*)
restored in 377; naval treaty with 377; hopes of using League against 380; Rhineland 385; air force 387; ineffective air strategy against 391; aids Franco 393, 394; anti-semitism 407; armaments as yardstick 409–10; Austria incorporated into 413, 424; attitudes towards 415–20; expected to be content after Munich 435; Bohemia becomes protectorate 439; expected to attack Rumania 442; problem of resisting 445; offers economic aid to 448–9; attacks Poland 451; war declared on 452; Second World War 453, 476; policy against 458; plans for attacking 460; economic strength 461; French wish to switch war to Russia 467; Churchill hopes to stop iron ore 468; Norway and Sweden refuse to provoke 469; backdoor wanted 481; invades Holland and Belgium 483–4; military strength 484; unconditional surrender demanded 489; fails to invade 498–500; mutual blockade 500; war at sea 504; British determined to defeat 514; supposed difficulties 515–16, 521; British bombing 517–19, 552, 562 — its effects 553, 571; Turks will not challenge 522; attacks Soviet Russia 528–9; Roosevelt does not assume war against 531; declares war on United States 532; private war ended 533, 536; no joint strategy with Japan or Italy 537; defeat put first 539; Churchill fights nationalist war against 560; unconditional surrender 561; Churchill wants backdoor 573; possibility of defeating (1944) 574; defeat sole Allied object 576–7; new weapons 578; problem of future 584; draws Allies

together 586; Morgenthau plan 587; discussed at Yalta 590; saved by Allied dissensions 593; occupied 594; reparations extracted from 596

Germany, Hansa of *see* Hansa of Germany

Germany, kings of *see* Adolf of Nassau; Albert of Austria; Richard of Cornwall; Rudolf of Habsburg

Germinilla **Ia** 688

Gerona **IV** 255

Gerontius **Ia** 428–39, 446, 469

Gerson, Jean Charlier de, Paris University chancellor **VI** 307, 311; address in Paris 93

Gertruidenberg **V** 156

Gervais, John, bishop of Winchester (1262–8) **IV** 186, 194, 195, 208

Gervase, merchant of Southampton **III** 423

Gervold, abbot of St Wandrille **II** 219–20

gesith *see* king's companion, thegn

Gessner, Conrad **VIII** 316

Gesta Dunelmensia **IV** 494–5

Geta, Emperor **Ia** 228, 230, 231, 250, 721

Gewisse, original name of West Saxons **II** 21

Ghana *see* Gold Coast

Gheeraerts, Marcus, of Bruges **VIII** 302; **IX** 374

Ghent (Flanders): monastery of St Peter **II** 448, 452–3; **III** 90, 91, 461; headquarters of Edward I (1297) **IV** 384; closed patriciate supported by Philip IV 659; thirty-six barrels of money shipped to (1297) 667; Charters confirmed 683; weavers **V** 120, 430, 432; van Arteveldt 128, 132; Edward II proclaimed king of France 162; Edward II at 167; birth of Prince John 267, 393; **VI** 72; **VII** 98, 404, 599; **VIII** 356–7, 364; **X** 233

Ghent, Simon of (de Gandavo),

bishop of Salisbury (1297–1315) **V** 10; *see also* Simon of Ghent

Gherbod, earl of Chester **II** 629

Ghilo de Picquigny **II** 629

ghosts **Ia** 679, 696

Gibbon, Edward (1707–70), father of the historian **XI** 93

Gibbon, Edward (1737–94) **XI** 52, 62, 431; aunt Hester 93; on William Law's *Serious Call* 94; on Charles Emmanuel III of Savoy 267; **XII** 145, 238, 250, 339, 534; at Oxford 40; historian 345, 347

Gibbons, Grinling (1648–1720), sculptor and wood-carver **X** 397; **XI** 402

Gibbons, Orlando (1583–1625), musician **VIII** 305, 306; **IX** 387, 389; **XI** 399

Gibbs, James (1682–1754), architect **XI** 401, 412

Gibbs, Joseph (1700–88), composer **XI** 417

Giberti, Giammateo, bishop of Verona **VII** 547

Gibraltar: Straits **III** 95; **V** 354; **X** 210, 230, 231, 348; **XI** 173, 198, 200, 207, 307; Spain's efforts to repossess 195; vulnerable to Bourbons 244; Admiral Byng 352; siege **XII** 212, 216, 241, 255; convoy (1917) **XV** 85; Gort its governor 486; French ships allowed to pass 516; Cunningham instructed to withdraw to 520; convoy (1943) 563; Hitler thinks of attacking 574

Gibson, Edmund (1669–1748), bishop of Lincoln (1717–23), of London (1723–48) **XI** 76, 323, 394, 415; quashes bill to relieve tithes 72; pressure on Sussex clergy 80; convocations cease 82

Gideon, Sampson (1699–1762) **XI** 73

Gien (Loiret) **VI** 240

Giffard, Bonaventura **X** 125

Giffard, Hugh, guardian of Edward, son of Henry III, father of bishops and abbesses **IV** 458

Giffard, John, of Brimpsfield **IV** 172–3, 199, 428, 438, 441; wife Maud Longespée, granddaughter of Llywelyn the Great 428; **V** 61, 74

Giffard, Walter, son of Hugh Giffard, chancellor and bishop of Bath and Wells (1265–6), archbishop of York (1266–79) **IV** 203, 225

Giffard, William, bishop of Winchester **III** 118

Giffard family **III** 404

Giffen, Sir R. **XIV** 104, 110, 273, 349

Gifford, Gilbert **VIII** 379, 380

Gifle **II** 43, 296

gift relationships **Ia** 166, 616–17, 662, 680

Giggleswick (Yorks.) **VI** 9, 337

Giglis (Gigli), John de, bishop elect of Worcester (d. 1498) **VII** 65

Giglis (Gigli), Silvestro de, bishop of Worcester (1498–1521) **VII** 176, 238, 289, 300

Gilbert, Adrian **VIII** 243

Gilbert, Alfred W. **XIV** 158

Gilbert, 'the Universal', bishop of London **III** 183

Gilbert, count of Brionne **II** 559, 631

Gilbert, earl of Lincoln **III** 188

Gilbert, Sir Humphrey: sent to Low Countries **VIII** 156; *Discourse to Prove North-west Passage* 240; planting of America 244–5; supports poor scholars 321; *Queene Elizabeth's Achademy* 323–4; **IX** 325

Gilbert, John (1693–1761), archbishop of York **XI** 81

Gilbert, John, bishop of Bangor (1372–5), of Hereford (1375–89), of St David's (1389–97), treasurer (1386–9) **V** 278, 429, 445

241

Gilbert, kinsman of Bishop Walcher **II** 613

Gilbert, son of Fergus, lord of Galloway **III** 278

Gilbert, Walter, Chaplain **VI** 131

Gilbert, William (1540–1603) **VIII** 307, 308; **IX** 369; and electricity **XI** 382

Gilbert, William Schwenck: collaboration with Sullivan **XIV** 159; plays 328

Gilbert Crispin, abbot of Westminster **II** 673

Gilbert de Gand **II** 629

Gilbert of Sempringham **III** 188

Gilbertines **III** 84, 188, 366

Gilboy, Mrs Elizabeth, *Wages in Eighteenth Century England* **XI** 127

Gildas **Ia** 403, 405, 419, 421, 456; plague 460, 472; Ambrosius Aurelianus 461, 483; Vortigern 468; Saxons 474, 490–1; lamentations 479; ruins 498; Christian church 721–2; *De Excidio et Conquestu Britanniae* language **Ib** xxv; appeal to Aetius 8; value of his book 8–9, 12–15, 19–20; *obsessio montis Badonici* 11, 158–60; life 13; Ambrosius Aurelianus 14, 158; devastation of Britain 14–15, 207–8; federate settlement 110; early Wessex 154–5, 158, 172; late Roman prosperity 162, 205–6; 'Groans of the Britons' 207; **II** 2–4, 6–8, 27, 64; before Mons Badonicus 12, 19; compared to annals 22–3; West Saxon conquest 30–1

Gildesburgh, Sir John **V** 405

Gildo **Ia** 420, 421

gilds: 'peace gild' of London **II** 354–5; *cnihtas* at Canterbury 527–8; merchant **III** 66, 71–2, 74–5, 87; chapmen's 74; knights' 74; craft 84–5; adulterine 85; weavers' 85, 87; craft **V** 311, 364, 369, 382–3; parochial and religious 311, 373; multiplication of

372–4; London 374–8, 435, 457; **IX** 285–6; *see also* urban economy

Giles, Master *see* Colonna

'Giles Chronicle' **VI** 14, 24, 46

Giles of Rome **V** 289–90

Gill, Eric **XIV** 540

Gillen, F. J. **XIV** 552

Gillis, Peter **VII** 259

Gillray, James (1757–1815) **XII** 346

gin-drinking **XI** 44, 133–4, 384

Ginkel, Godard van Reede, earl of Athlone **X** 189, 308, 309

Giotto **IV** 230

Gipeswic *see* Ipswich (Suffolk)

Girald the marshal **II** 630

Giraldus Cambrensis: satire of clergy **III** 224, 226; on diet of monks 228; importance of literature 236; *Topography of Ireland* 238; *Description of Wales* 256, 292; primacy of Welsh church 296; critic of John in Ireland 312; on Henry II 319, 332, 339; description of Longchamp 352

Giraud, General **XV** 560, 561

girls' schools **X** 417

Gironde, river **Ia** 653; **VI** 108, 364

Girtin, Thomas (1775–1802) **XI** 401

Girton **Ib** 41, 101; map 2 xxx

Giso, bishop of Wells **II** 468, 660, 680

Gisors (Eure) **VI** 183; *bailliage* 174, 189

Gisors (Vexin) **III** 124, 333; king's chamber 82; Robert of Bellême 112; interview with pope 125; Henry II overlord 323; Louis' loss 324; Philip's claim 342, 347, 363; Richard's victory 377

Gisors, John de **V** 81, 85

Gisors v. Anon **V** 197

Gissing, George **XIV** 331

Giustiniani, Sebastian, Venetian ambassador **VII** 286, 301, 305

gladiators **Ia** 214, 311, 579

Gladstone, Herbert, afterwards Viscount **XIV** 95; biography 38

Gladstone, William Ewart (1809–98): on Bishop Butler **XI** 90; economic policy 187; revival of office of Secretary of State, Scotland 273; **XIII** 90, 92, 93, 107, 111; and railways 42–3; opinion of Peel 109; opinion of Disraeli 116, 174; resigns over Maynooth grants 123; rejoins Peel 123–4; coalition government 160–1; protectionism 163; chancellor of the Exchequer (1852) 165–7, (1859) 179–81; committee of inquiry 168; Conservative Cabinet 170; relations with Palmerston 170–2, 177–8; character and ideas 173–8; biography 173; elected for South Lancashire 182; attacks Disraeli's Reform Bill (1867) 187; leader of Liberal party 188; views on Irish Church 189–90; disestablishment of Irish Church 189–90, 361–2; Irish Land Bill 190–1, 362–3; Crimean War 264; views on Italian question 299–300; High Commissioner in the Ionian Islands 300, 304; supports Palmerston 309; cotton famine 314; support for Denmark 320; Australia 384; divorce reform 473; opposes commission on the state of the universities 491; college aid 493; church rates 511; church reform 522; political duel with Disraeli **XIV** 1–2, 71; safeguards Belgian neutrality 3; alarmed about Alsace-Lorraine 6; passes University Tests Act 23; defeated on Irish University Bill 24; wishes to resign 25; reconstructs Cabinet and takes Exchequer 25; dissolution threat, defeated and resigns 25–6; retires from leadership 33; opposes Public Worship Bill 34; view of Eastern Question 41; campaign against Bulgarian atrocities 45; Midlothian campaigns 64; takes office again 66; treatment of radicals 66–7; Irish Land Act (1881) 73; delays over Gordon 82; short-sighted Egyptian policies 84–6; record in foreign affairs 85–6; defeated and resigns 90; looks to Lord Salisbury for Home Rule 93; communications with Parnell 93–4, 558–63; disclosure of conversion to Home Rule 95; mishandles colleagues 96; introduces first Home Rule Bill 97; defeat and resignation 99; last negotiation with Chamberlain 176; entertains Parnell at Hawarden 183; action in regard to Parnell divorce case 183, 184–5; Newcastle programme 207; forms fourth ministry 208–9; introduces second Home Rule Bill 211; last speech in parliament 214; resigns 214–15; last speech 238; death 264–5; religious side 23, 68, 137, 138; indifference to local government 23, 125, 126; views on Belgian neutrality 574; **XV** 195; direct taxation 124; Ireland 161; wishes to recommend a successor 204; MacDonald resembles 201; Snowden follows 212; constructionism 258

Glamorgan **Ia** 45, 137; **III** 288, 290, 297, 299; honour of house of Clare **IV** 406; Hubert de Burgh 43, 44, 396; revolt (1294) 440; King Edward (1295) 443; **V** 50, 58, 59, 61, 493; pursuit of younger Despenser 86; **VI** 58, 639; rising (1402) 42; Glyn Dŵr's authority 56; lordship 329; **VII** 57

Glamorgan, earl of see Somerset

Glanageenty, woods **VIII** 479

Glanvill, Gilbert, bishop of Rochester **III** 282, 446

Glanvill Rannulf **III** 4, 6, 337, 369, 414; *relief* defined 20, 21; *Investiture struggle* 180; lawyer 243, 247, 385; captured William the Lion

244

329, 547; as border county 44; parliament (1407) 84; Benedictine abbey 294, 501; cathedral 647; **VII** 35, 68, 400, 502, 518; Perkin's rebellion 145; Hooper was burnt (1555) 550; architecture 591; **IX** 132–3

Gloucester, abbot of **III** 181; *see also* Foliot; Gilbert; Serlo

Gloucester, bishops of *see* Brooks, James; Goodman, Godfrey; Hooper, John; Johnson, James; Wakeman, John; Wilcocks, Joseph

Gloucester, castle **VII** 57

Gloucester, countess of *see* Constance

Gloucester, duchess of *see* Cobham, Eleanor

Gloucester, duke of (1743–1805), marriage **XII** 155

Gloucester, duke of, proposed as commander-in-chief **XV** 554

Gloucester, dukes of *see* William, duke of Gloucester; Humphrey; Richard; Thomas of Woodstock

Gloucester, earls of **III** 76, 92, 157; *see also* Audley, Hugh; Clare, Gilbert de; Despenser, Thomas; Robert; William

Gloucestershire **Ia** 43, 59, 68, 103; Frampton 342, 725; villa and village 610; Lydney 686; **III** 82, 101, 148, 151–2, 162; system of fines 128, 355; **V** 192, 368, 492; **VII** 463, 504

Glover, Richard (1712–85) **XI** 22, 204, 421; with reference to Pitt 128, 355

Glyme, river, villas **Ia** 607

Glympton (Oxon.) **III** 388

Glyn, Eleanor **XV** 75

Glyn, Sir Richard **XII** 131

Glyn Dŵr, Gryffyn **VI** 37

Glyn Dŵr, Owain **VI** 30, 37, 38, 48, 51; inheritance 40; Welsh revolt 40; Mortimer plan 42; South Wales campaign (1402) 42; captures Grey and Mortimer 42; escapes Charlton (1401) 44; Towy valley (1403) 54; Carmarthen march 54; independent Welsh church proposals 56; French alliance 55; Tripartite Indenture 57; decline (1406) 58; Woodbury Hill (1405) 58; commissariat 58; loses Aberystwyth and Harlech (1408–9) 65; vanishes 65; family captured 65; in hiding (Sep. 1415) 66; and Prince Henry 101; rebellion 111; Southampton plot 146; **VII** 366

Glyn Dyfrdwy, district, gave name to Owen Glendower **IV** 424

Glyndyfrdwy (Merioneth) **VI** 37, 41, 66

Glynn, John (1722–79) **XII** 132, 142, 227

Gneisenau: sails through Channel **XV** 542; damaged 564

Goa **VIII** 242; Portuguese settlement **XII** 158

goats **Ia** 620

goblets, silver **VIII** 273

Goch, Iolo, poet **VI** 40

Goddard, Thomas (d. 1783), Indian general **XII** 315

Godeheu, director of French East India Company and successor of Dupleix **XI** 328

Goderich, Viscount *see* Robinson, Frederick John

Godesberg, meeting **XV** 427

Godfred, king of the Danes, murdered (810) **II** 241

Godfrey, bishop of Bath **III** 126

Godfrey, bishop of St Asaph **III** 224

Godfrey, Sir Edmund Berry **X** 93–4, 177

Godfrey, Michael **X** 177

Godfrey of Bouillon, king of Jerusalem **III** 189; **V** 123

Godgifu, daughter of King Æthelred II, married Drogo, count of the Vexin **II** 560

Godmanchester: town defences **Ia** 279, 389; *mansio* 568, 597

Godmunddingaham *see* Goodmanham (Yorks.)

Godmundeslæch *see* Gumley (Leics.)

Gododdin of Aneirin **II** 3, 77

Godolphin, Francis, 2nd earl of Goldolphin **X** 221

Godolphin, Sidney, earl of (1645–1712) **XI** 35, 420

Godoy, Manuel (1767–1851) **XII** 458

Godric **III** 94, 256

Godsalve, Sir Thomas **VII** 600

Godstow (Oxon.) **III** 237; **V** 279

Godwin, William (1756–1836) **XII** 534, 541

Godwine, earl of Wessex **II** 416–17, 420; origin 416–17; supports Harthacnut 420; arrests Alfred the Ætheling 421; prosecuted by Harthacnut 421; relations with Edward the Confessor 423, 424–6, 561–2; death 424, 569; expulsion and return 563–8; refuses to harry Dover 563; return 566–8; mobilizes family resources 567; its house position (1051) 568

Goering, H.: possible substitute for Hitler **XV** 458; approaches to 475; and *Luftwaffe* 486, 497, 498

Goertz, Baron Friedrich W. von (d. 1728) **XI** 153

Goffe, William **IX** 151, 153–4, 245

Goidelic language **Ia** 17

Golafre, Sir John **V** 437

Golconda **VIII** 242

gold: Irish **Ia** 16; British export 42, 58, 72, 540, 630; smelting 530, 658; bullion 532, 633; mining 632, 634; goldsmith's workshop 685; votive offerings 690; currencies **IV** 638; **X** 331; discovery —Australia **XIII** 125 —California 125 —South Africa 402

gold, Queen's: English Exchequer provides **VI** 184

Gold Coast **X** 332, 333; **XIV** 28, 35

gold reserves **XV** 337

gold standard: not abandoned (1914) **XV** 5; suspended (1919) 140; restored (1925) 222–5; refusal to abandon 290–2; saved 296; abandoned 297, 298, 370

Golden Age, foretold by Hoare **XV** 437

Golden House, Rome **Ia** 156, 161

Goldie, Sir George Taubman **XIV** 188, 189, 193, 194; military exploits 242

Golding, Mr **XII** 408

Golding, Louis **XV** 312

Goldolphin, Sidney, 1st earl of Goldolphin, account of **X** 114; lord of the Treasury 123, 180, 182; commissioner to William of Orange 141; view of parties 152; treated as a non-party man 180; involved in Jacobite plot 185; parliament (1702) 222; occasional conformity 224; Dr Sacheverell 226; dismissed 227; death 232; Jacobitism 240; 'prime minister' 256; East Indian Company 354

Goldolphin horse **X** 408

Goldsborough **Ib** map 6 88

Goldsmith, Oliver (1728–74) **XI** 62, 305, 407; *Deserted Village* 109, 141; *Vicar of Wakefield* 418; **XII** 40, 47, 328, 346, 349; biography 328

Goldsmith, Thomas, prior of Canterbury **VII** 19

goldsmiths **IX** 287

Goldsmiths' Row **VIII** 275

golf **XIV** 166

Golias, Goliad **III** 240, 258

Gollancz, Victor **XV** 396, 458

Gomez Suarez de Figueroa, count of Feria, Spanish ambassador **VII** 560

Grantley, Lord (Sir Fletcher Norton) **XII** 119, 120, 149, 235; lawyer 66; Speaker (1770) 102; sides with opposition 208; civil list 232; loses seat 240

Granvelle, cardinal de **VIII** 44, 59, 120, 121

Granvelle, sieur de *see* Perrenot, Antoine

Granville, earls of *see* Carteret, John; Granville, George; Leveson-Gower

Granville, George, Baron Lansdowne (1667–1735) **XI** 161

Granville, George, 2nd earl **XIV** 5, 6, 33, 37, 66; biography 4; Sudan mistakes 80, 81; Irish devolution 89; Gladstone's third ministry 97; Parnell's fall 183; African empire 190; and Bismarck 191; Home Rule 207

Granville, Countess Grace (*c.*1667–1744) **XI** 148, 204, 249

graphs **XV** xxi–xxvii; UK imports and exports by value (1914–45) xxi (fig. 1); UK imports and exports by volume (1919–47) xxii (fig. 2); gross national product (1914–48) xxiii (fig. 3); unemployment (1914–48) xxiv (fig. 4); national income (1914–48) xxv (fig. 5); prices and wages (1914–48) xxvi (fig. 6); expenditure of public authorities xxvii (fig. 7)

Grasmere (Cumbria) **V** 366

Grasse, de, French admiral **XII** 217

Grassi, J. L., on William Airmyn **V** 82

Grassington, Celtic fields **Ia** 621

Grateley (Hants) **II** 349

Gratian **III** 232

Gratian (I), the Elder **Ia** 351–3, 363, 369

Gratian (II), Emperor **Ia** 395, 400–3, 408, 435, 495, 691

Gratian (III), usurper **Ia** 426–7, 468

Grattan, Henry (1746–1820): identity of Junius **XII** 145; biography 223; in Ireland 223, 246, 389–96, 400, 422; foreign affairs 566

Graunt, John **X** 25

Gravamina, ecclesiastical **IV** 453–4, 456, 479, 480–4; taxation 456; English clergy's to the pope (1255–6) 503

grave goods **Ia** 652, 693–4, 703–5

Gravelines (W. Flanders) **III** 459; **V** 431, 432, 436; **VI** 73, 111, 178; **VII** 310; battle (1558) 559; **IX** 234; battle *see* Armada

Gravelot, Hubert François (1699–1773), engraver **XI** 406

Graves, Admiral **XII** 204, 217

Graves, Richard (1715–1804), *Spiritual Quixote* **XI** 97

Graves, Robert **XV** 61, 549

Gravesend (Kent) **VI** 23, 626

Gravesend, Richard, bishop of London (1258–79) **IV** 176, 208, 486–7; problem of pluralities 487

Gravesend, Richard, treasurer of St Paul's **IV** 486

Gravesend, Stephen, bishop of London (1280–1303) **IV** 486–7

Gravesend, Stephen, bishop of London (1319–38) **V** 93

Gravier, Charles, comte de Vergennes (1717–87) **XI** 375

Gravina, Admiral **XII** 425

Gray, Henry, Lord Powys **VI** 486, 516

Gray, John de, bishop of Norwich **III** 221, 315, 317, 444, 446

Gray, master of **VIII** 370, 386, 442

Gray, Richard, Lord **V** 90

Gray, Stephen (1696–1736), electrician **XI** 382–3

Gray, Thomas (1716–71) **XI** 129, 426, 429; **XII** 350; **XIII** 12

Gray, Sir Thomas (jun.), on Bannockburn **V** 35–9; on Gilbert Middleton 41

Gray, Sir Thomas (sen.) **V** 37, 38

Greenfield, William of, king's clerk **IV** 266

greengrocers **Ia** 657

Greenland, **VII** 227; whale fishing **IX** 51; fisheries **X** 317; **XII** 14

Greenwich (Grenewic) (Kent) **Ib** xxvi; **II** 384, 390; **V** 409, 508; king's palace **VI** 116; **VII** 78, 211, 229, 231, 312; Erasmus 249; William Roy and Jerome Barlow 343; Thomas Cranmer 348; death of Edward VI 524; palace developed 594; treaties (1543) 407, 483; hospital **X** 389; peerage **XII** 129

Greenwood, Arthur: biography **XV** 279; Housing Act 279, 344; opposes cuts in benefit 297; hopeful after reoccupation of Rhineland 386; defeated as Labour leader 393; opposes arms estimates 414; speaks for England 452, 606; meets Chamberlain 474; and Cabinet committees 482; ineffective 509; leaves War Cabinet 544; leads nominal Opposition 471; Beveridge wished on 567

Greenwood, Frederick **XIV** 38

Greenwood, Sir Hamar **XV** 157

Greenwood, John **VIII** 204

Greenwood, Walter **XV** 352

Greetham (Lincs.) **II** 518

Greetwell **Ib** 178, 182; map 4 xxxii

Gregory I, the Great, Pope **Ia** 735–6; **Ib** 115, 192; **II** 38, 59, 110, 167; dispatch of mission to Britain 103–4; replies to Augustine's questions 106–8; scheme for organization of English church 108–9, 226

Gregory II, Pope **II** 168

Gregory III, Pope **II** 145, 169, 175

Gregory VII, Pope (Hildebrand) **II** 586, 667, 675; **III** 180; reform of 169, 171, 176, 177

Gregory IX, Pope (1227–41) **IV** 45, 46, 89, 92; Frederick II 48, 59, 98,

106; sends legate Otto to England and Scotland 74, 583, 584; letter from Henry III on Peter of Dreux 97; Raymond of Toulouse 100; dies 100; Richard of Cornwall 106; decretals 449, 453; **VI** 265

Gregory X, Pope (1271–6): Kilwardy appointed Archbishop of Canterbury **IV** 225; policy 231–2; council of Lyons (1274) 232–3; Edward I 233; problem of Provence 247; crusade 264; taxation of clergy 266, 499; Welsh problems 406, 407

Gregory XI, Pope (1370–8) **V** 279, 285, 521

Gregory XII, Pope **VI** 91, 92

Gregory XIII, Pope **VIII** 158, 173–6, 352, 478

Gregory of Tours **Ia** 736; *History of the Franks* **Ib** 10; **II** 105, 195

Grein, J. T. **XIV** 329

Greindor, Grendor, Sir John **VI** 42, 103

Grenada: British capture (1762) **XII** 75; restored to England (1783) 255; free port (1787) 289

Grenadines: British capture **XII** 75; retention 85; restored to England (1783) 255

Grenewic *see* Greenwich (Kent)

Grenfell, Julian **XV** 61

Grentmesnil, Hugh de **III** 100–1

Grenvile, Sir Bevil **IX** 268

Grenville, 1st Baron *see* Wyndham, William

Grenville, Hon. George (1712–70) **XI** 224, 250, 353; George III's dislike of **XII** 79, 128; remained in office (1761) 74; treasurer of navy (1760–2) 557; secretary of state (1762) 79, 575; views on peace (1762) 79; views on domestic affairs (1762) 81; loss of power (1762) 82; economy campaigns 90, 92, 103–6; first lord of Treasury 93, 96–99, 102–9; fall 109–11, 147, 575, 577; criticism of

America under Rockingham 115; allegations 118; financial policy (1767) 126; Controverted Elections Act (1770) 139; identity of Junius 145; death 150; American policy 104–6, 164, 180, 182–7

Grenville, George Nugent-Temple, 2nd Earl Temple (1753–1813), son of George Grenville: downfall of Fox-North coalition **XII** 267; lord lieutenant of Ireland (1782–3) 579; secretary of state (December 1783) 579

Grenville, Sir Richard **VIII** 246, 412, **IX** 142

Grenville, Richard Temple, marquis of Buckingham (1784), 1st Earl Temple (1711–79) **XI** 49, 147, 354, 370, 413; lord privy seal (1757–61) **XII** 69, 74, 575; supporter of Pitt 69, 74; biography 74; connection with Wilkes 81, 98–100, 132; out of office 111, 118; and identity of Junius 145

Grenville, Thomas (1755–1846) **XII** 250, 418; president of Board of Control (1806) 582; first lord of admiralty (1806–7) 582

Grenville family: and Pitt **XI** 346, 376; opposed to Walpole 204, 238; **XII** 65, 439

Grenvillite whigs **XIII** 55, 68

Gresham (Norfolk), manor **VI** 344, 461

Gresham, John **VII** 412

Gresham, Richard **VII** 412

Gresham, Sir Thomas **VIII** 45, 48, 59, 240, 259–60

Gresham College **VIII** 320; **IX** 372

Greta Bridge **Ia** 522, 684

Gretna, munition works **XV** 37

Greville, Charles Cavendish Fulke **XIII** 56, 170, 239–40, 312; biography 20

Greville, Robert, 2nd Lord Brooke **IX** 90, 97, 338, 342

Grey, Arthur, Lord Grey de Wilton **VIII** 43, 177, 356, 478

Grey, Lady Catherine **VII** 524; **VIII** 95, 96

Grey, Charles, 2nd Earl (1764–1845) **XII** 363, 411, 499; proposals for parliamentary reform 301, 361, 439, 448, 450; biography 361; first lord of admiralty (1806) 435, 439, 582; foreign secretary (1806–7) 442, 445, 457, 582; out of office 484, 489, 491, 566, 572; **XIII** 56, 227, 230, 622; parliamentary reform (before 1830) 57–8, 65–6; biography 78; reform bills (1830–2) 78–9, 82, 84–6, 91; dislike of radicals 96; retirement 98

Grey, 3rd Earl **XIV** 12

Grey, Edmund, earl of Kent: grandson of Reginald **VI** 553; Edward IV supporter 557

Grey, Sir Edward, afterwards Viscount: success as under-secretary for foreign affairs **XIV** 219, 223; important declaration about Nile Valley 244; demurs to Campbell-Bannerman's premiership 384; foreign secretary 384–5; authorizes Anglo-French military conversations but not notified of Anglo-Belgian 399, 400; action in Bosnian crisis 410–11; demands House of Lords reform 420; action in Agadir crisis 434; speech on arbitration 448; difficulties over Persia 449; exchange of letters with Cambon 462; presides over London ambassadors' conference 466–8; negotiations with Lichnowsky and Kühlmann 471–2; visit to Paris 483; diplomacy in the final crisis 488–94, 496–7; relations to his party 572–4; biography **XV** 3; sends ultimatum to Germany 3; expects little suffering 4; council of war 6; runs foreign policy 14; remains foreign secretary 31; favours German offer to restrict

Grey, Sir Edward (*cont.*)
blockade 42; on war committee 47; takes up League 51; opposes conscription 55; supports Zionist plans 71; approves Lloyd George's war aims 97; demands reparations 127; Locarno fulfils hopes 221; First World War views 361; thinks Serbia should yield 370; Simon compared with 372

Grey, Lady Elizabeth, of Codnor **VI** 330

Grey, Elizabeth, wife of John (Elizabeth Woodville) **VI** 324; *see also* Woodville

Grey, Forde, Baron Grey of Werke **X** 105

Grey, Sir George, biography **XIII** 394

Grey, George, 2nd earl of Kent (d. 1503) **VII** 142

Grey, Henry, 3rd marquis of Dorset, duke of Suffolk (1551) (d. 1554) **VII** 488, 491, 492; Northumberland's defeat 527, 529; pardoned 530; Wyatt rebellion 538; death 539; portrait 599

Grey, Lord Henry, of Codnor **VI** 340

Grey, Henry George, 3rd Earl Grey, Viscount Howick **XIII** 16, 122; biography 270; colonial administration 367, 372, 382, 388–9, 399–401

Grey, Isabel, wife of Ralph **VI** 480

Grey, Lady Jane, *see* Jane Grey

Grey, Lord John (d. 1569) **VII** 543

Grey, Sir John, Lord Ferrers of Groby **VI** 324, 483; killed 535

Grey, John, gentleman **VII** 57

Grey, John de **IV** 402

Grey, Leonard, Lord: lord deputy of Ireland (1536–40) **VII** 365, 651; beheaded (1541) 418

Grey, Muriel, daughter of 2nd earl of Surrey, wife of John, 2nd Viscount Lisle **VII** 161

Grey, Sir Ralph **VI** 480; gives Alnwick to Lancastrians 530; Bamburgh holds out 531; beheaded 532

Grey, Lord Reginald, of Ruthin **VI** 37, 42, 51, 65; ransoms himself 46

Grey, Reginald de, justiciar of Chester **IV** 336, 436, 441; commission of inquiry into Welsh precedents 418; granted Duffryn Clwyd (later barony of Ruthin) 424, 430; Edward of Caernarvon (1297) 682

Grey, Lord Richard, of Codnor **VI** 87, 441; ambassador to France 141

Grey, Richard, son of Elizabeth **VI** 613

Grey, Richard de, castellan of Dover (1264) **IV** 187

Grey, Lord Thomas, executed (1554) **VII** 539

Grey, Sir Thomas, of Heton **VI** 272

Grey, Thomas, 1st marquis of Dorset (1451–1501) **VII** 50, 192, 288; arrested (1487) 73

Grey, Thomas, 2nd marquis of Dorset (1477–1530) **VI** 612; son of Elizabeth 276, 553; sanctuary at Westminster 614; Buckingham's revolt 627; **VII** 313

Grey, Sir William, 13th baron de Wilton (d. 1562) **VII** 484

Grey, William, bishop of Ely **VI** 270, 272, 301; books to Balliol 666, 679; John Free's patron 679

greyhound racing **XV** 313

Greystoke, John, Lord **VI** 323

Greystoke, Ralph, Lord **VI** 3

Greystoke, Ralph, Lord, grandson of Ralph **VI** 643

Greystoke family **VI** 319

Greystones, John, of Bottisham **V** 416

Grierson, General **XIV** 399, 400

Grievances, ecclesiastical *see Gravamina*

Griffin, Thomas (d. 1771), Admiral **XI** 262

Griffith, Arthur: plans non-violent resistance **XV** 154; heads provisional government 159; defends Irish treaty 161

Griffith, John **VII** 170

Griffith, Sir Rhys ap **V** 94

Griffith ap Nicholas **VI** 641

Griffith-Boscawen, Sir A. **XV** 205

Griffiths, D. W. **XV** 315

Griffo, Pietro **VII** 238

Griggs, Sir P. James: becomes secretary for war **XV** 479

Grilly, John de **IV** 243, 244, 279; seneschal of Gascony (1266 and 1278-87) 281, 254, 288-9, 306, 309; disgrace and later life (1287-1301) 289; transfer of the Agenais 292-3; seneschal of Edward's lands in Aquitaine (1279) 293-4

Grilly in Savoy **IV** 288

Grim, J. **III** 238

Grim, Simon **III** 410

Grimani, Marco, papal legate **VII** 407

Grimaud (Grimaldi), Reyner, Genoese admiral in service of Philip IV **IV** 655

Grimbald of St Omer **II** 271

Grim's Dyke **Ia** 561

Grimsby (Lincs.) **Ib** 179; **III** 88, 94, 96; **VI** 418

Grimshaw, Revd William (1708-63), of Haworth **XI** 88

Grindal, Edmund, archbishop of Canterbury **VIII** 17, 193, 194, 197, 198

Grindcob, William **V** 415, 416, 419

Grindon (Northumb.) **III** 283

Grinstead **Ib** map 5 68

Gristhwaite (N. Yorks.), manor **VI** 337

Groby (Leics.) **VI** 376; keep **VII** 38

Grocin, William **VII** 247, 250, 251; learning and scholarship 240-5

Gronlund, Laurence **XIV** 334

Grose, C. L. **X** 59

Grosmont Castle **IV** 43

Grosseteste, Robert, Bishop **VI** 277

Grosseteste, Robert, bishop of Lincoln (1235-53) **IV** 47, 57, 70, 78, 450-1; law of bastardy 70-2, 453; relations with Simon de Montfort 107, 113; at Lyons (1250) 114; tract on kingship 114; constitutions 452-3; legate Otto 453; *gravamina* of clergy 453-6, 460; anointing of kings 460; secular office held by ecclesiastics 461; attacks court of Canterbury (*sede vacante*) 466; advice on preaching 765

Grosseteste, Robert, Chancellor **III** 239

Grossstamm der Angeln **Ib** 108-9, 115

Grosvenor, Lord *see* Westminster, 1st duke of

Grote, George **XIII** 92, 452, 492; **XIV** 136

Grotius, Hugo **IX** 52, 217, 226

Ground Game Act (1880) **XIV** 86

Grove, Derek van **VII** 592

Grubenhäuser **Ib** 66, 99, 167, 208, 214

Gruffydd, of Llewelyn the Great **IV** 390; disinherited 393; Henry III and 398-9; death 399

Gruffydd, Rhys ap, of Cardigan (Rhys the Black) **VI** 65

Gruffydd, Sir Rhys ap **VII** 366

Gruffydd ap Cynan **III** 285-7, 291

Gruffydd ap Gwenwynwyn, lord of South Powys 398, 403; conspiracy against Llywelyn (1274) **IV** 406-7; baron of Wales 414, 417-19, 421, 427, 428; wife 326

Gruffydd ap Gwilym ap Gryffyd **VI** 39

Gruffydd ap Llywelyn, king of Gywnedd and Powys **II** 572-6

Gruffydd ap Madog, of Bromfield **IV** 382, 409-10, 424

Gruffydd ap Rhys ('Sir Gruffydd Llwyd') **IV** 441
Gruffydd ap Tudor, son of last Welsh seneschal, in Edward's service **IV** 441
Gruffydd Fychan, ancestor of Owen Glendower **IV** 424
Grundy, Felix (1777–1840), American politician **XII** 551
Grünfeld, Henry, papal protonotory **VI** 199
Guadeloupe **X** 325; **XI** 359, 364, 368, 372; returned to France (1763) **XII** 85; capture (1794) 369, 370
Guala, cardinal-priest of St Martin, papal legate: government of England (1216–18) **IV** 1–3, 11, 12, 16; seals first reissue of Great Charter 4; and Wales 393
Guallanc **Ib** 199
Gualo, papal legate **III** 77, 483, 484, 486
Gualter, Rudolf **VIII** 192
Guaras, Antonio **VII** 526; **VIII** 156, 163, 164, 338
Guardians of Scotland: Alexander III's minority **IV** 578, 582, 590–2; agreement with Welsh princes (1258) 582, 592; after death of Alexander III (1286) 597, 599, 604, 609; seal broken (1292) on Baliol's succession 609; court of justice 610; during the period (1298–1304) 694, 695, 696, 697, 709
'Gudemen' of Scotland **IV** 576
Gudendorf **Ib** 72, 193; map 1 xxix
Guelders, duchy **VI** 68, 572
Guérin, bishop-elect of Senlis **III** 467
Guernica **XV** 428, 437
Guernsey, Isle of **V** 119, 482; **VI** 593; see also Channel Islands
Guests, the ironworks, Dowlais, Worcs. **XI** 117
Gueux de mer (sea-beggars) **VIII** 127, 128, 155

Gui, Foulquois, legate **IV** 180; correspondence with English baronial leaders (1264) and becomes pope 195; see also Clement IV
Guiana **IX** 326; settlement (1814) **XII** 563
Guichen, Luc-Urbain de **XII** 215
Guienne: Normandy subsidies **VI** 468; **VII** 81, 172, 175, 220, 274; see also Aquitaine
Guienne Herald **VI** 124; **VII** 318
Guilden Morden, cemetery **Ia** 706
Guildford (Gyldeford) (Surrey) **Ia** 68; **III** 144; **V** 358; **VII** 142; parliamentary representation **XII** 52
Guildford, Sir Henry, comptroller of the household (1520) **VII** 600, 650
Guildford, Sir John **VI** 626
Guildford, Sir Richard (1455?–1506) comptroller of the household (1498) **VI** 626; **VII** 167, 169, 200, 210, 650
Guildown **Ib** 138; map 2 xxx; map 5 68
Guilford Court House, battle **XII** 216
Guillaume, count of Narbonne **VI** 244
Guillebaud, C. W. **XV** 514
Guilty Men **XV** 319
Guinea **VII** 561
Guinegate **VII** 268; battle (Battle of the Spurs) (1513) 279, 306, 599
Guines, count of **IV** 54, 214, 544, 545; **V** 140, 241; draft treaty of 137, 220; **VI** 641; county 106
Guines, Robert of **IV** 545
Guingamp **VII** 97, 104
Guiscard, Robert **III** 113
Guise (Aisne) **VI** 239; county 573
Guise, Charles, cardinal of Lorraine **VIII** 39, 46, 152, 374, 470
Guise, duke of see Francis
Guise, Francis, duke of: defends Calais **VIII** 36; inherits Crown 39; Catholic champion 54–8;

256

death 60, 74; Mary Stuart's uncle 71-2, 74

Guise, General **XII** 342

Guise, Henry, duke of **VIII** 157, 344, 357-8; enterprise against England 360-4; treaty of Joinville 365; Mary Stuart's execution 386, 388; conversion of James 391

Guise, Mary of, regent of Scotland **VIII** 39-40; proclamation against church 'reformers' 41-2; resists deposition 46-7

Guisnes **VII** 167, 310, 487, 493, 558

Guitalin (Vitalinus) **Ib** 164

Guiting (Glos.) **III** 42, 55

Guizot, F. **XIII** 117, 163, 224-5, 240-5, 247-8

Gulbenkian, Calouste **XV** 202

Gul's Hornbook **VIII** 293

Gumley (Godmundeslæch) (Leics.) **II** 205

gun-running: at Larne **XIV** 479; at Howth 481

Gundulf, bishop of Rochester **II** 671, 673, **III** 101, 260

Gunnhild, daughter of Cnut, German marriage **II** 408

Gunnhild, niece of Cnut **II** 405

Gunning, Elizabeth (duchess of Hamilton and Argyll) (1734-90) **XI** 148; **XII** 135

Gunning, Maria (Lady Coventry) (1733-60) **XI** 148

Gunpowder Plot **IX** 8

Gunthorpe, John, keeper of privy seal (d. 1498) **VI** 614, 616; **VII** 94, 203

'Guolloppum', battle **Ia** 471

Gurdon, Adam of **IV** 207, 208, 515

Gurk, bishop of *see* Lang

Gurney, Sir Thomas **V** 94

Gurney lordships **VI** 606

Gustavus Adolphus, king of Sweden **IX** 60, 209, 215, 401

gut, for artillery **Ia** 620

Guthberht, abbot of Wearmouth and Jarrow **II** 174

Guthfrith, Danish king of York **II** 262-3, 433

Guthfrith, Norse king in Ireland **II** 340, 342

Guthlac, St, founder of Crowland Abbey **II** 49, 158, 161, 178, 471

Guthrum, Danish king **II** 252-3; baptised 255, 257; king of East Anglia 257, 433; treaty with Alfred 260-2

Guy, count of Ponthieu **II** 577, **III** 105

Guy, count of Thouars **IV** 92

Guy, vicomte of Limoges **III** 466

Guy's Hospital, London, foundation **XII** 11

Gwaldus, wife of Reginald de Braose **III** 301

Gwalior, capture **XII** 315

Gwennllwyg, county of **V** 97

Gwent **Ia** 45; **II** 268, 615; **III** 287, 288, 291; three castles **IV** 20, 43, 52, 396, 401; Herbert stronghold **VI** 511

Gwent, Upper **III** 297

Gwenwynwyn **III** 298-9

Gwerthrynion, district **IV** 406

Gwilym, son of Tudor ap Goronwy **VI** 39

Gwithian **Ia** 8

Gwladus Ddu, daughter of Llywelyn the Great, wife of Reginald de Braose, later wife of Ralph Mortimer **IV** 395, 403

Gwynedd (Gwynnedd) (Snowdonia) **Ia** 45; kingdom **II** 80, 81, 576, 615-16; kings 330; **III** 294; resistance to Norman rule 285-8; primacy of princes **IV** 386; *see also* Owain; Llywelyn the Great; David; Llywelyn ap Gruffydd; Maelgwyn

Gwynionydd (Cardigan) **VI** 40

Gwynllwg **II** 268

Gyldeford *see* Guildford (Surrey)

Gyllenborg, Count Karl (1679-1746), and Jacobites **XI** 174

257

Gynewell, John, bishop of Lincoln (1347–62) **V** 301

gypsum, burial in **Ia** 700, 731

Gyrth, son of Earl Godwine **II** 565; earl of East Anglia 574; at Hast-ings 592; death 596

Gyruum *see* Jarrow (Co. Durham)

Gyrwe **II** 43, 294, 296; South Gyrwe 43; Tondberht *princeps* of 47

Gytha, wife of Earl Godwine **II** 417

H

habeas corpus **IX** 39

Habeas Corpus Acts **X** 99, 121, 185, 257; suspended (1794) **XII** 360

Habsburg: house of **VII** 113, 153, 187, 341, 474; Suffolk 183; death of Philip 184; Anglo-Burgundian treaties (1506) 186; quarrel with Valois 307, 535, 559; Maximilian's death 308; 'ladies' peace' of Cambrai (1529) 319, 328; Wolsey's downfall 320; Mary pledged to Philip (1553) 537

Hacha, President **XV** 439

Hacket, John **VII** 345

Hacket, William **VIII** 204

Haddington **VI** 35, 37; Hailes Castle 37; Scottish forces 587; **VII** 484-5

Haddock, Nicholas (1686-1746), Admiral **XI** 210, 226, 229, 236, 240; Spanish coastal patrol 233; retires from Mediterranean fleet (1742) 247

Haddon Rig, battle (1542) **VII** 405

Hadleigh (Essex) **VI** 654

Hadley, John **V** 401

Hadley, John (1682-1744), mathematician **XI** 382

Hadow report **XV** 211

Hadrian, abbot of St Peter and St Paul at Canterbury **II** 131-2, 191; as teacher 180-3

Hadrian, Emperor (117-38) **Ia** 154, 169-91; frontier policy 4, 169-71, 187, 242, 245 — security and policing 260 — Scottish policy 363-4; building of Wall 176-85, 198; town development 185-8, 232-3, 584; Fenland development 189-90, 243, 547-8, 644; compared with Antoninus 193, 198; evacuation of Pennine forts 199; plans for succession 204; provincial tour 301, 517;

architecture 326; control of lead and iron industries 635, 638; **VII** 264

Hadrian I, Pope **II** 176, 215, 217, 218

Hadrian's Wall: construction and purpose **Ia** 96, 166, 173, 175-85, 364; coastal system 177-8, 260; Offa's Dyke comparison 190-1; Antonine Wall comparison 193-5; settlement between walls 198, 385; 2nd cent. maintenance and recommissioning 202, 205, 206, 210-11, 222; outpost forts 206, 211, 226, 249, 352 — abandoned 377; Severan consolidation 223-9; civil settlements adjacent 247, 277, 385, 511, 594; communications 304, 383; Constantius and Constantine 312-15, 328-9; Theodosius 377-80, 398, 411; still held at end of Roman period 385, 405; Stilicho 420-3; Hadrian exercises command 528; water-mills 632; lead and iron 635, 638; shrines 666, 668, 683, 685, 708-9 — Mithras 711-12 — Carrawburg Mithraeum 734; burial club 696; **Ib** xxvi, 75, 77, 198; map 4 xxxii

Hæafuddene *see* Howden (Yorks.)

Hæddi, bishop of Winchester **II** 50, 134, 181

Hægel *see* Camel, river

Hæsten, Danish leader **II** 266-7

Haestingas **Ib** 43; map 2 xxx

Hæstingaceaster *see* Hastings (Sussex)

Hæthfeld *see* Hatfield (Herts.)

Hæthfeldland *see* Hatfield Chase (Yorks.)

hafod, hafota **IV** 384

haga **II** 526-7

Lichfield, keeper of privy seal **VI** 561

Hales, John, lawyer **VIII** 96

Hales, John, layman (d. 1571) **VII** 503, 504, 505

Hales, Sir Robert, treasurer (1381) **V** 407, 409, 410, 412

Hales, Stephen (1677–1761), scientist, author of *Vegetable Staticks* **XI** 384–5, 388, 391

Halfdan, Danish leader **II** 246, 252–3, 258, 271, 363

Halfdan, ealdorman under Cnut **II** 416

Halidon hill, battle **V** 117, 129, 205

Halifax (Yorks.) **VI** 366; **VII** 388; **IX** 132; **XII** 513; population **XV** 167

Halifax, earls of *see* Dunk, G. M.; Montague, Charles; Montague Dunk

Halifax, Lord *see* Wood, Edward Frederick Lindley

Halifax, marquis of *see* Savile, George

Halkett, Sir James **IX** 203

Hall, C. **XIII** 129

Hall, Chester Moor (1703–71), maker of achromatic lenses **XI** 382

Hall, doorkeeper to Gloucester **VI** 21–2

Hall, Edward (d. 1547) **VII** 27, 67, 75, 202, 580; Lambert Simnel 73; English success at Dixmude (1489) 99; Perkin Warbeck 140–2; Truce of Ayton (1497) 147; Arthur and Catherine 174; Henry VIII's early reign 235; English prose 266; Wolsey 295, 297, 303; Cloth of Gold 310; Anglo-Imperial alliance (1522) 311; Catherine and Henry's divorce 322; More 347, 363; Fisher 363; Henry VIII and music 589–90

Hall, Joseph **IX** 400

Hall, Richard (d. 1604) **VII** 322

hall-moot **II** 502

Hallam, Henry, *Constitutional History of England* (1827) **VII** 190; **XIII** 551

Hallam, John **VII** 392

Halle, Henry atte **V** 333

Hallé Orchestra **XV** 234, 314

Hallé, Sir Charles **XIV** 159, 327

Haller, Albrecht von (1708–77) **XI** 389

Haller, Dr Johannes **VI** 93

Halley, Bartholomew, MP Herts **VI** 417

Halley, Edmund (1656–1742) **X** 414; **XI** 379

Halley's Comet **III** 252

Halliwell (Lancs.), manor **VI** 323

Hallstatt culture **Ia** 9

Hallum, Robert, bishop of Salisbury **VI** 92, 169, 170; Arundel's auditor 93, 269

Halnaker **IV** 279

Halsbury, 1st earl of **XIV** 91, 224, 399, 428

Haltemprice, Austin convent **VI** 288

Halton, John, bishop of Carlisle (1292–1334): papal collector in Scotland **IV** 573, 584; **V** 61

Halton Chesters: tombstone **Ia** 696–7; **Ib** map 4 xxxii

Halyday, Robert **VI** 528

-ham **Ib** 33–5, 40–1, 43–4, 125

Ham **Ib** 102; map 2 xxx

Ham Hill **Ia** 93

Haman, Passfield likened to **XV** 276

Hamble, river **II** 23, 174

Hambledon, burials **Ia** 601, 696

Hambledon Club **XII** 337

Hamburg **Ib** map 1 xxix; **VI** 69, 359; **VII** 343; **VIII** 133, 239; bombed **XV** 570

Hamburg Company **XII** 25

Hamilton, Alexander (1757–1804) **XII** 471

Hamilton, Alexander (d. *c.*1732), traveller in the East **XI** 331–2

Hamilton, Anthony **X** 369

Hanau, negotiations at **XI** 243–4, 245, 269

Hanbury (Staffs.), monastery **II** 49

Hancchach, John **V** 416

Hancock, John **XII** 185, 202

Hancock, Thomas **XIII** 571

Handel, George Frederick (1685–1759) **X** 407; **XI** 10, 305, 399, 414–17; **XIII** 561

Handley, Tommy **XV** 549

handwriting: Carolingian **II** 189, 443; Hiberno-Saxon 191, 443: Irish 178–9, 184

Hankey, Sir Maurice: biography **XV** 3; suggests attack on Turkey 23; remark of Lloyd George to 62; organizes cabinet secretariat 75, 130, 196; urges convoy 84; Maurice debate 118; Chamberlain's war cabinet 456

Hankford, William, chief justice of the King's Bench **VI** 454

Hanmer, David **VI** 40

Hanmer, John **VI** 56

Hanmer, Philip, brother-in-law of Glyn Dŵr **VI** 37, 40

Hanmer, Sir Thomas (1677–1746), Speaker of House of Commons **X** 243–4; **XI** 154; edited Shakespeare 419

Hanney (Berks.) **III** 18

Hannibal, Thomas, master of the rolls (9 Oct. 1523) **VII** 648

Hannington, Wal **XV** 349

Hanotaux, G. **XIV** 242, 244

Hanover: early history **XI** 1–12; characteristics 11, 14–15; territories 12–13; population 13; 'Order of Government' 13–14, 40; relations with Britain 14, 19–21: royal visits 40–2; chaplains for 78; influence on British foreign policy 165, 174, 237–8, 240, 350; *see also* George I; George II; subsidies

Hanover, elector of *see* George I

Hans, painter **VI** 471

Hansa (Hansards, Easterlings, Al-mains) **III** 89, 91; records **IV** 687; German in London 621; Flemish merchants 621; German **VI** 69, 70, 352, 356; English goods 356; exports 356; relations with England 356–60; import restraints exemption 544; Warwick retaliation (1468) 554; steelyard closed 554; **VII** 102, 159, 183, 470, 476; Perkin Warbeck 124; monopolies challenged 188; treaty of Utrecht 220–1; privileges struggle with Henry 221–3; common cause against Turks 308; ousted by English merchants 471–5

Hansards **VI** 349

Hanse merchants **VIII** 239

Hanville, John de **III** 242

Hanway, Jonas (1712–86) **XI** 129, 136, 139; biography **XII** 11

Hanwell (Middx.): Jutish pottery **Ib** 67 [fig. 4(f)]; map 5 68

Harborne, William **VIII** 241

Harbottle **VII** 305

harbours **Ia** 26, 563–4; ports 57, 90, 95–7, 557, 563–4 — Gloucester and Cirencester 585 — exports 630; bases 97, 305–9, 528–30

Harclay, Andrew, earl of Carlisle (1322–3) **V** 66, 67, 73, 75, 87

Harcourt (Eure) **VI** 174, 207

Harcourt, 1st Earl (1714–77), lord lieutenant of Ireland **XII** 389, 577

Harcourt, Geoffrey of **V** 133

Harcourt, Jacques d' **VI** 242

Harcourt, Lewis V., afterwards Viscount **XIV** 234, 492

Harcourt, Simon, 1st Viscount (1661–1727) **XI** 150, 421

Harcourt, Sir William V.: biography **XIV** 25; opposed to relief of Gordon 82; won over to home rule 96; becomes chancellor of Exchequer 97; declines to appoint women inspectors 130; concerned in rupture between Liberals and

Harcourt, Sir William (*cont.*)
Parnell 184; returns to Exchequer 209; misses premiership 215; death duties 217–18; Raid inquiry committee 233–4; Liberal leader in Commons 239; resigns position 239; bill to reform London local government 297; on 'cleavage of classes' 333

Hardalio, slave, burial **Ia** 696

Hardie, J. Keir **XIV** 222, 265, 266, 397; biography 101; **XV** 382

Harding, John (d. 1725), printer of Swift's *Drapier's Letters* **XI** 302

Harding, Stephen **III** 187

Harding, Thomas **VIII** 11

Hardinge, Sir Alexander **XV** 400

Hardinge, Nicholas (1699–1758): and Journals of House of Commons **XI** 397

Hardinge, Sir Henry, Viscount Hardinge **XIII** 270; biography 424; governor-general of India 424–5

Hardknot, inscription **Ia** 203

Hardwick, Bess of, countess of Shrewsbury **VIII** 374

Hardwicke, 1st earl of *see* Yorke, Philip

Hardy, Sir Charles (1716?–80) **XII** 226

Hardy, founder of London Corresponding Society **XII** 358, 360

Hardy, Gathorne, Earl Cranbrook **XIV** 49, 62; biography 32

Hardy, Thomas **XIII** 559; **XIV** 160, 330, 331, 333, 549; **XV** 178

Hardyng, John, chronicler **VI** 4, 46, 224; **VII** 578, 580

Hare, Francis (1671–1740), bishop of Chichester **XI** 80

Hare, H. T. **XIV** 324

Hare, Sir Nicholas, master of requests (1537, 1552) **VII** 530, 646; speaker of House of Commons (1539) 654; master of the rolls (1553) 648

hare hunting **VIII** 277

Harewell, John, bishop of Bath and Wells (1366–86) **V** 389

Harfleur (Seine-Inf.) **VI** 149, 171, 189, 204, 206; port 33; siege (1416) 123, 124, 233; 'key to France' 149; English siege casualties 150; Henry V capture (23 Sep. 1415) 150–1; defenders depart 150; defenders 157; importance (1416) 157; operations 158; Armagnac blockade 163; French discussions 164, 165; critical position 165, 166; siege raised 168; debts 195; maintenance costs 204; prisoners ransomed 222; Bedford's relief expedition 327; embassy to France 474; Moleyns and Roos 480

Hargreaves, James (d. 1778) **XI** 110

Hargreaves' spinning Jenny *see* jennies

Harington, Sir C. **XV** 191

Harington, Sir John **VIII** 190, 438, 493, 494; **IX** 401

Haringworth Castle **VII** 38

Harlech **IV** 429; Welsh revolt (1294–5) 422; castle 430–2; borough 433; **VI** 44, 55, 422; falls to Talbots (1409) 65; Lancastrians 527

Harlesden (Middx.) **VI** 675

Harleston, Sir John **V** 24

Harlestone (Northants) **V** 345

Harley, Edward, 2nd earl of Oxford (1689–1741) **XI** 64, 181, 396; library 387

Harley, John, bishop of Hereford (1553–4) **VII** 545

Harley, Robert, 1st earl of Oxford (1661–1724): nonconformist **X** 24; reduction of the army 188; William III's view of 198; parliament (1702) 222; secretary of state 224; rise 225–7; out of office 227; and peace terms 233; Bolingbroke's jealousy of 239; dismissal 241, 247; Old Pretender 243;

culmination of Bolingbroke's quarrel 245–8; impeached 249; and the Cabinet 255; 'prime minister' 256; **XI** 38, 78, 155, 181, 183; impeached 24, 156; ignored by George I 154; South Sea concession 314; Royal Society 396; political writers 420

Harley, Thomas (1730–1804), lord mayor of London, MP **XII** 131, 247

Harman, Thomas **VIII** 264

Harmondsworth (Middx.), Winchester college living **VI** 496

Harmsworth (Middx.) **V** 337

Harmsworth, Alfred, Lord Northcliffe **XIV** 310, 311–15, 446, 532, 533–4; reading 550

Harmsworth, Harold Sydney, Lord Rothermere **XIV** 311, 480; biography **XV** 96; becomes secretary for air 96; at Ministry of Information 107; takes over Northcliffe's papers 187; sale of *The Times* 193; makes alliance with Beaverbrook 282; denounced by Baldwin 283; applauds British Union of Fascists 374; supports Edward VIII 401

Harnett, John **VI** 343

Harnett, Sir Nicholas, of Farleton **VI** 31

Harnett, Sir Thomas **VI** 516

Harney, G. J. **XIII** 136

Harnham Hill **Ib** 149; map 3 xxxi

Harold (Hein), king of Denmark **II** 611

Harold I, king of England **II** 420–2

Harold II, king of England **II** 466, 580; son of Earl Godwine 489; earl of East Anglia 561; expulsion and return 564–8; earl of Wessex 569; Welsh wars 572–4, 576; position in England 576–7, 579; oath to William of Normandy 577–8; administration 581–2; mobilizes forces 586–8; campaign against Harald Hardrada 588–

91; march from York 592–3; at Hastings 593–6; daughter 595–6, 687; illegitimate sons 600, 602; **III** 100

Harold, son of Swein, king of Denmark **II** 387, 401

Harold, son of Thorkell the Tall **II** 423–4, 427

Harold Fairhair, king of Norway **II** 348, 360, 406

Harold Gormsson, king of the Danes **II** 375

Harold Hardrada, king of Norway **II** 428, 432, 589; designs on England 560, 569, 575, 587; invades England 588

Harpsfield, John (1516–78) **VII** 575

Harpsfield, Nicholas, archdeacon of Canterbury (1519?–75) **VII** 247, 322, 324, 551, 571

Harriman, A. **XV** 529

Harringay (Middx.) **V** 450, 481, 488

Harrington, earl of *see* Stanhope, William

Harrington, James (1611–77) **IX** 250, 412; *Oceana* quoted **XI** 316

Harriot, Thomas **IX** 369

Harris, Sir Arthur T.: direct access to Churchill **XV** 480; advocates strategic bombing 483; commander-in-chief bomber command 520; conducts bombing offensive 552–3, 562; protests against diversion of bombers 564; conducts area bombing 570–1; day over 572; opposes precision bombing 580; defies Portal 591; not elevated to Lords 592

Harris, Dr Drew **XIV** 519

Harris, Howel (1714–73), and religious revival in Wales **XI** 97

Harris, James, 1st Earl Malmesbury (1746–1820) **XII** 368

Harris, James Howard, 3rd earl of Malmesbury **XIII** 166, 185, 186; biography 250; foreign secretary (1852) 250–1; (1858) 300

Harris, Renatus **X** 404, 405

Harris, Dr Rutherfoord **XIV** 231, 235

Harris, Wilson **XV** 310

Harrison, Frederic **XIII** 576, 613, 616; **XIV** 6, 132

Harrison, Henry **XV** 118

Harrison, James, inventor **XIV** 119

Harrison, John (1693–1776), clock-maker **XI** 381; inventor **XII** 17

Harrison, Thomas **IX** 158–9, 176, 242

Harrison, William **VIII** on inclosers 252; yeomen 256; vagabonds 264; fashion 267; beards 271; oak wood 272; tobacco 274; archery's decline 278; *Description of Britain* 283; election of scholars 321; **IX** 283, 385

Harrison, William Henry (1773–1841), president of U.S.A. **XII** 550

Harrogate **X** 409

Harrold **Ib** map 5 68

Harrow (Hearge) (Middx.) **II** 54, 101, 205, 732; **V** 414; **VI** 327

Harrow school **XV** 171

Harrowby, 1st Earl **XII** 484; foreign secretary (1804–5) **XII** 581; president of Board of Control (1809) 582; minister without portfolio (1809–12) 583; lord president of the council (1812) 583

Harston (Cambs.), Romano-Saxon pottery **Ib** 90 [fig. 7(c)]

Hart, Liddell: expects heavy casualties **XV** 438; economic weakness of Germany 461; indiscriminate bombing 534

Hartburn, settlement **Ia** 612

Harthacnut, son of Cnut and Emma **II** 402; king of Denmark 404–5, 406, 418; king of England 420–3, 554, 560; treaty with Magnus, king of Norway 421, 560; death 423

Hartington, Lord **XV** 204

Hartington, marquess of *see* Devonshire, 8th duke of

Hartlebury (Worcs.) **IV** 356

Hartlepool (Co. Durham) **IV** 705; **V** 32; **VIII** 140

Hartmann, son of Rudolf of Habsburg: betrothal to Joan of Acre **IV** 246, 247, 249

Hartshill **Ia** 645

haruspices **Ia** 680, 687

Harvard College **X** 347; **XII** 199

Harvey, Gabriel **VIII** 290, 294

Harvey, Revd James (1714–58) **XI** 88

Harvey, Martin **XV** 314

Harvey, William (1578–1657), physician **VIII** 312; **IX** 365, 371–2; **X** 376; **XI** 384

Harwich (Essex) **V** 162; **VI** 640; **X** 222; government influence **XII** 53

Harwich, Baron *see* Hillsborough, Viscount

Haseley (War.) **VI** 379

Haslemere, parliamentary representation **XII** 52

Haslingfield **Ib** map 2 xxx

Hassocks **Ib** 138–9; map 2 xxx

Hastings (Hæstingaceaster) (Sussex) **Ib** 43; circular brooch 60 [fig. 2(a)]; **II** 318, 432, 536, 566, 732; distinct from Sussex 18, 208; tribal names *Hæstingas* 18, 19; rape 19; battle 590–1, 593–6, 687; English and Norman armies 592–5; castle 591, 628; **III** 106, 264, 433, 434, 439; castle (king's chapel) **IV** 326; **V** 145; parliamentary representation **XII** 89

Hastings, Edward **VI** 473

Hastings, Sir Edward (later Lord Hastings of Loughborough), lord chamberlain of the household (1556) **VII** 649

Hastings, Gilbert of, bishop of Lisbon **III** 149

Hastings, Henry, 3rd earl of Huntingdon (1535–95) **VII** 524, 529, 538; **VIII** 95

Hastings, Henry of, defender of Kenilworth **IV** 208, 212

Hastings, Lord Hugh **V** 132, 133
Hastings, John, earl of Pembroke (1348–76) **V** 253, 268, 291, 384, 385
Hastings, John, earl of Pembroke (1376–89) **V** 260
Hastings, John, lord of Abergavenny **IV** 438; sister Ada, wife of Rhys ap Mareddud 438, 440; claimant of Scottish kingdom 606, 607; in Gascony 279
Hastings, Lawrence, earl of Pembroke (1340–8) **V** 145, 256
Hastings, marquis of, governorgeneral of Bengal **XIII** 403, 409–13; Gurkha war 411; central Indian campaign 411–12; annexation of Ceylon 412–13; purchase of Singapore 413; *see also* Rawdon-Hastings, Francis
Hastings, Sir P. **XV** 218, 225, 242
Hastings, Ralph, of Slingsby and Allerton **VI** 59, 325
Hastings, Richard, brother of William **VI** 325
Hastings, Warren (1732–1818) **XII** 417, 436; career in India 305–19, 161, 164, 169, 215 — Regulating Act 171 — and the French 255 — governor in Bengal 261, 264; attacks and impeachment 300, 319–22, 361; retirement 319
Hastings, William, Lord, chamberlain of Edward IV **VI** 325, 339, 501, 581, 612; with Edward at Olney 556; Edward at Pontefract 557; lieutenant of Calais (1471) 570; Gloucester's suspicion 570; Edward at Picquigny 577; Woodville reconciliation 589; master of Mint 590; Calais merchant of staple 591; Gloucester protector 611; Woodville limitation 612; council activity 617–18; executed 619; his sons 325
Hatclyf, William, king's secretary **VI** 555; **VII** 131, 132, 146
Hatfield, Thomas, bishop of Durham (1345–81) **V** 211, 372, 507
Hatfield Broadoak, priory **VI** 659
Hatfield Chase (Hæfeldland) (Yorks.) **II** 49, 296, 648, 732; battle 81, 116
Hatfield council (Hæthfeld) (Herts.) **II** 137; 732
Hatherley, Lord **XIV** 16, 17, 183
Hatherton, Lord *see* Littleton, E. J.
Hattin, battle **III** 343, 361
Hatton, Sir Christopher **VIII** 387
Hatton, Richard **VII** 167
Hattorf, John Philip, Hanoverian resident in Great Britain (1714–37) **XI** 14
Haughley (Suffolk), castle **II** 639
Hauksbee, Francis (1687–1763), mechanician **XI** 382
Havana **VIII** 369; British capture **XII** 76, 80; restored to Spain 86
Havart, Jean, Réné of Anjou's envoy **VI** 479
Havelock, Sir Henry **XIII** 436–6
Haverfordwest (Pembroke) **V** 471, 493; **VI** 57, 641; castle 641; **XII** 44
Haverhill (Suffolk) **VI** 647
Haverholme Priory (Lincs.) **III** 49
Havering (Essex) **IV** 512
Havering, John of, justiciar of Wales and seneschal of Gascony **IV** 279–80, 312, 436, 442–3
Haversham, 1st Baron *see* Thompson, John
Havre *see* Le Havre
Hawarden (Cheshire): castle **IV** 419; **VI** 38
Hawarden, Edward (1662–1735) **XI** 77
Hawke, Sir Edward, 1st Baron, 1st lord of admiralty (1766–71) **XI** 229, 248, 262, 349, 359, 368; victories over French fleets 262, 365–6; **XII** 153, 576
Hawkesbury, Lord *see* Jenkinson, Charles

Hawkins, Sir John **VIII** 146, 412; slave trade 123–5; challenges armada 399–400, 403; hinders Spanish treasure-fleet 412, 416–17

Hawkins, William **VIII** 123, 129

Hawksmoor, Nicholas (1661–1736), architect **X** 391; **XI** 402, 412

Hawkwood, Sir John **V** 346

Hawley, Henry, General (*c.*1679–1759) **XI** 218, 220, 255, 257

Hawley, John, junior, of Dartmouth **VI** 134

Hawley, John, senior, of Dartmouth **VI** 72

Hawley, Robert **V** 403–4, 513

Haxey, Thomas, king's clerk **V** 477; **VI** 286

Hay, Lord Charles (d. 1760): at Fontenoy **XI** 251

Hay, Edmund, Jesuit **VIII** 360

Hay, George, Viscount Dupplin, later earl of Kinnoull (d. 1758) **XI** 161

Hay, Ian **XV** 52

Hay, James, earl of Carlisle **IX** 337–8

Hay, Nicholas de la, castellan of Lincoln **IV** 11

Hay, Nicolaa de la **III** 485

Hay, William (1695–1755), social reformer **XI** 129, 136, 139

Hayashi, Baron **XIV** 352

Haydn, Franz Joseph **XII** 544

Haydon, Benjamin R. (1786–1846) **XII** 539; **XIII** 589

Hayle, river (Corn.) **II** 73

Hayling Island, shrine **Ia** 671, 750

Hayman, Francis (1708–76), painter **XI** 408, 413

Hayward, John **VIII** 283

Hazlitt, William (1778–1830) **XII** 542; **XIII** 14, 32, 38, 58, 530

Head, Sir Francis Bond **XIII** 380

Headda, bishop of Lichfield **II** 49, 50

Headington (Oxon.): kilns **Ia** 644; **II** 300

Heads of Agreement (1916) **XV** 57, 71–2

Heads of the Proposals **IX** 147–8

Heahberht, king of Kent **II** 206, 222

Healaugh (Yorks.), manor **VI** 63, 337; castle 47

healing **Ia** 238, 362, 466, 515, 686–8

Health, Ministry of: created **XV** 129; local authorities 147, 257; air raid casualties 411, 433–4; food standards 464

Healy, Tim M. **XIV** 183, 184, 451, 565, 566; **XV** 159

Heantune *see* Wolverhampton (Staffs.)

Heardred, son of Hygelac **II** 194

Hearge *see* Harrow (Middx.)

Hearne, Thomas (1678–1735), antiquarian **VII** 34; **X** 156; **XI** 395

hearth-tax **X** 175

Heath, Nicholas, bishop of Rochester (1540–3), Worcester (1543, 1551–3), Catholic archbishop of York (1555–9) **VII** 416, 518, 530, 555, 571; chancellor (1556) 646; **VIII** 20

Heath Row, temple **Ia** 671

Heathcote, Sir Gilbert (?1651–1733) **XI** 310

heathenism, Danish **II** 434

heathenism, Old English **II** 40, 54; authorities for 96–8; seasons and festivals 97–8; divinities 97–100; sites of worship 99–102; late survival 102–3, 128

Heathfield, George Augustus, 1st Baron (1717–90) **XI** 219

heating systems *see* hypocausts

Heber, Reginald **XIII** 539

Hebrew **IX** 350, 352

Hebrides **III** 88, 264

Hedges, Sir Charles **X** 222, 223

Hedingham Castle **IV** 9

Hedon (Yorks.) **III** 96

hedonism **XIV** 142–3, 305, 309–10

Heere, Lucas **VII** 601

Hefresham *see* Heversham (Westmorland)

Hegesippus **VI** 679

Heidegger, John James (?1659–1749), impresario **XI** 417

Heidelberg **X** 169, 171

Heidenheim, monastery **II** 175

Heinsius, Antonie **X** 202, 208

Heiu of Hartlepool **II** 119

Helena, Constantine's mother **Ia** 301, 340

Helgrim, Norwegian, brought gifts to Athelstan **II** 349

Helias of la Flèche, count of Maine **III** 112, 113, 119, 123

Heligoland **II** 167; **XIII** 194; **XIV** 193–4

Helinand, bishop of Laon **III** 233

Helinandus of Froidmont **VI** 306

Helles Beach **XV** 48

helmets **Ia** 74, 77

Helmstan, bishop of Winchester **II** 56

Helperby (Yorks.) **II** 496

Helsdon, Hellesdon (Norfolk) **VI** 289

Helston (Corn.) **VI** 419

Helvidius Priscus **Ia** 164

Hemming, brother of Thorkell the Tall **II** 382, 388

Hemming, king of the Danes **II** 241

Hende, John, draper of London **VI** 76, 86, 89, 440; loan (1413) 136

Henderson, Arthur: **XIV** 379, 439; biography **XV** 28; becomes Labour leader (1914) 28; joins first coalition 31; industrial conciliator 36, 39; Asquith 65; proposes conference 69; War Cabinet 75; reorganizes Labour party 91; leaves War Cabinet 96; defeated (1918) 128; agrees with Mac-Donald 136; attends industrial conference 139; Thomas on 144; returns to Commons 142; conditions in Ireland 155; delayed revenge 193; views on foreign policy 199; supports MacDonald 201; in first Labour government 210; Protocol 216; becomes foreign secretary 271; policy successful 272–3, 277; Egypt 276, 359; proposed cuts in benefit 288, 292–3; becomes Labour leader (1931) 294; opposes National government 297; relies on blockade 319; votes against exclusion of supporters of National government 323; forced to surrender papers 603

Henderson, Hubert **XV** 252, 269

Henderson, Mr **XII** 282

Henderson, Sir Neville **XV** 425, 451

Hendon (Middx.) **V** 414; **VI** 675

hendref, hendrefa **IV** 384

Heneage, Sir Thomas **VIII** 226

Hengest **II** 16–17; pedigree 8; son called Oisc or Æsc 9, 16–17

Hengestesdun *see* Hingston Down (Corn.)

Hengham, Ralph, chief justice of King's Bench **IV** 347, 356, 363, 373; investigates grievances of Rhys ap Mareddud 438; **V** 196

Hengist **Ia** 474, 483; **1b** 17, 55, 59, 109; Cantware kingdom 122; federate settlements 114, 124, 142; Frankish influence 126–8; appendix 1(a)

Hengistbury Head: mint **Ia** 44; port 57, 59

Henley **VII** 40, 142

Henley, Robert, earl of Northington (1708?–72) **XI** 60, 64; biography **XII** 112; lord chancellor (1761–66) 98, 112, 115, 576; lord president of council (1766–7) 117, 575

Henley, W. E. **XIV** 331

Henley, Walter of **III** 52, 53

Hennebon **VIII** 414

Henniker, Mr, MP **XII** 83

Henrietta, duchess of Marlborough **X** 221

Henrietta, duchess of Orléans, sister of Charles II **X** 63, 76

Henrietta Maria **IX** 143; marriage 60; French attendants expelled 65; Catholicism 72, 117, 128, 210; upholds Charles' prerogative 104, 123; arms royalists 130; encourages drama 264

Henry, archbishop of Dublin **III** 315

Henry III, count of Bar: marries Eleanor, eldest daughter of Edward I (1293) **IV** 264, 668; relations with Edward I 659, 668

Henry, count of Champagne and king of Navarre (1270–74): marries Blanche of Artois **IV** 238; relations with Edward I 238 *see also* Blanche of Artois; Jeanne

Henry, count palatine of the Rhine **III** 376, 449–51, 453; Henry, son of 451

Henry, duke of Brabant **III** 367, 450, 455, 464; honour of Eye 376–7, 453, 454; honour of Boulogne 440; suspected of treason 467

Henry, duke of Limburg **III** 367, 376, 454, 464; son of *see* Waleran

Henry (the Lion), duke of Saxony and Bavaria **III** 90, 215, 328, 339; Richard's link with Germany 362, 376

Henry, earl of Essex *see* Bourchier, Henry

Henry, earl of Huntingdon, son of David I, king of Scotland **III** 133, 141, 158, 281; granted honour of Huntingdon 270; earldom of Northumberland 271–2; death 275

Henry, earl of Lancaster **IV** 212

Henry, earl of Leicester (*c.*1281–1345) **V** 75, 153

Henry II, Emperor **III** 115

Henry III, Emperor **II** 428

Henry IV, Emperor **II** 586

Henry V, Emperor **III** 115, 126, 127, 128, 180, 295, 416

Henry VI, Emperor **III** 328, 360; Richard's deliverance to 362; desire for universal sovereignty 364; war with France 366–7, 374; death 377; coinage 415

Henry II (of Trastamara), king of Castile (1369–79) **V** 144, 145, 146

Henry III, king of Castile (1390–1406) **V** 464

Henry IV, king of Castile **VII** 326

Henry I, king of England (1100–35): marriage with Edith **III** 1, 114–15, 268; crown worn by 4; healing power exercised by 4–5; charter of liberties 5, 20–1, 190; household reform 7–8; 'counsel and consent' of barons 10; scutage payment 16; fondness for animals 19–20; knights Geoffrey of Anjou 24; forest under 29, 34; policy to towns 68–70; trade and commerce 76, 80, 85–6, 92; foreign trade 88, 94; his character 97, 99, 133; receives legacy from father 99; acquires Cotentin from Robert 104; part played in wars of his brothers 106–8; connection with death of Rufus 114; accession 114; Robert rebels against 115–17; conquest of Normandy 118–21; continental wars 122–6; marriage with Adeliza 126; relations with Germany 126–7; last days and death 129–30; results of his policy 130; his children 131; Roger, bishop of Salisbury 136; honour of Carlisle 141; Robert of Normandy 154; finance 155; few earldoms created 157; relations with the church 171, 182–4, 205; Anselm 194; conflict with Anselm 3, 177–80; monastic development 185–90; literacy 243 — and language 251, 252; entertainment 258; daughter, Empress Matilda 269; relations with Wales 287–290; Germany, England's ally 326; legislation 385–6,

438; administrative policy 388; Worcester Castle 389; revives capital punishment 404; assize of novel disseisin 408; punishes false moneyers 415; **VII** 325

Henry II, king of England (1154–89): attitude to royalty **III** 2, 3, 4, 5; as judge 7; his household 9; knight service 13–14, 370–1; travelling bear 19; control of castles 27; and the forest 29; reforms 44, 385–6, 388–90, 395–7, 406, 413; charters to towns 67, 75, 80; urban policy 68–70, 85; sons rebel against him 84, 332–7; policy to trade and commerce 85, 89, 91–2; acquires Maine and Anjou 112, 113; born 129; early visits to England 148, 150, 161–6; appeasement of Rannulf, earl of Chester 159; becomes Duke of Normandy 161; his education 161, 243, 321; marriage 162–3; control over Church 190, 219–20, 222; relations with Becket 198, 200; quarrels with him 202–215; reconciliation with Church 216, 218; monastic foundations 229; Adelard's treatise 244; interest in history 250; relations with Scotland 272, 275–9, 282–3; with Wales 291–5, 297, 301; with Ireland 303, 305, 306–12, 315; character 318–21; restores order after the Anarchy 321–2; acquires the Vexin 323–4 — and Brittany 324–5; invades Toulouse 325–6; relations with Germany 326–8; relations with his sons 329; makes treaty with Humbert, count of Maurienne 330; imperial ambitions 330–2; methods of finance 338–9, 350, 419; early relations with Philip Augustus 342; takes the cross 344; last war and death 344–6; burial 347; William II's legacy 360; Hubert Walter 369; general

eyre, exemption 400; relations with Wales **IV** 385, 386, 391; **V** 169, 196, 266, 364

Henry III, king of England (1216–72) **III** 4, 19, 31; his minority 76; foreign merchants 90; grand assize (1221) 151; Llywelyn's homage to infant king 301; homage of Flemish knights 464; 'foreigners' in administration 477; succession and first coronation **IV** 1; treaty of Kingston 14; second coronation (1220), minority and character 18–19, 21, 38, 59; patron saint *see* Edward the Confessor; in control of his seal (1223) 24–5; declares himself of age 38; quarrels with brother Richard 40–1; disappointed in Wales and Brittany (1228–31) 45, 92–7, 397; asks for papal legate (1230) 46; bid for power (1232) 48–59; relations with Ireland 54, 57–8, 563; political readjustment 59–63; marriage plans end in marriage to Eleanor of Provence (1236) 72–3; relations with great council (1236–58) 74–9, 132–4; period of hostility to papacy (1244–5) 133, 150, 499; relations with Scotland 138, 585–95; and with Welsh princes 382, 393, 397–404; ecclesiastical relations 460–1, 465–7, 468, 501; financial tour of monasteries (1235) 503; disregards conditions attached to lay subsidy (1237) 523; administration of royal demesne and boroughs 529–31; *foreign affairs*: claims Normandy (1233) **IV** 87; defends Gascony (1224–30) 90–1, 94–5; expedition (1242–3) 97–105; relations with Frederick II 97–8, 103; becomes friendlier with Louis IX 104, 106, 119–20; takes the cross (1250) 106, 116; Gascon affairs (1248–54) 107–8, 110–18;

271

Henry III, king of England (*cont.*)
returns to England through Paris
119; involved in affairs of Sicily
106, 120–3, 124, 125, 134–6;
makes peace with Louis IX (1257–
9) 84, 120, 122–8; new seal and
style 126; vassal of king of
France (1259) 126–8; and the baronial movement **V** 18, 20, 30, 196,
495; sworn agreement to change
(1258) 134–5; absence in France
(1259–60) and council of regency
150, 154–9; fears Edward's disloyalty 156–9; uncertain relations
with Simon de Montfort 154,
156–61; reasserts independence
(1261) 161–6; released by pope
from oath to Provisions of Oxford
163, 165, 168; breach with Simon
de Montfort (1262–3) 168–71,
174–5; in Paris (1262) 170–1,
173; serious illness 171; surrenders to new movement (1263)
172–7; references of difficulties to
Louis IX 178–84; from Oxford to
Lewes (1264) 185–90; honour-
able captivity 191, 193–4, 198,
200–2; restoration of peace
203–15; debts (1268) 220; seeks
papal aid 220; last days 224–5;
cloth industry 363; wool industry
364; Westminster Abbey **VI** 514;
VII 37

Henry IV (Bolingbroke), king of
England (1399–1413), earl of
Derby, Leicester and Lincoln
(1377–99), of Northampton
(1384–99), duke of Hereford
(1397–9), of Lancaster (1399–
1413) **V** 433, 441–2, 468,
473, 483; quarrel with Norfolk
265, 485–8; at Radcot Bridge
452–3; an appellant (1388)
454–61, 465; crusade in Prussia
463; quarrel with Arundel 469;
exiled 477, 487–9, 490; usurpa-
tion of the Crown 491–6; universities 503; Richard's deposition

522; John Gower 529; *as earl of
Derby*: disherison **VI** 1; sails from
Boulogne 1; prowess and position
2–3; Ravenspur landing 4; baronial council (1399) 4; increasing
welcome 5; parliamentary title to
throne 11, 14–17; claims throne
12–13; 'might and wilfulness' 15;
appointments (1399) 18; refrains
from subsidy demands (1399) 20;
vigilance against Lollardy 20;
East Prussia 326; *as king of England*: defeats earls' rebellion (Jan.
1400) 25–6; Richard II's pall
bearer 27; questions Franciscans
28; Scottish homage (1404) 34;
invades Scotland (1400) 34–5;
anger with Percy over prisoners
46; reinforces Percies 47; Percies
revolt (1403) 51; enters Shrewsbury (20 July 1403) 51; Percy
conciliation attempt 52; army at
Shrewsbury 52; attacks Northumberland 53; Hereford (11 Sep.
1403) 55; summons army (1405)
58; Scrope's death sentence 61;
enters York (1405) 63; diplomatic
activities 67; Rupert III marriage
negotiations 68; Hanseatic privileges (1399) 70; Joan of Brittany marriage (1403) 71; Ralph
Neville honour 72; financial position (1401) 75; collaboration with
Lords 80; Commons restrictions
85; 'sages de son Conseil' 85;
annual income 87–8; loans 88;
conciliar policy 90–1; General
Council 93; resistance to Arundel
98; illnesses 99, 480; collapses
and recovers 100; illness prevents
Channel crossing (summer 1411)
100, 112; Prince Henry and
Beaufort tactics 112; abdication
suggestion 112; parliamentary
'novelties' (Nov. 1411) 112;
Armagnac proposals (1412) 113;
Walsingham's verdict 117; Clifford temporalities refused 268;

Fotheringhay endowment 292; household 297; alien priories 300; liberty interpretation 308; **VII** 213, 424, 549

Henry V, king of England (1413–22), duke of Cornwall and earl of Chester: estimation **VI** 121; efforts for unity 121; French policy 123–4, 125; appearance 126; Oldcastle's revolt 116; French truce (Jan. 1414) 137; marriage proposal 138; claim to French crown (July 1415) 142; Armagnac attack (11 Apr. 1415) 148; Harfleur-Calais march 148; enters Harfleur (22 Sep. 1415) 150; Calais march 151; finds ford staked 152; Péronne, Ancre, and Canche 153; Agincourt 154, 155; enters London (Nov. 1415) 159; further French conquests urged 159; anti-French propaganda (early 1416) 159; Burgundy trade 159; encirclement of France 160; envoy to Sigismund 161; council of Constance 162, 170; to join Southampton forces (June 1416) 164; states terms 164–5; treaty of Canterbury 167; Constance instructions 167; Upper Seine 169; winters in France (1417–18) 171; Normandy attacks (1417) 172; reduces Falaise (Feb. 1418) 173; seizes Pont de l'Arche 175; sends herald to Burgundy 175; Normandy consolidation (Feb. 1419) 177; first sees Catherine (2 May 1419) 180; conference of Meulan 180; transfers headquarters 181; Montereau murder 182; French plan (Oct. 1419) 182; position in treaty 184; French heir 185; Treaty of Troyes (21 May 1420) 185; hangs Melun Scots 187; Corbeil 187; separate states 189; Normandy military administration 189; Normandy clerical appointments 192; home

government policy 193; loans (1421) 195; debts 195; hold on country 195; religious orders 196–7; chapter-general 196; return to France 200; Meaux siege 200; dysentery 200; hands over to Bedford at Corbeil (1422) 201; dying address 201; estimate 202; will and codicils 202, 213; lost will 213; Beaufort debts 227; Gloucester will, invalidity 233 — invocation 470; services 292; Sigismund advice 347; fleet 348; Lynn reconciliation 389; as Monmouth, prince of Wales **VI** 17, 18, 43, 69, 79; titles 23; Chester council 44; relations with Henry IV and council 45; wounded 53; short of money (1402) 77, 102; Commons subsidy 80; chamberlain 91; knighthood treatise 93, 305; Oxford residence 93; University reconciliation 98; Welsh household 101–2; constable of Dover, warden of Cinque Ports (1409) 104; Beaufort understanding (1408–9) 105; council (1410) 105; projected marriage 111; dismissed from council (30 Nov. 1411) 112; Bourges pact guarantor (1412) 113; declines to visit Aquitaine (1412) 115; slander 116; **VII** 210, 228, 425, 549, 593, **XV** 315; confessor *see also* Patrington, Stephen

Henry VI, king of England (1422–61): birth (6 Dec. 1421) **VI** 201; magnates exercise authority (1422) 212; care and instruction 213; Gloucester tutelage 214; Speaker welcomes (1423) 223; Burgundy's French truce letter 249; Paris coronation 250; coming of age 261; Papacy and see appointments 268–70; taken prisoner (1471) 310; *domini de consilio* 433; stops Bedford/Gloucester power discussion 435;

273

275

Henry VIII, king of England (*cont.*) England 433, 568–9; mainspring of state machine 434; character and achievement 441–3; cloth trade 462, 474; Navigation Act renewed 474; will 480, 493, 496, 499; burial 495; shaky finances 500–2; Somerset's commissions (1548) 505; religious legacy 510–11; Lady Jane Grey 523–4; Northumberland dilemma 527; marriage of Philip and Mary (1554) 541; public worship 544; Reginald Pole (1554) 547; Cranmer and Six Articles 551–2; reverence for the Crown 562; law of the Church 564; Trinity College 570; influence on universities 572, 573; English printers and fugitive pieces 579–80; music 588–90; English architecture 591; Hampton Court 595; portraits 599; Hans Holbein 600–2; coinage 605–7; earl marshal (1494) 651; **VIII** 1; supreme head of church 13, 14, 16; Elizabeth's title to succession 17–18; work in Ireland 462, 465, 469, 472; **XV** 2

Henry I, king of France **II** 560, 584, 619

Henry II, king of France (1547–9) **VII** 486, 487, 524, 534, 536; marries Catherine dei Medici (1533) 340; accession and ambitions 482; Elizabeth suspected of dealings with 540; treaty with pope (1556) 556; supports English malcontents 557–8; gains Calais (1558) 558; threat to Elizabeth **VIII** 1, 38; possession of Calais 1, 35–6; Franco-Spanish alliance 37, 39; Scottish protectorate 39, 41

Henry III, king of France: accession **VIII** 163; Anjou marriage 147–8, 152–3, 354–5; suspected assassin 157; threat from Spain 344, 346–7, 364–5; Henry of Valois 364–5

Henry IV, king of France **VIII** 408, 413–14, 415

Henry, Patrick (1736–99), governor of Virginia **XII** 173, 175, 184, 198; biography 173

Henry, prince of Wales **IX** 17, 34, 263

Henry, second son and (1271–4) heir of Edward I: plans for future (1273) **IV** 238; death (Oct. 1274) 238

Henry, son of King Henry II (the Young King): relations with Becket **III** 203, 214; crowned 212–13, 329; rebels against his father 220, 276, 332–7, 337; marriage 323–4; character 340–1; death 341–2

Henry, son of William I **II** 609, 620

Henry, Viscount Bourchier, earl of Essex *see* Bourchier, Henry

Henry of Bergen, bishop of Cambrai **VII** 117, 166, 181, 249

Henry of Canterbury **V** 114

Henry de Ferrars **II** 627, 629, 631

Henry of Grosmont, earl of Derby, Leicester, and Lincoln (1337–61), earl of Moray (1359–61), earl of Lancaster (1345–61), duke (1351–61) **V** 153, 185, 204, 238, 260; campaigns in Gascony 132, 133, 210, 362; in Brittany 138; loyalty to Edward III 148; hostage against Edward's loans 162; tries to prevent church-burning 246; piety 249, 257; knight of the Garter 252; career 254–5; no heirs 256; estates 259; patron of learning 507

Henry the Fowler, king of the Germans **II** 345–7

Henry the Treasurer **II** 644

Hentzner, Philip **VIII** 274

Heorotford *see* Hertford

Hepburn, James, earl of Bothwell

Hereford and Worcestershire **Ia** 43, 59, 255

Herefordshire **III** 394; **V** 192, 388, 520; **VI** 102, 194

heregeld **II** 412, 431, 650

heresy, acts against **VII** 424, 425, 432; repealed 513; parliament will not revive (1554) 546; revived 549; *see also* Arians; Christian culture; Pelagian; Priscillian

heretical books, holocaust of Lutheran books at St Paul's (1521 and 1526) **VII** 344–5

Hereward **II** 285, 605–6

Herfast the chancellor, bishop of Elmham **II** 642, 667

Herle, William **VI** 605

Herluin of Bec **II** 559, 662

Herman, bishop of Sherborne **II** 660

Hermann, General **XII** 379

Hermonymos, George **VII** 237

Herne the Hunter **Ia** 669

Hero and Leander **VIII** 288

Herodian **Ia** 218, 219, 221–2, 226–31, 247; Scottish campaign 318

heroic poetry **VIII** 286

Heron, John, merchant of London **VII** 145

Heron, John, treasurer of the chamber (from 1492) **VII** 218

Heron, Richard, Wiltshire's agent **VI** 540

Heron, William, household steward **VI** 80

Heronbridge **Ia** 631

Herrick, Robert **IX** 387, 401–2

Herries, Lord **VIII** 112–13

Herries, J. C. (1778–1855) **XIII** 75, 291

Herring, Thomas (1693–1757), archbishop of York (1743–7), of Canterbury (1747–57) **XI** 79

Hershell, Lord **XIV** 209, 211

Herstingas **Ib** map 2 xxx

Hert, William **V** 438

Hertford (Heorotford) **II** 324–5, 336; council 32, 133–4; shire 574; castle **IV** 9; **VII** 493

Hertford, earl of, 1st Marquis: lord lieutenant of Ireland (1765–6) **XII** 577; master of the horse (1766) 578; lord chamberlain (1783) 579

Hertford, earls of **III** 157; *see also* Clare, Richard of; Clare, Roger of; Seymour, Edward

Hertfordshire **Ia** 12, 33, 36, 43, 694; **Ib** 130; **III** 146; **V** 312, 414–15, 419; **VII** 504; **IX** 131

Hertzog, General **XIV** 345

Heruli, Late Roman unit **Ia** 361, 364, 381

Hervé, bishop of Bangor **III** 295

Hervelinghem (Calais) **VI** 106

Hervey, George William, 2nd earl of Bristol (1721–75): biography **XII** 75; envoy in Spain 75; lord privy seal 130, 575; lord lieutenant of Ireland 577

Hervey, John, Lord (1696–1743) **XI** 21, 26, 34, 147, 232; lord privy seal 231; on duke of Grafton 301; Pope 424; writings 428

Hervey, Molly (Lepel), Lady (1700–68) **XI** 148

Herzog, General **XV** 453

Hesdin (Pas-de-Calais) **VI** 5, 535; **VII** 312

Hesilrige, Sir Arthur **IX** 101, 122, 174, 186; republican leader 238, 243; attitude to the army 240

Hess, Myra **XV** 550

Hesse-Cassel, Landgrave **XI** 214; princess of 299; *see also* subsidies

Hethe, Hamo, bishop of Rochester (1319–52) **V** 78, 92, 93, 277, 301

Hetherington, H. **XIII** 133

Hève, Cap de la (Seine-Inf.) **VI** 158

Heveningham, Sir John **VI** 473

Heversham (Hefresham) (Westmorland) **II** 320, 732

Hewart, Sir G. **XV** 175

Hewins, W. A. S. **XV** 331

Hewitt, General **XIII** 433

Hewitt, Graily **XIV** 540

Heworth **Ib** 101, 196; map 4 xxxii; map 5 68

Hexham (Hagustaldesea) (Northumb.) **II** 81, 144, 732; diocese 109, 138–9, 146, 433; Scottish writs on behalf of canons (1297) **IV** 686; **V** 32; battle **VI** 494, 563; **VIII** 141; monastery 135–6, 138, 184, 433

Hexham, bishops of *see* Acca; Cuthbert; Eata; John; Tunberht

Hexham, Richard of **III** 270

Hexhamshire, franchise **VI** 134

Heybridge **Ib** 86; map 2 xxx; map 6 88

Heydon, John **VI** 344, 448, 491, 503

Heyle, Mr, MP **VIII** 229

Heyne (Heynes), William **VI** 379

Heysham (Lancs.), chapel at **II** 151

Heytesbury, Lord, biography **XIII** 416

Heywood, Thomas **VIII** 300, 301; **IX** 392

Hicce **II** 43, 296

Hickes, George (1642–1715), Bishop, non-juror **X** 156, 382; **XI** 75, 76

Hickey, William **XII** 157, 182, 220; **XV** 235

Hicks Pasha **XIV** 80

hide: meaning of term **II** 279; peasant holding 279, 476; survival in Danelaw 514; of assessment 646–7

Hide, Lawrence **VIII** 231

hides **Ia** 42, 58, 620, 630; *see also* leather

Hiesmois, county **II** 558

Higden, Ranulph (d. 1364), description of England **VII** 25

Higford, Norfolk's secretary **VIII** 151

High Commission, court of **VIII** 199, 202; **IX** 20–1, 78–9, 103; **X** 124

High Down **Ib** 131, 135, 138; circular brooch 60 [fig. 2(c)]; map 2 xxx; map 6 88

High Peak (Derby.) **V** 11

High Rochester (*Bremenium*): fort **Ia** 165, 211, 246, 352; *singulares* 521; Imperial Cult 683; tomb 701; **Ib** 76; map 4 xxxii

High Wycombe: military establishment **XII** 481; **XV** 480, 481

Higham, Sir Clement, speaker of the House of Commons (1554) **VII** 654

Higham Ferrers (Northants) **VI** 47; college church 292

Highingham of Yorkshire **VIII** 138

Highland Host **X** 270

highland zone **Ia** 4–5, 621–2

Highlands **Ia** 29, 149, 151, 211, 230; army involvement 261; tribes harried 319; cultural effects 612; *see also* Scotland

Highmore, Joseph (1692–1780), painter **XI** 408, 413

Highsted (Kent), Romano-Saxon pottery **Ib** 90 [fig. 7(b)]

highwaymen **VIII** 263–4; **X** 259

Hilary, bishop of Chichester **III** 195, 200, 203, 222

Hilary, dramatist **III** 258

Hilbadstow (Lincs.) **III** 6

Hild, abbess of Whitby **II** 119, 123, 162, 181, 196

Hildebrand, Hildebrandine Reform *see* Gregory VII, Pope

Hildebrand, Sir, of London **V** 345

Hildebrand of Saxony **III** 90

Hildegard, wife of Charlemagne and friend of Leofgyth **II** 173

Hildelith, abbess of Barking **II** 182

Hildesle, John **V** 113

Hill, John, Major-General **X** 230

Hill, Rowland **VII** 440

Hill, Rowland, 1st Viscount Hill (1772–1842) **XII** 494

Hill, Sir Roland: biography **XIII** 48; suggests penny postage 48–9; educational reforms 485

Hill, Wills, 2nd Viscount Hillsborough (1718–93): biography **XII** 129; secretary of state (1768–72) 129, 144, 183, 576; (1779–82) 225, 576; president of Board of Trade (1763–5, 1766, 1768–72) 578;

hill-crofts **Ia** 45

hill-forts **Ia** 45–6, 93, 121, 453, 485; Jobey's study 612–13; shrines 686, 738

Hilliard, Nicholas **VII** 601; **VIII** 302; **IX** 374–6

Hillsborough, 2nd Viscount *see* Hill, Wills

Hilsey, John (d. 1538), bishop of Rochester **VII** 382, 431

Hilton, Sir Reginald **V** 521

Hilton, Sir Robert **VI** 127

Hilton, Walter (d. 1396) **V** 526; writings **VI** 296

Hilton, Sir William **VI** 127, 128

Hindenburg **XV** 22

Hindon (Wilts.), manor **VI** 462

Hingeston, John **IX** 389

Hingston Down (Hengestesdun) (Corn.), battle **II** 235; 732

Hinton, David **Ia** 541–2

Hinton, priory (Carthusian) **VI** 296

Hinton St Mary, villa **Ia** 342, 725

Hipparchus (*fl.* 161–126 BC), astronomer **XI** 380

Hippocrates **III** 246; **IX** 364

hire purchase **XV** 300, 306

Hiroshima **XV** 96, 598, 601

Hispania Tarraconensis **Ia** 128

Hispaniola **IX** 337, 348

Historia Brittonum see Nennius

Historia Roffensis: on parliament (1327) **V** 88: on Londoners (1327) 92

historians **X** 378–81

Historical Register **XI** 31

history, vogue **VIII** 282–6; writing **IX** 408; study **XI** 139, 140, 393, 397, 430

History of England **VIII** 283

A History of the English-speaking Peoples **XV** 467

History of Great Britain **VIII** 283

History of Henry VII **VIII** 283

Hitchcock, Alfred **XV** 315, 633

Hitler, Adolf **VII** 263; Milner anticipates his programme **XV** 95; Chamberlain cheated by 206; rise 215; expects war (1943) 228; difficulties expected from 299; Churchill praises 317; condemned for unilateral repudiation 336; comes to power in Germany 347, 350, 351, 363, 373; leaves League 366; British attitudes towards 374, 417–19; effect of White Paper 376–7; British wish to enlist Mussolini against 384; reoccupies Rhineland 385; offers new treaty 386; claims air parity 387, 410; Spanish civil war 395, 398; cartoons by Low 408; armaments 413; Chamberlain treats as rational 414; problem of stopping 415; Eden 421; Halifax gives assurances to 422; claims to have overthrown Eden 423; enters Vienna 424; Czech crisis 425, 426–9; after Munich 431–2; expected to attack Soviet Russia 435–6; occupies Prague 439–41; negotiates with Poland 442; repudiates Anglo-German naval treaty 443; British-Polish alliance 443–4; efforts to deter 445–6; efforts to conciliate 448; attacks Poland 449–51, 453, 476; offers peace 454, 458; Mussolini's non-belligerence 460; orders scuttling of *Graf Spee* 462; Churchill says his path to east barred 467; French hope for his overthrow 468; conquers Norway and Denmark 470; Churchill 473, 475, 483; invades Holland and Belgium 483–4; halt before Dunkirk 486; offers peace 488–9; prepares invasion 490, 493, 498; orders bombing of London 499;

Hockwold (*cont.*)
    villa and village? 610; stock-raising 620, 627, 655; shrine 690; skeleton 696; ritual crowns 734
Hod Hill **Ia** 93
Hodges, Frank **XV** 146, 240
Hodgskin, Thomas **XIII** 130, 133
Hodgson, S. (1708–98), Brigadier **XI** 368
Hogarth, William (1697–1764) **XI** 9, 81, 399, 401–6, 409; *Gin Lane* 134, 410; portraits: Bambridge 135 — Captain Coram 408 — Lord George Graham in his cabin 225; *March to Finchley* 406; *Analysis of Beauty* 407, 410; *Sigismunda* 410; genre pictures 413; Foundling Hospital 416; **XII** 265, 346
Hogg, Sir Douglas, Lord Hailsham: in cabinet as attorney general **XV** 236; suggests agreement to differ 330; pushes Sankey off woolsack 378
Hogg, Quintin, champion of Munich **XV** 436
Hogue, La, battle *see* Barfleur
Hogue, sunk **XV** 13
Hohenstaufen, house **III** 362, 367, 449
Hoke, Robert, Lollard priest **VI** 283
Holand, Henry, duke of Exeter **VI** 508, 517, 523, 526; arrested (1454) 510; Flanders 530; attainder (1461) 539; Burgundy pension 562; opposition to Warwick 566; Newark route 567; Barnet command 568
Holand, John, duke of Exeter **VI** 1, 6, 21, 22, 25
Holand, Thomas, earl of Kent, duke of Surrey **VI** 6, 21, 22; rebellion 25
Holand Land *see* Palestine
Holbein, Hans, the younger (1479–1543) **VII** 232, 266, 592, 596; palace of Westminster 595; biography 599–602; **IX** 375, 378

Holborough, barrows **Ia** 698, 704
Holburn **VIII** 275
Holburne, Francis (1704–71) **XI** 359, 360
Holcot, Robert **V** 505, 510; **VI** 680
hold **II** 509
Holden, Charles **XV** 178
Holden, Robert **V** 93
Holderness (Yorks.) **II** 509, 588; **III** 109; **IV** 21, 634, 716; **V** 321; **VI** 2, 59; lordship 334
Holderness, 4th Earl (1718–78), secretary of state **XII** 67, 575; dismissal (1761) 69; *see also* D'Arcy, Robert
Holderness, Robin of *see* Robin of Holderness
Holgate, Robert, bishop of Llandaff (1527–45), and of York (1545–54) **VII** 545
holidays **XV** 305; during Second World War 551, 583
Holinshed, R., chronicler **VI** 8
Holinshed, Raphael **VIII** 5, 283
Holkar **XII** 385
Holland **Ia** 133, 369; flooding? 556; merchants **IV** 348; English wool trade organized by Edward I 659, 662–4; **V** 83; **VII** 470, 473; financial services **XII** 24; marines interned **XV** 11; William II 113, 134; German attack feared 437; Germans conquer 474, 483–5; liberation a British war aim 489; government in England 494; *see also* Batavians; Dutch people; Low Countries; Netherlands
Holland (Lincs.) **II** 49; **III** 409; **V** 337
Holland, 1st Baron *see* Fox, Henry
Holland, counts of *see* Dietrich; Florence; John; William
Holland, Eleanor, countess of March **V** 428
Holland, Elizabeth **VII** 421
Holland, Elizabeth, daughter of John of Gaunt **VI** 223

Holland, Elizabeth, Kent's daughter **VI** 8, 320

Holland, Henry (1746?–1806) **XII** 341

Holland, Henry Richard Vassal Fox, 3rd Baron (1773–1840): biography **XII** 363; opposition to Combination Acts 363; lord privy seal (1806–7) 582

Holland, John, earl of Huntingdon (1388–1400), duke of Exeter (1397–9) **V** 463, 465, 474, 481, 483; and affair of Carmelite friar 439; kills heir of Stafford 439; with Gaunt in Spain 441; admiral 469; with Richard II in Ireland 471; allowed crusading privileges 478; an appellant (1397) 479; granted Lancastrian lands 490

Holland, John, earl of Huntingdon **VI** 173, 183, 234

Holland, 3rd Lord **XIII** 57, 69, 75, 467

Holland (Holand), Lucy, Kent's widow **VI** 320

Holland, Philemon **IX** 406

Holland, Sir Robert **V** 50, 66, 204

Holland, Sir Thomas **V** 247

Holland, Thomas, earl of Kent (1380–97) **V** 428, 473

Holland, Thomas, earl of Kent (1397–1400), duke of Surrey (1397–9) **V** 474, 478, 481, 483; to lead expedition to Italy 476; an appellant (1397) 479; granted Lancastrian lands 490; king of Ireland rumour 491

Holland and Zeeland **VI** 475, 582

Holles, Denzil **IX** 38, 122

Hollingbourne **Ib** map 5 68

Hollis, Daniel, imprisoned (1709–58), for tithe debt **XI** 72

Hollis, Thomas (1720–74), art collector **XI** 405

Holmby House **IX** 145

Holme, battle **II** 322, 509

Holme, Richard, lawyer, French embassy (Mar. 1415) **VI** 141

Holme Cultram, abbey, chancery (1299) **IV** 702

Holmes, Charles (1711–61), Admiral **XI** 362

Holmes, Sir Robert: west coast of Africa **X** 63, 332; Anglo-Dutch war 65; attacks Dutch Smyrna fleet 77–8

Holofernes **VII** 441, 578

Holroyd, John Baker, earl of Sheffield (1735–1821) **XI** 52; **XII** 238

Holst, Gustav Theodore, composer **XIV** 545; **XV** 178

Holstein **Ib** 46–7, 50, 54–5, 63, 66; cemeteries 72; map 1 xxix; **VII** 159

Holstein, Adolf, count of **III** 327

Holstein, Baron **XIV** 197, 201, 233, 370, 432

Holt (Cheshire), tile factory **Ia** 631

Holt (Denbigh.) **VI** 38; castle **VII** 122

Holt, Richard **VI** 500

Holt, Sir John **V** 449

Holt, William, Jesuit **VIII** 360, 361

Holt-on-the-Dee **V** 469

Holy Island (Northumb.) **II** 76; **VI** 533

Holy Land **V** 123, 463; *see also* Palestine

Holy League (1496) **VII** 115–16; (1511) 273–5; (1524) 315

Holy Places *see* Crimean War

Holy River, battle **II** 403–4

Holybones (le) **Ib** 183

Holyrood **III** 274; abbey **V** 98

Holyroodhouse **VII** 161, 407

Home (Hume), Alexander, 1st Lord **VII** 141

Home (Hume), Alexander, 3rd Lord, great chamberlain of Scotland **VII** 280, 282

Home, castle **VII** 484

Home, earl of **XII** 135

Home, Revd John (1722–1808) *Douglas* **XI** 286, 287

Home, Lord *see* Dunglass

Home Guard: instituted **XV** 492; American rifles 496; stands to arms 499; continued 500, 503, 549

Home Office: runs factory acts **XV** 36; supervises watch committees 257; naturalization 420; prepares Air Raid Precautions 433; Home Security joined to 456

home policy committee **XV** 482

Home Rule: origin of phrase **XIV** 55; first Home Rule Bill 97–9; second 210–11; factors of population bearing on 270; third 450–2; Irish: placed on statute book **XV** 16–17, 155; proposals for (1916) 57, 71–2; promise renewed (1918) 104; only Ulster receives 156; all round 160

Home Security, Ministry of **XV** 456

Homfrays **XII** 506

Homildon (Hambledon) Hill, battle **VI** 45, 46, 47, 64

homilies, book of **VII** 431; **VIII** 31

homosexuality **XV** 170

Hondschoote, battle (1793) **XII** 367

Honduras **VIII** 248; bay of **X** 325; **XII** 85, 108, 255

Hone, William **XIII** 30

Honest Whore **VIII** 301

honestiores **Ia** 512

Honfleur (Calvados) **VI** 150, 189, 206

Hong Kong **XV** 151

Honorius, archbishop of Canterbury **II** 113, 115–16, 119, 121; date of death 129

Honorius, Emperor **Ia** 346, 415–49; barbarians in western armies 330–1, 417–19, 432–3, 487–8; family 417, 428, 447, 694; Goths 417–18, 423–5, 430–1, 447–9; relations with E. empire 417, 423, 426–7; Stilicho 417–26; last coins in Britain 424–5; Gaul and Britain under Constantine III 426–46, 501; provincial defence 427; administration 434–40, 443, 578; British expulsion of Roman administration 434–40, 443, 578; withdrawal of troops 437–9, 469–70; rescript 443–4, 469–70; paganism survives under 735; **Ib** 7

Honorius I, Pope **II** 115, 117

Honorius II, Pope **III** 182, 184

Honorius III, Pope (1216–27) **III** 191, 246; Albigensian crusade **IV** 87–8, 91; Henry III 16, 24; Fawkes de Breauté 26; rights of David of Snowdonia 393; taxation of the clergy 498, 501–2; and Ireland 568; allows election of *conservator* of Church of Scotland 583; forbids coronation and unction of Alexander II 594–5

Honorius IV, Pope (1285–7): conditions of peace with Aragon **IV** 256, 257; renews papal prohibition of Anglo-Aragonese marriage 258; crusade 265

honour: meaning of term **II** 627, 636–7; formation of honours 627, 683; different types 626–7

honours, political use of **XV** 175, 188, 265

Hoo (Hó) (Kent), monastery **II** 70, 160, 732

Hoo, Sir Thomas **VI** 474, 501

Hoochstraten, John, printer at Antwerp **VII** 344

Hood, Alexander, Viscount Bridport (1726–1814) **XII** 372

Hood, Samuel, 1st Viscount (1724–1816) **XII** 217, 275, 367

Hood, sunk **XV** 506

Hood, Zachariah **XII** 186

Hooe (Sussex) **V** 345

Hoogebeintum **Ib** map 5 68

Hooke, Robert **X** 42, 43, 390, 392

Hooker, Richard **VIII** 32, 458, 459, 460; **IX** 68

'Hooks' and 'Cod-fish', feud in Netherlands **VII** 85, 98, 108

Hoole, Charles **IX** 350

Hoon, Gaylon **VII** 592

Hooper, George (1640–1727), Bishop **XI** 77

Hooper, John (d. 1555), bishop of Gloucester (1551–2), bishop of Worcester (1552–3) **VII** 512, 516, 520, 545, 546; starts vestiarian controversy 518; simplification of ceremonies 519; arrested 543; burnt (9 Feb. 1555) 550

Hoover, President **XV** 335, 372

Hope, John, of Rankeillor (1725–86) **XI** 275

Hopkins, Harry **XV** 555

Hopkins, K. **Ia** 550

Hopkins, Matthew **IX** 371

Hoppner, John (1758–1810) **XII** 344

Hopton, Sir Ralph **IX** 133, 137, 142

Hopton, Walter de, president of Welsh judicial commission (1278) **IV** 415, 416, 417–18, 440; commission of inquiry into precedents in Wales 418

Horace (Horatius Flaccus, Q.) **Ia** 48, 52, 61

Horace (Orace) **VI** 360

Hore-Belisha, Leslie: insists on war **XV** 452; biography 459; sends Gort to France 459; dismissed 460

Horik, king of the Danes **II** 239, 241–2

Horley, Robert, of London **VI** 131

Horman, William (d. 1535) **VII** 246, 575, 577

Hormer hundred (Berks.) **II** 501

Hornby (Lancs.) **VI** 31

Hornby v. Close **XIV** 131

Horncastle (Lincs.) **Ib** 179–80; map 4 xxxii; map 6 88; **VII** 387, 388

Horndon (Essex) **II** 536

Horne, John **V** 410

Horne, John *see* Tooke, Horne

Horne, R. H. **XIV** 330

Horne, Robert, bishop of Winchester **VIII** 193

Horne, Robert, of Kent **VI** 599

Horne, Sylvester **XV** 169

Hornebolt family **VII** 599

Horneck, Anthony **X** 159

Horner, Francis (1778–1817), biography **XII** 437

Horniman, Annie **XIV** 548; **XV** 314

Horrocks, Miller & Co. of Preston **XII** 511

Horrocks of Stockport **XII** 510

Horsa, monument **Ib** 114, appendix I(a); **II** 8–9, 16

Horse Guards parade, occupied by mutinous troops **XV** 138

horse-racing **X** 408–9; **XV** 313; in Second World War 551

Horsea **Ia** 474, 483

horses **Ia** 84, 536, 563, 579, 620; war (*dextrarius*), value **IV** 549–50, 553; *see also* cavalry

Horsey, Dr William, bishop of London's chancellor **VII** 292, 293

Horsfall, T. C. **XIV** 518

Horsly, John (1685–1732), *Britannia Romana* **XI** 395

Horsman, E. **XIII** 183

Horton (Bucks.) **V** 337

Horton (Dorset), abbey **II** 414

Horton (Oxon.) **II** 381

Horton, Mrs **XII** 155

Horton, Thomas, abbot of Gloucester **VI** 647

Horwode, John **V** 428

Horwood (Bucks.) **V** 332

Hosidius Geta, Cn. **Ia** 73, 84

Hosier, Francis (1673–1727), Admiral **XI** 199, 222, 224

Hoskins, John (father) **IX** 376

Hoskins, John (son) **IX** 376

Hospital of St John of Jerusalem: Knights of (Hospitallers) **III** 190, 423; Grand Master 343

'Hospital Sunday' **XIV** 163

hospitalitas **Ib** 32, 211

Hospitallers **IV** 82; prior **VI** 77; possessions 82

hospitals **XI** 392; St Bartholomew's 64, 392; Foundling 69, 139, 408, 416; Chelsea 217; Bedlam 392;

hospitals (*cont.*)
  Guy's 392; London 392; Middlesex 392; St George's 392; St Luke's 392; St Thomas's 392; Westminster 392; Haslar 393; at York 392; **XII** 11
hospites **Ib** 14
hostages **Ia** 30, 31, 36, 37, 39; Constantine the Great 322; Aetius 475; **IV** 190, 193–4, 282–4, 647
hostis **Ia** 396
hostmen of Newcastle **VIII** 258
Hotham, John, Bishop of Ely (1316–37), treasurer (1317–18), chancellor (1318–20) **V** 22, 49, 57, 87, 152; envoy, Avignon and Middle Party 52; deputation, Edward II's deposition 90; Mortimer's interests 96; manor produce 320
Hotham, Sir John **IX** 129
Hotham, William of, Dominican, prior provincial in England, later archbishop of Dublin **IV** 261, 269, 675; letters to Henry Eastry 261–2; Edward I's agent at papal court (1289) 261–2, 265–6, 340; Scottish case 603; Edward I's representative during arbitration at Rome (1298) 651, 652, 678
Hotman, Jean **VIII** 206
Hötzendorf, Conrad von **XIV** 469, 482–3
Houghton, Adam, bishop of St David's (1362–89), chancellor (1377–8) **V** 389, 395, 402, 404
Houghton, John **X** 42
Houghton, Stanley **XIV** 548
Hounslow (Middx.): Heath **VII** 142; **X** 122
House, Colonel E. M. **XIV** 484–5, 571; **XV** 111
House of Commons *see* Commons, House of
House of Lords *see* Lords, House of
housecarles **II** 412, 430, 582
household, the king's **II** 305,

638–41; under William I 638–9; pre-Conquest 639–40; officers 639–40
household, royal **IV** 767; centre of administration 48, 60, 323–4, 662; steward 323; knights 545–6; estate organization **VI** 444; arrears (1433–49) 445; queen's personal government 514; sheriffs 514; Edward IV personnel 595; ordinance (1478) 598; Edward IV expenses 598; local government connection 598–601
houses: Bronze Age **Ia** 8; Iron Age 7, 125; town houses (*domus*) 142, 157, 158, 188, 233 — Verulamium 237, 658 — reconstruction 459 — Gloucester and Cirencester 585–6; strip-houses 159, 537, 595; stone huts 612–13; **VIII** 272–3, 303–5; **IX** 385–6; *see also* farms; *insulae*; towns; villas
Housesteads (*Vercovicum*): fort **Ia** 178, 184, 222; inscriptions 248, 314, 667, 671; *vicus* 595, 708; Imperial Cult 683; *Genii Cucullati* 708; murder 696; **Ib** 77–8; Housesteads Ware 77; map 4 xxxii
housing **XII** 522; **XIII** 10–11, 599; **XIV** 35, 127–8, 301–2, 509–10, 514; town planning 518; shortage due to First World War **XV** 122; Addison 147–8, 210; local authorities 257; boom in thirties 344; number of new houses 366; at general elections 367, 383, 596; effects of bombing 438; deterioration during Second World War 551
Housing Act: (1923) Chamberlain's limited subsidy **XV** 206, 210; (1924) Wheatley's long-term programme 210–11, 237; Greenwood's slum clearance (1930 and 1938) 279, 406, 408
Housman, A. E. **XIV** 40, 330

Howard, Thomas, 3rd duke of Norfolk (*cont.*)

(1544) 409; 'privy privy council' 414, 435; fall of Cromwell (1540) 415, 417; arrest and Henry's death (1546) 421–2, 530; approves Six Articles 426; Mary's council 531; becomes lord admiral (1513) 650; treasurer (1522) 646; earl marshal (1533, 1553) 651

Howard, Thomas, 4th duke of Norfolk (executed 1572), earl marshal (1554) **VII** 651; aid to Scots **VIII** 43–4; conference at York 113–15; marriage alliance with Mary Stuart 113; trade stoppage 132; plot against Cecil 133–4; imprisonment 137; Ridolfi plot 148, 149–50, 151

Howard, Thomas, 8th duke of Norfolk (1683–1732) **XI** 118, 182

Howard, Thomas, 2nd earl of Arundel **IX** 376–7

Howard, Thomas, earl of Suffolk **IX** 15–17, 22

Howard, Thomas, earl of Surrey **VI** 622

Howard, William, Lord of Effingham **VII** 363, 400, 418; lord chamberlain of the household (1558) 649; lord admiral (1553) 650

Howard, William, Viscount Stafford **X** 54, 95

Howard family **XI** 73

Howards, fall **VII** 380, 421, 422

Howden (Yorks.) **II** 495; **III** 352; chapter house **VI** 271

Howe, George Augustus, 3rd Viscount (1725–58) **XI** 218, 361

Howe, Richard, 1st Earl (1726–99) **XI** 362; biography **XII** 206; naval exploits 206–8, 212, 370, 373; first lord of the admiralty (1783) 267, 579, (1783–8) 580; treasurer of the navy (1765–70) 577

Howe, William, 5th Viscount (1729–1814): biography **XII** 202;

military exploits 195, 208–10

Howel, Rhys ap **V** 86

Howel ap Goronwy, archdeacon of Anglesey **VI** 38

Howick, Viscount *see* Grey, Charles; Grey, Henry George

Howletts (Kent): Jutish pottery **Ib** 67 [fig. 4(i)]; Quoit Brooch Style 118 [fig. 10(c, d)]; map 5 68

Howth, book **VII** 132, 133

Howth, Lord **VII** 74

Hoxne (Suffolk) **II** 248, 437

Hræglthegns **II** 643

Hramesig *see* Ramsey (Hunts.)

Hrani, earl under Cnut **II** 416

Hremnesbyrig *see* Ramsbury (Wilts.)

Hretha, Goddess **II** 97–8

Hrofesceaster *see* Rochester (Kent)

Hrothgar, king of Danes **II** 194

Hrothweard, archbishop of York **II** 436

Hrotsvitha of Gandersheim **III** 257

Hrypadun *see* Repton (Derby.)

Hrypum *see* Ripon (Yorks.)

Hubert, Cardinal Deacon **II** 664

Hubert, viscomte of Maine **II** 608

Huddersfield **XII** 513

Huddleston, John **X** 115

Huddleston, Sir Richard, Beaumaris and Anglesey captain **VI** 635

Hudson, George **XIII** 596

Hudson, Sir Henry, rector **VI** 403

Hudson, Sir James **XIII** 300, 303

Hudson, R. S. **XV** 475–6

Hudson, Thomas (1701–79), painter **XI** 400

Hudson Bay **VII** 227; coast and forts **X** 340–2; Company **X** 61, 170, 340; merchants **XI** 307; Company **XII** 25

Hugh, abbot of Bury St Edmunds **III** 228

Hugh, archbishop of Lyons **III** 177, 178, 179

Hugh IV, duke of Burgundy, countess Eleanor's claims **IV** 164

Hugh, duke of the Franks **II** 345–7, 360

Hugh II, earl of Chester **III** 335, 338

Hugh I, earl of Chester (1071) **II** 615, 628; **III** 100, 285, 288, 295

Hugh the Chanter **III** 181, 276

Hugh fitz Baldric **II** 633

Hugh de Grandmaisnil **II** 630

Hugh d'Ivry **II** 630, 639

Hugh de Montfort **II** 593, 630, 633, 639

Hugh Pierleone, cardinal and legate **III** 220

Hugh de Port **II** 633

Hugh, seigneur of the Thimerais **II** 609

Hughes, Revd Hugh Price **XIV** 184

Hughes, Thomas (1822–96) **XIII** 495–6, 613, 616; biography 495; **XIV** 132

Hughes, W. M. **XV** 82

Hughes, William, bishop of St Asaph **VIII** 190

Hughli **X** 349

Huguenots **VIII** 54–62, 157–9, 160–1, 344; **IX** 63–6; **X** 109

Huguet, Major **XIV** 400

Huitdeniers, Osbert **III** 197

Hull (Yorks.) **III** 96; **IV** 634; **V** 360, 381, 452; **VI** 221, 418; incorporation charter 386, 393; Hansa merchants 654; **VII** 40, 214, 219, 389, 392; **IX** 129, 133; workhouse **X** 53; **XII** 515; university college **XV** 308

Hull, Edward **VI** 451, 471, 600

Hull, General **XII** 552

Hull, river *see* Kingston-on-Hull; Wyke-on-Hull

Hulton, Messrs **XIV** 532, 533

humanism: **VII** Erasmus 26, 249–58; beginnings in England 235–48; *see also* Colet; Grocin; Linacre; More

humanissimi **Ia** 42; *see also* Romanization

humanitarian movements **XI** 94, 136–9, 144, charity schools 141–2

humanitarianism **X** 418–21

Humber **II** 587, 604–5; early political boundary 32–4

Humber, river **Ib** xxvi, 82, 174–7, 178, 180, 196, 199; map 4 xxxii; **II** 732; **III** 37, 80, 351, 469; **V** 116, 492; **VI** 2, 447

Humber Street **Ib** 189

Humberside **Ia** 45, 68, 95, 97; **Ib** 87

Humberston (Humberstone) **Ib** 183; map 4 xxxii

Humbert **III** 330, 332

Humbert, General **XII** 398

Humble Petition and Advice **IX** 182–5, 187

Humbre *see* Humber, river

Humbrenses **Ib** 174–5, 181–2, 185

Hume, David (1711–76) **XI** 6, 10, 85, 286, 429–31; **XII** 280, 345, 348; biography 327

Hume, David **IX** 117; **X** 292

Hume, Joseph **XIII** 74, 148, 173, 266

Hume Castle **VIII** 146

Humfrey, Pelham **X** 406

humiliores **Ia** 512

'humours', theory **VIII** 313

Humphrey, duke of Gloucester **VI** 180, 217, 218, 332, 334; inexperience (1414) 127; riding into sea 125; security for duke of Burgundy (Sep.-Oct. 1416) 169; Cotentin 173; petitions 193; Henry V's will 211, 216; parliament summons (9 Nov. 1422) 212; Great Council (5 Nov. 1422) 212; Henry VI's tutelage 214, 216; lords' attitude to claim (1422) 215; protector and defender 215; council chief 215, 224; remuneration as Protector 220; salary (1423) 221; council interview 224–5, 231–2, 509; marriage 225; Hainault expedition 225; illegal marriage contention 225; parliamentary support 226;

Humphrey, duke of Gloucester (*cont.*)
loan 226; Burgundy duel 226;
Beaufort defrauding charge 229;
Beaufort coup warning 229;
Henry VI to London (Nov. 1425)
229; complaint against Beaufort
230; compensation granted
(1427) 233; grievances petition
233; Protector's powers 233; parliament attendance 233; resists
Curia demands 236; Low Countries campaign 245; Beaufort
attack renewed (1431) 253; council consultation 431; Henry VI's
minority 433; Normandy governorship declined 467; leads
council (1435) 473; arrest and
death 482–4; Cade's rebellion
499; protectorship struggle recalled (1483) 612; tomb 650;
Oxford lectures founded 677–8;
classical authors 679; books given
to King's College 679; murdered
(1447) **VII** 236, 267

Humphrey, earl of Stafford, killed at
Shrewsbury **VI** 52, 53

Huncote (Leics.) **III** 404

Hundiby, John **VI** 457

hundred: late appearance **II** 292–3;
origin 297–300; court's functions
298–301; fiscal business 298–
300, 646–7; annexed to royal
manors 300; on the eve of the
Conquest 501; spiritual pleas 546;
Anglo-Norman 684; court **IV** 68;
private 67, 366; rolls 359, 360; *see
also* borough

hundred of silver **II** 510

Hungarians **VII** 98, 104, 156, 308

Hungary **III** 362; **X** 111; peace
with **XV** 132; Bolshevism 135;
Griffith's version of non-violence
154; Fiume 161; throne offered
282; inflation 289; does not operate sanctions 380; claims on
Czechoslovakia 427, 429; supports Germany 435; seizes Sub-
Carpathian Ukraine 439, 441;

economic resources 577; shared
(50–50) 588

Hungary, Count Palatine of *see*
Count Palatine of Hungary

Hungary, king of *see* Sigismund,
king of Hungary

hunger marchers **XV** 349–50, 395

Hungerford, Bear Inn **X** 142

Hungerford, Edmund **VI** 451

Hungerford, Robert, Walter's
grandson **VI** 331

Hungerford, Robert, Walter's son
and heir **VI** 519; freed 520;
attainder (1461) 539; estates 607

Hungerford, Sir Thomas **V** 395

Hungerford, Walter, Sir, later Lord
VI 179, 213, 218, 220, 234;
treasurer 31; ambassador to
emperor (July 1414) 161; Sigismund conversations 162; diplomat 219; Courtenay and Peverell
estates 331; son 331; Lancaster
steward/administrator 331–2;
acquisitions 331–2; Constance
ambassador 332; '*Libelle*' 346–7;
Henry VI's council 433–5

Hunmanby (Yorks.) **VI** 337

Hunne, Richard (d. 1514) **VII** 291,
292, 343, 521

Huns **Ia** 241, 257, 474–5, 481–3,
663

Hunsdon (Herts.) **VI** 507; house
VII 526, 595

Hunsdon, Lord *see* Carey, Henry

Hunt, G. Ward **XIV** 17; biography
32

Hunt, Henry **XIII** 21–2, 63–5, 92;
biography 21

Hunt, J. H. Leigh (1784–1859) **XII**
542

Huntandun *see* Huntingdon

Huntcliff: watchtower **Ia** 383; **Ib**
map 6 88

Hunte, Richard **VI** 626

Hunter, headmaster of Lichfield
grammar school **XI** 63

Hunter, John (1728–93), surgeon
XI 391, 392

Hunter, Sir Robert **XIV** 340

Hunter, William (1718–83), surgeon **XI** 391

Huntingdon (Huntandun) **II** 327, 338; castle 601; earldom 612; shire 296, 501, 732; **III** 85, 337; county 31; St Mary's priory 186; honour 269, 270, 275; weaver's gild 338; honour and earldom **IV** 594, 606–7; **V** 416, 418; abbey (Austin) **VI** 302

Huntingdon, earldom of **III** 157, 276, 279

Huntingdon, earls of, master of the horse **XII** 578; *see also* d'Angle; David, son of David I, king of Scotland; Clinton; Henry, son of David I, king of Scotland; Hastings, Henry; Holland, John; Simon de Senlis; Waltheof

Huntingdon, Henry of **III** 99, 249

Huntingdon, Selina, countess of (1701–81) **XI** 96, 99; biography **XII** 3

Huntingdonshire **V** 192, 416, 487; **VI** 497

Huntingfield Manor (Kent) **VI** 333

Huntley, earl of *see* Gordon, George

Huntsman, Benjamin (1704–76) **XI** 116; **XII** 31, 506

Hurdell, Richard **VI** 462–3

Hurst Castle **IX** 156

Hurstbourne **Ib** 147

Hurstbourne Priors (Hants) **II** 476

Hurstmonceaux (Sussex) **IV** 545; castle **VI** 651

Hus, John **V** 516

Husbandman **IX** 284

Husee, Henry **V** 236

Huskisson, William **XIII** 62, 75–6, 78, 367, 373; biography 70; commercial and fiscal policy of 70–2

Hussa **Ib** 199

Hussein, sherif of Mecca **XV** 71

Hussey, John, Baron (1466?–1537) **VII** 390

Hussey, Thomas **VIII** 138

Hussites **VII** 332

Hutcheson, Francis (1694–1746) **XI** 6, 84, 286

Hutcheson, Mrs, philanthropist, friend of the Gibbons and William Law **XI** 93

Hutchins, William, *alias* Tyndale **VII** 343

Hutchinson, A. S. M. **XV** 311

Hutchinson, Colonel **X** 380

Hutchinson, Lucy **IX** 185, 251, 265–6, 358

Hutchinson, Thomas (1711–1800) **XII** 177–9, 185, 195; biography 178

huts *see* houses

Hutten, Ulrich von **VII** 247

Hutton (Essex) **V** 328, 341

Hutton, James (1726–97), chemist and geologist **XI** 287, 387; **XIII** 571

Hutton, Matthew (1693–1758), archbishop of York (1747–57), of Canterbury (1757–8) **XI** 78

Hutton, R. H. **XIII** 183

Hutton, Dr Thomas, Brittany envoy **VI** 626, 634

Huxley, Aldous **XV** 179–80

Huxley, Julian **XV** 550

Huxley, Thomas Henry **XIII** 499, 574, 577; **XIV** 137, 142, 145, 146, 162

Huy (Flanders) **II** 541; **III** 83; **X** 171, 204

Huygens, Christiaan **X** 42, 43, 372

Huygens, Constantijin, the younger **X** 281

Hwiccawudu *see* Wychwood Forest (Oxon.)

Hwicce **II** 44–8, 134, 296, 337, 398; dual origin 44–5; underkingdom under Mercian lordship 45–6, 231, 305; rulers named 45–7

Hwitern *see* Whithorn (Wigtown)

Hyacinth, Cardinal **III** 211

Hydar Ali **XII** 159

Hyde (Winchester): abbey **III** 170; abbot **VI** 234

Hyde, Anne, afterwards duchess of York **X** 72

Hyde, Lady Catherine, duchess of Queensberry (d. 1777) **XI** 10, 148, 204, 421

Hyde, Douglas **XIV** 335

Hyde, Edward, 1st earl of Clarendon (1609–74) **VII** 295; **IX** 21, 121; quoted 66, 105, 130, 132, 134; on court of wards 84; parliamentary demands 92, 144; Strafford's execution 102–4; on Irish rebellion 117; becomes Charles' advisor 124, 257; on Hobbes 170; on Roman Catholics 210; on Cromwell 235; on social evils 271; on compounding 272; on education 357; *History of the Rebellion* 408–9; chancellor **X** 1–2, 8; view of prerogative courts 9; House of Commons 12; view of administrative machine 13; attitude to Church 20; position of parliament 56; religious debates 58; appropriation for war 67; impeachment and fall 72; taxation of clergy 157; Carolina 339; writings 380, 381

Hyde, Henry, 2nd earl of Clarendon **X** 139, 141, 181, 183, 302

Hyde, Henry, Viscount Cornbury (1710–53), on Scottish legal system **XI** 273

Hyde, Laurence, earl of Rochester: signs treaty of alliance with Dutch **X** 88; 1st lord of the treasury 98, 116; rivalry with Halifax 114; petition for parliament 141; toryism 181; lord-lieutenant of Ireland 222; parliament (1702) 222

Hyde, Thomas **X** 383

Hyde Park: disturbances (1866) **XIII** 184; **XV** 261

Hygeberht, archbishop of Lichfield **II** 218, 225, 227; resigned his see 228

Hygelac, king of Geatas **II** 194–5

Hyndman, H. M. **XIV** 100; **XV** 143

hypocausts **Ia** 603, 608–9, 631; furnace 459

Hypselantes, Prince Alexander **XIII** 214

Hythe (Kent) **II** 432, 567; **III** 433; **V** 243

Hythloday, Raphael, character in *Utopia* **VII** 259–60, 264

Hywel, son of Idwal **II** 369

Hywel Dda, king of Dyfed **II** 341; laws **IV** 388, 390, 416

Hywel ap Meurig, constable of Builth, career **IV** 411, 415

I

Iago, king of Gwynedd **II** 369

Iberian peninsula **VII** 219, 309

Ibrahim Pasha *see* Mehemet Ali

Ibsen, H. **XIV** 328

Icanhoh, monastery **II** 117

Icel, founder of Mercian dynasty **Ib** 185; **II** 39

Iceland **III** 88, 215; **VI** 348; fishery 363–4; merchants 364; **VII** 219, 222, 224–5; occupied **XV** 505

Iceni **Ia** 44, 531; attempt to disarm 47, 90; early revolt 101, 189; Boudiccan revolt 114; *civitas* and forum 186; **Ib** 97

Ickleford **Ib** 185

Ickleton **Ib** 185

Icklingham, fonts? **Ia** 730; **Ib** 185

Icknield Way **Ib** xxvi; map 3 xxxi; **II** 26, 597; **III** 78, 79

Ickwell **Ib** map 2 xxx

Iclingas **Ib** 185

Icocca **VII** 312

Iconium, sultan of **III** 339

Ida, king of Bernicia **Ib** 6, 20, 198–9; **II** 76

Ida, wife of Renaud of Dammartin, count of Boulogne **III** 440

Iddesleigh, earl of *see* Northcote, Sir Stafford

Iden, Sir Alexander **VI** 497

identity cards **XV** 464, 492

Idle, river **Ib** 182; map 4 xxxii; battle **II** 79

Idler **XI** 422, 431

Idrīsī **III** 149

Idwal, king of Gwynedd **II** 341

If Winter Comes **XV** 311

Iffley (Oxon.), church **III** 262; **VI** 370

IJssel, river **Ib** map 1 xxix

Ilbert de Laci **II** 627

Ilchester (Som.) **III** 101, 436; **VI** 392

Ilchester, Richard of, archdeacon of Poitiers and bishop of Winchester **III** 210, 211, 221, 222, 336; hostility to Becket 220; diet of Würzburg 329; Norman justiciar 340

Ilfracombe (Devon) **III** 436

Ilkley **X** 409

Illington **Ib** map 5 68

Illustrious, at Taranto **XV** 523

Illyria, Illyricum **Ia** 130, 316, 348, 350, 354; Caesar 31; British units in 404; Alaric and Stilicho 423, 426

Imber, Lawrence **VII** 591

Immanuel Case (1799) **XII** 473

Immingham (Lincs.) **III** 96

immunity **II** 307; *see also* bookland

Imola, bishop of **VII** 65

Impeachment, foreshadowed in Stratford's case **V** 177; (1376) 193, 390–2; of Alice Perrers 403; of Despenser and his captains 433; of Michael de la Pole 445, 448–9; (1388) 458; (1397) 482–3; under Charles II **X** 11; **XI** 23–4, 156–7, 203

imperator **Ia** 86, 199

imperial biographers **Ia** 205

Imperial Conference (1923) **XV** 209; (1926) 253; at Ottawa 333; (1937) 420; *see also* Colonial Conference

imperial control: appointments **Ia** 49–50, 165, *see also* patronage; procurator 89; imperial commissioners 122, 535–6, 576–9; town defences 261, 373; *correctores* not found in Britain 536; public works 575–8; economic intervention 614; mines 635–7; wine production 652, 654; Diocletian's price edict 655–6; *see also* administration

imperial courts **Ia** 301, 517–18;

293

imperial courts (*cont.*)
relationships of court, army, and senate 301–2, 347, 400, 417, 430; Constantine 323, 365; Byzantium-Constantinople 325, 365–6, 489; Milan 354, 403, 408; Trier 302, 402; Ravenna 425, 429, 451, 465; Arles 429, 449, 451; Ausonius at court 400, 435, 436; St Ambrose 408, 468; Theodoric 488

Imperial Cult **Ia** 515–16, 580, 682–3; deification 109, 193, 214, 296–7, 302; temple of Claudius 117, 674; Constantine 344; altars 674, 683, 713; provincial aristocracy 682; Domitian's brutality 715

imperial estates: administration **Ia** 89, 224, 337–8, 530–1, 591 —satellite villas 597; acquisition of land 104, 114, 200–1, 224, 227 —sold for cash 280 —district office 531; on both sides of *limes* 175, 284, 524; Brigantan territory 200–1; near Bath 280; gifts to churches 341, 730; scattered nature of some estates 600, 627, 629; ownership not always apparent 601–2; Fens 603–4; iron working 637

imperial family, imperial house **Ia** 49–50, 58; Julio-Claudians 48–50, 68, 69, 71, 109 —ancient aristocrats 155–6 —army loyalty 291; allegiance of army 68, 212, 428; Flavians 154; choice of Commodus 209, 212; Severans 228, 241, 249–50; Tetrarchy 290–1, 301; Carausius' claims 299; Constantine 328, 348, 359, 362, 369 —controls barbarians 428; Gratian 351, 400; Theodosians 400, 415, 428; Stilicho's connections 416–17; Galla Placidia 447; Ambrosius Aurelianus' imperial connections? 461–2; cult 515, 682–3; mausoleum 703

Imperial Federation League **XIV** 178

imperial freedmen *see* freedmen

imperial guards: body-guard, *scholares domestici* **Ia** 334, 488; élite troops replacing praetorians 350, 366–7, 411; *protectores* 351, 488; *see also comitatenses*; palatine troops; praetorian guards

imperial post (*cursus publicus*) **Ia** 565–8, 597, 724; *see also mansio*

imperial power: division **Ia** 204, 300–1; demands of politics 242; accessibility 518–19; limits 525; maintenance 532; *see also auctoritas; imperium*

Imperial Preference **XV** 207; at Ottawa 333; Atlantic charter 529

imperial regalia **Ia** 461–2; 486, 497

imperial succession **Ia** 154–5, 209, 290–1, 322–3, 348; importance of army 68–9, 131–2, 171–2, 212–14, 271–2; 'Gallic Provinces' empire 273; military insurrection 287; praetorian guard 324; Magnus Maximus 402; Constantine III 427–8; unreliability 439

Imperial War Cabinet **XV** 82, 150

imperialism, ideas behind **XIV** 163, 331–3

Imperium Galliarum **Ia** 244, 252, 273–6, 282, 289; compared with Carausius' system 301; restoration of Autun 314; dating probabilities 327; governorship duties 530; effect on British iron production 639–40

imperium **Ia** 49, 537, 573; *see also auctoritas*

Impey, Sir Elijah (1732–1809) **XII** 308, 314

Imphal, Japanese defeat **XV** 586

Import Duties Bill (1932) **XV** 330

imports **X** 251–2, 265, 299; and exports (1815–20) **XIII** 6–8; (1850–70) 606–7; graphs **XV** xxi–xxii; rise in prices 41; licensing 64; surpass pre-war figure 249;

maintained during Depression 284; effect of Protection 330, 339; still cheaper 336; fall short (1939–40) 463; shifted to west coast ports 506; cuts in (1941) 512; under lend-lease 513; reach lowest point 546; improve (1943) 564

impositions **IX** 11–14, 17

impropriation of churches **IV** 458–9; magnates of England's letter to Alexander IV 461

improvement commissioners **XIII** 460–2

Imworth, Richard **V** 412

In Gyrvum *see* Jarrow

Inchcolm, island in Firth of Forth **VII** 484

Inchkeith, island of **VIII** 44

Inchtuthil: nails **Ia** 76; fortress 149–51, 163

'incident' **IX** 106

Incitement to Disaffection Act (1937) **XV** 374

Incitement to Mutiny Act (1797): prosecutions under **XV** 218, 242

inclosures **VII** 263, 448–9; government attempts to check 450–1, 453; extent 452; denunciations 456–8, 504; Somerset's commission (1548) 505; repression after Kett's revolt 506; **VIII** 251–5; **IX** 83, 261, 279–81; **XIII** 8–9, 598

incolae **Ia** 117, 581–2

income tax: introduction **XII** 375; dropped 413; revived 414; **XIII** 15, 71, 113, 165–7, 180–1; increased by McKenna **XV** 40; further increase 41, 124; reduced (1922) 163; (1925) 237; increased (1930) 286; (Sep. 1931) 295; reduced (1934) 351; increased by 3*d.* (1936) 359; increased to 7*s.* 6*d.* 465; to 8*s.* 6*d.* 491; to 10*s.* 511; PAYE 573

Indemnity, Acts of **IX** (1660) 245–6; **X** 4; (1675) 272; (1920) **XV** 35

indenture, tripartite **VI** 57

indentures, military **IV** 520; **V** 235–6

Independent Labour party: founded at Bradford **XIV** 222; and UDC **XV** 51; negotiated peace 65; Leeds convention 89; ruined by reorganization of Labour party 91; refuses to join third International 143; Clydesiders returned 189; Labour party 199; Living Wage 237; declines 238; conflict with Labour party 264–5, 267, 283; local government 266; leaves Labour party 348–9; Popular Front 397, 435; opposes Second World War 457, 548; proposes negotiated peace 503; votes against government 542

independents: extravagances **IX** 106–8, 125; debt to Cromwell 189; oppose presbyterianism 192–5; growth 194–6

India **VII** 224, 474; **IX** 52, 321–5; British in **X** 348–54; **XI** 324–33, 347; merchants 307, 324, 332; factories 325, 331–2; Black Hole of Calcutta 328–9, 359; Seven Years War in 359, 372; struggle between English and French 326–31, 347, 366; **XII** 140, 215, 225, 282, 371; history (1760–74) 73, 85, 124, 157–72, (1773–85) 221, 261–9, 305–23, (1784–1805) 274, 322, 371, 382–6, 409 — military achievements 412; British military failures 454; Travancore 489; establishment of church (1815) 570; routes to **XIII** 178, 194, 213, 236; committed to war **XV** 3; Mesopotamia 49; represented at Imperial War Cabinet 83; deaths from influenza 112; represented at peace conference 132; first disturbances 152–3; Simon Commission 254; Round Table conference 275–6; National government 277, 355–6;

India (*cont.*)

Churchill's views 277–8, 319; trade 339–40; keeps politicians busy 359; receives last emperor 403; involved in Second World War 452, Churchill discredited by 466; sterling balances 514; contribution to British army 515; shipping 520; Middle East 524; Cripps mission 545; British defend from habit 546; servicemen 549; famine 563; secured from Japanese 586; *see also* East India Company, Indian Mutiny, and *under* names of governors-general and viceroys

India, governors-general of *see* Canning, Earl; Dalhousie, 1st marquis of

India, viceroy of *see* Lawrence, John

India Defence League **XV** 356

Indian Ocean: Japanese neglect **XV** 545; sailings reduced 563; Roosevelt wants operation in 574–5

Indian National army **XV** 586

Indians, North American **X** 345–7

Indies **VII** 226, 227; *see also* West Indies

indigo **IX** 323, 338; **X** 331

Indo-China **XV** 370, 531

Indre, river **III** 328; **VI** 114

indulgence: letters and declarations, Canterbury diocese (1428) **VI** 237; **X** 270, 272, 275

industries **Ia** 588, 618–59; mining 183, 633–6; location 188, 588, 597, 656; iron 188–9, 529, 559–70, 637–41; salt 189, 224, 531, 620; urban craftsmen 237–8; pottery 238, 258, 455–6, 641–51; villas 281, 602, 610, 624–5; service 302, 514; state-controlled 337, 387, 421, 423, 438 — monopolies 531 — mining 633 — wool and mosaics 656; decline 455–6, 496, 661–2; glass 456; metal-working 537; pewter 595–

6, 635–6; tiles 585; textiles 601–2, 655–6; manpower 618, 639; agriculture 618–29; building 630–1; timber 630–1; fuel 631; power 631–3; wine 651–5; mosaics 656–7; finance 659–64; wool manufacture **XI** 110–11; silk 111–12, 132; cotton 112–13, 122; iron 113–17, 122; coal-using 115, 118–20, 122; machinery used 115–17, 119; steel 116–17; pottery 118, 120–1, 414; metal 121; skilled 132; fishing 276, 337; *see also* agriculture; American colonies; coal; communications; gin-drinking; Ireland; lead; London; pottery; prices; Scotland; silver; trade; wages

industry **VIII** 257, 258; general state **IX** 285; economics **X** 39; development 41–2; industrial expansion **XII** 26–32, 332–5, 504–16

Ine, king of Wessex **II** 71–3, 203, 204; organizes West Saxon church 71–2; laws 71; laws quoted 73, 280, 290, 312–14, 317

infangenetheof **II** 497–501, 636; *see also* jurisdiction, private

Infant Welfare movement **XIV** 519

infantry **Ia** 335; *see also* legions; *auxilia*

inflation **VII** 447

influenza epidemic (1918) **XV** 112, 121, 152

Information, Ministry of: First World War **XV** 106–7, 130; Second World War 456; proposal to appoint Hore-Belisha 460; Duff Cooper 478; on German morale 519; regional government 569

Ingaevones **Ib** 49

-*ingas* **Ib** 36–44

Inge, John **V** 205

Inge, W. R. **XV** 235

Inge, Sir William **V** 27

Ingeborg of Denmark, wife of Philip Augustus **III** 363, 364, 379

Ingeld, ancestor of King Alfred **II** 65

Ingham (Lincs.) **Ib** map 5 68

Ingham, Sir Oliver **V** 96, 102, 114, 115, 152

Inglis, General **XIII** 437

Inglis, Sir Robert **XIII** 491

Ingoldsby, Richard **IX** 239, 245

ingots **Ia** 415, 532, 633, 636

inheritance of land **II** 317–18

inhumation *see* burial customs

Inishboffin, Mayo, English monastery **II** 124

injunctions, royal **VIII** 31

Inkel, Thomas **III** 33

inland **II** 484

Innocent II, Pope **III** 133, 135, 185, 192–3, 194

Innocent III, Pope **III** 76, 192, 222; faithful to king 221; curbs episcopal greed 223; impressed by Giraldus Cambrensis 224; frees Welsh insurgents from allegiance to John (1212) 300; quarrel with Philip Augustus 364; Henry VI's ambition 366; intervention in Brittany 384; episcopal elections 444; interdict (1208) 445–6; threatens to depose John 456; interdict withdrawn 457; John's ally 458, 468, 478; deals with insurgent barons 470, 478–9; **IV** 17, 24, 87; Lateran Council 449; writ of caption 465

Innocent IV, Pope (1241–54) **IV** 110; Frederick II 98, 448; Sicilian business 106, 121–2; Simon de Montfort 115; coronation and anointing of king of Scots 594; *unitas actus* 538

Innocent VI, Pope (1352–62) **V** 137, 254, 276, 278, 284

Innocent VII, Pope **VI** 33, 91

Innocent VIII, Pope (1484–92) Giambattista Cibò: mentioned **VII** 65, 105; bull against abuse of sanctuary (1487) 77; bull against rebels 79; sends Henry cap and sword (1489) 101, 156; compromise with Scotland 336

Innocent XI, Pope **X** 129, 130

innoculation, development **XII** 11

inns **Ia** 562; *see also mansio*

Inns of Chancery **VII** 247, 565

Inns of Court **VI** 311; **VII** 565; Furnivall's Inn 247; Gray's Inn 300, 344; Lincoln's Inn 247; **IX** 360; **XIII** 18, 30, 618

Inquiry, Commissions of **IV** 481, 698–9, 702, 703; in Champagne 240–1, 322; in Gascony 295–6; in Channel Islands 320, 322, 358; complaints against king's servants 322; in Wales 329, 415–16, 418; pleas of liberties 353; statutes and eyres 355–8; royal inquests 358–60; judicial delay 360–1; archi-episcopal, into diocesan rights 491–3; new coinage and fraud 633

Inquisitio comitatus Cantabrigiensis **II** 649

Inquisitio Geldi **II** 644

Inquisition **VI** 250–2

Inskip, Sir Thomas Walker Hobart: opposes revised prayer book **XV** 259; biography 390; minister for co-ordination of defence 390; increases proportion of fighters 391; succeeded by Chatfield 456

Institution, Royal Philosophical *see* Philosophical Institution, Royal

Instrument of Government **IX** 176–8, 198

insulae **Ia** 159, 534, 658

Insurance, National *see* National Insurance

Insurrection Act **XII** 446

intercommuning, letters of (1675) **X** 270

Intercursus Magnus **VII** 139, 150, 181, 187, 222

Intercursus Malus **VII** 186, 187

474; Richard II 470–3, 491–2; Mortimer's death 495; **VI** 2, 104, 221, 347, 351; expenditure for 75; financial demands 88; Anglo-Irish lords 425; royal captain 432; Clarence lieutenancy 561; York popularity 629; **VII** 28, 121, 300, 434, 500; Lambert Simnel (1487) 68–70, 79; the Pale and the White Rose 70–2; Henry VII 73, 78; Sir Richard Edgecombe in Ireland (1488) 79–80; Perkin Warbeck 116, 120, 125–34, 138, 144, 150; parliament at Drogheda (1494–5) 128; Poynings laws 129–31; finances 131–2; Kildare as deputy 133–4; estimate of Henry VII's policy 134; attainder of Kildare 138; Henry VII's army 210; revenues 215; trade links 219; Henry VIII as lord-lieutenant 234, 385; Kildare summoned to London (1533) 364; revolt of Lord Thomas Fitzgerald (1534) 364; his surrender and execution 364–5; Lord Leonard Grey deputy (1536), executed (1541) 365; Henry takes title of king of Ireland and head of the church in Ireland (1540) 366; Geraldine rebellion 370; Leonard Grey beheaded 418; inclosure 450; French plottings 482, 487; Mary queen of Scots 485; English statesmanship **VIII** 461–2; condition of the country, work of Henry VIII 462–4; ignorance of English tongue 465; Catholic Ireland a danger to Protestant England 466; first Irish parliament 467; Bishop Brady's diocese in Meath 468; Shane O'Neill 'captain' of Tyrone 470; Sidney's analysis of situation 471–2; suppression of native Irish dress 473; attempt at colonization of Ireland, and failure 474–6; James Fitzmaurice 476–8; Catholic propaganda 479; Tyrone's Spanish policy 481–2; ill-adapted for invasion by English 482; the crucial years (1594–6) 483–5; rising of the Irish *en masse* 485; arrival of Mountjoy 486; Spanish assistance to the Irish 487; blow falls in Munster 488; Kinsale occupied by Spaniards, besieged by English 488–9; Mountjoy's triumph 489–90; *Pacata Hibernia* 490–2; **IX** 176, 288; army 95–6, 99–100, 111–12, 116; plantation of Ulster 108–10; Wentworth lord deputy 110–15; church of 110–11; parliament 112–13, 115; massacre in 116–18; 'Cessation' in 134–5; Charles seeks aid from 134–5, 142–3, 161; effect in England 135, 143, 161; reconquest 161–3, 288; settlement 164–6; army **X** 122; fighting during French war 164, 169; land grants 189; relations with 294–324; industries after the Revolution 316; **XII** 303, 376, 417, 441, 444–6; lords lieutenant 33, 292–3; church 68, 299; Jacobites 79–80, 287, 291, 300; agriculture, industries, trade 122, 192, 276, 294, 296–8; concessions to Parliament 129; in foreign service 202, 290–2; army 214, 299–300; barracks 215; principal discussions (1760–81) 221–5, (1760–1801) 387–402; Rockingham's policy 245; Pitt's policy 276–8, 392–403; exploitation and restrictions 287–8, 292, 295, 299; Roman Catholics 287–92, 299; Anglo-Irish 288, 292, 303; Presbyterian 288, 292; land system 288, 297; schools 289; parliament 290, 292–6, 300, 303; lord justices 293–4, 300; Speakers 294; 'undertakers' 294–5, 303; legal system 295; finance 295–6; famine 296–8; emigration 297;

Ireland (cont.)

Protestant Association 300; civil list 300; currency 300–1; arts 304–6; books 306; Waterford glass 306; threat of foreign invasion (1797) 372, 396–9; hospitals 392; rising (1803) 421; Wood's halfpence see Wood, William; **XIII** 2–3, 16, 87, 96–7, 109; Catholic emancipation 76–7, 328–9, 340–4; tithes 97, 338–9; coercion acts 98, 334, 345–6, 356, 360; famine 122, 352; Fenianism 189, 359–61, 363; Gladstone's Irish policy 189–90, 361–4; reform bills 192; union 329–30; land question 329–335; Devon commission 331–2, 335, 350, 352; evictions 332; agrarian crime 333, 356, 359; failure of British parliament to deal with Irish problems 334–5, 337; manufactures 337–8; taxation 338; O'Connell's agitation 340–1; tithe bills 344–7; Drummond as chief secretary 347–8; 'Young Ireland' 349–50, 357; arrest and trial of O'Connell 350; Peel's measures 350–2; famine relief 353–5; emigration 355; encumbered estates act 356–7; O'Brien's rising 357; Russell's measures 358; movement for tenant-right 358–9; Cardwell's acts 359; beginnings of Home Rule movement 364; government **XV** 16; Kitchener 20; plans for (1916) 56–8, 71–2; convention to settle 83; proposed conscription 103–4, 112; casualties 120; general election (1918) 128; Lloyd George wishes to conciliate 131; treaty of Versailles 136; 'Troubles' 153–6; treaty with 158; unity ended 159; civil war 188; Anderson 242; supposed to be example of conciliation 275; English statesmen 358; bitter question 408; naval bases 504; see

also Carteret; Dublin; O'Connell; Peel; Russel

Ireton, Henry **IX** 147, 150–2, 163, 374

Irish agrarian revolution: origins **XIV** 56–7; jury 72–3; 'Plan of Campaign' 178–9

Irish Free State: created **XV** 15, 159; boundary 158, 162; Dominion status 253; repudiates treaty 357–8; Crown 403

Irish land annuities **XV** 358, 408

Irish land legislation: Gladstone's Act (1870) **XIV** 3, 56; Act (1881) 73–4, 450; Lord Ashbourne's (Purchase) Act (1885) 92; Balfour's (Purchase) Act (1891) 187; Wyndham's (Purchase) Act (1903) 358–9, 450

Irish language **Ia** 17, 507; **X** 323–4

Irish National Land League: formed **XIV** 57; funds from America and Australia 72; prosecuted for conspiracy 73; 'proclaimed' 179

Irish Nationalist party (1914) **XV** 15; insists on Home Rule 16; prepares to desert Asquith 27; against Kitchener 29; estranged from Asquith 57, 67, 71; withdraws in protest 104; traditional support of Liberal government 281

Irish (or National) volunteers: Kitchener **XIV** 475, 479; **XV** 21, 27; Easter rebellion 56; become IRA 155

Irish republic: proclaimed **XV** 56; restored 128, 154; ordered out of existence 158

Irish Republican Army: starts war against British **XV** 155; perhaps exhausted 157; opposes treaty 159, 161; assassinates Wilson 188

Irish Republican Brotherhood **XIV** 56; **XV** 155; see also Fenians

Irish settlers in West Scotland **II** 77, 86–7; missionaries 103–4, to Northumbria 119–20; to central

300

England 120; Latinity 178; script 178–80, 184; manuscript art 191–2

Irish University Bill (1873) **XIV** 24–5

iron: exported **Ia** 42, 58; industry 188, 529, 537, 559; punch 530; Wealden 570, 637–41; stool 605; mined 630, 686; **III** 81–2; smelting at Coalbrookdale **X** 50; Irish 317

Iron Age: British and Continental cultures **Ia** 6–19; continuity with Bronze Age 9, 46; Aylesford-Swarling 11; agriculture 13–16, 234–5, 554–5, 571–2, 621–3; art 15; Cornwall 44; North Grimsthorpe 46; houses 125, 159, 235, 609; settlement 159, 189, 554–5, 561, 585 —nucleated 589 —Fens 604 —Upper Thames Valley 607–9 —communal grazing 627; little evidence in Fens 189, 604; use of slaves 605; gift exchange 616; pottery 642, 646; cults 669–70, 681, 706; burial customs 670; shrines 671, 692; metalwork 679; cemeteries 694; **Ib** 49, 92; *see also* Hallstatt; La Téne

iron and steel industry **XII** 28, 31, 332, 334, 504–8; Pont Cysyslltau 519; production processes **XIV** 105–6, 277; relative decline in British production 277, 503; significance in First World War 504–5

Ironside, Lord: becomes Chief of Imperial General Staff **XV** 459; sent to Gort 485; commands home forces 497

Ironsides **IX** 140, 186

Irthing, river **Ia** 176–9

Irthlingborough (Yetlingaburg) (Northants) **II** 211, 734; college church **VI** 292

Irvine, agreement with Bruce (1297) **IV** 685

Irving, Henry **XIV** 328

Irvingites **XIII** 525

Isaacs, Sir Rufus, afterwards Lord Reading: Marconi Affair **XIV** 457–8; biography 457; **XV** 118, 225

Isabel, daughter of Richard of Clare, earl of Pembroke, wife of William Marshal **III** 314, 347

Isabel, daughter of King William of Scotland **III** 283

Isabel, queen of England, wife of Richard II: return to France **VI** 67; betrothal to Orléans' son 108; Henry IV 109

Isabel, queen of France, wife of Charles VI **VI** 179, 180, 226; Montereau murder 182

Isabel of Anjou **VI** 476

Isabel of Brittany, daughter of Duke Francis II **VII** 86

Isabel of Gloucester, first wife of King John **III** 297, 330, 348, 380

Isabel of Hainault, wife of Philip Augustus **III** 342

Isabel of Portugal, wife of Charles V **VII** 316

Isabel of St Symphorien, lady of Landivas **VI** 110

Isabella, daughter of Peter of Aragon **IV** 257

Isabella, daughter of Philip IV **IV** 652; affianced to Edward of Caernarvon (1303) 654

Isabella, queen of Spain **XIII** 230–1, 242–5

Isabella, sister of Henry III, marries Frederick II **IV** 72

Isabella of Angoulême, widow of King John and wife of Hugh de Lusignan, count of La Marche **III** 380, 430, 466; **IV** 89–91, 92, 95; later marriages 23, 40; French war (1242–3) 97, 102–3; dies (1246) 103; tomb at Fontevrault 119

Isabella of Aragon, first wife of

Isabella of Aragon (*cont.*)
Philip III of France, mother of Philip IV **IV** 239–40

Isabella of Castile, countess of Cambridge and duchess of York **V** 268; **VI** 535; **VII** 5, 81, 84, 103, 225; Medina del Campo treaty (1489) 96; Perkin Warbeck 117, 143–4; Prince Arthur and Infanta Catherine 148, 172; death 151, 154, 183; death of Arthur 174; Catherine betrothed to Henry 174–6; Henry and Catherine divorce 328; attitude to marriage 534; court painter 598

Isabella of France, queen of Edward II **V** 125, 152, 269, 381; betrothal and marriage 1, 4; grants 7–8; household 13; Gaveston 25; escape from York 56; conspiracy with Mortimer against Edward II 79–94; murder of Edward II 94–5; rule with Mortimer 96–101; retirement at Lynn 102; foreign policy 110–11; forests 207; secretary 278; dowry 292; staple 352; **VI** 137

Isabella of France, queen of Richard II **V** 147, 474, 491

Isabella of Scotland, wife of Roger Bigod, earl of Norfolk **IV** 73

Isandhlwana **XIV** 60–1

Iscoed (Cardigan) **VI** 40

Isenbert **III** 64

Isgenen, district **VI** 438, 440

Isherwood, Christopher **XV** 347

Isidore of Seville **VI** 667

Isis, temple **Ia** 254, 667

Iskennin, lordship of **V** 74

Islam **VII** 84

Islay, duke of *see* Campbell, Archibald

Islay, Lord *see* Argyll, 3rd duke of

Isle de France **III** 111, 122

Isle of Man **II** 80; part of Norwegian system in war and administration **IV** 596; later history (1266–1765)

596, 609; **V** 13, 24, 33, 482; **VI** 63; **XV** 19

Isle of Wight (Wiht) **Ia** 92, 308, 320; **Ib** 144–9, 152; **II** 9, 21, 23, 38, 67, 734; royal family 38; Cædwalla invades 69–70; exterminated 70, 138; Danish fleet 379, 381; Cnut takes ships to 401; harried by Vikings 428; harried by Godwine 566; Tostig appears 586; **III** 484; acquired by Edward I **IV** 518; **V** 8, 236; **VI** 74; French occupation 166; **VII** 87, 450, 487, 557; **IX** 152; **XV** 432; *see also* Forz; Quarr

Islep, Simon, archbishop of Canterbury **VI** 420

Isles, the (Scottish) **III** 268, 271

Isleworth (Surrey): Richard of Cornwall's manor **IV** 175; attacked by Londoners (1264) 186; **VII** 526

Islington **X** 409

Islip, John **VII** 585, 593

Islip, Simon, archbishop of Canterbury (1349–66), keeper of the privy seal (1347–50) **V** 211, 276, 289, 296–7, 299; founder Canterbury Hall, Oxford 507

Ismay, General **XV** 479

Issoudun (Berri) **III** 374, 375, 379

Istria **III** 362; **XV** 50, 161–2

Istria, Capo d', diplomat **XII** 563

Isurium Brigantum see Aldborough

Isvolsky, A. P., intrigue with Aehrenthal **XIV** 410

Italian duchies **XI** 201–2, 206, 244, 265, 267–8; Spanish claims and Quadruple Alliance (1718) 172–3; Philip sends Ripperda to negotiate alliance 194; Don Philip secures Parma and Piacenza 270

Italian merchants **VII** 218, 219, 220, 223; *see also* merchants

Italian Relation **VII** 16, 30–32, 259

Italianate vices **VIII** 279, 326

'Italians': movement against

(1231–2) **IV** 45, 46, 766; *see also* Romans

Italica, *municipium* **Ia** 155

Italy: invaded by barbarians **Ia** 11, 204, 207, 270–1; civil war 31, 129–31, 217, 348, 462–4 —Constantine's advance 433 —Aegidus' march prevented 491; declining importance 169; estates 193, 370, 575, 605; part of western empire 287, 348, 353, 409; Goths 405, 418, 423, 426, 430; government becomes detached from north-western empire 415, 431, 435, 438, 451, 453; influence in Britain 506, 662; attitude to army 508; wine trade 652; towns 658; coinage 660; paganism 687, 691, 735; Norman states **II** 559, 585–6; trade with **III** 86, 90; Robert Curthose in 113; English students 237, 241, 244; Henry II's ambitions 330–2; financial dealings 354, 423; Otto IV's plans to conquer 452; representation of cities **IV** 531; famine in **V** 49; Clarence 267; Hawkwood 346; trade 350, 354, 360, 364, 381; Despenser 431; Chaucer 530, 531; **VII** 157, 269, 535, 558, 600; single unitary state concept 83; French claims 84; political position (1494) 112–14; unites against Charles VIII (1495) 115; League of Venice 115–16; Franco-Spanish *entente* 149–50; Louis occupies Milanese (1499) 152; Treaty of Granada 152–3; Maximilian's advance resisted 154–5; Spanish conquests 172; Catherine and Henry VIII marriage contract 175; Louis and Ferdinand's alliance 177, 188; scholarship 236, 240, 242, 245, 257, 569; Erasmus 249–52; Thomas More 264–5; Julian trumpet 271; Louis hard-pressed 275; Ferdinand negotiates with France 276; Anglo-French treaty 285; France conquers 306; partition (1517) 307; common cause against Turks 308; Charles V 309, 314, 321; Battle of Pavia (1525) 315–16; peace of Cambrai (1529) 319; Pope and Wolsey 327; Reformation 338, 348; Thomas Cromwell 351; wool trade 449; merchants and trade 474–5; Spanish conquests 559; influence on English music **X** 406; completes her unity **XIV** 7; population 103, 269, 498; Lord Salisbury's Mediterranean pact 198; attacks Turkey to seize Tripoli 436; declines to join in attack on Serbia 469; small number of large towns 498; war debt **XV** 42; treaty of London 50; partition of Turkey 70; resists negotiated peace 115; Fourteen Points 119; Fiume 132, 161–2; and Kemal 190–1; debt settlement with United States 203; Locarno 221; currency depreciation 223; air force antiquated 231; demands naval parity with France 273; Manchurian affair 369, 370; attack on Abyssinia 380, 381, 384, 418, 421; Rhineland 386; aids Franco 393–4; leaves League 415; Chamberlain 414, 421–3; trains run to time 417; plans for attacking 460; leak in the blockade 461; aids Finland 468; declares war 488; invades Egypt 522–3; defeated in desert 524; British private war against 536; no joint strategy with Germany 537; Americans committed to fight 540; Eighth Army begins advance 560; unconditional surrender 561; surrenders on terms 562; proposed invasion of 563–4; victories against 564; armistice with 572–3; new effort authorized 575; eclipsed by greater events

Italy (*cont.*)
576; Americans refuse to reinforce front 587; German armies surrender 593
Itchen, river **Ib** 92, 151; map 2 xxx; map 3 xxxi
Itford Hill **Ia** 8
ITMA **XV** 549
It's a Long Way to Tipperary **XV** 8
Ivan IV the Terrible, tsar of Russia **VII** 561; **VIII** 239

Ivar the Boneless **II** 246–7, 250, 271
Ive v. Ash **XIV** 10
Ivo, bishop of Chartres **III** 118, 179, 183
ivory **Ia** 42; **X** 331
Ivory, Thomas (d. 1786), Irish architect **XI** 304
Ivry (Eure) **III** 340, 342; **VI** 239
Ivry, lord of *see* Charles, lord of Ivry
Ixworth (Suffolk): cruciform brooch **Ib** 58 [fig. 1(b)]; map 2 xxx

J

J. H. (?John Hall) **IX** 123

Jack of Newbury **VIII** 293

Jackman, Charles **VIII** 241

Jackson, Andrew (1767–1845), president of USA **XII** 551, 552, 555

Jackson, C. **XIII** 489

Jackson, Francis James (1770–1814) **XII** 456

Jackson, Mr **XII** 236

Jackson, Sir T. G. **XIV** 156

Jacobites and Jacobitism: plots (1690–6) **X** 183–5; and the Tory party 229; (1702–14) 240–8; impossibility of a restoration 242–3; ministry suspected 245; Scottish Jacobitism 279–80; Irish 312, 315; **XI** 42, 150, 156–8, 166, 174; rising (1715) 49, 55, 71, 79, 159–63 —estates forfeited 280; rising (1745) 49, 72, 79, 104, 251–7 —Pelham's triumph 259 —estates forfeited 282–3, 285; plots 55, 73, 151, 173, 182–3 —invasions 213 —Ormonde 236 —Marshal Saxe 248; Walpole's pacific policy 184–5; influence on foreign policy 195, 196; Pulteney 204; cotton 250; *see also* Ireland

Jacobsen, Theodore (d. 1772), architect **XI** 412

Jacobus Magnus *see* Le Grand, Jacques

Jacombe, Robert, Walpole's banker (*c.*1720): and South Sea Bubble **XI** 178

Jacqueline of Hainault **VI** 225, 245; release negotiated 226

Jacquerie **V** 140, 338, 422

Jacques de Guesle **VIII** 388

Jacquetta, dowager duchess of Bedford **VI** 535

Jade Bay **Ib** 54; map 1 xxix

Jaenberht, archbishop of Canterbury **II** 216, 218, 225–6

Jaffa **III** 361, 362

Jaffray, Alexander **IX** 168

Jagiello, Ladislas, king of Hungary and Bohemia (1490–1516) **VII** 104, 320

Jaille, Sire de la, Breton nobleman **VI** 72

Jak, Mother **VII** 479

Jamaica **IX** 232, 337, 349; **X** 59, 60, 325, 326, 330–1; sugar **XI** 192, 308, 313, 369; dispute with Crown 312; population 313; slaves 314; free port (1787) **XII** 289; constitution **XIII** 103, 374; rising (1865) 374; *see also* West Indies

James, duke of Hamilton **IX** 89, 91, 100, 155

James, duke of York **IX** 114, 246

James, earl of Desmond **VI** 629; father killed 629

James, Henry **XIII** 595; **XIV** 160, 531, 549

James, Sir Henry, later Lord James of Hereford: biography **XIV** 25; passes Corrupt Practices Act 87; opposed to Home Rule 96; refuses the Lord Chancellorship 97; joins Unionist Cabinet 224; retires 354; opposed to Chamberlain's fiscal policy 373; opposes rejection of the (1909) budget by the Lords 415, 417

James, John (d. 1746), architect **XI** 412

James I, king of Aragon **IV** 99–100, 102, 116, 252

James II, king of Aragon **IV** 263, 661

James I, king of Cyprus (Lusignan) **VI** 10

James I, king of England (1603–25): son of Mary Queen of

James I, king of England (*cont.*)

Scots **VII** 162; birth **VIII** 100; coronation 108; hostage 146; assumes power in Scotland 352; portrait 359–60, 442; Gowrie conspiracy 360–2; signs Treaty of Berwick 370; Bond of Association 375–7; English succession 388–9, 439, 442–51, 454; **IX** 266, 407; accession 1; relations with first parliament 3–9; attitude to Roman Catholicism 3, 205, 209; political theories 8–9; tries to unite England and Scotland 9–10; Scottish favourites 12, 16; on the Commons 18; curious letter to Rochester 19; loses prestige 20; favours Buckingham 21; tries to suppress political discussion 24; speech to parliament (1621) 24; tears up Protestation 27–8; last parliament 28; death 28; importance of reign 28; belief in divine right of kings 31–4, 411; views on foreign policy 47, 235; despises the Dutch 49; influenced by Gondomar 54–5; eager for Spanish match 55–8; views on Bohemian revolution 56; aids France 64; denounces puritans 70; says 'No bishop, no king' 70; Scottish policy 86–7, 91; court 263; colonies 326; interferes with trade 330–3; touches for the king's evil 367; writes on witchcraft 370; **XI** 5, 110; and Society of Antiquaries 394

James II, king of England (1685–8): joint stock companies **X** 61; in the English channel 63; marriage 81; attempt to limit his influence 95; in exile 97; question of succession 98, 102, 103; return 99; supports Catholics 109; accession 116; address to privy council 116; ecclesiastical policy 117, 122; opening speech to parliament 121; rules without parliament 122; lord high admiral 123; opposed by Oxford and Cambridge 124–5; declarations of indulgence 125, 126; and parliament 126; birth of an heir 127; relations with Louis XIV 130, 132; with William III 130–5, 140–2; his tardy concessions 136; at Salisbury 139; his flight 142–3; and the navy 164; English politicians relations with 182; death of 198; and Scotland 273–6; land grants to 297; and Ireland 302–9; **XI** 3, 75, 152; statue 398

James, king of Majorca **IV** 253, 255, 256, 260, 263

James I, king of Scotland (1406–37) **VI** 192; Scottish heir 64; Melun siege 187; **VII** 134

James II, king of Scotland (1437–60), Northumberland, Cumberland and Durham pledge **VI** 514

James III, king of Scotland (1460–88) **VI** 523, 585–9; **VII** 134, 162, 270; killed at Sauchieburn 76; relations with England 136

James IV, king of Scotland (1488–1513) **VII** 5, 120, 135, 285; marriage to Margaret Tudor (1503) 41, 157–62; Henry's peace attempts (1491–5) 137; truce of Aylon (1497) 147–8; Perkin Warbeck 137–44; invasion of England (Sept. 1496) 140, 142; relations with England (1506–8) 163; royal dignity 191; his son and Erasmus 252; relations with England strained 270–1; honoured by Julius II (1507) 271; misconduct 273; France urges to war (1512) 275–6; Leo X warns against war 277; killed at Flodden 280–3

James V, king of Scotland (1513–42) **VII** 162, 305, 314, 325, 418; marries Madeleine of France (1 Jan. 1537) and Mary of

Guise (June 1538) 363; war with England (1542) 404–5; death (14 Dec. 1542) 406; Mary's marriage 534

James VI, king of Scotland see James I, king of England

James, William **XIV** 531

James Francis Edward Stuart (the Old Pretender) (1688–1766) **X** 240–3, 246, 256; **XI** 15, 73, 150, 151, 155; court of 153, 158, 160; Jacobite rising (1715) 157–63; characteristics 158; French favour 165; Swedish plot 174; plot (1722) 183; Baron de Stosch 184; Ripperda 195, 196, 200; Walpole 212; invasion fleet 236; French repudiation 264; Clementine Sobieski 292

Jameson, Dr L. S.: conquers Matabeleland **XIV** 212; Raid 229, 231; trial 'at Bar' 233; cooperates in uniting South Africa 391

Jamestown **IX** 327–9

James the deacon **II** 116, 123

James Bay **X** 340

Jane (cartoon) **XV** 548

Jane Grey, Lady **VII** 481, 576, 583; scheme to marry to Edward VI **VII** 488; king's 'devise' in her favour (June 1553) 522–3; proclaimed queen (10 July 1553) 526, 527; in Tower 529; condemned (Nov. 1553) 530; execution (12 Feb. 1554) 539

Jane Seymour, wife of Henry VIII: marriage **VII** 380, 442; death (1537) 394

Jannys, Robert, of Norwich **VI** 368

Januaria (Briton) **Ia** 684

Janville (Loiret) **VI** 245, 247, 250

Janyns, artists **VI** 648

Janyns, Robert, Merton College mason **VI** 648

Japan: war with China **XIV** 219; forced to return Port Arthur 219; takes Singapore 230, 541; Anglo-Japanese alliance 352–3; Russo-Japanese war 368–9, 370; second and closer Anglo-Japanese treaty 370; supplies cotton goods to India **XV** 152, 182, 356; Washington naval treaty 150–1; still friendly 227; failure of naval talks 225; takes Singapore 230, 541; London naval treaty 273; in Manchuria 298, 299, 363; competition from 339; League of Nations 370–3, 384, 415; chiefs of staff 375, 380; renews war with China 420, 421; naval preparations against 432; gamble on neutrality 521; apprehension of attack from 531; attacks Pearl Harbor 532; no co-ordination of plans with Germany 537; fears that Americans will concentrate against 539; conquers Burma 544; neglects Indian Ocean 545; American casualties against 577; fails in Assam 586; Stalin promises to go to war against 590; war expected to last further eighteen months 595; surrenders 561, 562, 595; atomic bomb 601

Japanese wall-papers **X** 398

japanning **X** 398

Jargeau (Loiret) **VI** 245, 246, 474

Jarnac **IV** 124

Jaroslav **VIII** 239

Jarrow (*In Gyrvum*) (Co. Durham) **Ib** 175, map 4 xxxii; monastery **II** 159, 184–5; library 185; sack 239, 732; **XV** 351

Jaruman, bishop of Mercia **II** 130

Java **IX** 52; **X** 349; British acquisition **XII** 489; British cession 564

Java sea, battle **XV** 544

'javelin men' **Ia** 213

Javolenus Priscus, L. **Ia** 162, 526

Jay, John (1745–1829) **XII** 254, 290

The Jazz Singer **XV** 315

Jean d'Harcourt, count of Aumâle **VI** 242, 244

Jean le Bel on Edward III **V** 150

Jeanne, daughter of Louis XI, wife of Orleans **VII** 86

Jeanne, queen of France, daughter and heiress of Henry, count of Champagne and king of Navarre **IV** 238–41, 647

Jeanne, wife of William Clito **III** 127

Jeans, Sir James **XV** 169

Jebb, John (1736–86) **XII** 228, 231

Jedburgh (Scotland) **III** 278; **V** 463; **VII** 313, 407; **VIII** 144

Jedburgh Castle **III** 278; **IV** 707; **VI** 35, 319

Jefferson, Thomas (1743–1826): biography **XII** 205; part in declaration of independence 205; president of USA 474, 475, 550

Jeffrey, Lord Francis **XII** 541; **XIII** 31

Jeffreys, Colonel **X** 334

Jeffreys, George, 1st Baron **X** 120, 123, 143, 180

Jellicoe, Sir John Rushworth: biography **XV** 13; at Scapa Flow 13; battle of Jutland 63; first sea lord 76; opposes convoy 84; dismissed 86

Jena, battle (1806) **XII** 452

Jenins, Robert **VII** 591

Jenkins, Sir Leoline **X** 56

Jenkins, Captain Robert (*fl.* 1731–8) **XI** 208

Jenkinson, Anthony (d. 1611) **VII** 507, 561; **VIII** 238

Jenkinson, Charles, Lord Hawkesbury, 1st earl of Liverpool (1727–1808) **XII** 65, 97, 105, 120, 224; 'King's Friends' 118, 119, 258, 265; and North 204; Gordon riots 237; ambitions 251; plan for reform in India 262; president of Board of Trade 276, 580; maiden speech (1792) 298; Irish Union 401; state office holders 577; chancellor of Duchy of Lancaster 580; cabinet lists 581

Jenkinson, Robert Banks, 2nd earl of Liverpool, foreign secretary (1801–4) **XII** 408, 414, 581; first lord of Treasury (1812) 408, 498, 499, 500, 562; home secretary 435, 443, 581, 582; Curwen's act 449; war office 484, 487, 492; Cabinet 503, 560, 582; Napoleon 566; nationalism 569; plans church improvements 572; **XIII** 24, 59, 65, 67, 69; biography 53; character and ideas 53; resignation 74

Jenner, Edward (1749–1823) **XI** 392; biography **XII** 11

Jenner, professor of civil law, Oxford (1753) **XI** 62

jennies, Hargreaves' invention **XII** 29, 332, 509

Jennings, Sir John (1664–1743), Admiral **XI** 200

Jennings, Sarah *see* Churchill

Jenyns, Soame (1704–87) **XII** 337

Jermyn, Henry **IX** 101

Jermyn, Henry, 1st Baron Dover **X** 123

Jerome, St **Ia** 369, 452; **III** 206; **V** 531; **VI** 283

Jerome, William **VII** 427

Jersey **III** 462; **IV** 319, 320; **V** 119; *see also* Channel Islands

Jersey, 1st earl of *see* Villiers, Edward

Jerusalem: siege **Ia** 75; **III** 94, 215, 216, 343, 361–2; kingdom 344; capture (1244) **IV** 110; Latin kingdom 107, 134, 137; **V** 248; **VII** 114, 245; captured **XV** 47, 98; Peel commission 407

Jervas, Charles (?1675–1739), printer **XI** 400, 406, 409

Jervaulx (N. Yorks.), abbey **III** 428; **VI** 328; **VII** 392, 397

Jervis, Sir John (1735–1823), earl of St Vincent: naval campaigns **XII** 369, 372, 378, 428; at admiralty 408, 412, 414, 418, 581

Jessel, Sir G. **XIV** 17, 25

Jesuit missions: to Ireland **VII** 366;

to England **VIII** 173–5, 177–9, 180–4; intrigues in Scotland 360–1

Jesuits and seculars, controversy **VIII** 453, 454, 455, 456, 457

jet **Ia** 658

Jew of Malta **VIII** 297

Jewell, John, bishop of Salisbury: reform of church ritual **VIII** 17, 32, 193; *Apology* 32; church robbers 33; attack on pope 169; food supplies 253; on witchcraft 330

jewellers **Ia** 657–8

jewellery **Ia** 15, 705

Jewish disabilities, removal **XIII** 162

Jewry Wall **Ib** 183

Jews **Ia** 171, 174, 182, 199, 344; allegations 665; Christian associations 717–18; tallage of **III** 6, 422–3; attacks on 353–4; hatred of 353; supposed 'ritual murders' by 353; extortion of 410, 422; exchequer of 422–3; taxation 422–3, 471, 474; **IV** 36, 102, 768; attacks (1264) 184, 186, 191; statute (1275) 322; excluded from statute of merchants 625; sufferings during drive against silver speculation and coinage debasement (1278–9) 633; expulsion (1290) 513; **IX** 214; resettlement **X** 35; **XI** 69, 73–4, 137, 337; in England **XV** 168, 169; Palestine 71, 276–7, 312, 407; Hitler's treatment 375, 419, 436–7

'Jingo' song **XIV** 48

Joachim (Jochim), John *see* Passano, Giovanni Giovacchino di

Joachim, Joseph **XIV** 159

Joad, C. E. M. **XV** 362, 550

Joan, countess of Westmorland **VI** 464; Council summons 322

Joan, daughter of Baldwin **IX**, count of Flanders **III** 454

Joan, daughter of King Henry II **III** 215, 331, 360, 362, 376

Joan, daughter of King John **III** 282, 466

Joan, Henry IV's wife **VI** 72, 477, 482; Wressell Castle and Percy manors (1405) 63; accused of magic 480

Joan, queen of David II of Scotland **V** 79, 99, 117, 118

Joan, sister of Henry III and wife of Alexander II, king of Scots **IV** 89, 585; death (1238) 587

Joan, wife of Llywelyn the Great and natural daughter of King John **III** 298, 299, 428; **IV** 45, 391, 393; declared legitimate 393; intrigue with William de Braose 395

Joan of Acre, daughter of Edward I, married to Gilbert of Clare (1290) **IV** 268, 512

Joan of Arc **VI** 246–8; captured at Compiègne 248; passed into English hands 249; Inquisition trial 250–1; **VII** 361

Joan of Bar, Countess Warenne **V** 51

Joan of Kent, princess of Wales **V** 395, 404; order of the Garter 251, 252; John of Gaunt 396–7; Peasants' Revolt 412; Richard II 424–5; death 439; astronomical calendar 509; Wyclif 512, 514; Lollard knights 521

Joan of Ponthieu, affianced to Henry III, later second wife of Ferdinand III of Castile and mother of Eleanor of Castile **IV** 73, 235

Jocelin, bishop of Salisbury **III** 214

Jocelin of Wells, bishop of Bath **III** 446, 448

Jocelyn, Robert, Viscount (?1680–1756) **XI** 295

Jockey Club **XII** 339

Joffre, General: battle of Marne **XV** 10, 32; Antwerp 11; offensive plans of 21, 444–5; battle of Somme 60; dismissed 80; Kitchener 81

309

Johannes (John), usurper **Ia** 474–6

John, Archduke **XII** 426

John, bishop of Bath **III** 107

John, brother of Louis IX, king of France **IV** 93

John I, count of Armagnac **V** 114, 144

John, count of Armagnac **VI** 470, 471, 474

John, count of Holland, marries Elizabeth, daughter of Edward I (Jan. 1297) **IV** 665; Edward I entrusted with settlement of his disputes with Flanders and Brabant 665

John, Dauphin, son of Charles VI **VI** 164

John, Don of Austria **VIII** 340–8

John II, duke of Alençon **VI** 156, 174, 244, 246, 247; liberation of Orléans 474; ransom 651

John, duke of Bedford **VI** 168, 192, 211, 224, 225; veneration of Scrope, letter 62; at Melun 187; regency 191; constable of England 193; Bois-de-Vincennes 201; Henry V's instructions 201; tentative regent in France 213; betrothal 225; reconciles Beaufort and Gloucester 229–30; declares Beaufort a 'trewe man' 231; Henry V's will 233; siege of Orléans 238; French operations 241, 244–5; strategy (1423–30) 242–52; supports legitimacy of Henry VI of France 250; Good Rest Lodge 343; power limited 431; council interview 434, 509; court at Rouen 484; death (1435) 465; Booth poem 499; Oxford lecture fund 677

John, duke of Berry **VI** 108, 139, 163, 241; offer to Henry IV 112; homage for Poitou 113; proctor 114; renounces agreement with England 114; chapel at Bourges 115

John I, duke of Brabant, killed at tournament in Bar-le-Duc (1294) **IV** 664

John II, duke of Brabant (1294): married Margaret, daughter of Edward I (1290) **IV** 268, 512, 513, 664; military alliance with Edward I (1295) 661, 663–4, 679; **V** 22

John III, duke of Brabant **V** 121, 127

John IV, duke of Brittany **VI** 71

John, duke of Brittany, earl of Richmond (1306–34) **IV** 236, 283, 514, 649, 713; **V** 1, 3, 6, 48, 74; Gaveston 8; Ordainer 10; loyalty rewarded 11; witness against Thomas of Lancaster 67; Queen Isabella 79; Paris ambassador 81; invasion scare 82

John, duke of Brittany (1285–1305), married Beatrice, daughter of Henry III (1260) **IV** 97, 159, 235–6, 514

John, duke of Brittany, son of Peter of Dreux (d. 1285) **IV** 159, 235–6

John V, duke of Brittany (1399–1442) **VI** 71, 244, 249, 257, 492

John the Fearless, duke of Burgundy **VI** 90, 100, 108; negotiates for English help 111; meets English embassy at Arras 111; English to be expelled from Aquitaine 113; pact of Bourges (1412) 114; embassy in Canterbury (June 1413) 136; opposition to Sigismund 163; secret negotiations at Bourges and Lille (1413) 137; negotiations after ambassadors left Calais 137; Henry V to marry daughter 139; ready to attack sovereign 139; held key to situation (Sept. 1416) 168; attitude to Henry V at Calais 169; unreliable (1417) 169; activity on the Oise 172; captured Beaumont-sur-Oise, Pontoise and Seine towns (Sept. 1417) 172; enters Paris

Johnson, Dr Samuel (1709–84) **III** 5; **V** 250; **X** 252; **XI** 9, 63, 129, 140, 145; parliamentary reports 31; capital punishment 62; William Law 94; Whitefield's preaching 96; John Wesley 97; science 139; education 141; Lord Kames 274; Highlands of Scotland 285; Mrs Grierson's influence 305; Chevalier Taylor 390; Chambers' *Considerations* 395; *Harleian Miscellany* preface 397; Soho/Covent Garden 407; Shenstone's ground 413; edited Shakespeare 419, 430; Pomfret 420; literary fame 420, 431, 431–3; Cibber 421; *Rambler* 422, 431; *Vanity of Human Wishes* 422, 431; Pope's *Essay on Man* 423; Richardson 427; Hume 429; *Dictionary* 431–2; **XII** 40, 135, 151, 338, 353, 388, 473; pension secured by Bute 69; American colonies 185; on Scottish submission to authority 280; attitudes to life 328; biography 328; critical power 348

Johnson, Thomas, editor of Gerard's *Herbal* (1633) **XI** 388

Johnson, Sir William (1715–74) **XI** 321

Johnston, Sir H. H. **XIV** 190

Johnston, Tom: aids Thomas **XV** 284; opposes cuts in benefit 297

Johnstone, Charles (?1719–?1800), *The Adventures of a Guinea* **XI** 53

Johnstone, George (1730–87), Commodore, MP **XII** 211

Joint Chiefs of Staff's committee: set up **XV** 537–8; conducts campaign against Japan 598; atomic bomb 601

Joinville, treaty **VIII** 365

Jolly George **XV** 143

Jolson, Al **XV** 315

Jómsborg, Vikings of **II** 375, 380, 382, 384, 401

Jones, David **XV** 62

Jones, Ernest **XIII** 144, 146

Jones, G. D. B. **Ia** 89, 177, 184, 313

Jones, Henry Arthur **XIV** 328, 547

Jones, Inigo (1573–1652) **IX** 381–3; **X** 389, 391, 412; **XI** 399, 411

Jones, John Paul (1747–92) **XII** 222

Jones, Kennedy **XIV** 311, 312, 532; **XV** 66

Jones, Michael **IX** 162

Jones, Samuel, Presbyterian academy at Tewkesbury **XI** 89

Jones, Tom: and Irish boundary **XV** 162; writes Baldwin's speeches 205; succession to Law 224

Jones, Viriamu **XIV** 336

Jones, Sir William (1746–94) **XII** 308

Jonestone, Elias **IV** 278; **V** 113

Jonquière, marquis de la (d. 1752) **XI** 230

Jonson, Ben: on becoming a gentleman **VIII** 268; comparison with Shakespeare 299–301; **IX** 394, 398; on plantation in Ireland 110; realist and classical playwright 392; popularity 393; poet 400–2; **X** 412

Jordan, Abraham **X** 404

Jordan, Henry **V** 337

Jordan, Thomas **V** 337

Jordanes **Ia** 439, 477

Joseph, Archduke, afterwards Emperor Joseph I **X** 161, 206, 212–17, 231, 314

Joseph, Charles **VII** 292

Joseph II, Emperor (1765–90), election as king of the Romans **XI** 344, 345

Joseph, Michael **VII** 141–3

Joseph, William **VI** 508

Joseph Bonaparte *see* Bonaparte, Joseph

Josephus **Ia** 75, 85

Joubert, Piet **XIV** 68, 69, 255

Joule, James Prescott **XIII** 567–8

Jourdan, J. B. (1762–1833) **XII** 367, 558

journalism, literary **X** 356–7
journals: *Common Sense* **XI** 205; *The Craftsman* 204–5, 422; *Critical Review* 422; *Faulkner's Journal* 306; *Fog's Weekly Journal* 205; *Gentleman's Magazine* 31, 422, 431; *Historical Register* 31; *Idler* 422, 431; *London Magazine* 31, 422; *New York Weekly Journal* 322; *Pue's Occurrences* 306; *Rambler* 422, 431; *Spectator* 419; *Tatler* 420; *Universal Chronicle* 422
journeymen **IX** 286
Journey's End **XV** 361
Jovian **Ia** 369
Joviani (Ioviani), Late Roman legion **Ia** 292
Jovii, Late Roman field army unit **Ia** 381
Jovina **Ia** 688
Jovinus (I) **Ia** 380–1
Jovinus (II), usurper **Ia** 429, 446–7, 452, 453
Jovius (imperial family name) **Ia** 291
Jowett, Benjamin **XIII** 575; **XIV** 162, 407
Jowitt, Sir William **XV** 270, 294
Joyce, Cornet **IX** 146
Joyce, James **XV** 179
Joyce, William **XV** 516–17, 533–4
Joyful News out of the New World **VIII** 317
Joynour, Richard, London grocer **VI** 419
Joynson-Hicks, Sir William: biography **XV** 242; prosecutes Communists 242; and Arcos raid 255; opposes revised prayer book 259; promises flapper vote 262
'Joyous Entry' **XII** 295
Juan del Aguila, Don **VIII** 414, 415–16, 488, 489, 490
Juana, daughter of Ferdinand and Isabella (d. 1555) **VII** 104, 115, 148, 154; Henry VII's proposals 178, 187; Anglo-Burgundian marriage treaties 179, 185; Philip

of Burgundy 181, 184
Juana, sister of Ferdinand the Catholic, widow of Ferdinand I of Naples **VII** 175
Juana, widow of Ferdinand II of Naples **VII** 175, 177, 178
Jubilees: (1887) **XIV** 176–8, 304; (1897) 239; (1935) **XV** 307, 377–8
Judaea **Ia** 182
judges: on eyre **IV** 16, 22, 39, 68, 335; Hugh Bigod and his colleages on eyre 146, 150–1; baronial government (1259) 150; general eyre 162, 357; under Dictum of Kenilworth 212–13; council and parliament 334–5, 341, 355–6; on eyre (1278) 352, 357, 358; diocese of Norwich (1286) 481–2; law merchant 623, 626; *see also Capitula itineris*; of king's bench **V** 11; chief 16; of jail delivery 27, 200; of trailbaston 171, 200, 206; arrest of (1340) 175; statutes (1341) 177; of the peace 189, 200–3; statute law 196–8; in council and chancery 198–9; itinerant 199–200; of *oyer et terminer* 200, 206; corruptibility 205–6; Statute of Treasons 257; Statute of Praemunire 281; convocation house 289; of labourers 337; on Iter of Judges and justices (1321) 374; attacks (1381) 419; Richard II's questions 448–50, 485; impeachment 458, 477–8; new appointments 464; **IX** 81–2; **X** 106–7, 191; tenure of office **XII** 57
Judges, delegate, papal, in Scotland **IV** 584
Judhael of Totness **II** 629
Judicaturae, of the Agenais **IV** 302–3
Judicature Act (1873) **XIV** 16–19
judices at Chester **II** 532–3; *see also* lawmen
judiciary **XI** 57–60; characteristics 64–7; emoluments 63–4

314

Judith, niece of William I and wife of Earl Waltheof **II** 610

Judith, wife of Æthelwulf **II** 245

Judith, wife of Earl Tostig **II** 565

Julia Domna, Empress **Ia** 228

Julian, Emperor **Ia** 342, 347, 359–69, 373, 577; grain shipments 360, 618; religion 362–3, 401, 736; Paris vineyards 654

Juliers, William, count and (from 1336) margrave of **V** 119, 121, 159

Julio-Claudians **Ia** 48–50, 68, 69, 71, 109; ancient aristocrats 155; army loyalty 291; their record 682, 709

Julius, martyr **Ia** 718, 721

Julius, Modius *see* Modius Julius

Julius II, Pope (1503–13) (Cardinal Giulio della Rovere) **VII** 153, 156, 590; as cardinal 114; excommunicates Venice (Apr. 1509) 155; marriage of Henry VIII and Catherine of Aragon 175–6; Ferdinand and Louis alliance 177; Silvestro de'Gigli 238; warlike breath 270–1; Lateran council (1512) 272; Holy League (1511) 273; war with France 276–7; 'Bull executorial' 277; death 284; divorce of Henry and Catherine 326, 328

Julius III, Pope (1550–5) (Giovanni Maria del Monte) **VII** 535, 547

Julius Agricola, Cn. *see* Agricola

Julius Alpinus Classicianus, C. *see* Classicianus

Julius Caesar **II** 15

Julius Caesar, C. *see* Caesar

Julius Firmicus Maternus **Ia** 349

Julius Frontinus, Sex. *see* Frontinus

Julius Indus **Ia** 122

Julius Marcus, C. **Ia** 249, 250

Julius Nepos **Ia** 486

Julius Pollienus Auspex, T. **Ia** 254

Julius Severus, S. **Ia** 182–3, 205

Julius Verus, Cn. **Ia** 200, 202–3, 205, 206, 635

Jumièges, abbey **III** 185

Jung **XIV** 552

Jungingen, Conrad of *see* Conrad

Junius **XII** 145

Junius, Francis **X** 382

Junius Faustinus Postumianus, C. **Ia** 254

Juno **Ia** 515, 682; Lupicina 707

Junot **XII** 458–60, 486

Junquera, Charles of Salerno meets Alfonso of Aragon near **IV** 262

Junto (or Junta), the **X** 225

Jupiter **Ia** 515, 683, 689, 716; Diocletian 291, 716; 'Jupiter columns' 669, 682; Jupiter Dolichenus 667

Jurassic Ridge, iron ore **Ia** 637

Jurati ad arma **IV** 551–3

jurats **IV** 321

Jurin, James (1684–1750), physiologist **XI** 391

jurisdiction, private **II** 492–502; origins 492–4; pleas of the Crown mediatized 497; profits 492–3; relations to hundred courts 499–502; hall-moot 502; territorialized 517–19; boroughs 530–1; *see also* sake and soke; toll, team, and infangenetheof

jury: of presentment, in Danelaw **II** 510–13, 651–2; unknown to pure Old English law 511; employed by William I 650–2; origins 651–2; **III** 387; trial by 403; origin 405; in civil cases 405–6; in petty assizes 406–9

Jus spolii **III** 182, 190

justice, administration **II** 652

justices, local: observance of the Charters of Liberties (1300, 1301) **IV** 218, 701, 704

justices of the Central Court **VII** 193–5; of assize 194; of the peace 195; authority extended (1485, 1495, 1504) 196; controlled by council and Crown 196–7, 563

justices of the peace **IV** 218; **VI** 195, 452–5; authority extended (1485, 1495, 1504) 196; controlled by council and Crown 196–7, 563; **VIII** 24, 212–13; **IX** 275–7, 295, 298; **XI** 33, 68, 72, 133, 143; local government control 46–50; appointed by Crown 48; administrative and judicial powers 51–2; tyranny of some JPs 53–6; leniency over papists 74; regulation of wages acts (1721 and 1726) 192; **XII** 43–8; decline in importance **XIII** 457–8

Justinian, Digest and Code of **III** 247

Justinian, Emperor **Ia** 465, 490, 497; **Ib** 47; **II** 4

Justinianus (*praepositus*) **Ia** 384

Justus, bishop of Rochester **II** 109, 112–13; archbishop of Canterbury 113

Jutes: in Kent **Ib** 26, 126–7; continental origin 29, 46–9; relations with Westgruppe 55; characteristic brooches 59; characteristic pottery 64–6, 67 [fig. 4]; map 5 68; settlement in eastern England 86; part of Mischgruppe 107; origin and identity 113–19; related to settlers of Isle of Wight 146; **II** 9; in Wessex 9, 23–4, 70; in Kent 10; origin 14–15; relations with Franks 14–15, 59; close connections with Saxons 14

Jutland: location of Bede's Jutes **Ib** 46–7, 54–5, 66, 114–15; cruciform brooches from cemeteries 59, 66; pottery styles 63–6, 72, 126; **V** 359; **VI** 69; **XV** battle 63, 402, 506

Juvénal des Ursins, Jean **VI** 154

Juvenal **Ia** 165, 457, 506, 538; **III** 243

Juxon, William, Archbishop **IX** 100, 202; **X** 391

K

Kabul, massacre **XIV** 63
Kadzand **X** 78
Kaiseraugust, treasure **Ia** 532
Kaiserswerth, island **II** 166; **X** 203
Kalenberg, dukes of **XI** 11
Kalm, Peter (1715–79), Swedish botanist and traveller **XI** 321, 388–9
Kalmar, union **VI** 69
Kames, Henry Home, Lord (1696–1782) **XI** 6, 66, 274, 287
Kanin peninsula **VIII** 237
Kara Sea **VII** 507; **VIII** 241
Karikal, ceded to France (1783) **XII** 255
Karlille, Adam **V** 401
Kasbin **VIII** 238
Katherine, daughter of Hugh, earl of Stafford **VI** 8
Katherine, dowager duchess of Buckingham **VI** 525
Katherine, sister of Eric of Norway **VI** 69
Kattegat, German ships **XV** 470
Kaunitz, Wenzel Anton, Prinze von (1711–94) **VII** 321; **XI** 344, 351
Kay, John (*fl.* 1733–64) **XI** 110
Kay-Shuttleworth, Sir James (Dr Kay) **XIII** 479
Kay's flying shuttle **XII** 28
Kearley, H. E., afterwards Lord Devonport **XIV** 385, 395, 443
Keats, John (1795–1821) **XII** 535; **XIII** 32–3
Keble, John **XIII** 519–20, 576; biography 513; takes part in Oxford movement 512–13, 515, 519, 539
Keene, Sir Benjamin (1697–1757) **XI** 208
Keene, Henry (1726–76), architect **XI** 304
keepers of the peace **IV** 218; **V** 4, 189

Keeton, John, bishop of Ely (1310–16) **V** 42
Keighley, Henry of **IV** 704, 717
Keigwin, Richard **X** 350–1
Keith, George, 10th Earl Marischal (1693–1778) **XI** 163
Keith, James Francis Edward (1696–1758) **XI** 163
Keith, Sir Robert **V** 36, 38
Kellogg pact **XV** 260
Kells, Book of **II** 191
Kells (Ireland) **V** 43
Kelly, Atterbury's secretary **XI** 182
Kelly, George, 'one of the seven men of Moidart' **XI** 252
Kelly of Lanark **XII** 333
Kelso (Scotland) **III** 276; monastery founded 274; **IV** 689; burnt in English raids **VII** 313, 405; abbey destroyed by Hertford (1545) 407; **VIII** 144
Kelvedon **Ib** 94
Kelvin, Lord *see* Thomson, William
Kemal, and Chanak crisis **XV** 190–1
Kemble, J. M. **XIII** 551
Keme, John **V** 366
Kemp, John, archbishop of Canterbury **VI** 190, 211, 218, 231, 260; Gloucester interview 232; ambition 269; lords of the council 434; Eleanor Cobham's trial 485; books valuation 666
Kemp, Thomas, bishop of London **VI** 520; joins Warwick at Sandwich (1469) 555
Kemp, William, mayor of Coventry **VI** 547
Kempe, Margery **VI** 273, 296, 685
Kempley (Glos.) **III** 264
Kempsey (Worcs.) **IV** 202, 705
Kempston **Ib** 61; map 2 xxx
Kenarton, Kenardington (Kent), manor **VI** 333

Kenchester, town development **Ia** 586, 594

Kendal (Westmorland): earldom granted to John, duke of Somerset **VI** 366, 435; **VII** 462

Kendal, earl of *see* Foix, Jean de

Kendal, Ehrengard Melusina, baroness von Schulenberg, duchess of (1667–1743) **XI** 152, 177, 184, 300

Kendall, John, cofferer to Edward IV: servant of Richard III **VI** 636; King's secretary 634; killed at Bosworth 644

Kenilworth (War.) **III** 25; constable **VI** 1; honour 478; **VII** 73, 208; **VIII** 272–3

Kenilworth Castle: home of Simon and Eleanor de Montfort **IV** 107; Earl Simon at (1263–4) 181, 182, 184, 185; hostages 194; Edward agrees to pact of Worcester 197; Edward surprises the younger Simon de Montfort (July 1265) 202; operations against (1265–6) 206, 208, 213; issue of papal bull for taxation of clergy (1266) 221; **V** 26, 47, 67–8, 492; Edward II at 86, 89, 90, 92, 94; Ordinance of 351, 357, 366; *see also* Dictum of Kenilworth

Kenmure, William Gordon, 6th Viscount (d. 1716) **XI** 162

Kennedy, Gilbert, 3rd earl of, Cassillis **VII** 406

Kennedy, Sir J. **XV** 484

Kennedy, James, bishop of St Andrews **VI** 523, 526

Kennedy, Joseph **XV** 450

Kennedy, Margaret **XV** 311

Kennet, river **V** 208

Kenneth, king of Scots **II** 369, 570

Kennett, lord mayor of London **XII** 237, 239

Kennett, river **Ib** 43, 149, 161; map 3 xxxi

Kennett, White (1660–1728), bishop of Peterborough **X** 355;

XI 81, 95

Kenninghall (Norfolk): cruciform brooch **Ib** 58 [fig. 1(h)]; **VII** 421, 489, 526, 541; **VIII** 137

Kenningham, John **V** 511

Kennington (Middx.) **V** 396, 397, 424, 459

Kennington (Surrey) **VI** 327

Kensham, William of **III** 484; **IV** 10

Kensington Palace **X** 389

Kent **Ia** 12; Belgic kings 36, 42, 47; Catuvellauni 58, 68; Roman victory 83; Reculver 254; Lullingstone 465, 702; Springhead shrines 596, 671; Holborough barrow 698; early Saxon settlement 472, 474; **Ib** 37, 39–40, 47, 59, 66; settlement 4, 5, 10; written records of early history 10; Jutish phase 26, 72, 113–14, 146; Roman-Saxon pottery 91; Saxonia 106; descent of royal family 109, 127; burials 111; Romano-British craftsmen 116; continuity with Romano-British past 122–6; early Germanic remains 123–4; Frankish influence 126–8; South Saxons 134; social structure contrasted with that of Wessex 142; *laets* of Kent and comparable folk in East Anglia 142–3; no detailed political history before Æthelbert 173, **II** 26, 37, 243, 278, 379; distinctive culture and customs 10, 15, 58; laws 15; conquest 16–17; kingdom 36, 58; issued by Æthelberht 60; by Hlothhere and Eadric 62; by Wihtred 62; invaded by Cædwalla of Wessex 70; becomes Mercian province 206–7; revolts from Cenwulf 225–7; submits to Egbert 231; agrarian system 281–3; part of Leofine's earldom 574; military command 625; *see also* laws; **III** 53, 56, 142, 422, 457; tenurial system in 38, 49; Iron industry 82; Odo's earldom 101; William of Ypres 143, 321; offered to count of Flanders 333; Reginald of Cornhill, justice and sheriff 390; loyalty to John in civil war 484; **V** 64, 155, 314, 527, 530; sheriff of 170, 171; assessment of 192; eyres 199; keepers of the peace 201; farming 316–38; rising 204, 407, 408, 419, 420; **VI** 2, 7; heresy preached in churches 129; rebels 496; 'commons' 498; Warwick supporters 560; **VII** 108, 125, 142, 304, 379; inclosure 452; Wyatt rebellion 538–9; **IX** 133, 137–8, 154, 280; population **XV** 167; airfields 499

Kent, earls of *see* Edmund of Woodstock; Grey, Edmund; Grey, George; Holland, Thomas; Neville, William; *see also* Joan of Kent

Kent, kings of **Ia** 36, 42, 47; origin **II** 9; possess hall in London 57; Frankish affinities 60–1; later kings named 206, 209; end of dynasty 206

Kent, river: rural settlement **Ia** 613; **VI** 366

Kent, Simon, draper, Reading MP **VI** 418

Kent, Thomas, clerk of Council **VI** 501

Kent, William (1684–1748), architect **XI** 401, 403, 406, 412

Kentford (Suffolk) **II** 649

Kentigern, St **II** 86

Kentish Knock, naval battle **IX** 223

Kentish Petition **X** 195–6

Kenton, John **VI** 457

Kenworthy, Lieutenant-Commander J. M.: advises Lloyd George **XV** 84; opposes treaty of Versailles 136

Kenya **XV** 151

Kenyngale, John, Carmelite **VI** 297

Kenyon, Sir Frederick **XV** 18

Keogh, John **XII** 446

Kepler, Johann (1571–1630), astro-nomer **VIII** 307, 308, 309; **XI** 380

Keppel, Arnold Joost van, 1st earl of Albemarle **X** 189

Keppel, Augustus, 1st Viscount (1725–86) **XI** 229, 363, 368, 404

Keppel, George, 3rd earl of Albemarle (1724–72) **XI** 226

Keppel, Viscount **XII** 121, 344, 369; court martial 213; first lord of admiralty (1782–3) 243, 578, 579

Ker, John, 1st duke of Roxburgh (d. 1741) **XI** 33, 203, 272, 273, 278

Ker, John, of Kersland (1673–1726) **XI** 196

Ker, Mr **XII** 135

Ker, Sir Robert, warden of the Middle March **VII** 163

Ker, W. P. **XIV** 551

Kerr, Philip **XV** 117, 418

Kerr, William, 3rd marquis of Lothian (*c*.1690–1767) **XI** 273

Kerrera, island of **IV** 596

Kerry **V** 471; **VII** 125

Kerry (Ceri), district in Wales: campaign **IV** 395; *see also* Ceri

Kerry, county **VI** 425

Kerry, Lord *see* Fitzmaurice, Edmond

Kersey (Suffolk) **VI** 646; Austin priory 675

Keshwayo (Cetewayo) **XIV** 58, 60, 61

Kesteven (Lincs.) **II** 49

Keswick, mines **VIII** 236

Kett, Robert, rising and execution **VII** 489–91, 506

Kett, William: hanged **VII** 491

Kettering (Northants) **Ib** 41; xxx map 2; **III** 42

Keyes, Sir Roger: attacks Zeebrugge **XV** 103; attacks Chamberlain 472

Keymis, Lawrence **VIII** 280

Keynes, John Maynard: biography **XV** 136; attacks reparations 136–7; opposes debt settlement 203; opposes return to gold 222,

Keynes, John Maynard (*cont.*)
238; inspires Lloyd George 149, 213, 252, 269; misses the multiplier 268; Macmillan committee 287; comment on May report 288; wants revenue tariff 290; *New Statesman* 310; Conservatives 329; thinks rentier doomed 338; ideas 348, 354–5, 417; Labour shares view on Germany 373; 'the Ins' 408; Wood learns from 511; British sacrifices 513; reparations 596; takes gloomy view of future 599

Keynsham, Imperial Cult **Ia** 683
Keyworth, Simon of **III** 49
Khartoum **XIV** 80–3, 244
Khorasmians **IV** 110
Kidd, Captain William **X** 330
Kidderminster, Richard, abbot of Wynchcombe **VII** 291
Kiderlen-Wächter, A. von **XIV** 433, 435
Kidson, F. **XIV** 544
Kidwelly (Glam.) **III** 290, 295, 301; castle **IV** 409, 410; **VI** 54
Kidwelly, Geoffrey **VI** 606
Kidwelly, lordship of **V** 59, 61
Kidwelly, Maurice **VI** 606
Kidwelly, Morgan, Richard III's attorney **VI** 634, 641
Kiel (Germany) **Ib** xxvii; canal widening **XIV** 364, 470, 481
Kienthal **XV** 65
Kildare, Butlers of *see* Butlers of Kildare
Kildare, county **V** 232, 471; **VI** 425
Kildare, earldom **VIII** 464
Kildare, earls of *see* Fitzgerald; Gerald
Kildare, Geraldines of *see* Geraldines of Kildare
Kilkenny: statutes of (1366) **IV** 566; **V** 232, 472; **VII** 71, 72, 130; **IX** 135; **X** 322
Killala, bishop of *see* Clayton, Robert
Killibegs **VIII** 484

Killiecrankie, battle **X** 277
Killigrew, Henry **VII** 479
Killigrew, Sir Henry **VIII** 154, 161
Killingworth, Thomas **VII** 170
Kilmainham hospital **X** 389
Kilmarnock, earl of *see* Boyd, William
Kilmore, see of **V** 458
kilns *see* pottery
Kilpeck Church (Hereford) **III** 263
Kilsby, William, keeper of the privy seal (1338–42) **V** 157–9, 167–8, 170–1, 176, 210
Kilwardby, Robert, Dominican archbishop of Canterbury (1272–8) and cardinal: appointed archbishop by Gregory X **IV** 225; Edward I's succession 225; court of Canterbury 492; friendship with Thomas of Cantilupe 489; provincial assemblies 504–5; Llywelyn of Wales 408; difficulties, elevation to cardinalate and death 469, 470–1; register 471
Kilwardby, Thomas, archbishop of Canterbury **VI** 253
Kimberley, earl of **XIII** 384
Kimberley, 1st earl of **XIV** 28, 57; biography 219
Kimberley, siege of **XIV** 252, 253, 254, 255
Kimberley diamonds field **XIV** 58
Kimbolton Castle **VII** 38; **VIII** 188
Kimswerd **Ib** map 5 68
Kincardine, John Baliol surrenders kingdom of Scotland **IV** 615
King, American admiral **XV** 555
King, Anthony **Ia** 93, 123, 236, 258, 379; *comes* headquarters 381; woodland cover 613; Hayling Island excavations 671
King, Dr Edward, bishop, trial **XIV** 306–7
King, Gregory **IX** 282
King, Mackenzie: refuses support at Chanak **XV** 191; constitutional crisis in Canada 253, 261

King, Oliver, bishop of Exeter (1493); secretary to the king (1487) **VII** 648

King, Peter, Lord (1669–1734) **XI** 63

King, William (1650–1729), archbishop of Dublin **XI** 289, 294, 302, 305, 396

King, William, lawyer **VI** 462

Kinghorn (Fife) **IV** 597; **V** 116

Kinglake, Alexander William, biography **XIII** 553

King's Bench, court of **V** 11, 199, 339, 419, 449; Arundel's death sentence 481; JP relations to 454–5; removal of cases by *mandamus* 455

King's Book **VII** 429–30, 513, 568

King's Companions **II** 301–3; grants 302–4; at king's court 304–6; wergild 303

King's County **IX** 110

King's Friends **XII** 118–20, 258

King's Langley (Herts.) **VI** 27

King's Lynn (Bishop's Lynn) (Norfolk) **III** 67, 90, 96, 353, 435; John's last days 485; **IV** 481, 708; **V** 102, 504; **VI** 194, 296, 360, 401–2, 528; merchants 364; gild of Holy Trinity 388–9; mayor 611; **VII** 219, 220, 221, 464; **X** 53, 391

King's Milton (Middeltun) (Kent) **II** 732

King's spears **VII** 267

King's Worthy (Hants), council **II** 349

Kingsbury (Middx.) **VI** 675

kingship: theory of **III** 2–5; **IV** 59, 129, 145, 192; Charter of Liberties 7, 68, 216; royal rule and political rule 131–4; revision of Provisions of Oxford 179; Dictum of Kenilworth 216; local law 281–2; government and kingship 520–3; Grosseteste on 453; Walter Burley on 521–2; Scottish and the papacy 593–5, 693, 702,

705–6, 707–10; succession case (1291–2) 601–2, 605, 607–8, 610–11, 706; compared with civic republics 626; *see also* Crown

Kingsholm (Glos.), legionary base **Ia** 105

Kingsley, Charles **XIII** 495–6, 520–1, 531, 534, 559; biography 495

Kingsmill, William, scrivener **VI** 664

Kingston (Hereford) **VI** 292

Kingston (Surrey) **II** 339; West Saxon assembly 234

Kingston, Sir Anthony **VII** 554

Kingston, duchess of *see* Chudleigh, Elizabeth

Kingston, Sir William **VII** 332, 437

Kingston Deverell (Wilts.) **VI** 462

Kingston-by-Lewes (Sussex), circular brooch **Ib** 60 [fig. 2(b)]

Kingston-on-Thames (Surrey): conferences **IV** 76, 166; treaty (1217) 13–15; **V** 64; **VII** 538

Kingston-upon-Hull (Wyke-upon-Hull or Hull) *see* Hull (Yorks.)

Kingston-upon-Soar **Ib** map 5 68

Kingsweston, villa **Ia** 557

Kington (Hereford) **V** 520

Kington, Master John, canon of Lincoln **VI** 68, 70

Kinloss Abbey **IV** 709

Kinnoull, earl of *see* Hay, George

Kinross, Alexander III taken at (1257) **IV** 592

Kinsale (Ireland) **VII** 79, 80, 132; Spaniards at **VIII** 488; **X** 304, 308

kinship **II** 315–18

Kinver (Staffs.) **II** 40; forest **III** 29; **VI** 57

Kipling, Rudyard **XIV** 330–3, 527; at ministry of information **XV** 107; and Baldwin 205, 283; buried in Westminster Abbey 178

Kirby, John J. (1716–74), mathematician **XI** 379

321

Kirby Hall (Northants) **VI** 339; **VIII** 303

Kirby Hill (Yorks.), church **II** 151

Kirby Muxloe (Leics.), castle **VI** 381

Kirk, Sir John **XIV** 190

Kirk-o'-Field **VIII** 102

Kirk Leavington (N. Yorks.), manor **VI** 337

Kirkaldy, Sir William of Grange **VIII** 40, 48, 78, 161–2

Kirkbridge, fort **Ia** 165

Kirkby, Adam de **VI** 285

Kirkby, John, king's clerk, deputy chancellor, treasurer (1284), bishop of Ely (1286–90) **IV** 335, 507; financial tour 505–6, 559; 'quest' (1285) 359; judicial inquiry at Tower of London (1285) 626; during Edward I's absence (1286–9) 511; death (1290) 627

Kirkby, Roger de, vicar **VI** 285

Kirkby, William **VI** 285

Kirkby Moorside (N. Yorks.) **VI** 8

Kirkby Thore: fort **Ia** 392; inscription 685

Kirkcudbright **III** 274

Kirke, Lieutenant-General Percy **X** 306

Kirkeby, John **V** 406

Kirkham, Walter of, bishop of Durham (1249–60), and John Baliol **IV** 466

Kirkintillock Castle **IV** 707

Kirkliston **IV** 689

Kirkstall Abbey (Yorks.) **III** 187; chronicle **VI** 2

Kirkstead Abbey (Lincs.) **III** 230; **VII** 397

Kirkwood, David: deported **XV** 39; returns 40; imprisoned 139; his extensive expectations 199

Kirmington **Ib** 82, 180–1; map 4 xxxii

Kirtlington (Oxon.) **II** 300

Kirton (Lincs.), church of **III** 6

Kirton Kindsey **Ib** 111; map 4 xxxii

Kit-Cat Club **X** 358

Kitchener, Sir Horatio Herbert, afterwards Earl (1850–1916): biography **XIV** 243; reconquers Egyptian Sudan 243–4; meets Marchand at Fashoda 244; chief of staff to Lord Roberts in South Africa 254; commander-in-chief 256; criticism of officers 293; operations (1901–2) 344–7; dispute with Milner and desire to make peace 345; large share in Peace of Vereeniging 347; biography **XV** 7; council of war 6; becomes secretary for war 7; instructions to French 8, 10; fails to help Antwerp 11; runs war 14; appeals for recruits 20, 459; Ireland 21; supply 22; Dardanelles 23–4; shells scandal 26, 27, 29; retains War Office 30; opinion of the machine gun 35; takes King's Pledge 37; reinforces Gallipoli 44; Joffre 45; goes to Gallipoli 46; powers reduced 47; evacuation of Gallipoli 48; death 58; Joffre 81; prestige unmatched 480

Kitchin, Anthony, bishop of Llandaff **VIII** 19

Kitzingen, monastery **II** 173

Knaresborough, castle **IV** 52; **V** 29

Knebworth (Herts.), church of **III** 25

Kneller, Sir Godfrey (1646–1723) **X** 400, 401; **XI** 399, 405, 409

Knevit (Knyvet), Lady Joan **IX** 201

Knight, Dr William **VII** 307, 329; secretary to the king (1526) **VII** 648

Knight of the Burning Pestle **VIII** 301

knight service: in Normandy **II** 556–60; introduced into England by William I 557, 634, 680–2; imposed on bishoprics and abbeys 634–5; **III** 12–18, 370–1; inquiry into (1242) **IV** 102; changes in military aspects 542–3, 549–53; in Ireland 565;

L

La Charité-sur-Loire (Nièvre) **VI** 114, 240

La Fayette, marquis de **XII** 217

La Fère (Aisne) **VI** 239

La Ferté-Bernard (Maine) **III** 213, 345

La Haye (Le Havre) **VIII** 57

La Hire, French commander **VI** 107, 239, 241, 247

La Hogue (Manche) **III** 135; **VI** 559; battle *see* Barfleur

La Marche, counts of *see* Bourbon, Jean; Lusignan

La Marche, county **III** 379–80

La Marck **VIII** 1–8, 155

La Motte, Toussaint Guillaume Picquet, comte de (1720–91) **XI** 349

La Noue **VIII** 156

La Palice, Jacques de Chabannes, sire de **VII** 315

La Réole (Gironde) **III** 466; **V** 81, 109, 132; **VI** 113, 240

La Rey, General de **XIV** 254, 256, 346, 347, 348

La Roche-aux-Moines **III** 466–7, 480

La Roche-Derrien **V** 136

La Rochefoucauld, duc de **X** 361

La Rochelle (Charente-Maritime) **III** 64, 82, 92, 441–2, 465–7; **V** 141, 145, 244, 245, 383; **VI** 177, 348; **VIII** 133, 161, 344; **IX** 38, 63–6; **XV** 579; battle (1809) **XII** 478

La Téne culture **Ia** 9–10, 18, 23, 46

La Trémouille (Trémoille), Louis de **VII** 87, 315

Labienus, T. **Ia** 32–3

Labouchere, Henry **XIV** 210, 233

labour exchanges **XIV** 516

labour, First World War **XV** 38; conscription planned 375; direction prepared 479; Second World War 512; Beaverbrook seeks to control 543; running down 565

Labour, Ministry of: created **XV** 76; survives 129; abolition proposed 184; runs employment exchanges 257; not equipped for means test 352; Ministry of National Service 456; regional government 569

Labour and the Nation **XV** 267

Labour party: foundation **XIV** 265–6; attitude to First World War **XV** 15; becoming independent 27–8; against Kitchener 29; conscription 53–4; remains resolute for war 65; Asquith 67; supports Lloyd George 69–70; reorganized 96–7; makes statement on war aims 96; breaks with coalition 106; political levy 114–15; wants capital levy 125; leaves coalition 125; general election (1918) 128; condemns Treaty of Versailles 136; opposes intervention in Russia 138; by-election success 142, 189; rejects Communists 143, 200; Ulster 160; Black and Tans 161; *Daily Herald* 187, 251; against Lloyd George 193; drops capital levy 197; general election (1922) 198–201; MacDonald elected leader 201; condemns first Labour government 214; Zinoviev letter 219; Campbell case 225; armaments 227; confident of victory 237; hostile to Chamberlain 256; 'flapper vote' 262; general election (1929) 263–6; resists ILP 267; victorious 270; acquires Roman Catholic lobby 280; few dissensions 283; rejects Mosley's proposals 285; opposes National government 294–6; League 318–19; excludes supporters of National government

Labour party (*cont.*)
322–3; defends Free Trade 324; general election (1931) 325–7; MacDonald scapegoat 334; becomes more socialist 346–7; planning 354; Soviet Russia 359; foreign affairs 360–1; supports disarmament 362, 365, 368; wins local elections (1933) 367; League 369; Manchurian affair 372; anxious to appease Germany 373–4; Jubilee 378; Peace Ballot 379; conflict over sanctions 381–2; general election (1935) 383; opposes rearmament 393; Spanish Civil War 394, 396, 398; against Edward VIII 401; dominated by foreign affairs 408; abstains over arms estimates 413–14; wants Soviet alliance 416; sympathizes with Germany 417–19; Czech crisis 427, 430; Popular Front 435–6; seems to have been proved right 440; opposes conscription 445; turns against Stalin 456; refuses to join Chamberlain's government 456; enthusiastic for Finland 468; forces a division 472; prefers Halifax to Churchill 473; replies to Chamberlain 474; cheers Churchill 475; Churchill's government 478; opposes purchase tax 491; Cripps still excluded 543; Beveridge plan 567; wants electoral reform 568; owes victory to unreformed system 569; opposes intervention in Greece 589; eager to resume independence 595; general election (1945) 596–7

labour service, origin **II** 473

labourers **Ia** 235, 238, 457

Lacaita, Sir J. **XIII** 300, 303

Lackford **Ib** map 5 68

Lacock (Wilts.) **II** 632, 640; **VII** 596

lacquering **X** 398

Lactantius **Ia** 294–5

Lacy, Alice de, countess of Lancaster **V** 51, 69, 73, 96

Lacy, Francis Antony (1731–92) **XI** 291

Lacy, Henry de **III** 189

Lacy, Henry de, earl of Lincoln (1272–1311) **IV** 514, 517, 653; Welsh wars 409, 411, 421, 441; granted Rhos and Rhufoniog (later honour of Denbigh) 424; with King Edward in Paris and Gascony (1286–9) 283, 290, 362; Tarascon (1291) 263; leader of forces in Gascony (1296–7) 649; Scottish expeditions 690, 694, 697; proctor for King and Prince Edward (1303) 653–4; **V** 1, 8, 10, 11; loan towards Scottish campaign 33; death bed speech 69; no heirs 260; sheep stock 323

Lacy, Hugh de (I) **III** 310, 311, 312, 313

Lacy, Hugh de (II) **III** 311, 315

Lacy, Ilbert de **III** 271

Lacy, John de, constable of Chester **III** 258

Lacy, John de, earl of Lincoln (1232–40) **IV** 51

Lacy, Matilda de, heiress of Ludlow and Trim **IV** 517

Lacy, Peter, keeper of the privy seal (1367–71) **V** 258

Lacy, Roger de **III** 101, 109

Lacy, Roger de, constable of Chester **III** 258, 384

Lacy, Walter de, lord of Ludlow and Meath **III** 315; **IV** 3, 4

Lacy, William, clerk to council **VI** 634

Lacy family **III** 26

Ladbroke, MP for London *v.* Wilkes **XII** 131

Lady Chatterley's Lover **XV** 180

Ladysmith, siege **XIV** 252, 253, 254, 255

Læstingaeu *see* Lastingham (Yorks.)

Laetenhorizont **Ib** 180, 196

laeti **Ia** 335, 355, 386, 406, 429–40;

cultivation 549; **Ib** 79–82, 85, 99, 131, 138; and '*Laets*' 142; Silchester 156; burials 167–8, 178; Lincolnshire wolds 180–1; Thurmaston 183; Deira 187–9; Yorkshire 194; Bernicia 198; Saxon Shore 204, 206–7

Læwes *see* Lewes (Sussex)

Lafayette, Gilbert de, dauphin's marshal **VI** 244

Lagnay, comte de (Bastard of Vendôme) **VI** 248

Lagrange, Joseph Louis (1736–1813) **XI** 379

Laguerre, Louis **X** 400

lahslit **II** 507

Laigle (Normandy) **III** 179

Laigle, Richer de **III** 197

laisser faire policy: limitation **XIII** 15–16; views of economists 445–6

laity: ecclesiastical discipline **IV** 454–6; clerks 458; views on state of Church (1258) 461; attitude to religious settlement **VIII** 21, 22

Lake, General (1744–1808): Irish campaigns **XII** 397–9

Lake District **Ia** 4; saved from railway **XIV** 341

Lake (Dorset), fortress **Ia** 95

lake villages **Ia** 16

Lakenheath (Suffolk): cruciform brooch **Ib** 58 [fig. 1(i)]; **III** 78

Lakenheath, John **V** 416

Lalaing, Roderic de, Burgundian envoy **VII** 138, 139

Lally-Tollendal, Thomas Arthur, comte de (1702–66) **XI** 292, 330

Lamb, Mr **XII** 89

Lamb, Charles (1775–1834) **XII** 532, 542, 549; **XIII** 7, 32, 35, 38, 530

Lamb, William, Viscount Melbourne **XIII** 57, 92, 106, 132, 238; dislike of radicals 96; biography 98; character and ideas 98–9; first administration 98, 101; 'dismissal' 101; second administration 102–3; advises Queen Victoria 104–5; suggests Prince George of Cambridge as Queen Victoria's husband 107; sends Durham to Canada 380–1; returns to office 416; Palmerston letter 418; Hampden appointment 515; new peers 622

Lambaesis, Algeria **Ia** 513

Lambarde, William **VIII** 212, 213, 282

Lambe, John **IX** 370

Lambert, George (1710–65), painter **XI** 410

Lambert, Sir John (1772–1847) **XII** 555

Lambert, John **IX** 260; paper constitution 175–6, 252; opposes kingship 182–3; dismissed by Cromwell 242, 245; ill-gotten gains 243; on act of indemnity 245–6; petitions Rump 248–50; defeat in north 252–3; escape from Tower 256; landowner 273

Lambert, Mr, MP **VIII** 219

Lambert, William **VI** 460

Lamberton Kirk **VII** 159, 161

Lamberton, William of, bishop of St Andrews: election (1297) **IV** 684; returns to Scotland and becomes chief guardian (1299) 695, 696; in Paris (1302–4) 697, 710; takes oath to King Edward (1304) 710; compact with Bruce (1304) 714; appointed chief warden of Scotland by Edward I (1305) 713; joins Bruce, surrenders and confined in irons at Winchester 714, 71

Lambeth (Surrey) **III** 282; treaty (1212) 453; provincial council (1261) **IV** 457–8; consistory (Oct. 1279) 476; provincial council (1281) 478; convocation (1283) 507; archbishop's manor; **V** 62, 84, 176, 409, 518; chancery records burnt 470; Wyclif in ecclesiastical court 512; **VI** 116; **VII** 142, 173, 232, 362, 600

Landois, Pierre, treasurer of Brittany: **VI** 628; hanged (1485) **VII** 86

Landor, Walter Savage **XIII** 32–3, 530

landowners: in towns and cities **Ia** 159, 598; rural 159, 235; life-style 159–60, 398, 449–54, 596–7; dispossession 224, 477, 479, 653; *see also* confiscations; Fens 268; migration from Gaul to Britain? 278, 303; responsibility for town defences 279, 389; selling of landholdings 280, 302, 547, 600, 727; interest in economic development 299, 629, 662–3; temple property 341; Christians 343, 395, 600; continued domination of office 435; attitudes to conscriptions 439, 509–10, 548; property management 600–1; religious leadership 723, 726, 737

Landriano, French defeat (1529) **VII** 319, 328

Land's End (Corn.) **VI** 56

landscape **Ia** 12–15, 189–90, 234–7, 267–9, 553–62

Landseer, Sir Edwin **XIII** 591

land-tax **X** 175, 289–90

Lane, Ralph **VIII** 246

Laneham, Robert **VIII** 272

Lanercost (Cumbria) **V** xi

Lanercost, chronicle: on Gaveston **V** 22; Bannockburn 39; Robert Bruce 40; assembly (1327) 91

Lanercost, priory: Edward I at (1306–7) **IV** 717, 719

Lanfranc, archbishop of Canterbury **II** 633, 649–50; king's representative 610, 611; advice to Waltheof (1075) 612; early life 662–4, 672–4; relations with William I 662–4; conception of ecclesiastical reform 662–71; appointment to see of Canterbury 664; assertion of primacy in England 664–5; councils held 665–6; at Winchester (1072) 665–6; at

London (1075) 666; in Winchester (1076) 667–8; ecclesiastical statesman 669; modification of marriage law 670; supervision of monastic order 671–4; *consuetudines* 671–2; attitude to Old English saints 672; relations with the papacy 674–6; his influence in England **III** 98, 100; William II educated by 98; death 102, 170, 171–2; condemns the bishop of Durham 103; judgement on Bishop Odo of Bayeux 103, 368; constitutions 185; influence of his teaching 233; sends monks from Canterbury to Scotland 267; claims primacy over Irish Church 304

Lang, Matthew, bishop of Gurk **VII** 272

Langby, William, friar of Guisborough **VI** 39

Langdon, Dr John **VI** 199

Langeais (Indre-et-Loire) **VI** 628; **VII** 105

Langford (Oxon.) **II** 443

Langham, Simon, bishop of Ely (1362–6), archbishop of Canterbury (1366–8), chancellor (1363–7) **V** 211, 227, 280, 298; **VI** 253

Langland, William: the devil as a Frenchman **V** 151; the Templars 292; suffragan bishops 301; chantries 304; friars 309; poor man's wife 342; life and works 526–7; **VI** 277, 293

Langley (Bucks.) **V** 2, 47, 76, 267

Langley (Northumb.) **VI** 323, 337; castle 9, 54, 63

Langley, Edmund, earl of Cambridge (1362–1402), duke of York (1385–1402) **V** 185, 384, 440, 465, 473; Flemish alliance prevented 143; marriage to Isabella of Castile 268; assault on Quimperlé 386; expedition to Portugal 428, 430; on commission (1386)

Langley, Edmund (*cont.*)
446, 451; intercedes for Burley 458; keeper of the realm (1394) 471; (1399) 491; surrenders to Bolingbroke 492
Langley, Geoffrey of **IV** 401
Langley, Thomas, bishop of Durham **VI** 86, 105, 138, 139, 141; dean of York 33; dismissed and thanked (1411) 112; excommunicates disorderly tenants 128; Burgundian negotiations 179; chancellor 218, 433; see of York 269; councillor 429, 431, 434; council (1410) 430
Langlinus **III** 225
Langon (Gironde) **VI** 109
Langport (Som.) **II** 534; battle **IX** 141
Langres (Haute-Marne) **VI** 573
Langrishe, Sir Hercules, biography **XII** 393
Langstrother, Sir John: treasurer **VI** 556, 561; executed 569
Langsworth (Yorks.) **VI** 337
Langtoft, on Bruce and parliament of Lincoln (1301) **IV** 695
Langton, John, bishop of Chichester (1305–37): chancellor (1292–1302, 1307–10) **IV** 681; **V** 3, 10, 11, 52
Langton, Simon, brother of Archbishop Stephen, chancellor of Louis of France **III** 447; **IV** 8, 12, 14
Langton, Stephen, archbishop of Canterbury and cardinal **III** 242, 252; election as archbishop 445, 447; comes to England to negotiate 448; efforts to reconcile with John 451; recognized as archbishop by John 457; return to England 461; takes the lead and produces charter of Henry I 462; influence on the form of Magna Carta 473; Tower of London entrusted to 478; suspended 478–9; in Rome (1216) **IV** 1, 3,

17; procures Pandulf's withdrawal 18; co-operation with Hubert de Burgh 23–8, 47; constitutions 24, 421, 450–2, 472; death (1228) 47; Wales 393; clerical taxation 501–2
Langton, Thomas, bishop of St David's (1483–5), bishop of Salisbury (1485–93), bishop of Winchester (1493–1501) **VI** 582, 628; **VII** 53, 257
Langton, Walter, treasurer (1295–1307), bishop of Coventry and Lichfield (1296–1321) **IV** 335, 514, 517, 662; mission to Edward's allies 664, 665, 667; and Archbishop Winchelsey 717, 718; **V** x, 3, 9, 14, 23; removal from council 46; forfeited lands 76
Langton, William, clerk **VI** 62
language: in Britain **Ia** 17–18; importance **Ib** xxiv; study **VIII** 287; **X** 409–10; *see also* Celtic; Latin
Languedoc **VI** 240, 241
Langwathby (Cumbria) **III** 283
Lankhills: cemetery **Ia** 551; **Ib** 150
Lannoy, Hugh de **VI** 257, 473, 536
Lansbury, George: wants pensions **XV** 60, 285; biography 142; *Daily Herald* 142, 251; in local government 174; excluded from first Labour government 209; Poplarism 256; in second Labour government 271; Lido 272; assists Thomas 284; opposes cuts in benefit 297; retains seat 326; leads Labour party 327–8; extremist 347; excluded from confidential information 360; pacifist 369; opposes sanctions 381; denounced by Bevin and resigns 382; pact to keep papers 603
Lansbury's Labour Weekly **XV** 328
Lansdowne (Som.) **IX** 133
Lansdowne, Baron *see* Granville, George
Lansdowne, Lord: minister without

330

portfolio **XV** 31; successfully opposes Home Rule 57, 71–2; advocates negotiated peace 65, 94, 116

Lansdowne, 3rd marquis of **XIII** 75, 249, 356

Lansdowne, 5th marquis of **XIV** 16, 224, 267, 365; negotiates Anglo-French entente 366, 567; middle position in fiscal controversy 373; conflict with Sir Charles Eliot 381; declaration about Persian Gulf 382; plans with Balfour to use House of Lords against Liberal ministry 386–8; opposes Qualification of Women Bill 399; handicaps as leader 415; narrow views on Ireland 423–4; alternative plan to Parliament Bill 425; scheme to reform House of Lords 427–8; amendments to Parliament Bill 429; weakness against Diehards 429; joins in demand that the king should dismiss Asquith 473; joins in letter to Asquith promising party support for a pro-French policy in war crisis 493; sale of *The Mill* to America 543

Lansdowne, marquises of *see* Petty, Lord Henry; Petty, Sir William

Lanthony, canons of **III** 447

Lanx, Corbridge **Ia** 729

Laodicea **III** 94

Laon (Aisne) **III** 233–4, 244, 416; **V** 127; **VI** 184

Laon, Anselm of **III** 233, 234

Laonnois **VI** 239

Lapis Niger, Rome **Ia** 677

Lapley (Staffs.), priory of **II** 674

Lardner, Nathaniel (1684–1768) **XI** 88

Laredo **VII** 172

Larentum, villa **Ia** 597

lares and *penates* **Ia** 408, 685, 704, 707–8

Largs, Norse defeat (1263) **IV** 596

Larinum **Ia** 711

Larkin, James **XIV** 472

Larne (Antrim) **V** 43

Laroon, Marcellus (1679–1772), painter **XI** 406

Larwood, H. **XV** 378

Las Minas, Portuguese general **X** 213

Las Palmas **VIII** 417

Lasco (Laski), John À **VII** 509, 515, 516, 520, 543

Laski, H.: goes Left **XV** 348; Left Book Club 396; head of Gestapo 596

Lastage **IV** 628, 631

Lastingham (Læstingaeu) (Yorks.) **II** 732; monastery 121

lætas in Kent **II** 303, 315

Lateran, the **III** 176

Lateran council, 2nd (1139) **III** 135, 192, 194; 3rd (1179) 219, 224, 373, 409; 4th (1215) **IV** 403, 447, 449–50, 478; clerical taxation 222–3, 497, 507; (1512–17) **VII** 272, 291, 294

Latham, Isabel, wife of Sir John Stanley **VI** 64

lathes (of Kent) **Ib** 124, 126, 200; **II** 293–4, 503–4

latifundia **Ia** 605

Latimer, barony **VI** 8, 323, 325–6

Latimer, Elizabeth **VI** 325

Latimer, Hugh, bishop of Worcester (1535–9) **VII** 377, 382, 427, 449, 573; denounces inclosures 456; Lenten sermon (1549) 478; vehement sermons 504, 514; in Tower 544; academic condemnation at Oxford (1554) 546; condemned and burnt (1555) 550–1; polemic writings 583; **VIII** 29; **IX** 279, 300

Latimer, John **V** 434

Latimer, Lord *see* Neville, John

Latimer, Sir Thomas **V** 521

Latimer, Sir William, 4th Lord **V** 354, 385, 397, 521; impeachment 389–91; restoration 394; on council (1377) 400; **VI** 99, 325

331

332

Law, Andrew Bonar: elected Unionist leader in Commons **XIV** 446; reviews Ulster Volunteers 453; 'Blenheim pledge' 455; demands that King dismiss Asquith 473–4; interviews with Asquith 474; appeals to army to disobey orders 475; advocates that Lords shall veto Army Annual Act 477; doubtful how far his party will support war 493; joins with Lansdowne in letter of assurance to Asquith 493; speech (3rd Aug. 1914) 494; biography **XV** 15; (1914) 15; Free Trade conflict 17; briefed by Fisher 23; making of first coalition 30; colonial secretary 31; Curzon not loyal 34; urges withdrawal from Gallipoli 46; war committee 47; accepts Home Rule scheme 57; proposes Lloyd George as secretary for war 58; fears Liberals against war 65; conflict between Asquith and Lloyd George 67–70; in War Cabinet 75; does not challenge Carson 85; Flanders offensive 87; institutes National Savings 88; Robertson 99; Maurice debate 105, 117; agrees to continue coalition 112; rejects capital levy 125; coupon 126; against reparations 127; ceases to be chancellor of Exchequer 130; Lloyd George respects 131; Paris peace conference 132; forbids putting Ulster under Dublin 158; destroys coalition 192; prime minister 193; government 195–6, 236; repudiates Protection 197, 206–7; doubts physical capacity 202; American debt settlement 203; resigns and dies 204; committee of imperial defence 228; Beaverbrook lacks 282

Law, Edmund (1703–87), bishop of Carlisle **XI** 140

Law, Edward, 1st Baron Ellenbor-

ough (1750–1818) **XII** 57; biography 436; lord chief justice of the king's bench (1806–7) 436, 442, 582

Law, Edward, 1st earl of Ellenborough (1790–1871), 2nd Baron Ellenborough **XIII** 11; biography 420; governor-general of India 420–4; abandons Auckland's Afghan policy 420–1; annexation of Sind 423; attack on Gwalior 423; recalled 423

law, Old English, survival **II** 686

'Law Padowe' (Roman Law) **VI** 563

Law Society **XIII** 619

Law, William (1686–1761) **XI** 10, 75, 85, 89; career and characteristics 93–4; *Serious Call* 93; **XIV** 137

Lawes, Henry (1596–1662) **XI** 399; **IX** 387

Lawes, Sir John **XIII** 566

Lawling (Essex) **V** 322

lawmen **II** 533

lawn tennis, invention **XIV** 165–6

Lawrence, Charles (d. 1760), governor of Nova Scotia **XI** 311, 347

Lawrence, David Herbert **XIV** 550, **XV** 179

Lawrence, Sir Henry: biography **XIII** 425; administration of the Punjab 425–6; defence of Lucknow 435, 437; death 437

Lawrence, Lord John **XIII** 437, 439; biography 426; administration of the Punjab 426; viceroy of India 442–3

Lawrence, Stringer (1697–1775) **XI** 218, 327, 328, 332, 347

Lawrence, Sir Thomas (1769–1830) **XII** 543; **XIII** 590

Lawrence, Thomas Edward **XV** 49, 179

laws: Æthelberht of Kent **II** 60, 106, 276; Hlothhere and Eadric, king of Kent 62; Wihtred, king of Kent 62, 72; Ine, king of Wessex 71–2;

Lebuin (Leofwine), St **II** 169

Lecky, William Edward Hartpole: biography **XIII** 549; works of 549–50; **XIV** 161

Leconfield (Yorks.) **VI** 10, 337

Leczinski, Stanislaus (d. 1766), king of Poland **XI** 206

Ledbury (Hereford) **V** 86

Leddet, Christiana **III** 124

Lee, Edward, archbishop of York (1531–44) **VII** 389, 391

Lee, John, solicitor general (1783) **XII** 579

Lee, Matthew (1694–1755), founder of readership at Christ Church, Oxford **XI** 389

Lee, Rowland, bishop of Lichfield and Coventry (1534–43) **VII** 367

Lee, Sir William (1688–1754) **XI** 61

Lee, William (d. *c*.1610), inventor of stocking frame **XI** 110

Leeds (Kent), castle **V** 64; **VI** 23

Leeds (Loidis) (Yorks.) **II** 732; **VI** 366; **IX** 132–3; hope of enfranchisement **XII** 278; manufacture 513; population 517; **XIII** 2, 26, 64, 136, 148; Oastler letters 148; Reform Act (1867) 187; college of medicine 493; technical education 501; 'Rational Recreation Society' 624–5; convention **XV** 89

Leeds, duke of *see* Osborne, Francis; Osborne, Thomas

Leek (Staffs.) **III** 65

Lees-Smith, H. B. **XV** 297, 477

leets, East Anglian **II** 645, 648

Leeuwen, Jacob van **X** 135

Leeward Islands **X** 325, 329, 334, 337

Lefèvre, Jacques d'Etaples **VII** 338

Left Book Club **XV** 396–7, 416, 450

Left Book Club News **XV** 397

Leg. II. Aug. **Ib** 119, 121

Leg. XIV. Gemina **Ib** 75

Leg. XX. VV **Ib** 119, 121

Leg, Edward **III** 39

Legaceaster *see* Chester

legate, cardinal: work for peace between Edward I and Philip IV **IV** 662, 665, 673; procurations 673

legate, papal: Henry III asks for (1230) **IV** 46; baronial council's request (1258) 135, 136; in France (1283–4) 254–5; archbishop of Canterbury's authority 18, 491–2; *see also* Guala; Pandulf; Otto; Gui; Ottobuono

legates, *legati*, legal commissioner (*legatus iuridicus*) **Ia** 162, 227, 526, 533; legionary commander (*legatus legionis*) 73, 514, 526, 533; provincial governor (*legatus Augusti pro praetore*) 88, 251, 514, 516–17, 528

legatine commissions: (of 786) **II** 215–17, 218, 237; (of 1062) 468; (of 1070) 659; at Windsor 661; in Normandy to fix penances for Hastings 661–2; (of 1072) 665

Legenda **IV** 447

Leges Burgorum (Scottish law book) **IV** 577

Legge, George, 1st Baron Dartmouth **X** 136, 138, 141, 142

Legge, Hon. Henry Bilson (1708–64) **XI** 34, 347, 352; biography **XII** 67; chancellor of the exchequer (1760–1) 67, 577; dismissal (1761) 69

Legge, John **V** 407, 412

Legge, William, 2nd earl of Dartmouth (1731–1801): president of board of trade (1765–6 and 1772–5) **XII** 578; secretary of state for colonies (1772–5) 151, 576; lord privy seal (1775–82) 203, 575; lord steward (1783) 579

legions: **Ia** 34, 73–6; use by Caesar 27, 30, 34–5; prestige 34, 74, 162, 293, 335 — palatine forces 366–7; on Rhine 52, 71; Claudian conquest 73; recruitment 75, 508–10, 513; vexillations 95, 101, 118,

153, 204, 317; labour and *the famuli* 325; estate stability 336; wool 350; **VII** 35, 505; **IX** 280

Leigh (Lee), Dr Thomas **VII** 376–7, 398

Leigh-Mallory, Sir T. L. **XV** 579

Leighton, Alexander **IX** 72, 75

Leighton, captain **VIII** 60

Leighton, Frederick, afterwards Lord **XIV** 156

Leighton (Montgomery), fort **Ia** 105

Leighton, Richard, of Shropshire **VI** 134

Leighton, Sir Thomas **VIII** 343

Leinster **III** 303, 305–7, 310, 314, 316; Marshal's honour **IV** 53, 58, 561, 562, 563–4; **V** 472, 491; **VII** 125; **IX** 135

Leinster, county **VI** 425

Leinster, duke of *see* Fitzgerald, James

Leintwardine, forts **Ia** 255–6

Leipzig, battle (1813) **XII** 558

Leisler, Jacob **X** 335, 337

Leith (Edinburgh) **IV** 707; **VI** 34, 35; **VII** 279, 407; **VIII** 42, 43, 46, 47

Leitrim **IX** 110

Leitrim, Lord, murder **XIV** 57

Leix **V** 42, 471; **VIII** 462

Leland, John (1506?–52) **VI** 365; **VII** 11, 25, 174, 590; *Itinerary, Collectanea* 32–41; **XI** 395

Leliants ('men of the lily'), at Bruges **IV** 669

Lelighem **V** 432, 434

Lely, Sir Peter (1618–80) **IX** 375; **X** 400; **XI** 399, 409

Lemanis see Lympne

lend-lease: instituted **XV** 513; provisions 533; respective contributions 538–9; tobacco 531, 565; provides munitions 565–6; during Stage II 586, 598; Truman ends 599

Lenin, Vladimir Ilyich **XV** 91, 143, 300

Leningrad **XV** 447

Lennox, Charles, 3rd duke of Richmond (1735–1806) **XII** 343; secretary of state (1766) 117, 575; correspondence 125; on America 211; in favour of reform movement 230; master general of the ordnance (1782–3) 243, 578, 579; Pitt's new colleague (1784–95) 267 — dockyards 276 — list of Cabinets 580

Lennox, earls of **IV** 714; *see also* Stuart; Stewart, Matthew; Stuart, Esmé

Lennox, Lady Sarah, George III's affection for **XII** 6

Lenten Stuff **VIII** 294

Lenthall, William **IX** 252

lentils **Ia** 234

Lenton (Notts.), Cluniac prior (1421) **VI** 197; **VII** 398

Lenton (Yorks.), manor **VI** 337

Lentulus *see* Longinus

Leo V, king of Armenia **V** 441

Leo III, Pope **II** 94, 217, 218

Leo IV, Pope **II** 272

Leo IX, Pope **II** 465, 467, 585, 666

Leo X, Pope (1513–21) (Giovanni de' Medici) **VII** 255, 258, 272, 277, 314; Ferdinand and Henry 283; English/French relations 284–5; Wolsey 289–90, 300–1, 310–11; death 290, 312; Lateran council (1514) 291; terms with Francis at Bologna 306; Treaty of Noyon (1516) 307; common cause against the Turks 308; Anglo-Imperial alliance (1522) 311; concordat with Francis I (1516) 336

Leobwin, chaplain of Bishop Walcher **II** 613

Leofgar, bishop of Hereford **II** 573

Leofgyth, daughter of Dynne, friend of St Boniface, and of Hildegard, wife of Charlemagne, abbess of Tauberbischofsheim **II** 173

Leofric, bishop of Exeter **II** 199, 642, 660

338

Leveson, Sir Richard **VIII** 489

Leveson-Gower, Sir George **XIV** 183

Leveson-Gower, Lord Granville, secretary at war (1809) **XII** 582

Leveson-Gower, Granville George, 2nd Earl Granville **XIII** 172, 189, 250, 302, 325; biography 250; university chancellor 497

levies, local (1297–1307) **IV** 684, 689, 703, 708

Lévis, François, duc de (1720–87) **XI** 365

Lewellyn, John, Mayor of Cork **VII** 116

Lewes (Læwes) (Sussex) **II** 536, 732; honour and castle 628, 631; rape of 628; battle (1264) **III** 55, 188–90; battle 476; **IV** 187; Mise of 190, 191; 'Song' of 192; **VII** 397

Lewes (Læwes) (Sussex), priory **II** 673; **III** 16, 185; **V** 293, 294

Lewes (Læwes) (Sussex), prior of **III** 227

Lewis, C. Day **XV** 347

Lewis, Count Palatine of Rhine, duke of Bavaria, son of Rupert III **VI** 68

Lewis, duke of Bavaria **VI** 163; annuity granted by Henry V 222

Lewis, Sir George Cornewall **XIII** 167, 309

Lewis IV, king of Bavaria (1314–47), emperor **V** 119, 122, 124, 125, 130; gives refuge to William of Ockham 509

Lewis IV, king of Germany and emperor **IV** 661

Lewis II (Jagiello), king of Hungary, killed (1526) **VII** 320

Lewis, Wyndham **XV** 395

Lewknor (Oxon.): medieval market **Ia** 541; **III** 1; manor, Abingdon Abbey **VI** 371, 372

lex Iulia de vi publica **Ia** 422

lex provinciae **Ia** 87

Lexden, Colchester, burial **Ia** 56

Lexington, battle (1775) **XII** 201

Leyburn, Roger: Lord Edward's circle **IV** 153, 154, 157; quarrel with Edward and political opposition (1262–3) 172, 173; made steward of royal household 177; Pact of Worcester (1264) 197; rescues king at Evesham 202; Edward's lieutenant in Kent (1266) 207, 208, 422; activity (1267) 214; Edward's lieutenant in Gascony and death (1271) 275, 279, 635

Leyburn, William, 1st admiral of English fleet **IV** 655–6

Leyden **IX** 329

Leys, Agnes *see* Sandys

Leyva, Antonio de **VII** 315

libel: responsibilities of jury **XII** 57, 140, 302; Libel Act (1792) 302

Libelle of Englysh Polycye (1436) **VI** 346–7; Libourne (Gironde) **VI** 108, 109, 505; **VII** 218

Libellus famosus **V** 170, 171

Liber de Ephemera Britannica **VIII** 314

Liber valorum **VII** 372

Liberal National party (Simonites) **XV** 326, 334, 473, 596

Liberal party: formation **XIV** 2; friction between Whigs and Radicals in parliament (1880) 66–7; changes through loss of Whigs 206–7; strength **XV** 15; attitude to First World War 17, 65; first coalition 32, 34; welcomes Home Rule 57; Lloyd George's supporters 67, 74; equivocal attitude to Lloyd George's government 92; Maurice debate 105; coupon 126; general election (1918) 128; Black and Tans 161; causes of decline 172; coalition 188; by-election successes 195; general election (1922) 195, 197; reunited 208; Russian treaty 217–18; Campbell case 219; general election (1924) 220; Lloyd George leads 252; injured by increase of electorate

Lincoln (Lindcylene) (*cont.*)
liament (1301) 693, 695, 697,
701–5; **V** 47–8; association of
knights 251; staple 351, 353;
weavers 364, 367; decay 380;
government 383; **VI** 276, 387,
418, 575; archdeaconry 199, 277;
diocese 302; incorporation charter 392; **VII** 37, 67, 388, 389, 392;
battle of Stoke 75; miracle plays
586; newspaper **X** 356; **XV** 116
Lincoln (Lindcylene), cathedral **III**
261–3, 416, 422; **IV** 277, 515;
diocese 332; see 276
Lincoln, American general **XII** 215
Lincoln, bishopric **III** 53, 160, 181,
222, 446; mandate from John
before interdict 447
Lincoln, bishops of **Ia** 340, 562; **III**
13, 202, 239; *see also* Alexander;
Beaufort; Buckingham; Burgh-
ersh; Chadworth, John; Ches-
ney, Robert; Coutances, Walter
of; Grosseteste; Gravesend;
Gyneswell; Hugh, St, of Avalon;
Longland, John; Remigius;
Repingdon; Rotherham; Sutton
Lincoln, canons of **III** 99, 408
Lincoln, earldom **IV** 20
Lincoln, earls of *see* Blundeville;
Clinton, Edward; Gilbert; Henry
IV (Bolingbroke); Henry of Gros-
mont; John of Gaunt; Lacy; Pole,
John de la
Lincoln, John, broker **VII** 298
Lincoln, John of **V** 21–2
Lincoln, Lord: resignation **XII** 85
Lincoln, president of USA **XIII**
184, 304, 307, 309–10
Lincoln's Inn **X** 391
Lincolnshire: **Ia** 43, 258, 558, 562,
620; excavation 626; limestone
hills 637; **Ib** 87, 178; **III** 38–9, 48,
51, 53; centre of cloth trade 86;
estates of Rannulf, earl of Chester
141; Bishop Chesney, royal justiciar 387; William Basset, sheriff
390; revenue from fines 395;

barons at Stamford 469; John's
last days 485; **V** 13, 368, 510;
assessment of 192; fenland 312,
321; population 314; farming 315;
disturbances 337; wool 350;
manor in Richmond lordship **VI**
78; **VII** 34; rising (1536) 387,
388, 389–92; **IX** 134, 329; riots **X**
258; **XV** 183
Lind, Dr, experiments **XII** 11
Lind, James (1716–94), naval
surgeon **XI** 225, 392
Lindcylene *see* Lincoln
Lindemann, F. A., Lord Cherwell:
brawls with Tizard **XV** 392;
directs physicists 501; advises
Churchill 508; advocates strategic bombing 552; sceptical of
rockets 584; supports Morgenthau plan 587
Lindisfarena *see* Lindisfarne
Lindisfarne (Lindisfarena) **Ib** 175,
199; map 4 xxxii; monastery **II**
88, 92, 118, 120–1, 159, 732
— literary centre 184–5 — flight
of monks (875) 332; *Liber Vitae* 95;
sack of 93, 239; diocese 109, 136,
146; administered by Wilfrid 139;
cathedral 433
Lindisfarne, bishops of *see* Æthel-
wald; Aidan; Colman; Cuthbert;
Eadfrith; Eata; Finan; Tuda
Lindisfarne Gospels **II** 191
Lindissi *see* Lindsey (Lincs.)
Lindiswaras **Ib** 175, 181–2, 199
Lindsay, A. D. **XV** 436
Lindsay, Alexander **IV** 684, 685
Lindsay, Sir John **XII** 166
Lindsay, Robert of Pitscottie
(1500?–65?) **VII** 9, 51
Lindsey (Lindissi) (Lincs.): **Ib** 107,
140, 173, 175–8, 180–2; map 4
xxxii; **II** 120, 243, 378, 386, 398,
732; kingdom 36, 44, 48–9, 211;
disputed between Mercia and
Northumbria 37, 48, 85; kings 48;
effect of Danish invasions 48;
diocese 48, 134, 136, 146, 433;

boundaries 49; conversion 113, 115; Tribal Hidage 296; Swein's attack 385; ecclesiastical jurisdiction 437, 468; militia 587; assessment 648; **V** 192

Lindsey, bishop of **II** 138

Lindsey, earl of *see* Bertie

Lindum colonia **Ib** 178; *see also* Lincoln

linen, table **VIII** 272; industry **X** 49-50, 179, 300, 318-19

Lingard, J. **XIII** 551

Lingones **Ia** 126, 684

Linguae Latinae Exercitatio **VIII** 323

Linlithgow **IV** 689, 690, 692; Edward I spends winter (1301-2) 694, 706; **VII** 406

Linlithgow Castle **IV** 431, 694, 695, 701; **V** 11, 33

Linlithgow Palace, Henry VI and Margaret's residence **VI** 526

Linnaeus, Carl (1707-80), Swedish botanist **X** 376; **XI** 388, 396

Lionel, duke of Clarence (1362-8), earl of Ulster (1347-68) **V** 185, 260, 265, 386; regent 212; marriages 229, 267; in Ireland 231-3; knight of the Garter 253; death 384; **VI** 3, 312

Lionel, 1st duke of Dorset (1688-1765) **XI** 292

liquor trade, association with Conservative party **XIV** 21-2

Lisbon **III** 95, 149, 150; **V** 440, 529; **VI** 351; **VII** 225; **VIII** 177, 412; **IX** 228; **X** 206

Lisieux (Calvados) **III** 117, 118, 124, 368; **VI** 172; see 199

Lisieux, archdeacons of *see* Séez, John

Lisieux, bishops of *see* Arnulf; Fresnel, Pierre; Séez, John of

Liskeard (Corn.) **VI** 419

L'Isle, Adam, Seigneur de: deserts Armagnacs **VI** 172; joins Burgundians 173

Lisle, Baldwin de **IV** 153; Brian de 51, 52, 58

Lisle, barony (Wilts., Berks., North-

ants) **VI** 329, 335

Lisle, Thomas de, bishop of Ely (1345-61) **V** 198, 212, 296

Lisle, Viscount *see* Dudley, John

Lismore, bishop of *see* Christian, bishop of Lismore

Lister, Geoffrey **V** 345, 417-18, 419, 420

Lister, Joseph **IX** 203

Lister, Lord **XIII** 447, 464, 620

litany, English **VII** 432

litera excusatoria of Edward I to the Gascons (1294) **IV** 649

literacy **Ia** 507-8

Literary Club **XII** 328-9

literature: Elizabethan **VIII** 280-2; **X** 355; Scottish song writers 263; colonial 347-8; **XI** 402, 419-33; letters and memoirs 428-9; novels 422, 427-8; poetry 423-6; **XII** 347-53, 536-42; **XIV** 159-63, 328-31, 545-51; **XV** 179-80

Lithuania: **V** 521; accepts Soviet demands **XV** 468

Lithulf **III** 252

Litlington (Cambs.), cemetery **Ia** 695

Little Weldon (Northants) **V** 337

Little Wilbraham (Cambs.); cruciform brooch **Ib** 58 [fig. 1(e)]; Saxon pottery 70 [fig. 5(d)]; map 2 xxx

Little Woodbury **Ia** 7, 13-14

Littleborough (Tiouulfingascæstir) (Notts.) **II** 116, 733

Littleton, E. J., Lord Hatherton **XIII** 346

liturgy, English **VII** 583

Litus Saxonicum see Saxon Shore

Litvinov, E. **XV** 386

Liudger, bishop of Münster **II** 175, 189

Liudhard, Frankish bishop in Kent **II** 105

Liudolf, duke of Suabia **II** 346

livestock **XI** 103, 105, 110

Liverpool **VII** 40; workhouse **X**

Liverpool (*cont.*)
53; newspaper 356; trade and
population **XI** 121–2; trade **XII**
25, 466, 503, 515, 570; manufactures
39; local politics, also urban
development 49; population 517;
Liverpool **XIII** 2, 42–3, 45–7,
187, 458–60; water companies
463–4; school attendance 478;
health 600; municipal activities
XIV 128, 129; sacks requisitioned
XV 35; riots 43; Chinese 167;
repertory theatres 314; new roads
338; Scotland division 597
Liverpool, earls of *see* Jenkinson,
Charles; Jenkinson, Robert
Banks
Liverpool Street station **XV** 551
livery of seisin **III** 412
living wage **XV** 237, 264
Livingston, Peter van Brugh
(1710–90) **XII** 177
Livingstone, David (1813–73): slave
trade revelations **XIII** 370, 375;
biographical note 553; death **XIV**
136; Presbyterian 137; evangelicalism
138; discoveries in Africa
187; Kirk, co-explorer 190
Livio, Tito *see* Livius
Livius, Titus, de Frulovisiis (Tito
Livio da Forli) **VI** 116, 124, 213;
translator of 124, 125
Livonia **VI** 69, 359
Livre de Seyntz Medicines **V** 258
Livy **Ia** 66, 536
Lizard, the **VIII** 400
Llanbadarn (Aberystwyth), castle
VI 44, 45, 55, 65; *see also* Aberystwyth
Llandaff **III** 296
Llandaff, archdeacon of *see* Rushook,
Thomas
Llandaff, bishop of *see* Monmouth
Llandaff, Lord *see* Matthews, H.
Llandaff, see **VII** 294
Llandeilo Fawr, Welsh victory
(1282) **IV** 420, 422
Llandilo (Carmarthen) **VI** 54

Llandovery Castle **IV** 410, 428, 439;
VI 641
Llanfaes (Angle) **IV** 661, 664; Franciscans
VI 27, 39
Llanfyllin (in Powys), borough **IV**
433
Llangenith (Glam.), cell of St
Taurin of Evreux **VI** 301, 675
Llangollen (Denbigh) **VI** 40, 66
Llangorse Lake **II** 327
Llanmelin Wood **Ia** 138
Llewelyn, David ap (Davy Gam) **VI**
156
Lleyn (Caernarfon) **IV** 443
Lloyd, Charles (1735–73) **XII** 97
Lloyd, John **VII** 224
Lloyd, Lord **XV** 276, 359, 361
Lloyd, Robert (1733–64), poet **XI**
425
Lloyd George, David, 1st earl of
Dwyfor: first prominence in parliament
XIV 223; strong pro-
Boer 337; opposes Balfour's
Education Bill 357; president of
Board of Trade 385; biography
394; Merchant Shipping Act
394–5; Patents Act 395; Census
of Production Act 395; settles
railway strike 395; negotiates
formation of Port of London
Authority 395; favours women's
suffrage 398; becomes chancellor
of Exchequer 406; opposes naval
demands (1909) 412; budget
(1909) 413–15; Limehouse
speech 416; budget rejected by
Lords 417; carried in following
parliament 420; proposals to
Constitutional Conference 424;
Mansion House speech 434–5;
active in settling railway strike
(1911) 441; passes National
Insurance Act 445–6, 519; Marconi
Affair 457–8; anxious to
reduce naval estimates (1914)
472; plans postponing Home
Rule to Ulster for five years 474;
anti-interventionists in Cabinet

(2 Aug. 1914) 493; biography **XV**
5; financial measures on outbreak
of war 5; slain by Law 11; offers
money for munitions 22; favours
expedition to Salonika 23, 24;
press 26; supports war 28;
budgets 28–9; makes treasury
agreement 29, 413; first coalition
30; minister of munitions 31,
34–6; does not take King's
Pledge 37; conciliates South
Wales 39; favours withdrawal
from Gallipoli 46; on war committee 47; out-manœuvred by
Haig 48; capture of Jerusalem 49;
supports conscription 53, 55; conscientious objectors 54; secretary
for war 58; knock-out blow 62;
conflict with Asquith 66–9;
becomes prime minister 70; as
prime minister 73–6; answers
Wilson 79; supports Nivelle 80–1;
Imperial War Cabinet 82–3;
imposes convoy 83–5; fails to
prevent Flanders offensive 86–7;
polemic against him in official
history 87, 621; industrial discontent 88; Henderson 90; fears
'Squiffites' 92; parliamentary
reform 93; RAF 96; states war
aims 97, 116; conflict with
Robertson 98–100; German
offensive 101–2; conscription in
Ireland 103–4; Maurice debate
104–5, 117–18; Labour discontent 106; welcomes self-
determination 108; accepts Fourteen Points 111; has influenza
112; announces armistice 114;
general election (1918) 125–8;
new parliament 129; remakes
government 130–1; peace conference 132–5; criticism of 136–7;
ideas on reconstruction 139;
Sankey Commission 140; rail
strike 141; Russo-Polish war
143–4; miners 144, 146; housing
147; extends unemployment

insurance 148–9; moves towards
Empire Free Trade 150; settles
Irish Question 156–9, 161;
Fiume 162; relies on Nonconformist conscience 169; allows smok-
ing in cabinet 173; recruits Fisher
184; proposes to edit *The Times*
187; honours 188; at Genoa 189,
334; Chanak crisis 190–1; resigns
192; estimate of 193; treatment of
Curzon 195; party machine 197;
abandoned by Curzon 204; on
Baldwin 205; humiliates Neville
Chamberlain 206; Protection
issue 207; shackled to Asquith-
ians 208; brings wealth to the
wealthy 212; condemned by
Dalton 213; MacDonald 214,
217; attacks Russian treaty 218;
leads Liberals in Commons 220;
initiates ten-years' rule 228; starts
chiefs of staff's committee 229;
unsuccessful on radio 235;
general strike 242, 246; becomes
Liberal leader 252; on Neville
Chamberlain 256; finances
Liberal party 263; supplies new
ideas 266–71; causes of First
World War 274, 361; problems as
Liberal leader 281–3; ill 292;
National government 293, 321,
323; does not aid Liberal party
324; reduced to family party 326,
384; poll tax 346; and Keynes
354–5; eclipsed 356, 357; Stresa
last echo 377; Baldwin imitates
383; Mosley's proposals more
creative 385–6; opposes Baldwin
389; Irish ports 406; Samuel and
435; demands Soviet alliance 455;
Chamberlain has more powers on
paper 466; position early in First
World War 466–7; attacks
Chamberlain 472; Churchill on
472; war government contrasted
with Churchill's 477–9, 482–3;
Hitler projects as prime minister
489; becomes minister of fuel and

Lloyd George (*cont.*)
power 547; War Cabinet demanded by Cripps 558; Beveridge imitates 567; Churchill less flexible than 585; aftermath of rule 596; cabinet papers 603

Lloyd George Fund: origin **XV** 188; invested in *Daily Chronicle* 118; contributions to Liberal party 208, 220, 252, 263; no contribution (1931) 324, 334; subsidizes Councils of Action 357

Lloyd-Greame *see* Cunliffe-Lister

Lloyd's Coffee-house **X** 358

Llyn Cerrig Bach (Angle): hoard **Ia** 605, 679

Llywelyn ap Gruffydd, first 'prince of Wales' **IV** 161, 185; assumes Prince of Wales title 137–8; breaks truce and starts war 155–6; terms of peace 163; breaks loose again 171–4; truce 177; Earl Simon appeals for aid 201; treaty of Montgomery (1267) 215, 406–7; Edward I declares war 242, 243, 408; marriage 331, 414; relations with Crown 381–3, 416–19; Welsh law 392; recovery of power 400–5; submission (1277) 412–13; assents to David's rebellion 419; movements, negotiations and death 420, 424–8

Llywelyn ap Iorwerth, the Great, prince of Aberffraw and lord of Snowdonia (d. 1240) **III** 298–301, 314, 441, 455; **IV** 1, 20, 391–8; makes peace at Worcester (1218) 16, 393; sympathy with Fawkes de Breauté 27, 85; Hubert de Burgh 44–5, 394–7; Richard Marshal 53, 55–6, 57, 397; makes truce at Middle (1234) 60, 397; wife Joan *see* Joan

Llywelyn ap Mareddud, royal pensioner, career **IV** 440

loan, forced **IX** 37

Lobel, Matthias **VIII** 316

local administration **VIII** 212–15

local government **IX** 275–7; **XI** 33, 44–56; county officials 48, 53; municipalities 53, 55; parish 46, 130; in country **XII** 42–8; in towns 43, 58–61; origin of term **XIV** 124; developments (1870–86) 124–9; (1886–1900) 294–7; (1901–14) 521; authorities build houses **XV** 147–8; elected 174; and education 184; license theatres and cinemas 233, 316; N. Chamberlain reforms 256–7, 352; Liberal weakness 266; spending powers curbed 338; Labour victories 367; local defence volunteers 492; resist regional government 569; *see also* Justices of the Peace; London

Local Government Act (1894) (Fowler's) **XIV** 213–14, 295–6

local government board: creation **XIV** 23; initial defect 126; Belgian refugees **XV** 19; runs Poor Law 36; absorbed by Ministry of Health 129, 147

Locarno, treaty **XV** 221–2, 227, 255, 272, 359; Dominions 253; France 366; reoccupation of Rhineland 386

Locher, Jacob **VII** 584

Loches (Touraine), castle **III** 374, 383

Lochmaben (Maponus) **Ia** 685; castle of Bruces in Annandale **IV** 692, 694, 695, 696, 707, 715; Edward I's 'peel' 589

Lock, Daniel (*c.*1682–1754): statue **XI** 402

Lock, Michael **VIII** 240

Locke, John (1632–1704): **VII** 561; undergraduate **X** 30; philosophy 35; economic interests 42; secretary to council for trade and plantations 43; report on pauperism 53; and parliament 57; supporter of Shaftesbury 82; and Algernon Sidney 105; in Holland 114; theory of government 147–8;

Ralph; Basset (Fulk); Belmeis, Richard de; Bentworth; Bonner, Edmund; Braybrooke; Clifford, Richard; Courtenay, William; Fauconberg; Fitz Neal, Richard; Fitzjames, Richard; Foliot, Gilbert; Gilbert the Universal; Gravesend; Gravesend (Richard); Kemp, John; Kemp, Thomas; Maurice; Mellitus; Niger; Northburgh, Michael; Robert of Jumièges; Sainte-Mère-Église, William de; Sandwich (Henry); Sherlok, Thomas; Stokesley; Stratford, Ralph; Sudbury; Theodred; Tunstall, Cuthbert; Waldhere; Warham, William; William; Wine; Wingham

London, boroughs and place-names (1216–1307): Aldgate **IV** 214; New Temple 17, 136, 147–8; St Martin's-le-Grand 623; St Mary-le-Bow 492; St Paul's 129, 176, 177, 191, 219; Savoy Palace 249

London, boroughs and place-names (1307–1399): Aldgate **V** 530; Austin friary 264; Baynard Castle 218, 379, 412; Blackfriars 514, 517, 518; Cheapside 84, 125, 396, 397, 410 — Richard Imworth execution 412; Chester Inn 210, 410; Clerkenwell 410, 414, 453; Cornhill 84, 526; Fleet prison 410; Fleet river 379; Fleet Street 379, 410; Guildhall 84, 89, 90, 92; Highbury 411, 414; Hospital of St John 410; London Bridge 87, 409–10, 412, 413, 435; Marshalsea prison 409, 412; Mile End 253, 409, 411, 412, 413 — king's charter 415, 416 — ratification demand 418 — Richard II's destiny 426; New Temple 28, 67, 292, 410, 501; Newgate 102; Newgate prison 88; New Temple 28, 67, 292, 410, 501; Paul's Cross 12, 18, 84, 178; Port of 244,

530; St Clement Dane's 84; St Martin-le-Grand 227, 499; St Mary-le-Bow 379, 414, 499; St Paul's cathedral 12, 69, 78, 85, 397 — bishop of Exeter's murder — Chaucer on chantries 304 — Wyclif's trial 396 — Richard II 450 — school 499; Savoy palace 254, 289, 396, 410; Smithfield 253, 413, 426, 467; Steelyard 359; Temple 501; Temple Bar 67; Thames Street 359; Tower Hill 481; Tyburn 458

London, boroughs and place-names (1399–1485): Aldrichgate Street **VI** 132; Baynard's Castle 620; Bread Street 355; Crosby's Place 617; Guildhall 664; Holborn 593; London Bridge 53, 230, 497, 519; Neville Inn (Silver Street) 323; Smithfield 132–3; Paternoster Row 130; Tower 231, 508, 520, 617, 624; Thames Street 508

London, boroughs and place-names (1485–1558) **VII** 164, 181, 530, 560, 602; Aldgate 529; Blackfriars 195, 292, 328; Blackwell (Bakewell) Hall 462, 469; Bridewell 328, 595, 601; bridge 36, 142, 143, 173, 538; Cheapside 147, 184; Clerkenwell 596; counter in Bread Street 440; Craft gilds 458; glaziers 592; Fleet 299, 300, 411, 420, 543; Fleet Street 538; Flemings in 470; Gildhall 122, 165, 242, 267, 418 — Surrey's trial 421 — Suffolk dines after Mary proclaimed 529 — Mary's appeal to citizens 538 — library 579 — Holbein 600; Hackney 586; Hoxton 586; Hyde Park 586; Islington 586; Italian merchants 413, 470, 475; Jewel-House 378; King's Bench 530; Ludgate 538; Marshalsea 530; Marylebone Park 586; National Portrait Gallery 589, 599; Newgate 143, 440; St Bartholomew's

351

352

359, 370, 418; **III** 165, 268, 273, 275; Berwick burnt 277, 283; **IV** 695; justices 712

Lothian, Lord **XV** 418

Lothian, marquis of *see* Kerr, William

Lothian hills **V** 75

lotteries **X** 176

Loubet, President **XIV** 262, 367, 368

Loudon Hill, fort **Ia** 145

Loudun (Ayreshire), Bruce's success (1307) **IV** 719

Loudun (Poitou), castle **III** 324, 332

Lough Swilly, battle **VIII** 470; **XV** 159

Loughborough (Leics.) **VI** 376; **VII** 40

Loughborough, 1st Baron (1733–1805) **XII** 57, 66, 251, 402; and identity of Junius 45; solicitor general 150, 169, 225; lord chancellor (1793–1801) 396, 401, 580

Loughor Castle **V** 73

Loughrigg (Cumbria) **V** 366

Louis, Count Palatine of the Rhine **VI** 187

Louis, count of Tonnerre **VI** 244

Louis, Dauphin (d. Dec. 1415), French city loans **VI** 170

Louis, Dauphin, son of Charles VII (Louis XI) **VI** 470, 519; supports Edward of March 526

Louis II, duke of Anjou **VI** 140, 241

Louis, 2nd duke of Bourbon **VI** 33, 108, 152, 163, 222; renounces English agreement (1412) 114; brought as prisoner to England 157, 257; family 241

Louis, duke of Orléans **VI** 64, 73, 108, 111, 240

Louis the Pious, emperor and king of the Franks **II** 240–2, 247

Louis IV, king of France: interest in science **X** 29; and Portugal 60, 71; and Spanish Netherlands 67; supporters in Europe 75; policy towards Dutch 75–6; agreement

with Charles II 86–7, 90; master in Europe 109; 're-unions' 111; ambitions in Germany 113–14; revokes Edict of Nantes 121; failure with Germany 128–9; relations with James II 130; commercial measures against Dutch 132–3; designs against Germany and Holland 135; war with Spain 161–74; Spanish succession 192, 197; recognizes James II's son as successor 198; peace negotiations (1708) 216–17; unable to help Old Pretender 242; and the Huguenots 311; English literature 364; architecture 389; war 420–1

Louis VI, king of France: opposes William II **III** 112; visits Henry I in England 115, 118; his wars with Henry I 122–7

Louis VII, king of France **III** 276, 294, 342, 419: supports Stephen 135, 192; takes the cross 149; recognizes Geoffrey of Anjou as duke of Normany 161, 162, 323; war with Henry Plantagenet 162–3; divorce from Eleanor of Aquitaine 162–3; supports Becket 209–10; relations with Henry II 323–9, 332; supports Henry, the young king, against his father 333–7; last years and death 339–40

Louis VIII, king of France (1223–6) **III** 283, 301, 379, 383; seized St Omer and Aire 454; encounter with John 466–7; English barons offer him the crown 479, 480; arrival in England 483, 484; **IV** 73; previous occupation of part of England 1, 3–4, 8–15; makes peace at Kingston 13–14; returns to France 15; accession 87; maintains rights in Normandy 87; overruns Poitou (1224) 88, 90–1; Albigensian crusade 87–8, 91; death 91

356

Louis of Luxemburg, count of St Pol **VI** 475, 558, 573, 576

Louis d'Outremer, king of the West Franks **II** 345–7, 360

Louis Phillippe XVIII, king of France **XIII** 144, 208, 224, 226–8, 230–1, 233; and Palmerston 237–8, 247; Spanish marriage 242–5

Louisburg, Cape Breton Island, Nova Scotia **XI** 270, 319, 347, 357, 360; captured by New England forces (1745) 260–1; French prepare recapture attempt 262; relinquished in exchange for Madras 264

Louise, daughter of Francis I **VII** 307

Louise of Savoy, daughter of Philip II, duke of Savoy, mother of Francis I **VII** 177, 301, 315, 316, 319; attack on Vienna (1529) 341

Loundoun, earl of *see* Campbell, John

Lousiana: English acquisition of part of **XII** 85; American purchase from France 551

Louth (Lincs.), monastery **II** 225; **V** 41, 42, 232; county **VI** 425; riot (1536) **VII** 387

Louth, earl of *see* Bermingham, John de

Louth, Richard of, chamberlain of the exchequer **IV** 698

Louth, William of, keeper of the wardrobe **IV** 280, 305, 362

Louvain **V** 196, 476; **VII** 255, 258; **VIII** 28, 345

Louvain, duchess of **III** 368, 377

Louvain, Godfrey of, duke of Lower Lorraine, brother of Henry **III** 126, 454

Louvain, Jocelin of **III** 126

Louvet, Jean **VI** 188

Louviers: treaty **III** 375, 379; **VI** 173

Louvois, François, marquis de **X** 111, 170

Louvre, palace **VI** 201; **VII** 601

Lovat, Simon Fraser, 12th Lord (?1667–1747) **XI** 162, 256, 281; impeached 24

Love on the Dole **XV** 352

Loveden Hill **Ib** 111, 176, 181; Anglian pottery 65 [fig. 3(b)]; map 4 xxxii; map 5 68

Lovel, John, Lord **VI** 7, 8, 519, 617, 632; joins Margaret 520

Lovel, William, Lord **VI** 640

Lovel estates **VI** 327

Lovelace, John, 3rd Baron **X** 139

Lovelace, Kentishman **VI** 524

Lovell, Francis, 1st Viscount Lovell (1454–87?) **VI** 617, 634, 643, 644; at Bosworth **VII** 58; rising against Henry (1486) 67; in hiding 68; in Low Countries 70; in Ireland 72; death (1487) 74

Lovell, Henry, 8th Baron Morley **VII** 58; killed at Dixmude (1489) 98, 99, 208

Lovell, Maud, Lady Arundel **VI** 484

Lovell, Sir Thomas (d. 1524) **VII** 61, 74, 170, 200, 300; chancellor of the Exchequer (1485) 56; speaker of the House of Commons (1485) 59, 652; treasurer of the household (1502) 217, 649; named as scrutineer 229; preserving Henry VII's system 233

Lovell v *Morley* **V** 265

Lovelych, John, rector of St Alphage, Canterbury **VI** 279

Lovemede (Trowbridge, Wilts.) **VI** 365

Lovett, William: biography **XIII** 133; chartist activities 133, 135–42, 146–7

Low, David **XV** 131, 141, 408

Low Countries (Netherlands) **Ia** 8, 140, 174, 288, 305; **Ib** 48; **III** 88, 367, 376, 452, 464; **V** 105, 368; Queen Isabella in 83, 110; and origins of the Hundred Years War 119–22; Edward III's allies

Low Countries (*cont.*)
in 155, 162; trade with 349, 358; *see also* Batavians; Belgium; Holland; Netherlands

Lowbury Hill **Ib** 157; map 3 xxxi

Lowe, Robert, 1st Viscount Sherbrooke (1811–92) **XIII** 190; opposition to parliamentary reform 184; applies 'payment by results' in education 481–2; biography 481; **XIV** 16, 20; match tax 20; becomes home secretary 25; opposed to franchise extension 55; dropped by Gladstone (1880) 66; 'payment by results' 146, 349

Lower, Richard **X** 376–7

Lower Thames Street, London, house/amphora and other remains **Ia** 459, 495

Lowestoft (Suffolk), manor **VI** 472

lowland zone **Ia** 4–5, 47, 95, 98, 621–2

Lowther, J. W., Lord Ullswater **XIV** 341; decision as to Reform Bill amendment 461; presides at Buckingham Palace Conference 480

Lowther, James, earl of Lonsdale (1736–1802) **XII** 51; marriage 70; application for Portland lands 144; on America 218; support of Gordon 236

Lowthers, the **XI** 118

Lübeck **III** 89; **V** 359; **VI** 69, 356–9; **VII** 221, 475; bombed **XV** 553

Luca, Conference **Ia** 24

Luca Fieschi, Cardinal **V** 40, 52

Lucan **III** 374

Lucan, earl of *see* Bingham, George Charles

Lucas, F. L. **XV** 317

Lucca: *podesta* and commonalty **IV** 519; merchants 505, 633, 639, 641; *see also* Riccardi; Lucca **VI** 91; cathedral 93; firms' Southampton agents 354; **VII** 112

Lucca, Luke of **IV** 629, 632, 642

Lucca, Ptolemy of *see* Ptolemy of Lucca

Luci, Richard de, justiciar **IV** 71

Lucius II, Pope **III** 147

Lucius III, Pope **III** 225, 344

Lucretius **III** 235

Lucy, Sir Anthony **V** 231

Lucy, Geoffrey de **III** 436

Lucy, Godfrey de, bishop of Winchester **III** 221, 366

Lucy, Lord **VI** 9

Lucy, Matilda de, wife of Gilbert de Umfraville **VI** 54

Lucy, Richard de, justiciar **III** 2, 160, 211, 277; loyal to Stephen 322; failure of rebellion in England 334

Luddism **XII** 570

Ludeca, king of Mercia **II** 231, 232

Ludendorff, E.: offensive **XV** 60, 100–2, 104, 108, 109; and armistice 110

Ludford Bridge (Salop), battle **VI** 512, 516

Ludgate Hill, London, statue base **Ia** 533

Ludgershall (Bucks.) **V** 510, 511

Ludgershall (Wilts.) **III** 88

Ludlow (Salop) **V** 97; **VI** 366, 510, 520, 611, 612; **VII** 174, 204, 385

Ludlow, Edmund: on Nineteen Propositions **IX** 125; royalists 127, 171; king's execution 158; conquest of Ireland 163; new lords in parliament 185; and the army 239, 243–5; republicans 258

Ludlow, Laurence of, wool merchant **IV** 632, 663

Ludlow Castle **III** 26; **IV** 201; **VI** 503, 504, 516; lords of *see* Geneville

Luel *see* Carlisle

Lufham, Thomas de **III** 407

Luftwaffe: and battle of Britain **XV** 498–500; and Blitz 501; and attacks on shipping 504; and strategic bombing 517; squadron sent to Sicily 524

Lugard, Sir Frederick, afterwards Lord **XIV** 190, 243

Lugard, Lady **XV** 20

Lugotorix **Ia** 36

Luguvallium see Carlisle

Lugwardine, John of **V** 279

Luiz, son of King Emmanuel of Portugal **VII** 534

Lull, archbishop of Mainz **II** 93, 173–5, 206; correspondents 174

Lulli, J.-B. de **X** 406

Lullingstone villa **Ia** 465, 601; tomb 702–3; chapel 725; paintings 727

Lumley, John, 1st Lord **VIII** 131, 151

Lumley, John, Lord **IX** 376

Lumley, Marmaduke, bishop of Carlisle, treasurer **VI** 253, 270, 328–9, 491, 682; Scrope lands 328–9; son of Lord Ralph 328; wife 328; *see also* Scrope, Richard

Lumley, Richard, 1st earl of Scarbrough **X** 133

Lumley, Thomas, Lord **VI** 530

Lumleys, the **XI** 118

Luna, Petrus Martini de **IV** 269

Lunden *see* London

Lundy Island **V** 59, 86

Lune, river, settlement research **Ia** 613

Lüneburg, duke of **XI** 11

Lunéville, Peace of (1801) **XII** 386, 406, 410, 412, 422

Lunsford, Thomas **IX** 122

Lunt, the, Baginton near Coventry (War.), fort **Ia** 275, 312

Lupicinus **Ia** 361, 367–8, 373, 378, 381

Lupset, Thomas (1498?–1530) **VII** 255, 454, 457, 571

Lupus, abbot of Ferrières **II** 189

Lupus, Virius *see* Virius Lupus

Lupus of Troyes, bishop **Ia** 462, 464, 470

Lusignan (Vienne): castle **IV** 89, 102; Provisions of Oxford 135, 138–40; **VI** 113; *see also* Valence, William of

Lusignan, Aymer de, bishop-elect of Winchester **IV** 139, 140–1, 159, 162, 327

Lusignan, Geoffrey de, lord of Jarnac **III** 382; **IV** 124, 138–40, 157, 159, 162; compensated by Edward 274–5

Lusignan, Guy de, lord of Cognac **IV** 124, 138–40, 159, 162; planning to sail from Breton 157; escapes to Pevensey 190; compensated by Edward 274–5; pledge for Alphonso 283

Lusignan, Guy of, king of Jerusalem **III** 342, 361

Lusignan, house of **III** 379–80, 381, 466; **IV** 89, 97

Lusignan, Hugh the Brown of, count of La Marche **III** 380, 382; his son 466

Lusignan, Margaret of **IV** 100

Lusignan, Ralph of, count of Eu **III** 380

Lusitania, sunk **XV** 43

Lusitanians **Ib** 76

Lusius Sabinianus, Q. *see* Sabinianus

Lutetia Parisiorum see Paris

Luther, Martin **VII** 309, 340, 356, 357, 433; burns bull of excommunication (1520) 337; New Testament and pamphlets 338; discussed at Cambridge 343; Tyndale's work 344; Thomas More 346; Cromwell and the 'new' Bible 397; Cromwell executed 404; doctrine of consubstantiation 508

Lutherans **VII** 319, 331, 332, 556; Augsburg confession (1530) and League of Schmalkalde (1530) 340; influence in Cambridge 343; in London (1538) 395, 403; English Protestants seek alliance 413; fall of Cromwell 415; Henry's

Lutherans (*cont.*)
religious reforms 425; Francisco de Encinas 516; Treaty of Passau (1552) 535
Luthington, John, auditor for N. Wales and Chester **VI** 603
Luton (Beds.) **Ib** 61; Saxon pottery 71 [fig. 6(d)]; **XV** 167.
Lutterell, Sir Hugh **VI** 72
Lutterworth (Leics.) **V** 325, 431; Wyclif 511, 514–15, 520
Luttrell, Henry Lawes, 2nd earl of Carhampton (1743–1821) **XII** 136, 138, 155
Luttrell, Sir John **VII** 484
Luttrell, Narcissus **X** 379
Lutyens, Sir Edwin **XIV** 540, 541, 542
Lützen, battle (1813) **XII** 556
Luxembourg (Luxemburg) **XIII** 227–8, 230, 324–5; **XV** 494, 577
Luxembourg, John of *see* John of Luxemburg
Luxembourg, marshall duc de **X** 170–2
Lycia **Ia** 109
Lydd and New Romney **VI** 675
Lydford (Devon) **II** 265, 532
Lydgate, John (1370?–1451?) **VII** 584; **VIII** 286
Lydgate, John, monk **VI** 658
Lydney, sanctuary **Ia** 362, 384, 686, 733
Lyell, Sir Charles **XIII** 535, 549, 572–3; biography 572
Lyfing, bishop of Worcester **II** 422–3
Lygeanburg (Lygeanburh) *see* Limbury (Beds.)
Lyhert, Walter, bishop of Norwich **VI** 270, 682
Lyle, Robert, 2nd Lord (d. 1497) **VII** 136
Lyly, John **VIII** 292, 295, 296
Lyme Bay **XV** 498
Lyme Regis **X** 118
Lyminge (Liminiæ) (Kent) **Ib** 124; Quoit Brooch Style 118 [fig.

10(a)]; **II** 293; monastery 111; lathe 283
Lyminster (Sussex), council **II** 349
Lympne (*Lemanis*) (Kent) **Ib** 31, 83, 113, 124, 126; map 2 xxx; map 5 68; map 6 88; '*Limenewara*' 135; Saxon Shore 204
Lympne (Limen) (Kent), river **II** 266, 732
lynchets **Ia** 8
Lyndfield, John, dean of the Arches **VI** 287
Lyndhurst (Hants) **Ib** 213
Lyndhurst, Lord **XIII** 84–6
Lyndwood (*Provincale*) **IV** 456, 474
Lyndwood, William, canonist **VI** 96, 302; *liber provincialis* 265
Lyngever, John, of Kingston Deverell **VI** 462–3
Lynn *see* King's Lynn (Norfolk)
Lynom, Thomas, Richard III's solicitor **VI** 634
Lyons (Rhône): urban cohort **Ia** 162; battle 220–1; church 717; **III** 177; council (1274) **IV** 232–3; local reports discussed by English clergy (1273) 504; Edward I's proctors 460; Archbishop Pecham 451, 472–5; **VI** 191, 240; **VII** 114, 272, 312; treaty between Louis XII and Philip (1501, 1503) 153–4
Lyons, Admiral **XIII** 279
Lyons, archbishop of: joins league of Mâcon **IV** 248; *see also* Belmeis, John; Bourbon, Charles de; Hugh
Lyons, canon of, on bigamy **IV** 463
Lyons, Richard **V** 410, 415; evades wool staple 354; arrest and trial 389–91
lyrics, 15th cent. **VI** 661–3
Lys, river **VII** 279
Lyte, Henry **VIII** 316–17
Lyttelton, Alfred **XIV** 377, 386; biography 375
Lyttleton, George, 1st Baron (1709–73) **XI** 22, 94, 145, 147, 250; opposes Walpole 204, 238;

360

Pitt alliance 346; Royal Society 396; Stowe park 413

Lyttleton, Oliver: biography **XV** 172; minister of state 528; minister of production 544

Lytton, 2nd earl of **XIV** 417

Lytton, Edward Robert, 1st Baron, 1st earl of Lytton **XIII** 554; **XIV** 62, 69; biography 62

Lytton report **XV** 371

M

Maamtrasna (Netherlands) murders **XIV** 76

Maas, river **Ib** map 1 xxix

Maastricht **III** 90

Mabel, daughter of Robert Fitz Hamon **III** 290

Mabel, wife of Roger Montgomery **III** 105

Mac Murrough, family **VII** 125

McAdam (Macadam), John Loudon, engineer (1756–1836) **XII** 518; **XIII** 4

McArdell, James (?1729–65), mezzotint engraver **XI** 414

MacArthur, Douglas, General **XV** 598

Macarthur, John (1767–1834) **XII** 513

Macarthy More of Muskerry **VIII** 471

Macartney, George, 1st Earl (1737–1806) **XII** 107, 316, 320

Macassar, king of **X** 349

Macaulay, Lord Thomas Babington **XIII** 25, 154, 249, 270, 441; supports reform bill 82; opposes Chartists 141; views on Indian education 407; University of London 492; Chatham essay 530; biography 541; writings 541–2; influence 541–2, 545; **XV** 378, 488, 492

Macaulay, Zachary (1768–1838) **XII** 354

Macbeth, king of Scotland **II** 570; **III** 266

MacCarthy, Dermot, king of Desmond **III** 308, 313

McCarthy, Justin **XIV** 90, 184, 186

MacCarthys of Desmond **IV** 561, 565; **V** 472

McCleary, Dr G. F. **XIV** 519

Macclesfield (Cheshire): archers **IV** 411; forest 513; silk industry **XII** 511

Macclesfield, earls of *see* Gerard, Charles; Parker, Thomas

MacColl, Canon Malcolm **XIV** 561

McCulloch, J. R. **XIII** 74, 445

Maccus, son of Harold **II** 369

Maccus, son of Olaf **II** 362

Macdonald, Æneas, 'one of the seven men of Moidart' **XI** 252

Macdonald, Alexander **XIII** 614

Macdonald, Flora (1722–90) **XI** 257

MacDonald, James Ramsay (1866–1937) **XIV** 266, 296, 378, 441, 459; opposes First World War **XV** 3; resigns as Labour leader 8; biography 28; UDC 51; attends Leeds Convention 89; co-operates with Henderson 91; drafts statement on war aims 96; defeated (1918) 128; shapes Labour foreign policy 136; Inner Cabinet 197; ILP 199; on Baldwin 205; becomes prime minister 208–9; security service 213; condemns Poplarism 214; reconciles France and Germany 214–15; Protocol 216; Russian treaty 217; Campbell case 218–19, 225; leaves office 219–20; Locarno much in his spirit 221–2; Zinoviev letter 226; relations with Baldwin 227–8; unsuccessful on radio 235; prestige remains high 237; Bevin hostile 239; resists ILP 267; national figure 270; prime minister again 271; London naval treaty 272–3; India 275–6; Palestine 276; boneless wonder 280; beats down Bevin 283; takes over unemployment 285; financial crisis 288, 291; becomes National prime minister 294; reports to

George V 297; departs from Labour party 294, 295, 323; friendly letters to Mussolini 317; general election (1931) 322, 324-5; co-operates with Baldwin 326-7; dislikes Lansbury 328; sets up economic advisory council 329; not at Ottawa 333; degrading position 334; pious platitudes 335; Labour moderate under 346; ceases to be prime minister 351, 378; India 355; foreign affairs 359, 360, 364; League habit 368; initials White Paper 376; Stresa 377; Lansbury denounced more fiercely 382; election as Labour leader 383; returned for university constituency 384; prestige dwindles 389; resigns and dies 404; foreign affairs during his first National session 408

Macdonald, Sir John, one of the 'seven men of Moidart' **XI** 252

MacDonald, Malcolm: defends National government **XV** 294; member 378, 384, 405

Macdonald of Clanranald **XI** 253

Macdonald of Glencoe, Alexander **X** 280

Macdonalds, the **XI** 253, 256

Macdonalds of Glengarry and Glencoe **XI** 254

Macdonnell, Sir Antony **XIV** 358, 359

Macdonough **XII** 554

McDougall, Alexander (1733-86) **XII** 194

McDougall, Sir J. **XIV** 340

McDougall, W. **XIV** 551

Macduff of Fife, appeal from Scottish to English king (1293) **IV** 610

Macedonia **XV** 577

macellum see market halls

MacGregor (*or* Campbell), Robert ('Rob Roy') (1671-1734) **XI** 280

MacGregor, Robert (son of the above) **XI** 280

Machado, Roger, Richmond king of arms **VII** 94, 121

Machaut, Guillaume de **V** 531

Machen, Arthur **XV** 9

Machiavelli, Niccolo **VII** 38, 152

machine guns: British Expeditionary Force **XV** 8, 9; Lloyd George 35; generals dislike 391

Machyn, Henry **VII** 580

Machynlleth (Montgomery) **VI** 55, 642

Mack, General **XII** 426

Mackay, Major-General Hugh **X** 170, 277, 278

McKenna duties: instituted **XV** 40, 82; prolonged after war 150; abolished by Snowden 212; restored by Churchill 237; remain 330

McKenna, Reginald **XIV** 385, 393, 397, 398; puts forward admiralty's demand (1909) 412; conflict with war office and transferred to be home secretary 436; 'Cat and Mouse Act' 460; reforms naval punishments 524; biography **XV** 31; becomes chancellor of Exchequer 31; Lloyd George 34; budget 40; borrowing 41; war debts 42; war committee 47; conscription 54-5; refuses Exchequer from Law 196; opposes American debt settlement 203; fails to find seat 205; proposed as prime minister 209; disappoints Free Trade hopes 326

Mackenzie, Sir A. C. **XIV** 158

Mackenzie, George, 3rd earl of Cromarty (d. 1766) **XI** 256

MacKenzie, Stuart **XII** 110, 119

McKenzie, W. L. **XIII** 380

Mackesy, General **XV** 471

Mackinnon, Sir William **XIV** 188, 189, 190, 193, 381

Mackintosh, C. R. **XIV** 541, 542

Mackintosh, Sir James (1765-1832) **XII** 437; **XIII** 92, 470

Mackintosh of Borlum, William (1662-1743) **XI** 162

Maclane, Private **XII** 133
MacLarens, the **XI** 280
Maclauray, Private **XII** 133
MacLaurin, Colin (1698–1746), mathematician **XI** 286, 379
Maclay, Sir J.: controller of shipping **XV** 77; makes admiralty responsible for shipbuilding 79; increases transports to France 101
Maclean, Sir Donald **XIII** 395; **XV** 127
Macleane, Lauchlin, **XII** 130, 166, 312
Macleod, Fiona **XIV** 335
Maclise, Daniel **XIII** 591
Macmahon, Sir Henry **XV** 71
Macmillan, Lord Harold **XV** 120, 354; committee on finance and industry 287
MacMillan, Margaret **XIV** 520
McMurrough, Art **V** 471–2, 491
McMurrough, Dermot, king of Leinster **III** 302–3, 304–6
Macneill, Prof. John **XIV** 475
McNeill, John **XV** 21, 56
Mâcon (Seine-et-Loire): conference (1281) **IV** 248, 288; **VI** 249, 256; *bailliage* 191, 239, 240; county 263
McPhelim, Brian *see* O'Neill
Macpherson, Sir Ian **XV** 117
Macpherson, James (1736–96) **XII** 352
Macpherson, Sir John (1745–1821), MP **XII** 320
Macqueen, Robert, 1st Baron Braxfield (1722–99) **XII** 359, 361
MacTaggart, Ferquhard, 1st earl of Ross **IV** 580
MacWilliam, Cuthred **III** 283
Madagascar **XIV** 192
Madeira **VII** 224
Madeleine, daughter of Francis I **VII** 363
Mademoiselle from Armentières **XV** 549
Madison, James (1751–1836), president of USA **XII** 475, 550–2, 555

Madocks, Alexander (1774–1828) **XII** 448
Madog ap Llywelyn, rebel leader (1294–5) **IV** 440–3
Madox, Thomas (1666–1727) **X** 381; antiquarian **XI** 394
Madras **IX** 323; **X** 349, 353; **XI** 261, 264, 270, 325, 366; the English Company 325, 332
Madre de Dios **VIII** 413
Madrid **VII** 315, 601; **X** 213; **XV** 393, 478
Madrid, treaties: between Francis I and Charles V (1526) **VII** 316; (1630) **IX** 67
Madrigal **VIII** 306
Maeatae **Ia** 225–7, 230, 241
Maecilius Fuscus **Ia** 251
Maegla **Ib** 147, appendix II
mægth **II** 293
Mældubesburg *see* Malmesbury (Wilts.)
Mældun *see* Malden (Essex)
Maelgwn of Gwynedd, lord of Anglesey **II** 4, 76
Maelienydd, district (cantref) **IV** 394, 406; **VI** 42, 335, 510
Maenius Agrippa, M. **Ia** 529
Mærse *see* Mersey, river
Mafeking, siege of **XIV** 253, 255
Magee, Dr W. C., bishop, afterwards archbishop **XIV** 2
Magellan, Ferdinand **VII** 4
Magennis, house of **VII** 128
magic **Ia** 394, 679–80, 688–9
Magilros *see* Old Melrose
Maginot line **XV** 415, 460, 484
magister: *magistri militum* **Ia** 331–3, 350; cavalry (*magister equitum*) and infantry (*magister peditum*) 331; Vetranio 354; *praesentales, in praesenti* 367, 489; in Britain 361, 384; Germans dominant 374–5, 471, 736; Theodosius the Great 400; Alaric 423; Gerontius dismissed 432; Aetius 475
magistracies: *cursus honorum* **Ia** 77; control of elections 79; provincial

governors 88; colleagues 287; display expected 311, 323; Constantinople 365–6, 521; distaste for burdens 399, 537; local magistracies 535, 537, 567, 573, 576 — *res publica* 591–2; combined with priesthoods 676, 702

magistri **Ia** 535

magistri rei privatae **Ia** 338, 339

Maglocunus (Maelgwn) **Ib** 12

Magna Carta: its importance **III** 1, 11, 476–7; on castle-guard 18; sergeanties 19; feudal incidents 20–1, 22; the forest 29; protects villein's wainage 41; boroughs 74; fish-weirs 81, 473; measures 86; *mala tolta* 93; Scotland 283; Wales 301; appointment of itinerant justices 390; sheriff's tourn 395; writ *de odio et athia* 403; petty assizes 407; writ *praecipe* 410; common pleas 413; county farms 421; Jews 423; struggle for 468, 471–3; relation to the unknown charter of Liberties 471; judgement of peers 472; sealed 473; clauses analysed 474–6; consequences 477–9; **IX** 148; *see also* Charter of Liberties

Magnaghten, Sir William Hay **XIII** 417–19

Magnentius, Emperor **Ia** 345, 354, 357–9, 368, 411; silver ingots 532; toleration 726

Magnus, king of Norway **II** 406, 419–20; treaty with Harthacnut 421–2, 560; claim upon England and Denmark 423–4; death (1047) 424

Magnus IV, king of Norway: cedes Western Isles and Man to king of Scots (1266) **IV** 569

Magnus Barefoot, king of Norway **III** 286

Magnus Maximus, Emperor **Ia** 321, 401–9, 416, 424, 427; heresy-hunting 411, 714, 737; mint 532, 660

Magonsætan **II** 46–8, 134, 337;

members of ruling family named 47

Maguire, Alexander, titular baron of Enniskillen (b. 1721) **XI** 292

Mahadaji Sindhia **XII** 315

Mahdi **XIV** 80

Mahé, British attack on **XII** 316

Mahmud II, sultan of Turkey **XIII** 215; obtains help of Mehemet Ali against the Greeks 215; agrees to treaty of Adrianople (1829) 220; first defeat by Mehemet Ali 233; accepts Russian help 233–5; second defeat by Mehemet Ali 236–7; death 237

Mahon, Lord *see* Stanhope, Charles

Mahratta princes **XIII** 403–4, 411–12

Mahudus (the Mahudas) **Ia** 691; **Ib** 79

Maiden Castle: hill-fort **Ia** 93; pagan shrine 735–8

Maidenhead (Berks.) **VI** 25; **VII** 35

Maidford (Northants) **III** 33

Maid's Tragedy **VIII** 301

Maidstone (Kent) **Ib** 123; map 2 xxx; **V** 297, 408; **VII** 538, 566; **IX** 155

Maidstone, Richard **V** 468

Maie, river **V** 134

Maildubh, Irish scholar **II** 125, 182

Maine (New England) **IX** 327; **X** 337

Maine, counts of **II** 555; *see also* Helias of la Flèche; Herbert Wake-Dog; Robert, duke of Normandy

Maine, county: William I uses English troops in **II** 585, 608; **III** 102; Robert of Normandy attempts to recover 107–8; William II 111–12; absorbed in Anjou 112, 113; Henry's inheritance 112, 318, 329; count Fulk's claim to 123 — settled on daughter Sibyl 126; English overlordship recognized 124, 125; bequeathed to Geoffrey 324;

Malestroit, truce **V** 131, 219

Malet, Gilbert **III** 23

Malet, William **III** 23

Malines (Mechlin), English staple (1295) **IV** 663, 664; town and lordship **VI** 553; **VIII** 45, 357

Mallet, David (?1705–65), poet **XI** 421

Malmesbury (Mældubesburg) (Wilts.): abbey **II** 68, 125, 151, 182, 455, 732; **III** 154, 185, 263; castle 138, 163; abbot 404; *see also* Aldhelm; church porch **VI** 649; **VII** 462

Malmesbury, earl of *see* Harris, James Howard

Malmesbury, William of **III** 2, 63, 86, 89, 253; on William Rufus 98; Philip of France 105; shire-levies, training 116; conquest of Normandy coincidence 120; witnessed election of Empress Matilda 143; on Robert of Gloucester 148; account of the Anarchy 150; value of his narratives 248; on David I 269

Malone, Anthony (1700–76) **XI** 295, 303

Malone, Kemp **II** 13

Malory, Sir Thomas **III** 255; **VI** 656–8

Malplaquet, battle **X** 219

malt-tax (1713) **X** 292

Malta **XII** 423, 425, 454; French capture 378; settlement (1802) 409, 412; retained by Britain 1814) 563; **XIII** 194, 304; easternmost dockyard **XV** 230; Gort governor 486; naval force 520; attacks on enemy convoys 523, 559; in danger 531; weakness 541; out of action 554; Italian fleet surrenders 573

Maltby, Sir Nicholas **VIII** 478

Malthus, Revd Thomas Robert (1766–1834) **XI** 128; **XII** 531; **XIII** 61, 445, 449, 573–4

Maltoltes: on wool (1294–7) **IV** 630,

663, 669, 682, 683; **V** 15, 161, 163, 193, 221–3

Malton: military **Ia** 95, 136, 384; inscriptions 658, 685; burial 695

Malton **Ib** xxvi, 78, 186–9, 195–6; map 4 xxxii; map 6 88

Malton, Thomas de, chaplain **VI** 288

Malton, William de, mason **VI** 288

Maltravers, Sir John **V** 94–5

Maltravers, Lord, Arundel's heir **VI** 536

Malvern (Worcs.): priory **V** 526; priory church **VI** 655; **X** 409; **XV** 179

Malvern, John of, on Wykeham **V** 226

Malvern Chase **III** 32

Mameceaster *see* Manchester (Lancs.)

Mamillia **VIII** 293

Mamluks of Syria **V** 123

Man, Dr John **VIII** 129

The Man of Property **XV** 178

Mancetter: battle? **Ia** 120; industrial development 595, 645

Manchester (Mameceaster) (Lancs.) **II** 334, 732; **VI** 33, 558; **IX** 288, 351; cotton trade **XI** 122; local government 47; manufactures **XII** 30, 334, 503, 508, 570; local government 44; hope of enfranchisement 278; Corresponding Society 358; strikes 466; bankruptcy of firms 469; population 511, 517; **XIII** 2, 4, 10, 26–7, 42–3; railway 45–7; 'Peterloo' affair 64–5; parliamentary representation 76, 81, 187; Reform agitation 83, 85; Statistical Society 93, 478; '*Young England*' 115; corn laws 118; Chartists 128, 138, 140–1, 146; textile trade 209; Fenianism at 360; improvement commission 461–2; medical officer of health 464; education 479; science and technology 566; trade unions 615; municipal acti-

Manchester (*cont.*)
vities **XIV** 128; representation **XV** 116; population 167; newspapers printed 234; change from trams to buses 303; prosperous 304; Liberal-Labour alliance 266; no repertory theatre 314; Popular Front meeting 397

Manchester Guardian: during First World War **XV** 27; supports Lloyd George 28, 66, 252; contributions 61, 167; depends on Scott family 194; becomes national newspaper 234; points logic of Covenant 300; opposes intervention in Greece 590

Manchester Ship Canal **XIV** 280

Manchester Town Hall, Lloyd George **XV** 112

Manchester University **XV** 347

Manchester, 4th duke of **XII** 230

Manchester, earl of *see* Montague

Manchon, Guillaume **VI** 251

Manchuria: Japanese invade **XV** 298, 299, 363, 380; League 370–2, 384; affair discredits Simon 378

Mancini, Dominic **VI** 610, 611, 612, 613, 616; princes in tower 623; on Edward IV 546; **VII** 237

Mandagod, William de **VI** 666

Mandates, invented **XV** 133

Mandeville, Bernard de (1670–1733): *Fable of the Bees* **XI** 84

Mandeville, Geoffrey de *see* Geoffrey de Mandeville

Mandeville, Viscount *see* Montague

Mandubracius **Ia** 35–7, 47, 57

manes **Ia** 699

Manfred, natural son of Frederick II and king of Sicily (1258) **IV** 121, 122, 123, 532; marries Beatrice, daughter of Amadeus of Savoy 247; daughter Constance marries Peter of Aragon 252

Mangalore, Peace of (1784) **XII** 316

Mani Begum **XII** 311

'Manifest Destiny' **XII** 550

Manila (Philippines) **XI** 371; British capture of **XII** 76

Mann, Sir Horace (1701–86) **XI** 184, 428; **XII** 337

Mann, Tom **XIV** 205, 438

Manners, John, marquis of Granby (1721–70) **XII** 209; refuses promotion 110; and the king 119; commander in chief (1766–70) 121, 576; opposition (1770) 146; master general of the ordnance 577

Manners, Lord John, 7th duke of Rutland **XIII** 114–16, 118, 160–1; biography 114

Manners, Thomas, 1st earl of Rutland (d. 1543) **VII** 400

Manning, Cardinal **XIV** 24, 68, 89, 185, 206

Manning, F. **XV** 549

Manningham, Eleanor, wife of Oliver **VI** 325

Manningham, Sir Oliver **VI** 325

Manningham, Thomas (?1651–1722), Bishop **XI** 77

Manny, Sir Walter **V** 148, 167, 249; raid on Cadsand 128; in Brittany 131; in Gascony 132; with Edward III in Netherlands 159; addresses parliament 221; admiral 245; knight of the Garter 253; carver to Queen Philippa 269; addresses convocation 288–9

Mannyng, Robert **V** 526

manor: meaning of word **II** 480; types 480–8, 683; origin 306–7, 313–14; **III** 56; court of 57

Manorbier (Pembroke), castle **VI** 641

manorial life: villages and villagers **IV** 773–6; economy **VII** 445–6

manors: royal **II** 300, 482–3, 483–6; ecclesiastical 486–9

manpower **Ia** 390–1, 439–40, 457, 546–8, 618; mining 633; iron industry 639; budget **XV** 512,

371

Margaret, daughter of Edward I, wife of John II of Brabant **IV** 268, 511, 512, 664, 680

Margaret, daughter of Louis VII, king of France **III** 323–4, 342

Margaret, daughter of William, king of Scotland **III** 280, 283

Margaret, daughter of William the Lion *see* Burgh, Margaret de

Margaret, duchess of Burgundy **VI** 575; Calais arrival 576

Margaret, Lady Beaufort, countess of Richmond (d. 1509) **VII** 191, 234, 252, 570; Henry's battle for the throne 48–50; tomb 592; St John's College 594; portrait 598

Margaret, Maid of Norway **III** 281

Margaret, Philip the Bold's wife **VI** 73

Margaret, queen of England, sister of Philip IV of France: draft treaty (1294) for her marriage with Edward I **IV** 647; papal dispensation for marriage 652; treaty for marriage and marriage (1299) 653; resides at Dunfermline Abbey (1304) 709; watches siege of Stirling (1304) 710

Margaret, queen of Scots, daughter of Henry III *see* St Margaret

Margaret, queen of Scots, the 'maid of Norway' **IV** 512, 597; betrothed to Edward of Caernarvon 265, 268, 598–600; death in Orkney 268, 511, 513, 600–1

Margaret, sister of Edgar the Ætheling **II** 606

Margaret, Tudor ap Goronwy's wife **VI** 39

Margaret, wife of Conan IV, duke of Brittany **III** 281

Margaret, 2nd wife of Cranmer **VII** 356, 551

Margaret, wife of Malcolm Canmore **III** 115, 237, 266–8, 269, 273

Margaret of Angoulême, sister of Francis I, wife of Henry II of Navarre (d. 1549) **VII** 177, 187, 322, 323, 338

Margaret of Anjou, daughter of René, queen of England **VI** 397, 441, 465, 477, 494; seen by Suffolk 475; leaves France 476; dowry 477; marries 477; loses Pembroke (1450) 478; letter to Charles VII (Dec. 1445) 479; exile in Scotland 481; and Somerset 503; son's birth (13 Oct. 1453) 508; leader of Somerset's faction (1454) 508–9; bargains with Scots 514; Piers de Brézé lands 514; Warwick returns from Calais 515; York-London march 523; Welsh diplomacy 516; Denbigh refuge 520; confronted by Warwick and March 523; Coppini 523; offers to surrender Berwick 523; soldiers' St Albans riot 525; Londoners suspicious 525; Scottish flight 526; attacks on Yorkists 528–9; besieges Alnwick 529; Bamburgh and Flanders 530; Louis XI meeting 532; requests loan from Charles VII 532; lands in Brittany (1462) 532; meets Louis XI 532; English return (1471) 564, 567; Weymouth arrival 568; recruitment 569; battle of Shrewsbury 569; captured 579; Cambridge college founded 670; queen consort of Henry VI **VII** 191

Margaret of Burgundy, sister of Edward IV (1446–1503) **VII** 67, 70, 139, 181, 182; Perkin Warbeck 117–18, 120–1, 123–4

Margaret of Denmark, queen of Norway **VI** 69

Margaret Douglas, daughter of Margaret Tudor, wife of Matthew, 4th earl of Lennox **VII** 305, 381

Margaret of Flanders, duchess of Burgundy **V** 143

Margaret Parma, duchess of **VIII** 44, 59

Margaret of Provence, queen of France, wife of Louis IX **IV** 73, 119; English affairs (1261–5) 164, 178, 184; and Edward I 244, 248–9; claims in Provence 234, 239, 246, 248–9; invested by Rudolf of Habsburg 247; forms league of Mâcon (1281) 248; concern for relatives in Savoy 249–50; case of Gaston of Béarn 286; John de Grilly 288

Margaret of Savoy, daughter of Maximilian and Mary, wife of Philip II of Savoy **VII** 85, 105, 121, 273, 319; widowed (1504) 177; proposed bride for Henry VII 183, 185, 186, 187; Cloth of Gold meeting with Henry 310

Margaret Tudor (1489–1541) **VII** 41, 160, 162, 192, 406; proposed bride for James IV (1495) 137, 157; marriage treaty (1502) 158; married to James IV (1503) 161; betrothal to James IV (1501) 174; Henry refuses to hand over jewels 270; marriage to earl of Angus (Aug. 1514) 305; gives birth to daughter 305; ejected from Scotland (1515) 305–6; Albany's absence (1522) 313; hopes James will marry Mary 314; divorced from Angus (1527) 321, 326; portrait 598

Margaret of York, duchess of Burgundy **VI** 573, 582, 583; sister of Clarence 579

Margaret of York, Edward IV's sister **VI** 551

Margarot, president of London Corresponding Society **XII** 359

Margate (Kent) **V** 446; **VIII** 146, 397; **XII** 549

Margesson, D. R. **XV** 473, 474

Maria, Empress (Stilicho's daughter) **Ia** 417; burial 693–4

Maria Anna Victoria (b. 1718), Spanish Infanta **XI** 193

Maria Theresa, Archduchess (1717–80) **XI** 194, 199, 207, 236, 249; English support 237–8, 240–1, 245, 250, 265; with Emperor Charles VII 243–4; relations with Charles Emmanuel of Savoy 244–5, 263, 268; successes (1745) 261; aims 266–7, 269; grievances 343; reversal of alliances 344; French alliance 351; *see also* subsidies

Marianus Scotus **III** 249

Marie, duchess of Berry **VI** 241

Marie, wife of Philip of Namur **III** 464

Marie of Brabant, second wife of Philip III of France (1274) **IV** 239, 240, 647

Marie de France **III** 243, 256

Marie Galante: returned to France (1763) **XII** 85; British capture of (1794) 370

Marienburg (Prussia) **VI** 71

Marignano, French victory (1515) **VII** 306, 309

Marillac, Charles de, French ambassador **VII** 417, 418, 432

Marine insurance **X** 358

Marinus, Pope **II** 466

Marischal, 10th earl of *see* Keith, George

Marisco, de *see* Marsh

maritime law **IV** 620; disputes at sea **IV** 644–6, 654–5; *see also* Oléron

Marius, C. **Ia** 11–12, 22

Marjorie of Scotland, wife of Gilbert the Marshal **IV** 73

Mark, Philip **IV** 21

Markele, Haddington **VI** 37

market halls (*macella*) **Ia** 584, 608, 658–9

market towns: represented in parliament of Easter (1275) **IV** 532; taxation did not imply representation in parliament 532–3

548; rolls 548, 558, 559; *see also* Bigod

Marshal, John **IV** 26

Marshal, John the **III** 207, 208

Marshal, John, sheriff of Yorkshire **III** 353

Marshal, Richard the, earl of Pembroke: and Hubert de Burgh **IV** 51; war against Henry III and his death 53–5, 57–8

Marshal, William, earl of Pembroke **III** 15, 180, 250, 357, 484; property 297, 432, 441; ignores rebellion in Wales 301; shelters William de Braose 315; faithful to John 317, 486; marriage to Isabel 347; peacemaker 316, 430, 441

Marshal, William the, earl of Pembroke: *rector regni* **IV** 2–4, 6–17; death 17; division of Irish lands after death of last son (1245) 564

Marshal, William the, junior, earl of Pembroke **IV** 10, 15, 26, 40, 76; marries Eleanor, sister of Henry III 41; in Ireland and Wales 42–3, 394–6; command in Brittany (1230) 95; dies (1231) 96

Marshall, Alfred **XIV** 501

Marshall, court of **V** 96, 489; office of 53, 265, 394, 395; *see* Percy

Marshall, George: wants direct attack on Germany **XV** 553, 555; North Africa 560; wants to shift to Pacific 562; goes to Algiers 564; Churchill wrangles with 573; does not become supreme commander 575

Marshall, John, nephew of William Marshal, earl of Pembroke **III** 473

Marshall, William **VII** 432

Marshall, William, Lord of Hengham **V** 10

Marshalsea, prison **VI** 77

marshes **Ia** 83, 84, 101–2, 319

Marsiglio of Padua **V** 290; **VII** 423

Marsin, Marshal **X** 208

Marson, Revd C. L. **XIV** 544

Marston, John **VIII** 300; **IX** 392

Marston Moor, battle **IX** 136–7

Martel, Geoffrey, count of Anjou **II** 585, 607

Martel, Guillaume, lord of Bacqueville **VI** 141

Martel, Philip **IV** 278, 313, 652, 657–8

Martel, William **III** 156

Martiannius Pulcher, M. **Ia** 254

Martin (Hants, formerly Wilts.) **III** 54

Martin, David, bishop of St David's (1296–1328) **V** 10

Martin, Geoffrey **V** 455

Martin, Hugh **V** 429

Martin, Kingsley **XV** 310–11

Martin, Lord William of Kemys **V** 10, 22

Martin, Mr, MP **XII** 110

Martin IV, Pope (1281–5) **IV** 248; Peter of Aragon 251, 253–5, 258; issues general absolution for sacrilege in baronial and Welsh wars 434; Edward I's seizure of papal taxes (1283) 506

Martin V, Pope **VI** 135, 198, 200, 259, 268; campaign against Provisors 234–5; Archbishop Chichele 235, 236; *leges Anglia* suspects 236; subsidy appeal 237; Albergati named as French legate 257; bulls received 430; 'lords of the council' 434

Martin, Richard **XIII** 470

Martin, William (1696–1756), Admiral **XI** 240, 244

Martin of Bracara **Ia** 736

Martin Marprelate **VIII** 201, 202

Martineau, Miss **XIII** 543, 549; biography 549

Martinengo, papal nuncio **VIII** 27

Martinique **X** 325, 330; capture **XII** 75; returned to France 85, 410

Martinus, Flavius **Ia** 345, 358

Martyn, Richard, envoy to Charles the Bold **VI** 575, 576

Martyr, Peter **VIII** 192

Martyr Worthy, cemetery **Ia** 693, 694

martyrology, Catholic **IX** 208–11

martyrs: Roman Catholic **VII** 362, 401; Protestant 550–3

Martyrs, Book of **VIII** 283

martyrs **Ia** 466; tombs and shrines 695, 731; Caerleon 718, 721; St Alban 720; late, in Tyrol 735

Maruffo, money broker **VII** 241

Marvell, Andrew **X** 364, 367

Marx, Karl **XIII** 144, 191; **XIV** 100, 334; **XV** 260

Mary, abbess of Shaftesbury **III** 243

Mary, Baroness Boteler's coheiress **VI** 320

Mary, daughter of Edward I, a nun at Amesbury **IV** 268

Mary, duchess of Brittany **V** 268

Mary, Princess **IX** 218, 220

Mary, Queen: on George VI **XV** 402; goes to Badminton 457

Mary I, queen of England (1553–8), daughter of Henry VIII **VII** 299, 385, 479, 576; Thomas Linacre 242; council in Marches of Wales (1525) 297; to marry Dauphin (1518) 308; betrothed to Charles V (1522) 311, 312; suggestion of marriage to James V (1524) 314, 325; to marry Francis I or one of his sons 317, 324, 341, 404, 408; accounts of the Reformation 322; possibility of match with Richmond 325; Jane Seymour 380; Pilgrims wish to have legitimized 391; effects of dissolution 401; Act of Succession (1544) 413; Edward Seymour 420; Henry's *imperium merum* 422; steelyards 475; Edward's relationship with 480; Edward's death 481–2, 524–5, 526; secured in her Mass by Charles V 486; Edward's reign 488–9; extruded for rise of Protestantism 511–12; defies reformers 517–18; Edward's 'devise' and Lady Jane Grey 523–5; Northumberland plans *coup* 526; resolution on Edward's death 526–7; proclaimed queen and enters London 528–30; in council 531–2; at first moderate 533; character 533–5; determined on Spanish marriage 534–8; Wyatt rebellion 539; married to Philip (25 July 1554) 541, 548–9; restores Roman Catholicism 543–7; responsible for burnings 550; Latimer Ridley and Cranmer (1555–6) 551–2; unhappiness 553–4; dilemma between Pope and Pole 556–7; stricken by loss of Calais 559; death (17 Nov. 1558) 560; estimate 560–1; royal authority 562; alliance of Crown and Commons 566–7; tradition in religion 569; printers and patronage 578; educated in music 590; portrait 599, 601; coinage 607; her reactionary legislation swept away **VIII** 14, 17

Mary II, queen of England (1689–1694) (b. 1662) **XI** 15, 112

Mary, queen of Scots *see* Stuart, Mary

Mary, wife of Eustace of Boulogne **III** 115, 132, 268, 270

Mary, wife of William of Orange, afterwards queen **X** 88, 100, 146, 151, 184

Mary of Burgundy, daughter of Charles the Bold, wife of Maximilian **VII** 84

Mary d'Este, afterwards queen-consort **X** 81

Mary of Guelders, queen-mother of Scotland **VI** 523; loans to Queen Margaret 527

Mary of Guise, duchess of Longueville, wife of James V **VII** 363, 402, 484, 486

Mary of Hungary, sister of Charles V, governess of the Netherlands **VII** 412

Mary of Hungary, wife of Charles of Salerno **IV** 283

Mary of Modena, queen (1658–1718) **XI** 158

Mary Tudor, daughter of Henry VII, queen of France and duchess of Suffolk **VII** 183, 187, 599; betrothed to archduke Charles (Charles V) (Dec. 1507) **VII** 179, 180, 187, 300; marriage prepared (1513) 279; marries Louis XII of France (1514) 284; marries Charles Brandon (1515) 305

Maryland **IX** 343; **X** 334, 337, 338

Maryport (Cumbria): fort **Ia** 177, 260; *singulares* 521; burial of altars 683, 702; Christian symbols 733

Masaryk, T. **XV** 107, 439

Masefield, John **XIV** 549

Maseres, Francis, attorney-general of Quebec **XII** 212

Maserfeld, Maserfelth (possibly Oswestry), battle **II** 82, 203

Masham (N. Yorks.) **VI** 60; prebend 26

Masham, Abigail, Lady Masham **X** 225, 230

Maskelyne, Nevil (1732–1811), astronomer **XI** 381

Mason (Mazon), John le, merchant of Bordeaux, appeal to Edward I from king of Scots **IV** 610

Mason, major of Marines, and attacks on French settlements in West Africa (1758) **XI** 363

Mason College, Birmingham **XIV** 147, 321

masons **Ia** 514, 697; wages **VI** 380–2; master masons' style 648

masque, the **IX** 387

Massachusetts **IX** 302–3, 339–43, 346; **X** 333, 336, 337

Massachusetts circular **XII** 191

Massena **XII** 426, 485–8

Massey, Sir Edward **IX** 134

Massinger, Philip **VIII** 302; **IX** 394

Massingham, carving and sculpting family **VI** 648

Massingham, H. W. **XIV** 316, 401; and *Nation* **XV** 27, 252, 311

Masson, David, quoted on Scotland **XI** 285

Massue, Henri de, earl of Galway, marquis de Ruvigny **X** 89, 189, 213, 215

Master agreement **XV** 533

master of ordnance, office of **VIII** 407

Masters, Richard **VII** 361

Masulipatam **X** 349, 352

Matabeleland: conquest **XIV** 212; revolt after Jameson Raid 236–7

Matapan, battle **XV** 526

mathematics **IX** 356; **X** 373–5; **XI** 378

Mathew, Father **XIII** 348

Mathews, Thomas, Admiral (1676–1751) **XI** 226, 229, 247, 248

Matilda, abbess of Essen **II** 347, 461

Matilda, Cornish woman **III** 402

Matilda, daughter of Fulk V, count of Anjou **III** 123, 124, 126

Matilda, daughter of Henry II, wife of Henry the Lion, duke of Saxony **III** 90, 215, 328

Matilda, daughter of Henry the Lion, duke of Saxony **III** 279

Matilda, Empress **III** 69, 113, 115, 303; marriage with Emperor Henry V 126; with Geoffrey of Anjou 128–9; claim to the throne 131, 135; in Normandy 134; appeals to pope 135, 192–3; lands in England 138; strength of her position 138, 142; *Domina Anglorum* 3, 143; driven from London 143, 197; from Winchester 144; from Oxford 145; leaves England 148, 150; creation of earls by 157; monastic development under 186, 188; relations with Church 180, 191, 200; education 243; relations with Scotland 269, 272; later life 326

Matilda, Queen, daughter of Henry I **VII** 325

Matilda, wife of Henry, duke of Brabant **III** 440

Matilda, wife of Henry I (Eadgyth or Edith) **III** 2, 114, 115, 268

Matilda, wife of William I, Conqueror **II** 585, 601; **III** 128

Matilda of Boulogne, wife of King Stephen **III** 115, 132, 164, 270, 440; gains support 143–4; grants to Knights Templars 189; pacifies David 272

Matilda de Laigle, wife of Robert Mowbray **III** 109–10

Matilda of Ramsbury **III** 137, 183

Matlock **X** 409

Matres (goddesses) **Ia** 708; Matres Aufaniae 669

Matthew, count of Boulogne **III** 335, 440

Matthew, count of Flanders **III** 440

Matthew, Thomas: his Bible **VII** 397

Matthew Paris: on St Edmund of Abingdon **IV** 57, 58; interest in Exchequer 65; on kingship 72; on the crises (1238 and 1244) 76–9; Tartars 110; on the years (1201–50) 114; dispute between earls of Leicester and Gloucester (1259) 147; success of Llywelyn ap Gruffydd 401; Grosseteste's inquisitions into morals of laity 455; Henry III and the Scots 593

Matthews, Henry, Lord Llandaff **XIV** 181, 204; biography 172

Matthews, John **Ia** 399, 409, 419, 431–2, 435, 495; aristocrats 399, 447; rescript 443; rich survival 449–52; Roman expulsion 477; Loire upper-class 492–3

Maubeuge, British Expeditionary Force **XV** 7

Mauclerc *see* Dreux, Peter of

Mauclerc, Walter **III** 457, 468

Mauclerc, Walter, bishop of Carlisle, treasurer **IV** 48, 51

Maudelyn, Richard, priest **VI** 25

Maudit, John **V** 508

Maudslay, Henry (1771–1831) **XII** 508; biography **XIII** 5

Mauduit, I. (1708–87) **XII** 71

Mauger, bishop of Worcester **III** 445–6

Maule, Henry (b. ?1676) bishop **XI** 290

Mauléon (Poitou) **IV** 90

Mauléon, Savari de **IV** 3; seneschal of Poitou 90, 91

Mauléon, Savory de **III** 480

Mauley, Sir Edward **V** 40

Mauley, Peter de **IV** 22, 23

Mauley, Peter, Lord **VI** 320

Maupertius **V** 138

Maupertuis, P. L. Moreau de (1698–1759), mathematician **XI** 396

Mauretania **Ia** 110; estates 600

Maureux (Dordogne), Henry IV grants protection **VI** 110

Maureward, Thomas, ex-sheriff of Warwickshire and Leicestershire **VI** 131

Maurice, Sir Frederick: charges against Lloyd George **XIV** 29; **XV** 104–5, 117–18; debate on charges 74, 105, 126, 219

Maurice, Frederick Dennison **XIII** 495–6, 520–1; biography 495

Maurice, Prince **IX** 133

Maurice the Chancellor, bishop of London **II** 642; **III** 170

Maurice Tiberius, gold coin **Ib** 168

Maurienne, count of *see* Humbert III

Mauritius **XII** 166, 562; **XIII** 194, 365, 373

mausolea **Ia** 701–3, 731–2

Mauvillon, Jacob M. (1743–94): quoted on British officers **XI** 216

Mauvissière, Castlenau de **VIII** 86–7, 377

Mawer, Allen **II** 358

Max Emmanuel, elector of Bavaria **X** 197, 234

Maxentius, Emperor **Ia** 324–6, 340, 351

Maxey (Cambs.), villa **Ia** 604

Maximian, Emperor **Ia** 287–304; Caesar 287; Bacaudae 287; Augustus 288; Rhine-Danube frontier 288, 307; Carausius 288–93, 301; tetrarch 290, 293, 301; inscriptions 293, 314; settlement of Franks 303, 355; son proclaimed emperor 324

Maximilian, Archduke **VI** 583, 585, 588, 628

Maximilian II, Emperor **VIII** 169

Maximilian, Joseph, elector of Bavaria (1745–77) (b. 1727): makes peace with Maria Theresa **XI** 261

Maximilian, king of the Romans (1493–1519) **VII** 81, 89, 152, 191, 469; subjects refuse to accept as regent 84; treaty of Arras (1482) 85, 99; imprisoned in Bruges (1488) 87; Henry VII's dealings in Brittany 91–3; Flemish pirates 92; alliance with Henry 96; defence of the Netherlands 98–9; peace treaty with France over Netherlands 99–101; deserts Brittany 101; proxy marriage to Anne of Brittany (1491) 103; war against king of Bohemia 104; Anne ignores proxy marriage and marries Charles 105; fails to assist Henry in military preparation 106–7; Treaty of Étaples (1492) 109–10; wed to Bianca (1493) 113–14; death (Jan. 1519) 308; League of Venice (1495) 115; Perkin Warbeck 117–18, 121, 125, 138, 139; death of Charles VII 149; French gains in Italy 155; Turkish war 156; treaty terms (1502) 159; defence of Milanese against 163; supports White Rose 167–8, 170, 183; Anglo-Burgundian treaties (1506) 185; Henry and Margaret of Savoy marriage proposals 185–6, 187; Erasmus' *Praise of Folly* 255; Lateran council (1512) 272; joins Holy League (1512) 275; Lille treaty for war on France 276, 283; joins Henry at Thérouanne 279; adheres to truce with Louis (1514) 283–4; Anglo-French marriage treaty (1514) 284–5; attempts to recover Milan 306; treaty of Noyon (1516) 307

Maximilian of Bavaria **IX** 58

Maximin Daia, Emperor **Ia** 316

Maximus **Ib** 121

Maximus (I), Governor **Ia** 251

Maximus, praetorian prefect **Ia** 394–5, 400

Maximus (II), usurper **Ia** 432–3, 446

Maximus (III) Magnus *see* Magnus Maximus

Maximus (IV) of Turin, bishop **Ia** 735

Maxton, J.: Campbell case **XV** 225; great orator 235; extremist 347; supports Popular Front 397; blesses Chamberlain's mission 429

Maxton (Roxburgh) **IV** 230

Maxwell, Gordon **Ia** 201

Maxwell, Sir J. **XV** 56

Maxwell, James **IX** 99

Maxwell, Lord **VIII** 48

Maxwell, William, 5th earl of Nithsdale (1676–1744) **XI** 162

May, Sir George: economy committee 287, 288, 291; tariff committee 330

Mayday, the Evil **VII** 298, 468

Mayer, Tobias (1723–62), mathematician **XI** 381

Mayerne, Sir Theodore **VIII** 314

Mayflower **IX** 330

Maynooth **VII** 365

Maynooth College, grant to **XIII** 118, 123, 189, 351, 362

Mayo (Ireland), English monastery of Inishboffin **II** 124; **V** 233

Maypoles **IX** 76, 311

Mazarin **X** 76
Mazarin, Jules, Cardinal **IX** 212, 218, 230, 232–3
Mazzini, G. **XIII** 300, 349
M'Donald **XII** 206
Mead, Richard (1673–1754), physician **XI** 388; art collection 405
Meadows, Sir Philip, the elder **X** 69
Meagher, Thomas Francis **XIII** 349
means test **XV** 352–3, 367, 393
Meanware **II** 294
Mearcredesburna **Ib** 136; river, battle by 485; appendix I(b); battle by **II** 17
Measures, assize (1196) **III** 86
measures, of cloth **IV** 347
meat **Ia** 619–20, 627; refrigeration, invention **XIV** 119–20; gradual supersession of live cattle trade 120–1
Meath, bishop of *see* Payne, John
Meath (Ireland) **II** 88; **III** 302, 310, 312, 315; subinfeudation 316; **V** 41, 42, 43, 44; obedient shire 232; county **VI** 425
Meautis, John, French secretary to Henry VII **VII** 138
Meaux (Seine-et-Marne) **III** 123, 296; **VI** 175; *bailliage* 177; market 200, 666; siege 327
Meaux (Yorks.), Cistercian abbey **III** 84; **IV** 634; **VI** 295, 446–7
Mecca **VII** 225
Mechanics' Institutes **XIII** 14, 494–5
Mechlin **VII** 121, 186
Mecklenburg **VI** 69
medallions **Ia** 310–11
Medeshamstede *see* Peterborough (Northants)
Medford, Richard, bishop of Chichester (1390–5), of Salisbury (1395–1407) **V** 437, 474
Medford, Richard, bishop of Salisbury **VI** 271
Medford, Walter, dean of Wells **VI** 234
Medici, Caterina de', marries

Henry of France (Henry II, 1547–59) **VII** 340
Medici, Cosimo de' **VII** 212
Medici, family **VII** 319, 326
Medici, Giovanni de' *see* Leo X, Pope
Medici, Giulo de' *see* Clement VII
Medici, Lorenzo de' (d. 1492) **VII** 113
Medici, Piero de' **VII** 113, 114
Medici, society, loans to Edward IV **VI** 592
medicine: progress of **VIII** 311–14; **IX** 364–7; Edinburgh medical school **X** 264; and surgery **XI** 378, 384, 389–93; inoculation for smallpox 392; (1760) **XII** 11
Médicis, Catherine de **VIII** 63; assumed regency 48; treatment of Huguenots 54, 159; and Elizabeth's mediation 55, 57, 59, 344; Coligny's assassination 157; Alençon marriage proposal 158, 160; claimant, Portuguese succession 352
Medieval scholars, listing **VI** 3
medieval villages **Ia** 611
medieval world: periodization **Ia** 285–6, 493–4, 498; population estimates 544–5
Medina del Campo **VII** 104, 110, 148, 172, 221; signing and implications 94–6; treaty ratified by Spain (1489) 96; never ratified 97
Medina Sidonia, duke of: command of armada **VIII** 396, 400; his instructions 397, 401; difficulties 401; retreat to Spain 402, 404
Mediterranean **Ia** 37, 429, 500, 506, 667; **III** 88, 94, 95, 434, 435; warships from 436; origin of mariner's compass 437; law of the sea 439; **V** 122, 138, 242, 354, 358; imports 360; **VII** 83, 111, 220, 223, 306; Turkish threat 341; imports 470; British fleet (1694) **X** 171; shipping losses during

First World War **XV** 85; British claim mastery 384; fleet 400, 486; campaign 515, 520–2; Italian convoys 523; Hitler's ambitions 524; British losses 530–1; ABC-1 agreement 536; shipping 555; second front 558; further campaign 560, 563; Americans divert landing craft 572; Churchill wishes to persist in 573–4; British command 575; loses significance 576

Medway, river (Miodowæge), battle **Ia** 83, 92; **Ib** 75, 115, 123, 125; map 2 xxx; **II** 392, 732; **V** 408

Meerut, trial **XV** 255

Mees, William **V** 90

Megiddo, battle **XV** 110

Mehemet Ali, pasha of Egypt: early history **XIII** 215–16; sends an expedition to Greece 216–17; defeat of his fleet at Navarino 219; first attack on Mahmud II 233–4; second attack on Mahmud II 236–7; accepts conditions laid down by the Powers 238

Meighen, A. **XV** 261

Mein Kampf **XV** 95

Meinhard, duke of Schomberg **X** 60, 138, 180, 307; death 308

Melancthon, Philip **VII** 382

Melania **Ia** 600, 727

Melba, Dame Nellie **XV** 232

Melbourne, Viscount **XIV** 10, 137; *see also* Lamb, William

Melcombe Regis **VII** 171, 184

Melfi **VII** 319

Melfort, earls of *see* Drummond, John

Melisende, wife of Fulk V, count of Anjou **III** 128, 343

Melksham (Wilts.), hundred **VI** 365

Mellifont (Cistercian abbey in Ireland), and its daughter houses **IV** 568

Mellitus, bishop of London **II** 109, 112, 121

Mellor, William **XV** 142, 381

Melrose (Roxburgh): monastery **II** 85, 126, 678; **III** 274; abbey **V** 440; **VI** 36; **VII** 407

Melton (Surrey), priory **VI** 116

Melton, Nicholas **VII** 387

Melton, William, archbishop of York (1317–40), keeper of the privy seal (1307–12), treasurer (1330–1) **V** 3, 8, 103, 118, 154, 264; keeper of the wardrobe 46; royal emissary 47; in command at Myton 56; at Sherburn assembly 61–2; authorizes truces with Scots 75; protests against murder of Stapledon 93; wealth and benefactions 298–9

Melton Mowbray (Leics.) **Ib** 176; **II** 525; **III** 481; production of cheeses **XII** 34

Melun (Seine-et-Marne): council at **III** 483; **VI** 175, 187, 257; *bailliage* 177, 191

Melville, Sir James **VIII** 90, 92, 100

Melville, Robert **VIII** 104, 107

Melville, Viscount *see* Dundas

Membury, Simon de **VI** 288

Memoirs of an Infantry Officer **XV** 361

men-at-arms: mounted **IV** 547, 548–9, 553, 554

Menai Straits **III** 286

Menander **III** 257

Menaphon **VIII** 293

Menapii **Ia** 288

Menasseh ben Israel **IX** 214

mendicants **VI** 61, 296–9

Mendip, Lord *see* Ellis, Welbore

Mendip hills: metals **Ia** 595, 634–7; **III** 82; **V** 271; **VII** 36, 461

Mendoza, Bernardino de **VIII** 164; soldier 345, 392; witness to Anjou courtship 355; Jesuit conspiracy 360–2; expelled from England 363–4; English succession 390–1; Spanish armada 394–5, 403, 405

Meno, Pregent, Breton merchant **VII** 119

Menschikoff, Prince **XIII** 255-8, 264

Mensdorff, Count, Smuts negotiates with **XV** 115-16

Menteith, earldom **IV** 581

Meon, river **Ib** 148; map 2 xxx; map 3 xxxi

Meopham, Simon, archbishop of Canterbury (1328-33) **V** 297

Mepal (Cambs.) **V** 308

Merantun, battle **II** 249

Mercadier **III** 372, 377; **IV** 544

mercantilism **IX** 316; system discussed by Adam Smith **X** 44-5; **XII** 14-19, 23-5, 174, 180-2, 276; French trade treaty 289; private trade theories 330; Anglo-French conflict 463

Mercator, Gerard **VIII** 241, 318

mercenaries: Frankish **Ia** 303, 306, 311-12; increased use of 417, 440; hypothetical in Britain 386-8; Saxons in Britain 498, 500; *see also* foederati

mercenary troops in England **IV** 12-13; (1233) 54; (1260) 156, 157, 158; (1261) 163, 166; (1262) 171, 176, 181; (1265) 199; (1267) 214; *see also* Artois; Boulogne: St Pol; money fiefs

Mercers Company, Acts of Court **VI** 352

Merchant Adventurers **VI** 350-2; organization 351; London groups 352; **VII** 121, 124, 220, 221; origin and structure 472-5; voyages of discovery 507; **VIII** 239; **IX** 291, 319, 333; **X** 47

merchant law **IV** 620, 623, 625, 627, 630-2; common law 620, 625, 626; in London 626, 627

Merchant Staplers **VII** 472, 474

Merchant Taylors **VII** 460, 465; school **XII** 56

merchants **Ia** 57, 299, 457; with army 514; Barates 514, 659; London 582; in towns 584-6; wine merchants 653; guilds 659;

attracted to Mithraism 711, 712, 668; Christianity 717-18; home and foreign **IV** 191, 505-6; reconciliation with Portsmen 207; Italian 304-5, 519, 662, 670, 672; foreign cloth 347-8; land transactions 519; Flemish 648; Crown and merchants 618-37; English at Antwerp 663; German, and Scots 687; Spanish and Portuguese 644; **IX** 128, 286, 336

merchet, payment **III** 20, 38, 40, 41; **IV** 682

Mercia **Ia** 190; **Ib** 39, 42-3, 59, 86, 184-6; supremacy 141; Humbrenses 175; foundations 182; map 4 xxxii; **II** 28, 32; meaning of name 40; scholarship 178, 190, 270-1; nature of kingdom 202; influence of its supremacy on smaller kingdoms 208-9, 236; conquered by Egbert 232; revival under Wiglaf 233-4; Danish invasions 248, 250-2; divided between Danes and King Ceolwulf II, 254; Danish settlement in 254-5; English, boundaries 321-2

Mercian law, shires **II** 505-9

Mercians **II** 43; eminence of their dynasty 39, 232; ends in Ceolwulf I, 232; north and south 40

Mercier, Philip, painter (1689-1760) **XII** 3

Mercoeur, duc de *see* Emmanuel, Philip

Mercurius Politicus **IX** 413

Mercury **Ia** 669

Mere Castle (Wilts.) **IV** 716

Meredith, George **XIII** 559, 598; **XIV** 144, 145, 160, 331; **XV** 178

Meredith, William, MP (d. 1790) **XII** 102, 121, 213

Meresig *see* Mersea Island (Essex)

Mereworth (Kent), manor **VI** 333

Merioneth **VI** 40, 41

Merivale, Herman **XIII** 368

Merke, Thomas, bishop of Carlisle (1397–9) **V** 474, 494

Merke, Thomas, bishop of Carlisle **VI** 22, 26; conspiracy 25

Merleswein **II** 628

Merlin, prophesy **IV** 719

Merlin, yacht **X** 77

Merobaudes **Ia** 479

Merovech, Merovingians **Ia** 494, 496

Mers-el-Kebir **XV** 494

Mersea Island (Meresig) (Essex) **II** 266, 268, 732

Mersey (Mærse), river **II** 732; **III** 275

Mersey tunnel **XV** 338

Mersham, nr. Ashford (Kent) **II** 311

Merston Boteler (War.), manor **VI** 320

Merston, John, keeper of king's jewels **VI** 481

Merton, Walter de, king's clerk, chancellor, bishop of Rochester (1274–7) **IV** 157, 165, 176, 225, 486; **V** 500

Merton Priory (Surrey) **III** 186, 197; **IV** 50

Merton: legislation in council (1236) **IV** 69–71, 367, 370; provincial council (1258) 457; statute (1235) **VII** 448

Meschin, William, brother of Rannult, earl of Chester **III** 271

Mesopotamia **Ia** 169; campaign **XV** 49, 98; Anglo-French agreement 50, 70; inquiry on campaign 58; malaria 126; *see also* Iraq

messengers, king's **IV** 767

Messina **III** 354, 355, 359–60, 363, 438

Mestrell, Eloye **VII** 608

metal industries **X** 50

metal-work **X** 396–7

metals: hoard **Ia** 15, 605, 680; working 537, 540; transport 563; economic significance 617, 630; votive offerings 689; *see also* gold;

iron, etc.

Metcalf, John (1717–1810) **XI** 104

Metcalfe, Sir Charles Theophilus **XIII** 404–5; biography 404

Metham, Yorkshire family name **VI** 327

Methodism **X** 23–4; development and spread **XII** 38; in education 39; *see also* Wesleyanism

Methuen, John **X** 207

Methuen, Lord **XIV** 29, 253, 347

Methuen, Sir Paul (1672–1757) **XI** 168

Methuen Treaty **X** 207

Methven, Bruce routed (1306) **IV** 715, 716

Metilius Nepos, P. **Ia** 152–3

Metropolitan Water Board **XV** 257

Metternich, Prince Carl **XII** 556, 559, 563, 566, 570; **XIII** 117, 195, 197, 199, 203–4; Russia 208; first principles 224; Turkish reform 235; overthrown 245; influence 247; **XV** 177

Metz **III** 127; **VII** 535; capitulation **XIV** 4, 6, 7, 9; **XV** 109

Meulan (Seine-et-Oise) **VI** 111, 172, 183, 200, 205; conference 180; capitulates 239; seized and recaptured 241

Meulan, county **II** 620

Meulan, Robert, count of **III** 118, 179; *see also* Waleran

Meun, Jean de **V** 531

Meung (Loiret) **VI** 114, 245, 247, 250

Mewtas, Sir Peter **VIII** 71

Mexico **VII** 557, 561; **IX** 337; **XIII** 211, 314; **XV** 84

Mexico, Gulf of **X** 343

Meyerburg Züschen, Clara Elizabeth von, countess of Platen 'the elder' **XI** 354

Mézières **VII** 311

Michael Palaeologus, Emperor **IV** 231, 232, 253

Michelangelo Buonarroti **VII** 592

Michelborne, Sir Edward **IX** 334

Micheldever **Ib** 149; map 3 xxxi
Michelle of France, Philip of Burgundy's wife **VI** 256
Mickfield (Suffolk) **Ia** 561
Midas **VIII** 296
Middelburg **V** 128, 352, 355; wine staple 363; wool staple 430, 436
Middeltun *see* King's Milton (Kent); Milton Abbas (Dorset)
Middle, truce (1234) **IV** 60, 397
Middle Angles **II** 9, 40, 42–3, 49; conversion 120
Middle Anglia **Ib** 59, 82, 86–7, 100, 107; mixed cemeteries 112; Ceawlin saga 166–7; political history 173; Sancton pottery 193; map 2 xxx; map 3 xxxi
Middle Carlton (Lincs.) **V** 332
middle classes, the **IX** 286–7, 350–1
Middle East: new British empire **XV** 152; conflicts with France 215; RAF dominate 231; Wavell commands 460; Hitler has no plans in 522, 524; expansion of command 523; Americans condemn 529; Canadian forces 558
Middle Saxons **Ib** 174; map 2 xxx; **II** 38, 54–5; boundaries 54–5; Surrey a province 54
Middleburg, 'Midilburg' **VI** 351; **VIII** 239
Middleham (N. Yorks.), castle **VI** 8, 351, 557, 607; lordship and castle 321, 336; college 609; **VII** 67, 204
Middlesex **Ia** 43; **Ib** 106; **II** 54, 234, 574; **III** 69, 71, 146, 404; **V** 92, 337, 411, 456; **VII** 379, 528; **IX** 305; magistrates **XII** 47, 131, 140; Wilkes as candidate 131–7, 142, 149; election (1779) 227; hospital, London, foundation 11; population **XV** 167
Middlesex, earl of *see* Cranfield
Middleton (Lancs.) **VI** 33
Middleton, Alice **VII** 248
Middleton, Charles, 1st Baron Barham (1726–1813), first lord of

admiralty (1805–6) **XII** 420, 431, 581
Middleton, Charles, 2nd earl of **X** 123
Middleton, Conyers (1683–1750), *Life of Cicero* **XI** 85, 140, 393
Middleton, 2nd earl of *see* Charles
Middleton, Sir Gilbert **V** 40–1, 204
Middleton, John, earl of **IX** 169
Middleton, Nathaniel **XII** 309, 318
Middleton, Richard of *see* Richard of Middleton
Middleton, Sir T. H. **XIV** 511
Middleton, Thomas **VIII** 300; **IX** 392, 395
Middleton, William, bishop of Norwich (1278–88) **IV** 481–2, 487, 491
Midhat Pasha **XIV** 46
Midland bank **XV** 196
Midlands **Ia** 12, 14, 120, 386
Midleton, Alan Broderick, Viscount (1656–1728) **XI** 294
Midleton, Viscount *see* Brodrick, St John
midwifery **X** 419
Midwinter, William **VI** 361
Miele, Dr **XIV** 519
migration: British, to Brittany **II** 5; reverse, from Britain to the Continent 5–8; nature of English, to Britain 277–8
Miguel, Dom, of Portugal **XIII** 211–12, 231–2
Miguel, Master (Zittoz?) **VII** 598
Milan: battle **Ia** 270; edict 285; imperial court 354, 403, 425, 429; St Ambrose 401, 402, 408; **III** 331; **V** 267, 285, 476; **VII** 83, 84, 106, 404; position in politics of Italy 112–14; League of Venice (1495) 115; Franco-Spanish *Entente* (1489) 149–50; occupied by France (1499) 152; regained by Sforza (1500) but retaken by France 152; Louis XII invested (1505) 154; Louis seeks Scottish aid for defence 163; Julius II

military actions (*cont.*)
Rome (1526–7) 317; St Andrews (1546–7) 408, 483; Sluys (1492) 108; Tournai (1513) 279; Tournai (1521) 311; Tunis (1535) 341; Vannes (1487) 86; Vienna (1529) 320; Wark (1513) 280; Wark (1524) 313; Waterford (1487) 73; Waterford (1495) 132

military conversations: Anglo-French **XIV** 399–400; Anglo-Belgian 400

Military Co-ordination Committee **XV** 472

Military Cross **XV** 59, 61, 175

military equipment **Ia** 74–5, 77, 386–8, 412, 421–3; archeological finds 440, 461

military glory **Ia** 38–9, 52–3, 61, 70, 140; Hadrian 172, 364; social mobility 271; Roman ideal 304; Britain reorganized 315; lack of realism in Late Empire 419

military handbooks **X** 168

military insignia **Ia** 332–3, 381, 387, 390, 412; civil/military blurring 467, 520

Military Service Act: first (1916) **XV** 53; second (1916) 55; (1918) 103–4

militia **X** 168, 266–7; **XII** 365, 415

Militia Acts (1802) **XII** 415; (1803) 415

Milk Street, London, timber building **Ia** 233

Mill, James **XIII** 36, 368, 445, 452, 492; on purpose of imprisonment 468

Mill, John Stuart **XII** 331; **XIII** 10, 35, 38, 159, 188; South America 223; on E. J. Ayre 374; Indian trade 406; state action 446; Poor Law Amendment Act 452; school examinations 482; religion 533; *Political Economy* 535; works 543–6; biography 544; **XIV** 136, 145, 163; **XV** 176

Millais, Sir J. E. **XIII** 591–3; **XIV** 156, 167

Millbrook (Beds.), manor and advowson **VI** 330

Millenary Petition **IX** 7, 69–70, 78

Miller, Hunter **XIII** 326

Miller, Mr, publisher **XII** 141

Millington, William, King's College Provost **VI** 669, 671

Milman, Henry Hart **XIII** 507

Milner, Alfred, afterwards Viscount: biography **XIV** 217; Harcourt's death duties 217; character 245; Graaff-Reinet speech 246; 'helots' despatch 247; at Bloemfontein Conference 248; diplomacy criticized 248; disagreement with Kitchener 345; administration after war 348; adopts Chinese labour policy 377; retires from South Africa 389; supports Licensing Bill 409; biography **XV** 18; mentions evacuation from Gallipoli 18; War Cabinet 75; opposes Flanders offensive 87; favours compromise peace 95, 108; against Robertson 99; Doullens conference 101–2; secretary for war 104; Maurice debate 118; colonial secretary 130; Kindergarten 418

Milner, Isaac (1750–1820), mathematician **XI** 140

Milton (Berks.) **II** 25

Milton (Kent) **II** 266; council at 349; manor **IV** 10

Milton, John (1608–74) **IX** 125, 173, 390, 400, 403, 407; bitterness against Church 107; antimonarchical tracts 158–9; on toleration 194; on persecuting Catholics 206, 213; denounces army 249; on university education 356; on speculative thought 362; *Comus* 387; fondness for music 388; poet 403–5; pamphleteer 404; **X** 33, 357, 359, 363–6; **XI** 419, 433, **XV** 233

386

Milton, Viscount **XII** 498
Milton Abbas (Middletun) (Dorset), abbey **II** 451, 455, 732
Milton Abbot (Devon) **III** 227
Milvian Bridge, battle **Ia** 331, 340, 733
Milward, Mr **XII** 89
Minchinhampton Common, earthworks **Ia** 103
Minchinhampton (Glos.) **III** 45, 54; **V** 369
Mincio **VII** 271
minerals in England **VII** 36
Miners' Federation of Great Britain: Sankey Commission **XV** 140; strike (1920) 144; defeated 145–6; becomes National Union of Mineworkers 567
Minerva **Ia** 515, 659, 666, 682, 687
The Mines for the Nation **XV** 141
Mines, Royal School of **XIII** 156, 500, 565–7
miniature painters **IX** 374–6
mining **Ia** 224, 338, 546, 632–5; silver 39; tin 44, 595; lead 570, 595; coal 631; iron 686; **V** 241, 370–2; **VII** 461
ministerial changes during the French war **X** 186–7
Ministers of the Crown Act (1937) **XV** 409
ministers of state: growth of Cabinet **XI** 35–40; powers 33–4; prime minister 34–5, 211; ministers, relation to Crown **XIII** 23–5, 101, 248–50; *see also* Crown; George I; George II
ministries (1714) **XI** 153–6, 163–4; split (1717) 168; reconciliation 172; 'Broadbottom Administration' 250, 257–8; Pelham 259, 264, 334; changes (1725) 303; Newcastle (1746–54) 347–5; Pitt (1756) 354–5; Pitt and Newcastle (1757) 355 *see also* Walpole
Minkowski **XIV** 552
Minorca **X** 215, 218, 348; **XI** 195, 198, 207, 230, 368; British officers

216; emperor promises return to Spain 244; French landing 351; lost to French 352; Richelieu, 360; Britain exchanges for Belle Île; restored to Britain at peace of Paris **XII** 86; French capture 226; Spanish claim 255; British capture 379; as a base 381; returned to Spain 409
Minority movement **XV** 349
Minot, Lawrence **V** 150, 526
minster, *matrix ecclesia* **II** 148–9, 152–6, 668
Minster in Thanet, monastery **II** 47, 229; abbess of *see* Eadburg; Mildthryth
The Mint **XV** 186
mint and exchange **IV** 65; *see also* exchanges
Minting (Lincs.) **II** 49
minting places named **II** 336, 482, 527, 535–7, 581; *see also* coinage; currency
Minto, 2nd earl of **XIII** 245, 522
Minto, 4th earl of **XIV** 421
Minto, Gilbert, 1st earl of (1751–1814) **XII** 489
mints: Trier **Ia** 310, 429, 433, 446, 479; Continent 318, 661; London 327, 532; Arles 433, 446; British 660; **II** 336; coinage 482, 527, 535–7, 581; royal **VI** 590; archbishop's 590; *see also* coinage; currency
Miodowæge *see* Medway, river
Miosson, river **V** 138
Miquelon: ceded to France (1763) **XII** 85; British capture 212; ceded to France (1783) 255; restored to France (1802) 410
Mir Jafar, established as ruler of Bengal (1757) **XI** 329
Mir Jaffir **XII** 160
Mir Kassim **XII** 160, 164
Mirabeau Castle (Poitou) **III** 332, 381–2
Miranda, Francesco (1754–1816) **XII** 472

387

Mirandola **VII** 272

Miraumont (Pas-de-Calais) **VI** 153

Mirror of Justices **IV** 521

Mirror for Magistrates **VIII** 286

mirrors **Ia** 15, 599

Mischgruppe **Ib** 55, 107

Missenden, Little (Bucks.) **VI** 132

Missiessy, Admiral **XII** 425

missionaries, English: in Frisia **II** 166–9, 175; in Germany 168–72, 175–6; in Scandinavia 462

missionary societies **XIII** 369, 390, 395, 397, 505–6

missions **X** 157, 346

Mitcham **Ib** 102, 138; map 2 xxx; map 5 68

Mitchel, John **XIII** 349–50, 357, 542

Mitchell, General Billy **XV** 390

Mitchell, Chalmers **XV** 398

Mitchell, Sir Francis **IX** 25

Mitchell, James **X** 271

Mitchell, R. J. **XV** 391

Mitchelstown shooting **XIV** 180

Mithraism, Mithras **Ia** 668, 671, 681, 711–13, 716; British popularity 732–4

Mittelfranken **Ib** 82, 194

Mixbury (Oxon.) **III** 25

M'Mahon, Colonel **XII** 492

Modius Julius **Ia** 250

Moerheb *see* Morfe Forest (Salop)

Moesia **Ia** 150, 401

Møgelby **Ib** map 5 68

moghul **VIII** 242

Mogul Empire **X** 350–1

Mohacz, Turkish victory (1526) **VII** 320

Mohammad Ali, nawab of the Carnatic (*c.*1750) **XI** 327

Mohammed **VII** 151

'Moidart, the seven men of' **XI** 252

Moigne, Thomas **VI** 450

Moira, earls of *see* Rawdon, John; Rawdon-Hastings, Francis

Moissac, wine merchants **IV** 306

Moivre, Abraham de (1667–1754), mathematician **XI** 379

Mokha **X** 349

molasses *see* sugar

Mølbjerg **Ib** map 5 68

Mold (Flint): castle **III** 291, 298; **IV** 399

mole (harbour) **Ia** 305

Molesworth, Robert, 1st Viscount (1656–1725) **XI** 305

Molesworth, Sir William **XIII** 92, 95–6, 368, 386, 391; biography 95

Moleyns, Adam, bishop of Chichester **VI** 347, 474, 480, 483, 495; murdered 492; and Pecock 683

Moleyns, Anne, *née* Whalesborough **VI** 484, 485

Moleyns, Eleanor **VI** 332; father killed 332

Moleyns, John, Lord **VI** 491, 503

Moleyns, Sir John **V** 159

Moleyns, Robert, Lord **VI** 344, 461

Molière **X** 368

Molinet, Jean, chronicler **VII** 85, 87, 99, 117, 118

Molineux, Mr, MP **VIII** 219

Molineux, Nicholas, duke of Bedford's receiver **VI** 209

Molis, Roger de **IV** 442

Molotov, Vyacheslav Mikhailovich: becomes foreign commissar **XV** 447; signs Nazi-Soviet pact 449; demands second front 553

Moltke, Count Helmuth von, the younger **XIV** 482–3, 570; and Marne **XV** 32

Moltke, H. von **XIII** 236, 322

Molyneux, Sir Thomas **V** 453

Molyneux, William **X** 320, 322, 386, 391

Mompesson, Sir Giles **IX** 25

Môn *see* Anglesey

monarchy: conception **II** 545–6; elective element 551–2

Monash, Sir John **XV** 100

monasteries: influence on conversion **II** 149; diverse origin 157–60; acceptance of Benedictine rule 158; early monastic federations 159–60; family 160–1;

double 161–2; lords of 163; bishops as protectors of 163–5; papal privileges 165; expiry during Danish invasion 444–5; place of women in monastic revival 444–5; abuses of hospitality **IV** 375; in Wales 389–90; legal studies 485; books and articles of administration and economy 762; patrons 762; **V** 122, 246, 298, 316, 450; contributions for war in Scotland 33; peace terms with Scots 75; revenues 303, 305–9; wealth 311; **IX** 274; *see also* religious houses

monastic order: character of Irish **II** 119; character of English 157–65; influence on conversion of Germany 165; double monasteries in Germany 173, 175–6; monastic revival of 10th cent. 365, 367, 445; reaction against 444–6; foreign influence on 444–5, 450–1, 453; influence on episcopate 456; influence on parochial clergy 456–7; influence on English civilization 457; books 457–60; Latin literature 458–9; influence on church in general 468

monastic revival in northern England **II** 677–8

monasticism **Ia** 728, 734

Monboddo, James Burnett, Lord (1714–99) **XI** 287

Moncada, Ugo de **VII** 317; killed (1528) 319

Monck, George, 1st duke of Albemarle **IX** 242, 247–8; subdues Scotland 169; advises Richard 236; supports the Rump 249–51; marches to London 253; in the City 254; admits excluded MPs 254–5; overtures to Charles II 256–7; part in the Restoration 258–9; **X** 3–6, 64–7, 266, 339

Monckton, Robert (1726–82), General **XI** 218, 371

Mond, Sir Alfred **XV** 249

Mond, Ludwig **XIV** 110

money: money economy **Ia** 235, 237, 373, 625, 659–62; exchange equivalents **IV** 282; of Bordeaux, Morlaas, and Tours 306; fiefs 544–6

Money, Sir Leo Chiozza **XV** 140, 261

moneyers: centralized control **II** 535–8; measure of town size 537–8; English influence on Scandinavian currency 543

Mongols **IV** 110; *see also* Tartars

Monk's Kirby **V** 295

Monk's Risborough (Bucks.) **V** 345

Monkswell, Lord *see* Collier, Sir R.

Monkwearmouth (Co. Durham), church **II** 152, 678; *see also* Wearmouth

Monmouth: castle **II** 615; **III** 287; **IV** 201; **V** 86, 88; annexed **VI** 510

Monmouth, dukes and earls of *see* Mordaunt, Charles; Scott, James

Monmouth, Geoffrey of **III** 237, 242, 255; **IV** 515; *see also* Geoffrey of Monmouth

Monmouth, Humphrey **VII** 343

Monmouth, John of **IV** 3, 4

Monmouth, John de, bishop of Llandaff (1297–1323) **V** 10

Monnet, Jean **XV** 487

monopolies **IX** 24–5, 331–6

monothelite heresy, English declaration against **II** 137, 144

Monreale, cathedral **III** 215, 226

Monro, Alexander, *primus* (1697–1767) **XI** 287, 391

Monro, Alexander, *secundus* (1733–1817) **XI** 391

Monro, Alexander, *tertius* (1773–1859) **XI** 391

Monro, Sir Charles **XV** 46

Monroe doctrine *see* United States

Mons **VIII** 157, 346; **X** 169, 219

Mons, battle **XV** 9, 17–18; Angels of 9, 18

Mons Badonicus **Ib** 11, 14, 16, 19; Saxon federates 154; site 158–60;

Montagu, William, earl of Salisbury (1349–97) **V** 255, 260, 266, 474, 479; Knight of the Garter 252

Montagu Dunk, George, earl of Halifax (1716–71) **XI** 311, 317, 320, 348

Montague, C. E. **XV** 61, 549

Montague, count of *see* Rotrou

Montague, Sir Edward (d. 1557) **VII** 529, 530

Montague, Henry, Baron, executed (1538) **VII** 396

Montague, Henry, Viscount Mandeville, earl of Manchester **IX** 122–3, 136–9, 199, 258, 357

Montague, Lord *see* Brown, Anthony

Montague, Ralph **X** 97

Montague, Richard, bishop **IX** 74; his *Appello Caesarem* 44

Montague House **X** 393

Montaigu College (Paris) **VII** 249

Montalt (Mowat), family of, and Cromarty **IV** 575

Montauban (Tarn-et-Garonne): castle **III** 442; wine merchants **IV** 306; **VI** 108; **VIII** 162

Montcalm, Louis Joseph, marquis de (1712–59) **XI** 360, 365

Montdidier (Somme) **VI** 248, 256; *prévôté* 263

Monte, Giovanni Maria del *see* Julius III

Monte, Piero da, papal envoy **VI** 346

Monte Carlo **XV** 313

Monteagle, Lord *see* Spring-Rice, T.

Monteferrato, Alan de, merchant **VI** 591

Monteith **XII** 510

Montemer, Ralph de **V** 101

Montenegro **XIV** 41, 51, 463; conflict over Scutari 467, 468, 573; **XV** 119

Montereau (Seine-et-Marne) **VI** 181, 187; tracing murderer 183

Montesquieu, Charles de Secondat, baron de (1689–1755) **XI** 51, 396;

XII 55, 138, 338

Montevideo **XV** 462

Montferrand (Auvergne) **III** 330, 332

Montferrat **VII** 340

Montferrat, Boniface, marquis of **III** 367, 377

Montferrat, Conrad, marquis of **III** 361

Montferrat, William, marquis of **III** 343

Montfichet (London), castle **III** 63

Montford, Amauri de, clerk, son of Earl Simon **IV** 206, 212, 330–1, 408

Montford, Amauri de, student of Padua **IV** 212

Montford, Eleanor de, daughter of Earl Simon, wife of Llywelyn ap Gruffydd (Oct. 1278) **IV** 331, 408, 441

Montford, Eleanor de, sister of King Henry III, widow of William the Marshal *junior*, marries Simon de Montfort (1238) **IV** 76, 107; dispute about dowry 107, 125–6, 164, 169–70, 194; after battle of Evesham 204, 206

Montford, Guy de, son of Earl Simon: captured at Evesham **IV** 202; later career in Tuscany 225–6; murders Henry of Almain (1271) 226

Montfort (l'Amaury) (Seine-et-Oise): home of house of Montfort, lords of: Amaury, constable of France, elder brother of Earl Simon **IV** 75, 88, 105, 114; Simon II, grandfather of Earl Simon 75, 88, 115; Beatrice de, and claim of her grandson to Brittany (1341) 598; **VI** 239

Montfort (Seine-et-Oise), castle **III** 112

Montfort, Almaric de **III** 124, 126

Montfort, Henry de, eldest son of Earl Simon: knighted by Lord Edward **IV** 159; at Amiens 182;

391

392

armies 579–80; battle for Caen 581; Eisenhower urged to dismiss 582; attempts to take Arnhem 589; checks Ardennes offensive 589; disputes with Eisenhower 590; enters Ruhr 592; Germans surrender 593

Montgomery, earl of *see* Herbert

Montgomery, Hugh, earl of Shrewsbury **III** 101, 105, 288

Montgomery, R. (1738–75) **XII** 202

Montgomery, Roger, earl of Shrewsbury **III** 117, 286

Montgomery, Sir Thomas **VI** 547; pension 578

Montgommery, count de **VIII** 161, 162

months, heathen names **II** 97–8

Montils-les-Tours (Loir-et-Cher) **VI** 474–5

Montjoie **VI** 183

Montlhéry (Seine-et-Oise) **VI** 175, 239

Montlouis (Touraine) **III** 337

Montmartre (nr. Paris) **III** 212

Montmirail (Sarthe) **III** 212, 329

Montmorency, Anne de **VII** 558

Montmorency, Anne de, constable of France **VIII** 54, 56, 60, 61, 62

Montpellier **III** 38, 95; **IV** 99

Montpellier, university **V** 144

Montpellier, William of **III** 19

Montpensier, duc de **VIII** 354

Montpezat **V** 109

Montreal **X** 341

Montreuil, Jean de **IX** 218

Montreuil, Jean de, Aquitaine treatise **VI** 137

Montreuil-sur-mer **II** 608; **IV** 178; treaty between Edward I and Flanders (1274) 622–4; treaty (1299) 652–3; court of claims (1305–6) 657–8; **V** 1, 8, 112, 117, 140; process 108, 113; **VII** 409, 410, 421

Montrose, 3rd duke of, president of board of trade (1804–6) **XII** 581

Montrose, James Graham, 1st duke of (d. 1742) **XI** 33, 272, 280

Montrose, John Baliol's abdication completed **IV** 614, 615

Montrose, marquis of *see* Graham

Montsegur **V** 132

Montserrat **IX** 337; returned to Britain (1783) **XII** 255

monuments: celebratory **Ia** 326, 328, 534; funerary 699–704; *see also* burials; tombstones

Monypenny, Sir William, Scots envoy **VI** 536; information to Louis XI 536, 550

Moore, Arthur **X** 247

Moore, Francis **VIII** 231

Moore, George **VIII** 229; **XIV** 548, 549

Moore, Sir Graham (1764–1843), naval captain **XII** 422

Moore, Henry **XV** 179

Moore, Sir John (1761–1809), General **XII** 457, 460, 485, 554; biography 457

Moore, Dr Samson **XIV** 519

Moore, Thomas (1779–1852), author **XII** 536; **XIII** 38, 62, 349, 530

Moore-Brabazon, J. T. C. **XV** 528

Moore Island, British capture of **XII** 554

Moors, the **III** 149; **VII** 273

Moorstead, Thomas, doctor **VI** 287

Mor, Anthonis **VII** 601

Morant, Sir Robert L. **XIV** 318, 355, 356, 357, 358; Education Bills 392, 397, 536; National Insurance Act 520; **XV** 174

Moravia, Charles of *see* Charles of Moravia

Moray: district and shire **IV** 574–5; rising (1297) 580, 684; (1304) 709

Moray, Sir Andrew **V** 118

Moray, Andrew of **IV** 687; son (d. 1297 or 1298), leader of the risings (1297) 580, 684–7; grandson Andrew, heir of Bothwell 687, 694

Moray, bishop of, crusade on behalf of Robert Bruce (1306) **IV** 714

Moray, earls of *see* Dunbar, Thomas; Henry of Grosmont; Randolph; Stewart

Moray, William of, lord of Bothwell **IV** 687

Moray family **IV** 580, 687

Moray Firth **III** 273

Morcant, King **Ib** 199

Morcar, earl of Northumbria **II** 547, 579, 581, 587, 589–90; submission to William 597; government of England 599; heads north with Edwin 601; joins Hereward at Ely 606; King William's charters 623; crisis (1066) 687; **III** 100

Morcar, son of Arngrim, murder **II** 388

Mordaunt, Charles, 1st earl of Monmouth, 3rd earl of Peterborough (1658–1735) **X** 180, 211, 213; **XI** 424

Mordaunt, Sir John (1697–1780), General **XI** 360

Mordaunt, John, speaker of the House of Commons (1487) **VII** 652

'Morden, Lord' *see* Yorke, Charles

More (Moor Park), treaty (1525) **VII** 316

More, Hannah (1745–1833) **XII** 339, 353, 355; **XIII** 505

More, Henry **X** 32

More, Sir John **VII** 246, 247, 601

More, Sir Thomas (1478–1535) **VI** 608, 619, 624; **VII** 10, 18, 228, 231; image of Richard 52; Henry's taxation methods 216; revival of learning 240–1, 243; education 246–7; elected to parliament (1504) 247; marriages 248; under-sheriff of the city (1510) 248; embassy to the Low Countries (1515) 248; Erasmus 250–2; *Utopia* 258–66, 578; early optimism and liberalism 265; Hunne's heresy 292; Wolsey's peace negotiations (1518) 301; chosen as speaker (1523) 303, 653; Treaty of Noyon (1516) 307; chancellor (1529) 330, 352, 646; attitude to heresy 346, 347; resigns office as chancellor (1532) 355; relations with the March of Kent 361–2; attempt at attainder fails (1534) 362; imprisoned in Tower (1534) 362; executed (6 July 1535) 362–3; denounces inclosures 451, 456; hard upon ex-soldiers 455; Cranmer's intercession 552; writings 568, 583; scholarship 570, 572; *Historie of Kyng Rycharde the Thirde* 579–80; portraits 600–1; **IX** 279; **XI** 139

More, William de la **V** 292

Morea, the **VII** 151

Morel, E. D.: and UDC **XV** 51–2; Labour party 136; elected 198; kept out of Foreign Office 209; historians learn from 361; not in Dictionary of National Bibliography 606

Moresby (Cumbria), fort **Ia** 177

Moreville, Daniel of **III** 236, 245

Moreville, Hugh de **III** 214, 252

Moreville family **III** 273

Morfe (Staffs.) **II** 40

Morfe Forest (Moerheb) (Salop) **II** 733

Morgan, Sir Frederick **XV** 572, 577

Morgan, Sir Henry **X** 285, 328, 329, 334

Morgan, king of Morgannwyg **II** 341

Morgan, Philip, bishop of Worcester, later of Ely **VI** 141, 431, 432, 433

Morgan, rebel in Glamorgan (1294) **IV** 440

Morgan, Thomas **VIII** 378, 379, 380

Morgan, Trahaiarn, of Kidwelly **VII** 52

Morgannock county (Wales) **VII** 57

Mowbray, Thomas, earl of Nottingham (*cont.*)

294–5; victory at sea 446; at Radcot Bridge 452–3; earl marshal 453; appellant (1388) 454–60; warden of the Marsh and captain of Calais 469; mainpernor for Arundel 470; with Richard II in Ireland 471; expedition to Italy 476; appellant (1397) 479; murder of Gloucester 481–2; quarrel with Hereford 265, 485–7; exiled for life 488

Mowbray family **V** 63; **VII** 421

Moxon, Joseph **X** 42

Moyle, Sir Thomas **VII** 440; speaker of House of Commons (1542) 654

Mozaffar Jang (d. 1751), French nominee in the Deccan **XI** 327

Mozart **XV** 268

M'Quirke, Mr **XII** 133

Mr Britling Sees it Through **XV** 18

Mr Norris Changes Trains **XV** 347

Much Hadham **Ib** map 3 xxxi

Muchelney (Som.), abbey **II** 286, 455

Mucianus, C. Licinius **Ia** 513

Mucking (Essex) **Ib** xxi, 41, 52, 61, 102, 131; map 2 xxx; map 5 68; map 6 88

Mudania, pact **XV** 191

Mudford, W. H. **XIV** 533

Muggeridge, Malcolm **XV** 298, 348

Muhammed Ali **XII** 159

Mühlberg, battle (1547) **VII** 482, 483

Muir, Thomas, founder of Scottish Friends of the People **XII** 359

Mul, brother of Cædwalla **II** 70, 73

Mulberry harbours **XV** 579

Mulcaster, Richard **VIII** 323

'Mule', the **XII** 333, 509, 513

Mulgrave, 1st earl of: chancellor of duchy of Lancaster (1804–5) **XII** 581; foreign secretary (1805–6) 582; first lord of the admiralty (1807–10) 581, 583; master

general of the ordnance (1810) 583

Multon, Thomas, lord of Gilsland **V** 61

Mummius Sisenna, P. **Ia** 182

Mun, Thomas **IX** 316

Münchausen, Ph. Adolf, Hanoverian resident in Great Britain (1749–62) **XI** 14

Munday, Anthony **IX** 414

Mundeford, Osbern, earl of Dorset's lieutenant **VI** 480

Mundella, A. J. **XIV** 294

Mundt, Christopher **VIII** 46

munera **Ia** 463

Munfichet, Margaret of **III** 55

Munich: conference **XV** 426, 428–9; no Soviet representative 445; debate over agreement 430; Hitler claims as triumph 431; British increase of armaments 432; thought to have averted war 435; outcry against 436; discredited by German occupation of Prague 439; Chamberlain attempts to defend 440; Hitler's hopes 476; Duff Cooper true hero 478; agreement repudiated 494; men reform 591

municipal corporations **X** 107–8

Municipal Corporations Act **VI** 394

municipal councils **Ia** 279, 390, 575–7; recruitment to 372, 463, 511, 537; municipal services 372–3, 578–80, 663; local aristocracy 597; *see also* administration; *curiales*

municipal *origo* **Ia** 581, 583

municipal stock, issues **XIV** 129

municipal trading **XIV** 128–9

municipalities, reform **XIII** 459–60, 462

municipium **Ia** 235, 534, 574, 586, 589; Verulamium 112, 232; London? 156; Italica 155; York? 583; Caerleon? 586

munitions: slow expansion of labour

XV 465; production reduced 565; provided under lend-lease 566

Munitions, Ministry of: created **XV** 30–1; work 34–6; ended 130; Ministry of Supply repeats 444

Munro, Sir Hector (1726–1805) **XII** 161

Munro, Sir Thomas **XIII** 406–7

Münster (Germany) **VII** 340; **IX** 129

Munster (Ireland) **III** 312, 313; **V** 470; north **VII** 125; rebellion in **IX** 135; **X** 129

Münster, bishop of *see* Galen, Bernhard von; Liudger

Muntchenesy, Joan de, daughter of William the Marshal and mother of Joan, wife of William of Valence **IV** 139

Muntchenesy, Warin de **IV** 139

Murad III, sultan of Turkey **VIII** 241

Murat, Joachim **XII** 452, 459, 568

Murbach (Vosges), abbey **III** 247

Murdac, Henry, abbot of Fountains and archbishop of York **III** 191

murder **Ia** 696; fine for **II** 685; **III** 69, 392–3; **V** 197

Murdoch, William **XIII** 44

Muret, battle **III** 463

Murimuth, Adam, on commissions of trailbaston **V** 169; on crisis (1341) 173

Murmansk **XV** 138

Murphy, Arthur **XII** 350

Murray, Hon. Alexander (d. 1777) **XI** 32

Murray, Anne **IX** 203

Murray, Captain **XII** 133

Murray, David, Viscount Stormont, 2nd earl of Mansfield (1727–96): biography **XII** 225; secretary of state (1779–82) 225, 237; lord president of council (1783) 255, 579, (1794–6) 225, 580

Murray, earl of *see* Stuart, James

Murray, Lord George (?1700–60) **XI** 254–7

Murray, Sir George (1772–1846) **XII** 481

Murray, Gilbert **XV** 300, 368

Murray, Sir James **XIV** 329

Murray, Hon. James (*c.*1719–94), General **XI** 218, 356

Murray, Sir John (1768?–1827) **XII** 558

Murray, John (1778–1843) **XII** 541

Murray, John, 1st duke of Atholl (1659–1724) **XI** 280, 282

Murray, John, 4th earl of Dunmore (1732–1809) **XII** 202

Murray, John, 1st marquis of Atholl **X** 277

Murray, Sir John, of Broughton (1718–77) **XI** 254, 256

Murray, Hon. William, 1st earl of Mansfield (1705–93) **XI** 61, 64, 66, 340, 355; lawyer 10, 22; Pitt 36, 353; appeals anomaly 59; Protestant dissenters 71; checkweavers' strike (1758) 143; career ambitions 346; incompetence accusations 348; habeas corpus amendment 357; **XII** 57, 66, 79, 135, 577; judge in Wilkes case 133, 136; Junius 145

Mursa, battle **Ia** 355, 532

Muschamp, Geoffrey, bishop of Coventry **III** 446

Muscitto, agent of Philip IV **IV** 668

Muscovy Company **VIII** 237, 238, 239, 241

musculi **Ia** 60

Musgrave, Thomas **V** 206

music: English **VII** 266, 588–91; **IX** 358, 386–9; **X** 402–7; **XI** 398, 414–18; Academy of Ancient Music 417; Three Choirs Festival 418; **XII** 543; **XIII** 14, 560–1; revival of composition by Parry and Stanford **XIV** 158; influence of Joachim 159; advent in England of Wagner's music 159; Gilbert and Sullivan's partnership 159; increase of orchestral music and development of intelligent

music (*cont.*)
audiences 327; beginnings of Elgar 327; later work and rise of considerable school of British composers 545; recording of English folk-songs 544; **XV** 178, 234

Music, Royal Academy of **XIII** 560

music halls **XV** 313–14

Musschenbroek (1692–1761), inventor of Leyden jar **XI** 383

Musselburgh (Lothian) **VII** 484

Mussolini, Benito: MacDonald friendly **XV** 217; expects war 228; temporary difficulty 299; British statesmen friendly 317; at Stresa 377; attacks Abyssinia 380, 384–5; Franco not his puppet 395; Low cartoons 408; Austria 415; makes trains run to time 417; Chamberlain 414, 421–3; Munich 428, 429, 431; Chamberlain and Halifax visit 436; proposes conference 451; announces non-belligerence 460; attacks Greece 524; declares war on United States 532; does not enter Cairo 555; Churchill would welcome 560; overthrown 572; killed 593

mutationes, Imperial Post **Ia** 566

mutinies: Spanish troops **VIII** 339; French army **XV** 81, 85; British army 138

mutiny, Indian: character and origin **XIII** 429–33; military weakness of British position 431–2; outbreak 433; course 434–8; suppression 438–40; effect 440–1; **XV** 153

Mutiny Acts (1766) **X** 152; **XI** 122, 188; (1784) 268, 270; (1807) 441

Myrc, John **VI** 281

Mystery of Mary Stuart **VIII** 103

Mystery Plays **VI** 397–8

mystery religions **Ia** 667, 676, 698–9, 709–10, 715; burial rites 730; *see also* religion

Mytens, Daniel **VIII** 302; **IX** 374

Myton, battle **V** 56, 58, 298, 368

N

Naaman **VIII** 22

Naevius, imperial freedman **Ia** 280, 531, 597

Nafferton (Yorks.), manor **VI** 337

Nagasaki, atomic bomb **XV** 96, 598

nails: Inchtuthil **Ia** 76; in graves 705–6; manufacture **XII** 30, 508

Nairne, Carolina, Baroness (1766–1845), ballad-writer **XI** 425

Nairne, William, 2nd Baron (1664–1726) **XI** 162

Nájera, battle **V** 144, 150, 247, 424

Names of Herbs **VIII** 316

Namier, Sir L. **XV** 129

Namsos **XV** 471

Namur **III** 83; **VIII** 344; **X** 169, 173

Namur, Guy, count of **V** 119

Namur, Philip of **III** 381, 454, 464

Nana Farnavis **XII** 314

Nandakumar **XII** 311

Nanfan, Sir Richard (d. 1507) **VII** 57, 88, 94, 169, 170; Wolsey in his service 288

Nanstallon, fort **Ia** 93

Nantes **III** 324; **IV** 90, 95; **V** 131; **VII** 86, 104

Nantes, Edict of **X** 109, 121, 314

Nantucket, importance **XII** 18

Napier, Admiral Sir Charles **XIII** 231, 274

Napier, General Sir Charles: relations with chartists **XIII** 138; biography 421; conquest of Sind 421–3; administration 423; second Sikh war 426; views on India 429; checks sepoy mutiny (1849) 430; quarrels with Dalhousie 430–1

Napier, Sir George **XIII** 398

Napier, John **IX** 369

Napier, Sir Joseph **XIII** 358–9

Naples: bay of **Ia** 161; naval battle (1284) **IV** 253; **VII** 83, 84, 150, 252, 556; politics of Italy 112–13; French invasion 114; League of Venice (1495) 115; French ambitions 152; Treaty of Granada (1500) 152–3; Louis and Ferdinand make marriage treaty 154–5; Julius II mobilizes strength 271; treaty of Noyon (1516) 306; Charles V struggles with Francis 309, 319; **X** 215–16; taken **XV** 576

Naples, Ferdinand of *see* Ferdinand of Naples

Napoleon **VIII** 407

Napoleon I **XIII** 195, 197

Napoleon III **XIII** 164, 170, 178–9, 249, 251; eastern question 254–5, 258–9; English defences 268; Crimean war 275–6, 286, 290; Italian question 299–303; expedition to Mexico 314; Polish rebellion 316–17; Schleswig-Holstein question 321–3; Luxembourg 324–5; **XIV** 3, 4, 88

Napoleon Bonaparte **XII** 108, 396, 536; military campaigns 367, 371, 378, 381, 386; first consul 380, 410; emperor of France 421, 424, 446, 455, 555–62; invasion plans 421; Russian ambitions and duc d'Enghien affair 423; abandons invasion 425–7 — and Boulogne for Austria 431; inadequate forces for Channel control 433; refuses peace negotiations with Fox 437; subdues Prussia 443; Portland administration 451; goads king of Prussia 452; Alexander and Treaty of Tilsit 455; control of Iberian peninsula 458; redeployment of European forces 460; economic warfare 463–71; American trade 475; acknowledged by Wellington 488; conditions for

Napoleon Bonaparte (*cont.*)
French peace 496; war with Russia (1812) 496; return after exile 566–8; rule of luck **XV** 206; British memories 488; invasion of Russia 528; Mediterranean 522

Narbonne: villa near **Ia** 450; **V** 138; treaty between France and Spain (1493) **VI** 162; **VII** 110, 112

Narbonne, archbishop of **VI** 558

Narbonne, count of *see* Guillaume, count of Narbonne

Narcissus **Ia** 82, 94, 109

Nares, James (1715–83), composer **XI** 417

Narrenschiff **VII** 252

Narrow Seas, sovereignty **IX** 85, 216–18

Narvik: plans to seize **XV** 468; inadequate base 469; occupied by Germans 470; captured and evacuated 471

Naseby, battle **IX** 141

Naseby *see* Royal Charles

Nash, John (1752–1835), architect **XII** 546; **XIII** 581–2

Nash, Thomas **VIII** 203, 279, 282, 293–4, 311

Nasmyth, James **XIII** 5

Nassau, Lewis of **VIII** 153, 156

Nassau, Maurice of **VIII** 368, 416

Nassau, William, *see* Orange

Natal *see* Cape Colony

Natanleag **Ib** appendix II; map 3 xxxi

Natanleod **Ib** 148, appendix II; **II** 20

Nation: in First World War **XV** 27; foreign circulation banned 106; changed character 252; absorbed by *New Statesman* 310–11

National anthem **XV** 163, 164

National Art Collections Fund **XIV** 543

National Council of Labour **XV** 142, 143

National Council of Labour Colleges **XV** 347

National Debt **XII** 19; Price on 40; increase under Newcastle 73; under Grenville 105; under North 153, 220; under Shelburne 252; under Pitt 283, 290–3, 374; under Addington 413; **XV** 124; *see also* debt

national defence contribution **XV** 412

National Democratic Party **XV** 126, 128

National Fire Service **XV** 503

National Gallery **XIV** 135, 326

National government: proposed by Samuel **XV** 292; made 293; gold standard 296–7; hesitate at nothing 317; claim to have saved country 321; Protection 322–4; prolonged 326; rely on natural recovery 331; financial policy 332; economic policy 336; Hitler 377; Peace Ballot 379–80; now wish to go against Italy 380; liberal repute restored 381; general election (1935) 383, 389; pretence 404, 458; foreign affairs 408, 419; end 474

National Insurance **XIV** 445–6, 519–20; **XV** 1, 36, 77

National Labour party **XV** 326, 384, 473

National Liberal Club **XV** 128

National Liberal Federation **XIV** 55, 90

National Liberal party (Lloyd George's) **XV** 197–8, 208

national registration **XV** 464

National Savings **XV** 46, 88, 180, 459, 511

National Service, Ministry of **XV** 76, 79, 130; joined to Ministry of Labour 456

National Society for the Education of the Poor **XII** 525

National Trust founded **XIV** 340

National Unemployed Workers' movement **XV** 349

navy (1760–1815) **XII** 365, 418; support by independent MPs 15; supplies 24, 130, 153–5, 175, 203 — North cuts expenditure 153–5; copper-bottom ships 60, 203, 363; state of 203, 412–14; expenditure on 115, 276, 292; mutinies (1797) 361, 372; recruitment 472

navy (1815–70): British, condition (1815–54) **XIII** 271–3; introduction of steamships and ironclads 179, 273–4, 293–4; expeditions in the Crimean War 274, 287–8; reforms after the Crimean War 293–5

navy (1870–1914): development (to 1886) **XIV** 121–4; small scale at Jubilee (1887) 177; development (to 1900) 286–9; Fisher-Cawdor reforms 363–5; Dreadnought policy 364, 522–3; effects of naval policy on foreign policy 368; Campbell-Bannerman's retrenchments of the Cawdor programme 401, 402; alarm at German acceleration (1909) 412; 'we want eight' 413; effect on the budget 413; Anglo-French Entente over Mediterranean and Channel 462; Cabinet's neglect to make either Rosyth, Cromarty or Scapa Flow defensible 472; conversations with Russia 483–4; mobilization of the fleet and decisive action by Prince Louis 487; naval assurance to France 491

navy (1914–45): between wars **XV** 230, 232, 365; capital expenditure 375; will have to fight Italy alone 384; mobilized during Czech crisis 428; goes over to two-ocean standard 432; German attack feared 437; in Mediterranean 460; cannot operate without air cover 470; invasion 490, 497; French fleet 493; Roosevelt wants assurances 495; main fleet expected to arrive at Singapore

531; defied in Channel 542; ready to join Pacific War 586

Naworth Castle **VIII** 141, 142

Naylor, James **IX** 183, 196

Nazi-Soviet pact **XV** 384, 449; British not shaken 450; Hitler 451; blockade 461; causes anti-Soviet feeling 469

Neal, Daniel (1678–1743) **XI** 88

Neath, Cross, captured in Wales **IV** 369

Neath Abbey **V** 86

necessity, doctrine of moral and political **IV** 522–3, 528, 679, 704

Nechtanesmere, battle **II** 88, 92, 146, 187

Neckham, Alexander, abbot of Cirencester **III** 236, 239, 245–6, 437

Nectaridus **Ia** 378, 382

Neerwinden, battle (1793) **X** 171; **XII** 366

Nefyn: 'spectacle' and 'round table' **IV** 429, 515; princely residence 392

Negapatam: capture **XII** 161; retention (1783) 256

negotium **Ia** 81, 203, 399, 511

Nehru, Paudit Jawaharlarl **XV** 365, 545

Neil, Sir Richard **VI** 635

Neile, Richard **IX** 17–18, 42

Neisse, Western **XV** 594

Nelson, Horatio (1758–1805), 1st Viscount **XII** 412, 414; Cape St Vincent (1797) 372; Aboukir Bay (1798) 369, 378; Copenhagen (1801) 214, 386, 407, 456; campaign (1804–5) 427–33; biography 429; references to **XV** 13, 63, 102

Nelson, John (1707–44) **XI** 97

Nelson's Column **XV** 114

Nemeton, place-names **Ia** 673, 713

Nemours, (Seine-et-Marne) **VI** 200

Nemours, Louis d'Armagnac, duc de **VII** 153

nemus **Ia** 673

Nen *see* Nene, river

Nene (Nen) river: pottery industry **Ia** 258, 643–4, 718; Christians 730; **Ib** xxvii; map 2 xxx; **II** 26, 733; **III** 485

Nennius **Ia** 472, 490; *Historia Brittonum* **Ib** 15–17, 172, 199, 216; on Arthur **II** 3; pedigrees recorded 38; northern traditions recorded 75–6, 80, 83

Neoplatonists **III** 257

Neolithic period **Ia** 8, 13

Neophytus, archbishop of Philippopolis **X** 372

Neoplatonism **Ia** 698

Nepos, A. Platorius **Ia** 173, 179–80, 181–2

Nepos, Julius, Emperor **Ia** 486

Nepos, P. Metilius *see* Metilius

Neptune **Ia** 659, 666

Neratius Marcellus, L. **Ia** 163–5

Nero, Emperor **Ia** 108–23; destroys Julian credit 71; Boudicca's revolt 89, 111–21; client kings 91; policy towards Britain 98, 109–23; new building in London 124; deposition and death 128, 155, 271; Golden House 156, 161; Commodus compared 212; lead mining 634

Nerthus **Ib** 50

Nerva, Emperor **Ia** 153–4, 164, 169, 170; Gloucester 153, 157, 232, 262

Nesbit (Northumb.) **VI** 45

Nesjar, battle **II** 403

Nesle (Somme) **VI** 153, 239

Nesle, lord of **IV** 194

Nesse **Ib** map 1 xxix

Nesselrode, Count **XIII** 234, 257, 260

Nest, daughter of Rhys ap Tewdwr **III** 289

Neston, in Dee estuary **IV** 422

Nether Wallop (Hants) **VI** 562

Netherby, fort **Ia** 176, 245

Netherlands **VII** 72, 102, 279, 309; duchess of Burgundy hostile to Henry 67, 70; Lincoln takes flight to 70; diplomatic stage of northwest Europe 82, 83, 341; parties in 85; English restrict trade 92; English intervention in (1489) 98–9; cessation of French interference 101; Maximilian and civil war 105; commercial treaties with Henry 116, 179, 310; Perkin Warbeck 119–22, 124–5; Scotland and Warbeck 137–8; *Magnus Intercursus* (1496) and treaty (1497) 139, 150, 186–7; English commercial prosperity 157, 163; nursery of Yorkist plot 167, 171, 183; English trade 181, 183, 188, 214, 218–19; commercial treaty with England (1502) 183; Henry demands surrender of Suffolk 185; English cloth trade 186, 474; Steelyard attack (1493) 222; Thomas More on embassy to 248, 259; treaty at Lille (1513) 283; League of Cambrai (1517) 307; League of Cognac (1526) 317; truce with England (1528) 318; 'ladies' peace' of Cambrai (1529) 319; Lutherans 343; Tyndale's New Testament 345; Thomas Cromwell 351; settlement at Doncaster (1536) 392; Henry woos merchants 403, 474; Anne of Cleves 404; financial centre of Europe 412, 474; russel weaving 463; exports to England 470; Merchant Adventurers 472–3; Northumberland's attempted *coup* 526; Charles defends western borders (1553) 535; Mary pledged to Philip (1553) 537; Spain and religion 550; Philip quits Mary and takes up residence 553–4; England sends army (1558) 559; painters 598–9; **VIII** 119–20; English propaganda in 120–1, 125–6; Alva in 127–34, 155–7, 164; Elizabeth and 332–70; **X** 69, 114, 171, 214–18; *see also* Dutch, the; Holland

Netherwent **V** 59
Netley Abbey **VII** 596
Netter, Thomas, of Walden **VI** 297,
298; *Doctrinale* 683
Nettlecombe (Som.) **III** 15
Neubourg (Eure) **III** 131
Neufmarché, Bernard of **III** 11, 288,
290
Neufmarché (Seine-Inf.) **III** 328
Neuss **Ia** 411, 587; **VI** 575, 576
Neustadt **VII** 103
neutrality, pact (1870) **XIV** 5–6
Neuve Chapelle, battle **XV** 26
Nevers (Nièvre): Franco-Burgun-
dian meeting **VI** 259, 260
Nevers (Nièvre), count of *see* Philip
Nevers, duke of **VIII** 157
Nevers, Louis de, count of Flanders
V 120, 135, 143
Nevill, Ralph, Chancellor, bishop of
Chichester (1224–44) **IV** 16–17,
47, 50, 60, 66, 75; granted office
for life 48; elected archbishop but
rejected by the pope 56; com-
pared with Burnell 335
Nevill, Ralph, of Raby **IV** 708
Nevill, Robert, Scottish war (1303)
IV 708
Neville, Alexander, archbishop of
York (1374–88) **V** 450, 467; in
his diocese 299; on commission
(1386); becomes adherent of
Richard II 448; witness to judges'
manifesto 449; appealed (1387)
451; flight to north 452; condemned in Merciless Parliament
457; translated to St Andrew's
459; Urban VI translates to
St Andrews **VI** 267
Neville, Anne, Cecily's sister, duchess of York, married Humphrey
Stafford **VI** 464; captured after
Tewkesbury 571
Neville, Anne, Richard Neville's
widow **VI** 581
Neville, Anne, Warwick's daughter,
dispensation for prince of Wales's
marriage **VI** 564

Neville, Cecily, duchess of York **VI**
464, 555
Neville, Charles, 6th earl of West-
morland **VIII** 131, 137, 138
Neville, Sir Edward **VII** 396
Neville, Edward, Earl Ralph Nev-
ille's son **VI** 510
Neville, Edward, later Lord Aber-
gavenny, son of Joan, countess of
Westmorland **VI**
Neville, Edward, ninth brother of
Cecily, duchess of York, 4th Lord
Abergavenny **VI** 464
Neville, Eleanor, daughter of Joan,
countess of Westmorland **VI** 321
Neville, Eleanor (later Lumley),
wife of Sir Ralph Lumley **VI** 328
Neville, Eleanor, married (1)
Richard, Lord Despenser (2)
Henry Percy, 2nd earl of North-
umberland II **VI** 464
Neville, Sir George, 3rd Baron
Abergavenny (1461?–1535) **VII**
140, 142, 215, 216
Neville, Sir George, bastard son of
Thomas Neville **VII** 169
Neville, George, bishop of Exeter,
later archbishop of York and
chancellor **VI** 323, 326, 436, 516,
520; 'charitable subsidy' 543;
Edward IV suspects loyalty 552;
conspiracy against Edward IV
555, 557; Readeption 561; Warwick's parliament (Nov. 1470)
562; Hammes castle prisoner 572;
pardoned (11 Nov. 1475) 572;
release 608; **VII** 236, 237
Neville, George, brother of Richard,
earl of Warwick **VI** 270
Neville, George, claimant to barony
of Latimer, son of Joan, countess
of Westmorland **VI** 321
Neville, George, duke of Clarence
VI 436, 563, 595, 604; Edward
IV's wedding 536; joins Warwick
555; married 555–6; Edward IV
refers to warmly (1489) 557; stays
in north with Warwick 557;

enters London 561; associated with Warwick as protector 563; York's heir 563; queen's land 566; Edward IV's pardon 571; Warwick estates 571; throne conspiracy 571; contingent in France 575; Picquigny 577; not to marry Mary of Burgundy 579; absent from court 579; suspects wife's poisoning 579; king's council appeal 580; East Anglian plot 580; Edward IV charges 580; attainted (1478) 581; Tower death 581; son 581; Warwickshire estates 581; estates 582; accounts commission 597; exporting wool 591; Shakespeare on death 608

Neville, Sir Henry **VIII** 137

Neville, Hugh de **III** 12, 420, 473

Neville, Sir Humphrey, holds out in Bamburgh **VI** 531

Neville, Joan (Beaufort), countess of Westmorland **VI** 319, 320–3; revenue secured 320; Neville estates 321

Neville, Joan, eldest daughter of William, 5th Lord: marries Thomas Neville **VI** 324

Neville, John, eldest son of Ralph **VI** 326

Neville, John, impeached (1376) **VI** 319

Neville, John, Lord **VI** 526; with Margaret at York 523

Neville, John, Lord Latimer **VI** 326

Neville, Lord John, of Raby **V** 391, 392, 439; marriages **VI** 324

Neville, John, marquis of Montagu, second earl of Northumberland **VI** 525, 528, 529, 531, 536; deserts Edward IV 560, 561; death at Barnet 568

Neville, Katherine, daughter of Joan, countess of Westmorland, sister of Cecily, duchess of York **VI** 321; marries John Mowbray, duke of Norfolk 464

Neville, Lady Lucy, wife of Sir Anthony Browne **VII** 169

Neville, Margaret, daughter of Lord Neville of Raby **VI** 9

Neville, Ralph, earl (1) of Westmorland (1397–1425) **V** 483, 492; **VI** 19, 35, 53, 60, 65; Bolingbroke's landing 4; Bainbridge and Wensleydale rights 34; keeper of West March 54; Archbishop Scrope 61, 326; Cockermouth Castle and Isle of Man secured 63; prince's council 105; dismissal from council 112; summoned to parliament (1421) 211; council member 218, 433; and Henry Bolingbroke 319; daughters 320; second wife *see* Joan, countess of Westmorland; Henry IV grants 320; Fauconberg custody 324; Latimer estates 325

Neville, Ralph, earl (2) of Westmorland **VI** 321, 322, 419, 459, 508; bound over 322; complaints against and bonds 322; Beaufort undertaking 323; prince of Wales's marriage 523; parliamentary summons (Nov. 1461) 538

Neville, Lord Ralph, of Raby **V** 136

Neville, Richard, earl of Salisbury **VI** 321, 515; succession claim 323; Westmorland border war 322; chancellor nomination (1454) 509; Warwick's return 515; Ludlow march 515; invasion (1460) 518; besieges Tower 520; beheaded 523; attainder reversed 542

Neville, Richard, earl of Warwick: **VI** 489, 504; Glamorgan and Morganwg possession (1449) 510; St Albans battle (1) 511–12; captain of Calais 512, 561; life threatened 514; Easterlings and Italians attacked 515; Ludlow Bridge defeat 516; escape to Calais 516; invasion (1460) 518; Northampton march and victory 520; St Albans defeat (2) 524; joins March 524; great chamber-

Neville, Richard, earl of Warwick (*cont.*)

lain 525; besieges Berwick 529; impasse in north (1463–4) 530; Grey and Neville pardon exemptions 531; Bamburgh walls breached 531–2; Edward IV's marriage 535, 536; avoids Louis XI at Hesdin (1464) 535, 536; Elizabeth Woodville's marriage escort 536; Anglo-French alliance policy 536, 537, 552; personality 537; opposition to Edward IV 550; Louis XI agreement (1466) 551; Danish vessels 554; Edward IV displacement preparations (1469) 555; invasion preparations 556; London march (20 July) and king's capture 556; Edward IV transferred 557; lacks control of country 557; daughter's betrothal 557; moves to Exeter and Calais 558; Louis XI's advice 558; Louis meeting 559; homage to Queen Margaret 559; lands forces in Dartmouth and Plymouth 560; joint proclamation 560; London attack 560; enters London (6 Oct. 1470) 561; Henry VI to St Paul's 561; responsible for government 561; lieutenant 561, 563; protector 563 (Nov. 1470) 563; expenses for Margaret 564; fights Edward IV alone 568; marches to Barnet 568; loans and income (1469) 564; fall and death 565, 568

Neville, Richard, nephew of Cecily, duchess of York: marriage **VI** 464

Neville, Robert, fifth brother of Cecily, duchess of York, bishop of Salisbury, later bishop of Durham **VI** 266, 464, 496

Neville, Lord, son of earl of Westmorland, Gloucester summons to London **VI** 618

Neville, Thomas, Lord Furnival, second son of John Lord Neville of Raby **VI** 8, 9, 35, 53, 429;

marriages 324

Neville, Thomas, privy councillor: speaker of House of Commons (1515) **VII** 653

Neville, Sir William **V** 521

Neville, William, earl of Kent **VI** 538

Neville, William, Lord Fauconberg, sixth son of Joan, countess of Westmorland (Beaufort): **VI** 321, 322, 323, 492, 518; summoned to parliament 324

Neville family **VI** 319–25, 503; **VII** 169, 385, 414

Neville's Cross, battle **V** 99, 142, 210, 248, 298; David II captured 136; Edward III's victory 148

Nevis, restored to England (1783) **XII** 255; **IX** 337

Nevyn *see* Nefyn

New Albion **VIII** 249

New Amsterdam *see* New York

New Army **XV** 20–2

New Brunswick **IX** 326; **X** 337

New Deal **XV** 268, 286, 337, 348

New England **X** 333, 335–7, 347

New England Company **IX** 339–40; **X** 157

New England Confederation **IX** 342–3, 345

New English Art Club **XIV** 157

New Forest (Hants): pottery industry **Ia** 645, 649; **II** 18, 23, 284, 683; **III** 30, 34, 53, 113; **V** 312, 314; **VI** 295

New Fresh Wharf, London **Ia** 564

New Guinea, conquered **XV** 23, 133

New Hampshire **IX** 342

New Haven **IX** 342

New Jersey **X** 334, 340

New Lanark *see* Owen, Robert

New Minster *see* Winchester

New Model army, the House of Lords **IV** 521; *see also* army

New Monarchy, views of Hallam and Green **VII** 6, 23

New Netherland **IX** 342, 344–5; **X** 68, 339

New party **XV** 285, 295, 326, 348, 354

New Providence, free port (1787) **XII** 289

New South Wales, governorship **XV** 172; *see also* Australia

New Statesman: cannibalistic practice **XV** 310; character 311; supports dismemberment of Czechoslovakia 426

New Testament, German (1522) **VII** 338; French (1523) 338; English (1526) 343–5; Roman Catholic translation planned **VII** 556; translation **VIII** 23

'New Unionism' **XIV** 206

New York (originally New Amsterdam) **X** 334, 335, 337, 340, 341; acquired by English (1667) 68; recaptured by Dutch 81; Palatine settlers 344; printing press (1693) 348; open port (1770) **XII** 193; **XV** 533

New York Weekly Journal **XI** 322

New Zealand **XIII** 242, 389–90; formation of early New Zealand association 390–1; relations between the association and the Colonial Office 391; annexation of New Zealand 391–2; New Zealand company surrenders its charter 393; grant of responsible government 394; Maori wars 394–5; representation at peace conference **XV** 132; opposes alliance with Japan 150; and Chanak 191; anxious for appeasement 420; Munich 430; declares war 452; Far East 495, 521

Newall, Robert **XIII** 571

Newark (Notts.) **Ib** 176, 182; Anglian pottery 65 [fig. 3(h)]; map 4 xxxii; **II** 525; **V** 526; **VII** 36, 74, 161; representation **X** 12

Newark Castle **III** 137, 485; **IV** 11, 21

Newbattle (Lothian) **III** 274

Newbattle Abbey **V** 440

Newberry *see* 'Universal Chronicle' *under* journals

Newbery, John **VIII** 242

Newbery, John, publisher (1713–67) **XII** 40

Newbiggin (Cumbria) **VI** 459

Newbold, J. T. Walton **XV** 200, 347

Newborough (Newport), in Anglesey **IV** 433

Newburgh, William of *see* William of Newburgh

Newburgh Priory (Yorks.) **III** 158

Newburn, cannonade **IX** 96, 168

Newburn on Tyne (Northumb.) **II** 601; **VI** 337

Newbury (Berks.) **VI** 518; battles **IX** 134, 137–8; **XII** 527

Newcastle-under-Lyme, castle **IV** 198

Newcastle upon Tyne (Northumb.): fort **Ia** 179–80; inscription 206; map 4 **Ib** xxxii; foundation **II** 614; **III** 47, 67, 82, 96; armed against David 270, 277, 338; retained by Stephen 272; castle 338, 352; Anglo-Scottish treaty (1244) **IV** 587–8; John Baliol does homage for Scotland 608; base of war finance (1296) 619; feudal host summoned (1297–8) 687, 688; Edward I at (1298) 699; Bishop Lamberton examined (1306) 716; **V** 98, 463; Edward II at 11, 25, 29; musters 48, 56, 68; coal trade 349; staple 351, 353; Edward III's charter 380; **VI** 35, 37, 45, 53, 63; castle 9; Percy estates 337; merchants 351; population 368; incorporation charter 392; and Edward IV 526; **VII** 75, 161, 214, 219, 229; Scottish invasion (1513) 280; Henry and James V make truce 363; trade and gild power 461, 465; foreign trade 468; Merchant Adventurers 473; sees divided

Newcastle upon Tyne (*cont.*)
518; hostmen of **IX** 333–4; parliamentary elections in **XII** 48, 52; **XV** 245–6, 434
Newcastle, duchess of **X** 418
Newcastle, duke of **X** 380; *see also* Pelham-Holles, Thomas
Newcastle, 5th duke of **XIII** 356, 383, 481
Newcastle, marquis of *see* Cavendish
Newcastle, Propositions of **IX** 144, 146
Newcastle programme **XIV** 207
Newcomen, Thomas **X** 43
Newcomen, Thomas (1663–1729) **XI** 115
Newcomen's pumping-engine **XII** 27
Newells (Herts.) *see* Scales, Robert, lord of Newell
Newent (Glos.) **VI** 292
Newfoundland **VII** 225, 226, 227, 228; **VIII** 245; **IX** 325–6, 343; **X** 231, 338, 340–2; fisheries 304, 338; **XI** 261, 264, 307, 310, 368; population and government 310; Treaty of Paris 372–5; **XII** 16, 75; (1783) 253–5
Newfoundland, and Chanak **XV** 191; American bases **XV** 496
Newhaven **VII** 407
Newhouse Abbey (Lincs.) **III** 188
Newman, Cardinal **XIV** 137
Newman, Dr George, afterwards Sir **XIV** 397, 520
Newman, John Henry **XIII** 504, 506, 520, 530, 539; biography 513; character and ideas 513–14; assists in writing *Tracts for the Times* 515; attacks Hampden 515–16; writes Tract XC 517; leaves the Church of England 518–19; description of gentleman 623
Newmarket (Cambs.) **V** 416, 418; **IX** 146, 264; **X** 408; **XV** 551
Newnes, George **XIV** 145, 310–11, 313, 315–16, 532

Newnham (Glos.) **III** 307
Newport (Monmouth) **IV** 202; **V** 59, 61; **VI** 510
Newport (Salop) **VI** 642
Newport Articles **IX** 153, 258
News Chronicle **XV** 309, 442
News of the World **XV** 28, 172
Newsholme, Dr Arthur, afterwards Sir **XIV** 518
newsletters **IX** 413
Newsome, Newsholme (Yorks.), manor **VI** 323
Newspaper Publication Act (1798) **XII** 362
newspaper-tax **X** 239
newspapers (newsbooks) **IX** 23, 412–13; **X** 356; **XI** 422; **XII** 541; circulation **XIII** 30–1, 623; stamp duty 179; (to 1886) **XIV** 143–5; (1886–1900) 310–16; (1901–14) 532–6; *see also* journals
Newstead: fort **Ia** 145, 151, 165, 200, 206; kept in use 211; vital route 246
Newton, Sir Isaac (1642–1727) **X** 30, 373–4, 383; language science 360; religious scepticism 386; **XI** 140, 301, 378, 379, 382; James Jurin 391; Royal Society 396; statue of 402, 409
Newton, Sir John **V** 408
Newton, John, treasurer of York **VI** 286
Newton, Thomas (1704–82), bishop of Bristol **XI** 82
Newton, William **XIII** 157
Newtown (Monmouth) **VI** 642
Newtown Butler **X** 306
Ney **XII** 460, 482, 486
Niall of the Nine Hostages **Ia** 426, 463
Nicaea, Greek empire **IV** 233
Nicaea, theatre **Ia** 578
Nicaragua **X** 328
Nice (Alpes-Mar.) **VI** 163; **X** 170, 213
Nicene Creed **Ia** 357
Nicholas, abbot of Siegburg **III** 328

Nicholas, cardinal bishop of Tusculum, and legate **III** 221, 457

Nicholas, Sir Edward, secretary of state **X** 2

Nicholas I, emperor of Russia **XIII** 217–18, 229, 233–5, 237, 239; Stratford Canning 252; Turkish empire 254–7, 260–1, 263–4; death 289; *see also* Crimean war; Russia, policy towards Turkey

Nicholas, Grand Duke **XV** 23

Nicholas, Hungarian clerk **III** 238

Nicholas II, Pope **II** 436, 465, 468, 585, 663

Nicholas III, Pope: and Peter of Aragon **IV** 253; relations with Kilwardby and Pecham 469–71, 474

Nicholas IV, Pope (1288–92): taxation of **III** 227; denounces treaty of Oloron **IV** 260; refuses to honour Charles of Salerno's engagements 261; grants dispensation for marriage of Edward of Caernarvon to Margaret of Scotland 265, 268, 599; king's clerks and the Church in England 261, 265–6, 340, 460; plans a crusade 265–7, 513; assessment of English clergy for tax (1291) 498, 509; **V** 287

Nicholas V, Pope **VI** 270

Nicholas, Sir Edward **IX** 33, 108, 128

Nicholas II, tsar of Russia **XIV** 260, 261, 366, 369; signs Björkö treaty 370; grants a constitution 404; dissolves the Duma 404; *see also* Russia

Nicholas of Clamanges **VI** 679

Nicholas of Lynn **V** 509

Nicholas of the Tower, warship **VI** 494

Nicholl, Robertson **XV** 28

Nicholls, Colonel **X** 63

Nicholson, Ben **XV** 179

Nicholson, General Francis **X** 230, 342

Nicholson, H., remains seated **XV** 328, 329

Nicholson, John **XIII** 437–8

Nicholson, *or* Lambert, William **VII** 395

Nichomachus Flavianus **Ia** 409

Nicolas, Sir Harris **XIII** 550–1

Nicoll, Robertson **XIV** 308

Nicolson, William (1655–1727), bishop of Carlisle **XI** 79; bishop of Derry 298, 304

Nicopolis, battle **V** 476

Nidaros **II** 406; assembly at 404–5

Nidd, river **Ib** map 4 xxxii; synod near **II** 145

Nidingham *see* Girton

Nietzsche **XIV** 551

Nieuport (Flanders) **V** 431; **VI** 137; **VII** 98, 99; **VIII** 357, 402, 428

Niewe Herball **VIII** 317

Nigel, bishop of Ely **III** 133, 136, 137, 183; pupil of Anselm 234; treasurer 322

Niger, Ralph, critic of the third crusade **IV** 80

Niger, Roger, bishop of London **IV** 50, 55, 60

Nigeria **XIV** 188, 189, 242–3; enemy property **XV** 67, 192

Nightingale, Lady Elizabeth, Roubiliac's monument of **XI** 409

Nightingale, Florence **XIII** 285–6, 621; biography 285

Nijmegen, legion IX tiles **Ia** 174

Nîmes **VIII** 162

Nine Hours' Day **XIV** 133

Nineteen Propositions **IX** 125–6

Ninian, St **II** 86

Niort (Deux-Sèvres) **VI** 113

Niort (Poitou) **III** 441

Nipius Ascanius, C. **Ia** 634

Nith, river **Ia** 145

nithing **II** 429–30

Nithsdale, earl of *see* Maxwell, William

Nivelle, General **XV** 80, 81, 86, 99

Nivelles **II** 541

Niven, Dr James **XIV** 509

Nivernais **VI** 573; *bailliage* 191, 239
Noaillan, Gilles de **IV** 285
Noailles, A. D., duc de, maréchal (1678–1766) **XI** 242, 247, 393
Noailles, Antoine, sieur de, French ambassador **VII** 528, 536, 537
Noailles, marshal de **X** 171
nobility: by birth **II** 303–4; of royal descent 305
Noble, Frank **Ia** 5, 190, 559–60
Nodens: sanctuary **Ia** 362, 686; *see also* Lydney
Noiers, Geoffrey de **III** 261
Nolan, Captain **XIII** 281–2
Nollekens, J. **XIII** 587
Nollekens, Joseph (1737–1823), sculptor **XI** 408
Nollet, Jean Antoine, abbé (1700–70), electricity experiments **XI** 383
Nombre de Dios **VIII** 248, 417
Nominalists **VII** 254
Nominated Parliament **IX** 175
Non-intercourse Act (1809) **XII** 474–5
Non-intervention committee **XV** 394, 398, 421
non-jurors **X** 156; **XI** 75–6, 86, 93, 183, 395
non-recognition **XV** 371, 372
non-resistance, doctrine **X** 34
Nonant, Hugh of, bishop of Coventry **III** 103, 222, 258, 357, 368
Nonconformists: under Charles II **X** 21–5; numbers 27; under William and Mary 153–4; ecclesiastical settlement after revolution 153–62; occasional conformity 224; Schism Bill 247; **XV** 169, 266, 357, 440; *see also* Congregationalists; Presbyterians; Quakers
nonconformity **XII** 336; dissenting academies 40, 58; position in constitution 56, 156; bills for relief 156, 301; in favour of parliamentary reform 230; philanthropy 353, 358, 524; *see also* Methodism; Unitarians

Nonius Philippus **Ia** 251
Nonsuch (Surrey) **VII** 595
Nootka Sound, British settlement **XII** 296
Norbert, archbishop of Magdeburg **III** 188
Norbury, John, treasurer **VI** 1, 18, 34, 87, 429
Norbury, William of, justice **IV** 624
Nord-Baden **Ib** 194
Norden, John **VIII** 282; **IX** 195
Nordseeküstengruppe **Ib** 55, 63–4, 66, 193
Nore, naval mutiny (1797) **XII** 361, 373
Norfolk: Iceni **Ia** 44, 90, 114; communications 90, 563; fort 255; Hockwold 594, 690; **Ib** 87, 112; **III** 38–9, 134, 393; **V** 316, 317, 346; assessment of 192; marshland 312, 321, 347; rising 417–18, 420, 422; **VI** 7, 31, 288, 289, 344; Richmond manors 78; sheriffs 345, 449; local disorder 491; **VII** 489, 490, 527; **IX** 293, 314, 329
Norfolk, Adam of, king's clerk **IV** 309
Norfolk, Agnes, dowager duchess of, widow of 2nd duke of, sister of Sir Philip Tilney **VII** 418, 419; countess of Surrey 161
Norfolk, archdeacon of **IV** 186
Norfolk, dukes of *see* Howard, John; Howard, Thomas; Mowbray, John I; Mowbray, John II; Mowbray, John III; Mowbray, Thomas
Norfolk, earls of *see* Bigod, Hugh; Bigod, Roger; Brotherton
Norham (Northumb.) **III** 282; treaty (1212) **IV** 586, 594–5; Anglo-Scottish discussions and agreements (1291) 603–4; John Baliol swears fealty to Edward I 608; **VII** 147, 279, 389
Norham Castle, surrenders **VI** 531
Noricum **Ia** 427, 438, 460

Norman conquest, population **Ia** 545, 562

Norman, Montagu: American debt settlement **XV** 203; Snowden 212; helpless in face of unemployment 287; demands printing of ration books 290; bank rate 337

Normanby, marquis of **XIII** 249, 391, 463

Normand, Roger **V** 238

Normandy: coastal raids **Ia** 241, 283, 288, 375, 386; Bacaudae 283; Carausius 297–307; villas 303; town walls 327; Theodosius 382, 384; Magnus Maximus 402–3; British fear of barbarian attack from 427–8; settlement of Britons in 492–3; development of Frankish kingdoms 492–8; relations of Britain with N. Gaul 495, 497; **II** 319, 348, 375, 379, 540; relations with England under Æthelred II 375, 379; Æthelred departs for 386; priests receive English bishoprics 464–5; peasant society 479; condition (1050) 554–5; materials for this history 555–6; courts and councils 555–6; art of war 556–7; military organization 558–9; private warfare 559; succession in **III** 97; separated from England 100, 104, 115, 128; state under Duke Robert 105; William II's conquest of eastern 106–8; pledged to William II 110–13; wars resulting from occupation 111; Henry I renounces claims 116; his conquest of 118–21; Henry's insecurity 122, 124–30; King Stephen 134–5; Geoffrey Plantagenet's conquest 145, 160–1, 323; Henry Plantagenet does homage for 162; ecclesiastics imported 167; condition of the church 169; English spoken by aristocracy 252–3; influence on art and architecture 259, 260–2; rebellion (1173–4) 333–4; order re-established 340; barons resist occupation 363; Philip Augustus occupies part of 365; wars of Richard I and Philip Augustus 373–8; loss by King John 381–4, 430; effects of loss 431–2, 439; barons' obligation to serve in 471; **V** 114, 119, 138, 147, 247, 254; Edward III's invasion 133–4, 147, 149, 244, 246; cession 141; salt trade 349; **VII** 81, 110, 131, 172, 410; Medina del Campo (1489) 95–6; Henry and Catherine marriage negotiations 175; Edward Howard attacks 274–5; *see also* Armorica

Normandy, duchy: homage of dukes **IV** 382; demand for restoration to Henry III 14, 15, 84, 87, 93–5; Henry III surrenders claim (1259) 126, 127; fleet and war with Cinque Ports 644–5; Channel Islands and 319, 320; **VI** 135, 140, 142, 432, 475; Orléans captain-general (1404) 108; resistance to Henry V (1419–20) 183; Church 199; estates' taxation 206; income seized 206–7; Suffolk's part in loss 492; Edward IV's treaty 573; force of 10,000 (1475) 575; chancellor *see* Kemp, John; Louis of Luxembourg

Normandy, dukes of *see* Robert; William

Normans and Englishmen under William I **II** 680–1

Normanton on the Wolds (Notts.) **III** 49

Norreys, Sir Henry **VIII** 144

Norreys, Sir John **VIII** 368; expedition with Drake 411–12; campaign in Brittany 414–16

Norris, Berkshire family **VI** 600

Norris, Admiral Sir John (*c.*1660–1749) **XI** 36, 175, 226, 229, 232; Baltic 166; home fleet 210; naval adviser 231; fleet against Pretender 236; attack on French fleet 248

Norris, John I, treasurer and steward **VI** 600

Norris, John II: Coventry parliament **VI** 601; knighted 601; in Edward's favour (1467 onwards) 601; Buckingham's rebellion 601; attainted (Feb. 1484) 608; restored by Henry VII 601

Norris, Sir William **VI** 631

North, Council of the: organization and principles **VI** 638–9; **VIII** 136, 172; **IX** 103

North, Lord **XV** 192, 254, 317, 449

North, Lord **XII** 329; control of Banbury 52, 59, 147; refusal of chancellorship of Exchequer (1767) 124; paymaster of forces 577; chancellor of Exchequer (1767–82) 129, 135, 137, 142, 577; first lord of Treasury (1770–82) 147–57, 172, 203, 215, 239–42 — America and Ireland 213, 218–27 — petitioning movement 231 — decline 232–4 — state office holders 575; American policy 151, 193, 197–203, 206, 210; Indian policy 166–72, 196, 221, 312; Irish policy 222–5; in opposition (1782–3) 250–2, 257; secretary of state (1783) 258–61, 264–7, 579; in opposition to Pitt 269, 272

North, rising (Apr. 1489) **VII** 90

North Africa: war plans **XV** 460; French communications 520; hopes of bringing back into war 521; German air corps 531; early action proposed 540, 553; Churchill urges invasion 554; Roosevelt decides on invasion 555–6; Stalin welcomes invasion 557; landings 560; campaign 561–3; victories too remote 566

North America, Scots settlers **X** 281

North American colonies **X** 333–48

North Briton see Wilkes, John

North Carolina *see* Carolina

North Circular road **XV** 338

North East Passage **VII** 507

North Elmham **Ib** map 2 xxx

North of England, condition **VIII** 134, 135, 136, 137

North Foreland **XV** 498

North and Grey, William, 6th Baron (1678–1734) **XI** 182

North Grimthorpe, Humberside **Ia** 46

North Leigh, villa **Ia** 608

North Marston (Bucks.) **VI** 276

North Newbald **Ib** 189; map 4 xxxii

North Petherton forest **V** 530

North Sea **Ia** 78, 369, 556; **V** 359

North Walsham (Norfolk) **V** 418

North-western England: Norse invasions **II** 320, 331–2; British invasion from Strathclyde 332; northern Cumberland recovered by Earl Siward 417–18

Northallerton (Yorks.) **III** 272; **VI** 59

Northampton **II** 261, 321, 325, 327, 357; shire 338; Tostig occupied 579; earldom 512; **III** 33, 129, 277, 351, 462; earl of Chester arrested 147; meeting of Henry II and Becket 203; school 236; council meetings (1157) 327 — (1164) 207–9, 321 — (1176) 390; assize 338; revision (1176) of Assize of Clarendon 339, 398–9, 402; destruction of castles 398; punishment of mutilation 404; inheritance secured by 408; barons summoned to (1199) 430; army mustered (1205) 440–1; Pandulf meets John 456; castle besieged by barons (1215) 470; **IV** 11; captured by Lord Edward (1264) 186–7, 190; court and baronial government (1265) 200; crusade preached (1268) 219; congregation of bishops (1277) 471; assemblies of laymen and clergy (1283) 506, 507; treaty (Aug. 1290) 513, 600, 605, 608; **V** 337, 345, 453, 466, 521; parliaments 4,

352, 406; treaty 98–9, 115, 116; council 160; weavers 364; Lollards 520; **VI** 37, 556; Franciscans 29; treaty 35; St Andrew's Cluniac Priory 350; battle 520; River's arrest 613; **VII** 40, 267, 452, 462, 505; parish churches 39; treaty (1328) 157; riots **X** 258

Northampton, battle **VII** 37

Northampton, castle **VII** 37

Northampton, county **III** 31, 100

Northampton, earldom of **III** 157

Northampton, earls of *see* Bohun, Henry (Bolingbroke); Howard; Parr, William; Simon of Senlis

Northampton, Grey Friars' House **VII** 39

Northampton, John of **V** 377–8, 434–6, 437, 458, 466; denied king's pardon 489

Northamptonshire **Ia** 43, 637, 706; **Ib** 112; Frisian place-names; Geld Roll **II** 644; **V** 337, 345, 521; **VII** 452, 505

Northborough (Northants) **III** 407

Northbrook, 1st earl of **XIV** 11, 16, 62, 140

Northburgh, Michael, bishop of London (1355–61) **V** 211

Northburgh, Roger, bishop of Lichfield (1322–59), keeper of the privy seal (1312–16) **V** 40, 168, 210, 275, 277

Northcliffe, Lord: biography **XV** 26; power 26–7; attacks Liberal government 27, 29; death of Kitchener 58; offers employment to Lloyd George 69; Unionists bar 70; feared by Lloyd George 74; backs Milner 75; introduces Kenworthy to Lloyd George 84; Ministry of Information 107; sees no end to the war 110; drafts peace terms 127; Lloyd George attacks 135; Lloyd George identified with 137; death 186, 193; transforms press 187; dismisses Dawson 194, 418; sponsors

Melba 232; succeeded by Beaverbrook 234–5; hostility towards 282–3; presents better news 309; *Daily Mail* 548; *see also* Harmsworth, Alfred

Northcote, Sir Stafford, earl of Iddesleigh: biography **XIV** 32; budgets 33–4, 36, 40; leader of the House of Commons 40; antiobstruction rules 56; weakness in the Bradlaugh episode 68; becomes lord president with a peerage 91; foreign secretary 172; supersession and death 176; weak policy in Africa 189, 190; **XIII** 621

Northern barons (Norenses, Northanhumbrenses, Norois, Aquilonares, Boreales) **III** 462, 468, 469, 477

Northern Ireland, parliament **XV** 156; boundary 158, 218; Free State 159; rejects reunification 407; conscription does not extend to 444

Northfleet **Ib** map 5 68

Northington, 1st earl of *see* Henley, Robert

Northington, 2nd earl of, lord lieutenant of Ireland (1783–4) **XII** 579

Northleach (Glos.) **VI** 647, 649

Northumberland **Ia** 46; lead mines 634; royal site 675; **II** 503, 506; **III** 272, 276; William's claim to 280, 281, 282; purchase of sheriffdom 350, 351, 352; local levies (1297) **IV** 684; overrun by Scots (1297) 686; levies (1302) 708; Scots in **V** 32, 40, 98; sheriff of 187–8; assessment of 192; Sir G. Middleton 41, 204; coal-mine 302; county **VI** 35; forces 53; **VII** 385

Northumberland, countess of **VIII** 138

Northumberland, duke of *see* Dudley, John

Norwich, cathedral **III** 226, 261
Norwich, Geoffrey of **III** 427
Norwich, Sir Walter, treasurer (1314–17) **V** 46, 49
Nostell (Yorks.), priory of **III** 269
notaries **IV** 490
notarius **Ia** 357
Notfried **Ib** 77–8
Notiere, Walter le **V** 317
Notitia Dignitatum **Ia** 257, 321, 336, 346, 378; *vicarius'* insignia 381, 390; *dux Britanniarum* units 392–3; Illyricum 404; stations listed 412; limitations 418; *comes Britanniarum* 422; Saxon Shore 424; official records 437; western part 476; Tigris bargees 530; financial administration 531; weaving-mills 656; **Ib** 83–4, 121, 187, 217
notitia **Ia** 357
Nottingham (Snotingaham) **II** 248, 329–30, 334, 604, 733; castle 601; shire 254, 357; added to see of York 436; **III** 47, 79, 80, 85; weavers' gild 338; Greek fire used in siege (1194) 373; John's army at 455, 462, 480; **V** 246, 394, 418, 519; capture of Mortimer 101, 153; councils 101, 155, 193, 479; judges 448; **VI** 47, 53, 418, 556; Franciscans 29; incorporation charter 393; archers 508; Scottish delegation 629; Richard III's headquarters 639; **VII** 34, 67, 74, 391, 597; Richard at 50; rebellion over taxation 388; **IX** 129, 306; newspaper **X** 356; first steam engine in cotton mill (1785) **XII** 334
Nottingham, county **III** 348
Nottingham, 3rd earl of, and 8th earl of Winchilsea (1689–1769) **XI** 223; *see also* Berkeley, William; Finch; Howard; Mowbray
Nottingham Castle **III** 261, 348, 355, 366; its capture 368; treasure store 417; **IV** 11, 198
Nottingham coalfield **XV** 183

Nottinghamshire **Ia** 43; footsoldiers on Scottish campaign (1300) **IV** 693; **V** 27, 371; **IX** 329
Nova Scotia (Acadia) **VII** 226; **IX** 326; **X** 327, 337, 338, 343; English occupation 230, 231; held by French 338; Port Royal captured then recovered 341; **XI** 307, 310, 318–19, 347; population and government 311; *see also* Louisburg
Nova Zembla **VII** 561
Novara, battle (1500) **VII** 152
novel disseisin, writ and assizes **III** 157, 315, 406–8; **IV** 361
novelists **XII** 348, 536–9
Noveray, Thomas, of Leicester, Lollard propagandist **VI** 131
Novgorod **III** 89; **V** 359; **VI** 355; St Peter's court 69
Novikov, Madame **XIV** 45
Noviomagus Regnensium see Chichester
Novum Organum **VIII** 294
Nowell, Alexander (1507?–1602): dean of St Paul's **VII** 571, 577
Nowell, Charles **VI** 344
Nowell, Laurence **VIII** 283
Noxgaga **Ib** 141
Noyon (Oise) **VI** 250; treaty **VII** 306; Maximilian adheres to (Jan. 1517) 307; **VIII** 414
Nugent, Christopher (d. 1731) **XI** 291
Nugent, Richard, Lord Delvin: lord deputy of Ireland (1527) **VII** 651
Nugent, Robert (1702–88) **XII** 53; president of the Board of Trade 578
'Nullum Tempus' Bill **XII** 144
numen **Ia** 707; emperor 533, 682, 688, 713; individual 684; place 690
numeracy **Ia** 507–8
numeri (military units) **Ia** 248, 521; *Brittonum* 197; *Moesiacorum* 361; *Barcariorum Tigrisiensium* 530; *Hnaudifridi* 667; **Ib** 77, 79, 80, 187
Numerian, Emperor **Ia** 287
Numerianus (soldier) **Ia** 511
numerus Hnaudifridi **Ib** 77–8

Numidia, estates **Ia** 600

Nuneaton (War.), pottery near **Ia** 645

Nunna, alias Nothelm, king of Sussex **II** 58, 73

Nuremberg: alliance between Edward I and Adolf of Nassau (1294) **IV** 660; **VI** 356; **VII** 104, 340, 356; losses in raid **XV** 572; trial of war criminals 596

Nursling (Hants), monastery **II** 159, 168

Nutley (Hants), abbey **III** 180

nutrition **XII** 11–13, 524

Ny Parke, fort **VIII** 489

Nymphs **Ia** 684

Nymwegen, peace of **X** 83, 88, 95

Nyon agreement **XV** 421

O

oak houses **VIII** 272
Oakwood, fort **Ia** 165
Oastler, Richard **XIII** 135, 148
Oates, Captain **XIV** 553
Oates, Titus **X** 93–5, 106, 118, 302
oath-helpers **II** 316–17; in Danelaw 512
oaths: to maintain the Provisions of Oxford by king, barons and freemen **IV** 135, 140, 146, 152; crucial clause 161–2; papal dispensation 163, 165, 168; settlement (May 1265) 198; fealty sworn by the Scots to Edward I (1291 and 1296) 606, 615–16; sworn to Edward's son and heir (1297) 680; Edward I's to observe concessions (1297) 697, 703; of supremacy **VIII** 15, 16; *ex officio* 199
OBE **XV** 175, 265
Oberjersdal **Ib** 55; map 1 xxix
Obi, river **VIII** 241
Obrenovitch dynasty **XIV** 195
O'Brien, Charles, 6th viscount of Clare (1699–1761) **XI** 291
O'Brien, Conor **V** 233
O'Brien, Donnell, king of Thomond **III** 308, 313, 314
O'Brien, James Bronterre **XIII** 135–6, 139, 141, 143, 146; biography 135
O'Brien, Murrough, of Thomond **VIII** 465
O'Brien, Smith **XIII** 349–50, 357
O'Brien, William **XIV** 179, 180, 182, 184, 186, 451
O'Brien family **V** 472; **VII** 125
O'Briens of Thomind **IV** 561
Observants (reformed Franciscans) **VII** 191, 229; suppressed in England **VII** 376
Observations on a libel **VIII** 453
Observer **XV** 27, 66, 194, 573

obsessio Etin or *Etain* **Ib** 197; *see also* Edinburgh
obsessio Montis Badonici see Mons Badonicus
obstruction, parliamentary **XIV** 11, 56, 73
Occamists **VII** 254
Occasional Conformity **X** 224; Acts 12, 232, 254
occupations of the people (1815) **XIII** 3–5; (1850–70) 601–4
Ocean **Ia** 3, 38, 82, 85, 420; permanent stations 427
Oceanus, cult **Ia** 687
Ochino, Bernardino **VII** 515, 543, 556
Ochsenfurt, monastery **II** 173
Ochterlony, Sir D., major-general **XIII** 411
Ockham, John **V** 22, 49
Ockham, William of **V** 290, 509–10; *see also* William of Ockham
Ockwells (Berks.), nr. Bray **VI** 600, 652
Ocland, Christopher **VIII** 323
Oclatinius Adventus **Ia** 227
O'Connell, Daniel (1775–1847) **XII** 446; wins Clare election **XIII** 77, 343; relations with the Whigs 94, 96, 101–2, 330, 344–9; biography 340; character and ideas 340–1; founds the Catholic association 342; arrest and trial 350; **XV** 159
O'Connor, Feargus: character **XIII** 136; editor of the *Northern Star* 136; chartist leader 137, 139–46
O'Connor, Sir R. **XV** 524
O'Connor, T. P. **XIV** 184
O'Conor, Rory **III** 303, 305, 306, 308, 311–13
O'Conor family **V** 472
O'Conors in Connaught **IV** 561; Cathel (d. 1224) 568
Octavius Sabinus **Ia** 251–2, 275

419

Octennial Act (1786) **XII** 389

October Club **X** 238

Oczakov: Russian capture **XII** 295; British ultimatum 297

Oda, bishop of Ramsey, archbishop of Canterbury **II** 347, 357, 365, 366, 437; monk at Fleury 448; death 367, 448

Odd Down **Ib** 168; map 3 xxxi

Odda of Deerhurst **II** 550

Odell (Beds.): agriculture **Ia** 15, 608; well-shaft 692

Odenwald, *limes* **Ia** 175, 197

Oder **XV** 594

Odger, George **XIV** 132

Odhams Press **XV** 251

Odiham (Hants) **III** 53

Odiham Castle **IV** 22, 25, 48

Odo, abbot of Battle **III** 253

Odo, bishop of Bayeux **II** 623, 625, 630, 637, 649; made earl of Kent 599; acts as Justiciar 610; commands forces (1075) 612; harries Northumbria 614; arrest and trial 616; Anglo-Norman jury 651; knight's service 682; **III** 52, 66, 115; rebellion 100–4; trial plea and verdict 103, 138, 368; tapestry 264

Odo, count of Champagne **III** 109

Odoacer **Ia** 438, 460

Odofredo (d. 1265), utility, necessity and taxation **IV** 322

O'Dogherty, Sir Cahir **IX** 109

O'Donnel, Hugh (Duv) **VII** 128, 132

O'Donnel family **VII** 125

O'Donnell, Daniel (1666–1735) **XI** 292

O'Donnell, Hugh Roe **VIII** 480–1

O'Donnell, Rory, earl of Tyrconnel **IX** 108–9

O'Donnells, the **VIII** 464

O'Donnells of Tirconnel **IV** 561

Ofen (Buda) **X** 127

Offa, king of Angel **II** 13; ancestor of Mercian kings 39; draws boundary *bi Fifeldore* **II** 13

Offa, king of Mercia, overlord of southern English **II** 34–6, 46, 93, 95, 259; charters quoted 46, 287–9, 306, 309, 526–7; establishes Mercian supremacy 204–6, 206–12; relations with English kingdoms, Kent 206–8, Sussex 208–9, Wessex 209–10, Essex 210, East Anglia 210, Northumbria 212; regnal styles 210; relations with British peoples 214–15; relations with Charlemagne 215, 219–21; receives papal legates 215–19; provides for archbishopric of Lichfield 218; son consecrated king 218–19; daughters' marriages 220, 224–5; daughter 224; coins 222–4; significance of reign 224–5; laws 224, 276

Offaly, lord of **IV** 679

Offaly, tribal lands **VIII** 462

Offamil, Walter of, archbishop of Palermo **III** 321, 331

Offa's Dyke **Ia** 190–1; **II** 36, 212–15, 574

Officers, household *see* Appendix

Officers of state *see* Appendix

official of archbishop and the Court of Canterbury **IV** 491–2

official records *see notitia*

official residences: Fishbourne? **Ia** 161–3; London 162–3; York 325, 328; repair 398; Cologne 456; Folkestone? 529; satellite villas 597–9; Fen? 644; *see also* palaces; *principia*

Official Secrets Act (1911) **XV** 485, 603

Offord, John **V** 211

Oftfor, bishop of Worcester **II** 181

Ogbourne (Wilts.), alien priory **VI** 301

Ogbourne St Andrew (Wilts.) **V** 339, 345

Ogilby, John, *Britannia* **X** 51

Ogilvie, William, biography **XIII** 129

Ogle, Sir Chaloner (?1681–1750), Admiral **XI** 235

Ogle, Robert, Lord **VI** 511, 530

Ogle, William **V** 94

Oglethorpe, James Edward (1696–1785) **XI** 10, 95, 129, 135, 139; Fisheries Bill 277, 337; and Georgia 207, 309–10

Oglethorpe, Owen, bishop of Carlisle **VIII** 9, 10

O'Hanlon, Phelyme **VII** 128

O'Hely, James, bishop of Tuam **VIII** 480

Ohthere, voyage **II** 274

oil **Ia** 42, 641, 652

oil industry **X** 339

Oisc *or* Æsc, surname of Oeric, son of Hengist **II** 9, 16–17, 31

Oiscingas, name of Kentish royal house **II** 17

Oise, river **VII** 313

Oisel, Hugh, of Ypres **III** 423

Okehampton (Devon) **II** 632

Okehampton, honour **IV** 557

Okeover, John **IX** 387

Okey, John **IX** 273

Olaf, king of Norway, son of Harold Hardrada **II** 590, 617

Olaf Guthfrithson, king of York and Dublin **II** 342–3, 357–9, 362; treaty with Edmund 357

Olaf Haroldson (St Olaf), king of Norway **II** 402–5; cult 462; London churches dedicated to **III** 88

Olaf Sihtricson, king of York and Dublin **II** 340, 351–8, 361–3

Olaf Skattkonung, king of Sweden **II** 543

Olaf Tryggvason, king of Norway **II** 378, 380, 406, 462, 541

Olarius **VII** 276

old age pensions **XV** 1; *see also* pensions

Old Bill **XV** 62

Old Fortunatus **VIII** 301

Old Hall (nr. Ware) **VII** 588

Old Malton (N. Yorks.) **VI** 417

Old Melrose (Magilros) **II** 732

Old Sarum (Searoburh) **Ib** 149, 153, 162; map 3 xxxi

Old Sleaford **Ia** 43

Old Vic **XV** 314

Oldcastle, Sir John, Lord Cobham **V** 520; **VI** 25, 273, 298; Builth captain 103; marriage 129; convocation appearance 130; imprisonment and escape 130; Lollard Commissioners' indictment 132; retreats 132; sought for by Clarence (Feb. 4) 133; Almeley (1417) 133; Southampton Plot 146

Oldcastle, Sir Richard, of Almeley **VI** 103

Oldcastle, Sir Thomas, sheriff of Herefordshire **VI** 103

Oldenburg, Henry **X** 372

Oldfield, Joshua **X** 264

Oldfield (Middx.) **V** 365

Oldhall, Sir William, of Hunsdon (Herts.) **VI** 516; Speaker of Commons 500; attainted (1453) 507; outlawry annulled (1455) 507

Oldham **XII** 511; mills **XV** 122; population 167

Oldknow, Mr **XII** 511

Oldys, William (1696–1761), antiquary **XI** 396

Oléron, Isle of: laws **III** 439; **IV** 88, 92, 95, 103, 127; demanded by Hugh of La Marche; granted to Lord Edward 118; Edward's attempt to grant it away (1258) 275; law 620, 645–6

Olibriones **Ia** 439, 488

Olivarez, Spanish ambassador at Rome **VIII** 389, 390, 391

Oliver, Isaac **VIII** 302; **IX** 375–6

Oliver, natural son of King John **III** 428

Oliver, Peter **IX** 375

Oliver, Peter (1713–91), Massachusetts landowner **XII** 177

Oliver, Richard, alderman, MP **XII** 142

olives **Ia** 540

Olivier, Sydney, afterwards Lord **XIV** 334

Oloron, in Béarn: treaty (1287) **IV** 259, 260; Edward I at (1288–9) 283–4

Olympian gods **Ia** 665–6, 707

O'Madden Tract **V** 44

O'Mahony, Daniel (d. 1714) **XI** 292

Ombrière, nr. Bordeaux, provost **IV** 304

O'Neill, Brian, 2nd Baron Dungannon **VIII** 469

O'Neill, Brian McPhelim **VIII** 475

O'Neill, Con, 1st earl of Tyrone **VIII** 465, 469

O'Neill, house of **VII** 125, 133

O'Neill, Hugh, earl of Tyrone: Irish rebel **VIII** 428, 431–7, 441, 483; alliance with Spain 408, 480, 482, 483–9; objectives and strategy 481–2, 483–8; surrender 490; **IX** 108–9

O'Neill, Matthew ('Kelly'), 1st baron of Dungannon **VIII** 469

O'Neill, Owen Roe **IX** 134, 162

O'Neill, Shane **VIII** 464, 465, 469, 470, 471

O'Neill, Turlogh Luineach **VIII** 469, 481

O'Neill of Clandeboy **VII** 132

O'Neill family **V** 472

O'Neills, the **VIII** 464

O'Neills of Tir Owen **IV** 561, 565; Brian 561

Onslow, Arthur (1691–1768), Speaker of House of Commons **XI** 21, 145, 183, 184, 203; **XII** 64, 150

Onslow, George (1731–92), MP **XII** 150

Onslow family, seat in parliament **XII** 52

Opdam, Wassanaer, Dutch admiral **IX** 228; **X** 65

open-fields **II** 280, 315, 514

opera **X** 405–6; beginning **IX** 389, 398–9

Operation Dynamo **XV** 486

Oplontis, villa **Ia** 161

Oporto **III** 149

oppida **Ia** 92, 589; *see also* towns

Opposition: vanishes in First World War **XV** 32; in Second World War 477; leader gets salary 404

optimorum consensus **Ia** 449

optio **Ia** 666

ora **II** 510

Oran, action **XV** 494

Orange, William of *see* William of Nassau

Orange Free State: alliance with Transvaal **XIV** 233; declared annexed 255; self-government granted 390; in the Union of South Africa 390

orators *see* rhetoric

Orbec (Calvados) **VI** 174

ordainers (1310–11) **V** 10, 72–6, 179–80

Orde, Sir John (1751–1824) **XII** 428

Orde, Thomas, 1st Baron Bolton (1746–1807), Irish secretary **XII** 276

Orde-Powlett, Thomas *see* Orde, Thomas

Ordericus Vitalis **III** 111, 117; on Bishop Odo's rebellion 100; ballad on Henry's victory 118; historian 248; on Henry I's ministers 388

orders in council **XII** 465, 472–5, 476, 499, 551

Ordgar, ealdorman of Devon **II** 372

Ordinal (1550) **VII** 517, 521

ordinances (1311) **V** 12–30, 46, 48, 69; Middle Party 53; Lancaster 54; approved 55; repealed 71; Ordainers 72; under Edward II and III and Despensers 77–8; 'death-blow' 103; Islip and clergy 297; common petitions 403; issued by two houses **IX** 105–6

ordnance *see* military equipment

Orwell, George **XV** 395
Orwell, river **Ib** map 2 xxx; **II** 392, 731; **III** 336
Osbeck, John, father of Perkin Warbeck **VII** 119
Osberht, king of Northumbria **II** 247
Osbern, author of *De expugnatione Lyxbonensi* **III** 150
Osbern, bishop of Exeter **II** 642, 677
Osbern, brother of Swein Estrithson **II** 247, 602
Osbern of Burghill (Osbern fitz Richard) **II** 562
Osborn, Henry (1698–1771), Admiral **XI** 361
Osborne, Dorothy **IX** 284, 389
Osborne, Sir Edward **VIII** 241, **IX** 97
Osborne, Francis, 5th duke of Leeds (1751–99): biography **XII** 267; foreign secretary (1783–91) 267, 297, 300, 580; out of office 325
Osborne, Thomas, 1st earl of Danby, marquis of Camarthen and duke of Leeds; lord treasurer **X** 85–7; impeachment 96–7, 352; on bail 106; William III 133, 139; favours coronation of Mary alone 146; lord president of the council 180
Osborne case **XIV** 437–8; judgement **XV** 114
Oseney Abbey (Oxford), **III** 148, 186, 237, 248; Oseney Abbey **V** 50
Osfrid, Norwegian ambassador to Athelstan **II** 349
Osfrith, son of King Edwin **II** 81
Osgar, monk of Abingdon sent to study customs of Fleury **II** 448
Osgod Clapa **II** 430
O'Shea, Mrs, afterwards Mrs Parnell **XIV** 74, 93, 183, 186; correspondence with Gladstone 558–63; relations with Parnell 564–6
O'Shea, Captain W. H. **XIV** 74, 89, 183, 559, 564–6

Osiander (Andreas Hosemann) **VII** 356, 551
Osketel, archbishop of York **II** 436, 495–6
Oslac, father of Osburg mother of King Alfred **II** 23–4, 639
Oslaf **Ib** appendix II
Oslo, captured by Germans **XV** 470
Osmund the Chancellor, bishop of Salisbury **II** 642, 644, 667, 671
Osnabrück, bishopric **XI** 12
Osney, nr. Oxford **VII** 462
Osred, son of Aldfrith, king of Northumbria **II** 91, 93, 205
Osred, son of Alhred, king of Northumbria **II** 93
Osric, king of Deira **II** 81
'Ossian' **XII** 352
Ossory **III** 305
Oste, river **Ib** 62
Ostend (Belgium) **VII** 99; **VIII** 357, 364, 428; **X** 216; **XV** 11; attempt to block 103
Ostend Company **XI** 193, 195–201
Osthryth, wife of King Æthelred of Mercia **II** 83
Ostia, archbishop of **III** 331
Ostia, cardinal bishop of, and legate *see* Alberic
Ostia, shops and warehouses **Ia** 657–8; tombs 697
Ostmen **III** 303; Irish settlements 302, 316; admit Lanfranc as head of church 304; assault on Dublin 306–7, 308; decay in Ireland **IV** 565
Ostorius Scapula, P. **Ia** 66, 85, 90, 100–6, 112; battle against 101, 186; defeat of Caratacus 106; lack of political judgement 107, 113; Silures 534
Ostrogoths **Ia** 371, 417, 425, 438
O'Sullivan **XI** 271; *see also* 'Moidart, the seven men of'
O'Sullivan Beare of Kerry **VIII** 471, 489, 490
Oswald, James (1715–69) **XII** 79
Oswald, king of Northumbria **II** 81;

424

overlord of southern English 34, 82–3, 86, 118; obtains bishop from Iona 118

Oswald, Mr **XII** 282

Oswald, Richard (1705–84) **XII** 250

Oswaldslow hundred (Worcs.) **II** 496, 501, 650

Oswestry (Salop), possibly Maserfelth **II** 82; **III** 299; pleadings **IV** 417, 418; **VI** 335

Oswine, king of Deira **II** 83

Oswiu, king of Northumbria **II** 81, 83, 120–2, 130; overlord of southern English 34, 83–5, 87–8, 232–3

Oswulf, earl of Northumbria, son of Eadwulf **II** 362, 601

Oswulf, king of Northumbria **II** 92

Otford (Ottanford) (Kent), battles **II** 207, 210, 392, 733

Otho, Emperor **Ia** 128–30

Otis, James (1725–83), American lawyer **XII** 177, 185

otium **Ia** 81, 203, 728; *cum dignitate* 710

Otley (Yorks.) **II** 436

Otranto **VII** 113

Ottanford *see* Otford (Kent)

Ottawa, conference **XV** 333; agreement 339, 529, 535

Otterburne, battle (Chevy Chase) **V** 146, 463

Otto, cardinal deacon of St Nicola, papal legate in England, Scotland and Ireland **IV** 74, 76, 398, 583, 586; council and constitutions (1237) 451, 453, 473; clerical taxation 502

Otto IV, count of Burgundy, fief of the Empire **IV** 248, 667

Otto I, Emperor, English marriage **II** 346–7

Otto IV, Emperor **III** 280–1; made count of Poitou 376; elected king of the Romans 377, 381, 415, 499–53, 461, 464; defeated at Bouvines 467

Otto, L. G. (1754–1817) **XII** 409

Otto the Goldsmith **III** 414

Ottoboino Fieschi, cardinal legate, later Pope Adrian VI (1276) **IV** 180; commission 199, 207; in England (1265–8) 206, 207–8, 209; success as peacemaker 213–15, 218; Treaty of Montgomery 215, 383; statute of Marlborough 216; preaches crusade and holds legatine council 219; constitutions 451, 472–4; importance of legation 219, 220

Otway, Thomas **X** 368

Oudenarde **VIII** 356

Oudenarde, battle **X** 216, 241

Oudh **XIII** 403, 428, 433, 439–40

Ouestræfeld *see* Austerfield (Yorks.)

Oughtred, William **IX** 368

Oundle (Undulum) (Northants), monastery **II** 145; chapel of St Thomas **VII** 39

Ouse (Use), Great, river **II** 26, 28, 261, 733

Ouse (Use), river (Beds.) **Ib** xxvii; map 2 xxx; map 3 xxxi; **II** 733

Ouse (Use), river (Cambs.) **Ia** 268, 564; **II** 733

Ouse (Use), river (Sussex) **Ib** 138; map 2 xxx; **II** 733

Ouse (Use), river (Yorks.) **Ib** xxvi, 175, 196; map 4 xxxii; **II** 589, 733; **VI** 286

outlawry, law **IV** 60

Outram, Sir James **XIII** 421–2, 437–9; biography 421

ovation **Ia** 97, 394

Overbury, Sir Thomas **IX** 20

Overend and Gurney failure **XIV** 112, 114

Overhall (Suffolk) **V** 415

Overlord, Operation: British committed **XV** 563; given priority 572; Churchill fails against 573; Stalin recommends 575; landing craft 576

Oxford, church of St Mary **III** 238, 242; church of St George in the castle 148

Oxford, councils (1136): **III** 133, 134; (1139) 137; (1166) 230, 398; (1177) 312; (1197) 371; (1205) 441; (1213) 463; (1215) 478

Oxford, earls of *see* Harley, Edward; Harley, Robert; Vere, John de; Vere, Richard de; Vere, Robert de

Oxford, John of, bishop of Norwich **III** 210, 211, 219, 222, 329

Oxford, prior of St Frideswide **III** 67

Oxford and Asquith, 1st earl of *see* Asquith, Herbert Henry

Oxford Movement **XIII** 114; origins and course 512–18; effect 519–20

Oxford Union, and King and Country **XV** 362, 364; *see also* Collective security

Oxford University **IV** 56, 57, 70; dispersion from (1264) 186; Durham monks as students of law 485; training ground of ecclesiastics 486–8; inception of Thomas de Cantilupe at (1273) 489–90; chancellor summoned to parliament of Lincoln 701; **V** 26, 153, 212, 299; sermon before 85; Wyclif 290, 511–16; Islip educated and founder, Canterbury College 296–7; library 300; anticlericalism 310; schools for boys 500; supremacy 501; officers 502; quarrel with friars 503–4 —with Oxford town 504–5; importance of colleges 506–7; degree subjects 508; Ockham and Wyclif, philosophers 509–10; Lollards 517–24; university 507; **VI** 421; northern nation clerks 58; view on heresy 96; Arundel's visit (1411) 97, 129; chancellor and proctors 97; St Mary's church 98, 675; letter to Convocation of Canterbury

298; chancellor's steward 601; **VII** 236, 237, 242, 295, 576; printing press 238–9, 579; Thomas More 247; Erasmus 249, 257; reformers 343, 345; divorce and the Reformation 348; Cromwell's visitation (1535–6) 377; medicine and fraud prevention 467; Lutherans and Zwinglians 516; colleges founded 570, 594; Greeks and Trojans at 570, 571; public professorships and lectureships founded 570, 572, 573; scholarship and politics 572; John Skelton 585; **IX** 131, 353–5; politics **X** 103, 105–6, 119, 124; architecture 390–1; education 414–15; unequal treatment of women **XV** 166; Anglican chapels 169; modern universities 171, 309; New Bodleian 178; university grants committee 186; for superior classes 308; gives degree to P. G. Wodehouse 312; *see also* universities

Oxford University, colleges: All Souls **VI** 287, 301, 372, 654–5, 669 —graduates 673 —alien priories 675; **VII** 242, 257; Balliol **V** 507, 510; **VI** 279, 680; Brasenose **VII** 570; Canterbury **V** 297, 507, 510, 515; **VII** 246, 573; Cardinal (later Christ Church) **VII** 333, 516, 594; foundation 343, 570; Tyndale's New Testament 345–6; Wolsey and scholarship 571–3; Corpus Christi **VII** 570, 572, 575, 599; Divinity School **VI** 648; Durham **V** 507; **VII** 573; Exeter **V** 299, 500, 506; Gloucester **V** 507; **VII** 573; Lincoln **VI** 669; Magdalen **VI** 669, 674; **VII** 241, 242, 245, 570, 575; Wolsey as bursar 287–8; Tyndale 343, 346; architecture 592; Merton **IV** 486, 493; **V** 468, 500, 506, 508, 517 —John Wyclif, fellow 510; **VI**

427

Oxford University, colleges (*cont.*) 648, 674, 676; **VII** 242; New **V** 226, 294, 394, 500, 506 —astronomy students 509; **VII** 236, 241, 377, 575, 577; Oriel **V** 264, 506; Queen's **V** 500, 506, 510; **VII** 257; St Bernard's **VII** 573; St John's **VII** 601; St Mary's **VII** 250, 573; University 507

Oxfordshire: sergeanties **III** 19; forest in 30, 31

Oxfordshire **Ia** 43, 68; pottery 644–9; cemeteries 694, 705–6; **Ib** 139, 170; **II** 38, 350, 393; **V** 204, 316, 429, 453, 520; change in rural life 315; **VII** 452, 457, 489, 505, 528

oxgang **II** 514–15

Oxinden, Henry **IX** 283–4

Oxmantown Green **VII** 127

Oxnaford *see* Oxford

Oxus **VIII** 238

oxygen **XII** 334

Oye (Calais) **VI** 106; French negotiations 474

Oyster, Thomas, of London **VI** 76

oyster shells **Ia** 565, 630

Oystermouth Castle (Gower) **V** 73

P

paintings (*cont.*)
156–7; (1890s) 325–6; (1901–14) 542–3

Paisley, Cluniac priory **IV** 580

Pakenham, Sir E. M. (1778–1815) **XII** 481, 494, 555

palaces: governor's at London **Ia** 112, 156–7, 161, 530–1, 658; Nero's Golden House 156, 161; York? 229, 328, 583; trier 325; Diocletian 325, 452; Cologne 456, 493; bishop's at Trier 725; *see also* Fishbourne; official residences

palaeobotany *see* scientific analysis

Palaeologus, house of **VII** 114

Palafox, J. de (1780–1847) **XII** 460

Palais de danse **XV** 313

Palatinate, Spanish invasion **IX** 23, 54; cause of Anglo-Spanish rupture 58–9; Charles eager to recover 59; recovery 215; **X** 128, 169

Palatine Hill, Rome **Ia** 161

palatine troops (*palatini*) **Ia** 375, 366–7, 404

Palatines **X** 129, 344

Palatio, Octavian de, archbishop of Armagh **VII** 72, 80

Palavicino, Horatio **VIII** 260–1

Pale, the **VII** 70, 127, 132, 134; attempts to make secure for England 130–1; **VIII** 463

Palermo, archbishop of *see* Offamil, Walter of

Palermo **III** 102; **IV** 121

Palestine **Ia** 75, 131, 717; **III** 95, 111, 125, 128, 478; Duke Robert's crusade 110, 113; expedition (1147) 149; cult of St Thomas 215; Richard's crusade and capture 297, 359–63, 373, 434; knight-service obligations 370; Saladin Tithe 419; Anglo-French agreement **XV** 50; Balfour declaration 71, 98; conquered 98; Lloyd George 116; British mandate 152; Passfield 254, 276–7; conflicts 407–8; Middle East

command 523

Palestrina **VIII** 306

Paley, William (1743–1805), archdeacon of Carlisle: *View of the Evidences of Christianity* **XI** 85, 87; **XII** 333

Palgrave, Francis **XIII** 551

Palingenius **VIII** 323

palisades **Ia** 175

Palk, chaplain at Fort St David (*c.*1755) **XI** 332

Palladio **IX** 380; **X** 392

Palladius **Ia** 395

Palliser, Sir Hugh (1723–96) **XII** 213

pallium, archbishops visits to Rome **II** 467; presented by Holy See representatives **VI** 266

Palm, Count, imperial ambassador (*c.*1727) **XI** 200

Palmer, Sir Henry **VIII** 398

Palmer, John (1742–1818) **XII** 285

Palmer, Richard, bishop of Syracuse and archbishop of Messina **III** 331

Palmer, Roger, earl of Castlemaine **X** 130

Palmer, Roundell, 1st earl of Selborne: biography **XIV** 2, 11, 16; passes Judicature Act 17–19; attitude about Gordon 82; passes Married Women's Property Act 86–7; differs from Gladstone over home rule 96; religious cast 137, 139

Palmer, Thomas **XII** 359

Palmer, Sir Thomas **VII** 529, 530

Palmerston, 2nd Viscount **XII** 272, 335, 338, 490

Palmerston, Viscount **XIV** 1, 2, 5, 10, 137; parliamentarianism 186; Belgian neutrality 491, 574; *see also* Temple, Henry John

Palmyra, Barates **Ia** 514, 659

Palos **VII** 225

Palsgrave, John, tutor to Princess Mary (d. 1554) **VII** 299, 303

Pampeluna **IV** 238; **V** 144

Paris (*cont.*)
and treaty (1259) 84, 122, 123–8, 124, 135; later discussions, execution and changes in the treaty 170, 186, 273, 289–91; Henry III in (1262) 170–1; epidemic 171; Edward I in (1273) 226; truce between Philip III and Alfonso X of Castile (1280) 243; Edward I's second visit and treaty (1286) 255–6, 290–1; negotiations of Edmund of Lancaster (1293–4) 646, 647; Scottish embassy (1302–4) 697, 710; peace (1303) 653–4, 708; the Louvre **IV** 255; Saint-Germain-des-Prés, abbey 255; Sainte-Chapelle 119; Temple 82, 126, 281; **V** 61, 123, 138, 144, 212; Isabella and exiles 81–2; embassies 117, 118; treaties 105–7; Edward III's armies march against Philip 134; movement of Étienne Marcel 140; university 501, 504; **VI** 137, 139, 151, 163, 166; pro-Burgundian feeling 108, 111; John the Fearless moves to capture 172; Henry V's campaign 173, 177, 187, 200; Burgundians enter 174; gates 181; Henry V's reception 182; University 187; king's palace 193; Salisbury enters (1428) 245; charterhouse 296; and Henry VI 310; *parlement* 540, 559; **VII** 88, 242, 313, 404, 558; Erasmus 250–1, 255, 571; Reformers 338; Reginald Pole 547; coinage 608; université de 348; **VIII** 414–15; siege **XIV** 7; Commune 7; Exhibition (1867) 319; Kitchener **XV** 10; Battle of Marne 10, 32; Germans 102; Joyce 179; Hoare 394; Churchill 485–7; liberated 582

Paris, *parlement see Parlement* of Paris

Paris, Peace of (1763): negotiations **XII** 75, 80, 84–6; terms 85; reaction in England 86–8; (1783)

251–4, 256, 259, 261; (1814) 562–4; *see also* Augsburg, negotiations; peace conference **XV** 130, 132–6

Paris, archdeacon of **V** 248

Paris, bishop of *see* Stephen Poncher

Paris, Matthew **III** 338, 425, 443, 485; *see also* Matthew Paris

Paris, Simon de **V** 346

parishes: origin **II** 147–54; number of English **IV** 445; boundary disputes 464; part in local government **XII** 44; decline in administrative importance **XIII** 458–9

Parisi **Ia** 10; British 46, 135; Gallic 590

Parisii **Ib** 187, 189

Parisis **VI** 175

Park, abbey of **X** 171

Park, Sir K. **XV** 497

Park Street (Herts.), villa **Ia** 605

Parke, Lieutenant-General Daniel **X** 334

Parker, Henry, Lord Morley **VIII** 131

Parker, Sir Hyde, 3rd baronet (1714–82) **XI** 229

Parker, Sir Hyde (1739–1807) **XII** 214, 241, 386

Parker, John **V** 520

Parker, Master John, *medicus* **VI** 287, 288

Parker, Matthew, archbishop of Canterbury **VII** 600; **VIII** 29–32, 192–4, 205

Parker, Richard **XII** 373

Parker, Samuel, bishop of Oxford **X** 124

Parker, Thomas, 1st earl of Macclesfield (*c.*1666–1732) **XI** 20, 57, 63, 78, 203; impeached 24, 64, 203

Parker, Thomas, 2nd earl of Macclesfield (1697–1764): and reform of calendar **XI** 381

Parker, William, of London **VI** 76

Parker of Waddington, Lord **XIV** 457

represents Kent (1386) 530; ordinance, papal favours (Feb. 1388) 281; Middelburg staple removed to Calais (Feb. 1388) 355; popular support for Richard at Westminster (Feb. 1388) 454–61; Merciless Parliament, treasonable activities (1388) 477; condemned judges restored (1388) 478; pardons repealed (1388) 483 —issued 486; heretical writings, seizure (1388) 522; Cambridge statute restricting labour mobility (Sept. 1388) 339; Richard presides at Cambridge (Sept. 1388) 462; gilds enquiry (1389) 374 —(Jan. 1390) 465 —(Nov. 1390) 355; Lancaster, truce request (1391) 466; Statute of Praemunire (1393) 282; Arundel-Lancaster hostility (1394) 469; Ireland debate (1395) 472–3; Lollard manifesto (1395) 521; knightly classes (Jan. 1397) 475; Franco-Florentine war, Richard (Jan. 1397) 476–7; heresy death penalty (Jan. 1397) 522; Nottingham, bill of appeal against Arundel, Warwick, and Gloucester (Sept. 1397) 479–87; Richard's abdication, Henry's succession (1399) 493–6

parliament (1399–1485): 15th cent. functions **VI** 407; lords' attendances 408–9; common petitions 409–11; Commons, intercommuning with Lords 411; 'official' bills 411; Speaker 413–14; Cumberland, Buckinghamshire, and Huntingdon election disputes 415–16; lawyers' attempted exclusion 416; trading and mercantile interests 417–18; burgesses, household members returned 418–19; Merciless (1388) 20; legislation (1397–9), undone (Oct. 1399) 20; *notes on individual parliaments,* contention over meeting

(30 Sept. 1399) 16; Henry IV's first (6 Oct. 1399) 19; common petitions (1399) 23–4; Welsh revolt alarm (Feb. 1401) 43; 'unlearned' (Coventry, Nov. 1404) 51; grants (Jan. 1401, Michaelmas 1402) 51; grants (Jan. 1404) 32; grants (Oct. 1404) 74; grants (1406) 82; longest under Henry IV 82; financial measures (autumn 1411) 112–13; Westminster (May 1413) 133; Leicester (Apr. 1414) 133, 134; double tenth and fifteenth granted (Nov. 1414) 140; life customs grant to Henry V (Nov. 1415) 159; Commons petitions (2 Dec. 1420) 193; Treaty of Troyes inspection 194; (1 Dec. 1421) 195; Elections Act (1429) 415; Reading (1453) 502; financial resumption programme (by 1456) 513; Coventry (1459), attainders reversed (Oct. 1460) 522; York's claim and Lords' objections (7 Oct. 1460) 521–2; Commons annulment petition (Nov. 1461) 538; York's title vindicated 538; general resumption act 539; Lancastrians attainted 539; Staple claim (2 Nov. 1461) 540; wool petitions (1463) 544; prorogation (1463–Nov. 1464) 542–3; Henry VI declared king (26 Nov. 1471) 563; Edward IV's war grant (1473) 573; Commons reservations 573; Rotherham denounces Louis XI (20 Jan. 1483) 588; Russell sermon (23 Jan. 1484) 630; acts 631–4

parliament (1485–1558): control over law **VII** 12, 189, 194; development during Tudor period 566–7; list of speakers Appendix 652–4; *under Edward VI:* extent of governmental control 497–500; meetings 499,

parliament (1485–1558) (*cont.*)
513–15, 516, 520–2; *under Henry VII*: position and composition 197–9; Henry VII's use 194, 199–201, 208; meetings 59–65, 77, 89, 106, 123; *under Henry VIII*: extent of royal control 349–51, 414, 436–9; increase of parliamentary prestige 381, 441, 566; parliamentary privilege 438–41; emergence of two Houses 340, 436, 437, 499, 566; Reformation parliament —attack on sanctuary, probates, mortuaries, leases (1529) 353; supplication against ordinaries (1532) 354; Act in restraint of annates (provisional) (1532) 355–6, 440; Act in restraint of appeals (1533) 357, 358; Act in restraint of annates made absolute (1534) 358; Act for submission of the clergy (1534) 358; Act for first-fruits and tenths (1534) 359; Act of succession (1534) 359; Act of supremacy (1534) 359; treasons act 360; new Act of succession (1536) 381; minorities act 381; *under Mary*: attempt to control 532; growing difference with Crown 554–5; meetings 540, 544, 548, 560

parliament (1554–1603) **VIII** 215–34; constitution 215–16; bills not to touch prerogative 217; liberty of discussion —the four freedoms 217–18; matters on which free speech may be applied 218; marriage and succession questions 219; the queen on the royal prerogative 220; Strickland's bill on ecclesiastical affairs, and his detention 221–2; Peter Wentworth's vehement speech and his imprisonment in the Tower 222–3; Cope's bill touching ecclesiastical government 224; Peter Wentworth's 'questions', and second imprison-

ment 225; his pertinacity 226; Attorney Morrice and ecclesiastical courts 226–7; revenue and finance questions 228; great subsidy debate (1593) 229; last parliament of the reign 230–2; triumph of the queen 233–4

parliament (1603–60): sessions (1604–11) **IX** 3–15; (1614) 17–18; (1621) 24–9; (1624) 28; (1625) 34–6, 60; (1626) 36–7; (1628–9) 39–50; annulment of parliaments (1639–61); (1640) 91–3; (1640–53) 97–106, 118–26, 124–6, 130, 140; Propositions of Newcastle 144–9; Vote of No Address 155–6; Cromwell 171–5; breach with Charles 209–10; (1653) 175; (1654) 176–7; (1656–7) 180–6; (1659) 238–41; (1659–60) 244–57; (1660) 257–9

parliament (1660–1714): necessity after Reformation **X** 3; convention (1660) 4–5, 20–1; Long Parliament of Charles I 9 —dissolved 97; cavalier (1661) 9–12 —committees 14 —Nonconformist toleration 20–1; Long Parliament of the Restoration (until 1679) 55 —duration controversy 56–7; secret agreement, Charles and Louis 86–7 (1675) —Charles breaks agreement (1678) 88; Charles granted money for war 89; troops' pay-off delayed (1678) 90–1; Habeas Corpus Amendment Act 98–9; Charles refused grant for Tangier (1680) 102; Charles's last parliament (1681) 99, 103; desire for new parliament 106; under James II 116, 118, 121–2, 141; Declaration of Indulgence (1688) 125–6, 136; convention (1689) 144, 182; three-year parliaments, Triennial Act (1689–1714) 149–51; over-

436

seas trade monopolies (1695) 283; Ireland 313–14, 319–21; the colonies 336–7; separate trade committees (1696) 150; status of members under Act of Settlement (1701) 190 — Partition treaties 194–5, 198; analysis of parliament (1702) 222–3; general elections (1702, 1705, 1708, 1710) 227; landed property qualification for MPs 239; Schism Bill and education (1714) 247; under Queen Anne 254; character 261–2; Scots 266, 306, 313–14, 319–21

parliament (1714–60): composition **XI** 21–2; debates 2, 9, 22, 30, 211–12; powers 2, 8–9, 15, 21, 211 — Pitt 376; as to treaties 372–3; reforms 5, 376; Commons: composition and powers 26–30, 32; growth of authority 211; journals 397; and ministers 355; Lords: bishops in 80–1; judicial functions 23–4, 59–60; powers 22–6; *see also* Acts and Bills

parliament (1815–70): unreformed/defects **XIII** 25–9; composition (1832–68) 92

Parliament Act (1911) **XV** 16, 204, 269, 280

Parliament Bill: introduced **XIV** 420; contents 424–5; passes the Commons 427; passes the Lords 430

Parliament Hall **VII** 193

parliamentarians: analysis **IX** 127–9; army (1642) 131

parliamentary debates, publicity **XII** 141

parliamentary reform *see* reform movements

parliamentary representation **X** 11–12

Parma **III** 331

Parma, duke of *see* Farnèse, Alexander

Parma, Margaret, duchess of *see*

Margaret Parma

Parmoor, Lord **XV** 297

Parnell, Charles Stewart: hails the Ballot Act **XIV** 24; early militancy 55–7; prosecuted 73; imprisoned 74; Kilmainham treaty 75; relations with Mrs O'Shea 74, 564–6; shaken by Phoenix Park murders 75; presentation of £38,000 76; negotiation with Chamberlain 89; pact with Conservatives 90; interview with Lord Carnarvon 92; correspondence with Gladstone through Mrs O'Shea 558–63; pro-Conservative election manifesto 94; mistakes 95; unawareness of 'Ulster' 451; disapproves the 'Plan of Campaign' 179; attacked in *The Times* 179, 181; Pigott's forgeries and suicide 182; exculpated by special commission 182; visits Gladstone 183; O'Shea divorce case 183; breach with Gladstone 184–5; in committee room no. 15 158; by-elections, marriage, death and character 186; **XV** 159, 402

Parnell, Thomas (1679–1718) **XI** 305, 425

'Parnellism and Crime' **XIV** 179, 181–2

Parpaglia, abbot of San Salvatore **VIII** 27

Parr, Catherine, wife of Henry VIII **VII** 422, 431, 480, 510, 590; marriage to Henry (1543) 413, 419; marries Thomas Seymour (1547) 488

Parr, Gilbert, crown yeoman **VI** 481

Parr, Sir Thomas **VI** 459, 516

Parr, Sir William, 1st marquis of Northampton (1513–71) **VII** 490, 494, 529, 530

Parret (Pedridanmutha), river **II** 63–4, 733

Parris, George van **VII** 520, 549, 552

408, 500; general standard of conduct 63–5; loyalty to Crown 117–20; North and Indian crisis 172; attitudes towards America 203; North's government 220, 227, 232, 234, 251; relations between king and minister 274; after 30 years' political turmoil 327; government unity 356 —disunity 404

'Patriots' **XI** 29, 113, 204

Patrizzi, Francesco **IX** 363

patronage **Ia** 616–17; army 21, 164–5, 212; imperial 49–50, 78–80, 518–19; legal remedies from 143, 527, 533–4; of local communities 143, 153–5, 251, 279, 534; of Christians 342–3, 462, 725; and doctrine of Grace 462, 466; display of status 465–6, 469; king's ecclesiastical **II** 547; origin of lay 149–50; of monastic houses **IV** 762; to reward king's supporters **VII** 56; literary **X** 355; **XI** 28–30, 295, 311; *see also clientela*

Patten, William **VII** 483, 485

pattern construction **Ia** 541, 615

Patteshall, Hugh, treasurer, bishop of Coventry (1240–1) **IV** 60

Patteshall, Martin, judge **IV** 17, 68

Paul, abbot of St Albans **II** 673

Paul, earl of the Orkneys **II** 590

Paul, Sir G. O., Gloucestershire JP **XI** 52

Paul I, Pope **II** 161

Paul III, Pope (1534–49) (Alessandro Farnese) **VII** 340, 364, 396, 403; prepares bull against Henry (1535) 341; creates Fisher cardinal 362; dates bull of excommunication (1535) 370 —orders its execution (1538) 402; belated attempt to help Pilgrimage of Grace 392; summons a General Council 402; council at Trent (1545), later at Bologna (1547) 481–2; death (1549) 547

Paul IV, Pope (1559–9) (Giovanni Pietro Caraffa) **VII** 547, 551, 560; quarrel with Spain 556; **VIII** 7, 25, 26

Paul V, Pope **IX** 209

Paul of Caen, abbot of St Albans **III** 167, 249

Paul the Chain, Paulus *Catena* **Ia** 357–8, 532, 726

Paulet, Sir Amyas **VII** 288; **VIII** 344, 345; war with Spain 346; Mary Stuart's keeper 378, 379, 383, 385–7

Paulet, Charles, 3rd duke of Bolton (1685–1754) **XI** 204

Paulet, Harry, 6th duke of Bolton (1719–94): son's patronage of cricket **XII** 337

Paulet, Sir William, Lord St John (1539), earl of Wiltshire (1530), 1st marquis of Winchester (1551) **VII** 400, 492, 494, 519, 538; Northumberland party collapses 528; sworn of Privy Council 530; keeps post as treasurer 531; Netley Abbey converted 596; treasurer (1550) 647; lord chamberlain of the household (1543) 649; great master of the household (1545) 649; comptroller (1532) 650; treasurer of the household (1537) 650

Paulinus, bishop of York **II** 113–16

Paulinus of Nola **Ia** 737

Paulinus *see* Suetonius Paulinus

Paulus (*comes*) **Ia** 491

Pausanias **Ia** 194, 199, 200–1

pavage **III** 79

Pavia, battle (1525) **VII** 315, 321, 340, 341

Pavia, council (1160) 327

Pavia, William of, cardinal **III** 211

Pavlov, Prof. **XIV** 552

Paxton, Sir Joseph **XIII** 266

pay as you earn **XV** 473

PAYE *see* pay as you earn

Paymaster-of-the-Forces, salary **XI** 337–8

payment of members **XIV** 444

Payn, John **VI** 498

Payne, John, bishop of Meath (1483–1507) **VII** 80, 133

Payne, Peter, principal, St Edmund Hall **VI** 96, 97

Payne, Stephen, dean of Exeter **VI** 288

Payne, Thomas, grocer, London and Southampton **VI** 355

peace: wardens, in shires **IV** 176, 182, 354; proclamations 190, 204–5, 214, 708; negotiated projects **XV** 65, 92, 115; lamented 274; ILP proposes 503

Peace Ballot **XV** 379–81

Peacham, Edmond **IX** 19, 21

Peacham, Henry **IX** 386

Peachey, Sir John, sheriff of Kent **VII** 125

Peaclond *see* Peak (Derby.)

Peacock, Reginald, bishop of Chichester (1450–7) **VII** 239

Peacock, Thomas Love, biography **XIII** 531

Peada, son of Penda **II** 42, 84, 120

Peak: castle **IV** 118, 198; forest 513

Peak (Peaclond) (Derby.) **II** 733; **III** 80, 82

Peak District **Ia** 4

Peake, Robert **VIII** 302

Pearce *see* Pierce

Pearce, Zachary (1690–1774), bishop of Bangor and Rochester **XI** 78

Peard, Mr **XII** 54

Pearl Harbour, Japanese attack **XV** 532, 536, 539, 541, 578

Pearl, medieval poem **V** 525

pearls **Ia** 72, 630

Pearse, P. H. **XIV** 475

Pearson, C. Arthur, afterwards Sir **XIV** 532, 533, 534

Pearson, C. H. **XIV** 332

Pearson, J. L. **XIV** 325

Peary, Robert **XIV** 553

peasants **Ia** 236; no peasant militia in Britain 247, 385; revolts in

Gaul 283, 382, 444–5, 447–8, 451 — fortified villa 452; 'justice' in Armorica 492; communication in Latin 507; distance from towns 541, 597; landholding patterns 604, 611, 625, 628–9; free of Danish Mercia **II** 254; in early Kent 277–8, 470; in early Wessex and Mercia 278–9; basis of English society 414; society and Norman Conquest 472–7; depression of 470–1; military service 583–4; *see also* Bacaudae; *casarius*

Peasants' Revolt (1381) **V** 338–9, 342, 345, 378, 427, 442; Black Prince suppresses Cheshire rising (1353) 204; background 384; against tax-collectors, Essex and Kent 407; Wat Tyler leader 408; assault on London 409–10; Richard II's negotiations with rebels 411; rebels attack Tower 412; Richard hears Tyler's demands 413; Tyler killed, rebels follow Richard 413; widespread consequences 414–15; Cambridge University assault 416–17; Litster leads rebellion in Norfolk 417–18; after-effects 419, 438, 514; causes 419–22; John of Northampton, mayor 435; Oxford escapes violence 505; John Gower's poem 528; **VI** 452

Pecche, John, vintner **V** 391

Pecche, Sir John **V** 521

Pecche, Sir William, of Lullingston (Kent) **VI** 593

Pecham, John, Franciscan, archbishop of Canterbury (1279–92): career and papal appointment **IV** 469–70; provincial councils and constitutions 451, 472–5, 479–80; gives shape to convocation 505–8, 671, 672; summons council to express views on crusade (1291–2) 267; Thomas de Cantilupe 489–90;

criticism and grievances of suffragans about his exercise of authority 490-3; relations with king 476, 478-80; and the Welsh 391, 415, 421, 424-6, 427 — on Welsh depravity 383-4 — on Welsh law 418; Church in Wales 430, 433-5; at Westminster (1285) 369; Amauri de Montfort 331; last years and death (1292) 484-5; **VI** 280

Peche, Richard, bishop of Coventry **III** 183

Peckham (Kent), archbishop of Canterbury's manor **III** 111

Peckham, Edmund **VII** 496

Peckham, Sir George **VIII** 244

Pecock, Reginald, bishop of Chichester: forced resignation **VI** 272; Lollard 'trowings' 282-3; Lollard defence 298; on 'doom of reason' 684; on Doctors 684

Pecsætan **Ib** 185; **II** 41, 296

pedesequus **II** 305

Pedridanmutha *see* Parret, river

Pedro, Dom, of Portugal **XIII** 211-12, 231

Peebles **IV** 694, 696, 707

Peel, A. W., afterwards Viscount **XIV** 68

Peel, General **XIII** 185-6

Peel, Lord, commission on Palestine **XV** 407

Peel, Sir Robert (the elder) (1750-1830) **XI** 109, 187; **XII** 511, 530; **XIII** 13, 110-11

Peel, Sir Robert (the younger) **XIII** 24, 37, 57, 59, 115; biography 59; views on currency 59, 112; refuses to support Canning 74-5; joins Wellington's administration 76; agrees to Catholic emancipation 77; opposes Reform Bill 82; refuses to join Wellington in forming a ministry (1832) 85; policy in opposition 89, 94, 97-8, 102; first administration 95, 101-2; relations with Queen Victoria (1839) 104-6; second administration 109-22; character and ideas 109-11; fiscal policy 113; repeal of the corn laws 122-4; attitude towards his party 123-4; resignation 124; temperament 149; trade 152; death 160; and Gladstone 174; co-operation 240; defeated on first Tithe Bill 346; Irish policy (1841-6) 349-53, 356; Lord Heytesbury 416; workhouse reform 455; municipal corporations 460; water-supplies 463; introduces metropolitan police 466; reform of prison administration 468; reform of the penal code 470-2; civil marriages 473; Church reform 510; Scottish churches 527; Tennyson's pension 535; creation of peers 622; **XIV** 186, 349, 560, 561; **XV** 161

Peele, George **VIII** 296, 298

Peelites **XIII** 162-3, 165, 168, 175, 522

Peerage Bill (1714) **X** 192

peers: Peter des Roches on **IV** 55; of France 243; **V** 19, 184-7, 455-6; trials 27, 67, 73, 85-7, 101; trial of Edmund of Kent 100; concept of peerage 103; archbishop Stratford 173-4, 176; responsibilities 174; judicial powers 96, 193, 483; participation in elections **XIV** 417

Pefenesea *see* Pevensey (Sussex)

Pegolotti, Francesco, of the Bardi company, mercantile practice 637-8

Pegu **VIII** 242

Pelagian heresy **Ia** 443, 462-7, 470, 480, 720; power base 727; advance of Christianity 734; **Ib** 15, 17, 20; **II** 1

Pelhain, Wolfgang von **VII** 103

Pelham, Hon. Henry (1696-1754) **XI** 146, 264, 376; Treasury and Exchequer 17, 246; death 18, 345;

and Bamburgh 530; lets French in 530; Hedgely Moor 531
Percy, Richard **IV** 66
Percy, Sir Richard, Northumberland's son **VI** 508
Percy, Thomas (1729–1811), bishop of Dromore **XII** 353
Percy, Thomas, brother of 6th earl of Northumberland **VII** 386
Percy, Thomas, 7th earl of Northumberland **VIII** 131, 137, 140, 141
Percy, Thomas, earl of Worcester (1397–1403) **V** 474; crushes revolt at Billericay 418; association with Gaunt 441, 465, 468–9; proctor of the clergy (1397) 480, 484; deserts Richard II 493; Admiral of England **VI** 6, 10, 18, 34, 45; and Henry IV 46, 47; removes treasure 48; Shrewsbury treachery 52; tried and beheaded 53; return of Isabel 67; ward 320
Percy, Thomas, Marquis, then duke of Exeter **VI** 514, 516
Percy, William **III** 353
Percy family **III** 351; **V** 63; wealth and support **VI** 9–10, 336; manorial accounts 338; **VII** 204, 385
Peregrine Bertie, Lord Willoughby **VIII** 413
peregrini **Ia** 175, 525, 534, 583; *see also* citizenship
Perennis **Ia** 212
Perfeddwlad **IV** 400; *see also* Four Cantrefs
perfumes **VIII** 271
Pergamum **Ia** 114
Pergolesi, Giovanni Battista (1710–36) **XI** 417
Périgord, county (Guienne) **IV** 291–2; French and Aquitanian administration 300, 301, 303; **V** 140, 361; **VI** 108, 109, 135, 178, 240
Périgueux (Dordogne): temple **Ia** 671; **IV** 645; city and diocese 291, 292, 309; diocese and treaty of

Paris (1259) 126, 128, 280–1, 289; process (1310–11) 291, 292, 654; **V** 140; process 108, 113; **VI** 113, 135, 140
Perlberg **Ib** 62; culture 108; Saxon pottery 71 [fig. 6(e)]; map 1 xxix
Péronne (Somme) **III** 361, 379; **VI** 111, 152, 153, 256, 576; *prévôté* 263; treaty 558, 559, 565; Charles returns 577
Perotti, Niccolo **VII** 239
Perpetual Edict (*Paix des Prêtres*) **VIII** 341
Perpignan (Pyr.-Orient): death of Philip III (1285) **IV** 255; Charles of Salerno 262; **VI** 163
Perrenots, Antoine, sieur de Granvelle **VII** 429, 559, 560
Perrers, Alice **V** 384, 390, 397, 402–3
Perris, William **VII** 17
Perrot, Sir John **VIII** 472, 473, 474
Perry, O. H. (1785–1819) **XII** 553
persecution: Diocletian of Christians **Ia** 339–40; of pagans 356, 411; political 357–9, 446–7, 449, 531, 532 — rise of Christianity 715; Aurelian 715; in Britain 721; of Catholics **VIII** 185–8; *see also* martyrs
Pershing, General **XV** 101, 102, 111
Persia: rise of Shah **VII** 151; **XIII** 235, 237, 417–18, 431, 434; Anglo-Russian convention **XIV** 402–3; troubles (1911) 449; neutral zone **XV** 50; German ambitions 65; British protectorate 152; fears for 521, 531
Persia, khan of *see* Arghun
Persian Gulf **X** 349; exclusive influence claimed by Britain **XIV** 382
Persians (Sassanians) **Ia** 239, 363–4, 368, 490; Zoroastrianism 668; magic 679; *see also* Parthians
personal names: Danish, in Northumbria and Mercia **II** 253–4; in Danelaw 519–20

446

Philip V (*cont.*)
291; death 263; *see also* Philip, duke of Anjou

Philip, abbot of L'Aumône **III** 204

Philip, bishop of Durham **III** 377, 428, 446

Philip, count of Nevers, Nièvre **VI** 156, 475

Philip, count of Savoy (d. 1285) **IV** 248, 249, 250-1

Philip, Don (1720-45) **XI** 209, 232, 241, 244-5; marriage alliance with Vienna 194; in Italy 247, 263, 267; Parma and Piacenza 265, 270

Philip, duke of Anjou, afterwards Philip V of Spain **X** 194, 206, 211, 213

Philip (the Bold), duke of Burgundy (1363-1404), count of Flanders **V** 143, 146, 225, 430, 432; urges English invasion 442

Philip, duke of Orleans **X** 63

Philip, duke of Swabia and king of the Romans **III** 450, 451, 453

Philip, Emperor **Ia** 529

Philip, King, native chief **X** 346

Philip I, king of France **II** 585, 607, 608-9, 620, 638; **III** 107, 115; conquest of Normandy 104-5, 108, 112, 122

Philip II, Augustus, king of France **III** 250; accession and coronation 340-1; character 342; early relations with Henry II and Richard I 342-3; takes the cross 344, 347; makes war on Henry II 344-6; comes to terms with Richard I 347, 350; on crusade 359-61; intrigues with John 359, 363-4; alliance with Hohenstaufen broken 367; war with Richard I 369, 370, 374-7; recognizes Arthur as Richard's successor 378-9; barons of Poitou appeal 380; conquers Normandy 382-4, 426; confiscates lands of English 431; plans invasion of England 440, 456; Treaty of Le Goulet 449; Otto IV's hostility 450; allies with Frederick of Hohenstaufen 452; quarrels with count of Boulogne 453; relations with Flanders 454; negotiates treaty with Llywelyn of Wales 455; invades Flanders 459; defeated at Damme 461; war with John 464, 466-7; wins battle of Bouvines 467-8; joins barons against John 470-1, 483

Philip III, king of France (1270-85) **IV** 226, 234; relations with Edward 236, 285-6; makes treaty of Amiens (1279) 289; Eleanor of Castile's succession to Ponthieu 235, 244; quarrel with Alfonso X of Castile 242-4; arbitrates about mother's claims in Provence 249; executor of crusade against Peter of Aragon 251, 253-5; death 255; increase of royal domain in his reign 237-41, 272-3; **V** 107

Philip IV, the Fair, king of France (1285-1315): relations with Edward I **IV** 236-7, 271, 290-1; succession to Champagne and Navarre 240-1; Amadeus V of Savoy 251; negotiations with Aragon for release of Charles of Salerno 256, 260; meeting with Sancho of Castile at Bayonne 262; dispute with Edward I about Gascony and occupation of Gascony 644-54; alliance with Scots and Eric of Norway (1295) 612-13; naval plans 646; relations with Guy of Flanders 652, 653, 659, 668-9, 697; and with Adolf of Nassau 660, 661, 668; truces and peace with Edward I 649, 650, 653-4; Scottish wars 653, 669, 693-7, 710; propaganda 527; **V** 1, 4, 33, 68, 123; and Gaveston 22; relations with Edward I and II 107, 115; Templars 291

448

Philip the Good (*cont.*)
offered French regency 213; English alliance (after 1422) 218; challenges Gloucester to duel 226; capacity to work with English 240; Montdidier mobilization 248; French truce (1421), renewed (1423) 249; dissatisfied with England (1430) 249; considers *rapprochement* with France (after 1429) 256; meetings planned (1430) 257; Bedford' Brittany alliance 257; bad relations with Bourbons 259; conference of Nevers 260; Congress of Arras 261–3; sends de Lannoy to England 473; earls invade France 519; supports Edward of March 526; attitude towards Louis XI manœuvres (1462) 533; anxious for English help in crusade 534; offers Edward IV his niece 534; English envoys at Hesdin 535; prohibits English cloth and yarn imports 537; supports Hansa resistance to English reprisals 554

Philipoppolis **VI** 275

Philipot, Sir John **V** 264, 404; emissary to Richard II 397; loan to Richard II 401; treasurer of the subsidy (1377) 402; equips a fleet 403; commission (1380) 405; Peasants' Revolt 414; Gaunt 436

Philippa, Erik of Norway's daughter **VI** 326

Philippa, Henry IV's daughter **VI** 318; marriage 69

Philippa, Henry V's sister **VI** 196

Philippa, John of Gaunt's daughter **VI** 229

Philippa of Hainault, queen of Edward III **V** 127, 128, 167, 393, 530; betrothed to Edward as part of bargain 83; pole siege of Calais 136; hostage for Edward III 162; character and influence 269; appeal to 344; benefactor of learning 507

Philippa of Lancaster, queen of Portugal **V** 464, 529

Philippines **XV** 151

Philippsburg **X** 135, 161, 169

Phillips, John **IX** 313–14

Phillips, Sir Tom **XV** 540

philology **X** 381–2

Philosophical Institution, Royal **XIII** 564–6

Philosophical Society of Edinburgh *see* Edinburgh Philosophical Society

philosophy **Ia** 676, 698, 709–10, 715–16, 728–9; **X** 30, 885–7; *see also* Epicureanism; Stoicism

Philpot, John, archdeacon of Winchester **VII** 544, 546

Phipps, Sir William **X** 341

Phoebus, Gaston, of Foix **VI** 107

Phoenix Park murders **XIV** 75–6

photography, early development **XIII** 594

physical condition of population **Ia** 549–52

Physical Training Act (1937) **XV** 406

physicians **Ia** 234; **VIII** 314; college of 315; **X** 419

Physicians, College of **IX** 366

Physicians, Royal College of **XIII** 18

Physicians of London, Incorporated **VII** 466–7

physics **X** 374–5

Physiologus **III** 260

physiology **X** 376

Piacenza **III** 423

Picardy **II** 629; **V** 256; **VI** 73, 104, 108, 175, 177; Dauphinist revival 200; receipts 208; defence 249; **VII** 85, 98, 110, 275

Picasso **XV** 178

Pichegru, Charles **XII** 368

Pickering (N. Yorks.) **VI** 2

Pickering, castle **IV** 165; **V** 67

Pickering, Church of St Peter and St Paul **VII** 568

Pickering, Vale of **Ib** xxvi

Pickering, Sir James **V** 404; **VI** 516
Pickford, Mr **XII** 519
Pickwell (Leics.), church of **III** 25
Pickworth, Sir Thomas **VI** 104
Pico della Mirandola **VII** 242, 243, 582; life of John Picus **VII** 248, 347
Picot, Eugenia **III** 22–3; her son *see* Fitz Bernard, John
Picot, Ralph, of Kent **III** 22
Picot of Cambridge **II** 633
Picquigny, treaty (1475) **VI** 577–8, 628; **VII** 102, 108, 109
Picton, Sir Thomas **XII** 493
Picts: Constantius' victory **Ia** 318; raids 360, 369; barbarian conspiracy 375; Magnus Maximus' victory 402; Gildas' 'Pictish Wars' 403, 405, 419–23; Vortigern 472; St Germanus 470, 479; **Ib** 13, 15, 18, 109, 200; Ceawlin saga 172; raids 198, 207; kingdom **II** 86–92, 252; and Scots 2, 34; of Galloway **III** 271
picture-heirlooms, problem of saving **XIV** 327, 543
Pie, Hugh, Lollard **VI** 282
pieces of eight **X** 328
Piedmont: **III** 330; **X** 170; sends troops to Crimea **XIII** 286, 289, 301–2; *see also* Austria; Cavour; Napoleon III
Piepowder, court **III** 77; **IV** 625
Pierce (Pearce), Edward **X** 379
Piercebridge: fort **Ia** 255; civil settlement 379; plough model 622
Piers Plowman **III** 34–5
Pigot, George, Lord Pigot (1719–77), governor of Madras **XI** 329, 331; 1st Baron **XII** 221, 320
Pigott, Richard **XIV** 182
Pike Hill, signal tower **Ia** 571
Pilche, Alexander **IV** 580
Pile of Fouldry **VII** 73
Pilgrim Fathers **IX** 329, 339, 342
Pilgrimage of Grace **VII** 281, 363, 419; ineffective government in

north 385–6; Lincolnshire rising (Oct. 1536) 387; Yorkshire rising (Oct. 1536) 389; discussion at Doncaster (27 Oct. 1536) 390; settlement at Doncaster (6 Dec. 1536) 391; sporadic risings excuse for severity 392; council of the north established 393; cost 370
pilgrimages, royal: to shrines and relics **IV** 49, 57, 59, 369, 512; *see also* Pontigny
Pilgrims' Way **Ib** xxvi
Pilkington, James, bishop of Durham **VIII** 22, 193
Pilnitz, meeting at **XII** 298
Pincahala, synod **II** 218
Pindar, Peter *see* Wolcot, John
Pinero, A. W. **XIV** 328, 547
Pinerolo **X** 162, 171, 173
Pinkie, battle **VII** 485
Pinnendenn *see* Penenden Heath (Kent)
Pinnendon Heath (Pinnenden) (Kent), plea **II** 650–1, 733
pins **Ia** 7
Pipe Rolls **V** 77
Pipewell, council (1189) **III** 221
Pippin, king of the Franks **II** 170
Pippin of Heristal **II** 166–7
Pipton, treaty **IV** 201, 403
piracy **Ia** 240, 259, 455; Carausius 298, 305–6; defences against 320, 378, 384, 639; Saxons 500; **VIII** 126, 127
Piranesi, Giovanni Battista (1707–78), engraver **XI** 404
Pisa, council **VI** 91, 92; English participation 93; English wool staple **VII** 223; general council (1512–17) 272, 274
Pisa, Henry of, cardinal legate **III** 200
Pitcairn, Frank *see* Cockburn, Claude
Pitscottie, Lindsay of *see* Lindsay
Pitt, John, 2nd earl of Chatham (1756–1835): biography **XII** 408; first lord of admiralty (1788–94)

Ireland 276-8, 392-403, 441; and Adam Smith 329; out of office 411-13, 416; first lord of Treasury (1804-6) 417-18, 429, 434, 581; death 434; catholicism 440; slave trade 440; Spencer Perceval 444; trade agreement with France 504; **XIII** 28, 195, 207, 328; **XV** 137, 293

Pius II, Pope **VI** 256, 518, 519

Pius III, Pope (Sept.-Oct. 1503) (Francesco Todeschini (Piccolomini)) **VII** 175

Pius IV, Pope **VIII** 27, 28

Pius V, Pope **VIII** 88-9, 106; papal bull (1570) 166-71

Place, Francis (1771-1854) **X** 401; **XI** 104, 144; **XIII** 2, 37, 128, 459-60, 495; biography 73; and the repeal of the combination laws 72-4; and the third Reform Bill 85-6; assists in drawing up the People's Charter 133; on *Pilgrim's Progress* 534

place-names: discussed **Ib** xxii, 29-45; Frisian 48; Saxon and Anglian areas 106-7; Jutish 114; in Kent 123-6; containing the name Cerdic 147; survival of British place-names in N. Hampshire 149; in Northumbria 200; meaning of Ambresbyrig 160, 213; in Lincolnshire 176-7; in eastern England 185; Anglian, Saxon and Jutish **II** 9-10: of Sussex 18-19; in *-ing* 18, 23; in *-ingas* 318; illustrating dual origin of Hwicce 44; English beyond Offa's Dyke 46-7; Anglian, in Lindsey 48-9; early, in Essex 53; interest in East Anglia 53; in Middlesex 54; in Surrey 55; in Dorset 63; in Devon 64; in Durham and Cumberland 74-5; in Cumberland and Lancs. 78; of Kent 282-3; of Trent basin 285; *Danish*: grammatical structure 519-22; in -by and -thorpe 523-5; Yorkshire 253; Mercia

253-4; distribution 519-23; Scandinavianization of English 523-4; illustrating Danish heathenism 434; Norse-Gaelic, in North-west 331-3, 521

placemen **X** 253-4

Placentia bay, meeting **XV** 529-30

plague **Ia** 496-7; (of 166-7) 207, 552; (in 15th cent.) 460; **VII** 586; before Henry VII's coronation 55; Holbein 602; isolation of victims **IX** 299; causes and treatment 366-7; theatre closures during 395; Great (1655-6) **X** 65

plaint (*querela*) **IV** 143, 350-5; (1258-60) 142, 144-8

Plancher, Burgundian historian **VI** 263

Plantagenet, Arthur **VII** 277

plantation of Ireland *see* Ireland

plate: Roman **Ia** 532, 633; Hockwold 101; Traprain Law 386, 729; Mildenhall 373, 607, 687, 729; Esquiline 431; Water Newton, Chesterton 340, 718, 720, 726; Corbridge 729; silver **VIII** 272

Platen, countesses of *see* Meyerburg Züschen; Uffeln

Plato **III** 234; *Phaedo* 237; *Timaeus* 235, 245; **IX** 356, 361

Platonists, Cambridge **X** 32-3, 386

Platorius Nepos, A. **Ia** 173, 179-80, 181-2

Plautus **III** 235, 257

Playfair, Lyon, 1st Baron **XIII** 500-1, 570; biography 500; **XIV** 230, 319: biography 25

Playford, John **IX** 389; **X** 403

plays *see* theatre

pleas of the crown **II** 497-502, 507

Pleasantmaris, Kenilworth (War.) **VI** 194

Plebs league **XV** 347

Plegmund, archbishop of Canterbury **II** 270-1, 435, 438

plena potestas of proctors and representatives **IV** 536, 538-9

Pleshey (Essex) **IV** 9; **V** 305, 478; castle **VI** 26

Plessis-les-Tours, treaty **VIII** 353

Plessyngton, Sir Robert **V** 490

Plevna **XIV** 47

Plimsoll, Samuel **XIV** 37, 56

Pliny the Elder (AD 23–79) **Ia** 635, 679, 690; **Ib** 51; **II** 11; **III** 235, 237, 243

Pliny the Younger (AD 62–118): friends and patronage **Ia** 163–4, 518; villas 597, 614; status of slaves 505; Priscus and Classicus prosecuted 533–4; permits and travel 566, 569; building projects 577–8; farm management 530, 600–1, 605, 628

Plotinus **Ia** 716; **III** 257

plough land **II** 514; assessment 646–8

plough-alms **II** 152–3

ploughs **Ia** 622, 627; Iron Age 8, 622–3

'Plug Plot' **XIII** 141

plumbatae **Ia** 412

Plumbers' Hall **VIII** 200

Plumer, Sir H. **XV** 100

Plummer, Sir John, keeper of Great Wardrobe **VI** 561

Plumpton, Sir Robert (1453–1523) **VII** 62, 208

Plumpton, Sir William **VI** 61; Scrope's rising 59

Plumpton Plain **Ia** 8

Plunket, Oliver, Archbishop **X** 95, 302

Plunkett, Sir Horace **XIV** 451

Plural Voting Bill **XIV** 392–3

pluralism and pluralities **IV** 458–9, 474–5, 487–8; Hengham's 356; **VIII** 190; bill against 227

Plutarch **Ia** 164, 537

Pluto, **XV** 579

Plymouth (Devon): expedition to Gascony **IV** 649, 659, 662; **V** 378, 379, 481; prosperity 381; **VI** 72; incorporation charter 392–3; **VII** 172, 273, 276, 440, 477; Mary

pledged to Philip (1553) 537; **VIII** 124, 403, 412; Spanish bullion detained at 129; armada look-out 146, 398–400; Drake and Norreys' expedition 411; plunder of *Madre de Dios* 413; **IX** 133, 138, 385–6; **X** 53, 138; bombed **XV** 502

Plymouth (Massachusetts) **IX** 330; **X** 333, 337

Plymouth brethren **XIII** 525

Plympton (Devon) **VI** 309

Plymton **IV** 26

pneumatic tyre, invention **XIV** 281, 338

Po valley **XV** 592

Poccock, Sir George (1706–92), Admiral **XI** 226, 262, 330, 366

Pocklington (Yorks.), manor **VI** 337

Pococke, Edward **X** 382–3

Podio, Orlandino de **IV** 632, 633

Poel, William **XIV** 547

Poenius Postumus **Ia** 119–21

Poetaster **VIII** 301

Poetovio: conference **Ia** 131

poetry, Old English **II** 190, 192–9; Germanic traditions 192–5; heroic 192–5; religious 196–7; gnomic 197–8; reflective 198–200; MS transmission 199–200; **IX** 399–404; English **X** 363–8, 370–2; **XII** 350–2, 338, 537–41

Poggio Bracciolini **VI** 680

Poincaré, Raymond **XIV** 488; **XV** 203

Point Rich **X** 343

Pointblank directive **XV** 570

Poissy **V** 134

Poitevins, outcry against (1232–4) **IV** 52

Poitiers (Vienne) **III** 329, 333, 369, 381; **IV** 96, 100; battle **V** 138–40, 145, 147, 150, 248; use of longbow 241; prisoners ransomed 247; wool trade 350; **VI** 113; battle 123; town and castle 135; *parlement* established 240

454

Poitiers, Alphonse of *see* Alphonse
Poitiers, Arnold, bishop of **V** 29
Poitiers, bishop of *see* Belmeis, John
Poitou, county **III** 318, 383, 424, 484; wine from 92; fighting in (1173–4) 334, 336, 337; custom of 342; Otto IV made count of 376; barons rebel against John 380; Arthur of Brittany invested with 381; John's campaigns in 426, 435, 440–2, 461–3, 465–8; claims to **IV** 84; occupied by Louis VIII and retained by Blanche of Castile for Louis IX 88–93; Henry III's march through 95; Henry's last bid 97, 100–4; Alphonse of Poitiers installed as count 100; claim to surrendered by Henry III (1259) 126; **V** 140, 246, 254; **VI** 113, 135, 142, 178, 240; duke of Berry 241; campaigns 474; *see also* Alphonse of Poitiers

Poland **III** 458; **V** 254, 359; **VI** 161, 356; **X** 73, 192; suppression of republic of Cracow **XIII** 245; rebellion (1863) 315–17; German plans **XV** 65; independence supported 97, 107; ambition of Emperor Charles 115; Fourteen Points 119; Danzig not annexed 134; Lloyd George condemned 136–7; war with Russia 142; A. Chamberlain 222; French alliance 222; British coal industry 240; Labour thinks frontiers should be revised 373, 417; Germans attack 388, 415, 459, 476; treats Jews badly 419; claims on Czechoslovakia 427, 429; expected to desert France 435; guarantee to 442, 446; no financial aid 443; impossible to aid 430, 445, refuses to admit Red Army 447; British hope to forget 448; Hitler thinks he can attack 449; British alliance 450; conquered 454, 458; not within British range 470, 484; liberation a

British war aim 489; government in England 494; disagreement with Stalin 588, 590; provisional government recognized 591; *see also* wars

Poland, king of *see* Casimir IV
Polaroon (Pulo-Run) **X** 68, 349
Pole, Anne de la, Richard III's niece **VI** 629
Pole, Sir Edmund de la, earl of Suffolk, executed (1513) **VII** 185, 250; flees to Netherlands and threat to Henry 167–70; Maximilian signs commercial treaty (1502) 183; Netherland/English relations threatened 222; pardon withheld 232; executed 267
Pole, Elizabeth de la, sister of Edward IV, wife of John de la Pole, 2nd duke of Suffolk **VII** 167
Pole, Geoffrey **VII** 396
Pole, John de la **V** 168
Pole, John de la, 2nd duke of Suffolk (1442–91), William's son **VI** 332, 557, 575; **VII** 70
Pole, John de la, earl of Lincoln (1464–1487) **VI** 617, 629, 636, 638; at Bosworth **VII** 58, 69; joined in Lambert Simnel conspiracy 70; lands at Dublin (1487) 72; in Lancashire (4 June 1487) 73; killed at Stoke (1487) 74, 75, 167
Pole, John de la, Suffolk's son **VI** 492
Pole, Margaret *see* Margaret, countess of Salisbury
Pole, Michael de la, earl of Suffolk (1385–8) **V** 438, 440, 442, 458, 465; staple policy 355, 436; appointed governor of Richard II 426–7; granted Ufford lands 429; impeaches Despenser 433; opens parliament 437; jealousy over friendship with king 441; movement against him (1386) 443–9; appeal against him (1387) 451; flight 452; sentenced (1388) 457;

455

Pole, Michael de la, earl of Suffolk (1385-8) (cont.)
death (1389) 467; heirs restored 485; **VI** 7
Pole, Michael de la, earl of Suffolk (d. Agincourt) **VI** 473
Pole, Michael de la, earl of Suffolk (d. Harfleur) **VI** 472, 473
Pole, Reginald, Cardinal **VII** 166, 352, 402, 454, 481; Reformation 348; cardinal (Dec. 1536) 382; legate *a latere* to support Pilgrimage of Grace 392, 394; family ruined 396, 548; act of attainder 414; preaches authority of Rome 423; inclosure 457; prospective husband for Mary 536; arrives in England as legate (Nov. 1554) 541, 548; career and development 547-8; receives England back into Roman Catholic Church 549; heresy trials 549-50, 553; efforts at reform 555-6; deprived by Pope Paul IV (1557) 556; death (17 Nov. 1558) 560; scholarship and power 572; portrait 601; chancellor of Oxford and Cambridge 575; 'accursed' **VIII** 12
Pole, Richard de la, killed at Pavia (1525) **VII** 167, 171
Pole, William de la **IV** 634; **V** 156, 160, 162, 224, 385; arrest (1340) 168
Pole, William de la, arrested (1502) **VII** 168
Pole, William de la, Earl, marquis (1444), duke (1448) of Suffolk **VI** 191, 211, 244, 245, 258; power 270, 332, 441; assaults on clergy 289; trial 309; income 334; fall 448; grandfather 472; duke of Orléans custody 473, 484; Normandy and Cotentin service 473; French peace policy 473; French embassy 474; meets Margaret of Anjou 475; Henry VI's proxy at marriage 476; parliamentary

approval 477; Gloucester 481, 483-4, 487; personal ascendancy 487; East Anglian officials 487-8; parliamentary charges 492; allegations 493; banished 493; murdered (1450) 494-5
Pole, de la, family, estates **VI** 472
Pole family **VII** 414
Poleyn, John, of Titchwell **VI** 288
Poleyne, William **VI** 343
police **X** 259; attempts to organize **XII** 45; system reform **XIII** 465-7; strike **XV** 106; control 174, 251; Savidge case 261; cuts in pay 296, 331
Polichronicon, Whalley continuator **VI** 13-14
Politian (Poliziano Angelo Ambrogio de) **VII** 241
political levy, and Labour party **XV** 92, 114-15, 263; Baldwin defeats attack 236; contracting imposed 250-1
political parties **X** 179-87, 221-8; 'court' and 'country' 181; *see also* Tory and Whig
Political Register **XV** 186
political theory of constitution *see* constitutional theory
political thought **X** 33, 256, 378
political warfare executive **XV** 516
poll taxes **V** 192, 287, 312-13, 338, 396; supplement to government loans (1379) 405; cause of revolt (1381) 406-7, 422; excluded from charter demands 414; ended 423; **XV** 567
Pollard, Sir John, speaker of the House of Commons (1553, 1555) **VII** 654
pollen deposits **Ia** 553-5, 571-2, 613
Pollini, Girolamo **VIII** 453
Pollitt, H. **XV** 397, 458
Pollockshaws **XII** 510
Polly case (1800) **XII** 473
Polo, Marco **VII** 224, 226, 264
Polton, Thomas, bishop of Chiches-

ter **VI** 218, 219, 230, 235; bishop of Worcester 253

Poly-Olbion **VIII** 286

Polybius **Ia** 297, 665

Polyclitus, imperial freedman **Ia** 123–4

Pomerania, duke of *see* Eric, duke of Pomerania

Pomfret, John (1667–1702), poet **XI** 420

Pompeii, shops **Ia** 657

Pompeius Falco, Q. **Ia** 173, 174

Pompeius Magnus, Cn. **Ia** 20, 22, 24, 48

Pompeius, T., landowner **Ia** 608

Pompeius, Trogus **VI** 679

Pomponne, French foreign minister **X** 109, 111

Poncher, Stephen, bishop of Paris **VII** 308

Pondicherry **X** 170; **XI** 262, 325–8, 330, 369; British capture of **XII** 73, 161, 371; to France (1783) 255

Ponet, John (1514?–56), bishop of Rochester (1550–1), bishop of Winchester (1551–6) **VII** 502, 518, 521; flees abroad (1554) 543; see returned to Gardiner 544; education 571, 574

Ponod, Henry **VIII** 452

Ponsonby, Arthur **XV** 198, 226

Ponsonby, George (1755–1817) **XII** 446, 451, 490

Ponsonby, John (1713–89) **XI** 294

Pont-de-l'Arche (Eure) **III** 430; **VI** 174; Henry V seizes 175

Pont-à-Mousson (Meurthe-et-Moselle), St Antoine **VI** 476

Pont-Sainte-Maxence **V** 112

Pont de l'Arche, William **III** 133

Pontaudemer (Eure) **VI** 174

Pontefract (Yorks.) **VI** 35, 53, 61, 523, 613; Edward IV by-passes (1471) 567; **VII** 75, 280, 389, 390

Pontefract (Yorks.), castle **II** 360, 627; **IV** 2, 23, 27; **V** 51, 65, 69, 78, 492; Scottish advance 57; Thomas of Lancaster assembles

magnates 61; siege 66; Lancaster's death sentence 67; revenue collecting centre 68; **VI** 2, 23, 27; **VII** 37

Pontefract (Yorks.), priory **III** 189; **IV** 585

Pontefract, Gregory of, official of Lynn **IV** 481, 482

Ponteland, church **IV** 493

Ponthieu **II** 540, 577; **III** 377; count of *see* Guy

Ponthieu, county **IV** 73, 235, 244; seneschal 280; **V** 2, 4, 109, 112, 117; given to Isabella 7; Prince Edward invested with 82; Edward III's sovereignty under truce (1360) 140; **VI** 110, 142, 152, 179; *see also* Dammartin, Simon de; Eleanor of Castile; Joan

Pontiac's conspiracy (1763) **XII** 183

Pontigny: abbey **III** 211, 445; shrine of St Edmund of Abingdon **IV** 57; Henry III 119; Edward I 256; abbot of 12

Pontissara, John de, bishop of Winchester (1282–1304) **IV** 362, 471, 485, 651, 653; exempted (1297) by Boniface VIII from jurisdiction of Canterbury 717

Pontius Leontius, land-owner **Ia** 450, 452, 454, 728

Pontoise (Seine-et-Oise) **VI** 111, 172, 173, 180, 190; Henry V takes 181; *bailliage* 189; falls (1441) 470

Pontoise, castle **III** 108, 112, 127

Pontorson (Manche) **VI** 173, 177

Pool Castle **IV** 421, 438; *see also* Welshpool

Poole Harbour (Dorset) **II** 389, 390; *see also* Lake (Dorset)

pools, football **XV** 313

poor: sufferings **VIII** 355; **IX** 276, 296–310; welfare of **X** 52–4

Poor Clares **V** 102

Poor Laws **VIII** 265, 266, 267; **X** 52; administration of: unreformed Poor Law **XIII** 449–50; commis-

Poor Laws (*cont.*)
sion of inquiry 450–2; Act (1834) 127, 452, 455; Poor Law Commissioners 452–5, 463; Poor Law Board 453–6; Poor Law in Ireland 336; **XIV** 125, 517–18; **XV** 36, 149, 174, 256, 354

poor relief **X** 157–8; **XII** 45, 527–9

Poore, Herbert, bishop of Salisbury **III** 282, 446

Poore, Richard, bishop of Chichester, Salisbury and Durham **III** 61, 486; **IV** 3, 495; constitutions 452; **VI** 496

Pope, Alexander, poet (1688–1744) **IX** 403; **X** 356, 370–1, 373, 385, 401, 418; translation of Homer 356; **XI** 10, 129, 157, 183, 204; quoted on turnips 106; *Essay on Criticism* 153; Dublin literary taste 306; and Stephen Hales 384; physicians and surgeons 390; *Dunciad* 393, 415, 422; Kneller's epitaph 400; Lord Burlington 403; *Ode to St Cecilia* 417; edits Shakespeare 419; Scribblers' Club 421; on Walpole 421; *Homer* 422; criticized 423–5; and Swift 426; correspondence 429; Johnson's '*Dictionary*' 432; **XII** 350, 539

Pope, the **Ia** 462, 466

popes, registers **IV** 740; *see also* Agatho; Alexander II, IV; Benedict VIII, X; Boniface III, V, VIII; Celestine V; Clement IV, V; Constantine; Formosus; Grefor I, II, III, VII; Gregory IX, X; Hadrian I; Honorius I, III, IV; Innocent III, IV; John XV, XXI; Leo III, IV, IX; Marinus; Martin IV; Nicholas II, III, IV; Paschal I; Paul I; Sergius I; Stephen II, IX; Urban IV; Victor II; Vitalian; Zacharias

Popham, Sir Home Riggs (1762–1820) **XII** 315, 453

Popham, Sir John **VI** 468; **VIII** 204, 436, 440, 457

Popish plot **X** 92–4, 110, 366

Poplar, Red Flag flies **XV** 199; Poplarism 214, 256, 329, 353

Poppaea Sabina, Empress **Ia** 128; villa 161

Popular Front: first taste **XV** 89; in Spain 393; in France 394; campaign (1937) 397, 416; (1938–9) 435–6; its ghost raised 459

population **Ia** 542–552; of England and Wales **VIII** 235–6; **V** 347, 370, 407; estimates unreliable after Domesday book 312–14; causes of decline 329–32; urban areas 380–1; London 378–9; **IX** 261; **X** 38–9, 40, 263; **XI** 105, 120, 123–4; colonial 338, 343; **XII** 10, 13, 517; statistics **XIII** 1, 2, 600–2; comparison **XIV** 102–3, 269–70, 498–9; (1921) **XV** 164; (1931) 301; *see also* American colonies; Edinburgh; Glasgow; Hanover; Jamaica; Liverpool; London; Newfoundland; Nova Scotia; Scotland; slave trade; West Indies

Porcher, John, master of the king's money (1300) **IV** 633

Porchester (Porteceaster) (Hants), **II** 733; castle **IV** 716; **VI** 146

Porlock (Portloca) (Som.) **II** 567, 733

Porson, Richard (1759–1808), scholar **XII** 348

Port **Ib** 145, 147, appendix II

Port and his sons Bieda and Mægla **II** 20

Port Cyslltau **XII** 519

Port Darwin **XV** 540

Port Egremont, British port **XII** 154

Port Mahon **X** 206, 215, 230, 231

Port Nelson **X** 340–2

Port Royal **X** 326, 328, 341, 342

Portal, Sir C.: strategic bombing **XV** 570; does not dismiss Harris 591

458

Portal, Sir Gerald **XIV** 212
Portchester (*Portus Adurni*) (Hants):
  fort **Ia** 320, 404; coins 352; **Ib** 84,
  92, 145; map 2 xxx; map 3 xxxi;
  map 6 88; **II** 264, 733
Porteceaster *see* Porchester (Hants)
Porteous, Lieutenant (d. 1737) **XI**
  278-9
Porteous riots *see* Edinburgh
Porter, Endymion **IX** 335
Porter, Peter P. **XII** 551
Portesmutha **Ib** 145, 147, appendix
  II; *see also* Portsmouth (Hants)
Portfangos, Catalonia **IV** 253
porticoes (*porticus*) **Ia** 142, 160
Portland (Dorset) **II** 239, 567
Portland, case of manor of **IV** 327
Portland, duke of *see* Bentinck, William Henry Cavendish
Portland, earl of *see* Bentinck, William; Weston, Richard
Portloca *see* Portlock (Som.)
Portlock (Som.) **II** 733
Porto Bello **VIII** 417; **XI** 222, 234,
  235
Porto Novo, battle (1781) **XII** 316
Porto Praya **VIII** 369
Porto Rico **VIII** 417; **IX** 337
portoria **Ia** 618
Ports, Cinque *see* Cinque Ports
ports, English **VII** 219; *see also*
  harbours
Portsmouth (Portesmutha) (Hants)
  II 20, 733; **III** 116, 369, 436, 465;
  naval port built (1194) 437-8;
  fleet mobilized by John 440, 459,
  461, 463; **IV** 45, 117, 649; ship
  656; **V** 128, 132, 244; **VI** 166, 393,
  492; new tower 195; harbour 354;
  VII 107, 209, 211, 274, 512; show
  of naval strength (1539) 403;
  capture of Boulogne (1544) 409;
  IX 251
Portugal **III** 95, 149-50; merchants
  IV 644; **V** 266, 440, 529; Edmund
  of Cambridge 428; Castile
  alliance 433; John of Gaunt 464,
  489; **VI** 347, 594; **VII** 93, 119,

159, 226, 308; treaties (1489-90)
  102; conquest of **VIII** 352, 353;
  IX 53, 224-5, 322-3, 326-7; **X**
  47, 60-1, 62, 205-7; peace negotiations 219; and India 349; **XI**
  relations with Britain; trade with
  XII 23; affairs **XIII** 202, 231-2;
  XIV 232, 261; Dilke's convention
  with 191; Salisbury's agreement
  and convention with 191, 192-3;
  allows use of Azores **XV** 564
Portugal, prince of *see* Peter, prince
  of Portugal
Portuguese **VII** 224, 227, 228, 270,
  561; succession question **VIII**
  352, 353; monopoly: in Africa
  123; wines **X** 207; in the East in
  India **XI** 325; **XII** 22-3; and Far
  East 158
Portus Adurni see Portchester
Porzmoguer, Hervé de **VII** 275
Positivists **XIV** 6
Post Office **XII** 60, 61, 216, 285; and
  radio **XV** 232; distributes pensions 257; credit balances used
  290, 325
post-horses **VIII** 263-4
Post-nati **IX** 9-10
Postal Convention **XIV** 35
Postcombe (Oxon.) **VI** 371
Postel, Guillaume **VII** 114
Postumus Dardanus, Claudius **Ia**
  452, 453, 729
Postumus, Gallic emperor **Ia** 273-7
postwar credits **XV** 511
potato **XII** 10, 12, 388
Potitus **Ia** 463
Potsdam, conference **XV** 594
Pott, Percival (1714-88), surgeon
  XI 391
Potter, Gilbert **VII** 527
Potter, John (*c.*1674-1747), archbishop of Canterbury **XI** 78,
  140
Potter, Thomas (1718-59), supporter of Frederick, prince of Wales
  XI 339; **XII** 101
Potterne (Wilts.) **II** 439

pottery: industry **Ia** 641–51; Iron Age 8, 11; imported pre-conquest 42, 57, 59; amphorae 57, 459, 641–2; Samian 184, 202, 243, 259, 636 — Gaulish industry 642–3; difficulties for dating 196, 202, 206–7, 259, 312 — Hadrian's Wall 377 — Castor ware 643; factory-made 237; on native and Roman sites 237, 603; Reculver 254; Nene valley 258, 338, 562, 605, 643–4 — Oxford industry 649; Carpow 319; E. Yorkshire (Malton Crambeck) 386, 645; Hampshire (Alice Holt and Farnham) 455–6, 646–9; decline of factories 456; stratified late pottery in towns 457–9; transport and distribution 562–5, 649; coarse and fine wares 636, 643; supplied to army 641, 650–1, 659; mortaria and flagons 642, 645; Rhenish 642–3; Oxfordshire 644–9; Dorset (black burnished) 645–6, 650–1, 659; Nuneaton 645; as archaeological evidence **Ib** 28–9; differences in pottery traditions 63–73; evidence for Saxon settlement on Saxon Shore 87; of Fyn 108; links between Kent and Jutland 115; map 5 68; at Sancton 192–4; Marbled Ware 204; Argonne Ware 204; manufacture **XII** 29, 514

Pouget, – **X** 393

Poulett Thomson, Charles Edward, 1st Baron Sydenham **XIII** 382

Poullain, Valerand **VII** 516, 543

Pound, Sir Dudley **XV** 480, 520

Poundbury, cemetery **Ia** 551, 700, 704, 731

poverty **XI** 128–32, 137–9; education of the poor 141–2; **XIV** 301, 513–15; treatment of 5–6, 9, 44; Wesley's influence 100; poor-rates 126, 131; poor-relief 130–2, 137–8; work-houses 137–8; *see also* Bristol; charity schools *under*

education; London

Powell, Mr **XII** 260

Powell, Edward **VII** 427

Power, Transport and Economic department **XV** 329

Powerscourt, Edward Wingfield, Viscount (1729–64) **XI** 304

Powis, 4th earl of **XII** 85

Powlett, Charles, 6th marquess of Winchester; 1st duke of Bolton; earl of Wiltshire **X** 139

Powys **Ia** 45; kingdom of **II** 4, 78, 576, 616; Mercian conquest 230; **III** 285; house of 286; Montgomery Castle 288; warring princes 289, 298, 299; **IV** 393, 398, 402, 403, 409–10; Llywelyn's claim to district 417; Edward's allocation of districts 423–4; Madog ap Llywelyn's disastrous expedition 442

Powys, Lords *see* Charlton, Edward; Gray, Henry; Gruffydd ap Gwenwynwyn; Gruffydd ap Madog; Gruffydd Fychan

Powys, lordship of **V** 50

Powys Fadog, N. Wales **VI** 40

Poynings, Sir Adrian **VIII** 60

Poynings, Sir Edward **VI** 628; **VII** 124, 127, 128, 169, 300; joins Henry VII's council 56; success at Sluys 108; 'laws' for Ireland 129, 133; successes in Ireland 131–2; reforms limitations 134; administration under Henry VIII 233; expedition for Margaret of the Netherlands 273; lord deputy of Ireland (1494) 651; comptroller of the household (1509) 650

Poynings, estates **VI** 337

Poynings, Henry, Lord **VI** 508

Poynings, Robert, Lord **VI** 212, 234, 457

Poynings, Thomas, Baron Poynings (d. 1545) **VII** 419

Poynings' Law **VIII** 463; **X** 294, 305, 312, 336; **XII** 223

460

Pozzi of Lucca **IV** 305

Prado **XV** 394

praefecti see praetorian, prefects

Praemunire: Beaufort writs **VI** 253; statute **VII** 549, 568; clergy impleaded 353; Wolsey attacked 329; Gardiner appeals 513

praepositi: praepositus regionis (military appointment) **Ia** 536; chamberlain (*praepositus sacri cubiculi*) 373; diocesan financial controller (*praepositus thesaurorum Augustensium*) 317, 531–2

praesentales, in praesenti **Ia** 350, 367, 417, 489; *see also* imperial guards

praeses **Ia** 251, 316, 347; *see also* governor, *rector*

Praet, Louis de Flandre, sieur de **VII** 301

praetor (status) **Ia** 223, 231, 523–4, 526, 528

praetorian camp, Rome **Ia** 106, 131, 324

praetorian guards: political role **Ia** 68, 71, 116, 128, 131; Nerva proclaimed emperor 154; prefect removed 212–14; Maxentius proclaimed emperor 324; status 293, 508; disbanded by Constantine 331; *see also* imperial guards

praetorian prefects **Ia** 439, 516–17; political role in Early Empire 116, 154, 172; under Commodus 212–14; Papinian 229; under Tetrarchy 301, 303–4, 307, 316–17; fourth-century change of function 331–2; supply and secretariat 332, 390; assessment of taxes 338, 360, 448; regional prefectures 339, 353–4, 449, 496, 501 — civil official 516–17; imperial control 343, 360, 398, 407; political role in Late Empire 394, 400, 409, 446, 449 — Dardanus 452 — Gallic council 501; family tradition of service in this role 436, 469; office retained after western empire's collapse 486

Pragmatic Sanction **XI** 206, 236, 266, 268; Philip's guarantee 195; France's opposition 201

Pragmatic sanctions of Bourges (1438) and Mainz (1439) **VII** 336

Prague **VI** 96; Runciman sent to **XV** 425; undamaged 430; Hitler 439, 441

Praise of Folly, (Moriae Encomium) **VII** 252, 253–5, 265

Prance, Miles **X** 94

prata legionis **Ia** 536, 587; *see also territorium*

Pratt, Sir Charles, 1st Earl Camden (1714–94) **XI** 61, 357; **XII** 66, 112; in Wilkes's case 99, 102; on America 116, 185; lord chancellor (1766) 121, 123, 135, 143, 576; dismissal (1770) 146; president of council (1782–3) 243, 578, 579; (1786–94) 580

Pratt, Sir John, C. J. (1657–1725) **XI** 57

Pratt, John Jeffreys, 2nd Earl Camden, 1st Marquis (1759–1840), lord lieutenant of Ireland **XII** 397; secretary for war and the colonies (1804–5) 581; lord president of the council (1805–6) 581, (1807–9) 582, (1809–12) 583; minister without portfolio (1812) 583

Prayer Book, English **VII** 568; first 515, 519; second 521; Roman Catholic version 555; **VIII** 14, 16; revision **X** 21, 154; revised **XV** 242, 259

Pre-Raphaelite movement **XIII** 540, 547, 591–4

preaching, guides **IV** 765; **IX** 407

prebends **II** 441

precincts *see* sanctuaries

prefects (*praefecti*): camp commandant (*praefectus castrorum*) **Ia** 107, 120, 213; control of civil area (*praefectus civitatis, praefectus regionis*) 187, 535–6; urban

prefects (*cont.*)
(*praefectus urbis*) 214, 362, 365, 408, 447 — Sidonius 453; (*praefectus reliquationis*) 384; beyond frontier in Scotland? 385; Egypt (*praefectus Aegypti*) 398; auxiliary commanders (*praefectus cohortis*) 514, 711; naval (*praefectus classis*) 529, 637; *see also* praetorian prefects

prefecture of the Gauls **Ia** 317, 339, 353–4, 415, 516–17; administration moved from Trier to Arles 429, 496; increasing Gallic independence from Italy 449, 453, 491, 501; recruitment of officials 435–6

Premonstratensian canons (*prémontré*) **V** 184, 303; **VI** 295

Premonstratensian order **III** 84, 188

Prendergast, Maurice of **III** 305

Prerogative, the **IX** 10–13, 20–1

prerogative, royal **IV** 320–33; **XIV** 10, 12

Presbyterianism **IX** 125; Charles on 143–4; Charles accepts 146, 153; dealt heavy blow at Dunbar 168; position (1650) 172–3, 198–9; attempts to enforce 191–4; opposed to independency 195; converted to royalism 246–7; at the Restoration 258–60

Presbyterians: English **X** 4, 17, 19, 20, 23; numbers 27; Scottish 267–73; in Ireland 295, 315, 322

Presentment of Englishry **V** 163, 197

press: Restoration licensing act **X** 28, 155; freedom **XIII** 30–1; position of editors **XV** 27; Northcliffe transforms 187; effect of radio 234–5; during general strike 246; mostly Conservative 264; political influence 282–3; becomes dependent on advertisements 309; war for circulation 309–10, 351; Edward VIII 400–1; *see also* newspapers

Press Bureau **XV** 18, 106

Pressburg, treaty (1805) **XII** 434, 451

Prester, John **VII** 277

Preston (Lancs.) **III** 73; **V** 75; **VII** 504; battle **IX** 155; **X** 222; **XII** 511

Preston, Captain **XII** 193

Preston, Captain Amyas **VIII** 419

Preston, Robert, Lord Gormanston, lord deputy of Ireland (1492) **VII** 127, 651

Preston, Thomas **IX** 162

Preston, Viscount *see* Graham, Richard

Preston, Walter of **III** 33

Preston, William, son of Lord Gormanston, lord deputy of Ireland (1492) **VII** 651

Prestonpans **VIII** 46; **XII** 332

Pretender, 'Old' *see* James Francis Edward; 'Young' *see* Charles Edward

pretium victoriae **Ia** 33, 39, 72, 630, 633

Pretoria, capture of **XIV** 255

Pretylwell, John **V** 340

Price, Richard, dissenter (1723–91) **XI** 88, 123; **XII** 40, 180, 231, 291; biography 40

price movements **XIV** 11, 274, 502–3

prices **V** 50, 191, 219, 224, 334, 349–62; rises **IX** 262; **X** 39; tea **XI** 325; rise in First World War **XV** 41; control 78, 88; rise after war 140; fall 145, 163; fall during Depression 284, 290, 342; rise in Second World War 465

Pride, Thomas **IX** 156, 173, 273

priesthoods: political function **Ia** 343, 580, 676, 701; professional priests 676; ritual functions 673, 681; ritual purity 701–2; equipment 719, 730; exemptions 576

Priestley, John Boynton **XV** 301, 312, 489

Priestley, Joseph (dissenter) (1733–

Principe, II **VII** 264−5, 417
principia **Ia** 280, 531, 597
Pringle, Sir John (1707−82): and army medical services **XI** 221, 389, 392−3
printing: in England **VII** 578−9; **XI** 414; and engraving **XII** 265, 346
printing presses: Catholic **VIII** 182−3; Puritan 201−2; **X** 410, 414−15; colonial 347
Prinz Eugen **XV** 505
Prior, Matthew (1664−1721) **X** 230, 355, 356, 358; **XI** 400, 419, 425; writer 10; plenipotentiary 156; *Pamela, The Turkish Spy* 306
Priscian **III** 232; **VI** 670
Priscillian heresy **Ia** 411, 714, 727, 737
Priscus (I) *see* Helvidius Priscus
Priscus (II), legionary legate? **Ia** 212
Priscus (III), Marius, prosecution of **Ia** 533−4
Priscus (IV) of Parium **Ia** 457
prise: royal exercise in war (1294−7) **IV** 659, 662, 666; wool 680−1; confirmation of Charters (1297) 683; inquiry into grievances of collection (1298) 699; *articuli super cartas* (1300) 700, 704; wine and its commutation (1302−3) 629, 631; corrupt supervisor in Kent 698
prison administration reform **XIII** 467−9; **XIV** 520−1
prison system **X** 158
prisoners: ransoms **VI** 145; governing sale of ordinances 145; sale of Agincourt French 157; French, at Agincourt and Meaux 222
prisoners of war (1264−5) **IV** 190, 191
prisons **IX** 302−3; **XI** 97, 135−6, 309; **XII** 38, 437
Prisot, John, C. J. C. P. **VI** 491
Pritt, D. N. **XV** 468
privateering **X** 166, 171, 231, 251
privilegium fori **IV** 462−3

1804) **XI** 88, 385; **XII** 40, 231, 334
priests: Christian **Ia** 340, 576; pagan 401, 580, 735; and patron **II** 149−50; economic position 152−5; *see also* Christian Church; clergy
prime minister: office of **X** 256; development of office **XII** 95−8, 123−5, 127, 204, 273; Shelburne 257; Pitt, cabinet government 300; ministerial disagreements 439; seldom from aristocracy **XV** 172; university education 70; appointments 175; increased power 197; choice by king 204; nominates governors of BBC 233; general election to decide 270; dissolution of parliament 323; minister of defence 363−4; office mentioned in statute 404; military uniform 480
primicerius notariorum **Ia** 224, 336, 357, 474, 476; *see also notitia*
Primrose of London **VIII** 369
primus pilus **Ia** 522; *see also* centurions
Prince Imperial of France **XIV** 61
Prince Regent *see* George IV
Prince of Wales: damaged **XV** 506; sent to Singapore 532; sunk 540
Princeps **Ia** 50
princeps praetorii **Ia** 520
Princes Risborough (Bucks.) **III** 395
Princes in the Tower (Edward V and Richard, duke of York): responsibility for death **VI** 623; closer confinement 623; evidence for existence (1484) 625; Henry Tudor's silence 625
Princeton **XII** 199
Principal Navigations (Hakluyt) **VIII** 281, 283, 318
principalities, Danubian **XIII** 214, 220, 256−8, 262−3, 275; constitution 291; trouble for Sultan 316
Principate **Ia** 169, 576, 618
Principato **VII** 153

tive party 195, 197; Baldwin espouses 206–7; in general election (1923) 208; Snowden abolishes 212; Baldwin renounces 230; planning 299; of films 315; advocated by Churchill 321; National government 322–4; Runciman expected to oppose 326; Cabinet committee advocates 328–9; established 330–1; effects 339–40

protectorate: **VII** 481, 493–5; debts **X** 6

protectores see imperial guards

protectorship, Gloucester's: (1422) **VI** 215–16; (1454 and 1455) 217; (1483) 612–13

Protestants: naturalization **X** 238–9; in Ireland 295–9

Protocol, Geneva **XV** 215–16, 221

Provençal **III** 256–7

Provence, county **VI** 579; English demand moiety 140; **VII** 315

Provence: house of **IV** 73; problems (1239–43) 98–100, 103; effects of succession of Charles of Anjou 246, 250, 252; fleet (1285) 255; treaty of Oloron 259; marquisate of *see* Venaissin; count of *see* Alfonso II; *see also* Beatrice; Eleanor; Margaret; Raymond-Berengar; Sanchia

Providence, island of **IX** 338; **X** 326, 328

provinces **Ia** 402; Gaul and Germany 78, 89; Britain constituted (*proxima pars Britanniae*) 87–9, 101; frontiers 95–8, 109, 166, 525; alignment of British provinces in civil wars 128–32, 217–20, 273, 282 — Maximian's campaigns 288 — mutiny against Stilicho 426; provincial families 153–5, 272, 351, 400, 434–6 — St Patrick 462–3 — 'provincial clarissimate' 464 — Arbogast 496; Hadrian's interest in provinces 173; division into two provinces 222,

225, 227, 231; recovery 223, 307–15, 405; successive Romanization of provincials 272; Diocletian's reorganization 295, 301, 517; north-west provinces grouped 301–4, 317, 322; division into four provinces 317; provincial structure no longer tied to military organization 333; low state of Britain 360, 368, 377–9; Theodosian restoration 384, 397; Valentia 392–6, 411; Stilicho's British wars 419–22; expulsion of Roman administration 434, 442; collapse of military establishment 437–9; provincial self-sufficiency 454–5; senatorial and imperial control 524; administration of Britain 524–37; cost and gains of provincial structure to Britons 662–3; *see also* Antonine Wall; Carausius; Hadrian's Wall; Imperium Galliarum, prefecture of the Gauls; Romanization

provincial council: Britain **Ia** 112, 552–3; Gaul 501

Provins (Seine-et-Marne) **IV** 240; **VI** 177, 179

provisions, papal, movements in England against (1231) **IV** 45–6

Provisions of Oxford (1258) **V** 10, 17

provisors: first statute **VI** 267; second statute (1390) 266, 267; 'moderations' 94

Prudde, John, king's glazier **VI** 654

Prudential Insurance Co **XV** 287

Prudhoe (Northumb.), castle **VI** 9, 54, 63; barony 337

Prusa, Bithynia, baths **Ia** 577

Prussia **V** 248, 254, 359, 360, 468; **VI** 70, 356–60; east 326; Bolingbroke's expedition 68; **VII** 221; relations with Britain **XI** 175, 197–9; **XIII** 195, 197–8, 200, 203, 218; Belgian question 227, 229; eastern question 237, 288–9;

Prussia (*cont.*)
Cracow suppression 245; Bismarck 315–23, 324–5; *see also* Bismarck; Frederick II; subsidies
Prussia, king of *see* William I
Prynne, William **IX** 111; punishment for pamphlets 75; exclusion from parliament 253; readmission 255–6; puritan view of music 388; of the stage 396; use of Bible 407
pseudo-comitatenses **Ia** 367; *see also comitatenses*
Pseudo-Isidorian Decretals **III** 103
Ptolemy (geographer) **Ia** 98; **Ib** 49, 50; **II** 11–13; **III** 244; Ptolemaic system **VIII** 307–8; **IX** 356, 369
Ptolemy of Lucca **VI** 315
public assistance committees **XV** 256, 353
public health: legislation dealing with **XIII** 463–5; **XIV** 36, 125–6, 302, 518–20
Public Order Act (1936) **XV** 374
public schools, for children of privileged **XV** 171; eclipsed in first Labour government 209; cease to be reliable 260; restrict Jews 419
Public Weal, war of League **VI** 535, 550
publicity of parliamentary debates **XII** 141
publishing, book **X** 356
Puckeridge: cemetery **Ia** 694; hobnails 705
Puckering, Sir William, Lord Keeper **VIII** 226–7
Pucklechurch (Puclancyrcan) (Glos.) **II** 360, 733
Puclancyrcan *see* Pucklechurch (Glos.)
puddling iron *see* Cort, Henry
Puebla, Roderigo de, ambassador **VII** 137, 178, 179, 181; Flemish pirates 92; Medina del Campo (1489) 93–4, 96, 172; Perkin Warbeck 117, 144, 166; Ferdinand suspicious 149–50; Ed-

mund de la Pole 167, 171; papal dispensation for marriage of Henry and Catherine 176
Puerto Bello **X** 328
Pue's Occurrences **XI** 306
Pugeys, Imbert **IV** 143
Pugin, Augustus Welby Northmore: biography **XIII** 583; work 583
Puiset, Hugh de, bishop of Durham **III** 223, 334, 337, 350, 364; conflict with Longchamp 351–3, 357
Pulisangan (Hoen-Ho) **VII** 264
Pullen, Robert **III** 195, 237
Pulo Run (Polaroon) **IX** 323–4; **X** 68, 349
pulpit **IX** 23, 74–5, 143–4, 407
Pulteney, Daniel (d. 1731), brother of William Pulteney, earl of Bath **XI** 204
Pulteney, Sir James Murray, MP **XII** 329
Pulteney, Sir John **V** 264
Pulteney, Dr Richard (1730–1801), botanist **XI** 388
Pulteney, William, earl of Bath (1684–1764) **XI** 22, 31, 36, 140, 146; resigns ministry 168; Walpole 182, 191, 204, 211; quoted on barracks 215; accepts peerage 238; Carteret's friend 246; summoned by king 258
Pumpsaint, fort, lead mines **Ia** 634
Punch and Judy **XV** 314
Puntal, fort **IX** 62
Purandhar, treaty (1776) **XII** 314
Purbeck, Isle of **VII** 195
Purcell, Henry (1659–95) **X** 370, 398, 403–6, 417; his father 406; **XI** 399, 417; **XV** 178
Purchas, Samuel **IX** 406
purchase tax **XV** 491
Puritanism: meaning **VIII** 188; opposition to Anglican system 189; hostility to greed, materialism and corruption 190; Vestiarian controversy 191–2; produces disorder in the Church 192; attack on bishops 193; Parker's

difficulties with 192–3; influence of Thomas Cartwright 194–6; effect on parliament 195–6; 'prophesyings' 197–8; Whitgift's treatment 198–9; 'classical' movement (presbytery in episcopacy) 200; separatist movement 200–1; Martin Marprelate conflict 201–2; Bancroft's attack on Presbyterianism 202–3, 204; severity of law to extremists 204; on Anabaptists 204–5; numbers 457

Puritans: position (1603) **IX** 68; Hampton Court Conference 70; hostile to Arminianism 71–7; attitude (1640) 79–80; definition 125; attempt to enforce moral code 304–15; attitude to music 388; and the theatre 395–9

Purity, medieval poem **V** 525

Purvey, John, Wycliffite **V** 515, 520, 523; **VI** 94, 95, 96

purveyance **V** 15, 18, 24; control 21; limitations under Edward III 163, 195; resentment to demands of royal purveyors 221; in war 242, 253; Philippa's excesses 269; *De Speculo Regis* 296; bondmen

342; pretext for extortion 362; **IX** 4–6, 14

Purvis, Arthur **XV** 496, 532

Pusey, Edward Bouverie **XIII** 519; biography 514; takes part in Oxford Movement 507, 513–17

Putney **VII** 68, 351

Puttock, Stephen **V** 317–18

Puymirol **V** 114

Pyckeryng, John, chaplain **VI** 285

Pyel, John **V** 391

Pygmalion **VIII** 288

Pym, John **IX** 97, 267, 338, 351; attacks Arminianism 44, 75; leads Commons (1640) 92–3; Long Parliament 99–101, 118, 120, 122–3, 124

Pympe, John **VII** 131

Pynchbeck, Thomas **V** 196

Pynsent, Mr **XII** 106

Pynson, Richard, printer **VI** 306; **VII** 578, 579, 580

Pyrenees **Ia** 51, 432; **III** 318, 330, 376; **V** 49, 112, 114; **VI** 140; lordship 107; **VII** 272, 314; treaty **IX** 234; Peace of **X** 60; **XV** 488

Pytchley (Northants) **III** 31, 43

Pythagoreans **Ia** 716

Pytheas of Marseilles **Ia** 44

Q

Quadi **Ia** 207

Quadra, Alvarez de, bishop of Aquila **VIII** 27, 50, 52, 123, 124; estimate of Elizabeth 53; public distrust 122

Quakerism **IX** 195-7, 309-10

Quakers **X** 18-19, 22-4; schools 24; numbers (in 1661) 27; non-resistance 34; in Ireland 295; simplicity of language 361; war 421; **XI** 69, 137, 324; refuse to pay tithes 72

Quakers' Act **X** 22, 23

Qualification of Women Act (1907) **XIV** 399

Quarr Abbey (IOW), abbot of and Adam de Stratton **IV** 365

Quartering Act **XII** 197

Quarterly Review **XII** 541

Quebec, conference (1943) **XV** 572, 598; (1944) 586-7

Quebec, Wolfe's victory at **XII** 25, 86

Quebec Act **XII** 197-9, 235

Quebec expedition (1710) **X** 247

queen, George III's *see* Charlotte Sophia

Queenborough **VIII** 44, 398

Queenborough Castle (Kent) **V** 218, 437, 453

Queen's County **VIII** 462

Queensberry, duchess of *see* Hyde, Lady Catherine

Queensberry, dukes of *see* Charles; Douglas

Queensferry **VIII** 44

Queenstown **XV** 159

Quentavic **II** 132, 263

Quentin Durward **VII** 85

Quercy: French and English rights **IV** 127, 272, 273, 289, 291; ducal administration 302, 309; **V** 140; *see also* Cahors

Quercy, county **VI** 135, 108

querela see plaint

Quettius Severus **Ia** 669

Quiéret, Hughes **V** 128

Quignon, Cardinal **VII** 515

Quimperlé **V** 386

Quincey (Quincy), Saer de, earl of Winchester **III** 470; **IV** 8, 11, 51, 75

Quincitilius Varus, P. *see* Varus

Quincy, Roger de, earl of Winchester, Scottish lands **IV** 580

Quinn v. *Leathem* **XIV** 378

Quirina, voting tribe **Ia** 153

Quo warranto, writs and pleas **IV** 39, 376-9, 521

Quoit Brooch Style **Ib** 113, 116-17, 118 [fig 10], 119-22, 126; Sussex burials 136, 138

Quorndon (Leics.) **VI** 376

R

Raad **Ib** map 5 68

Rabastans, wine merchants **IV** 306

Rabban Cauma, emissary of khan of Persia **IV** 252

Rabelais **VIII** 64

Raby (Co. Durham) **VI** 8, 319; lordship 321

racing **IX** 180, 264

Radagaisus **Ia** 425–7

radar **XV** 390–2, 432, 491; decisive asset 497; for aeroplanes 501

Radbod, king of the Frisians **II** 167–8

Radcliffe, Sir Geoffrey **VI** 449

Radcliffe, Sir George **IX** 111

Radcliffe, Sir James, 3rd earl of Derwentwater (1689–1716) **XI** 161, 163

Radcliffe, Sir John **VI** 222

Radcliffe, John, 1st Baron Fitzwater (Fitzwalter) (d. 1496) **VII** 122, 215; great master of the household (1485) 649

Radcliffe, John (1650–1714), physician **XI** 390

Radcliffe (Ratcliffe), Sir Henry, 2nd earl of Sussex (1506?–57) **VII** 528

Radcliffe, Sir Richard (d. 1485), killed at Bosworth **VII** 58

Radcliffe, Robert **VII** 122

Radcliffe, Robert, 1st earl of Sussex (1483–1542), son of 1st Baron Fitzwalter **VII** 400

Radcliffe, Thomas, 3rd earl of Sussex (1526?–83): lord lieutanant of Ireland (1556–60) **VII** 652; **VIII** 301; queen's agent against northern rebellion 137–44; Shane's overthrow 469

Radcot (Oxon.) **III** 145

Radcot Bridge (Oxon.), battle **V** 453, 456, 460, 485, 488; **VI** 3

Raddington, Sir Baldwin **V** 428, 471, 475

Radfield, hundred of (Cambs.) **III** 23

radicals **XII** 203; *see also* London, radicalism of; Wilkes, Gordon riots and Reform movements

Radisson, Pierre Esprit **X** 340

radknights **II** 473, 475, 477, 478

Radnor **III** 288, 297, 301; lordship and castle **IV** 185, 397, 404; castle **V** 255; **VI** 42, 510

Raeburn, Sir H. **XIII** 590

Raeder, Admiral, insists on narrow front **XV** 498

Raedgeat **Ib** 171

Rædwald, king of East Anglia and overlord of southern English **II** 34, 50, 53, 60, 127; accepts baptism 112; entertains Edwin 78, 114; wins battle of the Idle 79

Rædwulf, king of Northumbria **II** 244

Rægeheafde *see* Gateshead (Co. Durham)

Rægnald I, king of York **II** 332–4, 338, 358

Rægnald II, king of York **II** 358, 363

Raeti gaesati **Ia** 249

Raetia **Ia** 175, 199, 288; evacuation of 467

Raffles, Sir Thomas Stamford (1781–1826) **XII** 564; **XIII** 413

The Ragged Trousered Philanthropists **XV** 352

Raghoba *see* Raghurath Rao

Raghurath Rao **XII** 314

Raglan (Gwent) **VI** 510

Raglan, Lord *see* Somerset, Lord Fitzroy James Henry

Ragman Roll **IV** 358, 616; **V** 99

Ragnar Lothbrok **II** 241; sons in England 246, 247

Raikes, Robert (1755–1811) **XII** 39

Raikes, Thomas (1774–1848), governor of Bank of England **XII** 419

railways **XII** 518; early railway building **XIII** 43–7; social and economic effects 41–2; objections to 46–7; development (to 1870) 595–6, 624; **XIV** 107, 279–80; effect on buildings and architecture 153; taken over (1914) **XV** 5; effects of war 122; electrification expected 130; strike 141; returned to private ownership 145, 183; derating 257; no new lines 303; taken over (1939) 461; crisis 506–7; cleared 510

Rainald I, count of Burgundy **III** 125

Rainald II, count of Burgundy **III** 125

Rainborow, Thomas **IX** 152

The Rainbow **XV** 180

Rainsborough, William **IX** 111, 223

Ralegh, Hugh of **III** 15

Ralegh, William, judge, later bishop of Norwich (1239) and Winchester (1244–50) **IV** 68, 70, 71, 75; monastic patronage 762

Raleigh, Sir Walter (?1552–1618) **VIII** 413, 419, 439–40; biographical notes 421; aid to Huguenots 131; manor of Sherborne 191; subsidy debate 229; American 'planter' 245–6; on Drake 247; attack on second armada 426; Munster colony 475; **IX** 2, 55, 69, 326, 408; **XI** 394; **XIV** 551

Ralf I (the Staller), earl of East Anglia **II** 426, 610–12

Ralf II, earl of East Anglia **II** 610–12

Ralf, son of Drogo, count of the Vexin; earl in England **II** 560, 564; earl of Hereford 569; death 569–70

Ralf de Limesy **II** 631

Ralf Paganel **II** 628

Ralf de Tancarville **II** 630

Ralf de Tosny **II** 593, 631

Ralph, archbishop of Canterbury **III** 127, 213

Ralph Niger **III** 319

Ralph Roister Doister **VIII** 296

Ralph of Shrewsbury, bishop of Bath and Wells (1329–63) **V** 501

Rambler **XI** 422, 431

Ramillies, battle (1706) **X** 212

Ramlah **III** 94

Rammekens **VIII** 365

Ramsay, Adam **V** 428

Ramsay, Allan (1686–1758), poet **X** 263; **XI** 286, 425; **XII** 351

Ramsay, Allan (1713–84), painter **XI** 404, 407

Ramsay, James Andrew Broun, 10th earl and 1st marquis of Dalhousie: biography **XIII** 425; governor-general of India 408–9, 430–2; annexation of the Punjab 426; 'doctrine of lapse' 427–8; annexation of Oudh 428; reforms 428–9; *see also* second Burmese war

Ramsay, Sir John, Lord of Bothwell (d. 1513) **VII** 136, 138, 158

Ramsay, Sir William (1852–1916): quoted on Joseph Black **XI** 385

Ramsay of Banff, Sir James **VI** 437, 640

Ramsbottom, Mr **XII** 513

Ramsbury (Wilts.) **VI** 496

Ramsbury (Wilts.), see **II** 439, 440; bishop of *see* Oda

Ramsey (Hunts.), abbey **II** 373, 375, 413, 455, 680; Oswald's fame 450; gift to Fleury 462; knight service 635; **III** 77, 147, 447; **V** 343, 416; **VI** 378; lease 372; Houghton manor 372

Ramsey, Admiral **XV** 579

Ramseye, William de **V** 252

Ramus, Peter **IX** 356

Ranby, John **XII** 448

Randolph, Friar **VI** 482

Randolph, German tutor to Edward VI **VII** 479

Randolph, Thomas, earl of Moray (1312–32) **V** 65, 115, 116; lands appropriated by king 35; Battle of Bannockburn (1314) 37; victory 38; Irish invasion 43

Randolph, Thomas **VIII** 67; Mary Stuart's marriage 75–82, 84–5, 87–8; warns of murder conspiracy 92–4; heralds diplomatic settlement 145

Rangoon **XV** 598

Ranjit Singh **XIII** 403, 416–18, 424

Rannulf I, le Meschin, earl of Chester **III** 12

Rannulf II, de Gernon, earl of Chester **III** 52, 141, 153; his revolt (1146) 147–8; attack on Coventry (1147) 151; appropriates rents 155; territory and treaty with Leicester 159–60; attack on York 162, 273; his right to honour of Lancaster 165, 275

Rannulf III, de Blondeville, earl of Chester **III** 34, 35, 258, 281, 486

Ransoms **V** 225, 247–8

Ranulf the Breton, treasurer of the chamber **IV** 48

Rapallo, Italian-Yugoslav treaty **XV** 162; German-Soviet treaty 189, 217

rapes of Sussex **II** 294, 504, 625, 628

rapiers **VIII** 278

Rastadt, peace **X** 242

Rastell, John (d. 1536) **VII** 228, 580, 586

Rastell, William (1508?–65) **VII** 583

Ratae Coritanorum see Leicester

Ratcliffe, Sir Richard **VI** 634, 643; killed 644

rates, assessment **XII** 46

Rates, Book **VII** 476–7, 477, 507, 559; **IX** 83

Rathlin, massacre of **VIII** 475

Rathlin Island **V** 42

Rathmines, battle **IX** 162

Rationale **VII** 431

rationalis summae rei **Ia** 306, 337, 339

rationalis vicarii **Ia** 337–8, 339

rationalism **XIV** 141–2

rationing: food, instituted by accident **XV** 77, 78, 95, 121 — continued (until 1921) 140 — ends 163 — plans for 375 — War Cabinet refuses to sanction 457 — introduced 464, 479; petrol 461, 544; clothes 510, 544; coal 547

Ratisbon, peace (1684) **X** 113, 114

Ravel, Maurice **XV** 179

Ravenna: imperial court **Ia** 425, 427, 429, 662; political confusion 430–2; relations with eastern empire 432; no control over Britain 442–3; relations with Arles 451; Aetius' political control 475–6; northern Gaul 491; no need for emperor 486; mosaics 465

Ravenna Cosmography **Ia** 45

Ravenna, French victory (1512) **VII** 274

Ravenscar (Yorks.), inscription **Ia** 384; **Ib** map 6 88

Ravenser **IV** 634

Ravenspur (Yorks.) **V** 492; **VI** 2

Ravenstein, Philip of Cleves, count of **VII** 108

Ravensworth (Yorks.) **VI** 326

Rawdon, John, 1st earl of Moira (1720–93) **XI** 304

Rawdon-Hastings, Francis, 1st marquis of Hastings and 2nd earl of Moira (1754–1826): biography **XII** 435; master of ordnance (1806–7) 435, 582; attempts at cabinet-making 491, 499

Rawlinson, Sir H. S., and Somme **XV** 60; at Versailles 100

Rawlinson, Richard **X** 156

Rawnsley, Canon H. D. **XIV** 340

Ray, John **X** 376

Rayleigh (Essex), honour of **II** 425

471

Raymond V, count of Toulouse **III** 326, 330, 341, 344

Raymond VI, count of Toulouse **III** 376, 381, 463

Raymond VII, count of Toulouse **IV** 87–8; treaty with king of France (1227) 92; wavering ambitions (1239–43) 99–103; makes peace at Lorris 103; dies (1246) 103; inheritance to lands and rights 127; daughter Jeanne *see* Toulouse, Jeanne of

Raymond, Sir Robert, Lord Raymond (1673–1733) **XI** 61, 64, 323

Raymond Berenger, count of Provence **IV** 98–100, 103, 112; **VI** 140

Raymond le Gros **III** 310–11, 313

Ré, Isle of **IV** 103; Buckingham at **IX** 38, 66–7

Read, Colonel **XII** 385

Read, Sir William (d. 1715), quack **XI** 390

Reade, Winwood **XIV** 29

Reade, Robert, bishop of Chichester, Dominican **VI** 272

Reading (Readingum) (Berks.), **Ib** 38, 41, 43, 111, 156; Thames 161; map xxxi; **II** 733; early burials 25; Danes 248–9, 381; manor 478, 486; **III** 134, 143, 239, 292, 357; abbey 130, 185, 188, 243; annals 247; Heraclius' meeting with Henry II (1185) 344; provincial council (1279) **IV** 472–5; **V** 455, 465; **VI** 204, 294; parliament (1453) 507; **VII** 35, 199, 398; **X** 139; university **XV** 308

Reading, John of, on Wykeham **V** 227

Reading, Lord *see* Isaacs, Sir R.

Reading, Robert of, on Edward II **V** 57

Readingum *see* Reading (Berks.)

Realists **VII** 254

reaping machine, relief of **Ia** 623

rearmament: to make Great Britain a Great Power **XV** 300; not pre-

vented by Labour party 365; tardy recommendations 364; barely moves 375; justified by White Paper 376; general election (1935) 383; effective beginning 389; steps 411–13; Chamberlain leads 414

Réaumur, R. A. Ferchault de (1683–1757), chemist **XI** 396

Rebecca **XV** 312

Rebecca riots **XIII** 597

rebellion, attitudes to **Ia** 66–7, 121–3, 147–8, 224–5, 296–9; Paul 'The Chain' 357–8; Jovinus proclaimed emperor 446–7

receptoria of Agenais **IV** 302

recluses **IV** 765–6; Westminster **VI** 296

Recognitiones feodorum in Aquitaine **IV** 295–6

reconstruction: ideas after First World War **XV** 139; demanded (1943) 567; Churchill wants agreed programme 595

Reconstruction, Ministry of: set up (1917) **XV** 93; ended 130; set up (1943) 567

record office *see notitia*

Recorde, Robert **VIII** 307

records: English **IV** 277; register of foreign, Gascon and other affairs 277; courts **IV** 334; king 330

recruitment *see* army and conscription

Rectitudines singularum personarum **II** 473–6; compared with Domesday Book 476–9

rector **Ia** 392–3; *see also praeses*

rectors **IV** 458–9; legate Otto 448, 502

Reculf *see* Reculver (Kent)

Reculver (Reculf) (Kent): fort **Ia** 253, 257–60, 281, 300, 320; comes into commission 530; **Ib** 31, 83, 91, 113, 126; map 2 xxx; map 6 88; cross **II** 151; monastery 111; abbots 142, 207, 733

Recusancy **VIII** 136, 185

Rempston, Sir Thomas **VI** 1, 22, 239, 244

Renaissance **VII** 165, 235, 237, 598; views 2, 21; French 162; English culture 266; realpolitik 266–7; Wolsey 286; heresy 343

Renard, Simon, Imperial ambassador **VII** 532, 536, 537, 540, 544, 548

Rendlæsham *see* Rendlesham (Suffolk)

Rendlesham (Rendlæsham) (Suffolk) **Ib** map xxx; **II** 51, 733

René, duke of Anjou **VI** 474, 475–6; at war with Metz 476; instructions to his envoys in England 479; urges surrender of Maine 479; rights in Anjou, Bar and Provence 579; **VII** 114

Renée, daughter of Louis XII: to marry Ferdinand of Austria (1513) **VII** 283, 305, 307, 323

Rennes (Ille-et-Vilaine) **III** 329; **VI** 627; **VII** 50, 88, 97, 104

Rennie, John (1761–1821) **XII** 507

Rent Act (1923) **XV** 205

Renwick, James **X** 275

reparations: demand **XV** 127; Paris peace conference 134–5; condemned by Labour party 136; Genoa conference 189; linked with war debts 203–4; Dawes plan 215, 255; Young plan 272; Lausanne conference 335; Labour wishes to end 373; Yalta conference 590; Potsdam conference 594; extracted from Germany 596

Repingdon, Philip, bishop of Lincoln (1405–19) **V** 517–18; **VI** 273, 686

Replevin **IV** 368, 377

representation: in Commons **X** 12; of towns in parliament **XII** 48, 51–4

Representation of the People Act (1918) **XV** 94, 115–16

representation and taxation **IV** 30;

of cities and boroughs to discuss tallage in council (1268) 222; and consent 117, 222–3, 501–8, 526–40, 675–8

reprisal, custom **IV** 620–1, 626, 644

Repton (Derby.) **Ib** 186; map 4 xxxii; **II** 251–2; monastery 161

Repton, Humphrey (1752–1818), estate improver **XII** 546

Republic: continuity of traditions **Ia** 80, 192, 199, 311, 524 — constitutional powers 287 — minor triumphs 394 — *hostis* 396; system of patronage 78, 533; neo-republicanism and opposition to Flavians 153, 164; religion 681, 709; migration to cities 598; *latifundia* 605; Britain's incorporation 618

republicanism **X** 57

Repulse: sent to Singapore **XV** 532; sunk 540

Requesens, Don Luis **VIII** 164, 338, 339

Res Gestae: Augustus **Ia** 47; *Divi Saporis* 273

res publica: local community **Ia** 138, 534–5, 580–1, 585, 590–2

Reschid Pasha **XIII** 252–4, 259

Resitutus, Bishop **Ia** 340

resolutioners **IX** 168

resorts, seaside **XII** 549

Restitutio Christianismi **VIII** 312

Restoration, the **IX** 259–60

Restormel (Corn.) **VI** 497

Restout, Jean, Rouen merchant **VI** 578

Resumption Acts **VI** 81, 500, 501–2

The Resurrection of Hungary **XV** 154

retainers **V** 68, 236, 258, 262–3; corruption 456; and Richard II 487, 497

Retford (Notts.) **III** 481

Retford, Henry de, Speaker (1402) **VI** 80

Retford, William **V** 217

Rethel, county **VI** 573

Rethondes, armistice signed **XV** 113

Rhine, counts palatine of **V** 121; (Rupert of Bavaria) 476; *see also* Conrad; Henry

Rhine, river: Caesar's campaigns **Ia** 22, 25, 38; communications with Britain 58, 304, 359, 429, 563; revolts on frontier 68–70, 116, 126, 128–9, 411; garrison 71, 73, 198, 220, 269, 273, 304; frontier 78, 89, 178, 274, 279; barbarian attacks 203; zone beyond frontiers 270, 274; campaigns 279, 288, 307, 359, 369–70 — Abogast 409 — Germanic takeover 476–9; Gallic prefecture 353; Rhineland 353, 387, 448, 480, 499; glass industry 456; barbarian kingdoms 456, 493, 496–7; Kaiseraugst treasure 532; migration from 582; market for iron 639; pottery 642–3; imports from 666, 669; cemeteries 695; Rhineland deities at Bath 713; late pagan temples in use 735; **Ib** 47, 79; map 1 xxix; **V** 105, 122, 476

Rhinegrave **VIII** 57

Rhode Island **IX** 342; **X** 334

Rhodes **VI** 326; **VII** 245, 314, 581

Rhodes, Cecil J. **XIV** 188, 189; cheque to Parnell 189; height of career 212; interests in the Rand 228; claims in Bechuanaland 228; Raid plan 229; resigns Cape premiership 232; severely censured by select committee 233; whitewashed by Chamberlain 234; persuades Matabele rebels to surrender 236; re-emerges as British leader in South Africa 246; siege of Kimberley 253; death 348; will 349

Rhodian Sea-Law **III** 439

Rhodocanakis, Constantine **X** 372

Rhondda, Lord, food rationing **XV** 77, 79

Rhône, river **Ia** 37, 587; valley **III** 330

Rhos: one of Four Cantrefs **IV** 400, 414; part of new honour of Denbigh 421, 424; **VI** 38

Rhos, Lord William **V** 90

Rhuddlan (Flint) **II** 576; **III** 293; army headquarters **IV** 422–6, 428, 429, 441; strength of forces 423; borough 432; statute (1284) 65, 359; statute of Wales issued at 429; **VI** 38; *see also* statutes

Rhuddlan (Flint): castle **II** 615; **III** 285, 291, 293, 300; **IV** 403, 412, 413, 430–1

Rhuddlan, Robert of **III** 285, 287

Rhuvoniog (Cantref of North Wales) **IV** 400, 414; part of new honour of Denbigh 421, 424

Rhwfoniog (Cantref of North Wales) **VI** 38

Rhyl, Canadians mutiny **XV** 138

Rhyn Park, fortress, fort **Ia** 103, 137

Rhys, Fychan (d. 1271) **IV** 411

Rhys, Lord, prince of Deheubarth (d. 1197) **IV** 385, 386, 390, 391, 392; descendants 398, 402, 410–11, 419 — principality of Deheubarth shared 393 — Rhys ap Mareddud 438

Rhys, Tudor ap Goronwy's son **VI** 39

Rhys, Wyndod, descendant of Lord Rhys **IV** 410, 438

Rhys ap Gruffydd **III** 284, 291, 293–4, 297, 298

Rhys ap Maredudd, of Dryslwyn **IV** 410, 419, 421; baron of Wales 438; rebellion and end 438–40

Rhys ap Tewdwr, prince of Deheubarth **III** 287, 291

Rhys ap Thomas, Sir (1449–1525) **VII** 52, 366

Rhys ap Tudor (the Black) **VI** 40

Ribbentrop, von, goes to Moscow **XV** 449

Ribble (Rippel), river **Ia** 208, 392; **II** 733; **III** 265, 275; **VI** 337

Ribblesdale (Lancs. and Yorks.) **VI** 337

ribbon-weavers, riots **X** 258

Ribchester (Lancs.): inscription **Ia** 203; Sarmatae 208, 536; fort 392; *singulares* 521

Ribe **Ib** map 5 68

Ricardo, David (1772–1823) **XII** 469, 531; **XIII** 58–61, 129–30, 211, 445; biography 58

Riccall (Richale) (Yorks.) **II** 589, 733

Riccardi, of Lucca **IV** 266, 632, 634, 641, 642

Rice, Sir John ap *see* John ap Rice, Sir

Rich, Sir Richard, 1st Baron Rich (1496?–1567) **VII** 428, 494, 531; speaker of House of Commons (1536) 654; chancellor (1547) 646; resigns Great Seal (1551) 492

Rich, Robert **IX** 389

Rich, Robert, 2nd earl of Warwick **IX** 63, 96, 338

Richale *see* Riccall (Yorks.)

Richard 'with the beard' **III** 407

Richard, bishop of Bangor **IV** 390–1

Richard, duke of Gloucester *see* Richard III

Richard I, duke of Normandy **II** 375, 558

Richard II, duke of Normandy **II** 379, 402, 408, 558; **III** 125

Richard, duke of York **VI** 217, 423, 435, 464–72, 507, 623–5; marriage purchased from Crown 321; brought up at Raby 322; income and inheritance 334–5, 465; lieutenant in France (1436) 465; not allowed proceeds of Norman taxation 466; affronted by Somerset's second mission 467; allowed payment of less than half his troops 467; money intended for, diverted to Guienne 468; receives only a fraction of the taxes granted by the Norman estates 468; Somerset intrudes on sphere 471; ordered to defend Rouen 471; asked not to demand more money 471; returns from Ireland (1450) 499; protests against half-hearted Resumption Act 502; heads struggle against the Somerset and Beaufort interest 502–3; assumes position of reformer 503; advances on London (1452) 503–4; avoids the king, crosses Thames at Kingston Bridge 504; charges against Somerset (1452) 504; forced to swear allegiance to Henry VI publicly 504; protectorship (1455) 507; not invited by Somerset to Great Council (20 Oct. 1453) 508; appointments in council (Mar. 1454) 509; weakness of his position (1454) 509; to be 'chief of the Kynges Counseill' 509; in north to suppress private war (1454) 510; concerts forces with the Nevilles and Warwick 511; first protectorship 512–13; assumes Somerset's title of constable of England 512; sends word to Warwick (1454) to return from Calais 515; escapes to Ireland after Ludford Bridge 516; attainted (1459) 516; manifesto (1460) drafted 518; leaves Ireland to claim the throne 520; lands Chester marches through Ludlow and Hereford 520; enters Westminster Hall 520; presents genealogical statement of his claim 521; reminded of his oath to Henry VI 521; and of statutes making against his title 521; assumed succession though Henry VI was to retain Crown for life 524; assigned half Principality of Wales 522; proclaimed heir-apparent and protector 522; killed at Battle of Wakefield 523; beheaded on walls of York 523; attainder reversed (1461) 542; **VII** 67, 71

Richard, earl of Chester **III** 287

479

Roach, Sir William **VII** 411

Road Traffic Acts (1930, 1934) **XV** 302–3

roads **Ia** 175, 183, 193, 255, 298; London hub of system 257, 309, 361, 564; Fen Causeway 258; dangerous to travel 379, 455; surveillance 523; Icknield Way 541; transport and marketing of goods 541, 562–3, 647–8; environmental effect of road building 555; Watling Street 568; Imperial Post and communications 568, 570–1, 597; maintenance 568–9; Akeman Street 607; minor roads 608, 626; Stane Street 647; cemeteries 694; state of **VIII** 263, 264; system **X** 51; **XII** 26, 518; upkeep 45; **XIII** 4, 47, 597; new **XV** 338; deaths 303; in blackout 454; *see also* communications; Dere Street; Fosse Way; Stanegate; transport

Roanne (Loire) **VI** 240

Roanoke Island **VIII** 246, 369

Rob Roy see Macgregor, Robert

Robert, archbishop of Rouen **II** 462

Robert, bishop of Hereford **II** 618, 671

Robert, bishop of Ross **VI** 275

Robert, count of Eu **II** 604, 633

Robert II, count of Flanders **III** 118, 123

Robert, count of Mortain **II** 604, 623, 630, 637; **III** 100–1

Robert, count of Séez **III** 384

Robert II, duke of Burgundy **IV** 248; daughters 250

Robert I, duke of Normandy **II** 559–60, 619; marries and repudiates Estrith, sister of Cnut 408–9

Robert, earl of Gloucester: supports Stephen **III** 133–4; renounces his allegiance 135; support of bishops 137; arrival in England 137–9; treaty with earl of Hereford 140; at battle of Lincoln 141–2; capture and release 144–5; Nor-

mandy 145, 160; rule in the west 146; death 148, 150; fighting during anarchy 151; supposed coinage 158; Geoffrey of Monmouth dedicates his history 255; marries Mabel, daughter of Robert Fitz Hamon 290; relations with Wales 291

Robert I, earl of Leicester **III** 12, 137, 153, 164; clash and treaty with Chester 159–60; pronounces sentence upon Becket 208; loyal to Stephen 322

Robert II, earl of Leicester (1118–68) **III** 335–7, 341, 363

Robert, eldest son of William I **II** 607; rebellions 608–9; invades Scotland 614; nominated Duke of Normandy 620

Robert, king of Naples, hostage in childhood **IV** 283

Robert I (Bruce), king of Scotland (1306–29) and Thomas of Lancaster **V** 24, 45, 68; Bannockburn campaign 32–41; in Ireland 42–4; campaign (1319) 56; northern England 75, 76, 298; treaty of Northampton 98–9; death 115

Robert II (Stewart), king of Scotland (1371–90) **V** 118, 142; *see also* Bruce

Robert III, king of Scotland **IV** 685; **VI** 34, 35, 64; Henry IV treats with (1400) 36

Robert, son of Wimarch **II** 425, 591–2

Robert de Beaumont **II** 630

Robert de Bellême, earl of Shrewsbury **II** 637

Robert de Comines, earl of Northumbria **II** 602

Robert Curthose, duke of Normandy, count of Maine **III** 97, 103, 154; on crusade 97, 102, 110, 113, 176; character 97–8; failure of his rebellion against Rufus 101; rule in Normandy 104–5; treaty with Rufus (1091) 107; war in

Robert Curthose (*cont.*)
Maine 108; aim of Robert de Mowbray's rebellion 109; rebels against Henry I 115–17; defeated by Robert of Bellême 118; defeated at Tinchebrai 119–21; imprisonment and death 120–1, 125; claim to Normandy 128; treaty with Edgar the Ætheling 266

Robert the Dispenser **II** 632, 639

Robert le Frison, count of Flanders **II** 607, 609, 617

Robert of Jumièges, bishop of London **II** 464, 560; archbishop of Canterbury 464–5, 467, 568

Robert of Lorraine, bishop of Hereford **III** 416

Robert Malet **II** 639

Robert de Mowbray, earl of Northumbria **II** 614, 637

Robert d'Oilli **II** 633

Robert de Rhuddlan **II** 615, 632

Robert of Stafford **II** 631

Robert de Tosny, founder of Belvoir Castle **II** 631

Roberts, Frederick S., afterwards Earl **XIV** 362, 433, 475; victories in Afghanistan 63; march from Kabul to Kandahar 70; victories in South Africa 254–6; evidence before royal commission 292

Roberts, John (1712?–72) **XII** 53, 88

Roberts, Sir William **X** 23

Robertson, Scottish smuggler, and Porteous riots (1737) **XI** 278

Robertson, T. W. **XIII** 554; biography 625; **XIV** 328

Robertson, William (1721–93), historian **X** 293; **XI** 286; **XII** 280, 348

Robertson, Sir William R. (1860–1933) **XIV** 16; biography **XV** 47; Chief of Imperial General Staff 47; strategy 48; wants Derby as secretary for war 58; gets Lloyd George 59; Lloyd George turns against 62; prospects for victory 66; dislikes breakfast with Lloyd George 73; supported by Derby against Lloyd George 76; and Nivelle 80, 81; doubts on Flanders offensive 86–7; conflict with Lloyd George 98–9; dismissed 100; Maurice 117; condemns Dardanelles 555; doctrine of the longest purse 559

Robesart, Lewis **VI** 184, 201

Robethon, Jean de (d. 1722) **XI** 152, 155

Robey, George: on Asquith **XV** 15; in *Bing Boys* 52; knighted 180

Robin of Holderness **VI** 555

Robin Hood **III** 34, 35; **V** 209

Robin of Redesdale **VI** 422

Robinson, Frederick John, Viscount Goderich (1827), earl of Ripon (1833) **XIII** 100, 346, 423; biography 71; administration 75

Robinson, Henry **IX** 213

Robinson, Sir Hercules, Lord Rosmead **XIV** 229, 231, 233, 245

Robinson, John (1727–1802) **XII** 66, 153, 171, 204, 224; Shelburne 252; plan for North 262; government change analysis 266; George Rose 270

Robinson, Sir Thomas (Lord Grantham) (1695–1770) **XI** 34, 323, 346, 348

Robinson, Thomas, MP **XII** 88

Robsart, Amy **VIII** 49–51

Rochdale **XV** 267, 314

'Rochdale Pioneers' **XIII** 617

Roche, Mr **XII** 136

Rochelle, La **IV** 88, 90, 96, 102, 103; sacked 644–5; **IX** 63–6

Roches, Peter des, bishop of Winchester: **III** 223, 452, 462; weekday markets ruling 77; John's justiciar 446, 464–5, 486; suspends Stephen Langton 478–9; crowns Henry III (1216) **IV** 1; charge of the king 2; at Lincoln 11–12; political position 17, 24,

26; return to England from crusade 45, 47; mediates in France (1231) 96; influence on Henry III (1231–4) 47–9, 51, 53–9, 72; death (1238) 74

Roches, William des **III** 378, 379, 383, 467

Rochester (*Durobrivae*, later Hrofesceaster) (Kent) **Ib** 123–5; map 2 xxx; **II** 206, 257, 526–7; coinage minters 536; **III** 153, 173, 300; Aristotle's *Organon* 235; **IV** 187, 191, 683; **VI** 159, 381; diocese 275; representatives in Parliament 417–18; **VII** 398, 399; Henry VII meets Anne of Cleves 404

Rochester, bishopric **III** 252

Rochester, bishops of *see* Bottlesham, J.; Brunton; Eardwulf; Ernost; Glanvill, Gilbert; Gundulf; Hethe; Hilsey, John; Justus; Merton; Rotherham; Sandford; Scory; Sheppey; Siward; Wells, William; Wilcocks, Joseph

Rochester, earl of *see* Hyde, Laurence

Rochester, Sir Robert (1494?–1557) **VII** 532; comptroller of the household (1553) 650; keeper of the privy seal (1555) 647

Rochester, see of **II** 109, 111–12, 116, 134, 146–7; compared with other sees 132; **VII** 518, 545

Rochester, Viscount *see* Carr

Rochester Castle: siege (1088) **III** 101–2, 333; siege (1215) 479–81, 483; **V** 408

Rochester Cathedral **II** 111; **III** 226

Rochford (Essex) **III** 55

Rochford, earl of *see* Zuylestein, William Henry

Rochford, Lady Jane, daughter of Henry (Parker), Lord Morley **VII** 418, 419

Rochford, Sir Ralph **VI** 168

Rochford, Viscount *see* Boleyn, George; Boleyn, Thomas

Rockbourne (Hants) **V** 325

rockets: Germans develop **XV** 578; attack by 584

Rockingham (Northants) **III** 7, 160; council 104, 174

Rockingham, castle **V** 204; **VII** 38, 57

Rockingham, forest **V** 209; **VII** 34; **IX** 83

Rockingham, 2nd marquis of *see* Wentworth, Charles Watson

Roding villages (Essex) **Ib** 42

Rodingas **Ib** 42; map 2 xxx

Rodney, George Brydges, 1st Baron (1719–92) **XI** 229, 365, 371; **XII** 215, 217, 218, 244; biography 215

Rody, Nicholas, MP Warwick **VI** 417

Roe, Sir Thomas **IX** 323, 326

Roebuck, J., MP (1833) **XIII** 92, 141, 148

Roebuck, John (1718–94) **XI** 116, 277, 285, 387; **XII** 31, 332

Roebuck and Garbett **XII** 31

Roeskilde, treaty **IX** 228

Roet, Philippa, Catherine Swynford's sister **VI** 473

Roger, archbishop of York **III** 190, 196, 213, 214

Roger, bishop of Salisbury **III** 128, 179, 183, 234; controls the administration 133, 136, 181; his fall 137; property seized by Stephen 154, 190; organises the exchequer 416

Roger, bishop of Worcester **III** 222, 229

Roger, earl of Hereford, son of William fitz Osbern **II** 610–12; **III** 188, 322

Roger, earl of Warwick **III** 137, 153, 159, 164

Roger II, king of Sicily **III** 331, 360

Roger *artifex* **III** 261

Roger Bigot **II** 625, 631–3

Roger de Busli **II** 626–7

Roger de Courselles **II** 632

Roger d'Ivry **II** 639

171, 240, 505, 514; moralists 240; historians 252, 319; fusion with barbarian 271–2, 355, 454, 486; pragmatism 431; law 457, 526–7; philosophy 710–11; state religion 714–15; *see also* barbarians; citizenship; Latin language; education; religion; Romanization

Roman law, study, in England **II** 181–2; **III** 246–7

Roman Ridge **Ib** map 4 xxxii

Roman Rig **Ib** map 4 xxxii

Roman Roads **Ib** 40, 101, 107, 138, 151–2; Mildenhall to Bath 155; Mons Badonicus 158–60; Dorchester 168; Winteringham 176–7; Deira 189; York 196; **III** 78, 79

Roman de la Rose **V** 531

Roman de Troie **V** 531

Romanesque architecture **III** 260–3

Romanization **Ia** 171, 240, 505–15; pre-Conquest influences in Britain 42, 56–7, 59, 81–2; colonies 104; urban and rural development 111–13, 124–7, 138, 142–3, 156–61 —provincial differences 185–9, 232–8 —pattern-construction 541; Imperial Cult 117; education 142–3; provincial senators 153–5; citizenship and 173, 271–3; Pennines 199; difficult to determine degree 236–7, 583, 605–7, 609–10; Rhine-Danube lands 270, 735; settlement of barbarians within empire 355; end of Roman Britain 434, 443

Romano-Britons: in countryside, difficulty of isolating Roman and native **Ia** 236–7, 604–5, 607–8; fifth-century town and villa life 458–61; aristocrats and Pelagians 462–7; leaders and factions 462, 468, 471–7, 480; relations with barbarians 477, 479; emigration to Gaul 491–4, 738; relations

with Gallo-Roman states 496–7; comparison with Gaul 498–501; upper classes, villas and towns 596; effect of army departure 662–3; burials 697–8; Christianity and paganism among 723–39

Romano-Saxon pottery **Ib** 89–96, 90 [fig. 7], 204

'Romans' **IV** 494; tract against 733; *see also* 'Italians'

romanticism **XII** 534–49

Rome: Republic and Empire **Ia** 20–3; attitudes to Britain 3–4; focus of social and political aspirations 3, 354, 364–6, 464, 489; sacked by Barbarians 11, 270, 430–1, 488; military successes celebrated at 31, 97, 106, 199, 208 —Severus' British victory 228 —Plautius' major victory 394; Britons' dedication at 51; power struggles at 128–31, 171–2, 214, 217; buildings and monuments 161, 325–6, 672; control exercised from 236, 294, 334; weakening of control 269, 301, 317, 366; defences 278, 327, 423; Altar of Victory 356, 401, 409, 682, 735; weakening of communications 425; surviving prestige 466, 488; polluted by foreigners 506; relationship with surrounding country 588, 597, 600–1, 614; besieged 632; religious focus 666, 672, 677, 687, 695; **Ib** 6–7; councils (679) **II** 136–7 —(680) 137 —(1050) 467, 662; visits of English kings to, Æthelwulf 245, 272 —Alfred 272 —Burgred 252 —Cædwalla 70 —Cenred 203 —Cnut 407–8 —Ine 72–3; last male descendant of ancient kings of Powys 230; payments 408; relationship of English Church 435, 465–9; English school 466; English trade 541; Norman claim to England presented 586; **III** 127, 183, 185,

cious of British imperialism 545; decides in favour of North Africa 554, 556; moves round world 557; at Casablanca 561–2; Churchill counts on relations with 566; Quebec (1943) 572; rebuffs Churchill 573; Cairo and Teheran 574; unconditional surrender 576; economic benefits from war 577; insists on Transportation plan 580; confident of future 585; Quebec (1944) 586–7; Yalta 590; loan to Soviet Russia 594; death 593

Rotherham, Thomas: bishop of Lincoln, keeper of privy seal **VI** 555; archbishop of York (1480–1500) 318, 403, 614; Picquigny 577; Lincoln College statutes (1480) 672–3; chancellor (1485) **VII** 645

Rothermere, Lord *see* Harmsworth, Harold Sydney

Rothes, earls of *see* Leslie, John

Rothesay, duke of: son of James III **VI** 629; *see also* David, duke of Rothesay

Rothley (Rothwell) (Leics.) **Ib** 48; **II** 525

Rothschilds **XII** 464; family member imprisoned in Vienna **XV** 419

Rothwell (Northants) **Ib** 48; **III** 76

Rotrou, count of Mortagne **II** 609

Rotterdam, bombed **XV** 485, 534

Roubiliac, Louis François (1695–1762) **XI** 401, 408, 416

Roucy, count of **VI** 156

Roucy, county **VI** 573

Rouen **II** 376, 540, 620, 631; tower 609, 639; trade **III** 75, 82, 91–2; during wars of Robert and William Rufus 106–8; Henry I at 129; surrenders to Geoffrey of Anjou 161; centre of Angevin Empire 323; Empress Matilda retires to 326; Louis VII attacks 337; Philip Augustus besieges 363; John invested with Normandy 378; Arthur of Brittany murdered 382; surrenders to Philip Augustus 384, 450; **V** 133, 337; **VI** 124, 157, 171, 173, 175; falls 142; *bailliage* 174, 189; Louviers road 174; Normans in garrison 176; poor citizens 176; siege and fall 176–9; Norman estates 189; council of Duchy 191; diocese and levy 192; mint 192, 205; ransom 205; Joan's trial 251; monies from England 466; **VII** 51; treaty (1517) 308; **VIII** 57, 60, 131, 183, 414; **X** 237; petrol depot **XV** 109

Rouen, abbey of Sainte-Trinité du Mont **III** 412

Rouen, archbishops of **III** 135, 137; *see also* Robert de Bellême

Rouen, bishopric **Ia** 462, 737

Rouen Cathedral **III** 347

Rouergue **IV** 272

Rouergue, county **VI** 178, 240

Rougheye, John **V** 339

Roumare, William de, earl of Lincoln **III** 141, 160, 188

'round table conference': between Unionist and Home Rule Liberals **XIV** 176; on India, first **XV** 275; second 276, 356; third 356; on Palestine 407

Roundway Down **IX** 133

Rouquet, J. B. (*c.*1755), quoted on English art **XI** 405; on social distinctions **XII** 36

Rous (Roos), John, chronicler and armorialist **VI** 103, 104, 368–9, 613

Rousseau, Jean-Jacques **XII** 327, 358

Roussillon province **IV** 255, 262

Rovere, Francesco Maria I Della, duke of Urbino **VII** 403

Rovere, Cardinal Giulio della, *see* Julius II, Pope

Rovezzano, Benedetto di **VII** 592

Rowe, John **VII** 300

Rowlands, Daniel (1713–90) **XI** 97

Rowlandson, Thomas (1756–1827) **XII** 346

Rowley, William **VIII** 302

Rowley, medieval poetry of *see* Chatterton, Thomas

Rowntree, B. Seebohm: **XIV** 513, 515; introduces factory canteens **XV** 37; on primary poverty 177, 237; works with Lloyd George 269

Rowntrees, cocoa magnates, relinquish *Nation* **XV** 252

Roxburgh **VI** 35, 36; **VII** 405, 407, 484

Roxburgh, duke of *see* Ker, John

Roxburgh Castle **III** 278, 405, 407, 484; surrendered and restored 277–9; David I and **IV** 574; Bishop Wishart imprisoned 685; Scottish wars (1297–1303) 686, 688, 689, 695 — Edward's army 707–8; Edward I's oath to Charters renewed (1298) 697, 699; **V** 33, 116; Westmoreland commands **VI** 49

Roy, James le, of Dixmude, suit against John de Redmere **IV** 623–5, 626

Roy, William **VII** 343, 344

Royal Academy **XII** 342, 344, 346, 347

Royal African Company of England **X** 61, 63, 332–3

Royal Air Force: inspired by Pemberton Billing **XV** 44; created 96; establishes its independence 229; Trenchard 230–1; war plans 232; opposes ban on bombing 365; capital expenditure 375; German challenge 387; faith in bombing 390–1; leaders cavalry officers 392; funding 411; fighter squadrons increased 432; retains independent supply 444; debarred from bombing civilians 454; drops leaflets 459; Ministry of Aircraft Production 478; strategy 480–1; losses at Dunkirk 487; Germans aim to destroy its air superiority 498; uses scientists 508; cannot attack German oil plants 514; strategic bombing 517; abandons daylight bombing 518; losses during first bombing offensive 519; defied in Channel 542; no aeroplanes for Dieppe raid 558

Royal Charles (formerly *Naseby*), battleship **X** 67

Royal College of Physicians **X** 419

Royal Commissions on Historical Monuments: Scotland **Ia** 201, 612; England, York 326

Royal Exchange **VIII** 275, 303

Royal Flying Corps **XV** 8, 96

Royal Institute of British Architects **XIII** 578

Royal Institute of International Affairs **XV** 274

Royal Institution of Great Britain **XIII** 501, 564–6

Royal Irish Constabulary **XV** 155

Royal Lancastrian Association **XII** 525

Royal Lutestring Company **X** 49

Royal Marriages Act (1772) **XII** 155

Royal Military College **XII** 415

Royal Oak, sunk **XV** 462

Royal Philosophical Institution *see* Philosophical Institution, Royal

Royal Society of Art **XIII** 500

Royal Society **IX** 373; **X** 29, 42, 360, 372, 376–7; meeting place for scientists 412; **XII** 28, 339; and Freud **XV** 420

royal titles **XIV** 39, 344

royalists **IX** 176; formation 118, 126–7, 129–31; treatment under commonwealth 170–1, 271–2; decimation tax 180; rising (in 1659) 246; moderation (in 1660) 257

Roye (Somme) **VI** 111, 183, 256; *prévôté* 263

Rubjerg Knude **Ib** map 5 68

Rudchester (Co. Durham) Mithraeum **Ia** 668; destruction 732; **Ib** map 4 xxxii

Rudolf, bishop in Norway and abbot of Abingdon **II** 463

Rudolf of Habsburg: elected king of the Romans **IV** 232; relations with Edward I and Charles of Anjou 246–50; form of peace with Charles of Anjou 247; *see also* Arles; Margaret of France; Philip of Savoy

ruffs **VIII** 270

Rufinus **Ia** 253–4; **III** 206

Rugby **III** 153; continuation schools **XV** 184; inadequate railway link 507; football 313

Rugeley (Staffs.) **VI** 654

Ruggles-Brise, Sir Evelyn **XIV** 521, 546

Ruhr, French occupy **XV** 203–4, 214, 240; British bombers cannot reach 391; Hitler apprehensive 483; bombed 485; dams breached 570; only great prize in Europe 577; British armies enter 592

Ruisseauville (Pas-de-Calais) **VI** 154, 155

Rumania: treatment at Berlin Congress **XIV** 51; defensive alliance with Germany and Austria 196; attacks Bulgaria 468; joins Allies **XV** 63; Fourteen Points 119; Jews 419; conquest by Germany not needed 435; Hitler expected to attack 441, 442; oil supplies almost exhausted 577; 90 per cent Russian 588

Rumbold, Richard **X** 104, 120

Rumcofa *see* Runcorn (Cheshire)

Rumelia, Eastern: constituted apart from Bulgaria **XIV** 51; united to it 195

Rumenea *see* Romney (Kent)

Rumon, St **VI** 372

Rump **IX** 170, 173–4, 243–57

Rump parliament **XV** 472

Run, island **X** 68, 349

Runciman, Walter (1870–1949) **XIV** 385; Education Bill 393; enters Cabinet 406; biography **XV** 15; negative attitude 15, 34; wishes to coerce workers 39; opposes conscription 54–5; helpless 64; no longer opposes convoy 92; hostile to Lloyd George 271; supports National government 323; raises alarm 325; becomes president of Board of Trade 326; says tariff will bring in revenue 329; at Ottawa 333; goes to

Prague as mediator 425; his report 426

Runcorn (Rumcofa) (Cheshire) **II** 326, 333, 733

Rundstedt, General **XV** 486

Runnymede **III** 71, 473; concord 477

Rupert III, duke of Bavaria **VI** 92; elected king of the Romans 67; orator 92

Rupert, prince of the Palatinate: **IX** 133, 136–7, 141, 225, 292; and science **X** 29; in battle fleet 63, 65, 81

Rupert's River **X** 340

rural development *see* agriculture; countryside; villas; etc.

Rush, Richard **XIII** 206, 209

Rushford (Norfolk), Saxon pottery 71 [fig. 6(f)]

Rushook, Thomas, bishop of Llandaff (1383–5), of Chichester (1385–8), of Kilmore (1389–93) **V** 426, 429, 448, 449, 458

Rushworth, John **IX** 100

Ruskin, John (1819–1900) **XIII** 265, 499, 531, 570, 577; biography 546; works 546–8; Gothic architecture 580–1; supports Pre-Raphaelites 592, 594; **XIV** 45, 157, 167, 340

Ruskin College **XIV** 538–9

Russe Commonwealth **VIII** 319

Russell, Bertrand **XV** 51–2

Russell, Sir Charles, afterwards Lord Russell of Killowen **XIV** 182

Russell, Edward, earl of Orford (1653–1727), admiral **IX** 168; and *Instructions* (1691) 229; and William III **X** 133; at La Hogue 166; in Mediterranean 172; impeached in connection with Partition treaties 195; member of the junto 225; 1st lord of the Admiralty 225

Russell, Elias, citizen of London **IV** 662

493

Russia (*cont.*)

with France 197; Trans-Siberian Railway 197; Lord Salisbury's approach (Jan. 1898) 259; seizure of Port Arthur 259; calls first Hague Conference 261; mythical troops **XV** 19; war debt 42; agreements with 50, 70; revolution 71, 89, 123; Henderson 90; peace with Germany 94; Allied intervention 108; Fourteen Points 115; civil war 135, review of successive policies 350–1; occupies Manchuria 351; war with Japan 368–9, 370; Dogger Bank incident 369; Björkö treaty 370; dropped 371; Anglo-Russian Convention 402–3; effects on Russian policy 403–4; interest in Balkans 464–5; naval conversations with Great Britain 483–4; army increases 484; mobilization 490; German ultimatum 490; *see also* Alexander I; Baltic Powers; Catherine the Great; Crimean war; Elizabeth, tsaritsa; Nicholas I; Peter I; Peter III; subsidies Soviet Russia

Russia Company **VII** 507, 561; **X** 47

Russia Row, London, timber house **Ia** 233

Ruthall, Thomas, bishop of Durham (1509–23) **VII** 216, 232, 297; secretary to the king (1500) 648; keeper of the privy seal (18 May 1516) 647

Rutherford, Ernest, Lord (1871–1937) **XI** 385; **XIV** 551; **XV** 259

Rutherglen, Scottish parliament (1300) **IV** 694, 695

Ruthin (Denbigh): barony **IV** 424; castle 431; **VI** 37; Gly Dŵr attacks 42

Ruthven Castle **VIII** 361

Ruthven, Patrick, earl of Forth **IX** 137

Ruthwell (Dumfries.), cross **II** 86, 150, 196

Rutilius Namatianus **Ia** 346, 435, 448; travel 569

Rutland: origin of the shire **II** 338, 502, 505; **V** 192; county **VI** 413; newspaper **X** 356; population **XV** 256

Rutland, 3rd duke of (1696–1779): influence in Grantham 52; defection from Newcastle 85; lord steward (1760–1) 578; master of the horse (1761–6) 578

Rutland, 4th duke of (1754–87): and reform **XII** 230; lord steward (1783) 579; lord privy seal (1783–4) 267, 580; lord lieutenant of Ireland (1784) 276, 580

Rutland, duke of *see* Manners, Lord John

Rutland, earl of **VIII** 433; *see also* Edmund; Manners, Thomas; York, Edward of

Rutupiae see Richborough

Ruvigny, marquis de *see* Massue, Henri de

Ruyter, Michael de **IX** 223; **X** 63, 81, 327, 332; **X** 63–5, 74–5, 81, 91

Ruytingen shoals **VIII** 402

Ryder family **XII** 54

Ryder, Richard (1766–1832): biography **XII** 484; home secretary (1809–12) 484, 582

Rydon (Roydon) (Norfolk) **VI** 449

Rye (Sussex) **III** 94, 96, 430, 433; **IV** 10; **V** 145; government influence **XII** 53, 89

Rye House Plot **X** 57, 104, 106

Rymer, Thomas (1641–1713), royal historiographer **X** 381; **XI** 394

Rysbrack, John Michael (?1693–1770), sculptor **XI** 401, 408

Ryswick, treaty **X** 174, 192, 193, 236, 342

Ryther, Augustine **VIII** 302

S

497

Ste Suzanne, castle **II** 608
St Symphorien, Isabel of *see* Isabel of St Symphorien
St Tatheus **Ib** 18
St Thomas Aquinas *see* Aquinus, St Thomas
St Thomas Becket of Canterbury *see* Becket, St Thomas
St Thomas's Hospital, London, foundation **XII** 11
St Tiron **V** 294
St Trond **III** 464
St Ursula's *Schifflein* **VII** 337
St Vaast-de-la-Hogue **V** 133
St Valéry (Somme) **II** 588; **III** 106, 377; honour **V** 80; **VI** 205; **X** 237; **XV** 487
St Venant **X** 220
St Victor, Hugh of **III** 243
St Victor: order of **IV** 761; Andrew of 761
St Vincent: capture **XII** 75; retention 85
St Vincent, earl of *see* Jervis, John
St Waldburg **II** 175
St Wandrille, abbot of **III** 432; **V** 295
St Wilfrid **Ib** 106, 135; **II** 161, 180; advocate of Roman usages 123; Synod of Whitby 123; bishop of Ripon 124, 132; sends proctors to council at Hertford 133; position in Northumbria 135; alienates King Ecgfrith and his second wife 135; deprived of property 135; first appeal to Rome 136; exiled from Northumbria 138; converts the South Saxons 138; joins Cædwalla of Wessex 138; reconciled to Theodore 139; returns to Ripon, but again exiled 139; in Mercia 143; last visit to Rome 144; death 145; character 145; Benedictine rule 145, 158–9; founder of monasteries 159; influence on northern culture 184
St Willehad **II** 92; bishop of Breman 176

St William de Calais, bishop of Durham **II** 632, 678
St William Fitz Herbert, treasurer and afterwards archbishop of York **III** 191
St William of Norwich, boy-martyr **III** 353
St Willibald, bishop of Eichstatt **II** 150, 169, 174–5
St Willibrord **II** 111, 158, 163, 189; missionary to Frisia 166–8; compared with Boniface 168; relations with Frankish rulers 166–7; ordained bishop by pope 166–8
St Winifred's Well **X** 408, 409
St Wulfstan, bishop of Worcester **III** 40, 101, 171, 253, 486
St Wulfstan, shrine **IV** 1
Saintes **III** 64; **IV** 90, 92; Henry III (1242) 103, 104; castle 301
Saintes, Peter of **III** 161
Saintes (Saintonge) **VI** 107, 140
Saintonge **III** 442, 466; southern **IV** 88, 647; Henry III's failure (1242) 101–2; French and English rights 127, 272, 273, 289, 291; administration 301, 303; **V** 14, 361; **VI** 108, 109, 140, 178, 240
Saints, The, battle (1782) **XII** 218; capture (1794) 370
'Saints' of Clapham *see* Clapham sect
Saintsbury, George **XIV** 551
sake and soke **II** 494–6, 636; meaning 494; first appearance 494–5; grant by Cnut 497–8; number of lords possessing 498–9, 502; *see also* jurisdiction, private
Saklatvala, S. **XV** 200, 259, 271
Salabat Jang, french nominee in Deccan (1751) **XI** 327, 328
Saladin **III** 344, 361; tithe 419
Salamanca, battle (1812) **XII** 494, 496
Salassi **Ia** 49, 51
Salden (Bucks.) **II** 489
Salem **IX** 339, 341

Salisbury Castle **VII** 57
Salisbury Plain **Ib** xxvi, 155, 170
Salkeld (Cumbria) **III** 283
Sallee **IX** 111
Salley **VII** 397
Sallust (Saluste) **III** 235; **VI** 306
Sallustius Lucullus **Ia** 150, 152
Salmon, John, bishop of Norwich (1299–1325), chancellor (1320–3) **V** 10, 24, 48, 52, 57; joint ambassador to Paris on Gascony 81, 109
Salonika: expedition urged by Lloyd George **XV** 23; futility of 25; urged by French 46; British forces 49–50; advance from 63, 110; malaria 121
Saloninus **Ia** 273
Salop *see* Shropshire
Salsette Island **X** 351; **XII** 158, 314
salt: making **Ia** 189, 224, 531, 620, 644; trade **V** 349, 360; tax in Scotland **IX** 294; **X** 289; industry 317; raking 331
Saltash (Corn.) **III** 96
Saltburn **Ib** map 4 xxxii
salted-fish industry **X** 237
Salter, Sir Arthur **XV** 461
saltpetre **IX** 323
Saltwood, Arundel's prison **VI** 95
Salutati, Coluccio **VI** 676
Salvation Army **XIV** 163, 335
Salvayn, Roger, treasurer of Calais **VI** 104
Salvianus **Ia** 480
Salvius Liberalis, C. **Ia** 162, 526
Salzburg, see **II** 61, 169; death of Eadbald, king of Kent, recorded 61
Samarobriva Ambianorum see Amiens
Samnium, estates in **Ia** 600
Samoa, conquered **XV** 23
Samothrace, see **VI** 26
Sampson, Richard (d. 1554), resident ambassador to Spain (1522–5), bishop of Chichester (1536–43), bishop of Coventry

and Lichfield (1543–54) **VII** 315, 414, 545
Sampson, Richard, musician **VII** 588
Sampson, Thomas **V** 118
Sampsona, Petrus de **VI** 666
Samson, abbot of Bury St Edmunds **III** 253, 371, 451
Samuel, Herbert, afterwards Sir Herbert **XIV** 385, 457; biography **XV** 241; refuses to join Lloyd George 70, 435; supports Zionist plans 71; heads coal commission 241, 243; proposals end general strike 247; high and dry 281; proposes National government 292; police pay 296; consults Lloyd George 333; condemns Cabinet committee 328; insufficient Liberal support 334; formal opposition 362; refuses to join Chamberlain 435
Samuelson, Sir Bernhard **XIV** 319
San Angelo, castle **VII** 317
San Domingo **VIII** 369; **IX** 232
San Felipe **VIII** 395, 402
San Germano, treaty (1235) **IV** 48
San Mateo **VIII** 397, 402
San Severino, princes **VII** 114
San Thome **IX** 326
San Vitale, Ravenna, mosaics **Ia** 465
Sancergues (Cher) **VI** 114
Sancerre **VIII** 162
Sanchia of Provence, first betrothed to Raymond of Toulouse (1241) then married Richard of Cornwall (1243) **IV** 100, 104, 105, 107, 119
Sancho, king of Castile **IV** 242, 244–5, 262, 644
Sancho VI, king of Navarre **III** 339, 360
Sancho VII, king of Navarre **III** 376, 381; **IV** 109
Sancho I, king of Portugal **III** 454
Sancho Panza **XV** 474

501

Sancroft, William, archbishop of Canterbury **X** 117, 124, 126, 141, 156

Sanctæ Albanes Stow *see* St Albans (Herts.)

Sanctæ Eadmundes Stow *see* Bury St Edmunds (Suffolk)

Sanctæ Germane *see* St Germans (Corn.)

sanctions: imposed on Irish Free State **XV** 358; on Soviet Russia 358; faith 369; not invoked against Japan 371; imposed on Italy 380; Labour 381; general election (1935) 383; Italian oil exempt 384–5; proposed by Litvinov against Germany 386; Communists support 397; Chamberlain against 414; shattered 415; effects exaggerated 418

Sancto Leofardo, Gilbert de, bishop of Chichester (1288–1305) **IV** 491

Sancton **Ib** 69, 81, 176, 189–96; map 4 xxxii; map 5 68

sanctuaries **Ia** 671, 672–6, 678, 719; **IV** 50, 60; **VII** 77

Sandal (Yorks.), castle **VI** 635

Sandal, John de, warden of the exchanges (1300) **IV** 633; treasurer of Scotland (1305) 713

Sandale, John, bishop of Winchester (1316–19), treasurer (1310, 1312–14, 1318–19), chancellor (1314–18) **V** 46, 52, 57

Sandby, Paul (1725–1809), painter **XI** 401, 408, 410

Sandeman, Sir Robert **XIV** 62

Sander (Sanders), Nicholas **VII** 320, 322, 323, 324, 325

Sanders, Liman von, General, controversy over **XIV** 471

Sanders, Dr Nicholas **VIII** 12, 22, 177, 478, 479

Sanderson, William **VIII** 243

Sandford, Henry, bishop of Rochester (1227–35) **IV** 60

Sandon, Lord **XIV** 39

Sandwic *see* Sandwich (Kent)

Sandwich (Sandwic) (Kent) **II** 244, 381, 382, 389, 733; King Swein's first landing 385; Cnut leaves hostages 386; plundered by Vikings 428; King's fleet 566; support for Godwine 567; occupied by Tostig 587; Danish fleet repelled 603; **III** 96, 214, 282, 367, 433; **IV** 156, 207, 669, 688; naval battle 13; hospital of St Bartholomew 13; **V** 243, 384, 431; **VI** 168, 353, 518; Yorkists land 498; Yorkists capture from Calais 517; Warwick's headquarters (June 1469) 555; **VII** 219, 310, 471, 566

Sandwich, earl of *see* Montagu, John

Sandwich, Henry of, bishop of London (1263–73), Montfortian **IV** 176, 189, 192, 194, 195, 208

Sandwich, Ralph of, constable of the Tower and warden of London **IV** 627

Sandwich, Thomas of, seneschal of Ponthieu **IV** 280

Sandy (Beds.): Saxon pottery 71 [fig. 6(b)]; map 2 xxx

Sandys, Baron, president of board of trade (1761–3) **XII** 578

Sandys, Duncan, flying bombs **XV** 584

Sandys, Edward (1516?–88), vice-chancellor of Cambridge **VII** 528, 529, 543

Sandys, Sir Edwin **IX** 10, 15, 328

Sandys, Edwin, bishop of Worcester **VIII** 190, 193, 195, 259

Sandys, Samuel (?1695–1770), chancellor of the Exchequer (1742–3) **XI** 238, 246

Sandys, Lord William of 'The Vyne' (d. 1540), lord chamberlain of the household (1526) **VII** 649

Sangatte **V** 137

sanitation **XII** 523

Sankey, Sir J.: commission on mines

503

Schism, Great **V** 279, 293, 405; papal war of succession (1378) 145–6; translations 277; benefices under Edward III 278; **VI** 267, 268, 295; **VII** 336

Schism Bill **X** 247

Schleswig **Ib** xxvii, 46–7, 54–5, 59, 63; cemeteries 72, 192; map 1 xxix

Schleswig-Holstein question **XIII** 317–23

Schlieffen, Count **XIV** 399, 405

Schlieffen Plan **XIV** 400, 470, 483, 492, 570; **XV** 32, 60, 484

Schmalkalde, League of (1530) **VII** 340

Schmidt (or Smith), Bernard **X** 404

Schnorkel **XV** 578

Schola Saxonum **II** 466

scholae domesticorum see imperial guards

Scholemaster, the **VII** 583; **VIII** 324–7

Schomberg, duke of *see* Meinhard

School Care Committees **XIV** 397

School Medical Services **XIV** 397

schools: at York **II** 90, 175; in East Anglia 116–17; in Kent 117; at Malmesbury 125; at Canterbury 180–2; schools for clergy, in cathedral churches **IV** 450; training ground of ecclesiastics 485, 486–8; literature on history of 763–5; **V** 304, 500–1; grammar **VI** 667; English schools **VII** 576–8; grammar 514; London 576; Shrewsbury, Berkhampstead, St Albans, Stamford, Pocklington, East Retford 576–7; **VIII** 323–7; **X** 415–18; **XII** 39; meals **XIV** 397; buildings 539–40; school-leaving age **XV** 211; proposals to raise 280, 406; raised 568; *see also* education

Schooneveld banks **X** 81

Schouwen, Island of **VIII** 338

Schulenberg, countess of *see* Kendal, duchess of

Schütz, –, Hanoverian envoy **X** 246

Schuyler, P. J. (1733–1804) **XII** 202

Schwarz (Swart), Martin **VII** 72, 75; killed at Stoke (1487) 74

Schwarzenberg, Prince von **XII** 561

Schweinfurt, bombed **XV** 570

science **X** 28–30, 42–3, 373–8, 412; study of **XI** 139; natural sciences 378, 381–9; its influence on thought **XIV** 142, 162, 551–3; *see also* astronomy; medicine; surgery etc.

scientific analysis: parasitology **Ia** 551; palaeobotany 553–5, 571–2, 608, 613; soil deposits 554–7; timber 557, 564; coastline surveys 557–9; bones 613, 620, 627; other organic remains 613, 626; gas chromatography 642

scientists **X** 360, 372, 374

Scilly Isles **VIII** 400; **XV** 551

Scindia **XII** 385

Scireburnan *see* Sherborne (Dorset); Sherburn in Elmet (Yorks.)

Scirwudu *see* Sherwood Forest (Notts.)

Scithesbi (Lincs.) **III** 188

Sclater-Booth, G., Lord Basing **XIV** 36

Scobell, Henry **IX** 203

Scofield, Miss Cora **VI** 535, 574

Scone: stone of abbey **IV** 615, 766; recognition of Margaret as heir to Scottish throne (1284) 597; Wallace and justiciar of Scotland (1297) 684; parliament (1305) 711; Robert Bruce installed king (1306) 713; abbot 716; **V** 99, 117; **VIII** 40; **IX** 168

Scone, monastery of **III** 269

Scorranstan *see* Sherston (Wilts.)

Scory, John, bishop of Hereford **VIII** 190, 259

Scory, John, bishop of Rochester (1552–9) **VII** 518, 543, 544

Scot, John **III** 61–2; *see also* John the Scot

Scot, Michael **III** 246

Scot, Reginald **VIII** 311, 329, 330; **IX** 371

Scot, Thomas **IX** 174, 186, 238

Scot, William **V** 168; **VI** 457

Scotby (Cumbria) **III** 283

Scoteigni, Lambert de **III** 14

Scotia and *mare Scotiae* (the Firth of Forth) **IV** 574

Scotists **VII** 254, 256

Scotland (Roman Britain) **Ia** 4, 16, 46, 184; Vettius Bolanus? 133; Agricola 144–51; Trajan 163, 165–7; Brigantes 166; Antonines' policy 194–202, 206, 208, 210–11, 254 — garrison withdrawn 352 — cenotaphs 701; Severans' policy 229–30, 231; Constantius' campaigns 318–19, 322; Constantine 324; Constans and *areani*, raids from 352, 369, 383, 386; Hadrian's policy 364; wool trade 656; *see also* Brigantes; Caledonia; Maetae; Picts

Scotland (Anglo-Saxon period) **II** 601; kingdom 332–3; later kings 340, 342, 359, 369–70; *see also* Constantine; Kenneth; Macbeth; Malcolm I, II and III

Scotland (1216–1307) **III** 265–83; trade with 88; campaign (1191) 108, 266; supports the young king's rebellion (1173–4) 250, 276–7, 334–5; boundary of 265; influence of Queen Margaret 267; reign of David I 269, 273–5; his invasions of England during the Anarchy 270–2; effects of William the Lion's capture 278; independence restored 279; John's relations with 281–3, 426, 449

Scotland (1286–96) **IV** 512, 597–617; Edward I as supreme lord 560, 597, 604–5; disturbances (1290) 600, 601; great case and documents 602–8; Edward I insists on right to hear Scottish petitions 608–12; reign of John Baliol 609–13; surrender of kingdom and union with England 613–16; records and regalia 614; pacification (1296) 615; loss of public records 750–1; *see also* council; guardians; Edward I; Philip IV

Scotland (before Alexander III's death) (1286) **IV** 571–85; Llywelyn ap Gruffydd (1258) 138, 592; problem of homage 381, 594–6; geography, races and population 571–5, 579; currency 573; formation of state 574–8; administration 575–9; barons, thanes and free tenants 576; justice 577–8, 584; taxation 578; Church 583–5; Border 588–9; Henry III's request for an aid from (1253) 589; council and guardians (1255–61) 590–2; parties in 593–4; papacy, king, and state 593–5; *see also* Alexander II; Alexander III; castles; Henry III; Edward I

Scotland (1297–1307): claims for damages after truce (1897) and peace (1303) 658; risings (1297) **IV** 669, 677, 678, 683–7; Andrew of Moray and William Wallace *duces* of the Scottish army 687; Edward I's first campaigns (1298–1300) and truce with Scots 689–93; campaign (1301–2) and control of Lowlands 693–4, 706 — defence and administration by Scottish guardians (1298–1304) 694, 696; by Edward I in Lowlands (1298–1303) 695, 706–7; subjection in the campaign (1303–4) 708–11; plan for government (1305) 711–13; *communa* meeting (1305) 712; emergence, defeat and reappearance of Robert Bruce (1306–7) 713–16, 718–19; petitions to king in par-

513

503; commissions and inclosure (1548) 504–6; royal supremacy 511–12; reformation 512; academia and politics 572, 574; treasurer and earl marshal (1547) 647, 651; becomes lord admiral 650

Seymour, Lord Henry **VIII** 402

Seymour, James (1702–52, animal painter) **XI** 409

Seymour, John **V** 429

Seymour, Sir John **VII** 380

Seymour, Lord Thomas, Admiral **VIII** 2

Seymour, Sir Thomas (d. 1549) **VII** 419, 421, 494, 496; ambitions and death 488; lord admiral (1547) 650

Sforza, Bianca Maria, consort of Maximilian I **VII** 114

Sforza, Francesco, duke of Milan (d. 1466) **VII** 113

Sforza, Francesco Maria (d. 1535) **VII** 340

Sforza, Ludovico (Il Moro), duke of Milan (1494–1500) (d. 1508) **VII** 103, 113, 114, 115, 151; attacked by France (1479) 152

Sforza, Massimiliano, duke of Milan (d. 1530) **VII** 316

Sha, Sir Edmund, mayoralty **VI** 623

Sha, Friar Ralph, St Paul's Cross sermon **VI** 620

Shackleton, D. J., afterwards Sir **XIV** 379

Shadworth, John, of London **VI** 429

Shaftesbury (Sceaftenesbyrig) (Dorset) **II** 536; nunnery 374, 445; **VI** 462

Shaftesbury, 7th earl of **XIV** 34, 127, 137, 164; *see also* Cooper, Anthony Ashley

Shah Alam **XII** 385

Shakell, John **V** 403–4, 512

Shakenoak: villa **Ia** 608; **Ib** 85; map 2 xxx

Shakespeare, William (1564–1616): *Henry IV, Part II* **VI** 116; **VIII** 289, 297–301; **IX** 68; **X** 367, 371; **XI** 128, 419, 425; **XII** rediscovery 542; festival **XV** 178; Chaplin 181; touring companies 314

Shamakha **VIII** 238

Shanghai: French concession **XV** 370; British interests defended 318, 371

Shannon, river **III** 314, 315; **V** 470

Shapur I **Ia** 273

Shapwick, hill-fort **Ia** 93

Shareshill, William **V** 219

Sharington Sir William **VII** 488, 501, 596

Sharnburn, Thomas **VI** 449

Sharp, Cecil J. **XIV** 544

Sharp, Granville (1735–1813) **XII** 230, 231, 354

Sharp, James, Archbishop **X** 267–9; murder of 271

Sharp, William **XIV** 335

Sharpe v. Wakefield **XIV** 360

sharpers **IX** 303

Shaw, Benjamin **XIII** 211

Shaw, George Bernard **XIV** 329, 334, 517, 546, 549; out of fashion **XV** 52; historic moment 125; becomes respectable 178; prophesy 305; has no successor 311; touring company 314; quoted 354–5

Shaw, Dr John **VII** 19

Shaw, Sir John, lord mayor of London (1501) **VII** 173

Shaw, Norman **XIV** 323, 324

Shaw-Kennedy, Major-General **XIII** 275

Shaxton, Nicholas, bishop of Salisbury (1485?–1556) **VII** 382, 427, 428

Sheaffe, Sir Roger **XII** 553

Shearplace Hill **Ia** 8

Sheen (Isleworth) (Middx.) **VI** 480; royal residence 196; Carthusian house 196, 295; Bridgettine

Sheen (Isleworth) (Middx.) (*cont.*)
house; **VII** 147, 594; council
69–70; *see also* Sion
Sheen (Surrey) **V** 397, 398, 470
sheep **Ia** 191, 281, 620, 627; objects
of distraint **IV** 372; breeding in
Ireland **X** 301, 318
Sheering (Essex) **V** 339
Sheffield (Yorks.) manor and town
VI 323; castle **VIII** 374, 376, 378;
manufactures **XII** 31, 507; hope
of enfranchisement 278; Corres-
ponding Society 358; **XIII** 2,
13, 26, 65, 182; People's college
495; trade unions 614–15; steel
works **XV** 122; shop stewards
142; registration for evacuation
434
Sheffield, 1st earl of *see* Hol-
royd, J. B.
Sheffield, lord of (Thomas Furnival)
V 61
Sheffield, Sir Robert, speaker of the
House of Commons (1512) **VII**
292, 293, 653
Sheffield Park **VII** 332
Shefford, East (Berks.) **II** 25
Shelburne, 2nd earl of *see* Petty, Sir
William
Shelburne, earl of *see* William
Sheldon, Gilbert, Archbishop, and
taxation of the clergy **X** 157
Shelley, Percy Bysshe (1792–1822)
XI 424; **XII** 534, 540; **XIII** 32–5,
38, 366, 533, 537
Shelley, Sir Thomas, treasurer of
household **XII** 121
shells: provided by Ministry of
Munitions **XV** 35; army demand
(1942) 509; excessive production
565
shells committee (1914) **XV** 22
shells scandal **XV** 26, 27, 29, 30
Shenley (Herts.) **VI** 276
Shenstone, William (1714–63), poet
XI 413, 420
Shenton (Leics.) **VI** 644
Shepheards Calender **VIII** 290–1

Shepperton **Ib** 102; map 2 xxx
Sheppey (Sceapig) (Kent) **II** 241,
243, 392, 733
Sheppey, John, bishop of Rochester
(1353–60) **V** 211
Shepstone, Sir Theophilus, annexes
Transvaal **XIV** 59, 62
Shepway *see* Cinque Ports
Sher Ali **XIV** 62, 63
Sherard, James (1666–1738), botan-
ist **XI** 388
Sherard, William (1659–1728), bot-
anist **X** 376; **XI** 388
Sheraton, Thomas, cabinet-maker
(1751–1806) **XII** 29, 340
Sherborne (Scireburnan) (Dorset):
diocese **II** 65, 142, 146, 376, 439,
733; founded by Ine 71; removal
of see 666; castle **III** 146; abbey
295; **V** 322, 333; **VII** 591, 596
Sherborne, bishop of **II** 231; *see also*
Asser; Herman; Wulfsige
Sherborne, Robert, dean of St Paul's
VII 176
Sherbrooke, Viscount *see* Lowe,
Robert
Sherburn in Elmet (Scireburnan)
(Yorks.) **II** 436, 496, 733; **V**
61–63, 351
Sheridan, Richard Brinsley (1751–
1816): biography **XII** 349; political activity 320, 322, 324,
363, 409, 491; impeachment of
Warren Hastings 320, 322; character 339, 548; plays 349
Sheridan, Thomas (1719–88), one of
'the seven men of Moidart' **XI**
252, 304
sheriff, high **XII** 43
Sheriff Hutton (N. Yorks.): lordship
VI 8, 321, 638; castle 336; **VII** 54
sheriffs: Old English: origin of the office **II** 548–9; responsible to the
king 549; financial duties 549–50
position in shire court 550; post-
Conquest, Englishmen employed
623; baronial 633; commission on
acts of 633; **III** 68–71, 83, 157,

387–90, 417; inquest (1170) 389; castles **IV** 20; inquiries into royal rights (1223) 28; taxation 29, 33, 524, 527; relations with Exchequer 62–5; bailiffs of lords 366, 368; *jurati ad arma* 551–2; scutage 33–4, 556–8; chosen from vavassors (1258–61) 144, 146, 150, 162; Henry III appoints new sheriffs (1261) 164, 165; arbitration about appointment 166–7; decrease of payments into Exchequer (1264–8) 220; shires in Ireland 563–4; in Scotland 574–9; in Wales 435–7; **V** 23, 24, 28, 33, 48; methods of appointment 16, 388; change (1314) 46; (1318) 55; Walton Ordinances 158, (1340) 163, (1341) 169; tax enforcement in Essex 166; judgement of Stratford 170, 171; letters repealing statutes 177, 178; parliamentary elections 187–8; parliament 188–9; judicial powers 200; corruptibility 206–7; impressment of masons (1360) 372; Richard II's appellants summoned (1388) 454; proclaim king's government (1389) 464; dealings of Richard II 447, 486–7, 489; retained men **VI** 341; duties 448; venality and private feuds 449; county court 449–50; obsolete farms 450; permission to declare account 450–1; criminal jurisdiction abolished (1461) 541; office of **VII** 196; power curbed 194, 563; **VIII** 212, 213, 214

sheriff's aid **III** 202, 388

sheriff's tourn **III** 57, 395–6

Sherlock, Thomas (1678–1761), bishop of Bangor (1727–34), of Salisbury (1734–49), of London (1749–61) **XI** 77, 80, 86; *Tryal of the Witnesses* 84

Sherrett, Mr **XII** 508

Sherston (Scorranstan) (Wilts.) **II** 391, 733

Sherwell (Devon) **VI** 68

Sherwood (Scirwudu) Forest (Notts.) **II** 42, 284, 733; **IV** 513; bands of the disinherited 215; **V** 207, 312, 314; **VI** 37, 330

Shetland Islands **Ia** 539; **II** 239; **IV** 596, 597

Shiel, Norman **Ia** 313

shields **Ia** 73–4

Shinwell, E.: imprisoned **XV** 139; on MacDonald 201; no substitute for Churchill 542

ship money **IX** 82, 84–5, 103, 216–18

shipbuilding **XIV** 107, 278, 504; given to admiralty **XV** 79; outstrips losses 85; excessive capacity 122; decline 305; planned destruction of capacity 340

Shippen, William (1673–1743) **XI** 204, 214

shipping: Scottish **X** 265; **XII** 14–18, 386, 466, 515; **XIV** 108, 279, 505; war risk insurance **XV** 5; shortage 43; problem (in 1916) 64; Maclay controls 77; losses 84; Allied control 99; losses repaired 122; glut 145; decline during Depression 287; diverted to west coast 463; Norwegian, added to British resources 471; allied 494; losses (1941) 505; saving by better agriculture 510; worse losses (1942) 546; in Mediterranean 555; urgent topic, little discussed at Casablanca 562–3; losses decline (1943) 564

Shipping, Ministry of: created **XV** 76, 456; ended 130; reduces imports 463; amalgamated with transport 510; further reduces imports 512

shipping and ship-building **XI** 119, 121; *see also* Scotland

ships: Veneti **Ia** 26, 57; invasions of Britain 27–33, 61, 306–7; burnt 308–9; grain transport 359; target for pirates 385; travel by

Sigismund, Emperor, king of Hungary **VI** 92, 125, 161, 165, 204, 219; Conciliar letter to Henry 161; planning alliance against Burgundy 162; French mediator 162; English envoys (Nov. 1415) 163; in Westminster Palace 164; *Gallicana duplicitas* 166; treaty of Canterbury (15 Aug. 1416) 166–7; writes to Germans at Constance 167; Calais meeting hopes 167; Trino alliance to Charles VI 167; Henry VI Calais greeting (Sept. 1416) 168; Anglo-French mediator 168; favours English at Constance 169; Henry V deserts 200; negotiating cost 204

Siglem, Roger **V** 437–8

signal stations **Ia** 570–1; **Ib** xxvi, 179, 187; map 2 xxx; *see also* watch-towers

Sigtuna, Sweden, church of St Peter **II** 463

Sigulf, abbot of Ferrières **II** 189

Sihtric, earl under Cnut **II** 416

Sihtric, king of York **II** 334, 338

Sikh wars: first (1845–6) **XIII** 424; second (1848–9) 425–6

Silchester (*Calleva Atrebatum*) Atrebates **Ia** 43; town 92, 96–7, 576; defences 112, 261–2; Allectus?, inscribed tile 507; amphitheatre 579; inscription 583; water-mills 632; wine barrels 653, 654; trade guild 659; gold ring 689; household gods 708; church? 724; **Ib** xxvi, 129, 149–50, 156–60, 164; road 168; desolation 172; map 2 xxx; map 3 xxxi

Silesia **XI** 231, 236, 246, 249, 261, 265, 267, 269; plebiscite **XV** 134

silk **IX** 323; industry **X** 49, 179, 339; **XII** 511; *see also* Spitalfield weavers

Silures: territory **Ia** 45; resistance and conquest of 102–3, 105, 109, 120, 135 — **II** Augusta 137 — decurions 534 — savage repu-

tation 585; Romanization 138, 159, 534; described by Tacitus 539

Silva, Don Guzman de **VIII** 105, 122, 124, 126

Silvanus, cult **Ia** 673, 684

Silvanus (I), praetorian prefect **Ia** 273

Silvanus (II), usurper **Ia** 358

silver: exploited in Britain **Ia** 39, 42, 58, 72, 540; ingots 532; production of 630, 633, 635; votive offerings 690; speculation **IV** 632, 633; *see also* plate

silver mines **III** 82

silversmiths **X** 397

Silvester of Evesham, bishop of Worcester **III** 486

Silvianus, curse **Ia** 689

Simcoe, John Graves (1752–1806) **XII** 553

Simeon, Charles (1759–1836) **XII** 354; **XIII** 505

Simier, Jean de **VIII** 349–50, 351

Simnel, Lambert (*fl.* 1487–1525) **VII** 76–7, 79, 80, 120, 125; imposture as Edward of Warwick 68–9; crowned King Edward VI at Dublin (1487) 72; Lincoln invades England (1487) 73; made a turnspit (1487) 74

Simon, bishop-elect of Liège **III** 367

Simon, Ernest D. **XV** 174, 266

Simon, Sir John (1873–1954): **XIV** 493; biography **XV** 54; resigns in protest against conscription 54; inner Cabinet 197; drafts vote of censure on Labour government 218; in Cabinet as attorney general 225; asserts general strike illegal 246–7; heads commission on India 254–5, 275–6; hostile to Lloyd George 271; moving towards Conservatives 281; not in first National government 293; for National government at any price 323; becomes foreign secretary 326; blamed for failure of

525

Soult, Nicholas (1769–1851) **XII** 461, 482, 485, 487, 493–5; leads French in Switzerland 380; Toledo 557

Sourdeac, governor of Brest **VIII** 414

South Africa: representation at peace conference **XV** 132; refuses to surrender German South West Africa 133, 137; Dominion status 253; Milner's kindergarten 418; neutrality certain (1938) 430; declares war after dispute 453

South African War: initial defeats **XIV** 252–4; Lord Roberts's victories 254–6; first stage of guerrilla warfare 256; second stage 345–6; third stage 347; losses on both sides 347, 382

South America **VII** 259; **X** 325; trade with (1760) **XII** 14, 466, 469; see also Buenos Aires

South Cadbury **Ib** 216; hill-fort **Ia** 121, 453, 485

South Carolina see Carolina

South Cerney **VII** 519

South Elkington **Ib** 176, 181, 193; Saxon pottery 70 [fig. 5(f)]; map 4 xxxii

South Newbald **Ib** 189

South Saxons **II** 9; see also Sussex

South Sea Bubble **XI** 41, 176–8

South Sea Company **X** 47, 249; **XI** 27, 176–8, 186, 207, 209, 265, 313–15; **XII** 25

South Shields: fort and granaries **Ia** 529–30; coins 313; inscriptions 511, 514, 697; South Shields, population **XV** 167

South Wales: discontent **XV** 39; new steel works 122; Red flag flies 199; unemployment 351; a special area 352; strike at Tonypandy 466; coal 506

Southampton (Hants): sea routes **Ia** 91, 308; ports 563; naval base 384; lead pigs lost 634; **Ib** 4, 38; **II** 243, 265, 390, 526, 531; min-

ters 536; **III** 79, 96, 434, 437; service to the crown **IV** 530; **V** 242, 307; French raid 128; trade 358, 360, 381, 406; **VI** 72, 146, 227, 640; Plot 72; Henry V's journey to (1415) 141; Genoese shipping 351; Italians 352; anti-Genoese resentment (1458–60) 355; aldermen 387; incorporation deed, county status 393; municipal authority 398; customs 477; Queen Margaret's dowry contribution 478; Britanny treaty 554; **VII** 145, 211, 219, 229, 274; war with France (1512) 275; Charles V sails from 312; cloth trade 462; 'Flanders galleys' 471; marriage of Philip and Mary (1554) 541; representation **XV** 116

Southampton, 4th earl of see Wriothesley, Thomas

Southampton, earls of see Fitzwilliam, William; Wriothesley, Henry

Southampton Water **V** 208

Southend-on-sea, population **XV** 167

Southey, Robert (1774–1843) **VII** 585; **XII** 417, 532, 534, 541; **XIII** 3, 32, 38, 114, 530

Southrop Church (Glos.) **III** 263

Southwark (Suthriganaweorc) (Surrey) **II** 564, 567, 596; **III** 64; **IV** 182, 213, 214; **V** 409, 527; borough **VI** 345, 422, 423, 498; see also London, boroughs

Southwell (Suthwellan) (Notts.) **II** 365, 436, 495; church 436; Wolsey at **VII** 331

Southwell, Edward (1671–1730) **XI** 298

Southwell, Sir Richard **VII** 421, 496, 531

Southwell, Robert **VIII** 187, 289

Southwell, Sir Robert, master of the rolls (1541) **VII** 648 (brother of above)

Southwold Bay, battle **X** 78
Southwold (Suffolk) **VI** 649
sovereignty: Scotland and Wales **IV** 381–2; the sea 655
Soviet Russia: Lloyd George wishes to conciliate **XV** 131; peace conference 132, 135; intervention 137; infectious example 142; war with Poland 143–4, 199; Genoa conference 189; Kemalist Turkey 190; Labour attitude 200; threat at Straits 202; abortive treaty 217, 219, 221; compared with Britain 227; diplomatic relations broken off 255; resumed 274; not democratic 317; Depression 336; sets example of planning 348; embargo on trade 358; little difference between parties 359; Hoare crusades against 374; submarines and Anglo-German agreement 377; joins League 381; aids Spanish republic 393–4; Neville Chamberlain's attitude 415–16; compared with Nazi Germany 418; alliance with Czechoslovakia 424; Hitler expected to attack 435–7, 441; included by Hoare 437; invited to make declaration of joint resistance 442; demands for alliance with 445; Chamberlain's distrust 446; negotiations 447–50; waits for Hitler to attack 453; hope of switching war against 458, 467, 469, 470; a leak in the blockade 461; attacks Finland 468–9; possible domination of Europe 475; rigorous neutrality 495; Germans draw resources from 500; Germans prepare to attack 501, 503, 504; Great Britain more socialist than 507; delays involvement in war 514; needed to defeat Germany 515; German attack 521, 524, 528; defeat expected 529; Atlantic Charter 530; defeat postponed 531; takes offensive 532; lend-lease 533; no co-ordination of plans 536; United Nations 537; working-class enthusiastic 542–3; Beaverbrook enthusiastic for 544; convoys 546; North Africa conquest 555; not left to finish Hitler 566; combines with United States to impose strategy on Great Britain 575; alleged plans to forestall in Balkans 576; does most of the fighting against Germany 577; post-war prospects 584–5; American alliance with Britain 586; Roosevelt non-committal concerning 587; Poland 588; aid offered in Far East 590; relations with Western Powers 594; use of atomic bomb 601

Sowerby (Cumbria) **III** 283
Sozomen **Ia** 428
Spa Fields meeting (1816) **XIII** 63, 66
Spaatz, General, wishes to attack German oil **XV** 580
Spagnola, Baptista **VIII** 323
Spagnuoli, Baptista (Mantuanus) **VII** 584
Spaight, J. M., on indiscriminate bombing **XV** 534
Spain: Caesar **Ia** 22; communications 37, 44, 425, 539, 540; origins of trading families 155, 397, 402, 428; legions 173, 200; confiscations 224, 604; Imperium Galliarum 273; Gallic prefecture 348, 353; barbarians under Constantine III 428–34, 446, 469, 488; recovery? 447; Majorian 490; estates unsaleable 600; wine trade 459, 652–3; mines 632, 635–6; pagan survivals 673, 736; Christians and heretics 714, 727, 737; **Ib** 76; **III** 244, 245; merchants **IV** 644; *see also* Aragon; Castile; Navarre; **V** 31, 146, 268, 430; Black Prince restores Peter to throne 144; raids on England 145;

empire 450–4, 457, 467–9; different economic rewards 662–3; *see also* aristocrats; army; citizenship; Christian Church; social classes; social mobility

statute law, growth **V** 194–8

Statute of Limitations **XII** 304

statutes: private collections **IV** 70, 370; *De heretico comburendo* (1401) 95; Lollard (1406) 95, (1414) 453; Provisors (1390) and Praemunire (1393) 198; Provisors' repeal 199; Jews (1275) 322; Wales (1284) 322, 429, 435–7; *Districciones Scaccarii* (1275) 325, 372; Mortmain (*de religiosis* 1279) 325, 372; Gloucester (1278) 328, 330, 353, 357, 372 —franchises 376–7; background 352–5; *de justiciis assignatis* 352, 358; Westminster I (1275) 353, 357, 361, 368, 379 —sheriffs 377 —debts 356 —law 371 —determined by king's will 372 —protection of personal rights 375 —tithe disputes 464 — 'second statute' 480; of Edward I 355–80; Acton Burnell (1283) 356, 375, 620, 625; merchants (1285) 356, 357, 367, 375, 711 —merchant controls 620, 627 —debts 625; Rhuddlan (1284) 356, 357; *Quia emptores* (1290) 357, 376, 379–80; Winchester (1285) 357, 369, 374, 543, 627 —provisions against marauders 570; *Quo Warranto* (1290) 357, 372, 376–9, 513; Labourers 453; Northampton 453; Westminster I and II 460; clerical objections 625, 627; **V** 163, 177–8, 197; Stamford 9; York (1322) 71–3, 104, 456; staples (1354) 195, 353; Winchester (1285) 201, 203, 237; Northampton (1328) 201, 203; Westminster IV (1331) 203; labourers (1351) 206, 222, 335, 411; sumptuary acts (1363) 228, 346; Kilkenny (1366) 232; treasons (1352) 257, 449, 456, 459, 485; (1388) 459–60; De Donis Conditionalibus (1285) 261; against livery and maintenance (1390) 262; provisors (1351) 273, 280; (1390) 282, 297; mortmain (1279) 307; Cambridge (1388) 339; against purveyance (1351, 1369) 363; Cambridge (1388) 339; *see also* Dictum; Marlborough; Merton; Westminster

Stavegni, Roger of **V** 123

Staveley, Ralph, Henry of Derby's steward **VI** 31

Stavensby, Alexander, bishop of Coventry (1224–40) **IV** 60

Stayner, Richard **IX** 233

Stead, W. T. **XIV** 170, 184, 310, 315

steam, industrial use **XII** 332, 334, 478, 505, 508; Cartwright's power loom 510; ships 515

steam-power, factories **XIII** 4–5; (1871) 603; Irish factories 357

steamships, early **XIII** 42

Steed, Wickham, at Crewe House **XV** 107; peace terms 127; urges Law to return 192; dismissed 194

steel: distorted by First World War **XV** 122; rationalization 340–1; burden on railways 506; set for expansion 600; *see also* iron and steel industry

Steele, Sir Richard (1672–1729) **X** 226, 357, 358, 418, 420; expelled from parliament 239; **XI** 10, 22, 419, 421, 427

steelyard (London) **VI** 69, 70, 357, 360

Steenkirk, battle **X** 170

Steevens, Charles (1705–61), Admiral **XI** 330

stehende Bogen **Ib** 69, 102

Steinberg, Ernst von, Hanoverian resident in Great Britain (1738–49) **XI** 14

Steinmore *see* Stainmore (Yorks.)

535

Stewart, Alexander, son of James IV, archbishop of St Andrews **VII** 252, 282

Stewart, Bernard, sieur d'Aubigny **VII** 153, 164, 174

Stewart, Francis, earl of Bothwell **VIII** 443

Stewart, Sir Herbert **XIV** 82

Stewart, house of **VII** 162

Stewart, James, duke of Ross, brother of James IV **VII** 136

Stewart, James, earl of Arran (1581) **VIII** 358, 361, 370

Stewart, James, 1st earl of Buchan (second creation) **VII** 136

Stewart, James, son of James IV, earl of Moray **VII** 252

Stewart, John, Lord Darnley, 1st earl of Lennox (d. 1495) **VII** 136

Stewart, John, duke of Albany (1481–1536) **VII** 305, 306, 326, 585; Scots ordered to expel 312; sails to France (1522) 313; leaves Scotland (1524) 313–14

Stewart, John, earl of Buchan **VI** 244

Stewart, Sir John of Grandtully **XII** 135

Stewart, Sir Malcolm **XV** 352

Stewart, Matthew, 2nd earl of Lennox (d. 1513) **VII** 282

Stewart, Matthew, 4th earl of Lennox (1516–71) **VII** 305

Stewart, Murdoch (Murdach), earl of Fife, son of duke of Albany **VI** 45, 46, 64

Stewart, Lord Provost of Edinburgh **XI** 283

Stewart, Robert, Viscount Castlereagh, 2nd marquis of Londonderry (1769–1822): **XI** 424; **XII** 402; biography 399; on Ireland 399, 444; president of Board of Control (1802–6) 408, 418, 581; charges of corruption 448; secretary of war and colonies (1807–9) 444, 454, 457, 483, 582 —peninsula decision 476–8;

opposition of Canning to 477, 483, 498; out of office 485; foreign secretary (1812) 495, 498, 552, 556, 559–66 —succeeds Wellesley 492; European settlement 568–70; lists of Cabinets 582–3; **XIII** 15, 28, 38, 224; biography 399; on Ireland 399; **XIII** 15, 28, 38, 224; biography 54; leader of the House of Commons 54–5; proposes Waterloo and Trafalgar monuments 193; principles of foreign policy 195–8; attitude towards European revolutions 198–204; death 69, 204

Stewart (Stuart), Henry, Lord Darnley (1545–67) **VII** 305; return to Scotland **VIII** 78, 81; wins queen's favour 81–2; marriage 83–5, 88, 89; promotion 84–5; 'rides whirlwind' 86; Rizzio plot 91–3, 99; fall from grace 99; divorce mooted 101; his murder 101–3

Stewart family (Royal) **III** 273; *see also* Stuart

Stewarts of Appin **XI** 254

Steyn Priory, near Gouda **VII** 249, 251

Steyning (Sussex) **VI** 418

Stiff, John, Henry V's minstrel **VI** 144

Stiffkey **XV** 316

Stifford (Essex), church **III** 25

Stifford, Michael of **III** 25

Stigand, bishop of Elmham (*c*.1052) **II** 426; bishop of Winchester 568; and archbishop of Canterbury 465–6, 568, 586, 599, 623–4; relations with William I 624; deposition 659–60; **III** 251

Stiklestad, battle 405

Stilicho, Flavius **Ia** 416–31; and barbarians 418, 425, 427, 429; political activity 419, 430; dealings with Britain 419–26, 435; disgrace and death 430–1, 486; military leadership 434, 489

Stilicho **Ib** 84

Stillington, Robert, bishop of Bath and Wells **VI** 553, 561, 616, 634; Edward IV's children illegitimate 618

Stilton cheese **XII** 34

Stimson, H.: myth of lost opportunity **XV** 372; wants direct attack on Germany **XV** 553

Stirling **VII** 138; **VIII** 40, 44, 108, 154; **IX** 168

Stirling, James (1692–1770), mathematician **XI** 379

Stirling Bridge, battle (1297) **IV** 669, 683, 686, 687, 690

Stirling Castle **III** 278; **IV** 574, 614, 686; parliament (1295) 612; captured by Scots (1299) 692; held till (1304) 695, 708, 711; siege and surrender (1304) 710–11; pact of Bruce and Lamberton (1304) 714; Dominican priory 692; **V** 33, 34–9, 70

Stock Exchange, barred to women **XV** 166

stock-raising **Ia** 14–15, 281, 613, 620–1, 627; stock-yards 604, 620; *see also* agriculture; cattle; sheep; etc.

Stockbridge (Hants) **III** 144

Stockholm, proposed conference **XV** 90

Stockmar, Baron Christian Friedrich von **XIII** 104, 243, 315; biography 104; education of Prince Albert 106; influence upon Queen Victoria and Prince Albert 107–8

Stockport: Corresponding Society **XII** 358; industry 510

Stocton, Adam **V** 512

Stoddard, George **VIII** 260, 272

Stoicism **Ia** 164, 203, 209, 710, 711; progression 716; persistence in Christian thought 728

Stoke: battle (16 June 1487) **VII** 8, 79, 86; crisis for Henry VII 74–5

Stoke-by-Clare (Suffolk), priory **V** 293; **VI** 301

Stoke near Hurstbourne (Hants) **Ib** 147

Stoke Lyne (Fethanleag, Fethanleag) **Ib** 169, appendix II; map 3 xxxi; battle, probable site **II** 29

Stoke by Nayland (Suffolk) **VI** 503, 647

Stokes, Dr John **VI** 161, 179

Stokes mortar **XV** 35

Stokesley, John, bishop of London (1530–9) **VII** 347, 570

stone: forts **Ia** 163; stonemasons 218, 697; buildings 233, 266, 458, 609; town walls 261–5; large objects 562, 654, 700; transport and supply 562–3, 630–1; dressed 603, 609

Stone, Andrew (1703–73), Newcastle's secretary **XI** 295, 340, 341

Stone, George (?1708–64), archbishop of Armagh **XI** 295, 303

Stone-by-Faversham **Ib** 126; map 2 xxx

Stonea Camp: battle? **Ia** 101–2, 189; villa 604; village 610

Stoneleigh (War.) **V** 325

Stonesfield, villa **Ia** 608

Stonor, Thomas **VI** 450

Stonor, Sir William **VI** 626, 631

Stonors, the **XI** 73

Stonot, Sir John **V** 168

Stony Stratford (Bucks.) **Ia** 689; **VI** 535, 613

Stools **Ia** 605, 698

Stop of the Exchequer **X** 85

Stopes, Dr Marie **XV** 165

Stopford, Sir F. W., at Suvla Bay **XV** 44–5

Stoppingas **II** 44

storage pits **Ia** 554, 621, 623

Stork, William, dietary experiments of **XII** 11

Stormont, Viscount *see* Mansfield, 2nd earl of

Stosch, Baron de, and Jacobite activities abroad **XI** 184

Strathclyde (*cont.*)
Eadberht's conquest 92; later kings 332, 334, 340, 342, 359–60; invaded by Edmund 359, 369; granted to Malcolm, king of Scots 359–60, 370; raided by Æthelred II 379

Strathorde **IV** 709, 713

stratores **Ia** 522, 597

Stratton, Adam de, career and downfall **IV** 364–5

Stratton, battle **IX** 133

Stratton, John de, Bordelais lands and rents **VI** 110

Strauss, Henry, resigns **XV** 591

Stravinsky, Igor **XV** 178, 268

Straw, Jack **V** 411, 414, 419, 420

strawberry, introduction **XII** 132

Streatley (Berks.) **Ib** 158, 168; map 3 xxxi; **II** 73

Street, George Edmund: biography **XIII** 584; work 584; **XIV** 155

street traction **XIV** 280–1, 508–9; effect on housing 509

Streeter, Robert **X** 401

streetlighting extinguished **XV** 454

Streonæshalch *see* Whitby (Yorks.)

Stresa, meeting **XV** 377, 380; military agreement 388

Stresemann, G. **XV** 255, 272

Stretes, Guillim **VII** 601

Stretton, Robert, bishop of Lichfield (1360–85) **V** 276, 300, 303

Strickland, 'one of the seven men of Moidart' **XI** 252

Strickland, Sir Roger, Admiral **X** 123, 136

Strickland, Walter **VIII** 196, 220–2; **IX** 219, 222

Strickland, William, bishop of Carlisle **VI** 271

Strickland of Sizergh, family **VI** 271

strikes and lock-outs: **XI** 143; in the seventies **XIV** 34, 37, 133; London dock strike 205–6; dispute at Manningham Mills, Bradford 221; miners' lock-out (1893) 298–300; engineers' strike (1897) 300; threatened railway strike (1907) 395; great series of strikes (1910–12) 438–44; Irish transport strikes 472–3; in First World War **XV** 39, 40, 106; rail 141; by miners 144; fewer 163; during first Labour government 213; further decline 239, 248; renewed (1943) 566

Strode, Richard **VII** 439

Strode, William **IX** 122–3

Strong, Caleb (1745–1819), governor of Massachusetts **XII** 554

Stroud (Glos.) **VI** 365

Stroud Valley **Ia** 68; broadcloth **VI** 365

Strozzi, Leo, prior of Padua **VII** 483

Strozzi, Philip **VIII** 160, 356

Strozzi, Piero **VII** 558

Strutt, Jedediah (1726–97) **XI** 109

Strykland, Richard, of Haversham (Bucks.) **VI** 419

Stuart, Arabella **IX** 3

Stuart, General Sir Charles (1753–1801): biography **XII** 379; capture of Minorca 379; correspondence 479

Stuart, Esmé, earl of Lennox **VIII** 358–61

Stuart, Henry, Lord Darnley *see* Stewart

Stuart, James ('Athenian') (1713–88), architect and draughtsman **XI** 404, 412

Stuart, James, 3rd earl of Bute (1713–92) **XI** 185, 323, 341, 355, 368; perpetuates misunderstandings under George III 271; influence on young prince 341; made secretary 367; dominant in king's council 371, 373; neglects Frederic's interests abroad 372; art 399; **XII** 65, 74; biography 1; rise to power 4–7, 32, 66, 69–71; first lord of Treasury (1762–3) 79–82, 88, 90, 92, 575; resignation 93, 147; continued influence

540

Sunday Express, created by Beaverbrook **XV** 235

Sunday newspapers, become respectable **XV** 168

Sunday observance: Mid-Victorian strictness **XIV** 140; relaxations towards the end of the 19th cent. 309

Sunday Observance Act (1782) **XV** 316

Sunday schools **XII** 39

Sunderland (Co. Durham) **VI** 127

Sunderland, earls of *see* Spencer, Charles; Spencer, Robert

Sundon, Lady *see* Clayton, Charlotte

Sunningas *see* Sonning (Berks.)

Sunninghill (Berks.) **Ib** 43; **II** 294

Sunningwell (Oxon.) **Ib** 43; map 3 xxxi

superbus **Ia** 66, 465, 468, 472

superstitions **VIII** 327–32

Supply, Ministry of: clamour for **XV** 389, 433; set up 444; ignores shipping limitations 463; Ministry of Aircraft Production 478; Beaverbrook 510; saved by its own blunders 512, 546; Cripps refuses 543; regional government 569

Supremacy, Act of **X** 270; *see also* Acts of parliament

supreme war council (1917–19): set up **XV** 99; accepts Fourteen Points 111; extension of British line 117; peace conference 135; Churchill persuades to intervene in Russia 137; set up (1939–40) 454; does not debate advance into Belgium 484; not revived between Great Britain and United States 537

Surat **IX** 322–3; **X** 348, 350

Surgeons, Royal College of **XIII** 18

Surienne, François de **VI** 491

Surigone, Stefano, Milanese **VII** 237

Surinam **X** 68, 327

Surinam, river **X** 325

Surreau, Peter de, Normandy treasurer **VI** 205, 207, 208

Surrey **Ia** 42–3; **Ib** 106, 113, 139, 141, 174; **II** 26, 58, 439, 574; meaning of name 54–5, 293–4; relations with Kent 55, 61; with Mercia 55; with Wessex 61, 70, 72–3; submission to Egbert 231; **III** 434; **V** 314, 316, 329; **VII** 504; population **XV** 167

Surrey, duke of *see* Holland, Thomas

Surrey, earls of *see* Fitzalan, Warenne; Howard, Thomas; Warenne I, William de; Warenne II, William de; Warenne III, William de; Warenne IV, William de

surveys, private **II** 472–3

Susa **IV** 250; treaty **IX** 66

Susa, Henry de, archbishop of Embrun **IV** 135–6

Sussex **Ia** 12, 42–3, 625, 637, 730; **Ib** 4–5, 37, 39, 92, 106; kingdom 134–40; **II** 379; kingdom 12, 36, 58, 61; conquest 17–19; Andredes leag (Weald) 18; royal families 38, 58; conquered by Cædwalla 69; invaded by Ine 72–3; becomes Mercian province 208–9; later kings, named 211; submission to Egbert 231; shire 294; pastoral farming **III** 48; iron industry 82; Pevensey Castle 101; estates in 165, 207; sheriff 222; loyal to John 484; **V** 312, 314, 414; **VII** 504; **IX** 137–8; *see also* Weald

Sussex, duchy of Lancaster lordships **VI** 332

Sussex, earl of **III** 157; *see also* Albini I, William de; Albini II, William de; Radcliffe, Thomas

Sussex, sheriff of **III** 222, 356

Sutangli **II** 32

Sutherland, earls of *see* Gordon, John

Suthriganaweorc *see* Southwark

Suthrige **Ib** map 2 xxx
Suthwellan *see* Southwell (Notts.)
Sutton (Cambs.) **V** 317
Sutton (Kent), lathe **II** 499
Sutton, Oliver, bishop of Lincoln (1280–99) **IV** 486, 490
Sutton Cheney (Leics.) **VI** 643; Stanley forces 644
Sutton Coldfield (War.) **VI** 379
Sutton Courtenay (Berks.) **Ib** xxi, 102; map 2 xxx; **II** 26
Sutton Hoo (Suffolk) **Ib** xxii; map 2 xxx; ship burial **II** 50–2
Sutton Place **VII** 596
Suvermerianism **VII** 509
Suvla Bay **XV** 45, 48
Suvorov **XII** 296, 380, 385
Suzanne, mistress of King John **III** 428
Sveaborg **XII** 295
Swabia, dukes of *see* Conrad; Frederick; Philip
Swæfred, king of Essex **II** 204
Swaffham (Norfolk) **VI** 650
Swaffham, John, bishop of Bangor (1376–98) **V** 449
Swaffham Priory, villa **Ia** 604
Swale, river **V** 56
swamps *see* marshes
Swan, Sir J. W., inventor **XIV** 151–2
Swan, Vivien **Ia** 93, 642, 649, 650
Swan, William, court of Rome proctor **VI** 269, 270
Swanage (Swanawic) (Dorset) **II** 254, 733
Swanawic *see* Swanage (Dorset)
Swanland, Thomas **V** 224, 353
Swans, feast (1306) **IV** 515–16
Swansea **III** 291; castle 298; **V** 59, 73; Chinese **XV** 167
Swansea, university college **XV** 308
Swanwick, Mrs H. M. **XV** 216
Swaziland **XIV** 227
swearing **IX** 305, 306–7
Sweden **III** 458; fisheries **VI** 69; **IX** 225–30; **X** 73, 74, 112, 162; iron ore from **XI** 114; relations with

Britain 165, 174, 201; with Jacobites 174; Anglo-French treaty (1855) **XIII** 289; Germans get iron ore **XV** 467; expedition to Finland 468–9; supplies Germany 500; *see also* Baltic Powers; Charles XII
Swedes **II** 194–5, 239, 403–4, 406
swedes, introduction **XII** 12
The Swedish Intelligencer **IX** 413
Sweetheart Abbey **IV** 229, 693, 702
Swein, brother of Eric of Hlathir **II** 403–4
Swein, son of Cnut and Ælfgifu, underking of Norway **II** 398, 405–6
Swein, son of Earl Godwine **II** 429–30, 563–4, 569; earldom 561
Swein Estrithson, king of Denmark **II** 423–4, 427–8, 429, 432, 560–1; relations with Confessor's court 427; war with Magnus of Norway 427; war with Harold Hardrada 428; sends army to England 602; comes into the Humber 605; death 611
Swein Forkbeard, son of Harold, king of the Danes **II** 338, 375, 396, 411, 462; invades England (994) 378; murder of Gunnhild, sister 380; invades England (1003) 380; invades England (1013) 384–6; recognized as King of England 386; death 386; regular currency introduction 543
Sweodora **Ib** map 2 xxx
Swereford, Alexander, Exchequer **IV** 65
Swettenham, Matthew **V** 428
Sweveghem, agent of Alva **VIII** 163
Swift, Jonathan (1667–1745) **VII** 258; **IX** 287; **X** 257, 313, 359, 360, 385; sides with Harley, undermining ministry 226; political pamphleteers 355; London literary clubs 358; *Battle of the Books* 384; **XI** 10, 38, 183, 204, 288; on Carteret in Ireland 293; *Modest*

T

Talbot, Sir Thomas, of Davington, nr Faversham (Kent) **VI** 131

Talbot family **VI** 103; lands 335

Talents, Ministry of All the **XII** 394, 412, 435–43, 466, 499

Talgarth, land of **V** 74

Taliessin **Ib** 17

tallage **III** 418–19, 474; **IV** 529–31; in Henry III's time 36; in (1268) 221–2; in (1304) 534; use of term (1297) 682; *de tallagio non concedendo* 681–2; **V** 155, 160, 163, 191; prior to Peasants' Revolt (1381) 342; reduced by bishop of Chichester during 'hard years' 343; miners exempt 370

Tallard, Marshal **X** 208

Talley Church **IV** 390

Talleyrand, C.-M. de (1754–1838) **XII** 426, 562, 566; **XIII** 225, 227–9, 231

Talleyrand, Cardinal Elias **V** 278

Tallington **Ia** 604

Tallis, Thomas **VII** 589; **VIII** 305

Talman, William **X** 391

Talmont **IV** 90

Talorcan, king of the Picts **II** 87

Talvas, house **III** 105

Tamar (Tamur), river **Ia** 44; **II** 65, 264, 341, 733

Tamburlaine **VIII** 297

Tame, river **Ia** 544; **II** 41

Tamoworthig *see* Tamworth (Staffs.)

Tamu *see* Thame (Oxon.)

Tamur *see* Tamar, river

Tamworth (Tamoworthig) (Staffs.) **Ib** 186; map 4 xxxii; manifesto **II** 326, 330, 336, 339, 357, 733; chief seat of Mercian kings 40, 526; council 351; honour 639; Henry VII at **VII** 52; **XIII** 95, 102, 367

Tamworth, John, Winchelsea mayor **VI** 418

Tancred of Lecce, king of Sicily **III** 360, 362–3

Tandy, James Napper (1740–1803) **XII** 396

Tanfield, Robert, Northants lawyer **VI** 481

Tangier **X** 60, 102, 172, 348

Tangku, truce **XV** 372

Tankerville, earl of **XII** 337

tanks, manufacture begun **XV** 35; in Flanders 87; battle of Cambrai 88; neglected 231; losses in Belgium 487; before invasion 497; cannot be substituted for bombers 515; too slow 525; Sherman, diverted to Suez 554; losses at Alamein 559; production tails off 565; Americans supply 566

Tanne, John of Lynn **VII** 220, 472

Tannenberg, battle **XV** 12

Tanner, Thomas (1674–1735), Bishop, antiquarian **XI** 394

Tanner, William **VI** 460

Tanshelf (Taddenesscylf) (Yorks.) **II** 36, 733

Tantaun *see* Taunton (Som.)

Tany, Luke de, seneschal of Gascony (1272–8): career **IV** 279; Gaston of Béarn 284–5; replaced by John de Grilly 288; operations and death in Anglesey (1282) 426–7

tapestry **VIII** 230; **IX** 381–2

Taranto **VII** 153; Italian ships sunk **XV** 523

Tarascon, treaty (1291) **IV** 261, 262

Tarbes (Hautes-Pyrénées) **VI** 140

Tarbes, bishop of (Gabriel de Grammont) **VII** 317, 324, 325

Tarde, G. **XIV** 551

tariffs: reform by Huskisson **XIII** 70–2; by Peel 113; by Gladstone 179–81; effect of foreign **XIV** 275–6

Tarleton, Sir Banastre (1754–1833) **XII** 215

Tarragona, archbishop of **IV** 252, 258

Tarragona, massacre **XII** 488

Tartars **IV** 110, 167; *see also* Mongols

Tartas (Landes) **VI** 108, 470

Tas, river **Ib** xxvii, 98
Tascovianus **Ia** 47, 55–6
Tasmania **XIII** 384–6
Tassis, Juan Battista de **VIII** 361
Tatberht, abbot of Ripon **II** 187
Tate, Sir Henry **XIV** 326
Tathaceaster *see* Tadcaster (Yorks.)
Tatler **XI** 420
Tattershall (Lincs.), Cromwell re-
  builds **VI** 651–2; bricks 652
Tatwine, archbishop of Canterbury
  II 145, 183
Tauberbischofsheim, monastery **II**
  173
Taunton (Tantaun) (Som.) **II** 71;
  VI 366; **VII** 145, 349; **IX** 141
Taunton, Viscount **XIII** 487
Taunus, frontier **Ia** 175
Taurogen, convention (1813) **XII**
  555
Tavannes, Gaspard de Saulx **VIII**
  157
Taverner, John (*fl.* 1530); musician
  VII 588
Taverner, John, ship-builder **VII**
  219
Taverner, Richard (1505?–75) **VII**
  571
Tavistock (Devon), abbey: knight
  service **II** 635; **III** 227; **VI** 309;
  balanced economy 377
Tavistock, abbot of **III** 14
Tawney, R. H.: on Sankey Commission **XV** 140; statement on
  education 211; drafts Labour
  programme 267; his teaching 278,
  331, 347
Tawton, Robert, keeper of the privy
  seal (1334–5) **V** 154
Taxatio papae Nicholai **IV** 498, 509
taxation: national **II** 412, 644–8;
  pre-Alfredian 286–7; methods of
  assessment: in East Anglia 645; in
  Wessex and English Mercia
  646–7; in northern Danelaw
  646–7, 647–8; in Kent 647; vir-
  tues of English methods 648; in
  Henry III's reign **IV** 28–37, 75,

78, 281, 535–6; in Edward I's
reign 37, 343–4, 513, 523–8,
534–6 — revenue for invasions
and defence 673 — Pope Boniface
insists on papal approval 674;
proposed (1258) 135, 142; clergy
220–4; of Chester, Wales and the
Marches (1290–2) 259, 443, 560;
consent and the sense of obligation 526–7; of Ireland 535, 560;
subsidy for wool purchase 680–1;
from boroughs 703; twentieth and
thirtieth granted 715; tables for
Henry IV's reign **VI** 118–20;
tenths and fifteenths for Henry
V's reign 203–4; clerical tenths
for Henry V's reign 203–4; **X**
6–8, 175–6, 239, 250, 289; Scottish dissatisfaction over malt-tax
(1713) 292; (1760) **XII** 12, 20, 26,
44, 60; under Grenville 20,
103–6, 126; cider tax 64, 91–3
— abolished 114; under Newcastle 72; under Bute 90–3; under
Rockingham 126; under Pitt 126,
476; under North 153–5, 208,
226, 286; under Shelburne 252;
under Pitt 287, 292, 299, 374–6;
under Addington 412–14; under
Portland 476; America *see* America, revolt and war of independence; parliament; representation;
revenue
taxation of clergy **IV** 478–9, 500–9,
675–7; by the pope for the king
220–1, 497, 498–500; provinces
of Gaul for crusade against Aragon 254; subsidies 448, 497, 499,
501; mandatory 264–7, 470, 472,
496, 641–2; Scotland 573, 583; in
parliament 673–4
taxes **Ia** 236–7, 535, 576–8; from
commerce 51, 57, 618; attitudes
to 116, 126–7, 283, 662; collection
122, 187, 224, 279, 337–8
— Julian 360 — delegation 535;
support for army 126–7, 283, 337;
increases 283, 405; paid in kind

taxes (*cont.*)
337; cost and difficulties of collecting 345, 433, 440; exemptions
345, 457, 546; threat of forced
levies 431; tax havens in Gaul
448, 452; paid in gold 530; economic effects of provincial system
662
Taximagulus **Ia** 36
Tay, river **Ia** 144, 146, 196, 319; **III**
266, 273; **VII** 484
Taylor, Brook (1685–1731), mathematician **XI** 379
Taylor, Sir Herbert **XIII** 104
Taylor, Jeremy **IX** 213
Taylor, John **VII** 120, 165
Taylor, Dr John (1694–1761): academy at Warrington **XI** 89
Taylor, John, bishop of Lincoln
(1552–4) **VII** 545; burnt (1555)
550
Taylor, John, 'Chevalier' (1703–
72), quack **XI** 390
Taylor, John, clerk of the parliaments **VII** 279
Taylor, John, prebendary of Westminster (1518), master of the rolls
(26 June 1527) **VII** 648
Taylor, Sir Robert (1714–88),
architect **XI** 412
Taylor, Rowland (d. 1555) **VII** 546
Taylor, Tom **XIV** 125, 126
Taylor, William, St Edmund Hall
principal **VI** 96, 97, 298; Chichele
arraigns 97
tea: drinking **XII** 12; taxation 105,
127, 143, 152, 192; price juggling
in America 196; Boston Tea
Party (1773) 197; smuggling 288
'tea-room party' **XIII** 187
team *see* toll
Tecumseh, Indian chief **XII** 550,
552
Tedder, Sir A.: air commander in
Middle East **XV** 526; in
Mediterranean 563; deputy to
Eisenhower 579; issues orders to
Harris 580; urges dismissal of

Montgomery 582; wants attack
on communications 591
Teddington (Middx.) **V** 317
Tees (Tese), river **Ia** 4, 255; **Ib** xxvi,
175, 187; map 4 xxxii; **II** 733; **III**
265, 271, 275, 280; **V** 40
Tefgeta *see* Teviot, river
Tegeingl *see* Englefield
Teheran, conference **XV** 574–5, 587
Teifi, river **VI** 57
Teignmouth, John Shore, 1st Baron
XII 354
Tel-el-Kebir **XIV** 79
telegraphy, development **XIII** 569,
597–8
telescopes **XI** 382
Telese, monastery of San Salvatore
at **III** 176
Telford, Thomas, civil engineer
(1757–1834) **XII** 518; **XIII** 4,
597
Teme, river **Ia** 265
temenos see sanctuaries
Temes *see* Thames, river
Temesanford *see* Tempsford (Beds.)
Tempest, Robert **VIII** 138
Templars, knights **III** 42, 447;
absentee landlords 45; estates in
England 55, 189; grand masters
of: Arnold de Turre Rubea 344;
Terric 344; money-lenders 423–
4; **IV** 27, 82, 761; **V** 29, 30, 76,
291–2, 298
temple: Colchester **Ia** 117, 674;
Agricola 142; temple-guilds 279;
sequestration of funds 341, 577,
730; rebuilding 342, 409; closing
of pagan temples 356, 408; Lydney 384; restoration 530; (Jupiter) 530; upkeep 580; Pliny builds
601; Springhead 667; Bath 687;
Romano-Celtic 670–1, 695, 701;
(Mithras) 711; still in use under
Honorius 735; on hill-forts 738;
see also pagan cults; sanctuaries;
shrines
Temple, Dorothy **X** 77
Temple, earls of *see* Grenville,

550

Richard Temple; Grenville, George Nugent-Temple

Temple, Dr F., bishop, afterwards archbishop **XIV** 307

Temple, Henry John, 3rd Viscount Palmerston **XIII** 77, 79, 101, 107, 122–3; Ten Hours' movement 150; supports Ten Hours' Bill 154; party politics 160–2, 164–5, 170–1, 175–6, 178–81; dismissal 164; home secretary 165; first administration (1855) 167–70; views on parliamentary reform (1852) 168–9; second administration (1859) 169, 172–3, 286; death 181; biography 222; character and ideas 222–5; policy in the Belgian question 227–30; forms quadruple alliance (1834) 231–2; Turkish policy (1830–8) 233–6, (1839–41) 236–9; efforts to suppress the slave trade 240–1; attitude towards the revolutions (1848) 245–6; defence of Don Pacifico 246–7; differences with Queen Victoria and Prince Albert 246, 251, 301–2; advises Malmesbury 251; eastern policy (1853–4) 258, 264; (1855–7) 286; army reform 268–70; conduct of Crimean war 286; relations with China 296–8; policy on the Italian question 300–3; attitude towards American Civil War 308–9, 313; expedition to Mexico 314; and the Schleswig-Holstein question 317–18, 320–4; colonial policy 367; Dardanelles 418; supports Auckland's Afghan policy 418; architecture 585

Temple, New, London **IV** 17, 82, 136, 147–8, 641; Master of, in England 3, 17, 112; in Paris 14, 126; clerical subsidy 677

Temple, Sir Richard, Viscount Cobham (1675–1749) **XI** 204, 238, 413

Temple, Sir William **X** 73, 85, 90, 98, 378; peace emissary to Louis IV 72; *Essay upon the Ancient and Modern Learning* 384

Temple Bar **VIII** 6

Templehurst, baron of *see* Darcy, Thomas

temporalities **IV** 498, 509, 513, 523

Tempsford (Temesanford) (Beds.) **II** 327–8, 733

'Ten Minutes Bill' **XIII** 186

Ten Year Rule **XV** 228; abandoned 364

tenancy **Ia** 78, 159–60, 237, 602, 605–6; farm management 625, 627

Tenby (Pembroke) **VI** 57; lordship 77; castle 641

Tencteri **Ia** 25

Teneriffe **VIII** 124; **XII** 426

Tenet *see* Thanet (Kent)

Tenison, Thomas, archbishop of Canterbury (1636–1715) **X** 255; **XI** 78

tennis **XV** 19, 313; *see also* lawn tennis

Tennyson, Alfred, Lord (1809–92) **III** 255; **XIII** 178, 261, 495, 529–30, 532; biography 535; assessment 535–8; and Mill 546; **XIV** 45, 136, 161

Tenterden **Ib** 126; map 2 xxx

tents **Ia** 620

Tenuie (Seine-et-Oise) **VI** 239

Teotanheale *see* Tettenhall (Staffs.)

Teowdor, king of Brycheiniog **II** 341

Teramo, Simon de, papal collector **VI** 234, 236

Terceira **VIII** 353, 356

Terence **III** 257

Termes, Paul de la Barthe, seigneur de **VII** 485

Termonde **Ib** map 1 xxix

Ternate **VIII** 249

Ternoise, river **VI** 153

Terpen **Ib** xxi, xxvii, 51–2, 59

Terrington (Norfolk) **V** 321

territorium **Ia** 115, 153, 523, 536–7, 586; army food production 622

339, 349; **XIII** 14, 553, 560, 625–6; **XV** 314
Thedwestry hundred (Suffolk) **II** 645
thegnlands **II** 489–90
thegns: socially identical with *gesith* **II** 486–7; hereditary rank 487; popular conception 487; scattered estates 487–9; king's 487–8; meaning of term 488; wergild 488, 508–9; military equipment 488–9, 550; thegns and their lords 488–90, 564; Northumbrian law 508–9; settled in boroughs 529–30; military service 583–4; post-Conquest depression 680–1, 684–5; medieval families descended from 684–5
Thelwæl *see* Thelwall (Cheshire)
Thelwall (Thelwæl) (Cheshire) **II** 333
Thelwall, John (1764–1834) **XII** 357, 360
Theobald, archbishop of Canterbury: forbidden to crown Stephen's son **III** 163, 212; treaty between Stephen and Henry II 165; appointed archbishop 190, 193; opposed to Stephen 192, 194; legate 194; household 196; relations with Becket 197, 199; promotes canon law 200; death 203; independence of Welsh church 296
Theobald, count of Bar **III** 453
Theobald, count of Blois **III** 122, 131–2, 135
Theobald IV, count of Champagne, king of Navarre (d. 1253) **IV** 104, 105, 111, 116, 237; ravages Bayonne lands 109
Theobald, Lewis (1688–1744), critic **XI** 419
Theobald V, count of Champagne, king of Navarre (1253–70) **IV** 237–8
Theodford *see* Thetford (Norfolk)
Theodore, archbishop of Canter-

bury **II** 44, 48, 120, 124, 128, 165; penances against heathenism 128; present to Pope Vitalian 131; journey to Britain 131–2; provincial visitation 132–3; holds council at Hertford 133–4; creates dioceses 134–6, 146; divides Northumbrian diocese 134–8; holds council against Monothelite heresy 137; reconciled with Wilfrid 139; death 139; historical importance 139–42; *Poenitentiale* 140–1; introduces charter to England 141; centralization of the Church 139, 143, 177; history of standing cross 150; teacher 180–4
Theodore of Gaza **VII** 237
Theodore of Tarsus **VII** 237
Theodoric **Ib** 199
Theodoric, Ostrogothic king **Ia** 376, 462, 478, 488
Theodosian family **Ia** 381, 400, 416–17, 428, 432
Theodosius, Count **Ib** 106
Theodosius (the elder, *comes*) **Ia** 361, 428; clearance of barbarians 381–2; restoration of defences 383–4, 388–9, 397–9, 407, 412 —Spanish aristocracy 714 —army/towns restored 722; Valentia 392–6, 411; abolition of *areani* 377; execution 400; Magnus Maximus 402; pottery supplies for army 645
Theodosius I, the Great, emperor **Ia** 381, 400–15; East–West relations 288, 409, 432; *magister militum* 400; Ambrose 401, 408; Magnus Maximus 402–4; recovery of Britain 405, 421–2; paganism 408–9, 708, 714, 735; defeat of Arbogast and Eugenius 409, 417; significance of reign and death 410, 415; Stilicho 416; dominance of military commanders 416, 475
Theodosius II, Emperor **Ia** 432
Theodred, bishop of London **II** 437, 444

tion 69–70, 78–9; dispersal of estates 73; judgement on 74; earldom of Leicester (1324) 75; extortion in weavers' trade 364; borrows a French bible 522

Thomas, F. Freeman, Lord Willingdon **XIV** 385

Thomas, James Henry **XIV** 478; biography **XV** 141; rail strike 141; coal lock-out 146; Inner Cabinet 197; during general strike 248; becomes first Dominions secretary 254; agrees to conquer unemployment 271; fails to do so 284; relinquishes task 285; economy committee 288; in National government 294; loses pension 295; ceases to be member of Labour party 323; last trade union leader in parliament 327; at Ottawa 333; Irish Free State 358; leaks budget secret 359

Thomas, John (1691–1766), bishop of St Asaphs, Lincoln and Salisbury **XI** 78

Thomas, Rhys ap **VI** 641, 642; joins Henry Tudor 642; lieutenancy of Wales 642; *see also* Rhys ap Thomas

Thomas, S. Gilchrist, inventor **XIV** 106, 151

Thomas, St *see* Aquinas, Becket

Thomas Aquinas *see* Aquinas

Thomas Becket, of Canterbury *see* Becket, St Thomas

Thomas of Brotherton (1300–38) **VII** 421

Thomas of Woodstock, earl of Buckingham (1377–97), of Essex (1380–97), duke of Gloucester (1385–97) **V** 185, 384, 399, 440, 447; *chevauchée* (1380) 146; hostility to French king 151; regent of England (1359–60) 212; protest against peace 248; library 258; marriage to Eleanor Bohun 268; college at Pleshey 305; constable of England 395; outburst against

Brembre 404–5; crushes rising at Billericay 418; outburst against Richard II (1384) 434; with Richard II at Eltham 443–4; parliament (1386) 445; commissioners (1386) 446; masses troops against Richard II 450; at Radcot Bridge 453; appellant 451, 454–61, 498; principal councillor 462–3; relations with Gaunt 464, 465; lieutenant of Ireland 468; rising on his estates 469; with Richard II in Ireland 471–3; relations with Richard 474, 485; arrest and imprisonment at Calais 478–9; appeal against 480; murder 481–2; his heirs 491; **VI** 3, 7, 22, 622; Trinity gild, Coventry 400

Thomists **VII** 254

Thomond **V** 41

Thomond, earl of **VIII** 471

Thomond, earldom **VIII** 465

Thompson, Francis **XIV** 330

Thompson, John, 1st Baron Haversham **X** 240

Thompson, Mr **XII** 141

Thompson, T. **XV** 167

Thomson, Sir Basil **XV** 261

Thomson, Sir J. J. **XIV** 551

Thomson, James (1700–48) **XI** 420, 421, 425–6; quoted 128, 136, 147

Thomson, William, Lord Kelvin **XIII** 563, 570–1; **XIV** 151

Thomworth, John **VIII** 85

Thoresby, John, bishop of St David's (1347–9), of Worcester (1349–52), archbishop of York (1352–73), keeper of the privy seal (1345–7) **V** 211, 220, 296, 299

Thoresby, John, of Warwick **VI** 580

Thorkell the Tall: invades England (1009) **II** 382; tries to save Archbishop Ælfheah 284; supports Æthelred II 384–6, 430; joins Cnut 388; earl of East Anglia 398–9, 416; regent of Eng-

Thorkell the Tall (*cont.*)
land 401–2; outlawry and reconciliation 401–2; son *see* Harold
Thorley, Robert, Calais treasurer, accounts **VI** 104
Thornburgh, William, of Meaburn **VI** 459
Thorndike, H. on religion and trade **X** 35
Thorne, Robert (d. 1527), merchant and geographical writer **VII** 225
Thorney (Thornig) (Cambs.): abbey **II** 452, 455; **III** 224; **V** 321
Thorney (Northants), Benedictine Abbey **VI** 682
Thorney Island (Bucks.) **II** 266
Thorneycroft, Peter **XV** 591
Thornhill, Sir James (1675–1734), painter **X** 401; **XI** 396, 401
Thornig *see* Thorney (Cambs.); Thorney Island (Bucks.)
Thornton (Lincs.), Austin Cluniac Abbey **VI** 301
Thornton, Samuel **XII** 354, 440
Thornton-le-Dale (Yorks.) **V** 526
Thornycroft, Hamo **XIV** 158
Thorold, Dr, bishop **XIV** 307
'Thorough', discredited by Puritans **IX** 212
Thorp, Sir Robert, Chancellor (1371–2) **V** 385
Thorp, Thomas, Commons Speaker (1453) **VI** 507, 509
Thorp, Sir William **V** 205, 215
Thorpe, John **VIII** 303
Thorpe, Sir Robert, chief justice and chancellor **III** 47
Thorpe, William, Wycliffite **VI** 97
Thorpland Close, Milton (Northants) **VI** 500
Thouars (Poitou) **III** 442; **IV** 91; **VI** 135; **V** 140
Thouars, Almaric de **III** 442
Thouars, count of *see* Guy
Thouars, Guy de, count of Brittany **III** 442
Thouars, Vicomte de **III** 453

Thouars family **IV** 87, 90, 91; later name of bastide of Baa 310
Thrace **Ia** 350; cult influence 712
Thrale's brewery **XII** 334
Thrandeston, John de **V** 120
Thrandheim **II** 405–6
Thrasea Paetus, P. Clodius **Ia** 164
Threckingham (Lincs.), monastery **II** 49
Three Ladies of London **VIII** 267
Threlkeld, Sir Henry **VI** 459
threshing machine **XII** 521
Thring, Edward **XIII** 486–7
Throckmorton, Elizabeth **VIII** 421
Throckmorton, Francis **VIII** 363, 376
Throckmorton, John **VI** 343, 416
Throckmorton, Sir Nicholas (1515–71) **VII** 540; **VIII** 64, 68, 90; war against French 46, 48–9; hears of Cumnor tragedy 51; dealings with huguenots 52–6, 60; treaty of Troyes 62; Condé accord 72; Darnley marriage 83–5; mission to Edinburgh 107–9
Throgmorton, Job **VIII** 202
Throxenby (N. Yorks.), manor **VI** 337
Thucydides **XIV** 7
Thugut, Austrian chancellor **XII** 369
Thunderclap **XV** 591
Thunderfield (Surrey), council **II** 349
Thunderidge (Herts.) **II** 99
Thunderley (Essex) **II** 99
Thunor, god **II** 98–9; centres of his cult 99
Thurbrand the Hold **II** 390, 509
Thurferth, Earl **II** 328
Thurgarton Priory **V** 526
Thuringia **IV** 660
Thuringians **II** 7
Thurkelby, Roger, judge **IV** 150
Thurketil, Earl **II** 325–6
Thurkill of Arden **II** 626
Thurloe, John **IX** 236, 258; **X** 58

Thurlow, Edward, 1st Baron (1731–1806) **XII** 57, 66, 156; attorney general 151; lord chancellor (1778–83) 169, 225, 243, 576; in opposition 266; lord chancellor (1783–92) 267, 300, 321, 578, 579

Thurmaston (Leics.) **Ib** 101, 183; map 4 xxxii; map 5 68; abbey **VI** 374

Thursley (Surrey) **II** 99

Thurstan, abbot of Glastonbury **II** 672–3; **III** 167

Thurstan, archbishop of York **III** 184, 271, 276

Thurstan, son of Rolf **II** 630

Thwaites, Robert **VI** 680

Thynne, Thomas, 3rd Viscount Weymouth and 1st marquis of Bath (1734–96) **XII** 65, 110; lord lieutenant of Ireland (1765) 577; secretary of state (1768–70) 129, 130, 133, 136, 576 — Spain 154; secretary of state (1775–79) 203, 213, 225, 576

Thynnes family **IX** 268

Tibberton (Worcs.) **III** 158

Tiber, river, water-mills **Ia** 632

Tiberius, Emperor **Ia** 52, 55, 80, 566; Druidism 677, 679; Germanicus 701

Tibet: Younghusband mission **XIV** 383; Anglo-Russian agreement 403

Tichborne claimant **XV** 311

Tickhill (Yorks.) **III** 25, 117; bishop of Durham arrested 352; **IV** 118

Tickhill (Yorks.), castle **II** 628; **III** 348, 355, 364; submission on Richard's return 368; **V** 66

Ticonderoga, battle **XII** 209

Tideman, Cistercian, bishop of Worcester **VI** 272

Tideman of Winchcombe, bishop of Llandaff (1393–5), of Worcester (1395–1401) **V** 474

Tierche **VI** 239

Tierney, G. **XIII** 56, 75

Tierney, George (1761–1830) **XII** 409, 451, 492; biography 409

Tifernum, sculpture **Ia** 601

Tihel de Helion **II** 649

Tijou, Jean **X** 397

Tilbury (Essex) **Ib** map 2 xxx; **V** 340; **VIII** 397

Tilbury, John of **III** 238

Tilea raises alarm **XV** 442

tiles **Ia** 603, 609; stamped 157, 174, 260, 529, 585; Austalis 507; tile factories 585, 631; distribution patterns 648

Tilgarsley (Oxon.) **V** 332

Till, river **VI** 45; **VII** 280, 281

Tillett, Ben (b. 1860): biography **XIV** 205, 222; wins by-election **XV** 95

Tillières (Eure) **III** 374

Tillotson, John, archbishop (1630–94) **X** 156, 362; **XI** 76

Tilney, Sir Philip **VII** 280

Tilsit, treaty (1807) **XII** 455, 463, 465, 496, 564

timber: buildings **Ia** 163, 233, 266, 602, 626; transport 563; industry 630–1; burials 696; coffins 700; Richborough 725; **XII** 522

The Times **XII** 541; **XIV** 144, 179, 181, 182, 446; in First World War **XV** 27; supports Lloyd George 66; leader offends Asquith 69; refuses letter from Lansdown 94; Maurice's letter to him 104; peace terms 127; death of Northcliffe 186; ownership 187; bought by Astor and Walter 193–4; anonymous article by Law 203; Delane 234; for top people 310; against Hoare-Laval plan 385; and Edward VIII 400; appeasement 418; supports dismemberment of Czechoslovakia 426; letter from Halifax 431; opposes intervention in Greece 590

Timperley, John **VI** 345

Timworth (Suffolk), Romano-Saxon pottery **Ib** 90 [fig. 7(f)] tin: Britain **Ia** 16, 44, 595, 630; Spain 636; mines **III** 83

Tinchebrai, battle **III** 99, 117, 120–1, 250

Tincommius, coins **Ia** 47, 56, 59

Tindal, Matthew (?1653–1733): *Christianity as old as the Creation* **XI** 84

Tinhead (Wilts.) **VI** 496

Tintagel Castle **V** 22, 435

Tintern Abbey **III** 290, 295

Tiowulfingacæstir *see* Littleborough

Tippecanoe, battle **XII** 550

Tipperary **III** 314; **V** 232; county **VI** 425; **VII** 125

Tiptoft, John, earl of Worcester, Northumberland (1427–70) **VI** 529; councillor (1461) and constable 538; executed 562; legal methods 549, 563; Oxford 562–3; marriage 563; treasurer (1452–5) 563; studies at Padua and speaks at Mantua 563; **VII** 125, 236

Tiptoft, Sir John, keeper of the wardrobe, treasurer (1408), then Lord **VI** 234, 253, 433, 435; Speaker (1406) 43, 82–3, 219, 562; Norman exchequer 191; steward of Gascony 222; Henry of Derby's servant 562

Tiptoft (Tibetot) family **VI** 562; Wrothe estates 562

Tipu **XII** 316, 382–4

Tirel, Walter, lord of Poix in Ponthieu **III** 113

Tirlemont **VIII** 345

Tirley (Staffs.), manor **VI** 320

Tirpitz, Admiral Alfred von **XIV** 258, 259, 262, 412, 461; building programme 462; envy of Britain 505

Tirpitz **XV** 506; damaged and sunk 564

Titanic **XIV** 511

Titchfield (Hants) **VI** 495; **VII** 596

Titchfield, Premonstratensian abbey **VI** 146

Titchwell (Norfolk) **VI** 288

tithes **II** 152, 153–7, 217; Cnut's letter (1027) 411; **IV** 464, 469; Elizabeth's exchange **VIII** 33

Titian (Tiziano Vecellio) **VII** 19, 601

Tito, Josip Broz, and Trieste **XV** 593

Titus, Emperor **Ia** 141, 156, 287; popularity in Britain 132

Tiverton (Devon) **XII** 54

Tiw, Tig, god **Ib** 77; **II** 98–9; centres of cult 99

Tizard, Sir Henry **XV** 390

tobacco **VIII** 274; **IX** 327, 337, 344, 346; industry **X** 299, 331, 339; trade **XII** 20

Tobago **IX** 337; **X** 327; British capture of **XII** 75; retention at Peace of Paris 85; French gain at peace (1783) 255; returned to France (1802) 410; retained by Britain (1814) 562

Tobias, bishop of Rochester **II** 181

Tobruk (Tubruq) (Libya): taken **XV** 524; held 525; retreat to 541; lost 554

Tock, Roger **III** 33

Tocotes, Sir Roger, comptroller of the household (1492) **VII** 650

Today and Tomorrow series **XV** 260

Todd, Anthony **XII** 61, 285

Todeschini, Francesco (Piccolomini) *see* Pius III, Pope

Tofeceaster *see* Towcester (Northants)

Togodumnus **Ia** 67–8, 70, 83, 85

Togoland conquered **XV** 23

Toki, son of Outi **II** 626

Tokio bay **XV** 598

Toland, John (1670–1722) **X** 386; **XI** 89

Toledo, Council of **Ia** 410

Toledo (Spain) **III** 245, 246

Toledo, treaties: (1254) **IV** 118, 120; (1539) **VII** 403

Toleration Acts **X** 154, 291; **XI** 292

toleration, religious **IX** 211–12; **XI**

6-8, 69, 74-5, 100-1, 170; in Ireland 292

toll and team, taxes **II** 497-8, 636; **III** 75-6; *see also* jurisdiction, private

Tolpuddle Martyrs **XIII** 132

tombs *see* burials; cenotaphs; mausolea

tombstones: Favonius Facilis **Ia** 94, 699-700; Classicianus 122, 630; evidence from 550, 729; Victor 696-7; bought ready-made 697

Tomen-y-Mur, fort and amphitheatre **Ia** 579

Tomes, Sir John **XIII** 620

Tomsætan **II** 41

Tomson, Robert **VII** 557, 561

Tonbridge, castle **III** 101; **IV** 187

Tone, Theobald Wolfe **XII** 395, 399

Tong (Salop), Vernon's tomb **VI** 650

Tongaland **XIV** 227

Tonge, Israel **X** 93

tonnage and poundage **IX** 42, 82, 92, 103

Tonneins **IV** 294

Tonnerre, count of *see* Louis, count of Tonnere

Tonson, Jacob **X** 358

Tonypandy discredits Churchill **XV** 466

Tooke, John Horne (1736-1812) **XII** 132, 139-41, 360

Tooke, William **XII** 132

Tooley, – **X** 258

Tooley, John **VII** 553

tools **Ia** 623, 638

toothpaste **XV** 52

Tooting (Surrey) **V** 329

Topcliffe **VIII** 137

Topcliffe (N. Yorks.), castle and manor **VI** 9, 59, 60, 337

Topcliffe, Richard **VIII** 150

Topsham (Devon), harbour **Ia** 95-7

Torbay **X** 138

Torcy, J. B., marquis de (1665-1746) **X** 217; **XI** 158

Toresbi (Lincs.) **III** 188

Torhtmund, minister of King Æthelred of Northumbria **II** 90

Tories: party name becomes current **X** 101; political views 181; and British naval power 223-4; during last four years of Queen Anne 229-33; moderate and extreme (1710-14) 238-9; fear of George I 242; not a Jacobite party 243; Hanover 243-5; and Anglican Church **XI** 77, 82, 150; eclipse 154, 155-6; and Jacobites 151-2, 160, 168-9; policy 3-4, 150-1; relations with Whigs 169; **XII** 16; definition 58, 441

Torigni, Robert of, abbot of Mont-St-Michel **III** 248, 249

Torksey (Turecesieg) (Lincs.) **II** 251, 388, 733

Toron, lord of *see* Philip

Toronto **XII** 553

Torpe, John, Carmelite **VI** 297

Torregiano **VII** 228, 230, 592, 601

Torres Vedras **XII** 486

Torricelli **X** 43

Torrington, earl of *see* Herbert, Arthur

Tortuga, island of **X** 326

torture, use of **VIII** 149, 210

Toscanelli, cartographer **VII** 224

Tostig, son of Earl Godwine **II** 565; earl of Northumbria 570-2; married kinswoman of count Baldwin of Flanders (Judith) 565; Northumbrians revolt against 547, 579; escorts Malcolm of Scotland to visit King Edward 570; Welsh campaign 576; expelled from England 579; harries English coast 586-7; joins Harold Hardrada 588; killed 590

Totnes (Tottaness) (Devon) **II** 532, 733

Toto, Antonio **VII** 601

Tottaness *see* Totnes (Devon)

Tottel, Richard **VII** 587

Tottenhall (Middx.) **V** 518

Tottenham (Middx.) **II** 391; **V** 337

Touchet, James, 7th Baron Audley (1465?–97) **VII** 141, 142, 143

Toul **III** 452; **VII** 535

Toulouse **III** campaign (1159) 200, 202, 208, 276; Henry's acquisition 323, 325–6; heretics 340; Richard's campaign 344, 376; **IV** 87–8; wine merchants 306; conference (1280) 253; **V** 109, 254; university 144; **VI** 70; **VII** 220; university 348; **X** 64, 206, 215; British expedition (1793) **XII** 367; French fleet scuttled **XV** 560

Toulouse, counts of *see* Raymond

Toulouse, Jeanne of, wife of Alphonse of Poitiers (d. 1271) **IV** 272

Touques (Calvados) **VI** 171; river 171, 174

Touraine **III** 318, 345, 365, 374; allegiance to Arthur of Brittany 378, 381; loss to France 440–1; **VI** 135, 140, 142, 180, 200; county 240 **VII** 105

Touraine, duke of *see* Arundel, Lord

Tourcoign, battle (1794) **XII** 368

Tourelles, Orléans fort **VI** 245, 246

Tourn, sheriff's **IV** 68

Tournai (Belgium): royal burial **Ia** 494; mill 656; **III** 467; **V** 129, 165, 256; **VI** 263, 573; **VII** 119, 120, 279, 284; surrendered to French 308; Anglo-Imperial alliance (1522) 311; treaty of Madrid 316; **VIII** 355; **X** 219

Tournai, bishopric of **VII** 294

Tournai, Stephen of **III** 206

Tournai fonts **III** 263

tournaments **III** 24–5; **IV** 515, 516, 770; Lord Edward 159

Tourneur, Cyril **VIII** 300, 301; **IX** 392

Tours **III** 244, 318, 346; Richard's pilgrimage 359; Arthur recognized 378; fall of garrison (1204) 383; **IV** 91; **VI** 474; merchant's dispensation for Anne Neville 564; traders in England 565; **VII** 154, 272

Tours, abbey of St Martin of **II** 189

Tours, archbishop of **III** 356

Tours, bishop of *see* St Martin

Tours, council (1163) **III** 197, 219

Toury (Eure-et-Loire) **VI** 250

Toussaint l'Ouverture **XII** 370, 337, 471

Tout, T. F. **XV** 200

Tovi the Proud **II** 413, 414, 423

Towcester (Tofeceaster) (Northants): head **Ia** 692; **Ib** map 2 xxx; **II** 327–8

Tower of London **IV** 52, 687, 716; justiciar's custody 20, 48; Earl Ranulf's demonstration against 24–5; Hubert de Burgh 50, 65; Henry takes refuge 76; during the years (1258–67) 187, 188, 203, 213 —Hugh Bigod made justiciar 137 —Hugh le Despenser justiciar 163 —Henry takes refuge 163, 165 —Earl Simon takes possession 176, 180 —fortified against rebels 214; Edward's procession from 369; Gruffydd detained 399; John and Edward Baliol in (1297–9) 615; Douglas's imprisonment and death 685; Henry of Keighley's captivity 704; William Wallace's execution 712; records in 277; **VIII** 3, 45, 137, 149, 151, 275; **IX** 99, 101, 148; *see also* London, Tower of

towers **Ia** 246, 262–3, 291, 325, 540–4; *see also* watchtowers

Towerson, William **VII** 561

Towgood, Michaijah (1700–92) **XI** 86

town councils *see* municipal councils

Town and Country Planning, Ministry of **XV** 568

town life: advantages to Britons **Ia** 159–60, 237–8, 596–7; Trier 302, 496–7; decline in prosperity? 397, 411–12; Noricum under barbar-

million mark **XIV** 298; tendency
to substitute industrial for craft
organization 300–1; tendency to
lower productivity 501–2

trade union legislation (1871) **XIV**
23, 132; (1875) 35, 133; *see also*
Taff Vale Case; Trade Disputes
Act

Trade Unions **XIII** 72–4, 128–9,
156–9, 612–17; Amalgamated
Society of Engineers 157–8, 613;
Amalgamated Society of Carpenters and Joiners 158–9, 613;
General Trades Union 128;
Grand General Union 128;
Grand National Consolidated
Union 129, 131–2; Miners'
Association 156–7, 614; National
Association of United Trades
157; Trades Union Congress 615;
declare industrial truce **XV** 28;
and munitions 38–9; changed
outlook of leaders 141, 239;
increased membership 142; effect
of general strike 248; Labour
party 265

Trades Union Congress: makes
statement on war aims **XV** 96;
sets up general council 142; *Daily
Herald* 187, 251; Communists not
barred 200; condemns Dawes
plan 216; civil servants' union
forbidden to affiliate to 250; not
informed by Baldwin 361; ready
to restrain Italy 381; dominated
by foreign affairs 408; relaxes
craft restrictions 413

Traelborg **Ib** map 5 68

Trafalgar, battle (1805) **X** 166; **XII**
432; **XV** 63

Trafalgar Square, disorders (1886)
XIV 100; (1887) 180–1; signs of
armistice **XV** 114

Tragedy of Biron **VIII** 301

Traietto, duchess of *see* Gonzaga,
Julia

Trailbaston **IV** 345–6

train-bands **IX** 90, 91–2, 96, 131

Trajan, Emperor **Ia** 154–70; Dacian
Wars 74, 165–6, 526; origins and
accession 154–6; traditional
values 164, 681; neo-republican
patronage and appointments 164,
170; Pliny 164, 219; loss of Scotland 165–7, 198; frontier policy
166–7, 169, 193; Pliny and fire
brigades 344; Eastern dreams
363–4; Flavius Longinus, civil
career 511; Pliny and prosecution
of Priscus and Classicus 533–4;
Pliny's control of local administration 535–6, 576–8; Pliny and
Christians 716

Trajan story **IV** 143

Tramecourt (Pas-de-Calais) **VI** 154

trams, peak and decline **XV** 303–4

translations, Elizabethan **VIII**
287–8

transport **X** 51–2; **XII** 26, 518

Transport, Ministry of: created **XV**
129; railways 141; abolition proposed 184; amalgamated with
Ministry of Shipping 510

transport and communications **Ia**
359, 562–70, 640, 645, 653–4; **XI**
122, 125; roads 46, 102–5, 118,
281; water 105, 118; bridges 281,
382, 391; *see also* communications

transport workers **XV** 140–1; call off
strike 146; union 478

transportation **X** 344; **XIII** 385–7,
469, 471

transportation plan **XV** 580

Transvaal: under President Burgers
XIV 58; annexed by Shepstone
59; revolts and regains independence 69; ambiguity over its subsequent treaty status 69, 249; Uit-
lander problem 226; Jameson
Raid 231; alliance with Orange
Free State 233; armaments 246;
Edgar murder followed by Uit-
lander Petition 247; Bloemfontein
Conference 248; subsequent
negotiations until the war 248–9;
ultimatum to Great Britain 251;

Transvaal (*cont.*)
 formal ceremony of annexation 256; Treaty of Vereeniging 347–8; self-government granted (1907) 390; entrance into Union of South Africa 390
Trapani **IV** 232, 253
Traprain, Haddington **VI** 37
Traprain Law, treasure **Ia** 386, 729
travel **Ia** 435, 541–2, 565–71; danger 379, 384, 455; pilgrimages 596, 739; **XI** 403–4; *see also* communications
Travers, Walter **VIII** 195, 458
Treante *see* Trent, river
treason **Ia** 80, 343–4, 377, 396, 411; changes in law **X** 184; *see also* persecution
Treasonable Practices Act **XII** 360
Treasury **III** 9–10, 414–17; imposes exchange control **XV** 456; limits dollar spending 462; lays bases for level economy 465
Treasury, 1st lord of **XI** 33
Treasury Agreement **XV** 29, 38, 39, 413
Treasury Board **X** 186
Treasury, Old English **II** 643; *see also* Winchester
treaties: Caesar's agreement with Britons **Ia** 37; Caledonians 225, 230; Constans? 352, 360; reliance on barbarian federates against Huns 482; Stilicho and Alaric 425; Theodosius the Great? 405; Visigoths unreliable 476; **IV** 84–7; and sworn compacts 48, 152; between European princes: Arras (1482), Louis XI and Maximilian **VII** 85; Arras (1499), Louis XII and Philip 152; Barcelona (1529), Clement VII and Charles V 319, 328; Blois (1504), Louis XII and Ferdinand 154, 177; Crêpy (1544), Francis I and Charles V 409; Frankfurt (1489), Charles VIII and Maximilian 99; Granada (1500), Louis XII and

Ferdinand 153; Lyons (1501, 1503), Louis XII, Charles and Maximilian 153–4; Madrid (1526), Francis I and Charles V 316; Narbonne (1493), Charles VIII and Ferdinand 110; Noyons (1516), Francis I and Charles V 306–7; Nice (1538), truce Francis I and Charles V 341, 402; Orthez (1513), truce Louis XII and Ferdinand 276; Orthez (1514 renewed) 283; Passau (1522), Charles V and German princes 535; Sablé (1488), Charles VIII and Francis of Brittany 88; Senlis (1439), Charles VIII and Maximilian 110; Toledo (1539), Francis I and Charles V 403; Francis I's treaty with Turks (1536) 341; Aix-la-Chapelle (1748) **XI** 213, 264–5, 270, 315, 327 — ill-kept truce 334, 347; Anglo-Prussian (1757–60) 361; Anglo-Russian (1742) 240 — (1755) 350–1; Baden (1714) 165, 172; Barrier (1713) 162 — (1715) 196 — (1716) 165; Belgrade (1739) 233; Berlin (1742) 240, 246, 249; Carlowitz (1699) 233; Charlottenburg (1723) 197–8; Dresden (1745) 261; Dunkirk demolition 372; Franco-Spanish (1761) 369–70; Union of Frankfurt (1744) 249; Peace of Füssen (1745) 261; Hanover (1725) 198; Convention of Klein-Schnellendorf (1741) 238; Convention of Klosterseven (1757) 21, 360; Limerick (1691) 290; Münster (1648) 196; Neuhaus (1750) 344; Nystad (1721) 176; Convention of the Pardo (1739) 209; Paris (1763) 213, 330, 372–5 — Preliminaries of 368–70, 371–3; Passarowitz (1718) 193, 233; Penn's treaty with North American Indians (1681) 320; Quadruple Alliance (1718) 173,

Trefnant, John, Doctor of Civil Law, bishop of Hereford (1389–1404) **V** 301; **VI** 12, 271, 666

Tregonwell, Sir John (d. 1565) **VII** 377

Trek, the Great *see* Cape Colony

Trelawney, Sir Jonathan, 3rd baronet (1650–1721), bishop **XI** 183

Trematon Castle (Corn.) **VI** 498

Tremellio, Immanuel **VII** 516, 574

Trémoille, Georges de la **VI** 241

Trench, Richard Le Poer *see* Le Poer Trench

Trenchard, Sir John **X** 184

Trenchard, Lord: offensive air strategy **XV** 96, 231, 310; a cavalry officer 392

Trenchemer, Alan **III** 434

Trent, council **VII** 402, 481, 482, 547; **VIII** 27, 88

Trent, river **Ia** 95, 101, 544, 564, 610; **Ib** xxvii, 175–6, 181–2, 185–6; map 2 xxx; map 4 xxxii; **II** 38, 40–1, 285, 385–6; battle 85; **III** 79, 80, 417; **V** 11, 22, 24, 67, 77, 136, forests south of 153; tax-collectors for north and south districts 164, 213; defence funds north of 222; 'kings of arms' north and south 265; wool staples 351; **VI** 57; **VII** 28, 35, 36, 385, 386; **XV** 167

Trent, treaty between Maximilian and Louis (1501) **VII** 154

Trent case *see* United States

Trentham Priory (Staffs.), canons **III** 447

Trentholme Drive, York, cemetery **Ia** 551

Trenton, battle **XII** 208

Tresco (Scilly Islands) **III** 433

Tresham, Isabel **VI** 500

Tresham, Thomas, of Sywell **VI** 417, 451, 508; executed 569

Tresham, William **VI** 500

Tresilian, Sir Robert **V** 419, 448, 449–51, 452; condemned for treason 457–8

Tressell, Robert **XV** 352

Trevelyan, Sir Charles **XIII** 621; **XV** 174

Trevelyan, Charles P. **XV** 91, 198; education 211, 279–80

Trevelyan, G. M., writes George V's speech **XV** 378

Trevelyan, Sir G. O.: biography **XIV** 66, 76, 88; resigns over home rule 97; rejoins Gladstone 176

Trevelyan, John **VI** 497, 501, 508; under-sheriff of Cornwall (1459–60) 498; attainted but pardoned (1462) 498

Treveri **Ia** 126, 590, 713

Trevisa, John **III** 250; **V** 524

Trevisano, Andrea, Venetian ambassador in England **VII** 150

Trevithick, R. **XIII** 44

Trianon decrees (1812) **XII** 468

tribal hidage **Ib** 42–3, 141; **II** 43, 295–7, 300–1, 648

tribes, British: use of term **Ia** 7, 45; Roman attitudes towards 23, 40; pre-conquest 40–8; surrender to Claudius 86; subdued by Vespasian 92; disarming of 101; constitution as *civitates* 111, 115; place-names 590; *see also civitas* and individual tribes by name

tribunes, military: *augusticlavii* and *laticlavii* **Ia** 73; Titus 132; Late Empire 466–7

tribute **Ia** 37, 39, 42, 50, 51; aristocratic exchange 58

triclinium see dining rooms

Trie (Vexin) **III** 124

Triennial Act **IX** 102–3; **X** 57 149; bills 149–50

Trier: imperial capital **Ia** 302–4, 370, 375, 400, 402–3; mint 310, 429, 433, 446, 479; Basilica 325; buildings 326; administrative centre 339, 354, 517–18; communications with Milan,

Ravenna 425; shift to Arles 429, 449; sacked 456; surviving late 479, 495–7; temples 590; wine 654; mill 656; cults 666, 668, 671; bishop's palace/church 725; **X** 211

Trieste **XV** 161–2; Joyce 179; Tito 593

Trilleck, John, bishop of Hereford (1344–60) **V** 276, 278, 279

Trim, liberty **IV** 517, 564; **V** 42, 232, 471; **VII** 125, 130

Trincomalee (Ceylon): British restoration **XII** 255; British capture 371

Trinidad **IX** 337

Trinity College, Cambridge, and Russell **XV** 52; *see also* Cambridge University, colleges

Trino, treaty **VI** 162, 167

trinoda necessitas **II** 289–90

Trinovantes: struggle with Catuvellauni **Ia** 35, 37, 43, 47, 55; Caesar's friendship 57; allied with Iceni 101; seizure of property 104; join Boudiccan revolt 114, 119; aristocratic burial 598; wine trade 652

tripartite agreement (Glyn Dŵr, Mortimer, Northumberland) **VI** 47

Triple Alliance (1788) **X** 73–6; **XII** 294–8, 368, 434; origin **XIV** 84; restored **XV** 140; not invoked by NUR 141; prepares to support miners 144; fails to do so 145–6

Tripoli **X** 172; bombarded **XV** 526; Rommel abandons 559

Trithemius **VII** 237

triumphs **Ia** 394; triumphal insignia 84, 94, 97, 106; triumphal monuments 86, 281

Trivet, Sir Thomas **V** 432

Trokelowe, John, on Gaveston, **V** 22; on Bannockburn 39

Trollope, Sir Andrew **VI** 526; attainder (1461) 539

Trollope, Anthony **XIII** 17; bio-

graphy 556; novels 531, 556–7

Tromp, Marten Harpurson **IX** 218, 222, 223

Trondheim, proposed attack on **XV** 471

Trondhjem, archbishop of **III** 88

Tropenell, Thomas **VI** 462–3

Trotsky, Leo Davidovich, expects Anglo-American war **XV** 255

Trotskyites, prosecuted **XV** 566

Trotter, Mr **XII** 418

Troubadours and politics **IV** 95–6, 99, 100, 102

trousers **Ia** 77

Troutbeck (Cumbria) **V** 366

Troutbeck (Westmorland) **VI** 497

Trowbridge (Wilts.): castle **III** 138; **VI** 365

Troyes (Aube) **VI** 177, 181, 184; preliminaries 183; terms forecast 184–6; oath 257, 260; régime 263

Troyes, bishopric **Ia** 462

Troyes, Chrétien de **VI** 657

Troyes, Jean de Dinteville, Bailli of: French ambassador **VII** 341

Troyes, treaty **VI** 188, 189, 194, 217, 248; **VIII** 62

Trubleville, Henry de **IV** 98, 318

Trubleville, Hugh de **IV** 275

Truman, Harry: anti-Soviet views 528; decides to use atomic bomb 589, 601; becomes president 593; no loan to Russia 594; ends lend-lease 599

Trumpington (Cambs.) **V** 302

Truro **III** 76, 401

Truso, port **II** 274

Trussell, Sir John **V** 521; **VI** 128

Trussell, Sir William **V** 87, 90–1, 154, 165; **VI** 455

Trusts and combines **XIV** 283–4

tsar *see* Alexander II, Alexander III, Nicholas II

Tuam, archbishop of **III** 308

tuberculosis **XV** 164

Tubney (Berks.) **III** 18

Tuccianus **Ia** 251

Tuchet, George, 11th Lord Audley **IX** 109

Tucker –, clothmaker **VII** 462

Tucker, Dean Josiah (Joseph) (1712–99) **XI** 95; **XII** 53, 253, 329; biography 329

Tuda, bishop of Lindisfarne **II** 124

Tuddenham, Sir Thomas **VI** 461, 491, 547; Household treasurer 514

Tudela, battle (1808) **XII** 460

Tudela, Benjamin of **III** 95

Tudor, Edmund, earl of Richmond (1430?–56), father of Henry VII **VII** 48

Tudor, Goronwy, son of Tudor ap Goronwy **VI** 39

Tudor, Henry, earl of Richmond, given Herbert's lands **VI** 562; Poole, Plymouth landings 626; marriage contract 627; Urswick to Charles VIII 628; driven to Brittany 639; Milford Haven landing 641; Shrewsbury 642; Talbot joins, Shrewsbury surrenders 642; Stanley's Atherstone meeting 643; Bosworth 643–4; White Moors camp 644; Northumberland's homage 644–5

Tudor, Jasper, earl of Pembroke and duke of Bedford (1431?–95) **VI** 422, 478, 507, 511, 516; Welsh diplomacy 511; Mortimer's Cross defeat 524; return at Reademption 527; aid to Lancastrians 527, 530; Bamburgh 529; attainder (1461) 539; Herbert lands 562; neglects Warwick's summons (1471) 567; Brittany 639; **VII** 48, 51, 61, 73, 108; joins Henry VII's council 56; crushes northern rising (1486) 67; lieutenant in Ireland (1486) 72, 651

Tudor, Owen: and royal house of **IV** 391; beheaded **VI** 524

Tudor, Rhys ap **VI** 44, 65; death 65; *see also* Rhys ap Tudor

Tudor, William ap **VI** 44

Tudor ab Ednyfed, seneschal of Llywelyn ap Gruffydd **IV** 391

Tudor family **VII** 47, 190, 230, 234, 385; achievement in the state 562–7; responsible for form of Church of England 567–9

Tuesley (Surrey) **II** 99

Tufnell, Mr, MP **XII** 227

Tugela, battles **XIV** 253, 254, 255

Tuidi *see* Tweed, river

Tuihanti **Ia** 667

Tuihanti cives **Ib** 77

tuitio **IV** 466, 492–4

Tull, Jethro (1674–1741) **XI** 275; **XII** 32

Tullibardine, one of the 'seven men of Moidard' **XI** 252

Tully, Robert, bishop of St David's **VI** 539

Tunberht, bishop of Hexham **II** 138

Tunbridge Wells **X** 409

Tungrians **Ia** 148, 683; **Ib** 75

Tunis: captured by Charles V (1535) **VII** 341; **XIV** 84; in Middle East command **XV** 523; Germans control 560; Rommel defends 5, 63

Tunis, villa nr **Ia** 452

tunnage and poundage **V** 221, 362

Tunstall, Cuthbert, bishop of London (1522–30), bishop of Durham (1530–52, 1553–9) **VII** 37, 248, 257, 259, 552; treaty of Noyon (1516) 307; Wolsey sends to Madrid (1525) 315; disapproves of Tyndale 343, 345; president of council 386; president of Council of the North (1537) 393; fall of Cromwell (1540) 414; deprived (1552) 518; released from King's bench on Mary's accession 530; Mary's council 531; keeper of the privy seal (1523) 647; master of the rolls (1516) 648; **VIII** 20

Tunstall, Sir Richard **VI** 529, 582; master of the mint 561

tutors **Ia** 507

Tuxford (Notts.) **VI** 510

Tweed, river **Ia** 144–5; **Ib** 175, 199; map 4 xxxii; **II** 615; **III** 265, 266, 270, 280, 283; English frontier 282; **V** 35; **VII** 140, 147, 313

Tweeddale, John, 4th marquis of (d. 1762) **XI** 33, 253, 272

Tweedmouth, Lord **XIV** 406, 407

Tweedmouth Castle **III** 282

Tweng, Robert **IV** 45–6

Twente **Ib** 77

Tweoneam *see* Christchurch (Hants)

Twickenham (Middx.) **II** 204; **V** 414

Twizel Bridge **VII** 281, 282

Twyford (Bucks.) **VI** 672

Twyn, John **X** 28

Twyning (Glos.) **III** 412

Tybetot, Robert **IV** 196; justiciar of west Wales (1281) 415, 422, 436; and Rhys ap Mareddud 438–40; sent to Gascony (1294) 441, 649

Tyccea, abbot of Glastonbury **II** 174

Tye, Dr Christopher (composer) **VII** 479, 589; **VIII** 305

Tyes, Sir Henry **V** 73

Tyler, Wat **V** 253, 338, 408–19, 420, **VII** 142

Tylor, E. B. **XIII** 577

Tymperle, John, of Hintlesham (Suffolk) **VI** 419

Tyndale, honour **IV** 587, 600, 610

Tyndale, Talbot lands **VI** 337

Tyndale, William, translator of the Bible (d. 1536) **V** 524; **VII** 352, 423, 550, 570; Wolsey and the divorce 322, 348; education 343; translation completed 343; controversial works 344; reception of New Testament and burning

344–5; More's attack 346–7; his Bible 397, 429, 432

Tyndall, John **XIV** 145, 162

Tyne, franchise **VI** 134

Tyne, river: Agricola's crossing **Ia** 144, 194; frontier 166, 176, 180, 202; fourth-century defences 383–4, 392, 511; crossing to Rhine 563; Tyne-Forth Province 612; **Ib** 175, 198; map 4 xxxii; **III** 165, 274; **V** 40, 349; **VI** 63, 528

Tynedale, franchise **III** 274; **VIII** 139

Tynedale, Sir Walter of **V** 188

Tynely, Robert, of Ludgershall **VI** 419

Tynemouth (Northumb.), church **II** 678; **III** 109; **V** 25, 87

Tyneside, Depression **XV** 352

Tyninghame, Haddingtonsh, monastery **II** 85, 357

type-fossils, type-sites **Ia** 7

tyranni **Ia** 462, 468–9, 471–2, 480

Tyrconnel **III** 308; **VII** 125

Tyrconnel, earls of *see* O'Donnell; Talbot, Richard

Tyre, archbishop of **IV** 12

Tyrell, Sir James **VI** 624, 632, 635, 641

Tyrell, Thomas **VI** 451, 635

Tyrell, William, Winchelsea rector **VI** 289

Tyrol **VII** 306, 447; **XV** 50, 161–2, 388

Tyrone **III** 308; **V** 42, 470; boundary **XV** 162

Tyrone, earls of *see* Beresford, Marcus; O'Neill, Con; O'Neill, Hugh

Tyronne, earldom **VIII** 462

Tyrrell, Anthony **VIII** 178

Tyrrell, Sir James, lieutenant of Guisnes **VII** 98, 99, 167, 168–70; executed (1502) 168

U

U-boats: Germans restrain use **XV**
43; begin unrestricted war 83;
campaign against 103; admiralty's confidence against 461; sink-
ings 462; attacks 504–5; sink *Ark
Royal* and *Barham* 530; Americans
sink 531; victory 564, 578; ineffective during invasion of France
581

Ubaldi, Frederico, duke of Urbino;
Garter offered by Edward IV **VI**
574

Ubba **II** 246

Udall, John **VIII** 204

Udall, Nicholas **VII** 512, 534; **VIII**
296

Udimore **IV** 681, 686

Uffeln, Sophia Caroline von, countess of Platen 'the younger' **XI**
152, 177, 185

Ufford, Isabella, countess of Suffolk
VI 472

Ufford, Robert de, earl of Suffolk
(1337–69) **V** 148, 153, 256

Ufford, William de, earl of Suffolk
(1370–82) **V** 260, 389, 394,
428–9

Uganda **XIV** 188, 193, 212

Uganda Railway **XIV** 381

Ughtred v. Musgrave **V** 206

Uguccione, Francis, cardinal and
archbishop of Bordeaux **VI** 91,
92, 109

Uhtred, earl of Northumbria **II** 390,
417–19, 509

Uhtred, John, of Boldon **V** 511, 513,
519

Uhtred, under-king of Hwicce,
charter quoted **II** 292

Ukraine: Poles attempt to conquer
XV 143; Sub-Carpathian, seized
by Hungary 439, 441

Uley, temple **Ia** 688

Ulf, bishop of Dorchester **II** 464–5,
568

Ulf, Danish earl: married Estrith,
daughter of King Swein **II** 382;
regent of Denmark 402; rebellion
and death 403–4

Ulf, Margery Kemp's husband **VI**
686

Ulf, son of Harold, king of England
III 100

Ulfila **Ia** 446

Ulfkell Snilling **II** 380–1, 383, 392

Ulfketel, abbot of Crowland **II** 671

Ullerston, Richard, canon of Salisbury **VI** 278, 305–7; *Petitiones . . .
ecclesiae militantis* 93; knighthood
treatise 93

Ulloa, San Juan de **VIII** 125, 128–9

Ullswater, Lord *see* Lowther, J. W.

Ulm **VII** 103, 110

Ulpian **Ia** 523, 590–1

Ulpius Marcellus **Ia** 210–11, 225,
250

Ulster **III** 311, 312, 313, 315; Anglo-
Irish liberty and shire **IV** 564; **V**
228, 229, 232, 470, 472; **VI** 425;
earldom 465; **VII** 125, 128, 130,
131; **VIII** 462, 464–5; **IX**
108–10, 113–14, 135, 161–2;
X 322; **XIV** 541–2; Agar-
Robartes's amendment to exclude four Ulster counties 454;
Covenant 456; Government's
eventual proposal 476; exclusion
from Home Rule Act **XV** 16;
Asquith's promise to 17; alleged
pogrom 30; proposed exclusion
51, 71–2; assurances 83;
obstinacy 103; no Sinn Fein victory 154; Government of Ireland
Act 156; boundary with Free
State 158; separates from Free
State 159; brings advantage to
Conservatives 160; Churchill
challenges 475; *see also* Carson

V

576

Valerius Crescens Fulvianus **Ia** 251
Valerius Marcellus, Sex. **Ia** 224–5
Valerius Maximus **III** 235
Valerius Messalla Corvinus, C. **Ia** 61
Valerius Pudens, C. **Ia** 227
Valery, Érard de **IV** 285, 312
validissimae gentes **Ia** 92–3
Valla, Lorenzo **VII** 239
Valladolid **VII** 94
Valle Crucis, Cistercian monastery in Powys **IV** 389, 410
Vallum **Ia** 178, 180–1, 183, 191, 195; causeways removed 202; civil settlements 247, 511; military zone removed 277; *see also* Hadrian's Wall
Valmont (Seine-Inf.) **VI** 157, 163
Valois **VI** 248
Valois, Charles, count of, second son of Philip III: declared king of Aragon by the pope **IV** 254–5; receives Angou and Maine 272; and the Gascon trouble 646; commands French troops in Gascony (1295) 649; **V** 109
Valois, Elizabeth **VIII** 37
Valois, Henry, duke of Anjou *see* Henry III, king of France
Valois, house of **VII** 319, 320, 328, 341, 559; quarrel with Habsburgs and Maximilian's death 307–8
Valois, Jeanne de, treaty for marriage with Edward Baliol (1295) **IV** 612, 613
Valois, Margaret **VIII** 74
Valor ecclesiasticus **VII** 371–2
Vampage, John **VI** 416
Van de Velde Willem (father and son) **X** 400
Van Dyck, Sir Anthony (1599–1641) **IX** 374–5, 377, 381; **X** 400; **XI** 399
Van Leemput, Remigius, his daughter **X** 401
Van Nost, John **X** 397
Van Schuurman, Anna Maria **X** 417

Van Somer, Paul **IX** 374
Vanaken (van Haecken), Joseph (?1699–1749) **XI** 400
Vanbrugh, Sir John, poet and architect (1664–1726) **X** 358, 370; architecture 390, 391, 395; **XI** 399, 402, 412
Vancouver Island, British settlement **XII** 296
Vandalia Company **XII** 198
vandalism **VIII** 33–4
Vandals: prisoners **Ia** 282; Stilicho 416; attacks by 426, 432; Africa 473; defeat by 481; sack Rome 488; **Ib** 79, 81
Vane, Hon. Anne (1705–36) **XI** 148
Vane, Henry, 1st earl of Darlington (?1705–58) **XI** 106
Vane, Sir Henry, secretary of state **IX** 93, 100, 102
Vane, Sir Henry, the younger: committee of eight **IX** 118; against established Church 173; the Rump 174, 243; ecclesiastical jurisdiction 190; republican 238, 243; expelled 253; trade commissioner 292, 347; death **X** 4
Vane, Sir Ralph **VII** 492
'Vanessa', Swift's; Vanhomrigh, Esther *see* Swift's 'Vanessa'
Vange (Essex) **II** 293
Vanloo, J. B. (1684–1745), painter **XI** 406
Vannes (Morbihan) **V** 131; **VI** 628
Vannes, Peter **VII** 238
Vansittart, Henry (1732–70), governor of Bengal **XII** 160, 165, 166, 492; biography 160
Vansittart, Nicholas (1766–1851), 1st Baron Bexley: biography **XII** 492; chancellor of Exchequer (1812) 492, 498, 583
Vansittart, Sir Robert: wishes to resist Germany **XV** 405; drafts proposal for Anglo-French union 487
Vargas, Don Juan de **VIII** 357

Venner, Thomas **X** 22

Venta Belgarum see Winchester

Venta Icenorum see Caistor-by-Norwich

Ventadour, count of **VI** 244

Venturini, Borghese **VIII** 122

Venus and Adonis **VIII** 288

Venutius **Ia** 108, 133, 136–7, 199

Vera Cruz **VIII** 125

Veranius, Quintus **Ia** 109–10

Vercelli, council **II** 467, 662

Vercelli manuscript **II** 199

Vercingetorix **Ia** 12, 32, 37, 47, 239; Caratacus compared 105–6; capture 669; Druids 677; execution 680

Vercovicium see Housesteads

Verden *see* Bremen

Verdun **VII** 535; Germans attack **XV** 60, 80

Vere, Aubrey de **III** 161

Vere, Aubrey de, death (Feb. 1462) **VI** 563

Vere, earls of Oxford, family **VI** 503

Vere, Sir Francis **VIII** 417–18, 419, 426

Vere, Francis, daughter of 5th earl of Oxford, wife of Henry Howard, earl of Surrey **VII** 420

Vere, George de **VI** 571

Vere, Lord Hugh de **V** 10

Vere, John de, earl of Oxford (1331–60) **V** 256, 260

Vere, John de, 12th earl of Oxford **VI** 211, 486, 538, 563

Vere, John de, 13th earl of Oxford (1443–1513) **VI** 562, 567, 568, 571, 572; imprisoned 640; Tudor invasion 641, 644; allegiance to monarch **VII** 14; James Blount, servant 50–1; clothing at Henry VII's coronation 55; joins Henry VII's council 56; becomes lord admiral (1485) 57, 650; constable of the Tower 57; king's lieutenant 73, 209, 215; Henry's letter to 97; commander of war in France 108; lord high steward 165

Vere, Richard de, 11th earl of Oxford **VI** 114, 571

Vere, Sir Robert de **V** 204

Vere, Robert de, earl of Oxford, knighted at Lewes **IV** 188

Vere, Robert de, earl of Oxford (1296–1331) **V** 1, 260

Vere, Robert de, earl of Oxford (1384–92), marquis of Dublin (1385–8), duke of Ireland (1386–8): **V** 185, 260, 442–3, 458, 467, 471; marriage to Philippa de Coucy 268, 425; favourite of Richard II 425, 438; affair of the Carmelite friar 434; attacked by Walter Sibill 437; expedition to Scotland 440; grants to him in Ireland 441; marriage to Agnes Lancecrona 447; justice of Chester and North Wales 447; witness to the judges' manifesto 449; appeal against 451; flight from London 452; flees abroad after Radcot Bridge 453; charges against 456; sentenced by Merciless Parliament 457; duchy of Ireland confiscated 463 —forbidden to go there 471; funeral at Colne 476

Vere, Robert de, 9th earl of Oxford **VI** 64, 472

Vere, Robert de, 19th earl of Oxford **IX** 266–7

Vere, Thomas de **VI** 571

Verecundius Diogenes, M. (*sevir*) **Ia** 580

Vereeniging, Peace **XIV** 347–8

Vergennes, Charles, comte de **XII** 254

Vergennes, comte de *see* Gravier, Charles

Vergil, Polydore of Urbino (?1470–1555) **VI** 482, 640; **VII** 52, 76, 182, 191, 580; background and *Anglica Historia* 26–30, 162, 578; John Leland's refutation 33; Perkin Warbeck 120, 166; pope preaches a crusade (1500) 151;

Vergil (*cont.*)
Warwick and conspiracy 166;
Curzon and Suffolk 168; Henry
VII's council 202–3; Empson
and Dudley 216; *perfectae literae*
237; renown and career 238;
imprisoned by Wolsey (1515)
300; Wolsey sends to Rome
(1514) 301; Wolsey and the
divorce 322; Ten Articles, the
Injunctions (1536) 383
Verginius Rufus, L. **Ia** 128–9
Verica **Ia** 56, 69, 83, 91
Verli, Hugh de **III** 9
Vermandois **III** 342, 361; **V** 127;
county **VI** 170, 208, 239
Vermigli, 'Peter Martyr' **VII** 515,
516, 520, 543, 556; professor of
divinity 574
Vernemeton **Ia** 675
Verneuil (Eure) **III** 335, 374, 384;
battle **VI** 191, 206, 239, 244, 651;
French casualties 244
Verney, Christiana **X** 401
Verney, Sir Edmund **IX** 126
Verney, Sir Ralph **VII** 132
Verney, Ralph, 2nd Earl (1712?–
91) **XII** 36, 165, 166
Verney, Sir Ralph **IX** 270, 359, 374
Vernon (Eure) **III** 377, 379; **VI** 172,
173; Norman estates 205
Vernon, Edward (1684–1757): ad-
miral **XI** 210, 224, 226, 229,
277; and Nacton House of Indus-
try 138; and smuggling 190; Porto
Bello captured 234; criticism of
government 234, 235; Cartagena
attacked (1741) 235, 236
Vernon, Richard de **VI** 53
Vernon, Sir Richard, tomb **VI** 650
Verona **Ia** 393; **III** 344
Verona, bishops of *see* Giberti,
Giammateo
Verona, Guarino da **VII** 236
Verrio, Antonio **X** 400
Versailles: Peace of (1783) **XII**
254–7, 259, 261; supreme war
council **XV** 99, 100; treaty, terms

133–5; accepted by House of
Commons 135–6; condemned by
Labour 136, 216; attacked by
Keynes 136–7; Anglo-German
naval treaty repudiates 377;
Rhineland 386; regarded as
unjust 417; in ruins 449; German
grievance a cause of war 453
Vertue, George (1684–1756), engraver **XI** 406
Vertue, Robert **VII** 591
Verturiones **Ia** 375
Verulamium (St Albans): Cunobelinus' coins **Ia** 55; fort 94; chartered 112, 575; massacre 119,
678; villa near 125; forum 137,
161, 167; houses 159, 195, 458;
fire 232–3; defences 261; gates
232, 262; theatre 372, 579, 675;
corn-drying 454, 458; late
occupation 458–9; St Germanus
466–7; military tribune 467;
macellum 584, 658; temple 675,
734; martyrdom of St Alban 720;
see also St Albans
Verus, L., Emperor **Ia** 192, 204,
206–7, 209, 287; plague 552
Vervins, treaty **VIII** 427
Vesalius, Andreas (1506–64) **VIII**
312; **IX** 364–5
Vesci, Eustace de, lord of Alnwick
III 455, 468, 470, 481
Vescy, Henry, Lord de **VI** 519
Vescy, Lady Isabella de **V** 13, 24
Vescy, John de, of Alnwick **IV** 173,
214, 257, 283
Vesey, Mrs Elizabeth (1715–91) **XI**
148
Vespasian: in Britain **Ia** 73, 84–6,
92–4; emperor 130–1, 271; Britain under 132–8; Agricola's
appointments 132, 138; rehab-
ilitation of Corbulo 140; equestrian origins 155; Colosseum 156;
legati iuridici 162; Titus' elevation
287; seals 531
Vespucci, Amerigo **VII** 228, 259,
264

Vesta **Ia** 707
Vestal Virgins **Ia** 401, 682
Vestiarian controversy **VIII** 191
Vestmann islands (Iceland) **VI** 363
vestry, election and powers **XII** 44
veterans **Ia** 21, 510–14, 574, 586;
    Colchester 104, 115; Gloucester
    585, 655; among Bacaudae 283;
    see also army; *colonia*
Vetranio **Ia** 354–5
Vettius Bolanus, M. **Ia** 130–4
Vettius Valens, M. **Ia** 526, 533
Veurne (Furnes), defeat of Flemings
    (1297) **IV** 669
vexillations *see* forts; legions
Vexin: district **II** 619–20; **III** 108,
    325, 335; castles 82, 112, 127,
    328; campaign of William Rufus
    111–12; battle at Brémule 124;
    conferred on William Clito 127;
    Norman territory 162, 323; re-
    covered by Henry 323–4; and
    claimed by Philip 342–3, 363,
    379; reoccupied by Richard 375;
    VI 181
Vexin, count of *see* Drogo
Veyse, William, Eton bricks **VI** 652
Vezelay (Yonne) **III** 211, 359, 360
Vezzano, Geoffrey of, papal collec-
    tor: administration of wills **IV**
    470–1, 504
Via Devana **Ib** 107
vicarages **VI** 278–9; deterioration
    279; Chichester return 279;
    improvement constitutions 279
vicarii: Diocletian's reforms **Ia** 295;
    responsibility and status 316–17,
    331–2, 516–17; London 317,
    516–17; civil functions, *rationales
    vicarii* 332, 337–8, 339, 390, 439;
    Martinus 345, 358; Chrysanthus
    346, 407; Victorinus 346, 435;
    class origins 351, 354, 434–5;
    military insignia 381; Maximinus
    (Rome) 394; appointments cease
    in Britain 443; official travel 568
vicars **IV** 458–9, 760; choral **VI** 289
Vicars, John **IX** 125, 408

Vicary, surgeon **VIII** 312–13
vice-admirals **VIII** 215
Vicenza **VII** 151, 402
Vichy, French government: Wey-
    gand loyal **XV** 521; Canada
    represented 495; forces in Syria
    loyal 527
Victgils **Ib** 146
Victor IV, anti-pope **III** 326, 327
Victor (I), freedman **Ia** 511, 697
Victor II, Pope **II** 465, 467
Victor (II), soldier **Ia** 552
Victor Amadeus II, duke of Savoy
    (1666–1732) **X** 190, 205, 213,
    215, 217; French invasion
    thwarted (1691) 170 — rejects
    further attempt 219; defeated at
    Pinerolo and Marsaglia 171;
    made viceroy of Milan 214; given
    Sicily by Charles 234; **XI** 165,
    173
Victores, Late Roman unit **Ia** 381
Victoria, Queen **XIII** 169, 172, 178,
    184, 187; biography 103; acces-
    sion 103–4; marriage 106–7;
    influence of Prince Albert upon
    the Queen 107–8; Irish church
    bill 190; relations with Palmer-
    ston 224, 246, 247–50, 301–2,
    315; queen of Tahiti's appeal 241;
    meetings with Louis Philippe
    243, 245, 254; eastern question
    257; naval reform 274; opposes
    Italian policy of Palmerston
    and Russell (1859–60) 301–2;
    Albert's death 315; Frederick of
    Augustenberg 319; attitude
    towards Schleswig-Holstein ques-
    tion 321, 322; visits Ireland 357;
    Etty's nudes 588; theatre patron-
    age 625; phase of unpopularity
    XIV 26; estrangement from
    Gladstone begins (Aug. 1871) 27;
    annoyance with liberal opposi-
    tion to new title 39; attitude in
    Russo-Turkish conflict 47, 48;
    surprise at Lord Beaconsfield's
    defeat 64; anger about Gordon's

Victoria, Queen (*cont.*)
death 83; horror at Chamberlain's radicalism 92; attitude to army 130; religion 137, 139; attitude to divorced persons 169; first jubilee 176–8; second 239; courage during war defeats 254; visit to Ireland 268; death 268; contrasts with Edward VII 342–3; savings 344; **XV** 21, 286, 398; Gladstone 204; George V 209; Jubilee 377

Victoria Cross, institution **XIII** 292

Victoria station: leave trains **XV** 52; troops march from 138; Haile Selassie welcomed 385

Victorinus (I), Gallic emperor **Ia** 276

Victorinus (II), Moorish officer **Ia** 282

Victorinus (III) (*vicarius*) **Ia** 346, 435

Victory, Altar of **Ia** 356, 401, 409, 682, 735

Victory programme **XV** 530

Victricius of Rouen, Bishop **Ia** 462, 737

vicus: use of term **Ia** 535, 591; status as birth place 590–2; on Wall 385, 594, 708; Vindolanda 380, 537–8; Cirencester 584; Brancaster 594; veterans prefer larger towns? 512–13; **Ib** 31–4, 36, 76, 86–7, 91; *regius* 35; Aldwych 133; Dorchester-on-Thames 167–8; *see also* civil settlements; towns

Vidame de Chartres **VIII** 57, 122

Vienna **III** 362; **VII** 83, 85, 118, 121, 598; Turkish threat (1529) 320, 341; Henry VIII's interest in war (1542) 408; **X** 112, 205; congress **XII** 564–70; **XV** 419, 424

Vienne, church **Ia** 717

Vienne, council (1311), material collected for **IV** 483–4

Vienne, Hugh de, king's clerk **IV** 519

Vienne, Jean de, Admiral **V** 439, 440

Vienne, Jean de (d. 1351) **V** 136, 137

View of the Present State of Ireland **VIII** 291

vigiles **Ia** 334

Vigo **VIII** 369, 412

Vigo Bay, battle **X** 204

Vilbia **Ia** 688

vilicus see bailiffs

Villa Viciosa **VII** 307

Villafranca **VIII** 356

villages: associated with villas? **Ia** 303, 610–11; fourth-century towns reduced to? 371; in Britain 588–9, 594–5; settlement in **II** 285–7; development **VII** 463

Villandraut (Gironde), castle built by Pope Clement V **IV** 444

villani **II** 477–80; vagueness of term 478–80; in Danelaw 515–16

Villars, Hector de, Marshal **X** 203, 219, 230

villas **Ia** 596–611; development in Britain 14, 92, 125, 158–61, 188 —owner increase 235 —city magnates 266–7 —Witcombe and Droitwich 276, 278 —immigration 280–2 —lack of fortifications 329; official residences 92, 529, 597, 599, 644; ownership 280–1, 600–3; Trier 302–3; Gaul 303, 329, 355, 610, 639; unfortified 329, 599; Christianity associated with 342, 450, 452, 702–3, 725–6 —cemeteries 730, 732; life in 397, 450–4, 596–7, 598–9, 609–11; fortified 450, 452–3; shrines 450, 690; settlements 461; not mentioned in Gildas 495; location 512, 557, 584–5, 587, 596–7 —ownership 601, 604–8 —salt and pottery 664; definition 603, 614; economy of 624–9; iron working 640; mosaic industry 656; **Ib** Roman 35–6, 87, 91, 138, 210–11; coin evidence from 212; *regalis* 35, 123,

170, 186, 189 — in Northumbria and Kent 199–200; *see also* agriculture; countryside; estates; farming; landowners; Bignor; Ditchley; Fishbourne; Lullinstone

Villefranche-de-Belvés **IV** 302; castle 301

Villeinage, extinction of **VIII** 251

Villeins **III** 36, 38–48, 51

villeins and villeinage **V** 314–48, 411, 413, 418, 419; revolt 422

Villeneuve, Admiral **XII** 425–8, 430–2

Villeneuve, marquis de *see* Sauveur, Louis

Villeneuve-de-Roy (Yonne) **VI** 200

Villéon, Jacques de la **VI** 576

Villiers, Edward, 1st earl of Jersey **X** 195, 243

Villiers, Elizabeth, countess of Orkney **X** 180, 189, 316

Villiers, George, 1st duke of Buckingham **IX** 34, 42, 268, 370, 400; rise 18–19; lord high admiral 22; grants monopolies 24; impeached 36; assassinated 43, 66; at Madrid 58; at Paris 60; foreign policy 64; at Isle of Ré 65–6

Villiers, George, 2nd duke of Buckingham **X** 77, 84, 420

Villiers, George William Frederick, 4th earl of Clarendon **XIII** 165, 190, 244, 245, 249–51; biography 249; eastern question 257–61, 263, 291; America 309; Schleswig-Holstein 321; Luxemburg question 324–5; West Africa 375; education 487

Vimieiro, battle (1808) **XII** 459

Viminiacium **Ia** 457

Vimy ridge **XV** 81

Vincent of Beauvais **VI** 679

Vincidianus **Ia** 384

Vindex, C. Julius **Ia** 128

Vindiciae contra Tyrannos **VIII** 336–7

Vinea, Peter de, in England **IV** 72

Vinegar Hill, battle (1798) **XII** 398

Viner, Charles (1678–1756), Vinerian professorship of law **XI** 57

vines **Ia** 540, 601; *see also* wine

Vinsauf, Geoffrey of **III** 236

Vipont, Robert de, of Appleby **IV** 173

Virconium see Wroxeter

virgate **III** 42–3; *see also* yardland

Virgil **Ia** 48, 66, 106, 468, 588; literary influence 297, 304, 507; **III** 257; **V** 531

Virginia **VIII** 246; **IX** 320–1, 327–9, 344–5, 347; **X** 334, 337, 339, 346

Virilis **Ia** 685; **Ib** 79

Virius Lupus **Ia** 220, 224–6, 228, 658

Viry, comte de (d. 1766), Sardinian ambassador in London **XI** 371

Visconti, Bianca, daughter of Filippo Maria Visconti, wife of Francesco Sforza **VII** 113

Visconti, claim to Milan **VII** 84, 113

Visconti, Filippo Maria, duke of Milan (d. 1447) **VII** 113

Visconti, Tedaldo *see* Gregory X

Visconti family **VI** 108

Visconti of Milan **V** 284, 346; Bernabo de 267; Giangaleazzo 476; Violante (duchess of Clarence) 267

Visigoths: Alaric their leader **Ia** 417; in Epirus 423; in Gaul 446–8, 450–2; attack Arles 476–7; support Romans against Huns 481; unreliability 482, 490, 491; driven out of Gaul by Clovis 494; compared with Saxons 663; install usurper at Rome 488; Arians 736; Gallo-Romans under Visigoths 450–2, 728; **Ib** 117

visitations, ecclesiastical **VII** 373; Cromwell's visitations (1535) 376–7; (1538) 398

Vita Christiana, De **Ia** 441

Vitalian, Pope **II** 131

Vitalinus *see* Guitalin

W

Walcheren expedition **XII** 366, 408, 422, 483, 554; **XV** 579

Walcote, Warin of **III** 153

Waldby, Robert, archbishop of Dublin (1391–5), bishop of Chichester (1395–6), archbishop of York (1396–8) **V** 474

Waldeck, prince of **X** 169

Waldegrave, James, 1st Earl (1685–1741) **XI** 187, 202

Waldegrave, James, 2nd Earl (1715–63) **XI** 342, 348, 376

Waldegrave, Lady **XII** 155

Waldegrave, Sir Richard **V** 422

Walden, Roger, archbishop of Canterbury (1398) **V** 297, 474, 480

Walden, Roger, king's secretary, archbishop of Canterbury **VI** 26, 271; replaced 21

Waldezeemüller **VII** 259

Waldhere, bishop of London **II** 204; letter to Berhtwald 142, 179

Waldhere, legendary hero **II** 193

Waldon, John, Canon **VI** 658

Waldric, bishop of Laon **III** 233

Waldringfield, Great and Little (Suffolk) **VI** 647

Waleran, count of Meulan, earl of Worcester **III** 12, 137; fled battle of Lincoln 142; took the cross 149; authority during anarchy 158; absentee landlord 159

Waleran, son of Henry, duke of Limburg **III** 455

Waleran the German **III** 471; **IV** 40

Walerand, count of St Pol **VI** 33, 73

Walerand, Robert **IV** 153, 163, 167, 196

Wales: terrain **Ia** 4, 45; borders 14, 16, 139, 255, 584; Claudian fortress 90, 95; conquest 105–10, 113, 137–9; garrisons 150, 188, 254–6, 261; town development 251, 372; naval defence 384; Cunedda? 404; unconquered by Saxons 484; mines 632, 634; Llyn Cerig influences 680; relations with Mercia **II** 212–15, 230, 327,

330, 339; West Saxon kings 330; Athelstan 340–2; Edward the Confessor 572–6; Normans 615–16; **III** 283–301; geography of 283–4; Norman penetration 284; into north 285–7; into southern marches 287–90; Owain Gwynedd and Thys ap Gruffudd 290–5; Henry II's campaigns 292–3, 322, 370; supremacy of Llywelyn ap Iorworth in 298–301; John's policy 298–301, 426, 449; music 256; church 226, 295–7; march, border 322, 371, 391, 394, 485; mercenary troops 141–2 —during the anarchy 154 —march to Carlisle 278 —employed by John 298, 300; Fitz Stephen's force in Ireland 305 —help to put down Louis 337 —accompany Henry in last campaign 344 —professional, paid soldiers 372, 373; mariners impressed 436; 'friendly' Welsh in **IV** 411, 421; archers and foot soldiers in Flanders 384, 679; in Scotland 689, 690, 694; **V** 25, 429; archers from 35; and Ireland 42; Llewellyn Bren 50; ambitions of Despensers 58–61, 73; parliamentary representation 71, 88; plot to rescue Edward II 94; Mortimers 97, 255; Bohuns 256; Black Prince 258, 259, 266; wool 350; staple 351, 353; de Vere 447; Richard II and 484, 493; Lollards 518, 520; Glyn Dŵr revolt expenditure **VI** 30; gwely system 38; labourers 43; residents in England 43; students 43; archers and men-at-arms 48; ports 56; castle garrisons 77; financial demands 88; York-Lancaster balance 527; **VII** 34, 37, 94, 385, 396; favours Henry but slow to rally 51–2; Perkin Warbeck 121, 145; shires and lordships 366; advantages of Tudorism 366;

Rowland Lee suppresses disorders 366–7; acts (1536 and 1543) 367–8, 436; estimate of Tudor policy 368–9, 436; religious houses 378, **IX** 14, 134; royalist stronghold 98, 153–5; council of Marches abolished 103; administration under Cromwell 179–80; cattle **XI** 103; charity schools 142; religious revival 97; trade 122; *see also* Anglesey; Deceangli; Ordovices; Silures

Wales, North **VI** 41, 44, 56, 101, 102; royal lands 77; tenants' arrears 221

Wales, South **VI** 221; royal lands 77; Glyn Dŵr 58; rebellion 101, 102

Wales, barons of, so styled royal vassals **IV** 398, 413, 417, 418, 420, 421, 424

Wales, Gerald of *see* Giraldus Cambrensis

Wales, Marches **IV** 368; social complexities 403, 409–10, 437, 443–4

Wales, prince of *see* Edward VII; Frederick, prince of Wales; for party of prince of Wales *see* Leicester House Party

Wales and the Crown **IV** 381–2; relations to Henry III (1216–47) 20, 54–5, 57, 60, 392–400 —Hubert de Burgh's power 43–5; princes and the Scots 138, 582, 592; statute and administration (1284–1307) 322, 429, 435–8, 443; in the 12th and 13th centuries 384–91; changes in princely nomenclature 385, 392, 393; Church 388–91, 406, 433–5; foreign descriptions of the Welsh 393–4; military geography in Marches 394, 406, 410–11; how divided and administered between the first two Welsh wars (1277–82) 412–19; centre and west overrun by David and Llywelyn and reoccupied 419–

23; absolution and bonds made by Welsh to keep the peace 421; castles and boroughs 430–3; last risings 438–43, 649

Waleys, Henry, merchant of London, mayor of London and Bordeaux **IV** 632, 635, 636

Walingaford *see* Wallingford (Berks.)

Walker, Emery **XIV** 325, 540

Walker, Henry the **V** 365

Walker, John **IX** 200

Walker, Obadiah, master of University College, Oxford **X** 124

Walker, Robert **IX** 375

Walker, Rotherham iron-founder **XI** 116

Walkers of Sheffield **XII** 31

Wall (Staffs.): fort **Ia** 105; *mansio?* 568; lead tank 729

Wall, Don Ricardo (1694–1778) **XI** 292

Wall, Richard **XII** 75

Wallace, Alfred Russell, biography **XIII** 574

Wallace, Edgar **XV** 180

Wallace, J., attorney general (1783) **XII** 579

Wallace, Sir Richard **XIV** 326

Wallace, Thomas **XIII** 71

Wallace, William **IV** 332, 333, 572, 576; rise to power (1297–8) 669, 683, 684, 686, 687; defeat at Falkirk 689, 690; later years (1299–1305) 694, 696, 709, 711, 712

Wallas, Graham **XIV** 334

Waller, Edmund **IX** 405; **X** 364

Waller, Sir William **IX** 131, 133, 137, 257

Wallingford (Welingaford) (Berks.): medieval market **Ia** 542; **II** 265, 336, 381, 385, 582, 733; foundation 529; William's arrival 597; **III** town's loyalty to Angevin cause 75; controversy over market rights 78, 406; Matilda's flight from Oxford 145–6; truce after

Wallingford (Berks.) (*cont.*)
Henry's campaign (1153) 163–4; treaty at Winchester 165; barons swear allegiance to infant king (1155) 212; northern barons reconciled 463; **V** 4, 22, 85, 492; honour 80

Wallingford, Richard **V** 508

Wallingford Castle **III** 138, 139, 146, 359; **IV** 40, 160, 170, 196; mayor 366; **V** 25; **VI** 492, 494

Wallingford House party **IX** 237

Wallis, John **IX** 368–9; **X** 30, 360, 381

Wallis, Samuel, explorer (1728–95) **XII** 17

Wallmoden, Amalie Sophie Marianne, countess of Yarmouth (1704–65) **XI** 42, 354

Wallop **Ib** 164; map 3 xxxi

Wallop, Sir John **VII** 409, 418, 421

walls: *coloniae* **Ia** 153; turf and timber 175–7; replaced with stone 179; town defences in Britain 218–19, 261–3, 264–5, 389–91, 411–12; repaired 222; town in Gaul 275, 283, 327; York 325–7; defence against barbarians 330–1, 391; walled and unwalled towns 380, 594, 608; Gildas' stone wall 421–2; walled villas 450, 454; river wall 531; as indicators of town size 586–7, 593; cemeteries outside 695–6 *see also* Hadrian's Wall; Antonine Wall; earthworks; town defences

Wallsend: fort **Ia** 179, 184, 383, 392; seal 570; **Ib** map 4 xxxii

Walpole, Sir Edward **XII** 155

Walpole, Horace (1717–97), 4th earl of Orford **XI** 10, 64, 146, 390, 396; with reference to Archbishop Blackburne 81; duke of Cumberland 217; St Malo raids (1758) 362; year (1759) 363; Henry Fox 373; *Historic Doubts on Richard III* 395; Richardson, the painter 400; sculpture 401; Paris 404; *Anecdotes*

of Painting 407; letters and Memoirs 428; **XII** 60, 98, 172, 233, 284; diaries reflect social life 339; on Gothic architecture 341; medievalism in literature 352

Walpole, Horatio, Lord Walpole of Wolterton (1678–1757) **XI** 155, 186, 194–5, 200, 202

Walpole, Sir Robert, earl of Orford **X** 233; **XI** 10, 22, 41, 50, 57; achievements 1, 146, 211–12, 402; political views 8, 22, 29; George II 17, 202, 206, 339; foreign affairs and policy 19, 86, 178, 195, 201 — Fleury's negotiations 206 — national humiliation 374; and Hanover 21; influence on MPs 27; customs and excise 29, 189–91, 273, 278; resignation (1742) 32, 210–11, 238; ministry (1721–42) 33, 122, 179, 186, 214; as prime minister 35, 375; relations with Queen Caroline 42, 202–3, 206, 374; religious toleration 71; religious intolerance 73; economic and financial policy 73, 121, 170, 176, 185–93 — interest reductions 336; ecclesiastical patronage 77; episcopal support 80; Bishop Berkeley 91; four course rotation 106; Eton and Westminster 140; placemen and bishops 147; opposition 150, 203–5; paymaster 154; Bolingbroke returns 157; at Treasury and Exchequer (1715) 164, 169–70; adviser 167; career and characteristics 169, 180–2, 203, 211–12, 334; Stanhope and Sunderland 169, 170–2, 177–8; Tories 169, 185; South Sea Bubble 177, 178; George I 180, 202; Townsend 181, 186, 193; Jacobite plots 182–5, 196; colonial policy 192–3, 311, 316; war with Spain (1739) 208, 231–2, 374; army and navy 214; war of Polish Succession 232, 237, 374; Carteret 238,

588

Walton-on-the-Naze (Essex) **V** 83, 158

Walworth, Sir William **VI** 664

Walworth, Sir William, fishmonger **V** 375; mayor of London 411; loan to Richard II 401; treasurer of the subsidy (1377) 402; commission (1380) 405; with Richard II at Mile End 411; knighted 413–14; hostility to Gaunt 436

Wampool, river **Ia** 177–8

Wandesford, Christopher **IX** 111

Wandsworth (Surrey) **V** 365

Waneting *see* Wantage (Berks.)

Wanley, Humfrey (1672–1726) **X** 382; antiquarian **XI** 394

Wansbeck, by-election **XV** 106

Wansdyke **Ib** xxvi, 152–3, 155–6, 160–4, 168, 170–1; map 3 xxxi

Wansford (Northants) **III** 25

Wansford (Yorks.), manor **VI** 337

Wantage (Waneting) (Berks.) **II** 245, 733; Wantage code 508–12; **III** 397

Wantone, Sir John de **V** 239

wapentake **II** 504–5; occasionally called hundred 505; fiscal unit 647–8

Waplington (Yorks.), manor **VI** 337

Wapping (London): signal station **Ia** 571; **Ib** 131; map 6 88; fire **X** 66

war *see* wars

war aims: first discussion **XV** 50–2; Allies define 79–80; German 65, 95; Lloyd George 97; Churchill defines 489

The War Book **XIV** 433, 526

War Book **XV** 3

War Cabinet: Lloyd George's set up **XV** 456; approves putting Haig under Nivelle 80; examines Haig 86; Henderson resigns 90; accepts franchise reform 93; committee on manpower 97–8; end of 130, 132; Chamberlain's set up 456; refuses to sanction rationing 457;

Churchill 467; Finnish problem 469; agrees to mine leads 470; insists on attacking Trondheim 471; Churchill's set up 477–8; service ministers excluded 479; Dowding appeals to 480, 485; its function 483; French fleet 494; battle of Bevin and Beaverbrook 509; sanctions bombing of civilians 519, 592; resolves to reinforce Egypt 520; hesitates to aid Greece 525; Lyttelton represents in Middle East 528; authorizes its agents 538; remade 544; Cripps wants more power 558; further changes 559; endorses unconditional surrender 561, 576; Woolton 567; objects to Transportation plan 580; criticizes Morgenthau plan 587; end of war 590; Labour ministers 597; not consulted on atomic bomb 598; dissolved 598; escapes attention of historians 621, 643

war committee (1915–16): set up **XV** 47; equivocates over Gallipoli 48; swept away 74

war council (1914–15): British Expeditionary Force **XV** 6; set up 23; approves Dardanelles expedition 24; resolves to reinforce Gallipoli 30; dissolved 44; demanded by Lloyd George 66, 68

war criminals: proposed trials **XV** 134; trials 596

war debts: in First World War **XV** 42, 123; Balfour note 190; settlement 202–3; reparations 215; repudiated 335–6, 373, 358

War Loan **XV** 41, 124; converted 332, 338

War Office, and shells **XV** 22; loses munitions 33; demobilization 138; Norwegian campaign 471; bombing 552

War Production, Ministry of **XV** 543–4

War Transport, Ministry of **XV**

510; attempts to stop cut-flowers 551; regional government 569

Warbeck (Osbeck), Perkin **VI** 594, 625; **VII** 202, 208, 215, 217, 598; leader of Yorkist cause 8; appears at Cork (1491) 80, 106, 116–17; support from abroad 120–2; fall of Stanley (1495) 123; failure at Deal (1495) 125; Irish and Scottish intrigue 128; failed attack on Waterford 132; in Scotland (1495–7) 134, 137–44; proclaims himself Richard IV (1497) 145–6; confessions and imprisonment (1497–8) 147, 150; James V's support 157; imposture 116–20; executed (1499) 116, 165–6, 171

Warborough (Oxon.) **III** 169

Warburton, William (1698–1779), bishop of Gloucester **XI** 395; *Alliance between Church and State* 87; *Divine Legation of Moses* 87; edited Shakespeare 419; **XII** 42, 101

Ward, Mrs Humphry **XIV** 331

Ward, John **XIV** 478

Ward, Joshua (1685–1761), manufacturer of antimony pills **XI** 390; of sulphuric acid 387

Ward, W. G. **XIII** 517–18

Warden (Beds.) **VII** 398

Wardlaw-Milne, Sir John **XV** 554

Wardle, Gwyllym Lloyd (1762?–1833) **XII** 447, 449

wardrobe, king's **IV** 767; centre of administration 337–8, 524, 662, 667; the great 698; **V** 218, 379, 412; king's 29, 77, 217–18; privy 218, 412; keepers *see* Droxford; Langton, Walter

wardship **III** 20, 21–2, 55, 418; **IX** 4–7, 14

Ware (Herts.) **VI** 27

Ware, Isaac (d. 1766), architect **XI** 403–4, 412

Ware, Master Henry, dean of the Arches (1415) **VI** 138

Ware, Richard, abbot of Westminster, treasurer (1280–3) **IV** 485

Wareham (Werham) (Dorset) **II** 253, 265, 373, 536, 734; **III** 121, 123, 136, 145

Warelwast, Robert, bishop of Exeter **III** 227

Warelwast, William, bishop of Exeter **III** 6, 174, 177

Warenne, Isabella de **III** 164, 202

Warenne, John de, earl of Surrey (d. 1304) **IV** 153, 154; marries Alesia de Lusignan (1247) 138; Provisions of Oxford 138, 140; views (1261) 164; joins new baronial party (1262–3) 173; rejoins Edward 177; in war (1264) 187, 190; land in Pembroke (1265) 200; at Chesterfield 209; takes the cross (1268) 219; granted Bromfield and Yale 424; legend of *quo warranto* 521; father-in-law of John Baliol, king of Scots 602; custodian of northern shires (1295) 613; defeats Scots at Dunbar (1296) 614; warden of Scotland 615, 685, 686, 688, 689, 704, 707; defeated at Stirling Bridge 669, 686; death 707

Warenne, John de, earl of Surrey, grandson and heir of John, married Joan of Bar (1306) **IV** 138, 517; father William 138

Warenne, John de, earl of Surrey (1307–47): **V** 1, 260; combines against Gaveston 6; grants to, by Edward II 11; makes terms with Gaveston 25; joins court party 28; private war with Lancaster 51, 67; fails to obtain divorce 51; joins Middle Party 52; campaign (1319) 56; Boroughbridge campaign 66; trial of Lancaster 67; Despensers 74; flees to the west with Edward II 84; makes peace with Queen Isabella 88; deputation to Kenilworth 90; protest (1341) 176; and John Stratford 178; death 256

Warenne, Reginald de **III** 14

Warenne, William de **II** 593, 630, 673

Warenne I, William de, earl of Surrey **III** 12, 100, 157

Warenne II, William de, earl of Surrey **III** 116

Warenne III, William de, earl of Surrey **III** 137, 142, 149, 164

Warenne IV, William de, earl of Surrey **III** 457

Warenne family **IV** 23, 51

Wargoon, surrender **XII** 315

Warham, William, bishop of London (1502–3), archbishop of Canterbury (1503–32) **VII** 330, 345, 361, 572, 600; Perkin Warbeck 124; marries Henry and Catherine 231; Erasmus 251–2, 256–7; Holy League (1511) 273; Wolsey's power 288–9, 293; resigns (1515) 295, 306; revolt against authoritarian finance 304; death (1532) 355–6; chancellor (1504–15) 645–6; master of the rolls (1494) 648

Warin, son of Gerold **III** 428

Wariner, William **V** 242

Wark (Northumb.) **III** 274, 283; **VII** 280, 313

Wark, manor, in Tyndale **IV** 587, 600

Wark-on-Tweed (Berwick), castle **IV** 20, 613; Henry III at (1255) **IV** 590, 591

Warkworth (Northumb.), castle **VI** 9, 53, 54, 317, 651; barony 337

Warkworth, John, chronicler **VI** 555

Warley, Ingelard **V** 22, 23, 33, 46; keeper of the wardrobe 11; baron of the exchequer 49

Warminster (Wilts.) **II** 482, 533

Warner, William **VIII** 243

Warr, Lord de la **VI** 234, 519; joins Yorkists 520

Warren, Sir Charles **XIV** 180, 181, 227

Warren, Commodore Borlase **XII** 399

Warren, Sir Peter (1703–52) **XI** 262; capture of Louisburg 260, 319

Warrington (Lancs.), Franciscan **VI** 130

Warrington, earl of *see* Booth, Henry

wars, Spanish and French justification **X** 420–1; Austrian Succession **XI** 218–19, 259–64, 265–70; Polish Succession 206, 207, 232, 237, 374; Seven Years 214, 216, 219, 319, 356–68 — preliminary phases 351–2 — Pitt's conduct 375; Spanish Succession **XI** 291; war (1718–20) 173, 315; war (1727) 200, 202, 207; war (1739) 207–10, 213, 231–6, 374; war (1762) 371

Wars of the Roses **VII** 37, 71, 443, 462

Warsaw: Red army marches on **XV** 143; bombed by Germans 430, 451, 534; fate expected for London 454; Russians halt outside 577

Warton, Thomas, poet (1728–90) **XII** 341, 350

Warwick (Wæringwicum) **II** 326, 335, 531, 535, 582; castle 601; shire 431, 549; origin 337; **III** 25, 164; **V** 26, 27; **VI** 557; St Mary's college church 291, 648, 667; castle 558

Warwick, countesses of *see* Anne; Elizabeth

Warwick, earls of *see* Beauchamp, Richard; Beauchamp, Thomas; Dudley, Ambrose; Dudley, John; Edward; Neville, Richard; Rich, Robert

Warwick, Henry **VI** 336, 563

Warwick, Roger *see* Roger, earl of Warwick

Warwickshire **Ia** 43; **III** 151–2, 159, 222, 368; **V** 27, 153, 325; **VII** 37, 452, 505; **IX** 306

592

Watteville, de, soldier in Canada **XII** 554
Wattignies, battle (1793) **XII** 367
Watton **IV** 716
Watts, G. F. **XIII** 593; **XIV** 156
Watts, Isaac (1674–1748) **X** 24; **XI** 84, 86, 88, 425
Waugh, Evelyn **XV** 180, 260
Waurin, Burgundian chronicler **VI** 152
Wavell, Sir Archibald Percival: biography **XV** 460; commands Middle East 460; in Cairo 520; small force 523; moves slowly 523–4; agrees to aid Greece 525; conquers Abyssinia 526; superseded 527–8; his desert victory 530; supreme commander South East Asia 537
Waverley Abbey (Surrey) **III** 187
Waweton, Sir Thomas, Norfolk sheriff **VI** 416
Waxhaws, battle **XII** 215
Wayland, Thomas de, chief justice of Common pleas **IV** 363
Wayneflete, William of *see* William of Wayneflete
We Can Conquer Unemployment **XV** 267
wealas in Ine's laws **II** 315
Weald (Kent) **IV** 10; archers 422; men 187; **V** 314, 316, 371
Weald (Sussex) **Ia** 42–3, 559, 570, 637, 640; **Ib** 135, 148; **II** 731
wealth: target for barbarians **Ia** 240; conspicuous display 449–51, 453, 465, 469; acquired in imperial property 530–1; redistribution of 599–643, 662–3; in large estates 600, 663; economic motivator 615, *see also pretium victoriae*; investment in Britain 659–60; estimates of **XIV** 104, 273–4, 500–2
weapons **VIII** 230
Wear, river **Ib** map 4 xxxii
Weardale **VII** 37
Weardburh (Weardbyrig) **II** 326, 336, 536
Wearmouth, monastery **II** 68, 89, 159, 184–5; library 185; abbots of *see* Ceolfrith; Guthberht; *see also* Monkwearmouth
Weatmorland **VII** 392
weavers: riots **X** 259; Irish 319; handloom **XIII** 5, 6, 12
weaving: mills **Ia** 602, 656; comb 7
Webb, Sir Aston **XIV** 326
Webb, Beatrice (Mrs Sidney Webb) **XIV** 329
Webb, Major-General John Richmond **X** 216
Webb, Philip **XIV** 155, 323, 324, 540
Webb, Sidney, Lord Passfield (1859–1947) **XIV** 320, 329, 334, 499; biography **XV** 90; drafts Labour programme 90, 267, 347; on Sankey Commission 140; buried in Westminster Abbey 178; on inevitability of gradualness 201, 219; combines Colonial and Dominions Offices 254, 271; becomes Lord Passfield 271; Palestine 276–7; the Depression 285; gold standard 297; discovers new civilization 348; Beveridge fulfils plans 567
Webbe, William **VIII** 286
Weber, Max **X** 25
Webern, A. **XV** 179
Webster, Daniel **XIII** 305
Webster, G. **Ia** 95, 100, 120, 389, 571
Webster, John **VIII** 300, 301; **IX** 391, 394
Webster, Sir Richard, Lord Alverstone **XIV** 182
Wedderburn, Alexander, Lord Loughborough (1733–1805) **XI** 287; *see also* Loughborough
Wedgwood, Josiah (1730–95), pottery manufacturers **III** 84; **XI** 118, 120, 121, 414; **XII** 29, 277, 347, 514; biography 29; **XIII** 6; **XV** 170, 213, 401

Wedmore (Wethmore) (Som.) **II** 257, 734

Wednesbury (Staffs.) **II** 40

Weede, Everard van, lord of Dykeveld **X** 132, 173

Weedon (Northants) **V** 344, 345

Weedon Pinkney (Northants) **II** 629

The Week **XV** 397

Weekend Review **XV** 310

Weelkes, Thomas **VIII** 306

Weeton (Yorks.), manor **VI** 323

Wege *see* Wey, river

Wehden **Ib** 72, 193; map 1 xxix

weights and measures, ordinances **IV** 620

Weinbaum, M. **II** 540

Weissenburg, battle **XIV** 7

Welbeck (Notts.), abbey **III** 225; **VI** 295

Weldon, Sir Anthony **IX** 268

Welf, house **III** 362, 376, 449, 452

Well, wapentake **II** 501

Welland (Weolud), river **Ib** xxvii; map 2 xxx; **II** 26, 254, 329, 385, 733; **III** 37, 469

Welles, Wells, Sir Robert, captured **VI** 558

Welles, William, bishop of Rochester **VI** 469

Wellesley, Arthur, 1st duke of Wellington (1769–1852) **XII** 478; biography 384; in India 384; career 479–83; forces in Portugal (1809) 476, 485–9; sieges in Portugal (1812, 1813) 493–6, 557–9; Spanish campaigns 555; Bourbon line 561; Waterloo 566–8; methods 566–81; **XIII** 24, 53–4, 69, 101, 105; on patronage 28; prime minister 75–8; attitude to Reform Bill 85–6; on the defeat of Peel 124; chartists 145–6; Derby ministry 164; Castlereagh 195–6; in command of the army of occupation in France 200; views on Spanish question (1820) 201–2; protests at the Congress of Verona 207–8; eastern question 218, 220, 237; army 266, 268; and Raglan 274; Ireland 343–4; India 417, 419; Poor Law administration 452; playing-fields of Eton 485; Winchelsea duel 492; **XIV** 9, 10, 11, 560; forgotten by Lloyd George **XV** 70; Montgomery comparison 557; endowed 592

Wellesley, Garrett, 2nd baron and 1st earl of Mornington (1735–81) **XI** 305

Wellesley, Pole W. **XII** 583

Wellesley, Richard Colley, Marquis (1760–1842): biography **XII** 383; governor general of India 383–6, 410; foreign secretary (1809–12) 484, 491, 583; out of office (?) 492, 498

Wellington, duke of *see* Wellesley, Arthur

Wellow (Wilts.), council **II** 349

wells **Ia** 729; as ritual shafts 669–70, 680, 691–2; pagan cult 735

Wells (Wyllum) (Som.): diocese **II** 439, 734; **III** 431; cathedral 262; hall of bishop **IV** 339; **V** 501; deanery 473; cathedral **VI** 291; **VII** 141, 232; *see also* Bath and Wells

Wells, bishops of *see* Duduc; Giso

Wells, Calvin **Ia** 550

Wells, Colin **Ia** 50, 52, 66, 90

Wells, Herbert George: **XIV** 331, 548, 549; and Mr Britling **XV** 18; takes up League of Nations 51; at Crewe House 107; world state 178; *If Winter Comes* 311

Wells, John, 6th Baron Welles, 1st Viscount Welles (d. 1499) **VII** 57, 209

Wells, Leo, Lord **VI** 494, 526, 558; attainder (1461) 539

Wellstream, the **III** 485

Welsers (of Augsburg) **VII** 412

Welsh disestablishment **XIV** 207, 350–1, 450; **XV** 16, 236

Welsh language **Ia** 507; **X** 410

Welsh national movement **XIV** 336–7

Welsh traditional poetry **Ib** 199

Welshpool (Salop): borough **IV** 433; **VI** 38, 44

Wembley, Cup Final **XV** 313

Wemyss, Rosslyn Erskine: biography **XV** 48; favours naval action at Dardanelles 48; signs armistice 113

Wenceslas of Luxemburg, king of Bohemia and of the Romans (1378–1400) **V** 146

Wenden (Essex) **V** 320

Wendover, Roger of *see* Roger of Wendover

Wenham, Jane **X** 418

Wenlock, Cluniac prior **VI** 133

Wenlock, John, later Lord, of Someries **VI** 474, 481, 516, 536; Yorkist 512; Commons Speaker 512; with invading earls 518; besieges Tower 520; killed 569

Wenlock, Much (Salop): monastery **II** 47, 161; abbess of *see* Mildburg

Wenlock Priory **V** 293

Wensleydale (N. Yorks.) **VI** 321

Wentworth, Charles Watson, 2nd marquis of Rockingham (1730–82) **XII** 62, 65, 108, 125, 394; first lord of Treasury (1765–6) 111, 113–17, 118, 120, 149 —Stamp Act 187 —act against indirect taxes 191 —state office holders 575; in opposition 128, 223, 230, 235, 240 —privy council and riots 238; first lord of Treasury (1782) 243–6, 574, 578; on America 105, 115, 191, 203, 210; Irish policy 223, 245

Wentworth, Paul **VIII** 219, 223

Wentworth, Peter **VIII** 215–16, 222–3, 224, 225, 226

Wentworth, Philip, sheriff of Norfolk and Suffolk **VI** 345, 531

Wentworth, Thomas, 1st Baron (d. 1551), lord chamberlain of the household (1550) **VII** 649

Wentworth, Thomas, 2nd Baron (1525–84) **VII** 558

Wentworth, Thomas (d. 1747), General **XI** 235

Wentworth, Thomas, 1st earl of Strafford (1593–1641) **IX** 6, 38, 91; urges war on Scots 95–6; on royal defeat at Newburn 96; impeachment 99–100; attainder 101; execution 102, 143, 415; lord deputy of Ireland 110–15; his Irish informant 413; **X** 299, 300; **XI** 183

Wentworth, Thomas, Baron Raby, 3rd earl of Strafford (1672–1739) **XI** 156; impeached 24, 156

Wentworth, Thomas, lawyer **IX** 12

Wentworth, William, 2nd Earl Fitzwilliam (1748–1833): biography **XII** 394; lord lieutenant in Ireland 393, 394–6; president of council 435, 580, 582

Wenzel, king of Bohemia **VI** 67

Weobly (Hereford), Lord Ferrers' manor **VI** 626

Weogorenaleag *see* Wyre Forest (Worcs.)

Weogornaceaster *see* Worcester

Weolud *see* Welland, river

Werburh, St **II** 49

Werferth, bishop of Worcester **II** 271, 545

wergild: Danes and Englishmen **II** 261, 262; ceorl 278, 282, 303; *gesithcund man* 303; intermediate class 303; *læt* 303–4; in later Northumbria 508–9

Werham *see* Wareham (Dorset)

Werken, Theoderic of Appenbroeck **VI** 679

Werwulf, Mercian scholar **II** 271

Weser, river **Ib** xxvii, 46–7, 51, 55, 59; Saxon population 62–3, 66, 72, 102, 105; *Mischgruppe* 107; map 1 xxix

Wesley, Charles (1707–88) **XI** 10,

Westerwanna **Ib** 62, 102, 193; Saxon pottery 70, 71 [fig. 5(c, e), 6(a)]

Westgruppe **Ib** 55

Westley Waterless (Cambs.) **V** 238

Westmacott, Sir Richard **XIII** 587

Westminster, treaty (1674) **X** 83; local government **XII** 47; parliamentary representation 52, 275

Westminster, 1st duke of, Lord Grosvenor **XIII** 184

Westminster (Westmynster): consecration **II** 580, 734; coronation of Matilda 601; councils 631; knight service 635; coronations **III** 4, 98, 143, 213, 349, 378, 430; seat of government and judicial administration 7, 27, 114, 222, 401, 482; palace of 64, 66, 338; courts 115, 133, 207, 413; council (1141) 145; treaty between Stephen and Henry II 165; council (1163) 203; provisions 393; treasury 412, 416–17; great councils (1233–4) **IV** 55, 57; (in 1237) 75; parliaments (1258–1259) 144–6, 148–50; Llywelyn ap Gruffydd does homage (1277) 412; Archbishop Pecham and parliament (1279) 476; Edward I's return (1285) 480; provisions (1259) 174, 194, 216, 217, 370 —legislative and administrative 146–9; **V** 12, 47, 63, 155, 159, 429; evasive on revenue problems 160; Stratford expounds king's needs 161; chancery 213; appanage 258; the Church 272; merchant assembly 351; staple town 353; government offices 379; Edward III's last parliament 394; chronicle 436; war discussion, Richard II 442, 447; lords' appeal against courtiers 450–452; Tresilian discovered hiding 458; Richard's special oath 488 —betrayal 493; **VI** 14, 26, 110; abbey church 128, 294; archdeacon 25, 133; sanctuary 133, 614; Vaughan's house 597; Chapter House 407; Hall 12, 193, 620; Palace 237, 287, 407; White Chamber 407; St Stephen's 292, 647; **VII** 403, 576; Perkin Warbeck 147, 165; wool trade 181; see 400, 502; united with London 518; Lady Jane Grey 526, 528; conference **VIII** 115–17; statutes *see* statutes

Westminster, abbot of **III** 58; *see also* Colchester, William; Crispin, Gilbert; Crockesley; Ware

Westminster, bishops of *see* Thirlby, Thomas

Westminster, chronicler, on Richard II **V** 436, 437; on earl of Warwick 450; on the appellants 452; on de Vere 453; on the proceedings against Brembe 457

Westminster, statutes (1285) **VII** 195; **XV** 254, 261, 277; opposed by Churchill 277; Irish Free State 357

Westminster Abbey: **II** 455, 497, 572, 598, 672; **III** 185; **IV** 18, 119, 222, 224; chapel of St Katherine 75; refectory 78, 113, 672; burglary (1303) 689; records 227; **V** 295, 298, 306, 317, 398; breach of sanctuary scandal 403–4; Imworth dragged from hiding 412; renewal of oaths 459; Gloucester's dispute with monks 463; Richard's portrait 498; Chaucer's house 530; abbot of 99, 306; **VI** 128; **VII** 301, 576; Henry VII's chapel 44, 591, 593; Henry VII's will 229; Henry VIII's death 510; Edward VI's death 533; John Skelton 585; Unknown soldier buried **XV** 163; Hardy buried 178; Northcliffe subscribes to restoration 187; Law and N. Chamberlain buried 204; Handley deserves place 549

Westminster Assembly of Divines **IX** 144, 191–4

Westminster Hall: Provisions of Westminster read (1259) **IV** 148; settlement (Mar. 1265) proclaimed 198; William Wallace tried (1305) 712; Feast of Swans (1306) 514–15, 715; proclamations about petitions 350; **VII** 227, 386, 391, 393; seat of power 44–5; Elizabeth's coronation 78; Warwick condemned 165; banqueting and revelry 192–3; great courts and justice 193–4; council of Henry VII 203, 296, 352; 'evil Mayday' (1517) 298; Wolsey's fall 329; fall of Cromwell (1540) 415; Mary pledged to Philip (1553) 537; Elizabeth refused admission 540; study of law 565; **XV** 378

Westminster Ordinances (1324, 1326) **V** 77

Westminster Palace **VII** 595; seat of power 44–5; Henry VII's first parliament 59; Elizabeth's coronation 78; Wyatt rebellion 538; Mary's death 560

Westminster School: Alexander Nowell headmaster **VII** 577; **X** 415; **XII** 39

Westmoringaland see Westmorland

Westmorland (Westmoringaland) **II** 503, 506, 734; **III** 265, 280; local levies (1297–8) **IV** 684, 688; **V** 32, 60, 192; see also Northwestern England

Westmorland, countess of see Joan, countess of Westmorland

Westmorland, earls of **XIII** 560; see also Fane, John; Neville, Charles; Neville, Ralph (1) and (2)

Westmorland, Neville estates **VI** 321; petitions to Chancellor 458

Westmynster see Westminster

Weston, Edmund, Jesuit **VIII** 183–4, 454

Weston, Richard, earl of Portland **IX** 42, 60; lord high treasurer 82

Weston, Robert **V** 265

Weston-under-Penyard, industrial settlement **Ia** 595

Westphalia **VI** 357, 359

Wet, General C. de **XIV** 254, 255, 256, 345, 346; European visit 348

Wetherby **VIII** 140

Wetherell, Sir Charles **XIII** 83

Wethmor see Wedmore (Som.)

Wetmoor (Staffs.) **III** 60

Wetterau **Ia** 175

Wetwang, Walter **V** 217

Wexford **III** 302, 305, 306, 307, 310; **V** 232; county **VI** 425; **IX** 110, 163

Wey (Wege), river **II** 55, 733; **III** 80

Weybridge (Surrey) **III** 80; **V** 253

Weygand, M.: becomes supreme commander 485; devises imaginary offensive 486; wants armistice 487; rules North Africa 521

Weymouth (Dorset) **VI** 310; **XII** 549; riots **X** 258

Weymouth, Viscount see Bath, marquis of

Whaetberht **Ib** 106

whale fisheries **X** 237, 301; northern **XII** 16; southern 16, 18

Whalley **VII** 397

Whalley, Edward **IX** 239, 245

Whalley, Richard (1499?–1583) **VII** 501

Wharfe, river **II** 589–90, 594

Wharton, 1st marquess of see Wharton, Thomas

Wharton, Philip, 4th Baron **X** 152

Wharton, Philip, duke of (1698–1731) **XI** 179

Wharton, Sir Thomas **VII** 400

Wharton, Thomas, 1st marquess of Wharton: member of the junto **X** 225; lord lieutenant of Ireland 225; protégés 254; Irish Catholics 315; *Lilliburlero* 403 —and music 405

wharves **Ia** 557, 564, 631

Whateley, Thomas (d. 1772) **XII** 127

Wihtgarabyrig **Ib** appendix II; *see also* Carisbrooke

Wihtred, king of Kent **II** 62, 203, 206; charters quoted 283; laws 62, 128, 142; quoted 317

Wihtwara **Ib** 145

Wii *see* Wye (Kent)

Wijk bij Duurstede **II** 166

Wijster (Looveen) **Ib** xxi, 52; map 1 xxix; map 5 68

Wike-by-Arlingham (Glos.) **V** 320

Wikeford, Robert de, archbishop of Dublin (1376–90) **V** 449

Wilberforce, Samuel **XIII** 575–6

Wilberforce, William (1759–1833) **XII** 370, 371, 492, 570; biography 271; MP for Yorkshire 271, 513; support of abolition of slave trade 301, 354, 358, 440; member of Clapham sect 354; **XIII** 15, 31, 68, 370, 505

Wilbye, John **VIII** 306

Wilcocks, Joseph (1673–1756), bishop of Gloucester, then of Rochester **XI** 78

Wilcox, Thomas **VIII** 195–6

Wilde, Oscar **XIV** 304, 323, 333, 527

Wilder, Philip van **VII** 479

Wildman, John **IX** 151

Wildman, William, 2nd Viscount Barrington (1717–93): biography **XII** 69; secretary at war (1755–61) 577; chancellor of the Exchequer (1761–2) 69, 577; treasurer of the navy (1762–5) 577; secretary at war (1765–78) 115, 136, 203, 577

Wilford, Ralph, claims to be Warwick (1499) **VII** 164

Wilford, William de **VI** 72

Wilfrid, bishop of Worcester **II** 485

Wilhelmina, Queen **XV** 485, 486

Wilkes, John (1727–97) **XI** 32, 67, 368, 396; and Foundling Hospital 408; 'Wilkes case' 57; **XII** 64, 270, 357; *North Briton* 81, 99–102, 133; character 98; lack of support 114; elections (1768–74) 131–43, 148–50; identity of Junius 145; Reform movements (1780) 230; Gordon Riots 238; **XV** 374

Wilkie, Sir David (1785–1841) **XII** 539; **XIII** 588

Wilkins, David (1685–1745), editor of *Concilia* **XI** 394

Wilkins, John **IX** 372

Wilkins, Dr John **X** 30, 360, 362

Wilkins, William (1778–1839): biography **XII** 545; **XIII** 581; work of 581–2

Wilkinson, John, industrialist and ironmaster (1728–1808) **XI** 109; ironworks 117; **XII** 32, 332, 507, 553

Wilkinson, Prof. Spenser **XIV** 147, 291

Wilks, Sir Thomas **VIII** 343

will *see* bequest

Willes, Edward (1693–1773), bishop of Bath and Wells **XI** 78

Willes, Sir John (1685–1761) **XI** 58, 63

Willes family **XII** 61

Willesborough (Kent) **III** 225

Willesden (Middx.) **VI** 675

William, bishop of Basel (1394–9) **V** 301

William, bishop of London **II** 464–5, 660

William, brother of King Henry II **III** 129, 202

William I, count of Burgundy **III** 125

William II, count of Hainault, Holland and Zeeland **V** 83, 119, 121, 127

William, count of Holland (Lincs.) **III** 464

William, count of Holland, Zealand and Hainault **VI** 164, 165

William, count of Mortain **III** 119, 120

William, David, master of the rolls (1487) **VII** 648

William III, duke of Aquitaine **II** 407

William, duke of Aquitaine **III** 112

William IV, duke of Clarence (until 1830) **XIII** 24, 77, 84–7, 95, 98; dismissal of Melbourne 101–2; Victoria's accession 103, 104; distrust of Russia 235

William, duke of Cleves, brother of Anne **VII** 403, 404

William, duke of Gelderland **V** 466

William, duke of Gloucester **X** 189–90

William, earl of Arundel **VI** 529, 538

William, earl of Gloucester **III** 12, 158, 348

William, 2nd earl of Shelburne (1737–1805) **XI** 123; quoted 356

William I, Conqueror, king of England, duke of Normandy: relations with council of duchy **II** 555–6; relations with English court 560; recognized as Confessor's heir 561; visit to England 565–6; relations with Brittany 577, 608; position (1066) 577, 585; as military commander 584; career in Normandy 584; marriage 585; conquest of Maine 585; case against Harold 586–7; concentrates his forces 588; invades England 591; tactics at Hastings 593–6; advance upon London 596–8; crowned king 598; visits Normandy 599; reduces Exeter 600; northern campaigns 601–5; disbands mercenaries 605; devastates North and Midlands 605; revolt of the three English earls 610–11; execution of earl Waltheof 612; relations with Philip I of France 608; relations with sons 609; representatives in England 610–11; relations of Normans with Welsh 615–16; preparations against Cnut of Denmark 617–18; last French campaign 619–20; contemporary descriptions 620–21; claims to rule as King Edward's heir 622–4; changing policy towards English subjects 625–6, 680; redistribution of land 626, 680; attitude to Archbishop Stigand 624; initiates Domesday Survey 617; ecclesiastical reformer 658–9; relations with Lanfranc 662–5; his ecclesiastical appointments 672–3; relations with papacy 674–8, 678; ecclesiastical supremacy 675–7; refuses fealty to pope 675; legislation 685–6; title **III** 1; crown-wearing 4; knight service 12; dispositions and last acts 97–100; the fyrd 102; exacts Danegeld 110; earldoms 157, 285; relations with the Church 167, 169, 201, 202, 205; relations with Scotland 265, 268; murder fine 393; abolishes capital punishment 404; monument 414

William II, Rufus, king of England **III** 1, 132, 154, 167; writ 6; extortions 20, 169–71; trade with Norway 88; character 98–9; suppresses rebellion of Odo 101–4; Norman wars 104–8, 119; rebellion against 109–10; buys Normandy 110; campaigns in Vexin and Maine 111–12; death 113–14; creation of earls 157; relations with Church 169–73; quarrel with Anselm 173–7; founds Bermondsey Abbey 185; trials of Anselm 194; income from Church 220; relations with Scotland 266, 268, 283; with Wales 286, 288, 289; Irish ambition not realized 302; respecter of property 408

William III, king of England (1689–1702): sets up Board of Trade **X** 44; Charles II and 62; stadholder 83–4; marriage 88;

William Clito, son of Robert Curthose **III** 121-2, 124-7
William the Englishman **III** 261
William d'Eu **II** 487, 632
William of Hesse, prince (d. 1760) **XI** 243-4
William Malet **II** 593, 630
William de Mandeville, earl of Essex **III** 351
William and Mary College **X** 348
William the miller **III** 404
William IV of Nassau, prince of Orange, right to issue naval commissions **VIII** 128, 155; Netherlands campaign 156, 164-5, 336-47, 351; his murder 364; stadtholder of United Provinces (1711-51) **XI** 260
William of Newark **VII** 589
William of Newburgh **III** 136, 158, 189, 203; opinion of Becket 209; of bishops 223; historian 248; extent of David's kingdom 274-5; view of Malcolm IV 276; of Richard's liberation of prisoners 349; on massacres of the Jews 354; **VI** 657
William of Ockham **IV** 523; **V** 290, 509-10; **VI** 677; Oxford reaction 680
William fitz Osbern, earl of Hereford **II** 593, 599, 602, 607; regency in King William's absence 610; conquests in Wales 615; King William's charter 623; organizes Hereford as military command 625; *dapifer* 630, 639; death 639
William de Percy **II** 632
William de Poitiers **II** 658
William de St Calais, bishop of Durham **II** 632, 678
William of Savoy, bishop-elect of Valence, uncle of Eleanor of Provence **IV** 74-5
William de Warenne **II** 593, 630, 673
William of Waynflete, bishop of Winchester **VI** 419, 504; East Meon tenants 540-1; treasurer 513; Magdalen College founder 674
William of Worcester **VI** 342, 350, 351; Maine petition 507
William of Wykeham, bishop of Winchester **VI** 271, 294, 342-3, 650
Williams, Sir Charles Hanbury (1708-59) **XI** 350, 425; *Old England's Te Deum* 24; *Isabella of the Morning* 148
Williams, Dr Daniel **X** 158, 264, 324
Williams, E. T. **XV** 508
Williams, Colonel L. Fenwick **XIII** 288
Williams, Mr, priest **VII** 592
Williams, Richard, Welsh castles **VI** 641
Williams, Roger **VIII** 357, 414; **IX** 213, 341-2
Williams, Vaughan **XV** 178, 398
Williamsburg **X** 348
Williamson, Sir Joseph **X** 56
Willikin of the Weald **III** 484; *see also* Kensham, William of
Willingdon, Lord *see* Thomas, F. Freeman
Willingham, watercourse **Ia** 268
Willoughby, Francis, 5th Baron **X** 327
Willoughby, Sir Hugh (d. 1554) **VII** 507; **VIII** 237
Willoughby, Lord *see* Peregrine Bertie; William
Willoughby, Sir Richard **V** 168, 204, 205
Willoughby, Sir Robert, 1st Baron Willoughby de Broke (1452-1502) **VII** 54, 55, 89, 145, 209; great master of the household (1488) 649
Willoughby, Robert, lord of Eresby **VI** 325, 494, 526
Willoughby, Sir Thomas **VI** 325
Willoughby, Sir William **VII** 57

Willoughby-on-the-Wolds **Ib** 182; map 4 xxxii; map 5 68

Willoughby de Broke, Lord **XIV** 428, 476

Willoughby Cole, William, 1st earl of Enniskillen (1736–1803) **XI** 298

Willoughton (Lincs.) **III** 59

wills, administration **IV** 470–1, 490–1

Wills, Sir Charles, General (1666–1741) **XI** 162

Will's Coffee-house **X** 358

Wilmington, earl of *see* Compton, Sir Spencer

Wilmot, Sir John Eardley (1709–92) **XI** 63, 65

Wilra, Conrad of, seneschal of Otto IV **III** 451

Wilson, Sir Arthur **XIV** 435, 436

Wilson, Benjamin (1721–88), painter **XI** 406

Wilson, Sir Henry (1864–1922) **XIV** 435, 475, 477, 478, 479; biography **XV** 6; British Expeditionary Force 6, 7; doubts whether troops reliable 38; becomes Chief of Imperial General Staff 100; expects victory only (1919) 108; urges conscription for Ireland 112; reconquest of Ireland 156; assassinated 188

Wilson, Sir Henry Maitland: tries to seize Aegean island **XV** 573; supreme commander Mediterranean 575; Washington

Wilson, Sir Horace: power **XV** 174; German rearmament 376; becomes Chamberlain's adviser 405; accompanies Chamberlain 426; sent to Hitler 428; conversations with Wohltat 475–6

Wilson, Richard (1714–82), painter **XI** 401, 403, 408, 410; **XII** 344

Wilson, Sir Richard (1777–1849), biography **XII** 489

Wilson, Richard, painter (1714–82) **XII** 344

Wilson, Scottish smuggler, hanged in Edinburgh (1737) **XI** 278

Wilson, Sir Thomas **VIII** 342, 347

Wilson, Thomas (1525?–81) **VII** 583

Wilson, Thomas (1663–1755), bishop of Sodor and Man **XI** 88

Wilson, Woodrow: protests at sinking of *Lusitania* **XV** 43; proposes negotiated peace 62; offers to mediate 79; declares war on Germany 84; Lloyd George appeals to 101; Germans appeal to 110; Fourteen Points 111, 116–19; Paris conference 132; League 133; German frontiers 134; Fiume 162

Wilton (Wiltun) (Wilts.) **Ib** 154; map 3 xxxi; **II** 250, 337, 380, 531; 734; council 349; nunnery 445; **III** 25, 143, 146; **IX** 381–2, 384

Wilton, abbess of **VII** 295

Wilton, Jacke **VIII** 294

Wilton, Joseph (1722–1803), sculptor **XI** 402, 408

Wilton, William of, judge **IV** 176

Wilton Diptych **V** 498

Wiltshire: county **VI** 68; archdeaconry 283; assessed 476; archers 508; **Ia** 43, 44, 75, 93; **Ib** 129, 139, 150, 152, 155; Mons Badonicus 159–60, 162; Cuddesdon 170; raiding 185; Saxon settlements 215; **II** 63, 65, 279, 439, 505; origin 41; meaning of the name 294–5, 337; **III** 48, 61, 86, 101, 393; fighting during the Anarchy 151–2; Angevin stronghold 162; John's hunting ground 431; **V** 67, 192, 226, 368; Edington's collegiate church 213; water power for fulling-mills 365; earl of *see* Scrope, Sir William; **VII** 145, 146, 462, 463, 504; **IX** 296

Wiltshire, earls of *see* Boleyn, Thomas; Butler, James; Paulet, William; Powlett, Charles; Scrope, Sir William

Wiltshire, sheriff of, amerced **VI** 513

Wiltun *see* Wilton (Wilts.)

Wimbish (Essex) **VI** 562

Wimbledon, Viscount *see* Cecil, Edward

Wimborne (Winburnan) (Dorset) **II** 250, 321, 734; monastery 173, 321

Wimborne, Lord **XIV** 543

Wimbush (Essex) **V** 239

Wimbush, John **V** 428

Winburnan *see* Wimborne (Dorset)

Wincanton **X** 139

Wincelcumb *see* Winchcombe (Glos.)

Winchcomb, Richard, New College sculptor **VI** 648

Winchcombe (Glos.), shire **II** 337; abbey 450, 677; **III** 164, 412; abbey **V** 322, 330; **VI** 367, 647; abbot (1421) 196

Winchcombe, John **VII** 462; **VIII** 258

Winchelsea (Sussex) **III** 96, 433; **IV** 10, 207; new town 635–7; Edward I's port of departure for Flanders (1297) 636, 668, 676, 678; **V** 87, 241, 243, 244, 380; Spanish shipping raids 137; Henry of Lancaster in sea-fight 254, 256

Winchelsea, earl of, lord president of council (1765–66) **XII** 575

Winchelsey, Robert, archbishop of Canterbury: (1294–1313) **IV** 488; character 673, 678, 717–18; election and arrival in England 671–3; debts 672, 718; dilemma in regard to clerical taxation by the king 523, 672–8, 680; takes papal letters about Scotland to the king (1300) 229, 693, 702; action in parliament of Lincoln (1301) 704, 705; strained relations with Edward I, suspension and departure from England 717–18; (1294–1313) **V** 5, 7, 295, 300; recalled by Edward II 3, 5, 6; opposes Edward II 7, 9, 288;

Ordainer 10; Ordinances 18; excommunicates Gaveston 24; death 30; Lancaster associated with 69; **VI** 420

Winchelsey, Thomas, Franciscan **VI** 298

Winchester (Wintanceaster) (Hants): *civitas* capital **Ia** 93; defences 261; burials 358–9, 386, 551, 694; Hampshire pottery distribution 648; state weaving-mill? 656; (*Venta Belgarum*) **Ib** xxvi, 4, 149–52, 159–60, 213; map 2 xxx; map 3 xxxi; map 6 88; **II** 264, 385, 426, 531, 631; see 122, 134, 146, 147, 438; king's council 349; treasury 420, 643–4, 655; minting and moneyers 436–8; cathedral 441, 445, 451; school of illuminators 443; New Minster 444–5, 451, 455, 462; ecclesiastical councils 449, 452–3; submission to King William 596; King William returns for Easter festival 602; Devon rising 603; Earl Waltheof beheaded 612; knight service 634; legatine councils (1070) 660, (1072) 664–5; provincial councils (1072) 665; (1076) 667–8; **III** 100, 116, 233, 396; Domesday Book 1, 36; crown-wearing 4; merchant gild 72; St Giles's fair 77, 155; cloth industry 85, 87; assize of customs 93; William II buried 113; council (1139) 136, 138; Matilda elected 143; 'rout' 144, 272; treaty between Stephen and Henry Plantagenet 165, 166; Anselm's homage to William II 173; council (1155) 303; quarrel between John and Longchamp 355–6; Longchamp venerated 358; Richard I crowned 369; false moneyers condemned 415; Christmas feast (1206) 427; conference with Simon Langton 447; John absolved from excommunication 461; John driven

legatine council (1070) 661; (1072) 665; (1179) 222; **III** 175, 357, 364, 473, 484; **V** 11, 22, 23, 131, 408; Suffolk jailed 446; Hereford and Norfolk dispute 487; **VI** 25, 553; forest 100; St George's chapel 164, 278, 292, 300, 639; liberties 393–4; castle 486; royal lodgings 648; bells, jewels and vestments 669; forest **VII** 34; heretics burned (1543) 427–8; Henry VIII buried 442, 495, 510; marriage of Philip and Mary (1554) 541; **VIII** 50; **IX** 153, 157

Windsor, treaties (1175) **III** 311; (1522) **VII** 312, 315, 316

Windsor, Sir William of **V** 386–7

Windsor Castle: **III** 18, 315, 352, 359; **IV** 22, 25, 48, 63, 118; council (1236) 74; knights of shire summoned (1261) 166; Lord Edward surrenders (1263) 176, 180, 181; restored to King Henry 203; ordinances issued (1265) 204–5; **V** 226, 252, 256, 373; Roger Mortimer commemorated in royal chapel 287; building conscripts 372; **VII** 88, 204, 390, 591; Sir Thomas Bourchier 57; Philip and Juana entertained 184, 186; feasts and splendour 191–2; Charles and Henry VIII sign treaties (1522) 312; fall of Wolsey 329; Northumberland plot 526, 528; St George's chapel 593; paintings 600

Windsor Park **III** 53

Windward Islands **X** 325

wine **Ia** 42, 224, 459, 651–5; in burials 704; barrels 653; **IV** 629, 631; trade with Gascony 276, 669; trade **V** 149, 360–3; **X** 358; *see also* Bordeaux, customs; Gascony

Wine, bishop of Winchester **II** 122, 124; bishop of London 132, 133

Wines, assize **III** 92

Wingfield (Suffolk) **VI** 472, 484, 494

Wingfield, Sir Anthony (d. 1552), comptroller (1550) **VII** 650

Wingfield, Humphrey, speaker of the House of Commons (1533) **VII** 198, 653

Wingfield, Sir John **V** 247; **VIII** 419

Wingfield, Katherine, Sir John's daughter **VI** 472

Wingfield, Sir Richard (1469?–1525), chancellor of duchy of Lancaster (1524) **VII** 315

Wingfield, Sir Robert, controller of the household **VI** 604

Wingfield, Roger **V** 292

Wingham, Henry of, king's clerk, chancellor (1255–60), bishop of London (1260–2) **IV** 112, 162

Wingham **Ib** map 5 68

Winstanley, Gerrard **IX** 197–8

Winston (Devon) **VI** 309

Winta (Wintra) **Ib** 176, 180

Wintanceaster *see* Winchester (Hants)

Winter, de, Dutch admiral **XII** 373

Winter (Wynter), Thomas **VII** 295

Winter, Sir William **VIII** 43, 44, 402, 478

Winteringham **Ib** 177; map 4 xxxii

Winterton (Humberside), excavations **Ia** 626; **Ib** 177; map 4 xxxii

Winterton, Lord **XV** 542

Winthrop, John **IX** 340

Wintoun, earl of *see* Seton, George

Wintringham, T. H. **XV** 347

Winwæd, river, battle **II** 84

Winwood, Sir Ralph **IX** 16

Wipped, Wippedes fleot **Ib** appendix I(a)

Wireker, Nigel, precentor of Canterbury **III** 223, 241, 242

wireless telegraphy **XIV** 510–11

Wirheulum *see* Wirral (Cheshire)

Wirral (Wirheulum) (Cheshire) **II** 734; **V** 418

Wisbech Barton (Cambs.) **III** 485; **V** 321, 326, 330

Wisbech Castle **V** 317; **VIII** 188

Wisby **III** 89

Wise, E. F. **XV** 349

Wise, Francis (1695–1767), editor of Asser's *Annals of Alfred* **XI** 394

Wiseman, N., Cardinal **XIII** 522

Wishart, George **VII** 407

Wishart, Robert, bishop of Glasgow (1273–1316), guardian of Scotland (1286) **IV** 597, 598, 606; vote in succession case 607; rising (of 1297) 684; imprisoned (1297–9) 685; swears fealty to Edward (1300) 710; defection, rebuked by Pope Boniface 709–10; later betrayals and imprisonment (1303–6) 710, 711–14, 716

Wissant (Calais) **VI** 106

Wissey, river **II** 295, 321

Witan, Witenagemot **II** 622; *see also* council, the king's

Witch, The **VIII** 301

witchcraft **IX** 370–2; **X** 418

witchcraft and witches **VIII** 329, 330, 331; **IX** 370–2; **X** 418; abolished as a crime **XI** 61

Witchley hundred (Rutland) **II** 505

Witcombe, villa **Ia** 276, 278

Witefeld, Robert de **III** 390

With, De, Witte Corneliszoon **IX** 223

Witham (Witham) (Essex) **II** 325, 335, 734

Witham (Withma), river **Ib** 181; map 4 xxxii; **II** 734; **III** 80

Witham Priory (Som.) **III** 86, 229

Wither, George **VIII** 302

Wither, William **IV** 46; *see also* Tweng

Withma *see* Witham, river

Witlanbyrig *see* Whittlebury (Northants)

Witney (Oxon.) **III** 463

Witsand (Pas-de-Calais) **III** 363

Witte, Count **XIV** 403

Wittelsbach, Conrad of, archbishop of Mainz **III** 367, 450

Wittenberg **VII** 343, 382

Witton (Norfolk) **III** 337

Witton-le-Wear (Co. Durham) **VI** 417

Wiuræmuda *see* Monkwearmouth (Co. Durham)

Wix nunnery (Essex) **III** 30

Wlencing **Ib** 137, appendix I(b)

Woburn **VII** 398

Woccingas **Ib** 43

Wode, John, Commons Speaker **VI** 614–15

Wodeforde, William **V** 511, 519; **VI** 297

Wodehouse, Pelham Grenville **XV** 312; proposal to prosecute 534

Wodehouse, Robert, treasurer (1329–30, 1338) **V** 158, 159

Woden, god **II** 19, 98–101; Grim an *alias* of 100–1

Wodnesbeorg (Wodnes Beorg, Wodnesbeorh) *see* Alton Priors (Wilts.)

Wodnesgeat **Ib** 160

Woffington, Peg (?1714–60), Irish actress **XI** 304

Wogan, Charles (?1698–1752) **XI** 292

Wogan, Sir John **V** 41

Wogan, John, justiciar of Ireland **IV** 535

Wohltat, conversations **XV** 475–6

Woking (Surrey) **Ib** 43; monastery **II** 160, 165

Wokingham **Ib** 43

Wolcot, John **XII** 350

Wolf, David, Jesuit **VIII** 468

Wolf Hall (Wilts.) **VII** 380

Wolfe, Revd Charles (1791–1823) **XII** 461

Wolfe, James (1727–59) **XI** 218, 221, 361, 363–4, 365; **XII** 25, 369; pictures of death 86, 345, 430

Wolfe, Reyner **VII** 578

Wolfenbüttel, duke of *see* Augustus William

Wolff, Sir H. Drummond **XIV** 52, 67

Wollaston (Northants) **II** 629

Wollaton Hall **VIII** 303

610

Wolseley, Sir Charles **X** 31
Wolseley, Sir G. J., afterwards Viscount **XIII** 436; **XIV** 11, 28–9, 61; Tel-el-Kebir 79; as commander-in-chief 291–2
Wolsey, Thomas **VII** 7, 232, 283, 350, 353; supposed creator of Star Chamber 207; origin 233, 287; Silvestro de' Gigli 238; Erasmus 257; vigour in preparing invasion of France (1513) 277; part in the volte-face (1514) 285; power and offices 286–7, 302–3; ecclesiastical promotion 289–90; bishop of Lincoln and Tournai (1514) 289; archbishop of York (1514) 289; cardinal (1515) 289; legate *a latere* (1518) 289, 308, 568; defends Church against lay interference in Hunne case (1514–15) 291–3; use of legatine council to control English Church 293–5; activity as chancellor (1515–29) 295–9; autocracy as first minister 299–302; failure of finance 303–4; foreign policy 305; encourages adventurousness of Henry (1515–16) 307; not discomfited by Treaty of Noyon 307; success in universal peace (1518) 308–9; furthers Anglo-Imperial alliance (1520–4) 310–15; disappointed of papacy 290, 312, 314; allies with France (1524–8) 315–18; policy fails with Peace of Cambrai (1529) 319–20; estimate of foreign policy 320–1; wrongly denounced as author of 'divorce' 322–4; dilemma 327; Henry and Catherine's divorce 328; fall 329–30; last venture 331; arrest and death (29 Nov. 1530) 332; failures and achievements 333–4; example to Henry 334; attitude to reformers 343–6; to heretics 347; Reformation 348; Thomas Cromwell 351–2, 370; Edmund Bonner 358; affairs in Ireland 364; Rhys

ap Gruffydd's execution 366–7; suppresses small houses for benefit of colleges at Ipswich and Oxford (1518) 375–6; Pilgrimage of Grace (1536) 385–6; English currency (1526) 412, 605; Commission on Inclosures (1517) 451; Staplers and the cloth trade 474; Cardinal College 570; Lutheranism 572; Joannes Ludovicus Vives 576; John Skelton 585; encouraged musicians 590; Hampton Court 592, 595, 597, 602; coinage 605; becomes chancellor (1515) 646
Wolverhampton **IV** 339
wolves **X** 409
Wolvesey, castle of bishop of Winchester **IV** 140
Wolvesey Palace, Winchester **III** 144
Woman Killed by Kindness **VIII** 301
women: contribution to monastic reform **II** 445; as labourers **IX** 297; fashions denounced 311–12; education 358–9; education **XIV** 148–50; First World War **XV** 38; suffrage 94, 115, 204; first MP 128; leave industry 139; high numbers 166; clothes 173; cinema-goers 181; vote attained 236; on equal terms 262; MPs force vote against Chamberlain 472; conscription 512, 548
women inspectors **XIV** 130, 294
Women's Institutes **XV** 264
Women's Social and Political Union (WSPU) **XIV** 397, 398, 459, 460
women's suffrage, bills (1911–13) **XIV** 459–61
Wood, Alderman **XIII** 67
Wood, Sir Andrew **VII** 136
Wood, Anthony (1632–95) **IX** 98; **XI** 394
Wood, Edward Frederick Lindley, Lord Halifax, Lord Irwin: biography **XV** 129; against conciliating Germany 129; Inner Cabinet

Wood (Lord Halifax) (*cont.*)
197; becomes viceroy 254; promises Dominion status 275; Simon
compared with 372; insists on
Hoare's resignation 385; historic
title 405; supports Chamberlain's
policy 420; visits Germany 422;
becomes foreign secretary 423;
accepts Franco's victory 424;
Czech crisis 427, 428; discusses
Munich with Chamberlain 431;
visits Mussolini 436; Hitler's
occupation of Prague 440; wishes
to keep Russia in play 446; does
not go to Moscow 448; outbreak
of war 449–52; War Cabinet 456;
objects to Hore-Belisha as minister of information 460; proposed
as prime minister 473; declines
474; George VI regrets 475;
speech on foreign policy 476;
Churchill's War Cabinet 478;
rejects Hitler's peace offer 489;
goes to Washington as ambassador 509
Wood, Sir Evelyn **XIV** 29, 564,
565
Wood, G. H. **XIV** 134
Wood, H. G. **X** 25
Wood, Mrs Henry **XIV** 160
Wood, John (?1705–54), architect
XI 402, 411
Wood, John (d. 1782), architect **XI**
402, 411
Wood, John, Murray's servant **VIII**
111, 114
Wood, John, Yorkshire manufacturer **XIII** 148–9
Wood, Sir Kingsley: biography **XV**
459; refuses to bomb private
property 459; Chamberlain's resignation 474; imposes purchase
tax 491; enters War Cabinet 509;
novel finance 511; ejected from
War Cabinet 544; death and
legacy 573
Wood, Robert (?1717–71), *Essay on
Homer* **XI** 394

Wood, Robert, under-secretary of
state **XII** 100
Wood, Thomas, MP **XII** 228
Wood, William (1671–1730) **XI**
115, 300–1; 'Wood's halfpence'
293, 300–3
Woodall, John **VIII** 313
Woodard, Nathaniel **XIII** 488
Woodchester, villa **Ia** 597, 731
Woodhead, Sir John, and Palestine
XV 407
Woodhouse, Henry, son of John **VI**
449
Woodhouse, John, of Kimberley
(Norfolk) **VI** 297; Castle Rising
constable 31; Suffolk MP 416;
Lancaster chancellor 449
woodland *see* forest(s)
woodland, treatment **II** 282–5
Woodlark, Robert **VI** 671
Woodlock, Henry, bishop of Win-
chester (1305–16) **V** 300
Woodstock (Oxon.): assize **III** 32;
park and forest 19–20, 236–7,
321; royal palace 88, 214, 279;
council at (1163) 202; homage of
Malcolm 276 —and Llywelyn
299; incorporation charter 321;
treaty (1247) **IV** 400, 412; **VI**
393; **VII** 148, 203, 329, 540; **X**
389–91
Woodstock, Thomas of *see* Thomas
of Woodstock
Woodville, Anthony, 2nd Earl Rivers (1442?–83) **VII** 15, 18
Woodville, Anthony, Earl Rivers
(d. 1469) **VI** 517, 570
Woodville, Catherine, wife of William Courtenay **VII** 169
Woodville, Edward, Lord Scales
VII 49, 88; killed at St Aubin du
Cormier (1488) 87
Woodville, Edward, Queen Elizabeth's brother **VI** 590, 612,
615, 616, 628
Woodville, Elizabeth (1437?–92):
sent to convent (1487) **VII** 69;
mentioned 49, 61

Woodville, Elizabeth, Edward IV's queen: ancestry **VI** 535; marriage 536; Edward IV's secrecy 546; Buckingham custody 553; lands confiscated 605; suspected by Protector 617–18

Woodville, John, executed **VI** 536

Woodville, Lionel, bishop of Salisbury **VI** 570, 604, 626, 627, 632

Woodville, Richard **VI** 626, 627

Woodville, Richard, Earl Rivers **VI** 517, 570; son 517, 570; queen's father 535; treasurer 553; Edgecot flight 556; Calais lieutenancy 570; sent to solicit Charles the Bold 575, 576; arrested 612; executed (1469) 613

Woodville family: Hastings enmity **VI** 570; success 553; **VII** 57; *see also* Woodville, Anthony, Earl Rivers; Woodville, Richard, Earl Rivers

wool **Ia** 620, 655–6; customs **V** 14, 155–7, 166, 179, 180; consent to increases 192–3; wages for Brittany campaign 235; enforcement of ordinance 354; subsidy granted to Edward III 392; accorded to Richard II 485; products **VIII** 237, 238

wool, fells, and hides: continental trade in English and Welsh **IV** 637–8; customs 532, 628, 629–31 — receipts from 630; embargo on export to Flanders (1290–8) and value of licensed exports 621–2; prices 629, 637–8; maltote (1294–7) 630, 663, 669, 682, 683; seizures and royal controls of sales as a war measure (1294–7) 648, 662–3, 666, 671; centralized control of exports and beginnings of the staple 663–4; assignation of customs to men of Bayonne (1299–1304) 650; prices and inquiries into 659, 680–1, 699

wool trade **V** 120–1, 143, 225, 305, 322–3; slump following Black

Death 336; becomes main export 349–56; endangered during Norwich crusade 432; **VII** 125, 186–7; **XIV** 278

Wooler **VII** 280

Wooler, Thomas Jonathan, biography **XIII** 30

Woolf, Virginia **XV** 311

woollen industry **V** 302, 356, 363–70, 505; **IX** 288–93; parliamentarian strongholds in Yorkshire 132; regulation 149, 293; clothing areas 261; export trade 289, 291–2, 317–18, 332–3; **X** 48–9, 178, 207, 317, 319; protected from foreign competition 45, 237; Ireland 301, 317–19

woollen manufacture *see under* textiles

woollen trade **XIV** 278

Woollett, William (1735–85), engraver **XI** 414; **XII** 346

Woolley, Hanna **X** 418

Woolman, Robert **V** 206

Woolner, Thomas **XIV** 158

Woolston, Thomas (1670–1733) **XI** 84

Woolton, Lord: non-party minister **XV** 478; favours points 510; reconstruction 567

Wootton (Oxon.) **III** 19

Wootton, John (?1668–1765), painter **XI** 401, 410

Wootton Bassett **Ib** 149; map 3 xxxi

Worcester (Weogornaceaster) **Ib** 3 xxxi; **II** 326, 422, 526, 529, 531, 733; diocese 44, 134, 146, 664; English and Danish Thegns in Worcestershire 413; cathedral 414; diocese annexed to see of York 436; borough, fortification, by Æthelred and Æthelflæd of Mercia 529; minters and moneyers 537; sacked by Harthacnut 563; knight service 634; dispute between bishop and abbot of Evesham 650; **III** 55, 102, 247; see 14, 172, 226; cloth

Worcester (*cont.*)

fair 86; during the Anarchy 136, 139–40, 153, 158; survival of English language 253; council (1218) 301; grievances in Inquest of Sheriffs 389; John buried and his memory observed 429, 486; King John buried in cathedral church **IV** 1; treaty (1218) 16, 393; stormed (1264) 196–8, 199; headquarters of Lord Edward (1265) 202; King Edward's armies 408, 441; **V** 462; diocese 283, 519; priory 418; **VI** 58, 102, 547; north gate 57; Woodbury Hill 58; **VII** 67, 68; castle 57; see 238, 294, 399, 596; **IX** 138, 169; riots **X** 258; workhouse 53; newspaper 356

Worcester, bishops of *see* Alcock; Barnet; Cantilupe, Walter de; Cenwald; Cobham, Thomas; Ealdred; Evesham, Sylvester of; Giglis, John de; Giglis, Silvestro de; Gray, Walter de; Hooper, John; Johnson, James; Latimer, Hugh; Lyfing; Oftfor; Mauger; Montague, Simon; Morton, Robert; Orleton; Pate, Richard; Reynolds, Walter; Roger; Silvester; Thoresby; Tideman; Werferth; Whittlesey; Wilfrid; Wulfstan I and II

Worcester, earls of *see* Somerset, Charles; Somerset, Edward; Somerset, William; Tiptoft, John; Percy, Thomas; Waleran, count of Meulan

Worcester, East Indiaman **X** 285

Worcester, Florence of **III** 249

Worcester, John of **III** 150

Worcester, marquis of *see* Somerset

Worcester, Philip of **III** 313

Worcester, prior (1421) **VI** 196

Worcester, Ralph of **III** 189

Worcester, William of *see* William of Worcester

Worcestershire: rising (1088) **III**

101, 102, 202; JPs **VI** 451, 452; **VII** 68, 464, 504; **IX** 280

Worde, Wynkyn de **VI** 665

Wordsworth, Dr John, bishop **XIV** 307

Wordsworth, William **X** 373; **XII** 534, 539; **XIII** 32, 35, 37–8, 267, 366; best work 530

Workers' Educational Association **XIV** 538; **XV** 267

Workers' Weekly **XV** 218, 225

workhouses **X** 53–4

working classes **IX** 294–5

workshops **Ia** 657–8

Worksop (Notts) **VI** 523

World economic conference **XV** 334–5

World War, First: declared **XV** 2–3; Great Britain loses independence 8; trench warfare 11; changed character 61–2; effects 52, 120–3, 163–4, 182; religion 169; MacDonald's attitude 214–15, 293, 382; makes Britain secure 227; memories 259; started by mistake 274, 370; memory erased 298; economic policy 268, 299; produces new ideas 322; obscures need for economic changes 345; books published 361; effects of blockade exaggerated 370; bombing believed unanswerable 390; generals disliked machine guns 391; legacy 417; misleading air casualty statistics 437; Simon opposed 452; for King and Country 459; hostility between civilians and fighting men 504; inspiring echoes 514; supreme war council 537; characteristic song 549; bibliography 620–6

World War, Second: few memorials **XV** 163; expected (1943) 228; air forces at outbreak 231; increase in birth rate after 302; film units in front line 316; Manchurian affair regarded as first step towards

370; Neville Chamberlain lays foundations of British strength 418; gas not used 427–8; fate of Czechoslovakia and Poland 430; air raid casualties 437; outbreak 452; causes 453; manpower policy 456; chiefs of staff 457; aims lacking 458; characteristic poster 459; co-operation 508; code names of campaigns 536; shape determined at Arcadia conference 539; strategic bombing 541; literature 549; more munitions produced than in First World War 565; three milestones 570; stimulates new industries 600; bibliography 642–8

Wormald, Patrick **Ia** 473, 501

Worms **III** 127, 364; Concordat 180; **VII** 343; diet (1521) 338

Worsley, royal surveyor **XII** 97

Worsley, William, dean of St Paul's **VII** 122

Worthing **XII** 549

Worthington, Gilbert, parson **VI** 669

Wortley *see* Stuart-Wortley-Mackenzie

Wotton, Edward (1492–1555) **VII** 571; **VIII** 315, 370

Wotton, Sir Henry **VIII** 441

Wotton, Nicholas, principal secretary (1549) **VII** 649

Wotton, Sir Henry **IX** 352, 377

Wrawe, John **V** 415, 416, 418, 419

Wray, Sir Cecil **XII** 275

Wray, Sir Christopher **VIII** 220

Wreak, river **Ib** map 2 xxx; map 4 xxxii

wreck, law **IV** 375, 620

Wrekin (Wreocen) (Salop) **II** 243, 734

Wren, Sir Christopher (1632–1723) **X** 30, 383, 388, 391, 393–7; **XI** 399, 407, 410, 411

Wreocen *see* The Wrekin (Salop)

Wreocensætan **II** 41, 44, 296, 337

Wressell (Yorks.): castle **VI** 10, 63, 337, 638; **VII** 389

Wright, Andrew **VII** 599, 601

Wright, Edward **IX** 368

Wright, Joseph, of Derby (1734–97), painter **XI** 401; **XII** 347

Wright v. Fitzgerald, case of **XII** 397

Wriothesley, Charles **VII** 580

Wriothesley, Henry, 2nd earl of Southampton **VIII** 151

Wriothesley, Henry, 3rd earl of Southampton **VIII** 433, 439, 441

Wriothesley, Sir Thomas, 1st Baron Wriothesley of Titchfield, earl of Southampton **VII** 491, 511, 512, 596, 648; monastery land 400; 'benevolence money' 411; principal secretary of state (1540) 414, 648; fall of Cromwell (1540) 415–16; out of favour 418; heretic persecutions 428; Crown and parliament 437; death of Henry VIII 442; made baron but deprived of chancellorship (1547) 493–4, 496, 646; readmitted to council (1548) 496

Wriothesley, Thomas, 4th earl of Southampton **X** 2–3, 7–8, 67

writ, king's: origin **II** 395–6, 415; Anglo-Norman 642–3

writ *de excommunicato capiendo* **VIII** 24

writ *de odio et athia* **III** 403

writ *praecipe* **III** 410, 475

writ of right **III** 387, 410, 411

writing tablets **Ia** 165, 531, 565

writs of caption **IV** 465, 467; *de tali saisina habenda* 15–16, 205; *rex relatu plurimorum* 468

writs, royal: control of new **IV** 78; of expenses 144; cases without 218; special 327, 330; return 366, 377–8; register of original, in Ireland and Wales 560; dated in Scotland to be admitted in England (1291) 560

Writtel, Godebold of **III** 147

Wroth, Sir Robert **VIII** 226, 231
Wrotham, William of, archdeacon
of Taunton **III** 224, 435
Wroxeter (*Viroconium* and *Civitas
Cornoviorum*) **Ia** 95, 105, 135; *civitas Cornoviorum* and town development 185–6, 584; communications 255; evidence for late
occupation 388, 397, 458; plague?
552; baths 185, 578; *macellum* 584;
pottery shop 658; **Ib** 22, 23
Wryght, priest **VIII** 451
Wuffingas **Ib** 97
Wulfhere, archbishop of York **II** 251
Wulfhere, king of Mercia **II** 55, 67;
overlord of southern English 34,
84–5, 202; sells see of London 57,
132; accession 84; charter quoted
294
Wulfnoth, brother of Harold, king of
England **III** 100
Wulfnoth of Sussex **II** 382, 417
Wulfred, archbishop of Canterbury
II 36; formerly archdeacon of
Canterbury 229, 440; induced
clergy of Canterbury to adopt
rule of Chrodegang of Metz 229;
quarrel with Cenwulf 229
Wulfric **III** 94
Wulfric, abbot of Newminster **II**
665
Wulfric, Saxon thegn **II** 488
Wulfric Spot **II** 496, 553
Wulfsige, bishop of Sherborne **II**
456, 459
Wulfstan I, archbishop of York **II**
357, 360, 361
Wulfstan II, archbishop of York **II**
394; bishop of Worcester 459;
writer of homilies and drafter of
laws 459, 546, 676; English works
457, 460
Wulfstan II, bishop of Worcester **II**
468, 546, 581, 597, 666; cooperates with Norman barons
612; dispute with abbot of
Evesham 650; position unchallenged 660; penitential code of

Ermenfrid 662; only English
bishop under Conquerer 680
Wulfstan, voyage **II** 274
Wulfwig, bishop of Dorchester **II**
468
Württemberg: cemetery **Ia** 695; **Ib**
82
Württemberg, prince-regent of **X**
170, 171
Würzburg, diet of **III** 210, 329
Wyatt, Sir Henry (d. 1537): treasurer to the king's chamber
(1524–8) **VII** 122, 131, 218, 600
Wyatt, James (1746–1813), architect **XII** 544, 545; biography
XIII 581; work 581
Wyatt, Margaret, Lady Lee **VII** 601
Wyatt, Samuel, architect **XII** 544
Wyatt, Sir Thomas, the Elder
(d. 1542) **VII** 266, 323, 418, 420,
587
Wyatt, Sir Thomas, the Younger
(1521?–4), rising and execution
VII 538–40, 545
Wyatt rebellion **VIII** 3
Wyatville, Sir Jeffry: biography
XIII 581; work 581
Wych, St Richard *see* St Richard
Wych
Wychboid (Worcs.) **II** 234
Wyche, Richard, Lollard **VI** 496
Wycherley, William **X** 369
Wychwood (Oxon.) **Ia** 608; forest **II**
44; **III** 19; **V** 322
Wyclif, John **V** 279, 284, 303, 503;
on Wykeham 227; French war
250; parliament (1371) 290;
career and works 290, 510–15;
and John of Gaunt 290, 404, 436,
489 — his ally 396, 400; on
bishops 296, 299; on monks 305,
308; character and importance
311, 515–17; summoned to St
Paul's (1377) 396; Gloucester
parliament (1378) 404; the Bohemians 427; on Norwich crusade
431; followers 517–22; English
Bible 522–3

X Y Z

Xaintrailles, Poton de **VI** 107, 239, 241, 247
Xanten, villa nr. **Ia** 587

yachting **X** 408
Yale **XII** 149
Yale (Ial) **IV** 410, 424
Yale, Elihu, and Royal Society **XI** 396
Yalta, conference **XV** 590–1
yardland **II** 474; meaning 313–14
Yare, river xxvii; map 2 xxx
Yarm (Yorks.) **III** 96
Yarmouth (IOW) **VII** 557
Yarmouth (Norfolk) **III** 94, 96, 420; disputes with men of Cinque Ports **IV** 645; ships in war time 655, 656; **V** 145, 244, 380, 391, 417; cause of violence 420; **VII** 198, 464, 468, 490, 528
Yarmouth, countess of *see* Wallmoden
Yates, Dornford **XV** 312
Yattenden (Berks.) **VI** 600
Yatton (Surrey) **VI** 419
Yaxley (Northants) **III** 75
Yaxley, Francis **VIII** 88
Yeading (Middx.) **II** 294
Year of Four Emperors **Ia** 128–35, 172, 677
A Year under the Terror **XV** 317
Yeats, William Butler **XIV** 330, 335
Yeavering (Northumb.): Anglian site **Ia** 675; **Ib** 199; map 4 xxxii; **II** 115
The Yellow Book **XIV** 304, 330
Yelverton, Mr, MP **VIII** 221
Yelverton, William, justice of Kings Bench **VI** 449, 491
Yeo, Sir James **XII** 553
Yeoman of the guard **VII** 58, 208, 267, 557
yeomanry **IX** 282–4
Yerman, John, of Exchequer **VI** 419

Yetham (Roxburgh) **VI** 36
Yolanda of Aragon ('Queen of Sicily') **VI** 241
Yolande, daughter of John of Brienne and heiress of kingdom of Jerusalem, second wife of Frederick II **IV** 107
Yolande of Brittany, daughter of Peter of Dreux **IV** 93
Yolande of Dreux, 2nd wife of Alexander III, king of Scots (1285) **IV** 597, 598; transmits the Montfort claim to Brittany 598
Yonge, George, secretary at war (1783) **XII** 579
Yonge, John, dean of York (1514): master of the rolls (1508) **VII** 648
Yonne, river **VI** 200
Yorck, Prussian general **XII** 555
York, Canada *see* Toronto
York (Eboracum, Eoforwic): legionary fortress **Ia** 136–7, 152, 163, 221–2, 325 — raiders 384; legion IX 137, 152, 174; Geta and Caracalla 229–30, 250; legion VI 231, 298, 412; provincial capital 231, 517; deaths of emperors 322–3; town and monuments 325–8, 581–3; military control from 384, 528, 564; Valentia 411; *colonia* 512, 575; governor's guards 521; altar to Britannia 531; *sevir Augustalis* 580; craft guild 659; jet 658; burials 700, 702, 704; Constantine proclaimed 713; **Ib** xxvi, 4, 80–1, 87, 89; cemeteries 101, 110, 178; road 176; and Brough 187; continuity 195–7; map 4 xxxii; map 6 88; **II** 340, 349, 388, 533, 563; school 90, 175, 187–9; archbishopric 108, 145–6; relations with Canterbury 108–9, 435, 664–5; seat of Paulinus 115; early see 124; Bede's influence

618

185, 187–9; Frisian colony 221, 526–7, 542; Danish invasions 247–8, 604, 611; see 433, 440, 659; foreign influence on art 443; minting and moneyers 537; divided into wards 540; Danish traders 542; revolt (1065) 578; castles 601, 602; revolts in Mercia 603; knight service 635; destruction owing to Conquest **III** 65; attempts to found a commune 70; seal 73; trade 75, 90, 96; weavers' gild 85; Stephen 162, 273; diocese 210; St Mary's Abbey 229; school 233; William of Scotland's oath of allegiance to Henry II 278; massacre of Jews 353–4; citizens fined 366; John (1216) 480–1; Henry III writes to archbishop and citizens (1260) **IV** 158; abbot of 165; royal council (1301) 316; court of archbishop 493–4; Minster 494; assemblies of laymen and clergy (1283) 506; convocations of clergy 506, 507; treaty (1237) 574, 579, 586, 593–4; archbishop's claim over Scottish bishoprics 583; castle 627; great hall 627; transfer of exchequer and bench to (1298–1304) 627, 688; administrative centre during Scottish wars 688, 695, 704, 711; summons to parliament (1298) 688; **V** 439, 522; council 9; Edward II at 11, 23; muster 51; Household Ordinance 55; escape of queen 56; parliaments 57, 67, 71–3, 190, 352; Scottish peace meeting (1328) 98; Edward III at 117, 154; frequent meetings under Edward III 155; convocation 155; archbishopric 184; assessment of 192; diocese 210, 332; see 210, 298–9, 301; Minster 277, 278, 299; trial of Templars 292; citizens 299; population 314, 378, 379; oats sent by sea 320; staple 351, 353; textile workers 367; Flemings 368; cloth-making 370; prosperity 380–1; government 382; disturbances 414; Richard II at 467; plays 526; **VI** 35, 53, 61, 63, 194; Micklegate Bar 53, 61, 402; merchant community 60; Bootham Bar 61; Minster 61 — windows 655; *Alma Curia* 62; St Mary's Abbey 234, 286, 447; diocese 269; Hospital of St Leonard 288; St William's College 292; value of estates 337; Merchant Venturers Hall 351; mercers 357; development 366; tax and population 368; division of citizens 387; incorporation charter 392; Gild and fraternity of Tailors 396; aldermen 399; Gild of Corpus Christi 402; Hospital of St Thomas of Canterbury 402; St Anne's Fossgate 403; St Michael le Belfry 403; Act books 403; All Saints, North Street 403; Richard's fall 523 — and Edward IV 528; Austin Friars, Kendal 608; Gloucester demands fencibles 618; St Michael, Spurriergate 655; Council of North 668; **VII** 35, 37, 40, 161, 405; greets Henry VII 67–8; battle of Stoke 75; Scottish threat (1512) 276; convocation summoned to (1530) 331; fall of Wolsey 332; convocation (1540) 417; gilds 458; cloth trade 462, 464; Whalley's embezzlement 501; mint 604–6, 607; 'conference' **VIII** 113, 114, 138–9, 140, 188; city **IX** 97, 129, 136–7, 351; newspaper **X** 356; primary poverty in **XV** 237

York (kingdom): Danish kingdom **II** 262–3, 323; Norse kingdom 329, 330, 338; Athelstan's relations with 339–40; Eric Bloodaxe, son of Harold Fairhair, acquired kingdom 360; King Eric killed on Stainmore 362

'York, Anonymous of' **III** 3, 181